POETRY
for Students

Advisors

POETRY
for Students

Presenting Analysis, Context, and Criticism
on Commonly Studied Poetry

VOLUME 36

Sara Constantakis, Project Editor

Foreword by David J. Kelly

GALE
CENGAGE Learning

Detroit • New York • San Francisco • New Haven, Conn • Waterville, Maine • London

GALE
CENGAGE Learning™

Poetry for Students, Volume 36

Project Editor: Sara Constantakis

Rights Acquisition and Management: Sara Crane,
Sari Gordon, Barb McNeil, Robyn Young

Composition: Evi Abou-El-Seoud

Manufacturing: Drew Kalasky

Imaging: John Watkins

Product Design: Pamela A. E. Galbreath,
Jennifer Wahi

Content Conversion: Katrina Coach

Product Manager: Meggin Condino

Gale
27500 Drake Rd.
Farmington Hills, MI, 48331-3535

ISBN-13: 978-1-4144-6703-0
ISBN-10: 1-4144-6703-6

ISSN 1094-7019

This title is also available as an e-book.
ISBN-13: 978-1-4144-7387-1
ISBN-10: 1-4144-7387-7
Contact your Gale, a part of Cengage Learning sales representative for ordering information.

Printed in Mexico
1 2 3 4 5 6 7 14 13 12 11 10

Table of Contents

Just a Few Lines on a Page

I have often thought that poets have the easiest job in the world. A poem, after all, is just a few lines on a page, usually not even extending margin to margin—how long would that take to write, about five minutes? Maybe ten at the most, if you wanted it to rhyme or have a repeating meter. Why, I could start in the morning and produce a book of poetry by dinnertime. But we all know that it isn't that easy. Anyone can come up with enough words, but the poet's job is about writing the *right* ones. The right words will change lives, making people see the world somewhat differently than they saw it just a few minutes earlier. The right words can make a reader who relies on the dictionary for meanings take a greater responsibility for his or her own personal understanding. A poem that is put on the page correctly can bear any amount of analysis, probing, defining, explaining, and interrogating, and something about it will still feel new the next time you read it.

It would be fine with me if I could talk about poetry without using the word "magical," because that word is overused these days to imply "a really good time," often with a certain sweetness about it, and a lot of poetry is neither of these. But if you stop and think about magic—whether it brings to mind sorcery, witchcraft, or bunnies pulled from top hats—it always seems to involve stretching reality to produce a result greater than the sum of its parts and pulling unexpected results out of thin air. This book provides ample cases where a few simple words conjure up whole worlds. We do

not actually travel to different times and different cultures, but the poems get into our minds, they find what little we know about the places they are talking about, and then they make that little bit blossom into a bouquet of someone else's life. Poets make us think we are following simple, specific events, but then they leave ideas in our heads that cannot be found on the printed page. Abracadabra.

Sometimes when you finish a poem it doesn't feel as if it has left any supernatural effect on you, like it did not have any more to say beyond the actual words that it used. This happens to everybody, but most often to inexperienced readers: regardless of what is often said about young people's infinite capacity to be amazed, you have to understand what usually does happen, and what could have happened instead, if you are going to be moved by what someone has accomplished. In those cases in which you finish a poem with a "So what?" attitude, the information provided in *Poetry for Students* comes in handy. Readers can feel assured that the poems included here actually are potent magic, not just because a few (or a hundred or ten thousand) professors of literature say they are: they're significant because they can withstand close inspection and still amaze the very same people who have just finished taking them apart and seeing how they work. Turn them inside out, and they will still be able to come alive, again and again. *Poetry for Students* gives readers of any age good practice in feeling the ways poems relate to both the reality of the time and place the poet lived in and the reality of our emotions. Practice is just another word for being a student. The information given here helps you understand the way to read poetry; what to look for, what to expect.

With all of this in mind, I really don't think I would actually like to have a poet's job at all. There are too many skills involved, including precision, honesty, taste, courage, linguistics, passion, compassion, and the ability to keep all sorts of people entertained at once. And that is just what they do with one hand, while the other hand pulls some sort of trick that most of us will never fully understand. I can't even pack all that I need for a weekend into one suitcase, so what would be my chances of stuffing so much life into a few lines? With all that *Poetry for Students* tells us about each poem, I am impressed that any poet can finish three or four poems a year. Read the inside stories of these poems, and you won't be able to approach any poem in the same way you did before.

David J. Kelly
College of Lake County

Introduction

Purpose of the Book

The purpose of *Poetry for Students (PfS)* is to provide readers with a guide to understanding, enjoying, and studying poems by giving them easy access to information about the work. Part of Gale's "For Students" Literature line, *PfS* is specifically designed to meet the curricular needs of high school and undergraduate college students and their teachers, as well as the interests of general readers and researchers considering specific poems. While each volume contains entries on "classic" poems frequently studied in classrooms, there are also entries containing hard-to-find information on contemporary poems, including works by multicultural, international, and women poets.

The information covered in each entry includes an introduction to the poem and the poem's author; the actual poem text (if possible); a poem summary, to help readers unravel and understand the meaning of the poem; analysis of important themes in the poem; and an explanation of important literary techniques and movements as they are demonstrated in the poem.

In addition to this material, which helps the readers analyze the poem itself, students are also provided with important information on the literary and historical background informing each work. This includes a historical context essay, a box comparing the time or place the poem was written to modern Western culture, a critical overview essay, and excerpts from critical essays on the poem. A unique feature of *PfS* is a specially commissioned critical essay on each poem, targeted toward the student reader.

To further help today's student in studying and enjoying each poem, information on audio recordings and other media adaptations is provided (if available), as well as reading suggestions for works of fiction and nonfiction on similar themes and topics. Classroom aids include ideas for research papers and lists of critical and reference sources that provide additional material on the poem.

Selection Criteria

The titles for each volume of *PfS* are selected by surveying numerous sources on notable literary works and analyzing course curricula for various schools, school districts, and states. Some of the sources surveyed include: high school and undergraduate literature anthologies and textbooks; lists of award-winners, and recommended titles, including the Young Adult Library Services Association (YALSA) list of best books for young adults.

Input solicited from our expert advisory board—consisting of educators and librarians—guides us to maintain a mix of "classic" and contemporary literary works, a mix of challenging and engaging works (including genre titles that are commonly studied) appropriate for different age levels, and a mix of international, multicultural and women authors. These advisors also consult on each volume's entry list, advising on which titles are most studied, most appropriate, and meet the broadest interests across secondary (grades 7–12) curricula and undergraduate literature studies.

How Each Entry Is Organized

Each entry, or chapter, in *PfS* focuses on one poem. Each entry heading lists the full name of the poem, the author's name, and the date of the poem's publication. The following elements are contained in each entry:

Introduction: a brief overview of the poem which provides information about its first appearance, its literary standing, any controversies surrounding the work, and major conflicts or themes within the work.

Author Biography: this section includes basic facts about the poet's life, and focuses on events and times in the author's life that inspired the poem in question.

Poem Text: when permission has been granted, the poem is reprinted, allowing for quick reference when reading the explication of the following section.

Poem Summary: a description of the major events in the poem. Summaries are broken down with subheads that indicate the lines being discussed.

Themes: a thorough overview of how the major topics, themes, and issues are addressed within the poem. Each theme discussed appears in a separate subhead.

Style: this section addresses important style elements of the poem, such as form, meter, and rhyme scheme; important literary devices used, such as imagery, foreshadowing, and symbolism; and, if applicable, genres to which the work might have belonged, such as Gothicism or Romanticism. Literary terms are explained within the entry, but can also be found in the Glossary.

Historical Context: this section outlines the social, political, and cultural climate in which the author lived and the poem was created. This section may include descriptions of related historical events, pertinent aspects of daily life in the culture, and the artistic and literary sensibilities of the time in which the work was written. If the poem is a historical work, information regarding the time in which the poem is set is also included. Each section is broken down with helpful subheads.

Critical Overview: this section provides background on the critical reputation of the poem, including bannings or any other public controversies surrounding the work. For older works, this section includes a history of how the poem was first received and how perceptions of it may have changed over the years; for more recent poems, direct quotes from early reviews may also be included.

Criticism: an essay commissioned by *PfS* which specifically deals with the poem and is written specifically for the student audience, as well as excerpts from previously published criticism on the work (if available).

Sources: an alphabetical list of critical material quoted in the entry, with full bibliographical information.

Further Reading: an alphabetical list of other critical sources which may prove useful for the student. Includes full bibliographical information and a brief annotation.

Suggested Search Terms: a list of search terms and phrases to jumpstart students' further information seeking. Terms include not just titles and author names but also terms and topics related to the historical and literary context of the works.

In addition, each entry contains the following highlighted sections, set apart from the main text as sidebars:

Media Adaptations: if available, a list of audio recordings as well as any film or television adaptations of the poem, including source information.

Topics for Further Study: a list of potential study questions or research topics dealing with the poem. This section includes questions related to other disciplines the student may be studying, such as American history, world history, science, math, government, business, geography, economics, psychology, etc.

Compare & Contrast: an "at-a-glance" comparison of the cultural and historical differences between the author's time and culture and late twentieth century or early twenty-first century Western culture. This box includes pertinent parallels between the major scientific, political, and cultural movements of the time or place the poem was written, the time or place the poem was set (if a historical work), and modern Western culture. Works written after 1990 may not have this box.

What Do I Read Next?: a list of works that might give a reader points of entry into a classic work (e.g., YA or multicultural titles) and/or complement the featured poem or serve as a contrast to it. This includes works by the same author and others, works from various genres, YA works, and works from various cultures and eras.

Other Features

PfS includes "Just a Few Lines on a Page," a foreword by David J. Kelly, an adjunct professor of English, College of Lake County, Illinois. This essay provides a straightforward, unpretentious explanation of why poetry should be marveled at and how *PfS* can help teachers show students how to enrich their own reading experiences.

A Cumulative Author/Title Index lists the authors and titles covered in each volume of the *PfS* series.

A Cumulative Nationality/Ethnicity Index breaks down the authors and titles covered in each volume of the *PfS* series by nationality and ethnicity.

A Subject/Theme Index, specific to each volume, provides easy reference for users who may be studying a particular subject or theme rather than a single work. Significant subjects from events to broad themes are included.

A Cumulative Index of First Lines (beginning in Vol. 10) provides easy reference for users who may be familiar with the first line of a poem but may not remember the actual title.

A Cumulative Index of Last Lines (beginning in Vol. 10) provides easy reference for users who may be familiar with the last line of a poem but may not remember the actual title.

Each entry may include illustrations, including photo of the author and other graphics related to the poem.

Citing Poetry for Students

When writing papers, students who quote directly from any volume of *PfS* may use the following general forms. These examples are based on MLA style; teachers may request that students adhere to a different style, so the following examples may be adapted as needed.

When citing text from *PfS* that is not attributed to a particular author (i.e., the Themes, Style, Historical Context sections, etc.), the following format should be used in the bibliography section:

"Angle of Geese." *Poetry for Students.* Ed. Marie Napierkowski and Mary Ruby. Vol. 2. Detroit: Gale, 1998. 8–9.

When quoting the specially commissioned essay from *PfS* (usually the first piece under the "Criticism" subhead), the following format should be used:

Velie, Alan. Critical Essay on "Angle of Geese." *Poetry for Students.* Ed. Marie Napierkowski and Mary Ruby. Vol. 2. Detroit: Gale, 1998. 7–10.

When quoting a journal or newspaper essay that is reprinted in a volume of *PfS*, the following form may be used:

Luscher, Robert M. "An Emersonian Context of Dickinson's 'The Soul Selects Her Own Society'." *ESQ: A Journal of American Renaissance* 30.2 (1984): 111–16. Excerpted and reprinted in *Poetry for Students.* Ed. Marie Napierkowski and Mary Ruby. Vol. 1. Detroit: Gale, 1998. 266–69.

When quoting material reprinted from a book that appears in a volume of *PfS*, the following form may be used:

Mootry, Maria K. "'Tell It Slant': Disguise and Discovery as Revisionist Poetic Discourse in 'The Bean Eaters'." *A Life Distilled: Gwendolyn Brooks, Her Poetry and Fiction.* Ed. Maria K. Mootry and Gary Smith. Urbana: University of Illinois Press, 1987. 177–80, 191. Excerpted and reprinted in *Poetry for Students.* Ed. Marie Napierkowski and Mary Ruby. Vol. 2. Detroit: Gale, 1998. 22–24.

We Welcome Your Suggestions

The editorial staff of *Poetry for Students* welcomes your comments and ideas. Readers who wish to suggest poems to appear in future volumes, or who have other suggestions, are cordially invited to contact the editor. You may contact the editor via E-mail at: **ForStudentsEditors@cengage.com.** Or write to the editor at:

Editor, *Poetry for Students*
Gale
27500 Drake Road
Farmington Hills, MI 48331-3535

Literary Chronology

365: T'ao Ch'ien is born in Ch'ai-sang, China.

c. 417: T'ao Ch'ien's "I Built My Hut Beside a Traveled Road" is written as part of a group called *Drinking Poems*.

427: T'ao Ch'ien dies in Ch'ai-sang, China.

1753: Phillis Wheatley is born in west Africa.

1773: Phillis Wheatley's "An Hymn to the Evening" is published in *Poems on Subjects, Religious and Moral*.

1784: Phillis Wheatley dies of complications from childbirth on December 5 in Massachusetts.

1792: Percy Bysshe Shelley is born on August 4 in Horsham, England.

1795: John Keats is born on October 31 in London, England.

1807: John Greenleaf Whittier is born on December 17 in Haverhill, Massachusetts.

1820: John Keats's "To Autumn" is published in *Lamia, Isabella, The Eve of St. Agnes, and Other Poems*.

1821: John Keats dies of tuberculosis on February 23, in Rome, Italy.

1822: Percy Bysshe Shelley died in a boating accident on July 8 while sailing between Livorno and Lenici, Italy.

1839: Percy Bysshe Shelley's "Song to the Men of England" is published.

1866: John Greenleaf Whittier's *Snow-Bound* is published.

1878: Carl August Sandburg is born on August 6 in Galesburg, Illinois.

1889: Anna Akhmatova is born on June 23 near Odessa, Russia.

1892: John Greenleaf Whittier dies on September 7 in Hampton Falls, New Hampshire.

1906: Léopold Sédar Senghor is born on October 9 in Joal, Senegal.

1909: Sir Stephen Harold Spender was born February 28 in Kensington, London, England.

1917: Robert Lowell is born on March 1 in Boston, Massachusetts.

1919: Carl August Sandburg is awarded the Pulitzer Prize for poetry for *Cornhuskers*.

1922: Anna Akhmataova's "I Am Not One of Those Who Have Left the Country" is published in *Anno Domini MCMXXI*.

1923: Mari Evans is born on July 16 in Toledo, Ohio.

1928: Anne Sexton is born Anne Gray Harvey on November 9 in Newton Massachusetts.

1931: Etheridge Knight is born April 19 in Corinth, Mississippi.

1933: Sir Stephen Harold Spender's "What I Expected" is published in *Poems*.

1938: Charles Simic is born on May 9 in Belgrade, Yugoslavia.

1940: Carl August Sandburg is awarded the Pulitzer Prize for history for *Abraham Lincoln: The War Years.*

1942: Joseph Bruchac is born on October 16 in Saratoga Springs, New York.

1945: Kay Ryan is born on September 21 in San Jose, California.

1945: Léopold Sédar Senghor's "Prayer to the Masks" is published in *Songs of the Shadow.*

1947: Robert Lowell is awarded the Pulitzer Prize for poetry for *Lord Weary's Castle.*

1951: Carl August Sandburg is awarded the Pulitzer Prize for poetry for *Carl Sandburg: Complete Poems.*

1963: Carl August Sandburg's "Moon Rondeau" is published in *Honey and Salt.*

1964: Robert Lowell's "Hawthorne" is published in *For the Union Dead.*

1966: Anna Akhmatova dies of a heart attack near Moscow, Russia.

1966: Anne Sexton's poem "Self in 1958" is published in *Live or Die.*

1967: Anne Sexton is awarded the Pulitzer Prize for poetry for *Live or Die.*

1967: Carl August Sandburg dies of heart failure on July 22 in Flat Rock, North Carolina.

1968: Etheridge Knight's "The Idea of Ancestry" is published in *Poems from Prison.*

1970: Evans's "When In Rome" is published in *I Am A Black Woman.*

1974: Anne Sexton commits suicide on October 4 in Boston, Massachusetts.

1974: Robert Lowell is awarded the Pulitzer Prize for poetry for *The Dolphin.*

1977: Robert Lowell dies of heart failure on September 12 in New York City, New York.

1978: Joseph Bruchac's "Birdfoot's Grampa" is published in *Entering Onandaga.*

1980: Charles Simic's "Prodigy" is published in *Classic Ballroom Dances.*

1991: Etheridge Knight dies of lung cancer on March 10 in Indianapolis, Indiana.

1995: Sir Stephen Harold Spender died of natural causes on July 16 in London, England.

1996: Kay Ryan's "All Shall Be Restored" is published in *Elephant Rocks.*

2001: Léopold Sédar Senghor dies on December 20 in Verson, France.

Acknowledgments

The editors wish to thank the copyright holders of the excerpted criticism included in this volume and the permissions managers of many book and magazine publishing companies for assisting us in securing reproduction rights. We are also grateful to the staffs of the Detroit Public Library, the Library of Congress, the University of Detroit Mercy Library, Wayne State University Purdy/ Kresge Library Complex, and the University of Michigan Libraries for making their resources available to us. Following is a list of the copyright holders who have granted us permission to reproduce material in this volume of *PfS*. Every effort has been made to trace copyright, but if omissions have been made, please let us know.

COPYRIGHTED EXCERPTS IN *PfS*, VOLUME 36, WERE REPRODUCED FROM THE FOLLOWING PERIODICALS:

America, v. 116, May 13, 1967; v. 148, January 22, 1983. Copyright © 1967, 1983 www.americamagazine.org. All rights reserved. Both reproduced by permission of America Press. For subscription information, visit www.americamagazine.org.—*American Poetry Review*, January/February, 1977 for "Robert Lowell: Learning to Live in History" by J. D. McClatchy; v. 38, July/ August, 2009 for "An Interview with Kay Ryan" by Grace Cavalieri. Both reproduced by permission of the respective authors.—*American Scholar*, v. 77, summer, 2008. Copyright © 2008 by the author. Reprinted by permission.—*ANQ*, v. 20, spring, 2007. Copyright 2007 Heldref Publications. Reprinted by permission of publisher (Heldref Publications, www.heldref.org).—*Antioch Review*, v. 54, autumn, 1996; v. 64, spring, 2006. Copyright © 1996, 2006 by the Antioch Review Inc. Both reproduced by permission of the Editors.—*Black American Literature Forum*, v. 14, fall, 1980. Reproduced by permission.—*Booklist*, v. 95, May 1, 1999. Copyright © 1999 by the American Library Association. Reproduced by permission.—*Books Abroad*, v. 38, spring, 1964. Copyright 1964 by the University of Oklahoma Press. Reproduced by permission.—*Callaloo*, v. 19, autumn, 1996. Copyright © 1996 by The Johns Hopkins University Press. Reproduced by permission.—*Chinese Literature: Essays, Articles, Reviews*, v. 20, December, 1998. Copyright © 1998 *Chinese Literature: Essays, Articles, Reviews (CLEAR)*. Reproduced by permission.—*College Literature*, v. 22, October, 1995. Copyright © 1995 by West Chester University. Reproduced by permission.—*Commonweal*, December 9, 1977. Copyright © 1977 Commonweal Publishing Co., Inc. Reproduced by permission of Commonweal Foundation.—*Emily Dickinson Journal*, v. 5, fall, 1996. Copyright © 1996 by The Johns Hopkins University Press. Reproduced by permission.—*The Explicator*, v. 65, fall, 2006. Copyright © 2006 Heldref Publications. Reprinted by permission of publisher (Heldref Publications, www.heldref.org).—*Hollins Critic*, v. XVIII, December, 1981; v. 21, June, 1984. Copyright 1981, 1984 by Hollins College. Both reproduced by permission.—

Robert Hightower. Translated by James Robert Hightower. Clarendon Press, 1970. Copyright © Oxford University Press 1970. Reproduced by permission of Oxford University Press.—Vossekuil, Cheryl. From "Embracing Life: Anne Sexton's Early Poems," in *Critical Essays on Anne Sexton*. Edited by Linda Wagner-Martin. G.K. Hall, 1989. Copyright © 1989 by Linda Wagner-Martin. Reproduced by permission of Gale, a part of Cengage Learning.

Contributors

Bryan Aubrey: Aubrey holds a Ph.D. in English. Entries on "I Built My Hut beside a Traveled Road" and "To Autumn." Original essays on "I Built My Hut beside a Traveled Road" and "To Autumn."

Catherine Dominic: Dominic is a novelist, free-lance writer, and editor. Entries on "All Shall Be Restored" and *Snow-Bound*. Original essays on "All Shall Be Restored" and *Snow-Bound*.

Charlotte M. Freeman: Freeman is a novelist, free-lance writer, and former academic who lives in Montana. Entries on "Birdfoot's Grampa" and "An Hymn to the Evening." Original essays on "Birdfoot's Grampa" and "An Hymn to the Evening".

Cynthia Gower: Gower is a novelist, playwright, and freelance writer. Entry on "Moon Rondeau." Original essay on "Moon Rondeau."

Joyce Hart: Hart is a published writer and creative writing teacher. Entries on "The Idea of Ancestry" and "Prodigy." Original essays on "The Idea of Ancestry" and "Prodigy."

Diane Andrews Henningfeld: Henningfeld is a professor emerita of English at Adrian College and writes widely on literature. Entry on "I Am Not One of Those Who Left the Land." Original essay on "I Am Not One of Those Who Left the Land."

Sheri Metzger Karmiol: Karmiol teaches literature and drama at the University of New Mexico, where she is a lecturer in the university honors program. Entry on "What I Expected." Original essay on "What I Expected."

Tyrus Miller: Miller has taught comparative literature and English and published a book titled *Late Modernism Politics, Fiction, and the Arts between the World Wars*. Entry on "Prayer to the Masks." Original essay on "Prayer to the Masks."

Rachel Porter: Porter is a freelance writer and editor who holds a bachelor of arts in English literature. Entry on "When in Rome." Original essay on "When in Rome."

Jon Richardson: Richardson is a writer and editor. Entry on "Hawthorne." Original essay on "Hawthorne."

Chris Semansky: Semansky is a widely published poet, fiction writer, and critic and has taught literature and writing. Original essay on "Prayer to the Masks."

Bradley A. Skeen: Skeen is a classics professor. Entry on "Song to the Men of England." Original essay on "Song to the Men of England."

Leah Tieger: Tieger is a freelance writer and editor. Entry on "Self in 1958." Original essay on "Self in 1958."

All Shall Be Restored

KAY RYAN

1996

California poet Kay Ryan achieved national recognition when she was asked by the Library of Congress to serve as poet laureate from 2008 to 2009. In 2009, she was asked to serve a second one-year term. Her poetry in general is characterized by its philosophical nature, its efficiency of expression, and by structures that often make use of internal rhyming. Her 1996 poem "All Shall Be Restored" exemplifies these characteristics. In this work, Ryan explores the notion that the world will one day return to its original state, a state in which all evidence of humanity's impact on the earth will be erased. The poem is brief, and in succinct terms Ryan offers a broad view of the natural world and the transient nature of humanity's place in this world. While many of Ryan's works are described as both pithy and playful, "All Shall Be Restored" has too much philosophical and emotional depth to be treated lightly. While the theme of restoration has positive overtones, in Ryan's poem the idea of restoration is ironically juxtaposed with the erasure of humanity from the planet.

Ryan's "All Shall Be Restored" first appeared in the 1996 volume of poetry *Elephant Rocks*, published by Grove Press.

AUTHOR BIOGRAPHY

Ryan was born on September 21, 1945, to Kay and Bessie Pederson, in San Jose, California. Kay

Kay Ryan (*John Lamparski / WireImage*)

Richard Pederson, Ryan's father, was an oil driller. Raised in the desert region of Southern California, Ryan graduated in 1963 from Antelope Valley High School in Lancaster, California. She went on to the University of California at Los Angeles, receiving a B.A. in 1967 and an M.A. in 1968, both in English literature. Ryan self-published her first collection of poems, *Dragon Acts to Dragon Ends*, in 1983, a work that was financed largely through the efforts of Ryan's longtime partner, Carol Adair. In 1985, the small press Copper Beech published Ryan's next volume, *Strangely Marked Metal*, but the publication of the work went unnoticed by critics. However, Ryan began publishing poems in major American literary journals following the publication of *Strangely Marked Metal*, and by the time her next collection, *Flamingo Watching*, was published in 1994, Ryan had established a critical reputation that earned the volume prominent and favorable reviews. *Elephant Rocks*, the volume that contains the poem "All Shall Be Restored," was published in 1996. Several other volumes followed, along with such awards as the

National Endowment for the Arts Fellowship, the Maurice English Poetry Award in 2001, a Guggenheim Fellowship, the Ruth Lilly Poetry Prize from the Poetry Foundation in 2004, and four Pushcart Prizes. Her works have been widely anthologized. In 2008 and in 2009, Ryan was asked by the Library of Congress to serve as the poet laureate. In 2010, she released the collection *The Best of It: New and Selected Poems*, published by Grove Press. Ryan lives in Marin County, California. Until her appointment as poet laureate, Ryan worked as an instructor of remedial English at the College of Marin in Kentfield, California, a position she held for over thirty years.

POEM TEXT

The grains shall be collected
from the thousand shores
to which they found their way,
and the boulder restored,
and the boulder itself replaced   5
in the cliff, and likewise
the cliff shall rise
or subside until the plate of earth
is without fissure. Restoration
knows no half-measure. It will   10
not stop when the treasured and lost
bronze horse remounts the steps.
Even this horse will founder backward
to coin, cannon, and domestic pots,
which themselves shall bubble and   15
drain back to green veins in stone.
And every word written shall lift off
letter by letter, the backward text
read ever briefer, ever more antic
in its effort to insist that nothing   20
shall be lost.

POEM SUMMARY

Lines 1–3
"All Shall Be Restored" is a twenty-one line poem with no stanzaic divisions. (A stanza is a unit of poetry that structurally divides the poem the way a paragraph divides prose.) In this poem, Ryan grounds her ideas in images and moves from one image to the next as she develops her themes. The first image is explored in the first three lines of the poem. She opens with the idea of grains, presumably of sand, that shall find their way together again from numerous shores. The movement this

image conveys is one of backward progression, as if the countless grains are almost magnetically drawn back to some original source.

Lines 4–10

In the next several lines, Ryan links a number of related images together. She speaks of the boulders rejoining with cliffs, and cliffs shifting until the earth's surface is no longer fractured. Her tone reflects the idea conveyed in the title of the poem, suggesting that the world is being mended, or restored through natural means. In lines 9 and 10, the poet asserts that this process of repair can only be achieved if it is thorough and all-encompassing. Once started, it will be taken to its extreme end, for true restoration can only be achieved if the task is completed fully, Ryan asserts in these lines.

Lines 11–16

Ryan moves from the idea of the natural world's restoration to exploring the fate of humanity in this process. To do so, in lines 11–16, Ryan employs the image of the bronze horse, a type of sculpture typically associated with ancient Greece and Rome, as well as with the Renaissance period of art in Europe during the fifteenth century. She speaks specifically of a bronze horse, once lost, mounting steps, presumably of where it had been displayed, once again. This bronze horse, like all the others, Ryan says, will be melted down. Her notion of a backward progression of time is once again invoked, as she speaks of the melted bronze being cast into useful things, such as coins and pots, and these being melted as well until they are once again simply veins of metal in the earth's rock. Through this series of images, Ryan seems to be suggesting that the efforts of humans, artistic and otherwise, will be erased in this process of restoration. The earth will be returned to an original state in which there is no evidence of the presence of humanity.

Lines 17–21

This idea of the absence of human life is reaffirmed in the final lines of the poem. The image Ryan now studies is that of the printed word on the page—her own artistic medium. She describes the backward march of time once again, how letter by letter the words will disappear in reverse order from the page, from last to first. Ryan's concise imagery conveys the notion that the message on the written page will become shorter and shorter, until all disappears, despite the insistence

of the text itself that it—and nothing—will be lost. This last series of images suggests that artists strive to attain something permanent with their creations. However, Ryan insists that nothing is permanent, despite one's efforts to create something lasting, like sculpture or poetry. The vision or message of the artist is as lost in this process of the restoration of the earth as anything else that has damaged, over time, the physical unity of the earth. Humanity's place in Earth's history, Ryan's poem suggests, is ephemeral. The poem's title indicates that everything will be restored, and Ryan's language and imagery at the onset of the poem describes the events that will bring about this restoration almost as a healing process. Yet, this process also involves the destruction or erasure of the mark of humanity upon the earth. All may be restored in one sense, but all is lost in human terms as well.

THEMES

Natural Cycles

In "All Shall Be Restored," Ryan explores the world's natural cycle of self-regeneration. She describes epic shifts in the earth's natural features, envisioning the world reforming itself over time and returning to an early, primitive, whole state. In an interview with Pulitzer Prize-winning composer Lewis Spratlan (commissioned to set to music poems by Ryan including "All Shall Be Restored") in a 2009 issue of the *Amherst Bulletin*, Bonnie Wells describes Ryan's poem as "a profound nod to the first law of thermodynamics, conservation of energy, or the way the stuff of the world continually recycles, with nothing lost." Ryan's language and imagery depict a process in which everything recedes, in a reverse fashion, to an ever-earlier state. The use of the word "restored" in the poem's title and within the verse itself suggests also a returning of the world to its original state. Ryan conveys a sense of reverse motion, almost as if time is moving backward, undoing what has been done.

Apocalypse

While Wells focuses on the regenerative nature of the process Ryan describes, the human element now present on Earth is envisioned by Ryan as eventually lost. Although this may be regarded as regenerative, it may also be considered an

TOPICS FOR FURTHER STUDY

- Ryan's poetry utilizes some elements of traditional structures, such as rhyme scheme and meter, and incorporates them into an overall form composed in a free verse style. Select a topic and compose your own poem in which you, like Ryan, employ elements of both formalism and free verse. Share your poem with your class either orally or on a Web page or other social networking site.

- Ryan's work is highly regarded by critics and poets alike and has been described as unique in the world of contemporary poetry. In its compact style and philosophical, lyrical treatment of themes, Ryan's poetry is also compared to that of Emily Dickinson. Using print and electronic resources, research the life and poetry of Emily Dickinson. Write a biographical essay in which you discuss Dickinson's personal history, as well as the literary and historical context in which she wrote. Make your essay available electronically as a blog or Web page. Be sure to cite all of your sources.

- The section "Energy" in the chapter "Mechanics" in *Fantastic Voyages: Learning Science Through Science Fiction Films*, written by Leroy W. Dubeck, Suzanne E. Moshier, and Judith E. Boss, and published in 1994 by the American Institute of Physics, explores the law of physics related to the conservation of energy. Ryan's poem "All Shall Be Restored" has been discussed within the context of this scientific law concerning the transformation of energy. Dubeck, Moshier, and Boss use science fiction films such as *The Empire Strikes Back* to explore this scientific concept. Read the section on energy in *Learning Science Through Science Fiction Films*. Does the explanation of the properties of energy open up further possibilities in understanding the process Ryan contemplates in her poem? More generally, can science help one to understand poetry? Write an essay in which you explore these issues. Your findings may be presented in a written essay or on a Web page accessible by your classmates.

- Ryan, in many of the poems in *Elephant Rocks*, deals with everyday subjects and emotional reactions. She contemplates the theme of community in "The Woman Who Wrote Too Much," for example, and the feeling of relief in "Relief," and she also includes various animals as her subject matter. Californian poet and author Gary Soto similarly contemplates the issues of daily life. In his collection of poetry for young adults, *Neighborhood Odes* (published in 1992 by Harcourt Children's Books and reprinted by Harcourt in 2005), he considers such themes from the perspective of a Hispanic California community. Read a sampling of Ryan's poems and Soto's poems, comparing them. Do the poets treat any similar themes? How are their styles alike? What are the major differences in their approach, in their language? Write a comparative essay in which you discuss your findings, or read the poetry with a book group and prepare an oral report for the class.

---

apocalypse. The term apocalypse refers to the destruction of life on Earth as it is currently known. Ryan does not appear to mourn this loss in the poem. Yet, the process by which the human literary effort is erased is described in terms that suggest a panicked, frantic human energy, one that protests the impending loss.

One may accept the fact that the human race will one day be erased from the planet, as time marches on, and that natural disasters such as those that have repeatedly reshaped the world over millions of years will one day recreate the earth's features yet again. This may be regarded as both a natural process and as an inevitable

The poem describes things that "shall bubble and drain back to green veins in stone." *(Image copyright A. Ryser, 2010. Used under license from Shutterstock.com)*

event. As such, it may likewise strike terror within the human heart. Yet in her verse, Ryan superimposes over the destructive process a sense of necessity and incorporates the idealized notion that the process is one that is healing, or restorative in nature.

Humanity

The place of humanity in the world is a subject of contemplation in "All Shall Be Restored." The natural world the poet describes, and Ryan's vision for the fate of the world, is interjected with a human element about a third of the way through the poem. From details concerned with grains of sand and boulders and cliffs, Ryan turns to man-made items, such as bronze horses, coins, cannons, and cookware. All the items humanity has fashioned for purposeful use, for warfare, for pleasure, will share the same fate, Ryan prophesizes. All shall return to their natural metallic state, lodged within the earth's rocky surface. Ryan's discussion of the written word is a meditation on the fate of the writer in the process of the world's restoration. The creations of artists, Ryan

states, will be erased, letter by letter, until nothing remains. Some may resist this process, Ryan suggests through her imagery of the text itself struggling to assert its permanence. The sense of inevitability that the poem conveys, however, dominates the poem and places the presence of humanity on Earth in perspective, highlighting its impermanent nature.

Ryan's tone throughout the poem is an impassive, nonjudgmental one. She does not characterize the human effort to create art, such as the bronze horse sculptures or the written words she describes, as futile. Nor does she suggest that works of art, or any human effort for that matter, are without value. They appear to possess no greater or less value than the grains of sand, the boulders, or the cliffs she describes. In Ryan's conception, all the world as we know it will be restored to a state that existed before natural forces broke the earth's surface, and certainly before humanity made its mark on the world. Human effort, in Ryan's view, appears to be a part of a greater whole, a part of the energy that will be not be destroyed, but rather, transformed.

STYLE

Meter and Structure

Like many of Ryan's poems, "All Shall Be Restored" is a short poem of mixed metrical structure. Meter is a consistent pattern of unaccented and accented syllables in a line of poetry. As Richard Halstead reports in a 2007 article for the electronic edition of the *Marin Independent Journal*, "Although the poems contain no regular meter—alternating between iambic and unmetered—Ryan says she doesn't write free verse." An iambic line of verse is one in which an accented syllable follows an unaccented one, and iambic meter is often compared to the rhythm of everyday speech. Halstead quotes Ryan as saying that she strives to insert "clunky passages" into her lines of poetry to avoid a regular metrical structure. "All Shall Be Restored" is reflective of this habit. Some lines possess the steady rhythmic flow characterized by the iambic meter, while other lines interrupt the fluid progression of the poem. The effect of this mixture of metered and unmetered verse is one of lyricism punctuated by shifts in rhythm, or pauses in which the reader may ponder the connections between the lines of poetry.

"All Shall Be Restored" consists of twenty-one lines. Ryan does not incorporate the use of stanzas in this poem. Stanzas are groupings of lines in a poem that divide it into thematically related units in which the metrical structure and rhyme scheme of the poem are repeated. Without this structure, the lines of Ryan's poem are set apart from one another in terms of imagery and through the transitions between metered and unmetered phrases. The pauses typically inspired by stanzaic structure are incorporated to a lesser degree by these other elements. Additionally, the absence of stanzaic structure lends to the poem a sense of thematic unity. Each line of the poem builds on the lines that precede it and culminate in a rich and complex, but focused, theme (in this case, the restoration, or healing, of the natural world).

Internal Rhyme Scheme

In "All Shall Be Restored," Ryan does not employ end rhyme, that is, a rhyme scheme in which a pattern occurs in the rhyming of the final syllables of the lines of verse. Rather, Ryan uses rhymes or off rhymes within lines of verse. An off rhyme, or near rhyme, is one in which the words possess similar sounds but do not rhyme perfectly. For example, Ryan uses words such as "thousand" in

one line of "All Shall Be Restored" and "found" in the next, rhyming the vowel sound of the first syllable of thousand with the word found. Coupled in this way, the repetition of sound links the lines and underscores the thematic link created by the imagery in the lines. In this case, the images of the gathered grains from the various shores emphasize the notion of the reunification of something divided, an idea underscored by the connection of the lines through internal off rhyme, and an idea that is built upon as the poem progresses.

Lyric Poetry

A lyric poem is a brief work in which the poet expresses personal feelings or emotional responses to a situation or an event. As such an expression, a lyric poem is not the kind of poem that tells a story. A broad category of poetry, it encompasses poems of various structures, but it is characterized by its subjectivity. Ryan's work is often described as modern lyric poetry. In that "All Shall Be Restored" captures the author's response to an event she foresees in a brief, compact format, the work may accurately be labeled as modern lyric poetry.

HISTORICAL CONTEXT

New Formalist versus Free Verse Poetry

Modern poetry is characterized by two distinct trends, one toward traditional forms and structures, and one toward freedom from these strictures. New formalism is a school of thought born in the 1980s as a response to the prevalence and popularity of free verse poetry that had held sway for a good portion of the twentieth century. New formalism seeks to revive traditional verse forms that employ the consistent use of meter, rhyme scheme, and stanzaic structure. Although poets who adhered to such ideals wrote alongside free verse practitioners in the 1960s and 1970s, it was not until after free verse had really taken hold of modern poetry and was upheld as the standard for the expression of poetic truth that the new formalists rallied in defense of traditional form. Well-known formalists include Dana Gioia and Timothy Steele.

Free verse is a type of poetry in which the regular pattern of unaccented and accented syllables known as meter is eschewed, as are rhyme patterns and the use of stanzas to order a poem. While free verse poetry had existed as a technical category in American poetry since the early nineteenth century, in the 1960s and 1970s, this category transformed into a movement. Traditional forms were seen by free verse poets, such as Allen Ginsberg and William Carlos Williams, as inhibiting to poetic expression. Recent, well-known free verse poets include Alice Walker, Susan Hahn, and Robert Hass. Poets like Ryan seem to bridge a gap between these two schools of thought, as she incorporates elements of traditional structures, including meter and rhyme scheme, into poems that are expressionistic and otherwise lacking in formalist structures.

Modern Californian Poetry

While Ryan's poetry does not always deal with subject matter unique to California or its history, her work has been placed within the context of Californian poetry. Dana Gioia, in his introduction to the 2004 *California Poetry: From the Gold Rush to the Present*, which he edited with Chryss Yost and Jack Hicks, delineates characteristics of the "Californian literary sensibility." Gioia describes as influences the Mediterranean Catholic tradition and the proximity to both Mexico and Asia. Also explored are class and land-use issues and the differences between California and the rest of the American West. Social and religious diversity are key elements in defining California's unique literary history, Gioia maintains. The poetry of the region is not to be characterized solely by its free verse traditions nor by its "persistent reinventions of formalism." Within this discussion of California's free verse and formalist traditions, Gioia places Ryan, stating that her work "is distinguished mostly by its lack of similarity to any other current poetry in form or free verse."

Warfare in the 1990s

"All Shall Be Restored" does not directly discuss contemporary political issues, but in it the poet does explore the notion of the world's end, or, restoration to an original, idealized state. The United States, during the time period in which Ryan's poem about destruction and healing was written, became involved in violent international conflicts. In the 1990s, the United States was involved in two prominent wars, one in the Persian Gulf region, and one in Bosnia. In the first war, in August 1990, the United States intervened when Iraq invaded Kuwait, sending troops to protect Kuwait from an Iraqi takeover. By February 1991, Iraqi forces abandoned Kuwait, and a gradual withdrawal of U.S. troops began. In the mid-

In the poem, a bronze horse represents history.
(Image copyright Claudio Zaccherini, 2010. Used under license from Shutterstock.com)

1990s, the United States and NATO (the North Atlantic Treaty Organization) similarly intervened in another region, sending troops to help end a civil war devastating the former Yugoslavia. The conflict began following the dissolving of Yugoslavia. As the region was redivided, violence between Croatians, Serbians, and Bosnian Muslims intensified. In both the Persian Gulf and the Bosnian conflicts, numerous civilians, as well as soldiers on all sides, lost their lives. In the first decade of the twenty-first century, the Persian Gulf region remains in conflict, and tensions are again mounting in what is now Bosnia-Herzegovina.

CRITICAL OVERVIEW

Critical attention to Ryan's work was slow in coming. She built up a small following for her poetry as it began being accepted in literary journals. After the publication of two volumes of poetry, one which was self-published and one which was published by a small press, and neither of which received much attention, *Flamingo Watching* was published in 1994. The volume was well received and was followed two years later by *Elephant Rocks*, the volume that contains "All Shall Be Restored." Andrew Frisardi reviewed that volume in 1997 in *Poetry* magazine. Frisardi is among the first of Ryan's reviewers to compare her work to that of Emily Dickinson, a comparison that is now repeatedly made in response to the insightful brevity of Ryan's work. In describing the volume as a whole, Frisardi states: "So original, so astute, so pleasurable are the poems in this book, it wouldn't be at all surprising if they're still being read long after the current critical fashions are dated."

Former chairman of the National Endowment for the Arts, the poet Dana Gioia was one of Ryan's earliest supporters. In an article for the Winter 1998–1999 issue of the *Dark Horse*, a poetry journal, Gioia offers a lengthy, laudatory assessment of Ryan's work. He commends her language as reflective of "the shaping hand of a quick and skeptical intelligence," and describes Ryan as a poet who is "refined, disciplined, and original." Gioia states that "Like Dickinson, Ryan has found a way of exploring ideas without losing either the musical impulse or imaginative intensity necessary to lyric poetry." Also admiring the compact nature of Ryan's poems, Gioia observes that the effect of Ryan's ability to endow a short poem consisting of brief lines with so much meaning "is complex but never annoyingly cluttered or overly elaborate." In an introduction to Ryan's work in *California Poetry*, editors Gioia, Chryss Yost, and Jack Hicks maintain that Ryan's *Elephant Rocks*, along with her 2000 volume of verse *Say Uncle*, "have confirmed her position as one of the finest poets of her generation."

In another anthology, the 2005 *100 Essential Modern Poems*, editor Joseph Parisi introduces Ryan by stating that her "witty poems are bright distillations of her precise observations of the world and the vagaries of humankind." Parisi goes on to observe that "For her wry, idiosyncratic take on life and her use of compact, seemingly simple forms, Ryan is often compared with Emily Dickinson." The Dickinson comparison comes up again in a 2008 *American Scholar* essay on Ryan by Langdon Hammer, who states, "Critics compare her poems to those of Robert Frost and Emily Dickinson—Frost because of their moral seriousness and playful skepticism, and Dickinson because of their small-scale lyric intensity, the power the poems gain from compactness." Hammer goes on to explore Ryan's unique style and language, finding that her "language is plain but crowded with internal rhymes that create complex networks of sound, and the syntax is compressed, making those short lines extremely dense." Since Ryan's work began to be treated seriously by literary critics, it has been lauded for its ability to capture in compact language and efficient structure the weight of emotional and philosophical responses to the world.

CRITICISM

Catherine Dominic

Dominic is a novelist, freelance writer, and editor. In the following essay, she studies the language, imagery, and tone of Ryan's "All Shall Be Restored," demonstrating the ways in which the poem's uplifting title contrasts sharply with its apocalyptic content.

In Ryan's "All Shall Be Restored," the poet develops a sense of gravity and inevitability that belies the sense of hope that the poem's title implies. It is possible to view the process Ryan describes in the poem as a regenerative natural cycle, and Ryan's use of the term restoration suggests healing and a return to an ideal state. However, the process of restoration that Ryan outlines in the course of the poem is detailed as a series of destructive events, events that erase the course of the world's history. In language and rhythm, Ryan's poem is suggestive of biblical prophecy. The work is imbued with a sense of inevitability and tinged with a hint of horror at the fate of humanity. While the title of the poem and the repeated usage of the notion of restoration nudge the reader toward an interpretation of the poem that is positive and hopeful, the work also possesses apocalyptic overtones that cannot be ignored.

From the first line of "All Shall Be Restored," Ryan employs the language of biblical prophecy. (A prophecy is a prediction about the future.) Repeatedly, Ryan uses a future verb tense to convey what will happen in the future. Notably, Ryan does not use the verb "will," but rather, the more poetic, and more biblical, "shall." Immediately

WHAT DO I READ NEXT?

- Ryan's *The Best of It: New and Collected Poems*, published by Grove Press in 2010, provides a comprehensive retrospective of Ryan's highly praised poetry.

- Native American poet and writer N. Scott Momaday's *In the Bear's House*, published by St. Martin's in 1999, is a collection of art in literary and visual forms. Like Ryan, Momaday experiments with both free verse and formalist approaches to poetry. The poetry section of *In the Bear's House* includes works written in both free verse and formal styles, along with poetry composed as native chant.

- Morton D. Paley's *Apocalypse and Millennium in English Romantic Poetry*, published by Oxford University Press in 1999, explores the prominent themes of prophecy and apocalypse in the work of nineteenth-century romantic poets, such as Lord Byron, Percy Bysshe Shelley, and John Keats.

- In Errol E. Harris's book *Apocalypse and Paradigm: Science and Everyday Thinking*, published in 2000 by Praeger, Harris studies the way people think about the threats to the survival of the human race, such as global warming, and the social, ethical, and moral impact of scientific investigations of these problems on contemporary thought and action.

- One of the sustained images in "All Shall Be Restored," is of bronze statuary as an emblem of human creativity. Carol C. Mattusch in *Classical Bronzes: The Art and Craft of Greek and Roman Statuary*, published in 1996 by Cornell University, offers a detailed exploration of the early history of this art form.

- Jeanne DuPrau's young-adult novel *The City of Ember* is described as a post-apocalyptic novel geared toward a teen audience. Like Ryan's poem, it envisages the result (a new type of world) of a destructive process (an apocalyptic event). The work was adapted into a 2008 film as well. *The City of Ember* was published by Random House Books for Young readers in 2003.

---

she establishes a tone in which the reader is alert to the prognostication (prediction) being made and the seriousness with which the poet is making it. The rhythm and repetition Ryan uses in the poem's first eight lines, like her verb choice, invites comparison to the opening verses of the Bible. Ryan uses the word "and" to connect the various natural features that will return to an original state. The use of this list format with the word "and," along with the repetitive nature of this list making, brings to mind the biblical book of Genesis, in which the writer narrates the story of the creation of the world. Ryan's unmaking of the world is thus linked with a reference to its creation. As Genesis opens, the writer lists what God has created, employing the word "and" often in this inventory. For example, in Genesis 1:3, the writer states "And God said, Let there be light: and there was light." The words "and," "God,"

and "light" are repeated several times in subsequent passages. The writer of Genesis, in describing the process of creation, repeats details and the word "and," establishing patterns and rhythms that are carried through the rest of the chapter. Ryan similarly, in describing the process of restoration, repeats details and the word "and," constructing patterns and rhythms that inspire a comparison to the Bible. This comparison underscores the scope of the process that Ryan describes. The restoration of the world, as she envisions it, is actually its undoing. As a destructive process, Ryan suggests, it is as monumental as the creative process of forming the world. Whether or not that creation occurred through divine or natural means is beside the point Ryan is making; the grand scale of formation and destruction is the comparison to which Ryan's poetry points. What must be emphasized here is that

> WHILE THE TITLE OF THE POEM AND THE REPEATED USAGE OF THE NOTION OF RESTORATION NUDGE THE READER TOWARD AN INTERPRETATION OF THE POEM THAT IS POSITIVE AND HOPEFUL, THE WORK ALSO POSSESSES APOCALYPTIC OVERTONES THAT CANNOT BE IGNORED."

Ryan's vision is not one pertaining specifically to religion. The allusion to the tone and style of the book of Genesis serves as a means of underscoring the gravity of the situation. Ryan uses a general familiarity with the Bible, rather than specific references to details contained in it, in order to suggest to the reader the grand or epic nature of the process she is describing, and its inevitable outcome.

The discussion of the process of restoration through destruction that Ryan imagines moves from details concerned with the earth's natural, physical features to facets of the realm of human existence and endeavor. Ryan next considers the bronze horse sculpture, in lines 11–13. In exploring her prophecy regarding the restoration of the world, Ryan continues to employ the notions of undoing, of reversals. Just as in the first lines of the poem when the grains of sand are collected together, rejoining after being separated on various shores, the man-made bronze sculpture is likewise undone, melted, cast into more commonplace objects, and then transformed back further into its original state as a vein of metal in the earth. Through these images, Ryan traces details of human existence. She lists commonplace items—money and cookware—as well as weapons of war, as the uses to which bronze was put before being crafted into art, into a sculpture of a horse. In doing so, Ryan touches on many aspects of human existence, creating images in the reader's mind of what it means to be human. With a few well-chosen images, Ryan conveys a wealth of information about human activity on Earth. She captures familial and communal existence, commerce, and the inhuman way humankind behaves when engaged in warfare. Just as the reader begins to grapple the significance of these images, Ryan turns in the next lines to the ultimate reversal. She outlines the erasure of humanity from the world, and humanity's resistance to this undoing.

In the final five lines of the poem, Ryan describes the process by which evidence of creative endeavors will be obliterated. She utilizes again the image of the reversal of time, as she has done throughout in the poem in images of the grains of sand returning to one another, boulders returning to cliff faces, cliffs reforming an unbroken landscape, and metals foundering back into pure forms in the earth's crust. In this reversal, letters disappear from lines of texts from the end back to the beginning. If this process is imagined, the last letter to appear on the page of a book would be the first to disappear, and the first letter of the first word typed would be the last to be erased. This imagery summons to mind the familiar biblical text as expressed in Matthew 20:16, "So the last shall be first and the first last." While Ryan does not implicitly make this connection, the image of the text suggests it, and this imagery supports the weighty, apocalyptic tone that has been developed through the course of the short poem.

While the end of the penultimate line of the poem and the last line of the poem include the idea that nothing will, in the course of the process the poem describes, be lost, the sentiment is only affirming if taken out of the context of the final five lines of the poem. In these lines, Ryan describes the way in which the letters of written words shall be removed one by one, in reverse order, from the pages of texts. The imagery here suggests that ultimately the efforts of writers will be undone; their works will disappear. As this process continues, Ryan states, the line of text grows shorter and shorter, the message of literary artists disappearing but nonetheless insisting on its own permanence. Ryan's language in these lines points to the way this insistence appears distorted, even grotesque, as the erasure of literary history ensues. Marking the writer's efforts at immortality in this way, as a bizarre spectacle, Ryan signals to the reader the horrific nature of this loss. The position in the poem, as the last element Ryan explores, underscores the significance of the destruction of human creativity. The suggestion, perhaps, is that creative expression is what makes us human, and the loss of human artistic expression is all the more tragic. The resistance of humanity to this horrific erasure is all the more understandable. Ryan depicts the apocalypse—an end to the world as it is now

The poem describes a boulder being restored to its cliff. *(Image copyright slavapolo, 2010. Used under license from* *Shutterstock.com)*

known—as a process in which all that has been created through human agency, and all that has been formed in the natural world through the passage of time, is returned to an original state, is healed, is restored. The process is not described in violent terms, nor are the images Ryan uses graphic. Yet through subtle word choices, through language that evokes the notion of an event of biblical proportions, Ryan suggests both the panicked horror of humanity and the inevitability of the restoration, or destruction, of the world. When one considers the destructive process that Ryan outlines in "All Shall Be Restored," the hopeful, positive, uplifting slant of the title can only be taken ironically.

Source: Catherine Dominic, Critical Essay on "All Shall Be Restored," in *Poetry for Students*, Gale, Cengage Learning, 2011.

Grace Cavalieri

In the following excerpt, Cavalieri interviews Ryan about her poetry, awards, and life experiences.

This interview was recorded at The Library of Congress, September 2008, for distribution on public radio stations.

GRACE CAVALIERI: Kay Ryan will begin with an opening poem.

KAY RYAN: This is thinking about who my audience for poetry would be. "Ideal Audience":

Not scattered legions,
not a dozen from
a single region
for whom accent
matters, not a
seven-member coven,
not five shirttail
cousins; just
one free citizen—
maybe not alive
now even—who
will know with
exquisite gloom
that only we two
ever found this room.

GRACE: Everyone will want to know this one thing: What did you feel when you were called and asked to be the Poet Laureate?

KAY: I felt completely unequal to the task. I thought, no, never in a million years.

"

I THINK IT'S, IN A SENSE, LAUGHABLE TO SAY THAT ANY POETRY IS IMPERSONAL, BECAUSE THE MOTIVE IS TERRIBLY PERSONAL."

GRACE: What would "equal to the task" be?

KAY: Well, I have lived a life that hasn't, intentionally hasn't, required me to opine about poetry very much, or to represent poetry. I've found it comfortable to represent my own poetry. I feel confident talking about it and thinking about it, but I feel really shaky when I have to generalize beyond my own private, selfish, obsessive interests.

GRACE: Maybe being yourself was good enough.

KAY: Well, it got me here! We'll see how much farther it gets me.

GRACE: In the Niagara River poems, you do mention "limelight sunlight." And so the challenge will be how to manage that, won't it? How to bring sunlight to the limelight.

KAY: It's called "Lime Light," and I've found in my writing life, an interesting truth. And that is I have to write about things that are going to be really important to me later, far before they're really important. I have to write when I'm just starting to get an inkling of them. Like this whole business about worrying about being in the limelight; well, I wasn't in very darn much limelight when I wrote this.

GRACE: But you knew there was danger in this.

KAY: I knew there was danger in limelight. Here, I found it. Now, I want to tell you; we use that term lime light, and we all know it means being in the spotlight. But in fact, the term lime light comes from before there was electrical lighting in theaters, and they would have these cans of lime or something at the, what are they called, the footlights, you know, where the footlights would be. And so that would be lime light. But you could see it would mean, you're the person who's lit up. Being in the lime light is being lit up, and in an artificial way. It's not regular life.

GRACE: It was probably phosphorescence.

KAY: I bet it was very phosphorescent. And it was some kind of lime itself. Okay, so here's the little poem. "Lime Light":

One can't work
By lime light.

A bowlful
right at
one's elbow

produces no
more than
a baleful
glow against
the kitchen table.

The fruit purveyor's
whole unstable
pyramid
doesn't equal
what daylight did.

… GRACE: But, Kay, what we see is that, it is the balance in your work, that you are always finding through paradox. You get paradox, which results in balance. And that poem is a perfect example of finding balance indirectly. And look at the irony. Well, I'm going to just read you—rattle off a few things that are said about you, and you can raise your hand if you don't like them. They're just things I picked up, and I think they're right, for the most part: "Big little poems," "things are not what they seem, but the reverse," "succinct," "not personal," "the closer you look, the more you see," "hidden rhymes," "poems are magnifications," "tangible realities of intangible states of being," I made that up, I like that one.

Kay: That was my favorite so far.

GRACE: Oh! "Sly." I do not believe that, because "sly" to me is not totally honest, and your poems are entirely honest in thought, word and deed.

Kay: Well, you know, maybe when that writer used the word "sly," they wanted to say "oblique," you know, at an angle. We use "sly" and it has negative connotations, but it also means, "coming at something from a new angle."

GRACE: But "cunning" is not the same as "elucidating," and you don't do it just to trick us, and that's the whole point.

Kay: No, never! No, no, no. No, no.

GRACE: It's about intention.

Kay: No. To amuse. To briefly mislead, and then correct.

GRACE: You're intellectually mischievous.

Kay: Yes, I would say that I am mischievous.

GRACE: And so my two and a half cents says, you're always balancing the material and the non-material, and therefore, it really is always about relationships. Always. So it's always personal. It's always about you in relation to this space, or the periphery, or the edge.

KAY: Well, you know, I would utterly agree. I think it's, in a sense, laughable to say that any poetry is impersonal, because the motive is terribly personal. And if you wind up writing about a cup, there is some personal reason that you're writing about that, and some personal way that you're approaching its dimension, or color, or placement in the universe. We can't hide ourselves. That's the truth. No poetry, however apparently impersonal, allows us to hide. And if you have hidden, you've really failed. It means that you've been opaque. It means that you have perhaps written something that's already been written. Because, then your words would be hidden directly behind somebody else's words. They wouldn't exist independently. There's no hiding.

GRACE: There's nothing better within these marble halls, having poetry alive and throbbing, something unsure. I love that.

KAY: Well, you know what, I think I'll read—I just picked up another book; an earlier one—this is *Flamingo Watching*, and I think I'll read a poem called "This Life." It has some funny rhymes in. I used to think, when I was younger, that I, could maybe avoid trouble in life by making myself small. You know, I think a lot of people try to get little and get out of the path of bullets, and this is a poem that kind of thinks about that. "This Life."

It's a pickle, this life.
even shut down to a trickle
it carries every kind of particle
that causes strife on a grander scale:
to be miniature is to be swallowed
by a miniature whale. Zeno knew
the law that we know: no matter
how carefully diminished, a race
can only be half finished with success;
then comes the endless halving of the rest—
the ribbon's stalled approach, the helpless
red-faced urgings of the coach.

GRACE: What I like is, after you read, you literally frame the poem in silence. And there's a kind of a pulse beat which you add to the poem, which is a silence, and I'm going to remember that.

It adds to the aesthetic of the poem. (pause) You won the gold medal for poetry from the San Francisco Commonwealth Club, the Ruth Lilly Poetry Prize, a Guggenheim—that was the same year I think—an Ingram Merrill Award, a fellowship from NEA, the Union League Poetry Prize, the Maurice English Poetry Award, three Pushcarts, and your work has many times been selected for The Best American Poetry, *and it was in the major volume from '88 to '97. Also, you've been in the funnies. On subways, and in the* New Yorker. *So you've been around. But there's one thing I wonder if you know. There is a website that counts your words. It is hilarious. Did you see that? "The Poetry of Kay Ryan: Comments by J. Zimmerman," it's called. And it takes each one of your books, and has a chart, and it counts the number of sentences in a book, number of words, and then most frequently used words. Is that the oddest thing?*

KAY: There never seems to be a surface equal to the needs of these people. It's a kind of a mad, obsessed quality that one feels in looking at much outsider art. It isn't adjusted, you know. It isn't "wholesome" the way we think "Folk Art," you know; a nice quilt of the American Flag, or something. There's something urgent, and hungry, and restless in it, and savage in a way. And I thought, when I was writing this poem, that I really was talking about the kinds of images I'd seen in this book of "folk" art. But I eventually realized that the laugh was on me, because I was really talking about myself, too.

GRACE: Well, we don't want to lose that rawness. As much as we create the poem and burnish it, if there isn't that rawness underneath, forget it.

KAY: You are right. You are right.

GRACE: Paradox and argument, I mentioned before, and your poems are called little arguments. I was wondering about the dialectic in your head. How were you raised so that you questioned yourself? You questioned, and you turned the world on edge, and then you turned it upside down, and then you saw inside of it. That dialectic is a way of thinking. Where do you think you got that? You weren't raised in a monastery where you had to argue St. Thomas Aquinas. Where did that come from?

KAY: You know, that's a very good question. Nobody's even come close to asking me that before. And I really appreciate a good question, and a new question, because it requires new thinking. I imagine that I developed this kind of "but" response, you know, "but wait a minute," or "look at the other side," from being a reader. From the fact that most of the writing that I do is not directly in response to something that I've read, necessarily, although some poems have an epigraph. But that, it is through reading something difficult, something exciting, that my mind comes to some new little perception; some new little thing. So that I'm in conversation with what I read, what I have read. Lots of times in the morning, I read something really difficult, really thrillingly intellectual.

Source: Grace Cavalieri, "An Interview with Kay Ryan," in *American Poetry Review*, Vol. 38, No. 4, July/August 2009, pp. 43–47.

Langdon Hammer

In the following essay, Hammer explains how Ryan's poetry is a model of the experience or idea it investigates.

When she reads her poetry in public, Kay Ryan does something unusual: she reads poems, at least some poems, twice. Few poets write poems short enough to permit that repetition, or interesting enough to reward it, but Ryan's invite (and demand) rereading: they are that intricate and quick. They are built like jokes that create a pause after the punch line (wait, is that all there is?) before we start to laugh, ask to hear the joke again, and ask for another.

Critics compare her poems to those of Robert Frost and Emily Dickinson—Frost because of their moral seriousness and playful skepticism, and Dickinson because of their small-scale lyric intensity, the power the poems gain from compactness. They unfold as brief trials or "essays" (in the etymological sense of the word) in which the poet tests an idea, explores the implications of a pun or image, takes a figure of speech literally, or activates the figurative suggestions latent in a phrase we are used to taking literally, in order to see what knowledge that starting place—often declared in the title—might yield about the world and how we live in it.

Ryan's poems have a consistent look and feel. They tend to happen in the space of 20 lines or fewer, and those lines are very short, seldom more than three words per line, as if they had been composed in a tiny hand on the fortunes of Chinese fortune cookies or typed on strands of ribbon. Their language is plain but crowded with internal rhymes that create complex networks of sound, and the syntax is compressed, making

those short lines extremely dense. This combination of simplicity and complexity is part of the poetry's off-center, idiosyncratic approach to the commonplace. The mind at work in them is both familiar and eccentric. There is no 'I' in them—Ryan is concerned with what "we" do and how "we" think and speak, or what "you" see and feel. If her perspective is impersonal, it is also quirky and individual.

Ryan is a Californian. She grew up in small towns in the Mojave Desert and San Joaquin Valley, and she has taught basic English skills at the College of Marin since 1971. She makes a point, she says, of living "very quietly." Nonetheless, awards committees have sought her out (her body of work won the Poetry Foundation's Ruth Lilly Prize), and she is a chancellor of the American Academy of Poets. *The Niagara River*, her sixth and most recent book of poetry, was published in 2005.

Ryan's poems reflect back on their own activity in ways that make the poem itself a model of the experience or idea it investigates. Take "It Cannot Be Said for Certain." Here Ryan wonders whether the patterns we discover in experience are imposed ("self-flattering"). If not, then those patterns of meaningfulness are like a fork—an ordinary object, but a strange one to bring forward in a metaphysical argument like this one. How did she get there?

The poem's logic goes something like this. The frisson of recognition we feel when experience discloses a pattern gives us a "shiver." That word suggests to Ryan its neighbor "silver," which, put together with "shiver," neatly describes the kind of light spine tingle she means. These words together give concreteness to the feeling: it is almost something definite and objective. The feeling occurs periodically, regularly enough for the poet to hold it up as proof against the vacancy and randomness that she experiences when there is no "silver shiver" of coherence. Doing this mentally, she decides, is like holding up . . . a fork. What is a fork exactly? It consists of those tines and the spaces between them, those absences being "the necessary black." Even the random dark, Ryan reasons, is part of a necessary design.

Ryan develops this idea through a series of associations in which the sound of words is prominent. The key word "pattern" suggests "self-flattery" and "matter" (not true rhymes, but close); the "velvet dark" turns into the "silver shiver," and the "v" returns in "vacancies." As in other Ryan poems, sound seems essential to this poem's way of making meaning—while sound is also resistantly arbitrary here, not reducible to sense. But Ryan is redefining the random as necessary. Prepared by the end of the poem to trust not only the "silver shiver" of epiphany but also those gaps "between the tines," we can reread the poem, paying attention to the potential for meaning in seemingly random wordplay—and in everything else that happens between the lines.

Yes! We can bet that Ryan wants us to hear the cliche between (or behind) her final line, an old saw which she has ingenuously warped and sharpened, giving it back some bite. Every Ryan poem involves some pleasingly confounding confluence of sound and sense, thought and feeling, life and art. To get that silver feeling, we need to read between the tines.

Source: Langdon Hammer, "Confluences of Sound and Sense: Kay Ryan's Idiosyncratic Approach to the Commonplace," in *American Scholar*, Vol. 77, No. 3, Summer 2008, p. 58.

Craig Morgan Teicher

In the following review, Teicher traces Ryan's poetic career.

Kay Ryan's career as a poet began in 1976 on a "bikecentennial" ride from Oregon to Virginia. She'd taken time off from her job at the College of Marin (where she still teaches remedial English) to cycle across the country and also maybe figure out whether or not she really wanted to be a writer. Six books later, with last year's *The Niagara River* (Grove, 2005) capping off many honors including *Poetry* Magazine's $100,000 Ruth Lilly Prize and a Chancellorship from the Academy of American Poets, it seems that bike ride was a smart move.

DO YOU LIKE IT?

Ryan's interests always involved physical exertion; at 60, she's still an avid jogger and cyclist. "I had an image of myself that didn't go with 'poet' at all. I liked to think of myself in a pickup truck." The daughter of a ranch worker turned oil driller and a teacher from Nevada, Ryan grew up rough in the small towns of California's San Joaquin Valley, with its agriculture and oil economy. But she had an intellectual bent, and she was passionate about poetry. "I did want to be a writer", she says, "but I didn't want to expose the depths that you have to expose. I was the class clown and I wanted to stay a funny person."

Always, though, she was compelled to write. In her 20s, she sent an early manuscript of poems printed on "chunky brown kindergarten paper" to Dell, which was essentially a comic book publisher. She was doing everything wrong or, as she says, "trying to do it and not do it."

But, near her 30th birthday, poetry began to pull harder at her. "One night, I was reading a novel, and the prose started rhyming, and I thought, 'this is getting very strong.'" And then there was the epic bike ride with the seminal moment when it all became clear.

Pedaling up a steep pass in Colorado, Ryan had "almost the only metaphysical experience of my life." She felt incredible mental power, a sort of transcendent state of athlete's high: "I was permeable—everything could go through me and I could go through everything." This was the perfect time, she realized, to ask herself the life-defining question: should I be a writer?

The answer was: *Do you like it?*

And the answer to that was a resounding "yes."

Ryan had solved one of her life's major problems with that uphill climb. But, once the bike ride was over, she knew she had a lot more work to do.

ATHLETIC TRAINING

"I still didn't know how to write when I came home," Ryan remembers. "I was still writing funny, highly protected poems." Not knowing what else to do, she took another semester off from teaching and worked every day at transcribing the journal she had kept during her cross-country ride. "That gave me the habit of writing," she says. Like an athlete training every day to master a sport, Ryan was getting her writing muscles in shape, teaching herself how to dig deep and be vulnerable.

Next, she upped the ante, setting a daily ritual that taught her that she could write about a wide array of subjects: writing a poem in response to a randomly drawn card from a tarot deck. "Things came up like love, like death," subjects she would never have tackled before. This ritual "made me do things I didn't want to do."

From there, it was a matter of working like an athlete, sticking to her practice, heading up to her writing room and writing and revising poems. She believed that if she applied the same determination to her writing that had kept her in top physical shape, she would get where she wanted to go. And while she didn't start to publish poems in magazines until well into her 30s, and her first non-self-published book, *Strangely Marked Metal* (Copper Beach, 1985), wouldn't come out until she was 40, she was right.

A BATTERING RAM

Ryan lives in a small house in Fairfax, about 20 minutes north of San Francisco over the Golden Gate Bridge, a place she describes as "almost unbearably picturesque," with Carol, her partner of 27 years, to whom all of her books are dedicated, and their black cat Ubu.

The five-room house displays the same fastidiousness with which she has conducted her writing life. An orange tree leans over the garden fence, violets squeeze through the slats, and on the front stairs there's a blue, orange and white tile mosaic that Ryan made herself. Ryan writes in a loft over the living room. Mementos and gifts from friends are everywhere, including a battery-operated cardinal that chirps and bobs its head when anyone passes by. Ryan calls it "cute" and says it was a present from the poet Jane Hirshfeld, whom she calls "her only poet friend."

A small library crowds the bookshelf in Ryan's office. Volumes by the English poet Stevie Smith, the Romanian writer E.M. Cioran (given to her by Cioran translator and poet Richard Howard), Emily Dickinson and William Bronk stand beside collections of Krazy Kat comics. Stacked on the desk are poems in progress, written on pages torn from yellow legal pads. Ryan keeps all her drafts stapled together so she can see the progression. She writes complete drafts in one sitting, then revises again and again, describing her method as "using a battering ram to knock a little start of a hole, then using that distance to get a little further. I just keep going over those lines and making them find the next line."

Ryan's poems have always been short, usually no more than half a page of tiny, jagged lines. Her poetic voice crystallized while she was writing her second book, *Flamingo Watching* (Copper Beach, 1994). The speaker is detached—descending from those early, protected poems?—but mischievously wise, wanting to instruct and help, but also to get us a bit lost to see if we can find our way out. Ryan describes it as a voice "with a blade in it someplace."

Her writing is never overtly autobiographical, but it is rife with the kind of vulnerability that she worked so hard to coax out. "In art," she says, "experience goes through some kind of 'chillifier' that makes it touchable. Then it goes into us and we reheat it. It took me a long time to figure out how to cool it."

The Niagara River shows Ryan at the top of her form. With her trademark pith, tough love and humor, she treats subjects such as her ideal reader—"one free citizen— / maybe not alive / now even— who / will know with / exquisite gloom / that only we two / ever found this room."—the way we make the best of meager circumstances, and ominous last chances. "It's not that I really know those things, but if I'm going to go forward I must know them, briefly."

Source: Craig Morgan Teicher, "Pedaling up Parnassus," in *Publishers Weekly*, Vol. 253, No. 15, April 10, 2006, pp. 39–40.

Daniel McGuiness

In the following review of Elephant Rocks, *McGuiness describes Ryan's style of poetry as "far out."*

"Poetry is like a strong explosion in the sky. She makes a mushroom shape of terror and drops to the ground with a strong infection. Also she is a strong way out. The human creature is alone in his carapace. Poetry is a strong way out. The passage out that she blasts is often in splinters covered with blood; but she can come out softly."—Stevie Smith.

Ryan's poems have been far out all her life, and not feeling but thinking. This, her third book, is of a piece with her others: miniature five-paragraph essays, something like those little books the Brontës wrote for their dolls. They're epigrams or digestifs or, better, aphorisms if we remember the source of such things: Hippocrates making little pills of pithiness, haiku with punch lines, prescriptions not meant for the pharmacist.

Here's "Apogee"; "At high speeds / we know / when an orbit / starts to go / backwards: / on fair rides / like the Hammer / or in airplane disasters, / our brains are / plastered to / one wall of the skull / or another; / we comprehend reverse / through the / sudden compression / of matter. // In a way it's worse / when the turn's wider—/ say a boat on a soft tide / in mild water—/ we hardly knew / that we were floating out. / The sense of turning back / seems like our fault."

If John Skelton had been Emily Dickinson's tutor instead of Jane Scrope's, these poems would not surprise us. But they do. And their miniaturized size fits a recent trend in *New Yorker* poems: Virginia Hamilton Adair Sapphire. What's the deal, you ask? I was told once of another's shock years ago at discovering that the *Saturday Review* filed its accepted poems by line length, to use to fill the holes when layout was complete. It's all proverbial, of course. It always is.

Source: Daniel McGuiness, Review of *Elephant Rocks*, in *Antioch Review*, Vol. 54, No. 4, Autumn 1996, pp. 486–97.

SOURCES

Atkinson, Rick, "Chronology," in *Crusade: The Untold Story of the Persian Gulf War*, Houghton Mifflin, 1993, pp. 509–12.

Beyers, Chris, Introduction to *A History of Free Verse*, University of Arkansas Press, 2001, pp. 1–12.

"A Brief Guide to New Formalism," in *Poets.org: From The American Academy of American Poets*, http://www.poets.org/viewmedia.php/prmMID/5667 (accessed January 9, 2010).

Cohen, Patricia, "Kay Ryan, Outsider with Sly Style, Named Poet Laureate," in *New York Times*, July 17, 2008, http://www.nytimes.com/2008/07/17/books/17poet.html?_r=1&scp=2&sq=kay%20ryan&st=cse (accessed January 9, 2010).

Frisardi, Andrew, Review of *Elephant Rocks*, in *Poetry*, Vol. 170, No. 2, May 1997, pp. 101–104.

"Genesis," and "Matthew," in *The Bible: The Authorized King James Version*, edited by Robert Carroll and Stephen Prickett, Oxford University Press, 1997, *The Books of the Old Testament*, pp. 1–64, and *The Books of the New Testament*, pp. 3–43.

Gioia, Dana, "Discovering Kay Ryan," in *Dark Horse*, No. 7, Winter 1998–1999, pp. 6–9.

———, Introduction to *California Poetry: From the Gold Rush to the Present*, edited by Dana Gioia, Chryss Yost, and Jack Hicks, Heydey Books, 2004, pp. xix–xxix.

———, Chryss Yost, and Jack Hicks, eds., "Kay Ryan," in *California Poetry: From the Gold Rush to the Present*, Heydey Books, 2004, pp. 258–61.

Halstead, Richard, "Kay Ryan Rises to the Top Despite Her Refusal to Compromise," in *Marin Independent Journal*, September 23, 2007, http://www.marinij.com/ci_6975060 (accessed January 9, 2010).

Hammer, Langdon, "Confluences of Sound and Sense: Kay Ryan's Idiosyncratic Approach to the Commonplace," in *American Scholar*, Vol. 77, No. 3, Summer 2008, pp. 58–60.

Holden, Jonathan, "American Poetry: 1970–1990," in *A Profile of Twentieth-Century American Poetry*, edited by

Jack Elliott Myers and David Wojahn, Southern Illinois University, 1991, pp. 254–76.

Lake, Paul, "Kay Ryan," in *Dictionary of Literary Biography*, Vol. 282, *New Formalist Poets*, edited by Jonathan N. Barron, Thomson Gale, 2003, pp. 258–64.

"Librarian of Congress Appoints Kay Ryan Poet Laureate," in *News from the Library of Congress*, July 17, 2008, http://www.loc.gov/today/pr/2008/08-127.html (accessed January 9, 2010).

"Library of Congress Appoints Kay Ryan to Second Term as U.S. Poet Laureate," in *News from the Library of Congress*, April 13, 2009, http://www.loc.gov/today/pr/2009/09-073.html (accessed January 9, 2010).

Parisi, Joseph, ed., "Kay Ryan," in *100 Essential Modern Poems*, Ivan R. Dee, 2005, pp. 263–65.

Ryan, Kay, "All Shall Be Restored," in *Elephant Rocks*, Grove Press, 1996, pp. 12–13.

Von Hallberg, Robert, "Politics," "Rear Guards," and "Authenticity," in *The Cambridge History of American Literature*, Vol. 8, *Poetry and Criticism, 1940–1995*, edited by Sacvan Bercovitch and Cyrus R. K. Patell, Cambridge University Press, 1996, pp. 23–55, 56–82, and 123–59.

Wells, Bonnie, "Singing the World Poetic: Da Camera Marks Milestones with World Premiere by Local Composer," in *Amherst Bulletin*, January 23, 2009, http://www.amherstbulletin.com/story/id/126175/ (accessed January 9, 2010).

Whitlock, Craig, "Old Troubles Threaten Again in Bosnia," in *Washington Post*, August 23, 2009, http://www.washingtonpost.com/wp-dyn/content/story/2009/08/22/ST2009082202479.html?sid=ST2009082202479 (accessed January 9, 2010).

FURTHER READING

Erkkila, Betsy, *The Wicked Sisters: Women Poets, Literary History, and Discord*, Oxford University Press, 1992.

Erkkila examines the lives and poetical works of five prominent female poets throughout history: Emily Dickinson, Marianne Moore, Elizabeth Bishop, Adrienne Rich, and Gwendolyn Brooks. Erkkila's study, which is informed by the unique challenges faced by women writers, and by feminists, investigates the power struggles, political conflicts, and general discord historically present within the community of women poets.

Matterson, Stephen, and Darryl Jones, *Studying Poetry*, Hodder Arnold, 2000.

Matterson and Jones offer students a path toward understanding poetry, focusing on technical aspects such as form, structure, symbolism, and rhyme schemes, as well as the way these elements contribute to the poem's meaning.

Additionally, the authors examine the relationship between poetry and literary theory, and they also discuss various types of poetry, such as political poetry.

Redfern, Ron, *Origins: The Evolution of Continents, Oceans and Life*, University of Oklahoma Press, 2001.
Redfern explores the geographic history and evolution of the planet, placing human life within the context of the ever-changing physical world. The work is relevant for students of Ryan's "All Shall Be Restored" in its exploration of the processes Ryan's poem depicts.

Ryan, Kay, "Laugh While You Can: A Consideration of Poetry," in *Poetry*, Vol. 188, No. 2, May 2006, pp. 148–59.
Ryan discusses her philosophy concerning the purpose of poetry and delineates the elements necessary for a poem to be suffused with energy and meaning and to be regarded as a success in terms of the reader's interaction with and appreciation of the poem.

Webb, Jack, ed., *The Best of Border Voices: Poet Laureates, Pulitzer-Prize Winners & the Wisdom of Kids*, Level 4 Press, 2007.

Webb's collection gathers together poetry from fourteen years of the San Diego Border Voices Poetry Festival. The work features poetry from prominent contemporary poets and poet laureates, as well as work by students and teachers. Biographical notes are included for the major poets.

SUGGESTED SEARCH TERMS

Elephant Rocks AND Ryan

All Shall Be Restored AND Ryan

Kay Ryan

Kay Ryan AND free verse

Kay Ryan AND poet laureate

Kay Ryan AND new formalism

Kay Ryan AND Californian poetry

Kay Ryan AND Emily Dickinson

Birdfoot's Grampa

JOSEPH BRUCHAC
1978

Joseph Bruchac first published "Birdfoot's Grampa" in 1978 in the collection *Entering Onandaga*, published by Cold Mountain Press. It is currently available in the collection *Translator's Son*, published by Cross-Cultural Communications in 1994.

In a 1996 interview with Meredith Ricker published by the *Society for the Study of the Multi-Ethnic Literature of the United States (MELUS)*, Bruchac stated that the poem came out of his experience traveling with an elderly Pueblo Apache storyteller named Swift Eagle. "One night we were late for a storytelling program I was supposed to give and Swifty kept making me stop so he could pick up...toads." Bruchac said the old man's insistence on saving them, described in the poem, was like a lightbulb going off: "The poem really is about being stupid and having your eyes opened by an elder."

Bruchac's life work has been bringing Native American stories and wisdom to as many audiences as possible. His vibrant oral storytelling has made him a popular speaker in schools, and the many children's books he has published have made him a familiar figure to many young people. Of mixed Abenaki and Slovakian heritage, Bruchac prefers the French-Canadian term for mixed-blood peoples, *metis*, because as he explains in his essay "Translator's Son," *metis* "means that you are able to understand the language of both sides, to help them understand

Joseph Bruchac *(Photograph by Michael Greenlar. Reproduced by permission of Joseph Bruchac.)*

each other." This process of cross-cultural translation has been Bruchac's life work, and he has taken it to schoolchildren, prisoners, college students, and audiences all over North America.

AUTHOR BIOGRAPHY

Bruchac was born on October 16, 1942, in Saratoga Springs, New York. At a young age he went to live with his maternal grandparents, Jesse and Marion Dunham Bowman. They had a little general store where Bruchac helped out. His grandmother had a law degree from the Albany Law School, and although she never practiced law, she made sure the house was full of books. His grandfather, who was of Abenaki descent, could hardly read or write, but was, Bruchac wrote in a biographical piece for *Scholastic.com*, "one of the kindest people I ever knew. I followed him everywhere. He showed me how to walk quietly in the woods and how to fish." However, as Bruchac recalls in a profile in *Publishers Weekly*, his grandfather

was "visibly Indian but wouldn't talk about it" because prejudice was still very strong in that part of the country against Native peoples.

In the same profile in *Publishers Weekly*, Bruchac says that although he originally wanted to be "a park ranger, or one of those interpretive naturalists who goes and gives tours in national parks" he found himself becoming more and more interested in writing. He attended Cornell University in Ithaca, New York, and then completed a master's degree in creative writing at Syracuse University. Inspired in part by his grandfather's heritage and his reluctance to discuss that heritage, Bruchac found himself delving deeper and deeper into Native American literature and folklore.

After graduating from Syracuse, Bruchac and his wife Carol went to Africa, where they spent three years teaching in a secondary school in Ghana. It was an experience that left him convinced, as he told Meredith Ricker at *MELUS*, that there is a "quality of sweetness and gentleness both in Native American communities and in native communities in Africa." His experience in Africa later influenced Bruchac's work in the prisons in New York, where he applied Native American ideas about storytelling as a means to connect prisoners back with their own communities and their own stories. When they returned from Africa, Bruchac and his wife moved back in with his grandfather, and he taught for four years at Skidmore College, where he founded the prison program at Great Meadow Correctional facility.

Bruchac published his first book of poetry, *Indian Mountain and Other Poems,* in 1971, and in 1976 he published his first book for children, *Turkey Brother and Other Iroquois Stories.* Since then, he has published more than seventy works of poetry, fiction, nonfiction, and picture books. He has won the American Book Award, the Cherokee Nation Prose Award, the *Scientific American* Award for Young Readers, the Hope S. Dean Award for Notable Achievement in Children's Literature, the Writer of the Year Award from the Native Writers Circle of the Americas, the Paterson Award, and the Knickerbocker Award. He and Carol founded and run the Greenfield Review Press. Bruchac travels extensively, performing as a storyteller and working with schoolchildren across North America.

POEM TEXT

The old man
must have stopped our car
two dozen times to climb out
and gather into his hands
the small toads blinded   5
by our lights and leaping,
live drops of rain.

The rain was falling,
a mist about his white hair
and I kept saying   10
you can't save them all,
accept it, get back in
we've got places to go.

But, leathery hands full
of wet brown life,   15
knee deep in the summer
roadside grass,
he just smiled and said
they have places to go to
too.   20

POEM SUMMARY

Stanza 1, Lines 1–7

The first stanza of this narrative poem introduces two characters, the old man and the narrator; places them in a setting (a car driving on a dark road at night through a rural area); and introduces a conflict. The narrator is not specifically identified but may for convenience be identified with the poet himself and therefore referred to as "he" rather than "she." Similarly, since the other person is called "old," readers may understand that the narrator is considerably younger. The narrator grows impatient with the frequency with which the old man stops the car in order to rescue toads blinded by the headlights of the car. To the narrator, the toads are an inconvenience. They are both too numerous and too tiny to bother with. To the old man, though, the toads are a part of nature, like the raindrops that have called them up out of the woods. The narrator is metaphorically aligned with the vehicle: he wants to get to their destination even if the car in which they travel, with its blinding lights, will crush the toads. Toads swarm just after the tadpoles grow limbs, so the confrontation in this stanza is between many tiny, vulnerable creatures that have just emerged from infancy and the brute force of mechanized human civilization. By stopping over and over, the old man insists that it does not matter that the toads are so tiny and

MEDIA ADAPTATIONS

- Many of Bruchac's children's books are available as audiocassettes or audio downloads.

numerous that it is impossible to save them all; there is merit in trying.

Stanza 2, Lines 8–13

In the second stanza, the narrator remains inside the car, observing the old man outside in the rain. The old man's white hair, like the mist, is illuminated in the headlights. Because of his position, the narrator is metaphorically aligned with the automobile, with the forces of modern life, with machines. The narrator argues for expedience (practicality); impatient with the many stops, he tells the old man they do not have time, they have to get to their destination. The narrator represents the voice of human progress, willing to sacrifice nature when it is inconvenient. He tells the old man that it is impossible to save all the toads. The narrator values progress; he wants to reach their destination, despite the fact that in order to do so in a timely manner he must sacrifice the lives of the vulnerable toads that have just emerged into the world from infancy. He is impatient with the old man and with the forces of nature that stand between himself and his destination.

Stanza 3, Lines 14–20

The old man, however, is not agitated by the narrator's urgency. In this final stanza, the adjectives used to describe the old man indicate that unlike the narrator, whose position inside the car allies him metaphorically with the forces of mechanized civilization, the old man is allied with nature. He is compared to natural substances such as leather and is portrayed standing up to his knees in the long grass. He represents the opposite forces, the forces of a nature wild enough to send toads out in swarms in order to ensure that some of them will survive. It is only when the narrator really looks at the old man, when he sees him knee-deep in nature, that he can hear the old man's message: the toads' lives are as valid as those of the human beings. Smiling, the old man reminds the impatient narrator that the toads' journey is as important to them as the men's journey is to them. Until the moment when the old man speaks, the narrator has been metaphorically stuck inside the car—stuck in a mindset that says it is natural for human beings to dominate nature, in the same way that the car dominates the night, with its dangerous headlights and great speed. Even the existence of the road, built specifically for cars, seems to indicate that it is normal for human beings to disregard the world outside their machines when that world is inconvenient to them. From his position outside the car, knee-deep in nature, the old man gently reminds the narrator that the toads have a destination also. This reminder causes the narrator to realize that his impatience and his reliance on the machinery of modern life are dividing him from the natural world.

THEMES

Nature

The question of the proper relationship of human beings to nature is at the core of "Birdfoot's Grampa." The poem is narrated by a speaker who is separated from nature. He observes the nighttime and the rain from inside an automobile. Meanwhile, the old man with whom he travels keeps impeding their progress by insisting that they stop the car so he can go out into the rain to move swarms of toads off the road. The narrator is metaphorically allied with the automobile because he remains inside it. There is perhaps no more powerful metaphor for the contradictions of modern technology than the automobile. It has been a force for mobility, allowing people to travel farther and faster than was previously possible, and yet it has also been an incredibly destructive force against the natural world. Automobiles pollute, they necessitate the paving of roads through natural areas, and of course, they cause the deaths of countless animals that are hit and killed by cars. The narrator of the poem is anxious to reach his destination, and yet he is mindful of the old man, who insists that they stop and do what they can to mitigate the destructive power of human technology. The old man is not hiding from the forces of nature,

as the narrator does. He gets out of the car and into nature. His hair, like the mist of rain, is white in the headlights, and his hands are described as resembling hide. Finally, it is the sight of the old man, fully immersed in nature, up to his knees in the long grass, along with the old man's gentle admonishment that the toads have as much right to their journey as the people do, that wakes the narrator from his technology-induced blindness and allows him to see the importance of the natural world around him. The toads are tiny and vulnerable emblems of the natural world, so tiny and so vulnerable that one is tempted to believe that it is impossible to save them all, but they have as much right to live and to travel as the human beings do. The natural world is not something out there over which humans have dominion, but is a community of which humans are a part.

Native American Literature

Bruchac is a major figure in what has come to be known as the Native American renaissance, a surge in literature by Native American writers that has taken place since the early 1970s. One of the key factors of this movement has been that these writers are not only of Native American descent but are writing Native American worldviews, beliefs, and myths into the larger body of American literature. Some of the characteristics of a Native American approach to poetry include the mixing of genres, reference to Native American myths and song forms, use of intensely visual imagery, and a concern with the relationship of human beings to the natural world. Bruchac is known as a poet of narrative directness. Many of his poems, like "Birdfoot's Grampa," sound like a person telling a story or relating an incident that has happened, and often the narrator learns a lesson over the course of the poem. In "Birdfoot's Grampa," the narrator addresses the audience in a conversational tone. When he tells the audience in lines 2 and 3 how many times they stopped, the tone is one of someone telling an anecdote to a friend. This mixing of genres, combining the elements of poetry, storytelling, and fable, is typical of Native American poetry as it has been written in the last several decades. However, it is in the poem's concern with the proper relationship of human beings to the natural world that the poem embodies one of the central characteristics of Native American poetry. The central concern in the poem is a restoration of balance in the relationship of human beings to the natural world. In the

TOPICS FOR FURTHER STUDY

- Select another poem by a Native American poet and write an essay in which you compare and contrast it in terms of style and theme with "Birdfoot's Grampa." Possible poems for comparison include "Grandfather at the Indian Health Clinic" by Elizabeth Cook-Lynn, "Pow-wow Polaroid" by Sherman Alexie, "Travels in the South" by Simon Ortiz, or another poem of your choice.

- When Bruchac does storytelling workshops, he often asks students whether there is a story that one of their elders tells them over and over again. The reason the old people keep retelling the story, he tells students, is that it is important to them, There is a lesson they are trying to teach. Make a video of an older relative telling you a family story. Then do a video interview with your relative about why that story is important. Why does your relative love that story? What is important about it? What lesson does he or she want to teach with the story? Edit the videos into a presentation for your class.

- Teenagers often feel alienated from the cultures of their families as they come to adulthood. Compare the alienation experienced by the protagonists in *Parrot in the Oven: Mi Vida* by Victor Martinez, *The Absolutely True Diary of a Part-Time Indian* by Sherman Alexie, and *American Born Chinese* by Gene Luen Yang. Write a paper explaining what is similar and what is different about the experiences of these three characters.

- Research the Native American history of your area. Find out about the history and traditions of the Native Americans who inhabited your geographic location and visit a historical site. Make a PowerPoint presentation, complete with maps, historical illustrations, and photographs of the historical site, that explains the history of the Native Americans of your area.

- Research the natural history of your area and write a poem in which a person has an encounter with an animal or other representative of the natural world. The poem can be narrative (story) or lyric (expressing feelings directly), but it must be at least fourteen lines long. Over the course of the poem, the protagonist or narrator must experience some kind of realization.

- Find a traditional Native American story, preferably one from your geographic area. With a small group of your classmates, write a dramatic adaptation of that story, assign roles to everyone in the group, and act it out for your class. Since most Native American stories are intended to teach a lesson, make sure that your drama contains a recognizable lesson for your classmates.

- Interview your parents and grandparents about your own ethnic background and the roles that stories, poetry, or music play in those cultures. Research the place of the oral tradition in your ethnic background and build a Web site with elements that include video interviews with your family, visual representations of the story, recordings of traditional performers, and links to research about ethnic organizations working to keep those traditions alive.

- Many families have traditional dishes or ways of preparing food that have been passed down from one generation to the next. Interview your parents, grandparents, aunts, or uncles and ask them to tell you about a family dish. Ask them to teach you how to cook their favorite family dish. Write a recipe for it, complete with ingredients, measurements, and instructions. Pretend you are producing a cooking show, and create a video presentation that explains the origins of this recipe and that can be used to teach someone else how to make it.

The poem is set in a car driving through rain. (*Image copyright Dgrilla, 2010. Used under license from Shutterstock.com*)

beginning of the poem, the narrator views the tiny, numerous, and vulnerable toads as merely an inconvenience. There are too many of them to save, and he has places to go. He is in a hurry, and he is closely identified with the automobile, a symbol of the technological worldview that values human life over the lives of natural creatures. However, through the lessons of an elder—another important part of Native American literature—the narrator comes to see the error of his ways and is restored to a more balanced relationship with the natural world. Balance, and the restoration of balance, is often a central concern of Native American literature, and the addition of this worldview has been an important contribution to American literature as a whole.

Storytelling

Although narrative poetry has a long history, beginning with ancient epic poems (long poems telling a story of legends or heroes), Native American poets such as Bruchac tend to call on the voice of the storyteller to animate much of their work. In Native American culture—especially as Bruchac has tried to document it,

not only in poetry, but also in fiction and children's literature—the voice of the elder is deeply important. It is the elders who teach the younger members of the community how to live in proper relationship not only with the natural world, but also with one another. In "Birdfoot's Grampa," Bruchac presents a community of two human beings, an elder and a younger man, who are in a car on a journey. The younger man is impatient; he is focused on the destination rather than the journey. The older man ignores the impatience of the younger, insisting that they must stop as many times as necessary to help the vulnerable toads across the road. Over the course of the poem, the old man teaches the younger one by his actions what his proper relationship to the natural world should be. In turn, the narrator addresses the audience in order to pass the lesson along to the larger world. Although the poem is narrative in nature, it is not a story but a poem, and it uses poetic forms to help create meaning. In particular, poems can use line breaks to draw attention to what is important. Line breaks in this poem tend to occur both outside the automobile and after gerunds (-*ing* verbs) that draw attention to the actions of both the old man and the toads out in the natural world. All the action in this poem happens outside the car. The outside world is characterized by images that could be considered alien or hostile: rain, a plague of toads, nighttime. However, because the old man is consistently portrayed as not only comfortable, but happy outside in the nighttime rain with the toads, we come to see that it is that outdoor world of nature, not the protected indoor world of the technological automobile, that is the true home for these characters. Bruchac skillfully uses both the techniques of poetry and the direct address of narrative in order to teach a lesson about the proper relationship between human beings and the natural world.

STYLE

Imagery

One of the hallmarks of Native American poetry is its use of concrete visual imagery, especially images of the natural world, to guide the reader's attention to what is important. Although the narrator of the poem is positioned inside the car, the car itself is hardly described. The poet mentions is that it is a car, that it has headlights that both blind the toads and illuminate the old man's white hair, and that while the old man keeps getting in and out, the narrator remains inside, impatient to continue the journey. On the other hand, the imagery of the natural world is very concrete and specific, which indicates that this is where the poet wants to draw our attention. The poem describes a rainy night, when headlights blind small animals, an occurrence that readers might take for granted. The road is covered with very small toads, for a long enough distance that the narrator is forced to stop over and over again. The toads are as numerous as the raindrops; they are compared to life itself, and in their smallness and wetness they are very vulnerable. The contrast between the image of a tiny toad, just past the transition from tadpole, and the tires of a speeding automobile could not be starker. While saving the toads, the old man appears to the narrator to be up to his knees in the very essence of nature itself. The specificity of the images of the natural world compared to the lack of specificity of images of the car is a clear indication of where the poet wants the audience to direct its attention. Just as the old man draws the narrator's attention to the importance and vulnerability of the natural world, so too does Bruchac draw the audience's attention to the same thing.

Didactic Poetry

A didactic poem is one in which the author wants to impart a lesson to the audience. With the romantic and aesthetic movements of the nineteenth century, which declared that the most important purpose of poetry was to create an elevated emotional state or to illuminate a particular aspect of beauty, didacticism fell out of favor. However, to Native American poets like Bruchac, who view the sharp separation of genres as an artificial construct alien to their culture, the use of poetry as a teaching tool is a natural extension of the Native American oral tradition. In an interview with Meredith Ricker published in *MELUS*, Bruchac noted that "Birdfoot's Grampa" is a poem "about learning from your own mistakes." In Native American traditions, stories are the means by which elders teach younger people how to live in correct relationships, and in the same *MELUS* interview, Bruchac explains that the incident he describes in "Birdfoot's Grampa" is one that he experienced. What he wanted to describe was the lesson that he learned that night, from an older Pueblo storyteller named Swift Eagle. One reason that poets, beginning with the romantics in the early nineteenth century, rebelled against didactic poetry was because it was so lacking in humor; it forced poetry to serve the lesson rather than living up to its true potential. In the Native American tradition, stories that contain a message are often told by self-deprecating (modest or self-criticizing) narrators, like the one in "Birdfoot's Grampa." Although Bruchac is open about his desire to use his writing to teach his readers something, he is also clear that it is crucial not to alienate his audience while doing so. Humor, especially the sort of self-deprecating humor that illustrates a moment of enlightenment, is a hallmark of Native American literature and a crucial tool for imparting a message without alienating the audience.

Metaphor

Metaphor is a figure of speech by which one thing, idea, or action is referred to by a word or expression that normally denotes something else in order to suggest some common quality shared by the two. Although Bruchac is known for the direct narrative style that he uses in "Birdfoot's Grampa," he not only uses several direct metaphors in the poem but also builds an implied metaphor. Direct metaphors that occur in the poem include the statement that the toads are living drops of rain. If this was a simile, he would have said that the toads were *like* drops of rain, but instead, by asserting that they *are* live drops of rain, he is making a comparison between the number and density of the toads on the road and the rain falling in the night. Just as one cannot count the number of raindrops, it is impossible to count the number of small toads on the highway. The metaphor also draws a parallel between two natural events: the rain and the swarms of toads that sometimes occur in early summer when the tadpoles emerge from the wetlands. Another direct metaphor is the description of the old man whose hands are actually full of toads, but who is described as holding life itself in his cupped hands. With this metaphor, Bruchac makes clear what is at stake in this poem. It is not simply the lives of a few small toads, it is life itself, the life of the natural world. Not all metaphors need to be direct; poems can also create an indirect metaphor. Bruchac does this by juxtaposing the automobile and the toads. On the one hand, there is the automobile, a symbol of the technological world of human beings, a world that subordinates the individual to the collective in much the same way that each individual worker on the assembly line that built the car is subordinated to the larger product that is the car itself. The car travels along a road, a straight line between two points, and the poem's narrator is so focused on the destination that he is willing to sacrifice the lives of the toads to reach this linear goal. Western European history and culture considers time to be linear, to proceed in a straight line until it reaches a goal, while Native American history and culture considers time to be circular, in much the same way that the seasons are circular, repeating themselves year after year. Hence we have an extended metaphor at work; the Native American driver of the Western automobile must be reminded by the old man that it is not the destination but the journey that is important. He must be reminded that the respect for life at the heart of Native American tradition must be honored, even if it is inconvenient.

HISTORICAL CONTEXT

As the mixed-blood critic and novelist Louis Owens notes in *Other Destinies: Understanding the American Indian Novel*, before 1968 only nine novels written by Native American writers had been published; however, since the late 1960s and early 1970s, Native American writers have, if not flourished, at least managed to secure themselves a position among the many voices that make up multicultural American literature. This is due in part to the manner in which in public interest about Native Americans grew during the early 1970s. As Donald Parman notes in an article published in the *Organization of American Historians Magazine of History*, during the turbulent era that encompassed the Vietnam War, the civil rights movement, and the beginnings of the environmental movement, "many Americans turned to Indian life as an attractive alternative." Native American ideas such as the circularity of time and history, the importance of living in harmony with the earth rather than dominating it, and the communal nature of Native American societies all sparked the imaginations of many Americans seeking either a return to a more traditional and pastoral time or a new age of spiritual harmony.

It was during this time period that the first Native American studies programs were formed. The first one was at San Francisco State University in 1968, followed shortly by the establishment of programs at the University of California at Berkeley, the University of California at Los Angeles, and Dartmouth University. By the year 2000, there were 112 Native American studies programs in the United States and Canada. Many Native American studies programs were designed not only to study Native Americans but to foster the success of Native American students in the universities. Some Native American writers, such as the novelist Louise Erdrich, who was one of the first students in the Dartmouth College program, gravitated toward these programs, while others, such as Louis Owens, felt that it was only by doing their degree work on established American writers, in his case, John Steinbeck, that they could prove that they were as qualified as their non-Native American classmates.

The general surge of interest in Native Americans and their points of view, however, did encourage many new writers. Poets such as

COMPARE
&
CONTRAST

- **1970s:** After occupying a series of sites (including Alcatraz Island, the headquarters of the Bureau of Indian Affairs in Washington, D.C., and Mount Rushmore), the American Indian Movement (AIM) protests the light sentence given two white men for killing an Indian on the Sioux reservation by occupying the small town of Wounded Knee, South Dakota, in early 1973. Wounded Knee was the site of a massacre in 1873, when troops led by General Nelson Miles killed 146 men, women, and children. The 1973 standoff lasts for 71 days, during which two AIM members are killed and one federal marshal is wounded by gunfire. On May 5, 1973, a negotiated settlement is reached, and the standoff ends. By the end of the 1970s, AIM's popularity fades as its militant tactics become controversial, and its leaders are imprisoned. However, it remains a powerful source of pan-Indian pride and unity long after its immediate political power wanes.

  Today: Although AIM is a smaller organization than it once was, it remains active in the International Indian Treaty Council, the National Coalition on Racism in Sports and Media, the American Indian Opportunities Industrialization Center, and the ongoing fight to free their imprisoned leader Leonard Peltier.

- **1970s:** The American Indian Religious Freedom Act is passed. This federal law states that the U.S. government must take Native American religious practices into account when making land and policy decisions.

  Today: Although the American Indian Religious Freedom Act faces serious challenges, overall it contributes to gains for Native Americans, including the 1996 Executive Order recognizing Sacred Sites and the 2000 Religious Land Use and Prison Act, which adds further protections for sacred lands while also granting legitimacy to Native American spiritual practices for federal prisoners.

- **1970s:** N. Scott Momaday's Pulitzer Prize for *House of Dawn* ushers in a new era of Native American publishing for writers of all genres. The 1970s see the emergence of writers such as Joy Harjo, Linda Hogan, Simon Ortiz, Gerald Vizenor, Joseph Bruchac, and Luci Tapahonso.

  Today: Native American studies programs become mainstream in many colleges and universities, providing not only teaching jobs to support Native American writers but forums in which Native American writing is studied with sensitivity to cultural context.

Simon Ortiz, Luci Tapahonso, and Joy Harjo began to find outlets for their work and, in some cases, teaching positions in universities to support themselves. In 1969, N. Scott Momaday won the Pulitzer Prize for his novel *House Made of Dawn*. Novelists such as Owens, James Welch, and Gerald Vizenor brought the conventions of Native American storytelling to the novel form, in some cases significantly reinventing it, and Louise Erdrich became the first Native American writer to routinely break into the best-seller lists. Joseph Bruchac joined them, not only writing everything from poetry to novels to children's books but also publishing many of his fellow Native American writers through Greenfield Review Press, which he runs out of his home. Native Americans not only began writing, in their own voices, about their experiences starting in the 1970s but began publishing themselves and one another, and teaching students (Native American and not) how to read and interpret works written from a native point

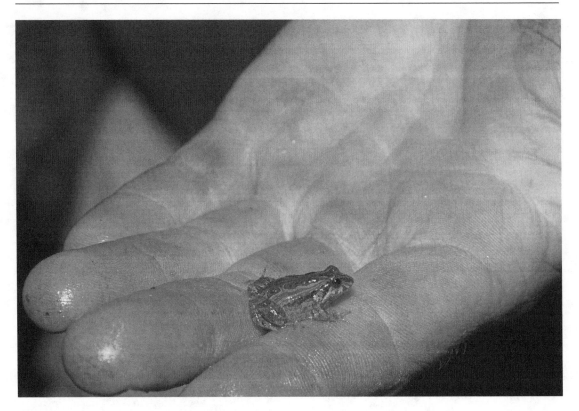

Grampa stops to rescue frogs out of the road. *(Image copyright clearviewstock, 2010. Used under license from Shutterstock.com)*

of view. Progress has not been perfect, and Native American viewpoints are still far from being universally understood, but the work of these elders who blazed the trail in the early 1970s has gone a long way toward making Native American viewpoints comprehensible to a majority culture who were previously unable to interpret them at all.

CRITICAL OVERVIEW

Although the collection in which "Birdfoot's Grampa" was originally published attracted almost no critical attention, Bruchac states that "Birdfoot's Grampa" is his most widely anthologized poem. Originally published in a small-press chapbook titled *Entering Onandaga*, the poem attracted additional attention when Bruchac used it to close his autobiographical essay "Translator's Son." The poem's conversational tone, simple language, and clear lesson have contributed to the poem's popularity in anthologies and as a teaching tool.

Bruchac's work as a storyteller and translator of Native American folklore and wisdom has taken him into thousands of schools across North America. "Birdfoot's Grampa" was published toward the beginning of his thirty-year career in which he has published fiction, poetry, and nonfiction for both adults and children. He has won many awards, including the American Book Award, a Horn Book honor, the *Scientific American* Children's Book Award, the Hope S. Dean Award for Notable Achievement in Children's Literature, the 2005 Virginia Hamilton Literary Award, the 2001 Parents Guide to Childrens' Media Award (for *Skeleton Man*), the 2000 Parents Choice Gold Award (for *Crazy Horse's Vision*), the 1999 Lifetime Achievement Award from the Native Writers Circle of the Americas, the 1999 Jane Addams Children's Book Award, the 1998 Writer of the Year Award from the Native Writers Circle of the Americas, the 1998 Storyteller of the Year Award from the Native Writers Circle of the Americas, the 1997 Paterson Award, the 1996 *Boston Globe* Book Award, and the 1995 Knickerbocker Award.

CRITICISM

Charlotte M. Freeman

Freeman is a novelist, freelance writer, and former academic. In this essay, she addresses how in "Birdfoot's Grampa," Bruchac uses many literary techniques characteristic of the modern Native American literary renaissance.

Since 1969, when N. Scott Momaday won the Pulitzer Prize for *House of Dawn*, the United States has seen a renaissance in Native American literature. Although the Native American point of view has by no means become commonplace, and although Native American writers from Louis Owens to Bruchac himself continue to critique mainstream publishers for lagging in their support of Native American literature, in the last forty years the Native American voice and viewpoint has become a pervasive, if minority, presence in American literature. When asked by Eliza T. Dresang about what characteristics distinguish Native American writing for an interview published by the *Cooperative Children's Book Center* of the School of Education at the University of Wisconsin, Madison, Bruchac noted, "It is important to recognize that Native people are not locked into the past. That those called American Indians have living traditions." He also pointed out that Native Americans are not monolithic, that different tribes have their own distinct traditions and values. However, he noted, there are common traits that distinguish contemporary writing by Native American writers, including "the strength of oral traditions, an informed awareness of the process which is now called ecology and the place that human beings play within that circle of life." He also noted later in the interview that Native American writing is "characterized by a mixing and blurring of genres." Bruchac's most widely anthologized poem, "Birdfoot's Grampa," provides an excellent example of these characteristics of Native American literature.

Bruchac's poem is not set in the far-distant past of mythical American Native Americans, but in the present where actual Native Americans must exist and negotiate all the complications of modern life. The poem consists of two Native American men traveling in an automobile. There is no more powerful symbol of the modern reliance on technology that characterizes American life than the automobile. Cars are subject to nearly as many myths and stereotypes

as Native Americans themselves, and indeed, Native American tribal and place names have been appropriated as names for both car models and car companies. In addition, the road trip remains a central American myth: the idea that when the going gets tough, we can just jump in our automobiles and drive off into the sunset in search of a better or different life someplace else. Automobiles are a powerful symbol of the contradictions of technology. On the one hand, they give us freedom and flexibility of movement, they have enabled us to build suburbs and highways, they have provided jobs for millions and are one of our biggest exports to the rest of the world. On the other hand, they pollute the air and the water, they necessitate the building of roads and the mining of oil in natural areas, and they kill thousands of people and millions of animals each year. That the poem begins with two Native Americans in a car, modern Native Americans in that most modern of American symbols, sets up the core tension of the poem. How are Native Americans, and by extension the rest of us, to live with the technological contradictions that confront us in the modern world?

The poem is told in a direct narrative style, as if is narrator was speaking directly to his audience. As Bruchac notes, the centrality of the oral tradition is common to all Native peoples and is the primary method by which the culture is transmitted. The poem opens in a conversational tone, with the narrator complaining lightly about how many times the old man made him stop the car. This is not the formal way of speaking of premodernist poetry but the sort of conversational tone that one uses when telling a story to a friend or acquaintance. In the first stanza, the narrator is not quite complaining about the old man, but his impatience is clear. In the second stanza, he finally loses his patience

WHAT DO I READ NEXT?

- *Songs from This Earth on Turtle's Back* (1983) is a poetry anthology edited by Bruchac and composed of poems from many different Native American nations, including such acclaimed poets as Paula Gunn Allen, Diane Glancy, Joy Harjo, Adrian Louis, N. Scott Momaday, and Gerald Vizenor. This anthology is a terrific starting place for readers interested in Native American poetry.

- In Bruchac's young-adult novel *Code Talker* (2006), Ned Begay tells the story of his life. Beginning at age six, when he is sent to an Anglo (white) boarding school, the Navajo language and customs are forbidden. Begay grows up to serve with the U.S. Marines during World War II as a "code talker," sending encrypted messages. The code talkers' contribution to the war effort was so crucial that they were not allowed to tell their stories until the code was declassified in 1969.

- Bruchac's first novel, *Dawn Land* (1993), is the story of Young Hunter, set 10,000 years ago in the territory that will become New England. Young Hunter is dispatched on a journey to confront and defeat the enemy. Although written for adults, this book is suitable for young adults, as is its sequel, *Long River* (1995).

- Louis Owen's collection of critical essays, *Mixed-blood Messages* (1998), takes on the question of how we recognize an "authentic Indian." Are only full-blood tribal members qualified as authentic, or do mixed-blood writers such as Owens and Bruchac also qualify as Native Americans? A far-ranging collection of literary criticism that examines literature, film, and Owens's own family history, this has become a core text in Native American studies.

- *Fool's Crow* (2001) by James Welch is a novel set during the waning days of the Lone Eaters clan of the Blackfeet Indians. Fool's Crow witnesses the incursions of white settlers while struggling to save his tribal way of life.

Welch's invention of an English syntax that brings to life the Blackfoot worldview without ever falling into cliché is one of the great achievements of modern Western literature.

- *Buried Onions* (1997) is a young-adult novel by Gary Soto. Set in Fresno, California, it is the story of a Hispanic teenager trying to escape from both the poverty and the gangs that call his neighborhood home. It is a story about cultural cross-pressures similar to the themes in Bruchac's works.

- In *Aurelia: A Crow Creek Trilogy* (1999), Elizabeth Cook Lynn follows Aurelia, a Lakota woman, and her family from the 1930s to the 1990s. This series of three novellas traces the challenges of a Dakota Sioux woman who watches as her partner struggles to win reparations for his stolen cattle, who battles for her people as hydroelectric dams flood their territory, and who seeks to raise her children in a world where justice and equality always seem just out of reach.

- *Miko Kings* (2007), by Leanne Howe, is set in Ada, Oklahoma, in 1907, when Oklahoma was still Indian territory. The story follows Hope Little Leader, a Choctaw pitcher for the Miko Kings baseball team. The narrative shifts between characters and time periods, and it includes historical documents such as diaries and newspaper clippings in order to dramatize the clash of cultures that characterized Indian Territory.

- Arranged chronologically, beginning with Plymouth Rock, Dex Brooks's *Sweet Medicine: Sites of Indian Massacres, Battlefields and Treaties* (1995) is a photographic record of important sites in the history of white and Native American interactions. In many cases, Brooks's record documents how the presence of Native Americans has been erased from the American landscape.

and objects, telling the old man that there are too many toads to save and that he should get back in the car so they can keep moving. The poem contains a dialogue between the two people, the one insisting that they stop to move the tiny, numerous toads off the road and the other impatient to reach his destination. The old man's actions stand as a gentle rebuke to the narrator, but it is his statement at the end of the poem, that the toads' destinations are just as important to them as the humans' destination is to themselves, that forms the epiphany (the sudden realization of something important) of the poem. Like all good jokes, or good stories, this poem has a punch line, a moment when the speaker makes a point.

Here is an example of the mixing and blurring of genres that Bruchac identifies as a characteristic of Native American literary technique. The poem is clearly written using poetic form and technique, and yet it is also a classic lesson story. The narrator addresses the audience directly and tells a story in which the joke is on him. The use of humor, especially this sort of self-deprecating humor, is also a characteristic of Native American literature, as well as a blurring of genres. We tend to think of humor as belonging to the realm of poetry that is not considered serious—limericks, jokes, nursery rhymes—and yet in the Native American tradition, humor is often used to make exactly the sort of serious point that "Birdfoot's Grampa" is making. What better way to show people the error of their ways than to tease them into realizing it? At the poem's end, the old man's statement shocks the narrator out of his complacency and reminds him once more that he is not more important than the toads, that the toads have every bit as much right as he does to attempt to reach their destinations. The mixture of serious message and humorous vehicle, as well as the blurred line between storytelling and poetry, marks this poem as existing right in the center of the modern Native American literary tradition.

"Birdfoot's Grampa" is a deeply ecological poem, thus fulfilling another of Bruchac's characteristics of Native American literature. It poses a conflict between the natural cycles of amphibian reproduction and the technological forces of modern life, as embodied in the automobile. The toads in the road are small and very numerous. They are easily squashed, and they are very inconvenient to the human beings. The narrator begins in a frame of mind in which he seems merely puzzled that the

old man insists on stopping, but after many such stops, he becomes annoyed. His attitude seems to be that they are just toads; there are a lot of them, and running over a few will not hurt the survival of the species. The old man, however, keeps getting out in the rain to safely move the toads off the road. His position is a more radical one than the narrator's. He operates from a position that all life is sacred; all life has value, even the lives of thousands of little toads. The old man is, by his actions, demonstrating that he does not think that his busy life as a human being, in his fast, technologically advanced car, is more important than the lives of the toads. The toads are alive, and they need help to keep from being killed, and so the old man takes it as his responsibility to get out and help them. This position of ecological equality is one that is central to the Native American worldview, and some of the humor in the poem comes from the fact that the narrator, who is also Native American, has forgotten this. He must be reminded by an elder, who teaches him a lesson by example.

That it is an elder who is teaching the younger man a lesson about the rightful place of human beings in the natural world is also a hallmark of Native American literature. In an oral tradition, it is the older people who teach the younger ones how to behave responsibly. In this case, the lesson is how to exist in a responsible relationship with the natural world. The toads dramatize how difficult it can be to remain in the right relationship with the natural world. They are inconvenient; there are so many of them, and they are so tiny that to stop and move them off the road seems futile. The narrator has forgotten how to live with nature. He is willing to sacrifice the lives of those smaller and more numerous than himself, creatures that are inconvenient to him, in order to get to his destination on time. He has made the error of thinking that he is not a part of nature but that, in his automobile, he is somehow superior to other, smaller life forms. The old man, through his gentle example, reminds the narrator that just because the toads are small and weak and in the way, they are no less alive and no less worthy of life than he is. The frogs, the poem reminds us, are as wet and brown as life itself.

Bruchac's short poem, just twenty lines long, conveys a powerful message about how not just Native Americans but the rest of us too should live in the right relationship with both one another

Native American elder (*Image copyright ecliptic blue, 2010. Used under license from Shutterstock.com*)

and the natural world. The poem mixes the genres of joke, story, and poetry in order to induce in the reader the same kind of realization that takes place in the consciousness of the narrator. No matter how important we think we are, driving along in our fast cars, in a hurry to get to our destinations, we are still no more important than the tiniest toad trying to cross the road. We are all connected, and it is when we forget those connections that we become cut off from our relationships with the natural world and with one another.

Source: Charlotte M. Freeman, Critical Essay on "Birdfoot's Grampa," in *Poetry for Students*, 2011.

Meredith Ricker

In the following excerpt, Ricker interviews Bruchac and discusses his autobiographical poem, "Birdfoot's Grampa," and the importance of storytelling to preserving his Native American ancestry.

If the past thirty years encompass what has been called a Renaissance period in Native American literature, Joseph Bruchac, who has devoted his life to translating one culture to another through his writing and teaching, must surely be considered a Renaissance man. He has taught English in Africa and African American and Native American literature in this country. As the editor of The Greenfield Review Press, dedicated to the publication of multicultural material, he has published anthologies of poetry from American prisons—collected during seven years of teaching in the prison system—as well as anthologies of Native American, Asian American and African American poets. Greenfield Press has published early works by many writers who have gone on to become quite well known, such as Linda Hogan, Barney Bush, and Beth Brant, and an instructional volume for other small press publishers. Bruchac's writing includes poetry, novels, short stories, essays, and retellings of traditional Native American stories. Yet, he is perhaps best known for his award-winning storytelling. Much of his time is devoted to telling stories in schools, and his stories have been published in more than twenty books and numerous magazines, and in both audio and video formats. Bruchac's contributions to the educational process are numerous. Among his notable works of children's literature are his praised collaborations with Michael Caduto, *Keepers of the Earth* and *Keepers of the Animals*. In these books, traditional Native stories serve as a centerpiece for lessons about environmental concerns. Motivated by a belief that the world is in need of saving, Bruchac says: "My writing . . . give[s] me a chance to share my insights into the beautiful and all too fragile world of human life and living things we have been granted. Which is one of the reasons I write—not to be a man apart, but to share" (*Albany Times Union* 1 [June 1980]).

Born in upstate New York, Bruchac is of Abenaki and Slovak heritage. In his essay "Notes of a Translator's Son," Bruchac translates the French-Canadian term for a person of mixed blood, metis, into English as "translator's son." Unlike half-breed, a terms he finds insulting, metis "means that you are able to understand the language of both sides, to help them understand each other" (203). His poem "Birdfoot's Grandpa" is an example of the creation of such an understanding and part of Bruchac's quest to discover himself within his "confused heritage."

> 'BIRDFOOT'S GRANDPA' IS VERY MUCH A
> POEM ABOUT LEARNING. IT'S ABOUT LEARNING
> FROM YOUR OWN MISTAKES AND RECOGNIZING
> YOUR SIGNIFICANCE REALLY HAS TO BE MEASURED,
> NOT JUST AGAINST WHAT YOU THINK YOU ARE, BUT
> AGAINST A WORLD THAT'S LARGER THAN YOU."

His lack of personal Native history has led him not to anger, but to a celebration of learning. Unable to "remember" his Native heritage, he has learned it anew, has gained strength and a sense of continuance by learning traditional values from the simple lessons that come to you "when you least expect them" (204).

In keeping with the universal belief that the future of our world rests with our children, Bruchac makes traditional Native American stories available to children of all cultures. He says:

> When stories are told...they always serve a double purpose. Stories entertain and they instruct. They delight and they teach. Stories work best when they are told either to the very young or to those who have not forgotten the child within them, who open themselves without preconceptions to the possibility of other worlds than their own everyday reality, who accept that even everyday life—if seen through different eyes—may be suffused with magic. ("I Become Part of It" 2)

When asked what he wishes children to take away from his stories, Bruchac says simply that he wants them to take the stories. He believes that the future of the world depends upon a return to traditional Native values. To that end, he wants children to internalize the Native sense of community with nature, the spirit, the past, and each other through the medium of stories. Like Leslie Silko, Scott Momaday, and other Native American writers, Bruchac believes that the telling of stories is one of our most powerful weapons in the struggle for cultural and physical survival.

Storytelling's most important role, for Bruchac, is found in the urgent need to restore harmony and balance to the world. He writes often and eloquently about the role Native American stories play in reminding people that all life is a circle, dynamic and moving in a continuous cycle, in contrast to the European view that life is linear, and that the goal is progress. In his retelling of the Abenaki story of Gluskabe and the Wind Eagle, Bruchac explains how a simple story illustrates a severe environmental problem caused by human shortsightedness and shows the necessity of seeking wise counsel and a remedy to make things fight again. "It is this process which the stories teach us, a process we must follow as individuals, as leaders, as nations.... A feeling of guilt does nothing. Only action to restore the balance is the proper response" ("Rooted in Survival" 35). We must realize our errors and turn to traditional Native wisdom to learn how to correct them. Always optimistic, Bruchac maintains that it is not too late to listen and to learn.

This interview, Bruchac's first of full length on the receiving end of the questions, was conducted over a series of telephone calls for which he generously made time on his few days of rest during an extensive book tour. Much in demand as a speaker, he has recently published *Dawn Land*, a novel based on ancient Abenaki oral tradition, as well as two children's books. He speaks thoughtfully, in the compelling and rhythmic voice of a master storyteller, about the importance of stories and the need to teach traditional Native American beliefs to our children in order to ensure our survival.

> The old man
> must have stopped our car
> two dozen times to climb out
> and gather into his hands
> the small toads blinded
> by our lights and leaping,
> live drops of rain.
>
> The rain was falling,
> a mist about his white hair
> and I kept saying
> you can't save them all
> accept it, get back in
> we've got places to go.
>
> But, leathery hands full
> of wet brown life
> knee deep in the summer
> roadside grass,
> he just smiled and said
> *they have places to go to*
> *too*
>
> ("Notes of a Translator's Son")

Interviewer: I first discovered your work in Swann & Krupat's I Tell You Now: Autobiographical Essays by Native American Writers. *While most of the essays had a tone of anger in them, yours was the only one I found to be completely optimistic. Where does your optimism come from, in contrast to writers like Wendy Rose who often seem to write from anger?*

Bruchac: I suppose one place where I'm fortunate is that I was raised by my grandparents. I was taken out of what was an abusive situation to a small degree, or a large degree, I really can't say because my memory isn't that clear, with my parents, and raised by grandparents who gave me a lot of unconditional love. I think being around elders is a natural thing for human beings. Human beings thrive as little children if they're around caring elderly people who give them that kind of care and understanding. Very often the generation of our parents hasn't learned yet that kind of nurturing. Families are so split up in Western culture where you no longer have the extended family, but instead you have a mother and a father literally marooned on a little island with their children, often in situations where they don't know what to do. The results are often devastating for the kids, and it keeps getting passed on from generation to generation. I think that what I had in an upbringing was something closer to what a traditional upbringing should be in that I had that kind of support from elderly people. Maybe that's one reason for my optimism. A lot of other Native writers were denied that and are suffering from the same problems as all of Western society. The only difference is we're suffering from it as outsiders in our own land, with a memory of traditions so nurturing that in some ways we become bitter when we see those traditions denied us, or when we see our very existence defined as unnecessary or at least pointless by the overall majority culture. I think Wendy Rose's anger is a good example of that.

Interviewer: Why did you choose to end the essay with your poem "Birdfoot's Grandpa," rather than with "Translator's Son"?

Bruchac: "Birdfoot's Grandpa" is very much a poem about learning. It's about learning from your own mistakes and recognizing your significance really has to be measured, not just against what you think you are, but against a world that's larger than you. The poem is autobiographical, a lesson I really did learn, Not with my grandfather,

but with an elderly man named Swift Eagle who was a Pueblo Apache storyteller and musician who used to travel around with me. One night we were late for a storytelling program I was supposed to give and Swifty kept making me stop so he could pick up those damn toads. And finally when he said that, it was like a light went on in my head and I said to myself "Dummy?" I knew I had to write a poem about this. You know, the poem really is about being stupid and having your eyes opened by an elder.

Interviewer: I'm glad that poem is about something that really happened to you.

Bruchac: Oh, it truly is one of the gifts I was given. As you know from the essay, my grandfather would not talk about his Native ancestry. As I've grown older I've found that there was also Native ancestry on my grandmother's side of the family, even more deeply hidden. And my son has lately discovered, through his research, that my wife's family also has Abenaki ancestry that has been kept hidden for years. A lot of times I've wondered if I just imagined things from my childhood because it was such a deep secret. I got a letter recently from an elderly man named Don Bowman who knew my grandfather. Out of the blue he wrote me this letter describing what my grandfather was like when kids came to his general store. He would give kids a penny if they would bring in a frog or a toad or a turtle they'd found on the road and rescued. He kept a filled bathtub to put them in, and when things weren't too busy he'd carry them back to the lake or down to the creek. When I read this I thought, "my gosh, it's Birdfoot's Grandpa."

Interviewer: I think there may be another poem there.

Bruchac: Oh, yes. So you see there are circles that are very strong. Other people have commented on my optimism, and my response is that it's always turned out to be justified. And even if weren't justified, I've had a good time being optimistic while everyone else has been walking around being down in the mouth.

Source: Meredith Ricker, "An Interview in *MELUS*," in *MELUS*, Vol. 21, No. 3, Fall 1996, pp. 159–78.

Kit Alderdice

In the following essay, Alderdice discusses how Bruchac's impressive career has taken a bend toward children's books with Native American themes, themes that Bruchac has worked to make known in the literary world.

I THINK WRITING, LIKE STORYTELLING, HAS A DUAL PURPOSE. AT *LEAST* A DUAL PURPOSE. THE FIRST IS TO ENTERTAIN. BECAUSE IF IT ENTERTAINS, THEN PEOPLE WILL REALLY PAY ATTENTION TO IT. THE SECOND IS TO TEACH."

"It wasn't really a matter of choice. It was a matter of finding what road I was supposed to be on and then staying on it" is Joseph Bruchac's characteristically down-to-earth description of his work as poet, editor, professional storyteller and scholar of Native American culture. The most recent bend in his career path has led the multitalented Bruchac to the publication of more than a dozen children's books revolving around Native American themes.

Though merely one part of an already impressive career, this latest development is surely worthy of note: since 1988, Bruchac's books for children have been published by such major houses as Philomel, Bridgewater, Fulcrum, Harcourt Brace, Dutton and Dial. Among the honors he has garnered are the American Book Award, the Cherokee Nation Prose Award and the *Scientific American* Award for Young Readers. Most recently, his telling of the story of Sitting Bull, *A Boy Called Slow*, issued by Philomel (Children's Forecasts, Jan. 9), won the Mountains & Plains Booksellers Association's 1996 Regional Book Award for children's literature.

PW's interview with Joseph Bruchac starts off with a tour of his home in Greenfield Center, N.Y., several miles outside Saratoga Springs. Filled with books, mementos and a profound sense of personal history, the Bruchac family residence was originally two separate buildings: the house where the author was raised, and his grandparent's gas station/general store. Clever renovation joined the two structures in a single space which serves not only as home, but also as office and warehouse for The Greenfield Review Press, the independent publishing house founded by Bruchac and his wife, Carol. As our house tour evolves into an animated conversation, the lanky, ponytailed author returns repeatedly to the themes of nature, story-telling and Native American culture—the interconnected passions that have given form to so much of his career and life.

Certainly Bruchac—who is of Abenaki, English and Slovakian descent—has found his own Native American heritage to be a great source of inspiration. Raised by his maternal grandparents (his lawyer grandmother and his grandfather, who was "visibly Indian but wouldn't talk about it"), Bruchac grew up hoping to become "something like a park ranger, or one of those interpretive naturalists who goes and gives tours in national parks and explains what things are." But as a young adult, he gravitated toward literature and, intrigued in part by his grandfather's reticence, felt drawn to his Native American roots.

"Even when I was in college [at Cornell University], my fast poems ... were about American Indian themes," he observes.

In the mid-1960s, after completing a masters degree in creative writing at Syracuse University, Bruchac set off with his wife for Africa, where for three years they taught in a secondary school in Keta, Ghana. At the end of this stint, the Bruchacs returned to upstate New York and moved in with Bruchac's grandfather, settling in Bruchac's childhood home.

It was in 1971 that Joseph and Carol Bruchac started the *Greenfield Review*, a multicultural literary magazine devoted to publishing what he describes as "an equal blend of established and lesser-known writers." Though the magazine ceased publication six years ago, its book publishing arm, The Greenfield Review Press, and a spin-off project, the North American Native Authors Catalog, are still going strong. Given his strong sense of responsibility to his heritage, it's not surprising that Bruchac continued his commitment to education as well. After four years of teaching ethnic literature at Skidmore College, he founded—and for eight years directed—the school's program at the Great Meadow Correctional Facility, a maximum-security prison in Comstock, N.Y.

Bruchac was known as a poet before he branched into other genres. His first book was a volume called *Indian Mountain and Other Poems*, issued by Ithaca Press in 1971, and he has been prolific ever since. "I think I've been published now in 500 different poetry magazines," he says. He was one of the judges for the poetry panel of the National Book Awards in 1995.

Bruchac's close relationship with his two sons, Jim and Jesse, now in their mid-20s, was the catalyst for his work both as a professional storyteller and as a children's author. "When the boys were very little, I started telling them stories," he recalls. "And the stories I chose to tell were the traditional stories that I had grown up with, read in books and then, as an adult, been hearing from elders. I began seeking out more stories, so I could share them with the kids."

This private pursuit gained a wider audience thanks to Bruchac's friends John and Elaine Gill of Crossing Press, who asked the poet to write down some of the tales he told his sons. The end result was Bruchac's first book for children, *Turkey Brother and Other Iroquois Stories*, first published in 1976 and in print ever since.

Publication led in turn to Bruchac's now flourishing career as a professional storyteller. An invitation to read from *Turkey Brother* at an elementary school precipitated Bruchac's first storytelling performance, when, he recalls, "I got out in front of a group of kids with a book in my hand." Spontaneously, he remembers, "I just put the book down and said, 'Let me *tell* you these stories.'"

The transition from reader to storyteller is easy enough to imagine: even in casual conversation, Bruchac's gently resonant voice is persuasive, and he seems to possess an intuitive notion of the internal formation of even the smallest anecdote.

Propelled as he has been from one accomplishment to the next by a happy combination of good fortune and hard work, it's small wonder, Bruchac says, that he is a "strong believer in things occurring when they're meant to happen. That it's very different if you try to force things…but if you follow a sort of natural flow, the results are usually much better—for yourself, and for other people, too."

Certainly this idea of a natural flow is borne out as Bruchac describes how he started writing picture books. Familiar with Bruchac's work as a poet, Paula Wiseman, then senior editor at Philomel, had contacted the writer with the idea of a future project. Meanwhile, author Jonathan London, the writer's longtime friend and correspondent, asked Bruchac to collaborate with him on a collection of Native American-inspired poems and stories about the seasons. When London pitched this idea to Wiseman, the project became *Thirteen Moons on Turtle's Back* (Philomel, 1992),

illustrated by painter Thomas Locker, with whom Bruchac has continued to work.

Bruchac's work with London is just one of several occasions on which collaboration has led to publication. A fruitful association with Dial Books for Young Readers (three picture books published to date, with a middle-grade novel, *Children of the Longhouse*, in the works for this spring) began when a mutual acquaintance introduced Bruchac to the illustrator Anna Vojtech, who told Bruchac she was interested in illustrating a Native American story involving flowers. Bruchac recalls that he wrote down a version of a Cherokee tale. As he remembers it, Vojtech "did a few illustrations and showed them to me, and I thought, 'Those are really nice.' And then more than a year went by, and she called and said, 'Joe, our book is accepted!' and I said, 'What book?' I had no idea that she was sending it out. I'm sure she mentioned it to me, but it just didn't register." Dial published the book, titled *The First Strawberries*, in 1993.

Serendipitous encounters of this sort notwithstanding, not all Bruchac's efforts have met with such stress-free success. *Keepers of the Earth*, written in collaboration with storyteller and naturalist Michael Caduto, "was rejected more than 40 publishers" before being accepted by Fulcrum. An ambitious collection of Native American stories and environmental activities related to each tale, *Keepers of the Earth* (first released in 1988) and its sequels are all still in print, having sold more than 800,000 copies.

These days, Bruchac is much sought after. As he readily admits, "Virtually everything I do tends to be an idea that's been suggested to me by a publisher, rather than something I've come up with. I really don't have a lot of time to spend thinking up ideas and pitching them to people."

With his various talents very much in demand, Bruchac has the luxury of being able to pick and choose his projects. "I honestly don't want to do anything unless I can put myself into it fully: intellectually and spiritually," he says. This attitude enables him, he says, to promote other Native American writers. "Although I continue to do a lot of books, I'm constantly referring projects to other people. I can think of probably a dozen different books I could have done, over the last two years, or the next few years, that are being done by other Native writers whom I've recommended for those books. Which makes me feel very good."

A DEEPLY APPRECIATIVE AUDIENCE

Writing for children is exceptionally satisfying, Bruchac says. "It's an audience who really, deeply appreciate what you do. They're not just reading you because you're the latest best seller and everybody else is buying the book. And then there's the whole aspect of what I think writing should do. I think writing, like storytelling, has a dual purpose. At *least* a dual purpose.

"The first is to entertain. Because if it entertains, then people will really pay attention to it. The second is to teach. To provide lessons. And not to do so in an overly preachy way, or in a way which is forced, but to do it within the flow and the rhythm of the tale itself."

One lesson that seems to crop up in all Bruchac's books is a reverence of nature. "Unless we become part of the land, the land will reject us. It will continue without us, but it will reject us," he says. "No one will convince me that this is not the case. It's as clear as the fact that breathing in gives you life. And when you cut off the breath, the body dies."

Nowhere is this message more evident than in *Between Earth and Sky*, his latest collaboration with Thomas Locker, due out from Harcourt Brace this April. Beautifully designed, and filled with luminous paintings and haunting poetry, this picture book explores 10 places in North America that are sacred to Native peoples.

Powerful though his vision of the natural world is, it is not for this reason alone that Bruchac's work has captured a wide audience. Describing his success, he says, "I don't think it is just because, as some people have said, Indians are 'hot' right now. I really think that what people are seeing are those basic values: of family, of environment and community and storytelling. Values that all come together so clearly in the Native American traditions. But these are basic human values. And you don't have to be an Indian, or even interested, per se, in American Indian culture, to appreciate a book like *Between Earth and Sky*."

Despite the time and energy Bruchac has dedicated to making Native voices and visions better known to the world at large, he gently shrugs off any suggestion that he might be seen as a spokesperson for the Native American community. "There are more than 400 different living American Indian cultures in North America," he points out. "No one knows them all. And what I can say is that I know a bit, to some detail, about a couple of them."

Rather than assume the lofty title of spokesperson, Bruchac has a simple vision of his role. "I want to be able to speak clearly and well," he says, "and to say things in a way that I hope people will listen to." Given the receptiveness of his audience, the eagerness of his editors and the volume and quality of his writing, Bruchac is well on his way to achieving his goal.

Source: Kit Alderdice, "Joseph Bruchac: Sharing A Native-American Heritage," in *Publishers Weekly*, Vol. 243, No. 8, February 19, 1996, pp. 191–92.

Patricia Craig

In the following article, Craig examines the importance of Bruchac's storytelling as a traditional teaching method in the Native American culture and as a means to transmit history from generation to generation.

Joseph Bruchac, an Abenaki storyteller from the Adirondack Mountain region in New York, took an unusual approach to get ready for his Nov. 17 lecture at the Library: He burned a small bundle of sage leaves to purify the air and prepare a sacred space for his stories and audience. The American Folklife Center event was part of LC's celebration of Native American Heritage Month.

"We burn sage when we are about to begin something special," Mr. Bruchac told the audience, and holding up a small, tambourine-like drum, he explained that it symbolized the circle that draws all people together. "When we hear this sound, it is the sound of the heartbeat. This sound honors women; it honors the earth."

The traditional time for storytelling is between the first frost and last frost, he said. Tales would be shared while sitting around a fire. "Someone would stand up and ask it others wanted to hear a story," Mr. Bruchac said.

He then told the story of how the world came into being. The legend involved Glooscop, an Abenaki spirit who found himself lying on the earth. He wanted to get up to see where he was. He pushed hard with his arms, forming the mountains. When Glooscop tried to pull himself up by grabbing the tops of the mountains, his fingers gouged the rivers and streams. "He tried to stand before he had legs," explained Mr. Bruchac. The audience laughed when he wryly added, "Somehow Washington, D.C., seems like a good place to tell this story."

More tales followed, and Mr. Bruchac demonstrated a Native American storytelling device used to keep an audience attentive: Intermittently, throughout the story, he would interject the exclamation, "Ho!" The listeners would immediately respond, "Hey!"

Storytelling among Native American cultures was a traditional method for teaching. A particular story might be selected for a specific audience. Stories also served as learning tools for children when they misbehaved. A moral lesson, embedded in the tale, showed the consequences of bad actions. "A story goes into the heart—a beating stops at the skin," he said.

Native American storytelling was a means of transmitting the history of the group from generation to generation. The storyteller formed the link between the traditions of the past and those of the present.

Mr. Bruchac continues the line of storytelling in his family. He was raised by grandparents in the Adirondack region. His grandfather, who was also a storyteller, operated a general store where friends and family gathered to trade stories about their childhood and regional history and to tell tall tales. But Mr. Bruchac heard few Native American stories until he was in his teens. His grandparents kept secret their Abenaki lineage.

An accomplished writer and poet, Bruchac has turned to his Native American heritage for creative inspiration. The author of more than 20 books, including *Keepers of Life, Keepers of the Earth*, and *Dawn Land*, he helps keep the tradition of Native American storytelling alive.

He reminded his audience, "You all have stories. Celebrate the stories of your family and your life."

Source: Patricia Craig, "Sage Spirit: Abenaki Storyteller Joseph Bruchac Tells Tales," in *Library of Congress Information Bulletin*, Vol. 53, No. 22, November 28, 1994, p. 448.

Madeline Bodin

In the following review, Bodin examines Keepers of the Earth *and* Keepers of the Animals *as effective tools created by Bruchac and Michael J. Caduto to teach natural history and environmental sciences.*

Though *Dances with Wolves* has long since waltzed off the big screen, its enormous popularity is testament to a reawakening of pride in and respect for Native American heritage that has been sweeping the country for the past several years. Fulcrum Publishing, with its books of Native American stories, *Keepers of the Earth* (1988) and *Keepers of the Animals* (1991), is happy to be at the heart of this multicultural rebirth, even if by sheer coincidence.

Fulcrum is not a house known for producing children's books. Yet the Keepers series is its biggest sales success to date. The series has had a warm reception from critics, booksellers, teachers and children as well. A teacher's guide, story collection and audiotape are also available for each title; in all, the series has 300,000 books and tapes in print.

The books, written by environmental educator Michael J. Caduto and storyteller Joseph Bruchac, use Native American tales to teach and illuminate natural history and the environmental sciences. The series appears to be an ideal marriage of Caduto's and Bruchac's talents. Caduto's 15-year career in environmental education includes a book written for UNESCO on environmental education training. During his research he found that stories from indigenous peoples were particularly helpful as teaching tools. "Soon after I began working on *Keepers of the Earth*," Caduto says, "it became clear to me that it was important to include a native voice, and to have the storyteller in the book be of native North American ancestry."

The voice he asked to join him was Bruchac, the author of more than 20 books of poetry and native stories, and a nationally known storyteller. Bruchac is of both Native American (Abenaki and Czechoslovakian ancestry. Bruchac initially approached the project with caution, "because I want to make sure, if traditional materials are going to appear in a public format, that they appear in a way that is respectful and proper," he says. "But as I got to know Michael better I realized he had a sincere interest."

Bruchac chooses stories and puts them into an English that is easily readable. Caduto writes the discussion sections and the activities. Both authors are quick to add that the carefully researched black-and-white illustrations by John Kahionhes Fadden, a Mohawk artist, are also a vital element of the collaboration.

However, the road to publication has not all been smooth. *Keepers of the Earth* hit a bump when its first publisher, Prentice Hall, was acquired by S & S in 1984, and the house decided not to publish the book. Twenty-four rejections later, Caduto and Bruchac received three offers.

Caduto says they chose Golden, Colo.-based Fulcrum because of the enthusiasm the firm showed for the book.

Fulcrum began publishing books in 1986 with its first list of eight books; these days the house produces about 40 books per year. Up until now, according to publisher Bob Baron, the list has been heavily oriented toward nature, Western themes, travel and Native American books. But the Keepers series has brought attention to the company as a children's book publisher, and next spring it will publish its first work of fiction, Bruchac's novel *Dawn Land.*

Stephen Bond Garvan, Fulcrum's director of sales, says the Keepers books sell best in the Northeast, where the authors live, but also do well wherever there is interest in Native American themes. Although teachers have always been a major market, the books are now available from a variety of outlets, including museums, nature centers and specialty retailers. "The combination of the Native American stories, and the science and nature is so perfect—especially for teachers. They can build a whole unit around it," says Martha Jackson, children's book buyer at A Clean Well-Lighted Place for Books in Larkspur, Calif.

Linda Stark, Fulcrum's director of marketing, credits much of the books' success to the children's booksellers who supported them early on. Sheila Wilensky-Lanford of Oz Books in Southwest Harbor, Me., agrees. "Children's booksellers have been handselling this book for years," she says. She notes that when *Keepers of the Earth* was first published neither the environment nor Native American studies were particularly popular subjects. Current trends have caught up.

The Keepers story doesn't end here. The authors are hard at work on the third book in the series—on plants—due in '94. And looking even further ahead, perhaps Mdawilasis, an Abenaki elder and one of Bruchac's former teachers, puts it best when he says, "There are stories in everything around us. You just have to know how to look in order to see them."

Source: Madeline Bodin, "Keeping Tradition Alive," in *Publishers Weekly,* Vol. 239, No. 54, December 14, 1992, p. 23.

Nick Di Spoldo

In the following essay, Di Spoldo describes Bruchac's work promoting aspiring writers who are incarcerated.

" YES, OF COURSE, THERE CERTAINLY IS AN ABUNDANCE OF TALENT IN PRISON. I'D GUESS THAT THERE ARE AT LEAST SEVERAL HUNDRED PEOPLE DOING WORK WHICH IS AS GOOD AS THAT BEING DONE BY POETS AND FICTION WRITERS IN, FOR EXAMPLE, M.F.A. COLLEGE PROGRAMS IN CREATIVE WRITING."

Joseph Bruchac III goes in and out of prisons so often I am always afraid they are going to give him a number and a pair of blue denims.

As Lon Charley was the "Man of Many Faces," Joseph Bruchac is the man of many facets: poet, publisher, professor at Swarthmore College, literary mentor to hundreds of aspiring prison writers and a man who knows more about the Native American Indian than Geronimo knew about Apaches.

The name Joseph Bruchac will not appear in the usual soporific studies of prison reform and rehabilitation, but Professor Bruchac has entered the prisons of New York, Connecticut, Maine, South Carolina, South Dakota, Arizona, Oklahoma, California, Ohio and Pennsylvania, often at his own expense, to teach creative writing, establish workshops, provide esoteric market and manuscript information and encourage convicts to creativity. He has given fresh motivation to countless men and women, developing and nurturing tender talents and fragile egos, with the sincerity of a saint and the dedication of Dr. Dooley. I began corresponding with Joseph Bruchac in 1973 while incarcerated in the Louisiana State Prison at Angola. I was a writer, as yet unpublished, and an ad in a national prison paper claimed that the Greenfield Review Press would provide free books and other materials for prisoners. An organization called Committee of Small Magazine Editors and Publishers (COSMEP), of whose board Mr. Bruchac was a member, was assisting prison writers whose work demonstrated literary merit or potential.

Mr. Bruchac induced COSMEP to establish the prison project which initially did little more than send books to prisoners. Within two years, however, the project established *Prison Project Newsletter* (a twice-yearly publication consisting of prisoner poetry, prose, letters, graphics and art) and sponsored numerous seminars and workshops in Eastern prisons.

COSMEP created a causeway of communication that certainly served to nullify the despair and awesome sense of alienation prison imposes. Writers now had a link with the world of publishing, and before the 1970's would expire, prison writings would appear almost as frequently as Ann Landers's columns.

In 1975 Mr. Bruchac received a National Endowment for the Arts (N.E.A.) grant, and this funding enabled him to edit, publish and distribute the first edition of *Newsletter* which, according to *Corrections Magazine*, is "a forum, clearing house and gathering place for 1,000 prison writers and workshop instructors across the country."

Joseph Bruchac, along with wife Carol and two young sons, lives in a charming two-story house that was converted from a country grocery store-gas station in Greenfield Center, a few miles from Saratoga Springs, N.Y. and near the foothills of the Adirondack Mountains.

The front porch is screened-in, and it is fortunate that it is for there are so many stacks of books, ranging from tabloids to chapbooks and tomes, that they could pour from the porch and create a paper path all the way to Saratoga Springs. Recently, the Bruchacs formally opened a small press library, filled with small press memorabilia, which is free to the public.

Carol Bruchac, slender and sensitive, is a perfect complement to Joseph. She handles the "business end of things" at the Bruchacs' Greenfield Press, helps with proofreading and assists in editorial decisions.

The Bruchacs led me through their home and the office archives, which are lined with filing cabinets that bulge with years and years of correspondence with prisoners in every state.

I opened a drawer and could not help but wonder about all the pain, passions, dreams, frustrations and joys these drawers contain. For nearly seven years I had written such letters to the Bruchacs, and I knew that my own correspondence was some small part of this rich repository.

Joseph, gentle and genial, has a deceptive but distinctive strength, and the moral muscle that comes from quiet but considerable accomplishment.

We sat on lawn chairs, watching Carol pick vegetables from the garden, and discussed the value of prison literature, writers and the *Newsletter*.

"Since 1976," Mr. Bruchac began, "only one issue of the *Newsletter* received a grant for $800, and all the other issues have been paid for out of our pockets."

"Each issue costs about $1,000," he continued, "but postage for it is paid through the N.E.A. grant insofar as copies are sent free to inmates. The subscription rate for non-inmates is $5 per year. We get occasional donations for $5 or $10, here and there, a total of about $50 a year."

Mr. Bruchac contends that "some of the finest writing I have seen in the last few years has come from American prisons."

As a convict-author, and one who has been extensively published in both the establishment press and the alternative "underground" publications, I have often been condemned by prison-support groups for my criticism of the mainstream of prison prose and poetry.

Gregg Mitchell, writing in *Corrections Magazine*, pointed out that the essential criticism of prison writing is that the writers do not know anything else and are unimaginative. It is an assessment that is often applicable to contemporary prison writing. The genre of prison prose and poetry is characterized by an emotional hypercriticism and redundant political rhetoric wherein writers attempt to use an art form to vent personal hostilities. In the late 1960's and early 1970's a good many "underground" newspapers courted prison writers and published countless counterproductive articles and letters from prisons condemning society and the judicial system for their personal problems and for their imprisonment.

Publications like *Great Speckled Bird* (Atlanta), *Berkeley Barb*, *Los Angeles Free Press* and *Fortune News* (NYC) helped to create and sustain a sort of artistic anarchy among prisoners. The writing was invariably pseudopolitical in nature, and more often than not ideas were expressed in a language one reads on subway walls.

I am especially impatient and displeased with what is generously identified as "prison poetry." Joseph Addison, being led through the poets' plot in the cemetery at Westminster Abbey, was apologetically informed by a caretaker that some of the poets had no headstones. Addison, peering at the names on graves that were marked, observed: "Yes, and some of these headstones have no poets."

While every prison in America contains men and women writing poetry, most prisons, like Addison's headstones, contain no poets. A prison poet is a writer who attempts to dress gripes with grace and delights small press editors with an ability to rhyme "bail" with "jail."

There are exceptions, of course, and no one is more pleased than I when I am able to read the work of a fellow convict-author that is meaningful or attempts to do something new with form and language.

Michael Hogan, winner of the 1975 American PEN Prison Writing Award, is a notable exception. An ex-inmate of Arizona State Prison, he has published five books of poetry and today often joins Mr. Bruchac in conducting prison workshops.

John Paul Minarik is another notable exception. In 1974, Mr. Minarik, an inmate serving a life sentence at Pennsylvania's Western Penitentiary, formed a small writers' group that soon attracted the attention of community groups. The program grew and became known as the Academy of Prison Arts. Academy poets on supervised leave from the prison hold readings in the Pittsburgh area.

In 1978, after receiving several local and state grants, this academy of prison writers won the first of what was to become yearly N.E.A. grants. With these funds Mr. Minarik has been able to invite poets such as Bruchac, Hogan and Diane Wakowski for readings and seminars.

"The Academy of Prison Arts is not the first inmate-led writing program, but it is the only one sponsored by the N.E.A. It's one of the best workshops underway in the United States," Joseph Bruchac says.

Regardless of prevailing criticism, Mr. Bruchac is quite adamant about the number of legitimate literary talents in the nation's prisons: "Yes, of course, there certainly is an abundance of talent in prison. I'd guess that there are at least several hundred people doing work which is as good as that being done by poets and fiction writers in, for example, M.F.A. college programs in creative writing. There are at least that many who have been released from prison. Of those people there are several dozens, both inmates and ex-inmates, whose work I would rank as extremely powerful. You and Mike Hogan are two examples. Others include Jimmy Baca, ex-inmate with a very good book of poetry out from Louisiana State University Press called

Immigrants In Our Own Land. There are several more currently in prison I see as strong individual voices making an active contribution to American writing. There is Michael Knoll, now in prison in Arizona, whose first book, *The Woman at the End of the Mattress* just won the first COSMEP Harry Smith Award for best small press literary book of 1981."

Mr. Bruchac points to other prison writers whose work he has examined or considered for publication by his own Greenfield Press: Pancho Aguila (California), William Welch (Pennsylvania), Jerome Washington (New York), Steven Todd Booker (Florida's death row), Philip Brasefield (Texas), Diane Bickston (California).

COSMEP, of course, is not the only creditable organization actively engaged in promoting and disseminating prison prose and poetry. In 1973, The American PEN Center established the first annual prison writing awards. In 1976 PEN published its first *Prisoner Writing Information Bulletin.* "We're not literary agents," explains John Morrone, PEN's prison program coordinator, "but we do refer writers to people who can help get them published. Basically, we're just trying to provide information and encouragement."

Mr. Morrone agrees with this writer that the mainstream of prison prose and poetry lacks originality and substance. He has read thousands of inmate manuscripts submitted in PEN writing contests and says the fiction is by far the most interesting. "The nonfiction tends to be gripe essays or looks like term papers with footnotes and all. The poetry is mostly vague and chaotic," he says.

The first 1982 issue of *Newsletter* features women writers in prison, workshops in progress, with biographical notes by the authors. Prisons in the spotlight include Louisiana Correctional Institute for Women, Women's Unit of Oklahoma State Prison, Women's Annex of New Mexico State Prison.

The poetry of these women, as a whole, is romantic: whining at its worse and wistful at its best. They lament life, former lovers, the children they abandoned at one time or another, or a life of prostitution which, most of them feel, society condemned them to for some reason.

Still, I think it pointless to offer an extensive critique of their poetry. No one, I'm sure, expects to discover Emily Dickinson in the Women's Annex of New Mexico State Prison. But the very act of creativity is to be encouraged, since the creative endeavor, one hopes, will motivate writers and eventually replace self-destructive impulses with more positive and socially acceptable values.

A shedding of the old orientation and a first groping for new values is offered in the compact concept of Linda Gallegos of the New Mexico workshop.

A man, a human body.
A tattoo of skeletons, devils, saints, etc.
Why must you do this?
Does it give some kind of power?
A role in life you play?
Maybe the macho man?
Where's your head at?
Sure they're beautiful,
But why can't you be proud to
just be who you are?

Lorri Martinez, a fellow workshop writer of Miss Gallegos, realizes that simple things we often take for granted are often the very things that provide us with the only sense of happiness we are likely to ever know:

I still remember
the San Luis Bar,
and you ordering
Margaritas.
Do you remember
walking through

Mercado, and the
Man trying to get
Our attention
"Muchacho—a pretty
Piñata or a guitar
To serenade your sweetheart?"

The night we had a
Fiesta on Tacos and Salsa
Dripping from your mouth,
Bridge on Whittier Park in
El Paso painted our picture.

You acted like a clown,
And when they asked you
To state your citizenship,
You answered in a thick
Phony accent, "American—"
But you were proud to be.
Your smile, the Tequila,
Mariachis—moments on a
Soft pillow to remember.

I Am Waiting to be Free is a collection of women's writing from New Mexico State Prison and is available from Koyemsi Press, P.O. Box 2472, Santa Fe, NM 87501.

This collection is one of many in a recent boom of prison anthologies. Joseph Bruchac is pleasantly anticipating a new anthology that his press will publish in 1983. "It will be a major anthology by writers in prison, tentatively titled *Breaking Out With a Pen*. It will be at least 240 pages in length with eight pages devoted to each poet, including a photo, a page of biography or a statement of poetics and six pages of poetry."

Mr. Bruchac adds: "I am hopeful it will be the sort of collection that will represent the diversity and strength of the recent poetry being written by those men and women in a community traditionally ignored or looked upon as socially or intellectually irredeemable."

A valid and consistent question arises in any discussion of prison writers and the realization of literary success: Is writing conducive to rehabilitation? The question is a subject of contemporary controversy. Jack Henry Abbott, a Utah prisoner, began a long correspondence with Norman Mailer that resulted in Mr. Abbott's early parole (he had killed a fellow inmate) and a job in New York City as Mr. Mailer's research assistant. The Abbott Mailer correspondence was published under the title *In The Belly of the Beast* and very nearly made the best-seller lists. Mr. Abbott was courted on the cocktail circuit and introduced into the world of New York's literati.

Everything was coming up sevens for Jack Henry Abbott. Almost everything. On the morning of July 17, 1980, he stabbed a waiter to death. The Abbott case inspired denunciations of Norman Mailer and other literary "stars"—for using convicts to get cheap "outlaw thrills." Mr. Mailer was criticized in *The New York Times Book Review* for his "tendency to glorify and romanticize violence" and for "helping to obtain the release of a dangerous man."

Corrections Magazine said, "The Abbott case reaffirms an old truth—that success in learning to write (or weld or repair autos) does not mean an inmate is rehabilitated."

Joseph Bruchac agrees: "A lot of inmate-authors are just playing a game, it is true. They're con men. They'll do it with poetry as easily as with bad checks."

Source: Nick Di Spoldo, "Writers in Prison," in *America*, Vol. 148, No. 1–3, January 22, 1983, pp. 50–53.

SOURCES

Alderdice, Kit, "Joseph Bruchac: Sharing a Native-American Heritage," in *Publishers Weekly*, February 19, 1996, pp. 191–92.

Baldick, Chris, "Didactic" and "Metaphor," in *The Oxford Dictionary of Literary Terms*, Oxford University Press, 2009, pp. 89–90, 205.

Boyer, Paul S., "American Indian Movement" and "Wounded Knee Tragedy," in *Oxford Companion to American History*, Oxford University Press, 2001, pp. 32, 850.

Bruchac, Joseph, "Biography," in *Scholastic Teachers: Where Teachers Come First*, http://www2.scholastic.com/browse/contributor.jsp?id=1784 (accessed January 10, 2010).

———, "Birdfoot's Grampa," in *Unsettling America: An Anthology of Contemporary Multicultural Poetry*, edited by Maria Maaiotti Gillan and Jennifer Gillan, Penguin, 1994, pp. 266–67.

———, "Translator's Son," in *Growing Up Native American*, edited by Patricia Riley, Harper, 1993, pp. 237–46.

Cuddon, J. A., "Didactic" and "Metaphor," in *The Penguin Dictionary of Literary Terms and Literary Theory*, Penguin, 2000, pp. 224–25, 507.

Dresang, Eliza T., "An Interview with Joseph Bruchac," in *Cooperative Children's Book Center*, School of Education, University of Wisconsin, Madison, http://www.education.wisc.edu/ccbc/authors/bruchac.asp (accessed January 12, 2010).

"Native American Religious and Cultural Freedom: An Introductory Essay (2005)," in *The Pluralism Project at Harvard University*, http://pluralism.org/reports/view/176 (accessed January 10, 2010).

Owens, Louis, *Other Destinies: Understanding the American Indian Novel*, University of Oklahoma Press, 1994, p. 24.

Parman, Donald, "Twentieth-Century Indian History, Achievements, Needs and Problems," in *Organization of American Historians Magazine of History*, http://www.oah.org/pubs/magazine/west/parman.html (accessed January 10, 2010).

Preminger, Alex, and T. V. F. Brogan, "American Indian Poetry," in *The Princeton Encyclopedia of Poetry and Poetics*, Princeton University Press, 1993, pp. 42–43.

Ricker, Meredith, "A *MELUS* Interview: Joseph Bruchac," in *Society for the Study of the Multi-Ethnic Literature of the United States (MELUS)*, Vol. 21, No. 3, Fall 1996, pp. 159–78.

Wittstock, Laura Watterman, and Elaine J. Salinas, "A Brief History of the American Indian Movement," *American Indian Movement Grand Governing Council*, http://www.aimovement.org/ggc/history.html (accessed January 25, 2010).

FURTHER READING

Alexie, Sherman, *The Lone Ranger and Tonto Fistfight in Heaven*, Grove Press, 2005.
Alexie is a noted, accomplished, and funny Native American writer. In this collection he chronicles modern life on the Spokane Indian Reservation through the eyes of Victor, a smart and nerdy protagonist.

Momaday, N. Scott, *House Made of Dawn*, Harper, 1999.
Momaday won the Pulitzer Prize for *House Made of Dawn*. The story of a returning veteran named Abel, torn between his father's Native American world and the industrial world of urban America, this book is a classic of American literature.

Ortiz, Simon, *Woven Stone*, University of Arizona Press, 1992.
This collection of three of Ortiz's previous books, *Going for the Rain*, *A Good Journey*, and *Fight Back: For the Sake of the People, For the Sake of the Land* is a great introduction to the work of this important Native American poet.

Owens, Louis, *Wolfsong*, University of Oklahoma Press, 1995.
In Owen's novel *Wolfsong*, Tom Joseph returns home to attend his uncle's funeral and discovers that the wilderness he loves is endangered by a mining operation. He throws all his energy into defeating the mining project, with surprising results.

Smith, Paul Chaat, and Robert Allen Warrior, *Like a Hurricane: The Indian Movement from Alcatraz to Wounded Knee*, New Press, 1997.
This highly readable history of the American Indian protest movement of the early 1970s begins with the occupation of Alcatraz Island and follows the movement through the siege at Wounded Knee, South Dakota.

Tapahonso, Luci, *Blue Horses Rush In: Poems and Stories*, University of Arizona Press, 1997.
Tapahonso celebrates the joys and sorrows of everyday Native American life in the Southwest in this collection.

SUGGESTED SEARCH TERMS

Joseph Bruchac

Joseph Bruchac AND poetry

Joseph Bruchac AND storytelling

Native American AND poetry

American Indian AND poetry

American Indian AND nature

mixed-blood AND literature

metis AND literature

Hawthorne

ROBERT LOWELL

1964

"Hawthorne," published in 1964 in *For the Union Dead*, is a poem by Robert Lowell about the impact and works of the nineteenth-century American writer Nathaniel Hawthorne. At the time of its publication, Lowell was one of the most important poets in the United States and was spearheading the literary movement known as confessional poetry, which centered around the poet's personal and intimate reflections on his or her life and experience. Though "Hawthorne" is not one of his most confessional poems, it addresses the role of the artist in society, the relationship between the public and private, and creativity—all common themes in confessional poetry.

The poem looks at Nathaniel Hawthorne's life and career and references passages from his works "The Custom-House" and *Septimius Felton; or, the Elixir of Life*. Lowell sets the poem in Salem, Massachusetts, where Hawthorne lived and worked for a time, oscillating between Hawthorne's time and the present to show the lasting impact of his career and works. Lowell's own reflections and commentary in "Hawthorne" bring in his signature confessional voice and convey his reverence for this influential artist.

AUTHOR BIOGRAPHY

Lowell was born Robert Traill Spence Lowell IV on March 1, 1917, in Boston, Massachusetts, to a an established family of the Boston elite, having

Robert Lowell (The Library of Congress)

descended directly from signers of the U.S. Constitution, famed theologians, *Mayflower* passengers, and the poets Amy Lowell and James Russell Lowell. Lowell began his formal education at the prominent Massachusetts preparatory school, St. Mark's, where he studied poetry under Richard Eberhart before following in the Lowell tradition of attending Harvard University in Cambridge, Massachusetts. He would remain at Harvard for only two years before transferring to Kenyon College in Ohio to study under John Crowe Ransom, the former teacher of southern poet and friend Allen Tate, where he would graduate summa cum laude with a degree in the classics. While at Kenyon, Lowell met fellow writers Randall Jarrell and Peter Taylor. He also briefly studied under Robert Penn Warren and Cleanth Brooks at Louisiana State University.

In 1940, Lowell converted to Roman Catholicism and married the novelist Jean Stafford. Lowell's conversion to Catholicism in spite of his own strong Protestant heritage caused much inner strife, adding to his already tumultuous and manic personality. Lowell and Stafford lived with Allen Tate in the mountains of Tennessee between 1942 and 1943, where Lowell did much

of his early writing until he was jailed as a conscientious objector during World War II in 1943. His first work, *Land of Unlikeness*, was published in 1944 and featured an introduction from his friend and mentor, Tate. In 1946 he published *Lord Weary's Castle* for which he was awarded the Pulitzer Prize in poetry in 1947, firmly establishing his place in the American literary scene. Featuring one of his most famous poems, "The Quaker Graveyard in Nantucket," the work would also earn him a National Institute of Arts and Letters Award and a Guggenheim Fellowship. It was with the publication of *Lord Weary's Castle* that Lowell seemed to develop a particularly effective voice, especially when addressing history and place, namely New England. In 1947-1948, Lowell held the position of Poet Laureate Consultant in Poetry to the Library of Congress, a title now known as U.S. Poet Laureate.

Lowell abandoned the Catholic Church and divorced Stafford in 1948 and married the novelist Elizabeth Hardwick in 1949. The two moved to Italy, where they remained through the publication of Lowell's next work, *The Mills of the Kavanaughs*, in 1951 and the death of his mother in 1954, which prompted a temporary relocation to Boston. During the latter half of the 1950s, Lowell taught at different universities and traveled to California, where he met many writers of the Beat generation, before finally publishing *Life Studies* in 1959 and settling in New York in 1960 with Hardwick and their daughter Harriet (born 1957). *Life Studies* contains what is generally accepted as his mostly widely-read poem, "Skunk Hour," and earned him the 1960 National Book Award. With this publication Lowell began to develop an intensely personal and intimate poetic voice, arising initially as a form of therapy while recovering from a nervous breakdown, that led to the creation of the confessional poetry movement.

After winning a Bollingen prize for his collection of translations *Imitations* in 1962, Lowell began his next work of poetry, *For the Union Dead*, which took its name from a poem Lowell read at a Boston arts festival. Published in 1964, *For the Union Dead* continues in Lowell's now characteristic confessional voice but with more emphasis on the social and political climates of the past and present, the puritanical history of his own family, and his own spiritual conflicts. He was commissioned to write "Hawthorne," which appears in this volume, for the centenary edition of Nathaniel Hawthorne's works.

He published *The Old Glory* in 1965, featuring adaptations of short stories by Hawthorne and Melville, before becoming very involved in activist politics. He declined President Lyndon Johnson's invitation to the White House Festival of the Arts in 1965 as a protest against the Vietnam War and published the very political *Near the Ocean* in 1967, which featured the most formally structural works since his early career. *Notebook, 1967–68* was published in 1969.

In 1970, Lowell moved to England to teach at Kent University and the University of Essex, and eventually divorced Hardwick to marry another author, Caroline Blackwood, in 1972. The next year, Lowell published *For Lizzie and Harriet*, *History*, and *The Dolphin*, the last earning him a second Pulitzer Prize in 1974. He kept writing translations and produced works for the theater, and his *Selected Poems* was published in 1976. His final work, *Day by Day*, was published only days before his death in 1977 and earned him a National Book Critics Award in 1978.

MEDIA ADAPTATIONS

- The Poetry Foundation has a small collection of audio poetry criticism about Robert Lowell and his work at http://www.poetryfoundation.org/archive/poet.html?id=4181.

- The Academy of American Poets has a recording of Robert Lowell reading "Skunk Hour" and "The Public Garden" at http://www.poets.org/poet.php/prmPID/10.

- A compact disc recording of a 1963 presentation of Lowell reading from *Life Studies* can be ordered at http://www.poets.org/viewmedia.php/prmMID/17047.

- There is a recording of Robert Lowell reading one of his other works, "Old Flame" on YouTube at http://www.youtube.com/watch?v=hdx6VU07eIQ.

POEM SUMMARY

The setting of "Hawthorne" is significant to the meaning of the poem in that Nathaniel Hawthorne wrote his seminal work, *The Scarlet Letter*, and its introductory essay, "The Custom-House," while living and working in Salem. Hawthorne's history with the city influenced much of his writing, and there is now a commemorative statue of the author in Salem.

Stanza 1

The poem begins with a description of the landscape of Salem, Massachusetts, in lines 1 and 2. Lowell directs his audience to follow a sleepy, lazy street set between the alms house, which functioned to feed and care for the poor and aging, and Gallows Hill, the site of many hangings during the legendary Salem Witch Trials. Notably, Nathaniel Hawthorne was actually related to John Hathorne, one of the principal judges during the trials, and added the *w* to his last name to dissociate himself from this man. Lines 3 through 6 describe more of the flat, lifeless street and the houses that are so aged they resemble the mangy fur of an old dog. In line 7, Lowell suggests that the city holds no great answers or meaning within

its borders and buildings. This description of the city references lines from Hawthorne's essay "The Custom-House."

Stanza 2

In a stanza composed of only one line, Lowell employs a metaphor to suggest that Salem is stained by the history of persecution and executions associated with the Salem Witch Trials, and it can never be redeemed and return to the gleaming object that it once was. (A metaphor is an analogy or comparison of two objects or ideas.) This too is a reference to a line from "The Custom-House."

Stanza 3

Lowell brings the scene back to Salem, professing his respect for Hawthorne by kneeling. Lines 10 through 14 describe Hawthorne during his tenure as a customs officer (one who collects tariffs on imports) for the city. Lowell portrays him as measuring out amounts of coal to burn in the furnace, attempting to keep him warm in his office on the South-end dock. Outside the office is a short, black ship covered with persistent ice which seems to grow like mold on the ropes, crab traps, and buoys piled along the docks. Lines 15 through 18 paint a very different picture of the other side of town with the hustle and bustle of ordinary business people along State Street. Much like Hawthorne measures out his coal, the professionals measure out their weary day by the hours on the glowing clock tower that looms above them.

Stanza 4

Lowell here employs another metaphor. Even Hawthorne, though shy and doubtful as he was, has walked on a burning roof, and his brain has been singed. The placement of this metaphor, between Lowell's discussion of the mindless professionals of the third stanza and the poets of the fourth, suggests a balancing act between the professional world and the artistic one. Hawthorne, he suggests, has held and maintained the delicate balance between artist and professional, barely missing the pitfalls which could have dulled his mental edge and creativity or mired him in routine. This is evidenced by his post at the customs house right before he published *The Scarlet Letter*.

Stanza 5

In lines 23 through 25, Lowell commands his audience to look at four men: Henry Wadsworth Longfellow, James Russell Lowell, Oliver Wendell Holmes, and John Greenleaf Whittier, all contemporaries of Hawthorne. These poets, known as the fireside poets, favored formal rhyme and meter and American legends and politics as subjects. Hawthorne moved away from formalism and pushed boundaries in American literature, writing about personal responsibility, the importance of expression, and the relationship of man to the natural world. Since Hawthorne had dark hair, Lowell's reference to his blonde hair suggests that the poet is looking not at a picture of Hawthorne, as he states, but rather at the statue of Hawthorne in Salem and the gleam of bronze in the light. His coat and mustache remind Lowell of General George Custer from the Civil War, known for his blond hair. (Custer would go on to become a tragic hero after his defeat at the battle of Little Big Horn in the Great Sioux War of 1876–77.) Lowell draws a distinction here between a pioneering author, immortalized and forever young as a statue, while his contemporaries are left behind, graying with their literary tradition.

Stanza 6

Lowell personifies the statue in lines 32 through 38, stating that by watching and waiting, Hawthorne

can be observed deep in thought, pondering some wooden chip, rock, leaf, or any commonly found object as if it held some deeper answer or meaning he was trying to decode. The final four lines of the poem describe the moment when his frustrated eyes rise from their contemplation on something so small and genuine, still without answers. This image not only references Hawthorne's love of the natural world, but refers to his final work, *Septimius Felton; or, the Elixir of Life*. In it, the main character is searching for the elixir of life and immortality. Hawthorne has found exactly that through his writing; he is immortalized as a statue. Lowell depicts Hawthorne focusing on things which would seem unimportant, trivial, or meaningless to the fireside poets or the businessmen on State Street, seeking truth and meaning in common objects from the natural world. It is in this statement that Lowell draws an ironic divide between the perceptions of Hawthorne, the individual and immortalized writer, and his contemporaries' values and perceptions of poetry.

THEMES

Art in Society

Lowell was a poet who admired other great writers and artists. He was one of the last American poets who saw the role of the artist as a romantic and heroic pursuit that needed to be elegized or paid tribute to. The artist occupies a niche role in society while simultaneously helping to shape and define it. Although Lowell's poem does not take the typical laudatory tone of an homage, Nathaniel Hawthorne is the most important aspect of "Hawthorne." In stanza 4, Lowell depicts Hawthorne's ability to balance his artistic output while working in the professional world as a customs officer, comparing it to walking along a narrow beam on a burning roof. He notes the disastrous and even deadly consequences of falling into the encompassing flames of a dehumanizing work routine. The balancing act portrayed in the poem reflects the balancing act in Hawthorne's personal life, leading the reader to imagine the number of influential artists who had felt the fire and could not take the heat, falling in with the mechanized professionals across town on State Street. A distinction is also drawn between Hawthorne and his contemporaries, the fireside poets, in stanza 5. While the fireside poets were stylistically similar to British writers of the time, writing Romantic poetry in standard form and rhyme that was

TOPICS FOR FURTHER STUDY

- Pick one writer or poet whom you admire and then choose one of their works. Like Lowell did with Nathaniel Hawthorne and *The Scarlet Letter*, write a poem about your author using selections and passages from the work you have chosen. When writing your poem, insert yourself into the time and place of the selected work and consider the author in relation to other artists or writers of the same period, as Lowell did with the fireside poets.

- Go online to http://www.flickr.com and create an account. Search the Internet and find pictures of artists, writers, or poets who have had statues made of them around the world and save them to your Flickr account. Use the pictures to create a slideshow and prepare a presentation for your class detailing who these statues commemorate, what they did, and where the statues stand today.

- Robert Lowell founded the confessional poetry movement, forever changing the landscape of American and world poetry in the twentieth century. Research key writers, dates, and publications in the confessional poetry movement, and create a weblog on http://www.blogspot.com. Create a new entry every day for one week over one confessional poet, including a brief biography, a discussion of his or her significance, and one or two of the person's poems.

- The history of the Salem Witch Trials influenced Robert Lowell's view of Salem, Massachusetts, and it was particularly important to Nathaniel Hawthorne, who was a descendant of one of the principal judges. Read either the young-adult novel *Witch-Hunt: Mysteries of the Salem Witch Trials* by Marc Aronson or *A Break with Charity: A Story about the Salem Witch Trials* by Ann Rinaldi. Then, like Hawthorne did with *The Scarlet Letter*, write a short story or essay about a major event in your own family or community's history and why it is very important to you.

- Read the poem "Homage to the Empress of the Blues" by the twentieth-century African American poet Robert Hayden, dedicated to the great blues singer Bessie Smith. Find at least three academic-quality sources online and write a brief essay discussing Hayden and Smith, some of their contemporaries, and their lasting influence today. While writing your essay, consider an artist, be it musician, writer, or visual artist, who has influenced you greatly as well.

extremely popular for memorization, Hawthorne pushed the envelope and conventions of literature. The resilience and formality of their prose is dated and reflected by their gray beards. Hawthorne has instead been modeled in bronze, standing forever immortalized as a statue in Salem, his dignified look and dress even resembling that of Civil War general George Custer. In stanza 6, Lowell quotes Hawthorne's last work *Septimius Felton; or, the Elixir of Life* (1872), comparing him to his main character who sought a method for immortality; Hawthorne, however, has found it. Through his years of work and writing, Hawthorne has found immortality in the form of a statue, his lasting works, and poems like Lowell's.

The Relationship between the Private and the Public

The private and the public, more specifically the biographical and historical, were two key dimensions of Lowell's poetry. Since much of Lowell's work is confessional and therefore intimate, his personal history and the events that shaped him are just as important as the social and political climates that shaped his time and his experience in it. Likewise, the biography and history of Nathaniel Hawthorne is essential to "Hawthorne." When Lowell references "The Custom-House" in stanza 1, it is not only to give the reader a sense of place, but also to touch on Hawthorne's own life and submerged in reflection, but also a part of the public world, a part of Salem.

STYLE

Lyric Poetry

Lyric poetry is the classically preferred form for expressing emotions and feelings. Sonnets, villanelles, and ballads are all forms of lyric poetry involving a single speaker's thoughts and expressions. The confessional nature of Lowell's work, which takes on intimate and private subjects, naturally lends itself to the lyric style. As evidenced in "Hawthorne," Lowell is one of the few poets who uses the lyric poem as a vehicle not only for personal expression, but also to comment on the social and political. Lowell's reflection upon the city of Salem in line 9 and his tribute to Hawthorne throughout stanza 3 would be typical of lyric poetry. However, his shift to the working professionals on State Street in lines 15 through 18 exemplifies Lowell's twist on the style.

Free Verse

"Hawthorne" has no discernible rhyme scheme, form, or meter, and can therefore be classified as a free verse poem. Lowell, like many poets who used free verse, began his career by writing with very strict form and structure and much attention to rhyme. Like most free verse poetry, "Hawthorne" does not use end rhyme, meaning a defined rhyme scheme at the end of each line. In stanza 1, each line ends with enjambment, that is, without end punctuation, and therefore causes the reader to take a mental breath at the end of each line. Since there is no rhyme or meter to dictate why the line should break, Lowell forces the reader to consider why exactly a line ends after a particular word.

Personification

Personification means giving human traits or characteristics to inanimate or nonliving things or objects. Lowell asks us to follow Salem's lazy main street in line 1, though a street cannot actually be lazy. The use of personification here conveys a certain idea or mood that is associated with lazy things upon the setting of the main street. In stanzas 6, the personified statue of Hawthorne is described as being deep in thought and his eyes become sad, though a statue is inanimate and does not have thoughts or feelings. In contrast, in stanza 5 Lowell does not personify the statue when describing light's reflection against it. It is as if further observation brings the statue to

Nathaniel Hawthorne statue in Salem, Massachusetts (Image copyright Pierdelune, 2010. Used under license from Shutterstock.com)

work. Lowell devoted his life to literature and many of his works have these sorts of allusions, or references, seamlessly woven into them. Notably, "The Custom-House" is autobiographical in nature. Hawthorne wrote "The Custom-House" after being dismissed from his position as a customs officer due to political turmoil and uses it to introduce *The Scarlet Letter*. Its acknowledgement of the Puritanical history of Salem and Hawthorne's own family history makes it a perfect touchstone for Lowell's homage. Though perturbed at his removal, Hawthorne was nevertheless relieved at the loss of his post, as it gave him time to finish *The Scarlet Letter* and he had begun to fear that his immersion into the stifling realm of the public was impacting his personal creativity. Lowell's tone also shifts in "Hawthorne" from a public tour-guide sort of description of Salem in stanza 1, to the personal reflections of stanzas 2 and 3. Finally, the public and private converge in stanza 6, where Hawthorne is forever deep in thought and

COMPARE
&
CONTRAST

- **1850s:** Though Hawthorne is not an abolitionist, as racism is a common ideology and slavery an institution of the times, the anti-slavery movements gain momentum in the 1850s with the publishing of *Uncle Tom's Cabin* by Harriet Beecher Stowe in 1852 and in the wake of the landmark *Dred Scott v. Sandford* Supreme Court decision in 1857.

    1960s: Robert Lowell is deeply interested in the civil rights movement of the 1960s. *For the Union Dead* is published the same year the Civil Rights Act of 1964 is passed and only one year after Martin Luther King Jr.'s famous 1963 "I Have a Dream" speech. It is written one hundred years after the Civil War.

    Today: Today, African Americans experience equal rights and opportunities in the United States and are influential figures in the media, sports, the arts and literature, the armed forces, and government. Barack Obama is elected as the first African American president of the United States in 2008.

- **1850s:** Hawthorne writes *The Scarlet Letter* recounting the history of Puritanism in New England and the heavy religious influence throughout culture. Though it has lost much of the strict Calvinist doctrines by the mid-1800s, religion in the United States still revolves largely around the protestant ideas on which it was founded.

    1960s: Although he is from one of the first families of New England and is therefore tied to the history of Puritanism, Robert Lowell converts to Catholicism and eventually departs from that as well. This sense of spiritual abandonment greatly influences his later works.

    Today: According to a 2007 Pew Research Center survey, 78.5 percent of the American population practices Christianity, with 51.3 percent being Protestant. Though Christianity is not as predominant a theme in American poetry as it has been in the past, religion is still a major force in American culture and continues to influence American poetry.

- **1850s:** Poetry is a popular form of storytelling, and narrative poems like those by the fireside poets are often memorized and recited for entertainment.

    1960s: With advent of the confessional poetry movement, poets begin to convey intimate personal details in their writing. Poetry is a therapeutic endeavor for poets like Anne Sexton and Sylvia Plath.

    Today: Slam poetry, while not a mainstream form of entertainment, is growing in popularity and combines the traditions of poetry as performance and poetry as a means of personal revelation and exploration.

---

life, and the reader must wonder if the statue's observations of the inanimate things around him have a similar life-giving effect.

HISTORICAL CONTEXT

Hawthorne's Salem and Puritan History
When Hawthorne wrote *The Scarlet Letter* and "The Custom-House," he had just been removed from his post as a customs officer in Salem,

Massachusetts. After the presidential election of 1848 and the installment of the Whig president Zachary Taylor, the Democrat Hawthorne was removed from his post, but not before finding an account of a woman named Hester Prynne left over from a past surveyor and wrapped in scarlet cloth, as noted in "The Custom-House." Hester Prynne lived in Puritan New England. This society believed that the English Reformation was not strict enough and strove to establish a model community, a bastion for Christian ethics and piety. When sailing from

The poem describes Hawthorne standing near a schooner and dock. (*Image copyright Karin Lamprecht, 2010. Used under license from Shutterstock.com*)

England in 1630, John Winthrop, the first governor of the Massachusetts Bay Colony, envisioned the colony to be built in America "as a city upon a hill," standing as a pure model of Christianity. Puritans were very conservative in their beliefs and customs, stressing humility and private study and preferring plain dress in a statement of opposition to Catholic decadence and the corruption of the Anglican Church. The adultery of Hester Prynne, novelized in Hawthorne's *The Scarlet Letter*, was a tremendous offense and crime in Puritanical Salem, Massachusetts. This period overlapped with the controversial Salem Witch Trial hearings in 1692 and 1693, where many women and men were executed after being accused of witchcraft. Hawthorne was related to John Hathorne, one of the principle judges of the trials, and even changed his name dissociate himself from the name's darkened history. Hawthorne felt a sense of shame for the actions of his ancestors, as well as the political hypocrisy that framed the trials. After reading the account of Prynne and being fired for political reasons, Hawthorne was inspired to create *The Scarlet Letter*.

Lowell and Confessional Poetry

The confessional poetry movement, a movement whose name originated in a review of Lowell's *Life Studies*, was prominent during the 1950s and 1960s. Confessional poetry centers around the intimate and private details and experiences of the individual, subjects previously considered unfit for serious poetry. Many poets such as Delmore Schwartz and John Berryman had made steps towards a more confessional style, but it wasn't until a review of *Life Studies* by critic M. L. Rosenthal that, according to Deborah Nelson in her essay "Beyond Privacy: Confessions Between a Woman and her Doctor," the term was first employed. Lowell began writing confessional poetry as a means of therapy while being institutionalized after a nervous breakdown, exploring his own personal history and insights. By the time that *For the Union Dead* was released, other poets such as Sylvia Plath, Theodore Roethke, Anne Sexton, and William Snodgrass were already being identified under the banner of confessional poetry. Lowell's divorce, growing interest in the civil rights movement of the 1960's, and departure from the Catholic church left him looking for an outlet. Naturally, he turned to poetry. The work in *For the Union Dead* deals not only with Lowell's personal life but also with his feelings of isolation in modern society and his admiration for artists such as Nathaniel Hawthorne.

CRITICAL OVERVIEW

When *For the Union Dead* was published, Lowell was already a celebrated and decorated American poet. He won the Pulitzer Prize at the young age of thirty for *Lord Weary's Castle* and redefined himself in *Life Studies* with the development of his confessional style. *For the Union Dead*, therefore, was widely anticipated. "More than any contemporary writer, poet or novelist," states critic Richard Poirier in the collection *Critics on Robert Lowell* by Jonathan Price (quoted on the *Poetry Foundation* Web site), "Lowell has created the language, cool and violent all at once, of contemporary introspection. He is our truest historian." This description was apt, as Lowell's work was becoming increasingly centered on the individual as a part of history and the relevance of the past to the present. His confessional style allowed him to interweave and entwine these different perspectives and subjects without the structural restraints of his earlier works. His biographical poems began to take on new life in *For the Union Dead*, drawing vignettes of influential figures in culture and history and, as George W. Nitchie asserts in his essay "The Importance of Robert Lowell," finding "its human center in 'Hawthorne.'" Jonathan Raban, in a review in the *Observer* (quoted on the *Poetry Foundation* Web site), writes of Lowell's development that he "found a style in which he could write, not just about Cousin Harriet and Uncle Devereux but about that spacious mental world where the living share their quarters with the vivid dead."

CRITICISM

Jon Richardson

Richardson is a writer and editor. In this essay on "Hawthorne," he argues that Lowell's homage to Nathaniel Hawthorne's legacy reflects his desires for his own literary legacy.

Robert Lowell was one of the last American poetic heavyweights to view writing as a heroic and romantic pursuit, one that required the dedication and work of a lifetime. Throughout his prolific and diverse career, he wrote about many artists, paying homage to his contemporaries and those who had carried the torch long before him; "Hawthorne" from *For the Union Dead* is one such poem. However, through close reading and looking at his later works "Epilogue" and "Reading Myself" in relation to these odes, it becomes clear that Lowell's reverence for literature and other artists points back to his own longing to be recognized and uncertainty about where he will stand in the pages of history. "Hawthorne" is about the works and impact of Nathaniel Hawthorne, but it also stands as a peephole into Lowell's own desires for how he and his work will be remembered.

Commissioned for the centennial publication of Nathaniel Hawthorne's collected works by the Ohio State University press, Robert Lowell's poem celebrates Hawthorne's life, career, and literary legacy. Throughout it, Lowell draws on his vast knowledge of Hawthorne's works and inserts passages from them, specifically from "The Custom-House" and *Septimius Felton*, into his verses. He seamlessly weaves these references into the poem, using Hawthorne's autobiographical work to frame his portrait, from the coal furnace of the customs house to the bustling State Street. Robert Lowell was a bibliophile to the core, and his collected works reads like an annotated history of Western civilization. He devoured and pored over more volumes of history, philosophy, and literature than almost any other twentieth-century poet and was able to recall lines nearly at will from his vast stores of memory. Therefore, "Hawthorne," like many of his works, is jigsawed with quotations and allusions that would go unnoticed by the untrained eye. This assimilation of Hawthorne's texts into his own is one of the first connections that Lowell draws between himself and his subject, positioning the astute reader to view him with relative equality to Hawthorne.

WHAT DO I READ NEXT?

- Robert Lowell's *Collected Poems*, which was revised in 2007 by Frank Bidart and David Gewanter, features all of his works and even some of his unprinted manuscripts and translations. This volume not only contains the breadth of Lowell's entire literary career, showing his own evolution and adoption of the confessional style, but also has an extensive glossary of annotations and notes.

- *Words in Air: The Complete Correspondence between Elizabeth Bishop and Robert Lowell* (2010) is a compilation of almost thirty years of intimate conversation through letters between two of the twentieth century's most influential American poets. This collection not only shows Lowell's brilliance in a non-poetic setting, but also provides a unique insight into his personal life.

- Nathaniel Hawthorne's *Septimius Felton* was published in 1880, after Hawthorne's death in 1872. It is the haunting love story of a young scholar who tries to create an elixir of life from a rare flower, using a formula given to him by a dying man. Lowell quotes this work in addition to "The Custom-House" throughout "Hawthorne."

- *Live or Die* by Anne Sexton was published in 1966 and won the Pulitzer Prize the following year. Sexton helped to carry the torch of confessional poetry along with Lowell, and this volume is considered one of her best.

- *The Absolutely True Diary of a Part-Time Indian* by Sherman Alexie was published in 2007. It is a novel for young adults told from the viewpoint of a young Native American teenager that is confessional in nature, detailing the hardships of growing up on a modern reservation.

- *My Father's Martial Art: Poems* was published in 1999 by Stephen S.N. Liu. His intimate and expressive poetry reflects on his Chinese history and culture in relation to his modern experience of American life.

> THROUGHOUT THE POEM, LOWELL BOWS TO HAWTHORNE WHILE BLURRING THE LINES BETWEEN THEM. WHEN THIS IS CONSIDERED IN RELATION TO TWO OF HIS LATER POEMS, 'EPILOGUE' AND 'READING MYSELF,' LOWELL'S LONGING IN 'HAWTHORNE' FOR HIS OWN LITERARY MONUMENT BECOMES CLEAR."

Lowell applauds Hawthorne's ability to retain his creativity in the working world. Lowell himself came from a wealthy Boston-Brahmin family, having direct lineage back to *Mayflower* passengers and the earliest of the American social elite. Coming from a family whose name was synonymous with high society, he was able to pursue his literary career without too many financial pressures. These aspects of his background no doubt informed his view of the working world. He depicts Hawthorne's working week in stanza 3, carefully setting up a distinction between the writer's career and those of the professionals working across town, who measure out their weary days by the hashes on the ominous clock that looms above like an overseer. This distinct contrast mirrors the one shown in stanza 1 between the poor house, where those in need could receive aid through charity, and the site of the gallows, where many innocents were hung during the Salem Witch Trials, helping the reader to draw a greater divide between the artist and society. In stanza 4, Lowell's word choice creates ambiguity for the reader and allows for another comparison to Hawthorne. He remarks on the dangers and pitfalls that surround the line between a professional career and the life of an artist, as one false step could lead to a creative death, all while referencing one of Hawthorne's passages from "The Custom-House." The reader might believe Hawthorne to be the subject of this passage, but the wording leaves room for another interpretation. The ambiguity of the word "this" lends itself to both writers, as Lowell could just as easily be referring to himself as to Hawthorne, possibly referring to one of his many teaching stints.

The reverie of Hawthorne returns in stanza 5, as Lowell positions him above his contemporaries, the Fireside Poets, through the image of the statue. Lowell has been known to reference statues and other pieces of art in his poetry, most notably the frieze in "For the Union Dead," the title poem of the volume in which "Hawthorne" appears. Hawthorne stands golden in his triumph while the others are silvered and second best, graying in the pages of history. In the final stanza, Lowell again refers to *Septimius Felton*, which focused on a man pursuing the elixir of life that would grant him immortality. Lowell suggests that Hawthorne has done exactly this through his art; he will stand forever young. He is golden and will not tarnish or diminish in value; he has become a part of history. For the creative and artistic risks that he has taken, he has been immortalized in a statue, and as much as Salem's history was a part of Hawthorne, he has likewise become a part of Salem's history. Throughout his life and career, Lowell too was a driving and singular literary force. Not only was he prolific, but his writing style was pioneering. He moved from the formal, highly-stylized technical iambic pentameter to free verse, inspiring the confessional poetry literary movement, and then eventually back to formal structure; his literary career stands as a narrative in and of itself.

In the final stanza of the poem, Lowell once again references *Septimius Felton*, describing the public's perception of a writer or artist. While the public only sees a man bent over staring at some trivial or miniscule object, the artist is privately seeking a truth that cannot be found within file cabinets or ledgers. That the last two lines themselves present a puzzle—how the true can at the same time be insignificant, and why a great man would meditate on something that is insignificant—adds an air of exclusivity separating men like him and Hawthorne from the unenlightened, the non-artists.

Throughout the poem, Lowell bows to Hawthorne while blurring the lines between them. When this is considered in relation to two of his later poems, "Epilogue" and "Reading Myself," Lowell's longing in "Hawthorne" for his own literary monument becomes clear.

In "Reading Myself," which appeared in his volume *History* (1973), Lowell questions his place in the broader scope of art and literature. He characterizes his work as mere smoke and bang, built of tricks that led to quick celebrity and fame, but nothing that would endure. Lowell dips into his vast knowledge of history and mythology, mentioning Mount Parnassus, the classical Greek home to the muses and poetry, and wondering if he has earned the right to be within mere proximity of it. He sees his works as only transient and ephemeral vignettes and likens himself to a bee, building his own tomb around him with his volumes of poetry, hoping to last just long enough to be torn down and sacked by the hungry voracious beast of time. "Epilogue," the final poem in his last book *Day by Day* (1977), expresses Lowell's doubt about the lasting impact of his works. Once again, he remarks that the literary and poetic devices which he had mastered and utilized so well for so long seem lackluster, only allowing him to explain what is already in plain sight to the world. Lowell is nearing the end of his life and in these poems that are far more confessional in nature than "Hawthorne," he openly questions the permanence of his life and art. The poet and the man who is so transfixed by the narrow space where the personal, public, and historical meet is looking for exactly that—his own place in history.

Upon reading these later poems, "Hawthorne" begins to take on new meaning. The troubled eyes depicted in the final stanza bring to mind the manic behavior and even institutionalization of Lowell as well the romantic Hawthorne, whose Puritanical roots led to an obsession with man's burden of guilt and sin. In stanza 2, Salem's history has been tarnished and stained for both Lowell, who is haunted by his own upper-class New England heritage, and Hawthorne, who even changed his name in an attempt to dissociate himself from an unapologetic ancestor who was a magistrate in the Salem Witch Trials. Lowell's poem celebrates a writer who has been immortalized and cast in bronze, whose private introspection has become a piece of public history. Lowell, the Byronic Brahmin, rebelled against his own family history, helped to forge a new literary movement, and established himself as major literary force, winning a Pulitzer Prize and being appointed the U.S. Poet Laureate at the age of 29. His immense and challenging body of work stands on a pedestal in twentieth-century American poetry. Nevertheless, he remained insecure about his own standing in the world of literature and in the

Lowell alludes to times of darkness at Gallows Hill, where people accused of being witches were hung in Salem. (*Image copyright Sinisa Botas, 2010. Used under license from Shutterstock.com*)

realm of history. Thus, while celebrating the legacy of the artist in complicated odes like "Hawthorne," he also attempts to secure his own.

Source: Jon Richardson, Critical Essay on "Hawthorne," in *Poetry for Students*, Gale, Cengage Learning, 2011.

J. D. McClatchy

In the following review, McClatchy discusses why Lowell was described as "our truest historian" by Richard Poirer, who stated that Lowell's volumes displayed the character of a generation.

Whatever else it may signify, the fact that there have now been published more books about Robert Lowell than by him testifies to his rank as our preeminent contemporary poet. And the appearance of his *Selected Poems* is summary evidence of his further position as our representative national poet—not in the sentimental manner Frost was so designated, but in the sense that the work of Auden's career once

captured the shifting currents of his time, both in its public manifestations and its unconscious motivations. In much the same way, Lowell's successive volumes have not only displayed the character of our generation, most often revealed in the details of his own personality, but have also transcended that character to embody, in his art's voice and vision, its animating conscience. He is, in Richard Poirier's decisive phrase, "our truest historian." (p. 34)

What makes his *Selected Poems* so intriguing is that the book provides Lowell's own sense of his career.... *Selected Poems* affords us an adjusted vantage on his extraordinary art. His impulse toward existential narrative, his calculated use of surreal imagery, his deployment of historical allusion—all of these emerge with a heightened resonance. Likewise, his confessional method, first announced in *Life Studies* and later reaffirmed in *The Dolphin*, is revealed with new force.

THE THERAPEUTIC AND CRITICAL SUCCESS OF *LIFE STUDIES'*S REVELATIONS SEEMS TO HAVE OCCASIONED A SELF-CONSCIOUSNESS THAT DEMANDED BOTH RELEASE AND RESTRAINT....*FOR THE UNION DEAD,* IN OTHER WORDS, IS THE EFFECT OF *LIFE STUDIES.*"

As in his career, so too in his *Selected Poems* is *Life Studies* given a centering pride of place.... Not only has the book been regarded as a profound influence on American poetry generally and as both the origin and sanction of the confessional movement, but it has been represented as the radical, decisive reversal of Lowell's early style and subject, so that the poet discovered significance at once in and for himself.... His earliest and best critic, Randall Jarrell, quickly perceived the pattern of concern in the poet's development, and his judgment of *Lord Weary's Castle* was prophetic for the career itself: "Anyone who compares Mr. Lowell's earlier and later poems will see this movement from constriction to liberation as his work's ruling principle of growth."... That progress is at once tortuous and simple: a king's through the guts of a beggar. Its literary modes of expression—from the symbolic to the mythological to the historical—reflect his personal deconversion from faith to fiction to fact. In his *Notebook,* there is a line that could be used to graph the intention and effect of all his work: "I am learning to live in history."

...In his Introduction to Lowell's first book *Land of Unlikeness* (1944), Allen Tate offered an important observation about the early poems—one that applies equally to *Lord Weary's Castle* (1946) which incorporates the best of *Land of Unlikeness* and so is the convenient focus for a discussion of Lowell's beginnings. There are, Tate noted, two types of poems in the collection, "not yet united." The first are "the explicitly religious poems" with their intellectualized and often satirical Christian symbolism, and the second are those "richer in immediate experience," "more dramatic, the references being personal and historical and the symbolism less willed and

explicit." Together, they comprise what Hugh Staples calls a "poetry of rebellion."... But rebellion was less the reason for than the result of the informing vision and voice of these poems. The epigraph from St. Bernard affixed to *Land of Unlikeness* offers the cause in a comparison: *Inde anima dissimilis deo inde dissimilis est et sibi* (As the soul is unlike God, so is it unlike itself). This alienation, suspended from "the jerking noose of time," is masked behind a Catholic mysticism that holds the poet apart from both unredeemed nature and the burdens of history. (pp. 34–5)

Lowell's militant faith served him also as a defiance of and defense against the "sewage" that "sickens the rebellious seas" ("Salem")—his own past and that of his family, which emerge only emblematically in *Lord Weary's Castle.* (p. 35)

The *Selected Poems* rather self-consciously minimizes the impacted apocalyptic aspect of *Lord Weary's Castle,* in favor of those poems Tate referred to as "richer in immediate experience."... Stripped of its mystical contortions, it is easier now to see the book's treatment of concentric alienations as the prelude to Lowell's versions of the theme, under different guises, in subsequent collections. But what disturbs me is that the same argument that may have resulted in that decision may also have occasioned the poet's grievous cuts from his next book, *The Mills of the Kavanaughs* (1951). Perhaps Lowell has come to agree with the majority of his critics who, unlike myself, seem to consider the book an uncertain exercise in verbal self-indulgence.... Though these mythic monologues remain dramas of remission and evasion, they indicate that Lowell no longer wished to transform or transcend his personality, but to integrate its conflicting motifs. Poems like "Falling Asleep over the Aeneid" and "Mother Marie Therese"... seem self-absorbed in a gorgeous display of the form itself, but generally in this book Lowell, like one of his characters, has "gone underground/ Into myself." The voice is subdued to a new control, the scope narrowed from cultural to personal decline, from civilization to the family, from the Church to a marriage.... Each poem in *The Mills of the Kavanaughs* deals with a present relationship to the past, and as one critic says, the book "shares with *Life Studies* this intensity of memory."...

During the eight years that intervened before his next book, *Life Studies* (1959), Lowell's philosophy of composition underwent a radical revaluation. The influences on that process were multiple: some of them personal (the death of his mother in 1954, and his subsequent hospitalizations and private psychotherapy), some of them literary. The poet himself began to think that the style of his early poems was "distant, symbol-ridden, and willfully difficult," and occluded their sense. His exposure to the Beats and to the peculiar responsibilities of communication demanded by reading poetry aloud, interested him in a more colloquial approach to diction and the dynamics of narrative, while his simultaneous immersion in prose studies—especially the subdued, realistic precision of Chekhov and Flaubert—confirmed him in the need for a more relaxed rhythm and line, for a syntax responsible to voice and a tone that would both prompt and project his subject. . . . Replacing the strictures of imposed form, Lowell's new voice worked with subtle modulations of stanza, varying rhythm, unobtrusive rhyme and sharp detail, to achieve an effect of "heightened conversation." . . . So the mystical commitment of the early symbolist verse becomes a moral commitment in the confessional verse; honesty replaces devotion, fact replaces faith, in the poet's shift from ideology to history, from Catholicism to psychoanalysis as a method of self-interpretation, from apocalyptic rebellion to ironic detachment. . . .

Life Studies begins with a renunciation of the consolations of culture and religion that had previously sustained Lowell's art and life: "Much against my will/I left the City of God where it belongs." Will surrenders to experience, eternity to history, as Lowell sets out to discover where *he* belongs. In this modern, parallaxed *Prelude*, the poet arranges his significant spots of time, pausing at moments of crisis like infernal circles, into the definition of himself that presents a life in which the only innocence is insanity, the only resolution a scavenging survival. (p. 36)

The sins of the father revisited in *Life Studies* revealed a helpless and ironic repetition in his life that Lowell was determined to avoid in his art . . . *For the Union Dead* (1964), with the grand public manner of its title poem, is the "more impersonal matter," the retreat from self to sensibility: "I am tired. Everyone's tired of my turmoil." . . . His guilts become figures in an "unforgivable landscape," his neuroses change the studied confessions into impulsive, lyrical meditations. The therapeutic and critical success of *Life Studies*'s revelations seems to have occasioned a self-consciousness that demanded both

release and restraint. . . . *For the Union Dead*, in other words, is the effect of *Life Studies*. (p. 37)

The political poems that are the positive achievement of *For the Union Dead* are the reason for Lowell's subsequent book, *Near the Ocean* (1967), which draws on his previous talents for elegy and imitation to complete—along with his staged poems *The Old Glory* (1965) and *Prometheus Bound* (1967)—his Juvenalian indictment of mid-century American political and spiritual failure. Written during the period of Lowell's own most active political involvement, the book sheds a good deal of personal malaise coincident with the national. . . . [Critics] were disappointed by *Near the Ocean*—except for its interesting reversion to a strict prosody, presumably to emphasize the severe moral tone these poems adopt. After *Life Studies* Lowell seems to have experienced a difficulty—or possibly a diffidence—in combining the confessional and political modes. The large experiment he next undertook to overcome that difficulty—*Notebook 1967–68* (1969)—created difficulties of its own, as evidenced by the constant recycling of its format and contents, first as *Notebook* (1970) and then as *History* (1973. . . . The poet here resumes history by recording it, not by narrowing it to the slant of private vision but by opening his vision to the rush of outer accidents, tempered only by the seasonal cycle that underlies it and the involuntary memories that intrude upon it. It is his effort to accommodate a life in history and the life of history—though many of its first readers found it merely one damn poem after another. . . .

It is an unfortunate necessity that the present book cannot reproduce *History*'s convulsive particularity and sacrifices its scope to a fine sample from his catalogue of tyrants and saints, artists and criminals, each a variation on the type of the monster, so that his meditations are really personalizing studies of the themes, of will, authority, breakdown, and recrimination in his own history. . . .

His portrayal of a discontented civilization derives from the late Freudian model, whose sense of instinctive aggression is finally suicidal—itself an illuminating comparison with Lowell's confrontations with both himself and his society. . . .

[The] more congenial if painful struggles of "becoming" are the subject of his most intimate and controversial book, *The Dolphin*, an account of his divorce from [Elizabeth] Hardwick, his remarriage to Caroline Blackwood and the birth of their son Sheridan.... With the melodrama diluted, we are not offered glimpses of the wrenching affair, which leaves it with an appropriate immediacy yet lends it a retrospective quality of accomplishment.... [Lowell has said of] his own acknowledged precursors—Pound, Eliot, Williams, and Hart Crane among them—... [that they wrote] in "styles closer to the difficulties of art and the mind's unreason." There is no better descriptive praise for Lowell's own work than that, and his *Selected Poems* are both the abstract and particulars of the successful risks he has taken to bring the mind's unreason to the orders of art, to bring the difficulties of art to the history of human experience. (p. 38)

Source: J. D. McClatchy, "Robert Lowell: Learning to Live in History," in *American Poetry Review*, January/February 1977, pp. 34–38.

Don Bogen

In the following review, Bogen offers a positive evaluation of Lowell's Collected Prose *and adds that his "free verse confessions and diary-like musings in poems were news in a way that no poet's are today."*

Robert Lowell was probably the last American poet who might be described as formidable. His stylistic transformations—from dense formal elegies to free verse confessions, blank sonnets and diary-like musings—were news in a way that no poet's are today. Immersed in aesthetic debates and the controversies of public life, he held a commanding place in American culture even after his move to Britain in the late 1960s. That prominence has declined in the decade since his death. Lowell's choice of subject may be partly to blame here. A poet who writes a lot about his life is at the mercy of his biographer after his death, and Lowell was not served well by his. Ian Hamilton's *Robert Lowell: A Biography* is an exhausting compendium of letters, anecdotes and narration which presents, finally, a stock image of the poet as inspired madman: frenzied, often cruel, living life at superhuman intensity and, in the current version of the myth, a victim of his own aberrant brain chemistry. Lowell's *Collected Prose* should help correct that image. It reminds us that what matters is not how often the poet was in mental hospitals or how many affairs he had but what he wrote and thought.

Lowell seems to have struggled with his writing more than most, revising, as he put it,

> HIS REVIEWS AND ESSAYS HAVE AN ALMOST OLD-FASHIONED ELEMENT OF INTELLECTUAL RESPONSIBILITY TO THEM. THEY REFLECT A TIME WHEN CRITICS ACTIVELY INTERPRETED POEMS AND POETS ACTUALLY READ WHAT CRITICS WROTE."

"endlessly." In his elegy for Lowell, the Irish poet Seamus Heaney compared him to a retiarius, the gladiator who fought with a net. Knotting, weaving, casting and recasting his mesh of words, Lowell produced a body of poetry that makes most poets' careers look facile and self-imitative. Though he wrote relatively little prose, the range of Lowell's net in this mode was wide. His *Collected Prose* contains autobiographical studies; essays on American, European and classical literature; reviews of contemporary poets and critics from I. A. Richards to Sylvia Plath; and two interviews. Not all the material is equally well crafted or illuminating—sometimes the net has big holes in it. But what Lowell manages to capture in these pieces is well worth the occasional passage through empty air.

Lowell's prose was edited by his friend and publisher Robert Giroux, who provides a good introduction and careful, unobtrusive notes. A bit more than a quarter of the book consists of previously unpublished material, most of which is unfinished and still rough. The ideas are often fascinating here, especially Lowell's scattered comments on American writers in "New England and Further" but we can see why the poet didn't find this work ready for print. A few of the unpublished pieces should probably not have been printed at all. The inclusion of Lowell's prep-school essay on the Iliad, for example, serves no purpose. Lowell was no Rimbaud; his term-paper, style sounds as windy and adolescent as any school boy's. Publishing the letter of protest Lowell wrote to President Roosevelt when he refused induction during World War II is perhaps more understandable, as there may be some biographical interest in seeing the actual "manic statement" mentioned in Lowell's *Life Studies*. But though his poems brilliantly capture the public climates of our time—particularly the cold war and Vietnam eras—this letter shows a muddled anticommunism that does him little credit. Like Yeats, Lowell used the ambiguities and tensions of verse to thread through the labyrinth of political life. Without them, he seems as lost as any of us.

But Lowell is not lost in the critical essays and reviews he wrote for publication. The *Collected Prose* brings those together well, juxtaposing his early and later pieces on central modernist figures such as T.S. Eliot and William Carlos Williams and poet-critics such as Randall Jarrell and John Crowe Ransom. In most of these pairings the first piece is an analytical review from the late 1940s, the second an overview and elegy some twenty years later. What's perhaps most striking in Lowell's criticism is his generosity of spirit. In dealing with poets' lives he has kind things to say about everyone. Even Robert Frost, a man possessing what Lowell termed "a heart of stonemason darkness," is treated with sympathetic understanding. Likewise his judgments of writers' work are appealingly eclectic, reminding us that the kinds of oppositions that shape a literary history—Williams versus Eliot, Stevens versus Frost—should not keep us from enjoying different kinds of poetry. Although he considered his essays "much sloppier and more intuitive" than standard criticism, Lowell rarely indulges in the bland poets' shoptalk that crops up all too frequently in literary magazines today. Rather he combines scholarly breadth and rigor with an insider's attention to the significant aspects of poetic practice. In his essay on Williams, for example, Lowell pinpoints the essence of the poet's free verse technique—"quick changes of tone, atmosphere, and speed"—which has escaped William's ubiquitous imitators. And his review of Elizabeth Bishop's first book, *North & South*, in 1947 defines the precise values that remained central throughout her career: variety and the ability to let description and reflection feed each other, to build poems that simultaneously show and think.

If Lowell as critic is perceptive in his praise, he is equally insightful in his put-downs. Here he is on a new translation of Ovid in 1955:

> A. E. Watts's translation of the *Metamorphoses* into five-foot couplets is admirable, steady, civilized—and impossible. Watts, you have to conclude, has chosen the wrong poem in the *Metamorphoses* because this work, as he says in his preface, is "the most complete exploration in verse of the resources of rhetoric." Unfortunately, the resources of rhetoric cannot be explored by academic piety and a photostat exhibition of devices and tropes. Once started on the job, however, Watts chose the wrong meter. No English poet has ever translated hexameters into adequate pentameter couplets. No poet since Chaucer has done a translation even of couplets into couplets that has turned out to be comparable to the original. No one *not* a poet has ever written readable couplets. No one in our century has written an interesting long poem in couplets. To make sure of mortally crippling himself, Watts has chosen to mix a gushing run-on line with the divided, antithetical, and end-stopped line of Pope and Dryden. The Watts couplet is freakishly stiff and floppy, a Minotaur, uneasy in both its natures; it brays without emphasis.

You can tell Lowell is having a good time here: a breezy wit animates the piece from the opening reversal through all those *no*'s below. But this is no cheap shot. Turning from what he calls "Watts- baiting" a paragraph later, Lowell spends the bulk of his review defining what makes Ovid so elusive in English. His discussion of what's wrong in just the first lines of English versions by Watts, Dryden and the Elizabethan translator Arthur Golding is an engaging tour de force, and his sense of Ovid's subtleties illuminates the entire essay. It's common enough to see a work of verse as untranslatable, but Lowell's review is finally encouraging to those who would attempt an English Ovid. By describing the original in all its protean energy, its shifts, as he puts it, "from Vergilian wonder to the flippant, forceful, jabbing worldliness of a letter writer," Lowell whets our appetite for a good translation. His concern with the intricacies of Ovid and Vergil is not merely antiquarian. For Lowell, modern America was a version of Augustan Rome: a republic gone to seed, peevish, imperialist, in constant search of reminders of its own greatness. In this regard the classics are as fresh as ever.

If the net of Lowell's verse caught much of our imperial petulance, it also dragged in great swaths of his own troubled life. It is interesting to see him examining parts of that life in two previously unpublished autobiographical essays from the late 1950s, "Antebellum Boston" and "Near the Unbalanced Aquarium." Though they complement the brilliant prose piece "91 Revere Street," which Lowell included in *Life Studies*, they are not as well written. Their structures seem a little clunky, their ironies not as sharp as they could be. Instead of revising them extensively for publication, Lowell appears to have mined these essays for poems. In one section of

"Near the Unbalanced Aquarium," for instance, all the details of what will later become the poem "Father's Bedroom" arise in one dense paragraph. To read this is to appreciate Lowell's sheer craft in converting a mass of description and speculation into an incisive and purposeful work of verse. Elsewhere in these essays are some vivid depictions of illness: a childhood bout with croup, pervaded by the smell of benzoin and the hallucinations of three days without sleep; and Lowell's stay at the Payne-Whitney Clinic in 1954, which alternates between manic pranks and the medicated lethargy of "a diver in the full billowings of his equipment on the bottom of the sea."

But the best autobiographical piece in the *Collected Prose*—one of the finest essays of its sort in the last forty years—is "91 Revere Street." Weaving memories of boyhood incidents with family history and sketches of his parents and their friends, Lowell captures not just one life but a whole context of experience. The central event is Lowell's father's decision in 1927 to acquiesce to his wife's demands and resign his commission in the Navy. In tracing the man's pathetic attempts at explaining his action to his Navy buddies, Lowell builds a devastating vision of balding "boys" still checking out one another's "*figger* and waterline," frozen in adolescence by nostalgia and the petty rules and rewards of service life. Though the boy Lowell's sympathies are clearly with his mother (there is no shortage of Oedipal overtones here), the essay exposes her much-valued Old Boston taste as "middle-of-the-road," her social pretensions as laughable and her marital tactics as unscrupulous. Any pity we might feel for the only child of this union between New England snobbery and Annapolis juvenility is held in check by Lowell's depiction of himself as alternately aggressive and thick-skulled, enjoying his mother's attention and his role as a pawn in his parents' fights. As a study of the intricacies of domestic discord, "91 Revere Street" is cold, accurate and ferocious.

Lowell was a great poet of description, and one thing that makes the tensions so vivid in "91 Revere Street" is his startling treatment of inanimate objects, especially clothes and furniture. His picture of the Victorian furnishings the Lowells inherited from relatives is typical:

> Here, table, highboy, chairs, and screen—mahogany, cherry, teak—looked nervous and disproportioned. They seemed to wince, touch elbows, shift from foot to foot. High above the highboy, our gold National Eagle stooped forward, plastery and doddering. The Sheffield silver-plate urns, more precious than solid sterling, peeled; the bodies of the heraldic mermaids on the Mason-Myers crest blushed a metallic copper tan. In the harsh New England light, the bronze sphinxes supporting our sideboard looked as though manufactured in Grand Rapids.

Precise, evocative and ironic, Lowell gets *things* to say more about family life than most writers do with whole pages of dialogue. But domestic *angst* is, of course, not the only subject here. "91 Revere Street" is a study in mismatches: between furniture and its setting, between taste and wealth, between a husband and wife, and between the past and the present. The story of a naval engineer who decides to work for Lever Brothers has its interest, but the fact that the man's surname is Lowell gives his decline obvious ramifications. In taking apart his family history, exposing the shoddiness and awkward displacement behind the lofty facade, Lowell dissects the complex tissue of our New England "aristocracies." Puritan moral rectitude and family-tree exclusiveness go out the window. In a perfect touch near the end of the essay, Lowell imagines his great-great-grandfather Major Mordecai Myers (who, we are told, "had never frowned down in judgment on a Salem witch") announcing to his descendants, "My children, my blood, accept graciously the loot of your inheritance. We are all dealers in used furniture."

Latter-day Romans, inheritors of claptrap and loot—Robert Lowell was able to define better than most writers what we as Americans are. His reviews and essays have an almost old-fashioned element of intellectual responsibility to them. They reflect a time when critics actively interpreted poems and poets actually read what critics wrote. Lowell's attention to tradition, social issues and the subtleties of craft gives his *Collected Prose* energy and lasting value.

Source: Don Bogen, "Perfection of the Work," in *Nation*, April 11, 1987, pp. 475–76, 478.

John Druska

In the following essay, Druska provides an overview of Lowell's literary career, artistic development, and major themes in his poetry.

1. HIS CAREER

The speaker of Robert Lowell's "In the American Grain" (*History*) announces at the close of the poem

> **AND THE FARTHER WE FOLLOW LOWELL THROUGH HIS CAREER THE MORE WE SEE HIS OWN MIND, INSOFAR AS IT ASSIMILATES THE HISTORY AND CULTURES OF WESTERN CIVILIZATION AS WELL AS THE DATA OF HIS OWN EXPERIENCE, BECOMING HIS REAL CHURCH."**

(')I am not William Carlos Williams. He knew the germ on every flower, and saw the snake is a petty, rather pathetic creature.'

Whether or not the speaker is Lowell—the poem is a direct quote, perhaps a letter to him— the sentiment is rarely his. Snakes, dragons, other biblical and/or allusive figures haunt Lowell's pages. In the early poems of *Land of Unlikeness* and *Lord Weary's Castle* he writes this most emblematic. "No ideas but in things," Williams proclaimed. Lowell's first works, for which he has lionized by much of the critical establishment, might well be saying, "Nothing but within my ideas of things":

> ... I fear
> That only Armageddon will suffice
> To turn the hero skating on thin ice
> When Whore and Beast and Dragon rise
>   for air
> From allegoric waters.
> ("To Peter Taylor on the Feast of the
>   Epiphany," *Lord Weary*)

The self-assurance of Lowell's poems in *Lord Weary* impressed. The difficulties they posed to be puzzled through impressed. Only a few objections have been recorded. Hayden Carruth dismissed the motifs in *Lord Weary* as lifeless tokens and many of the poems as "set pieces in a high style," a young poet's homage to his older masters; though among the purely "sententious" specimens Carruth discovered poems that include, under their "high gloss of artifice," urgent and moving autobiographical elements ("A Meaning of Robert Lowell," *Robert Lowell: A Portrait of the Artist in His Time*, 1970). And the artifice of Lowell's third volume, *The Mills of the Kavanaughs*, caused Williams to temper a favorable review:

In his new book Robert Lowell gives us six first-rate poems of which we may well be proud. As usual he has taken the rhyme-track for his effects. We shall now have rhyme again for a while, rhymes completely missing the incentive. The rhymes are necessary to Mr. Lowell. He must, to his mind, appear to surmount them. ("In a Mood of tragedy. . . . ": ibid.)

Did Williams's objection to rhyme echo a bit his lament that T.S. Eliot had set back irreparably the course of poetry in an American idiom?

Just as critics have stressed Eliot's religion, which never was more than a convenience to his poetry, many have made much of Lowell's temporarily-adopted (and adapted?) Catholicism and its influence on his early poetry. In retrospect, though, Lowell's true faith appears to have been in the Western tradition, T.S. Eliot pastor, rather than in the Catholic Church, which became, for a time, the exoskeleton of his emotions, ideas and images. And the farther we follow Lowell through his career the more we see his own mind, insofar as it assimilates the history and cultures of Western civilization as well as the data of his own experience, becoming his real church. Under its vault he worships not only the occasional order its rituals conjure, but the cracks in its walls, the dissolution implicit in accepting one's self in the world as the manifest sign of poetry. Thus his titles evolve from the symbolic prominence of *Land of Unlikeness* and *Lord Weary's Castle* to the pop-tune lyric, *Day by Day*.

Wondering over the course of his poetry, Lowell says in one of his last poems ("Unwanted," *Day by Day*)

> I was surer, wasn't I, once . . .
> and had flashes when I first found
> a humor for myself in images,
> farfetched misalliance
> that made evasions a revelation?

If those first poems were evasive, they were evading an audience already tantalized. If Lowell's marriage to his emblems was far-fetched, not many seemed to have noticed. Or his revelation sufficed.

But Lowell himself, long before his nostalgia in *Day by Day*, had reacted against the lineal descendants of his highly-praised *Lord Weary* works, in commenting upon poems he had been writing in the 1950's: "Their style seem distant, symbol-ridden and willfully difficult . . . my own poems seemed like prehistoric monsters dragged down into the bog and death by their ponderous armor." ("On Skunk Hour," *The Contemporary Poet as Artist and Critic*, 1964.) Later, after

Lowell closed out the 50's with *Life Studies*, which made him as popular as any legitimate poet is likely to become today, and especially after his poems of the 1960's had accumulated in *Notebook 1967–68* some critics saw a devolution in his poetry and enshrined *Lord Weary* as Lowell's masterwork. Others (including those for whom he became a confessional darling), and Lowell apparently came to regard *Lord Weary*'s mode as some archaic-baroque shell of the poet's past.

Between the publications of *Life Studies* and *Notebook 1967–68*, Donald Hall, writing the introduction to the Penguin *Contemporary American Poetry* (1962), concluded: "When he wrote *Life Studies*, Robert Lowell sent his muse to the *atelier* of William Carlos Williams (from that of Allen Tate)." To Williams's *atelier*, though, just for diction lessons. Even after the shift from "rhetorical stanzas" to "common speech" (as Hall puts it), Lowell keeps us in a world skewed by his mind's impositions, an introverted mythos, rather than in the sort of garden of realized common-place that Williams gives us. As after his exit from Catholicism, figures of that faith (or the faith of his puritanical forebears) keep slithering through his lines, pets of the tradition he extends).

Following Lowell's break from rhetorical stanzas, his movement into freer verse forms, and his settling for a long while on blank verse sonnet-sections, he suffered less drastically from distaste for his own work. Change became a matter of shuffling lines, replacing words: rewriting became a prime writing method. Through the 60's, into the 1970's, Lowell rewrote incessantly, his poetry suggests, and the nature of this revision implies some amount of disintegration, off-centeredness in his evocations of the past, present and himself in relationship to himself—a difficulty in getting the equations right, a lack of perception. Yet it implies too Lowell's immense care for getting the poem right, his attention to focusing better, pooling his work, and so perhaps himself, together. Sometimes the changes perplex. Lines and sets of lines move from one poem to another in consecutive volumes; changing contexts as well, from historical to private or vice-versa. Lowell insists on our staying in his flux while he manipulates for us the data of history and memory in order to fix (but just momentarily?) his vision of his (our?) world. This is not Williams's *Paterson* regenerating itself beyond its designed end, but Lowell's notebook-history-life—Lowell's life become poem life, as Stephen Yenser claims—rehearsing as if unready to be apprised of its end.

In "Randall Jarrell" (*History*) Lowell has his fellow poet tell him, "You didn't write, you *rewrote*." Lowell himself admitted to spending hours, days, choosing the proper word for a line. Farther and farther away from the devotional structures of his early poetry could Lowell hope to invest his work with any of the certainty whose lack his later poetry, as we've seen, seems on occasion to lament, in spite of his dismissing the "prehistoric monsters"?

Those blessed structures, plot and rhyme—
why are they no help to me now
I want to make
something imagined, not recalled?
. . .
We are poor passing facts,
warned by that to give
each figure in the photograph
his living name.

From effects of stained glass to the snapshots with which Lowell ends "Epilogue," last poem of *Day by Day*, his last book.

II. HIS LIFE, HIS DEATH: HIS POETRY

As much as history, legend and myth overshadow Lowell's work, he remains at the center of his poems, in the context of his life, from childhood to death and caught inextricably between.

Lowell's "childhood, closer to me than what I love" ("Returning," *History*) draws him, throughout his poetry, in its direction, at times back to encounters with his parents, at other times toward a life-force in his work, as well as in others': "the supreme artist, Flaubert, was a boy before the mania for phrases dried his heart" ("Les Mots," *Notebook*).

His fascination for childhood in places recalls Jarrell's. Even some of the same yearning for a child-like love occurs, as in Jarrell's brother-sister poems, or the folk tales he used to render:

Here nature seldom feels the hand of man,
our alders skirmish. I flame for the one
    friend—
is it always the same child or animal
impregnable in shell or coat of thorns
("Long Summer," *Notebook*)

And all Lowell's visions of childhood root in his own memories of Boston during the 1920's. In "91 Revere Street," a rare piece of Lowell prose which serves as Part Two of *Life Studies* in the American edition, Lowell precisely details his family life as a child. The sketch ends a joke, as obliquely as it began, neatly sliced. A joke, however, that aptly completes the poet's portrayal of himself. Lowell's father, in the piece, has been forced by his superior to spend nights away from home at the naval compound, and he is ribbed about this by an old Navy buddy: "I know why Young Bob is an only child."

But drawn in one direction by his childhood, Lowell is drawn even within the memories of his childhood in the other direction by death. "(A)lways inside me is the child who died," he says in "Night Sweat" (*For the Union Death*), "always inside me is his will to die—" And, Lowell avers in "Death and the Maiden" ("Circles, 19," *Notebook*), "A good ear hears its own death talking."

Death is the simple fact ("You were alive. You are dead.": "Alfred Corning Clark," *For the Union Dead*) that opens to the common mystery, the ultimate poet's question: "'But tell me, / Cal, why did we live? Why do we die?'" ("Randall Jarrell," *History*). It becomes in fact part of Lowell's grim bond with his fellow poets and the souce of a wry recapitulation of his career:

> Ah the swift vanishing of my older
> generation—the deaths, suicide, madness
> of Roethke, Berryman, Jarrell and Lowell,
> 'the last the most discouraging of all
> surviving to dissipate *Lord Weary's Castle*
> and nine subsequent useful poems
> in the seedy grandiloquence of *Notebook*.'
> ("Last Night," *History*)

Consistently through Lowell's *corpus* death supplies a haunting keynote:

> Fifty-one years, how many millions gone—
> . . . hear it, hear the clopping
> of the hundreds of horses unstopping . . . each
> hauls a coffin.
> ("Half a Century Gone, 5," *Notebook*)

And at an extreme death grows to an embodiment of the poet's work. In "Reading Myself" (*Notebook 1967–68*) Lowell shifts the metaphor of his work as honey-comb—"circle to circle, cell to cell, / the wax and honey of a mausoleum"—through that last image to the analogy, "this open book . . . my open coffin."

Even though his poetry virtually embalms him before our eyes, Lowell is not averse to gallows humor. Or is this the undertone of an unearthly wish?

> sleep is lovely, death is better still,
> not to have been born is of course the miracle.
> ("Heine Dying in Paris, I: Death and
> Morphine," *Imitations*)

Impossible miracle for the child already born into life's continuum, prey to its inevitable changes: "They say fear of death is a child's remembrance / of the first desertion." ("During a Transatlantic Call," *The Dolphin*).

Yet even while chronicling his own aging in his poems, (while indulging in the delight and detritus of his marriages), Lowell retains an adolescent élan, at least wistfulness:

> . . . it's the same for me
> at fifty as at thirteen, my childish thirst
> or the grown-ups in their open cars and
> girls. . . .
> ("Through the Night, 1," *Notebook 1967–
> 68*)

Growing old he does not, perhaps, grow adult. Writing for his adolescent daughter, Lowell sees her growing "too fast apace, / too fast adult; no, not adult, mature." ("Growth," *Notebook 1967–68*) He too, perhaps, matures without calcifying.

Born and bred of good Boston stock, Lowell set out, like Yeats, to do just one thing, to write poetry well, according to Hugh B. Staples, the first critic to deal with Lowell's poetry at book-length. Equipped with the wherewithal to live, and so the leisure to write, appropriately bull-headed (skeptical indeed of Yeats's achievement; what did Yeats really accomplish, he once told Staples, aside from leaving us "about four-hundred lyrics"), Lowell became a poet, discovering in the process that "Poets die adolescents" ("Fishnet," *The Dolphin*).

Are we, in fact, to regard him as a chronic adolescent? His precocious success with *Lord Weary*, his circling through his works the last decade, writing and rewriting, self-absorbed (insecure?), so seriously cocooning himself in the orbit of his psychic concerns—America's grand adolescent laureate?

III. HIS REPUTATION

Robert Lowell's persistent rewriting might have made us wonder at one time whether he would ever surpass the "four-hundred lyrics" he credited to Yeats. Yet today the critical writing on Lowell's position in American letters grows redundant. He has become for some a kind of American Yeats, not only bridging poetic tradition and the ragbone present, but turning out as well dramas that recast for us Classical and American myths, plays like those of the *Old Glory* trilogy that test our ancestral beliefs against our ancestors' and our own actions. In our present mood of eulogy, as in the wake of his lionization three decades ago, to evaluate Robert Lowell's work in a mode other than speculative is to attempt the common and the impossible.

What will come of the intellectual tradition that many have taken Lowell to represent? What of Robert Bly, called by some Lowell's most intransigent critic? Are his attacks on the *Kenyon Review* clique, Lowell included, and the anti-surrealist academics, along with his advocacy of "leaping poetry" (see *Leaping Poetry*, 1975), part of communist plot, or has Bly revealed the arc that will carry American poetry into its future? What of some voices who have been plainly showing us truths all along: Denise Levertov, David Ignatow, William Stafford, all poets in our world? And what do the Irish think of Yeats today anyway?

In its obituary of Robert Lowell last September 14, the Bangor (Me.) *Daily News* remarked, "James Russell Lowell, foremost American man of letters in his times, was Robert Lowell's great-grandfather...." Born in 1819, James Russell Lowell died in 1891. In our time we remember too that Walt Whitman lived from 1819 to 1892.

So we might do well, at least for now, to think of Robert Lowell as a person and a poet in his own age, instead of as an idol for the ages.

While he attended Kenyon College in Gambier, Ohio, after a requisite year at Harvard, Robert Lowell roomed with Peter Taylor, today one of our finest storytellers. During their time under the tutelage of John Crowe Ransom (Jarrell appearing as Instructor for a year as well), Taylor, Lowell and a handful of hardy fellow-artists also survived the rigors of watching the frat-jock parades down Kenyon's famed Middle Path, where every Tuesday night's songfest included a lyrical toast to "The first of Kenyon's goodly race / ... that great man Philander Chase." A friend who has just graduated from Kenyon assures me that not only was Philander Chase a real personage, but the parading and singing still go on along the Middle Path. As in Taylor's story of double romantic disillusionment, "1939," Lowell and his friends, reprobates all, continue to haunt Kenyon.

Lowell has written: "In truth I seem to have felt mostly the joys of living; in remembering, in recording, thanks to the gift of the Muse, it is the pain." ("Afterthought," *Notebook*)

Thanks to "1939" we see Lowell, even before he knows the harsh reality of love lost in Manhattan, in the self-consumed, self-consuming, sober

attitude of the artist as youth that pervades his work, that causes us perhaps to call him a latter-day and peculiar Romantic, in this case the adolescent the father of the man:

> *We walked the country road for miles in every direction, talking every step of the way about ourselves or about our writing, or if we exhausted those two dearer subjects, we talked about whatever we were reading at the time. We read W.H. Auden and Yvor Winters and Wyndhan Lewis and Joyce and Christopher Dawson. We read The Wings of the Dove (aloud!) and The Cosmological Eye and The Last Puritan and In Dreams Begin Responsibilities.* (Of course, I am speaking only of books that didn't come within the range of the formal courses we were taking in the college.) On our walks through the country—never more than two or three of us together—we talked and talked, but I think none of us ever listened to anyone's talk but his own. Our talk seemed always to come to nothing. But our walking took us past the sheep farms and orchards and past some of the stone farmhouses that are scattered throughout that township. It brought us to the old quarry from which most of the stone for the college buildings and for the farmhouses had been taken, and brought us to Quarry Chapel, a long since deserted and 'deconsecrated' chapel, standing on a hill two miles from the college and symbolizing there the failure of Episcopalianism to take root among the Ohio country people. Sometimes we walked along the railroad track through the valley at the foot of the college hill, and I remember more than once coming upon two or three tramps warming themselves by a little fire they had built or even cooking a meal over it. We would see them may be a hundred yards ahead, and we would get close enough to hear them laughing and talking together. But as soon as they noticed us we would turn back and walk in the other direction, for we pitied them and felt that our presence was an intrusion. And yet, looking back on it, I remember how happy those tramps always seemed. And how sad and serious we were.

Source: John Druska, "Aspects of Robert Lowell," in *Commonweal*, December 9, 1977, pp. 783–88.

SOURCES

Altieri, Charles, "Robert Lowell and the Difficulties of Escaping Modernism," in *Enlarging the Temple: New Directions in American Poetry During the 1960s*, Bucknell University Press, 1979; originally published in *Contemporary Literary Criticism*, edited by Sharon R. Gunton and Laurie Lanzen Harris, Vol. 15, Gale Research, 1980, pp. 53–77.

Brown, Ashley, "Robert Lowell," in *Dictionary of Literary Biography*, Vol. 5, *American Poets Since World War II, First Series*, edited by Donald J. Greiner, Gale Research, 1980, pp. 24–33.

Flanzbaum, Hilene, "Surviving the Marketplace: Robert Lowell and the Sixties," in *New England Quarterly*, Vol. 68, No. 1, March 1995, pp. 44–57.

Lowell, Robert, *Selected Poems: Expanded Edition: Including Selections from Day By Day*, Farrar, Straus and Giroux, 2nd ed., 2007, pp. 299, 338.

McCall, Dan, "Robert Lowell's 'Hawthorne,'" in *New England Quarterly* Vol. 39, No. 2, June 1966, pp. 237–39.

McClatchy, J. D., "Robert Lowell: Learning to Live in History," in *American Poetry Review*, January/February 1977, pp. 34–38.

Nelson, Deborah, "Beyond Privacy: Confessions Between a Woman and her Doctor," in *Feminist Studies*, Vol. 25, No. 2, Summer 1999, pp. 279.

Nitchie, George W., "The Importance of Robert Lowell," in *Southern Review*, Vol. 8, No. 1, Winter 1972, pp. 118–32.

"Robert Lowell (1917–1977)," in *Poetry Foundation*, http://www.poetryfoundation.org/archive/poet.html?id=4181 (accessed January 22, 2010).

"Robert Lowell," in *Poets.org*, http://www.poets.org/poet.php/prmPID/10 (accessed January 22, 2010).

Schneidermann, Josh, "Pilgrim's Blues: Puritan Anxiety in Robert Lowell's *For The Union Dead*," in *Journal of Modern Literature*, Vol. 31, No. 3, Spring 2008, pp. 58.

Scott, A. O., "A Life's Study: Why Robert Lowell is America's Most Important Career Poet," in *Slate*, June 20, 2003, http://www.slate.com/id/2084651/ (accessed March 15, 2010).

Spiegelman, Willard, "The Achievement of Robert Lowell," Review of *Collected Poems*, in *Kenyon Review*, Vol. 27, No. 1, Winter 2005, pp.134–69.

Thurston, Michael, "Robert Lowell (1917–1977)," in *Modern American Poetry*, http://www.english.illinois.edu/maps/poets/g_l/lowell/lowell.htm (accessed March 15, 2010).

"U.S. Religious Landscape Survey: Report 1: Religious Affiliation," in *The Pew Forum on Religion & Public Life*, http://religions.pewforum.org/reports (accessed April 16, 2010).

Woodson, Thomas, "Robert Lowell's 'Hawthorne': Yvor Winters and the American Literary Tradition," in *American Quarterly*, Vol. 19, No. 3, Autumn 1967, pp. 575–82.

FURTHER READING

Kirsch, Adam, *The Wounded Surgeon: Confession and Transformation in Six American Poets*, W. W. Norton, 2005.
Kirsch's book explores the works of the six major American confessional poets of the fifties and sixties using close reading and analysis as well as providing individual biographies. Kirsch puts an emphasis on their ability to relate personal experiences and transform them into art.

Davison, Peter, *The Fading Smile: Poets in Boston from Robert Lowell To Sylvia Plath*, W. W. Norton, 1994.
This book offers a snapshot of the vivid poetry scene in Boston in the 1950s, looking at poets from Robert Lowell to Anne Sexton and even Robert Frost. This personal and historical account shows the inner workings and dynamics of one of the most important literary and intellectual groups of the twentieth century, one which helped lead to the rise of free verse and confessional poetry.

Axelrod, Steven, and Helen Deese, eds., *Robert Lowell: Essays on the Poetry*, Cambridge University Press, 1986.
Featuring twelve essays from a range of diverse and distinguished literary critics, this volume chronologically analyzes Lowell's poetic career, giving attention to his famous, prize-winning works as well as his later and often neglected ones.

Mariani, Paul L., *Lost Puritan: A Life of Robert Lowell*, W. W. Norton, 1994.
Providing a personal rather than academic look into the tumultuous life and works of Lowell, Mariani's biography stretches from Lowell's roots in Boston high society to his failed marriages, and even details his manic behavior and institutionalization. Mariani's accessible approach to one of the twentieth century's most challenging and influential poets breathes new life into Lowell's legacy and impact today.

Wineapple, Brenda, *Hawthorne: A Life*, Random House, 2003.
This compelling biography details Nathaniel Hawthorne's personal life and career while illuminating nineteenth-century New England, offering insight into one of America's most important authors.

SUGGESTED SEARCH TERMS

Robert Lowell

Robert Lowell AND For the Union Dead

Robert Lowell AND For the Union Dead analysis

Robert Lowell poems

Hawthorne AND poem

confessional poetry

Robert Lowell AND confessional poetry

Robert Lowell AND artist in society

Robert Lowell AND Nathaniel Hawthorne

Nathaniel Hawthorne

An Hymn to the Evening

PHILLIS WHEATLEY

1773

Phillis Wheatley's poem "An Hymn to the Evening" was published in 1773 in her only book, *Poems on Various Subjects, Religious and Moral*. The book was published in London after efforts to raise sufficient funding in Boston failed. Wheatley had been writing poems since she was twelve, and her first poem "On Messrs. Hussey and Coffin" was published in 1767. Wheatley began regularly publishing in the Boston newspapers. In 1770, she published the poem that brought her international fame, "On the Death of the Reverend Mr. George Whitefield." Reverend Whitefield was a prominent evangelical preacher in New England and also the Countess of Huntingdon's personal chaplain. The Countess of Huntingdon was active in abolitionist affairs in England and provided the patronage needed for to publish Wheatley's book in 1773. She also brought Wheatley's poetry to a larger audience, including the French philosopher Voltaire, who, as Vincent Carretta notes in his introductory essay to Wheatley's *Complete Writings* wrote to a friend "that Wheatley's very fine English verse disproved [the] contention that no black poets existed."

"An Hymn to the Evening" is one of three hymns that appear in *Poems on Various Subjects, Religious and Moral*. The hymn was a common poetic form that poets used to draw a portrait of natural wonder and praise God as the cause. Although *Poems on Various Subjects, Religious and Moral* consists primarily of elegies, it also contains several odes, as well as meditations on

Phillis Wheatley *(The Library of Congress)*

subjects such as imagination and virtue. Wheatley did write a second collection of poetry, but it was lost when she could not find a publisher and her husband sold the manuscript to pay his debts.

AUTHOR BIOGRAPHY

Wheatley was born in approximately 1753 in West Africa, probably in either present-day Ghana or Gambia. Taken by slave traders, she was brought to Boston in 1761 aboard the slave ship *Phillis* and was purchased by John Wheatley. Her name derives from the name of the slave ship and the surname of her owner. She is estimated to have been about seven or eight years old, because she was missing her front teeth at the time of purchase, and she was a thin, sickly child.

John Wheatley had twin children, Nathaniel and Mary, who were eighteen when Phillis was purchased. Mary taught Phillis to read and write English. By the time she was twelve, she was also reading Greek and Latin classics in their original languages. The Wheatleys were active in Boston's literary and evangelical circles, and through them Wheatley was exposed to a wide variety of literary,

religious, and political ideas. She was often called upon to write occasional verse (poems prepared for a special occasion), and her many elegies (poems of mourning for the dead) for Boston's prominent citizens only added to her literary reputation. Her 1770 elegy for the Reverend George Whitefield, a popular clergyman, made her a sensation in Boston. In those days, books were published by subscription; that is, a person would advertise in the newspaper and raise money from subscribers in advance of publication. Despite her literary prominence, the Wheatleys were unable to raise sufficient funds to publish her poems in Boston; however, the Countess of Huntington, an English aristocrat who was interested in evangelical and abolitionist causes, invited Wheatley to come to England and promised to help her find publication support there. Susannah Wheatley and Countess Huntington arranged for the publication of *Poems on Various Subjects, Religious and Moral.* Archibald Bell agreed to publish the book on the condition that Wheatley's owners and distinguished patrons testify in the introduction that she did indeed write the enclosed poems. This represented only the first of many doubts that would be raised over the years about the ability of a young female slave to write such works.

In 1773, Wheatley sailed for England in the company of Nathaniel Wheatley. In England, she intended to meet her aristocratic patron and to see her book through publication. Although she did not have the opportunity to meet the Countess, who had retired to her country estate in Wales, Wheatley caused a sensation in London, where only a year before, a lawsuit brought by a slave had made it illegal for an owner to force an enslaved person back to the colonies. Since slavery was outlawed in England itself, this meant that any slave on English soil was essentially free. Some have argued that Wheatley would have been better off if she had remained in England. She returned to nurse the ailing Susannah, and after her death and the deaths of John and Mary Wheatley, she found herself a free woman with no means of supporting herself. She married John Peters in 1778, but the marriage was not a success. After the deaths of her two children, he deserted her, and she died in 1784, at the age of 31. Her third child died hours later. Despite her literary fame and her emancipated status, without patrons Wheatley could not survive as a black female poet in colonial America.

POEM SUMMARY

Stanza 1, Lines 1–6

Wheatley opens the poem by establishing a pastoral and rustic setting. The sun has just set, and although thunder can be heard, it does not overwhelm the fresh breeze of spring that carries the sound of running water and birdsong. The first stanza is characterized by images of nature, including the sunset itself, thunder, a breeze, the scent of springtime, the sound of a stream, birdsong, and music. These images are typical of a classical pastoral poem, such as the *Ecologues* of Virgil, which Wheatley would have been familiar with because of her study of the Greek and Latin classics. Although this poem does not celebrate the lives of shepherds as a strict pastoral would, the rural setting and the emphasis on the beauty of nature show that this is the tradition from which she draws.

Stanza 2, Lines 7–10

The second stanza, with four lines (two couplets, or pairs), is shorter than the first and third stanzas, each of which is six lines (three couplets) long. In this stanza, Wheatley celebrates the colors of the sunset, noting that the sky has been stained as if with dye, although the most beautiful color lies in the far west, where the deepest colors glow. In line 9, she makes the transition from describing nature outside as she sees it to urging her reader to take that natural beauty as inspiration for virtuous behavior. Just as the sunset reflects the brighter light of the sun, Wheatley advises her readers to remember that the glow of virtue that fills their hearts is always only a reflection of the much greater light that comes from God. She asks her readers to cultivate virtue not only for its own sake but as a reflection of the much greater virtue that comes from God. This cultivation of virtue will reflect God's glory back to him as though from a multitude of temples. This emphasizes that the virtue belongs not to the individuals but to God. Its presence in the heart of an individual is a reflection of God, just as the color of the evening sky is a reflection of the sun.

Stanza 3, Lines 11–16

In stanza 3, the poet moves the poem indoors. Wheatley indicates that just as a person might draw the curtains at night, so God, who controls the universe, draws the curtains of nighttime across the earth. The poet urges those inspired by the metaphorical glow of virtue that the sunset

displayed in the previous stanza to be sure to give praise to the God from whom such virtue flows before going to sleep for the night. The person who does so will experience sweet sleep and will be guarded from the temptation of sinful dreams; this person will awaken in the morning ready to begin the day's work with a heart and mind that have been refreshed by the virtues of God. It is by consigning oneself in trust to God before risking the dangers of sleep and dreams that one can be sure of a sleep that will refresh and restore the soul. Wheatley is a religious poet, and hence, her poem urges the reader to trust in God, from whom all good things come.

Stanza 4, Lines 17–18

In the final couplet, Wheatley returns to the classical imagery with which she began the poem. Although Wheatley is a deeply Christian poet and the title designates this as a hymn whose purpose is to praise the Christian God from whom she claims all blessings flow, her reference to a Aurora, the Roman goddess of the morning, symbolically returns the poem to the tradition from which she began. By referring to the imagery of classical literature, Wheatley demonstrates that she is an educated poet and is authorized to join in the long line of poets, beginning with Virgil, who have written pastoral poetry.

THEMES

Neoclassicism (Literature)

The rediscovery in the sixteenth century of Aristotle's *Poetics* inspired the neoclassical movement of the seventeenth and eighteenth centuries. Because the mark of an educated person was the ability to read and write Latin and Greek, most poets had an intimate knowledge of the classics of Greek and Latin literature. The neoclassical movement, which was in part a reaction against the emotionalism of the romantic movement, posited that poetry should imitate the masters of Greece and Rome and that poetry should be characterized by clarity, restraint, and decorum. The neoclassicists believed that because the classical poets had already attained perfection, modern poets were tasked with imitating them. Wheatley's knowledge of Greek and Latin defined her as an educated person. That she had been taught these languages was doubly unlikely, since most girls were almost never taught these languages and Wheatley was the first American slave girl known to have learned

TOPICS FOR FURTHER STUDY

- Wheatley's poem is written in heroic couplets, which are rhyming pairs of lines written in iambic pentameter. Research poetic meter (the rhythm and pattern of stressed and unstressed syllables in a poem) in which this poem is written and then scan (that is, read for the rhythm) "An Hymn to the Evening." Follow up this exercise by writing a paper in which you explain how the research and scanning have increased your understanding of the poem's meaning. Share your comments and allow classmates to add comments on a Weblog site.

- Read the following two young-adult novels: *The Secret Soldier: The Story of Deborah Sampson* by Ann McGovern and *A Voice of Her Own: A Story of Phillis Wheatley, Slave Poet* by Kathryn Lasky. Compare the challenges that Deborah Sampson faced as an impoverished white girl to those that Phillis Wheatley faced as a young slave girl. Write a paper comparing and contrasting the challenges each girl faced and how she dealt with them.

- Wheatley's poem relies on specific images of nature. Team up with a partner to find online images that illustrate the poem. Find one illustration (in the public domain or available under a Creative Commons noncommercial license) that represents each line of the poem and use a program such as iPhoto or PowerPoint to create a slideshow. Then, using a music mixing program such as GarageBand, create audio to accompany your slideshow in which you describe each slide and read or sing the line of poetry it represents.

- Wheatley declares in the title that her poem is a hymn. In common usage, a hymn is a song with a religious message. With two or three other classmates, set Wheatley's poem to music, then use a music program such as GarageBand to record a music video of your song. Play the video for your class.

- Choose a place in nature that you particularly love and, setting a timer, do a free writing exercise for ten minutes in which you describe it in as much detail as you can remember. Using that free writing exercise as a starting place, write an eighteen-line poem about your place. Then rewrite the poem in rhyming couplets.

---

them. Although the Christian message of "An Hymn to the Evening" is not neoclassical, its use of the pastoral setting metaphorically allies it with Virgil's *Ecologues,* which were considered the model to which all other pastoral poetry should aspire. Although much of the poem concerns itself with giving praise to God for any personal virtue the poet or reader might have acquired, by making a reference to Aurora in the final couplet, Wheatley reminds her audience that she is familiar with the figures and tropes (conventions) of classical literature; she thus returns the poem to its neoclassical purpose. That neoclassicism is a conservative movement, one that looks backward to a golden age of perfection and advocates an imitative style, might be one cause of the criticism

Wheatley's poetry attracted from some quarters. She was accused of not being original, of writing derivative poetry and merely copying the masters; however, if she was indeed writing in the neoclassical tradition, this would have been her intention all along. It was only by demonstrating her familiarity with the tropes of classical poetry that Wheatley proved her status as an educated person when brought before the panel of Boston's intellectuals and thereby gained their signatures on the attestation required by her publisher before he would print her book of poetry.

Christianity
Wheatley was raised among the most prominent Christian thinkers in the Massachusetts colony, and

The poem opens by describing a sunset. *(Image copyright Galyna Andrushko, 2010. Used under license from Shutterstock.com)*

her poetry consistently shows Christian themes. In "An Hymn to the Evening," she is at pains to remind her readers that the glories of nature exist only as an imitation of the much greater glories of God. In the second stanza, she metaphorically creates the idea that as the sunset is a fading reflection of the sun's bright light, so too any virtue that resides in the human heart can only ever be a pale reflection of the dazzling virtue of God. In the third stanza, she claims that it is only those who go to sleep with hearts filled with praise for the God who created both day and night, who wake the next morning rested, refreshed, and ready to once more take up their work, which is also properly understood to be for the greater glory of God. The poem states in its title that it is a hymn, and therefore its very purpose is to praise God. Wheatley's Christian faith was seen as another marker of her exceptional status. It was widely believed that just as Africans could not learn to read or write or reason, they were not capable of Christian faith. Wheatley's Christian virtue was an important factor in her role as ambassador to the white world, and it was one important reason that she gained the patronage of so many important people of her day. She demonstrated by her example not only that Africans could learn and could create literature but that they could enter into Christian salvation just like any white person. Because conversion to Christianity was at the root of the Somerset case, which emancipated slaves in the British Isles, Wheatley's Christianity was deeply important to her cause. If the humanity of Africans, and blacks in general, was in doubt during the eighteenth century, it was the model provided by writers like Wheatley that was largely responsible for convincing the white elites that slavery was, in the final analysis, wrong and unacceptable.

Nature

The neoclassical movement was very much interested in the imitation of nature. The first stanza of "An Hymn to the Evening" is marked by its nature imagery. Wheatley paints a picture of a fresh evening in springtime, with a brilliant red sunset, a breeze, thunder in the distance, and the sounds of running water and birdsong. This is both a very effective evocation of a natural scene and the beginning of an extended metaphor about the greatness of God. The power of a metaphor, however, stems from the strength of the images used to carry the metaphorical meaning, and "An Hymn to the Evening" begins with a clear, strong evocation of the natural world. Even as the poem moves indoors in the third stanza, it maintains its concrete imagery of the natural world. One of the tensions that Wheatley faced as a woman and a slave in the eighteenth century was that those categories were considered to be absolutely outside of the categories of rationality and intellect that defined the civilized man. Men were considered superior to women because women were considered to be at the mercy of their natures. Early scientists thought that the biological processes that define womanhood—menstruation, childbirth, and nursing in particular—precluded women from intellectual thought by sapping their vital energy. Wheatley was also African and black; in those early days of scientific classification, these groups were also considered to be at an intellectual deficit. Blacks were originally classified by European science as not entirely human and were given a lower status than whites on the Great Chain of Being, an eighteenth-century idea that placed God as the highest being, then men, then women, and then the other animals in descending order of importance. One of the many challenges facing Wheatley was demonstrating through her poetry that she was not, due to her biology, the inferior of the white male poets of her day. One way that she did this was by using nature imagery in a manner that those poets would recognize as skillful. By writing poetry that was recognized as exceptional,

Wheatley sought to disprove those critics who denied her intellect and humanity on the grounds of what we now know was faulty scientific theory.

STYLE

Hymn

The literary hymn is a form of lyric poetry in which the primary point is to praise or honor a deity. The form has a vibrant history in the Greek and Hebrew traditions, and hence it would have been attractive to Wheatley because of her neoclassical style. As a poetic form, the literary hymn, especially as it was reconstructed by the neoclassicists, usually begins with an invocation of some sort; the body narrates some moral or philosophical point, and then the poem ends with a prayer or farewell. "An Hymn to the Evening" contains all of these features. She opens the poem with a sort of invocation to nature, painting a picture of natural beauty that she then, in the second stanza, attributes to God. The body of the poem illustrates her position, which is that all beauty and virtue stem from and reflect the glory of God. Like many hymns, Wheatley's ends with a farewell, telling the reader goodbye until the morning breaks.

Iambic Pentameter

Iambic pentameter describes poetry in which each line contains five *iambs*, or metrical feet (units). Each iamb consists of one stressed and one unstressed syllable, and so a line of iambic pentameter contains ten syllables, alternating between the stressed and unstressed. When iambic pentameter rhymes at the end of each pair of lines, it is known as heroic couplets, and when it does not rhyme, it is called blank verse. Many scholars feel that the iamb is the central rhythm of English speech, which would explain its common use in English poetry. It is very easy to create any number of ordinary sentences that scan as iambic pentameter; for example, "I'll have a Whopper and a glass of Coke" is iambic pentameter. Iambic pentameter is the most common metrical line in poetry, and it is also the most common form in William Shakespeare's plays. For a poet like Wheatley, who was very concerned with demonstrating a thorough knowledge of and familiarity with the conventions of English poetry and who had a deep love for both Pope and the great English poet John Milton, writing in iambic pentameter would have seemed like the best way to ensure that her poetry was taken seriously.

Heroic Couplets

Heroic couplets are lines written in iambic pentameter that are paired by their end rhymes, which are usually masculine and usually closed. Masculine rhymes are those that rhyme only on one syllable, usually the last, and that syllable is usually stressed. Closed couplets are those in which the unit of meaning comes at the end of the line. In "An Hymn to the Evening," the punctuation appears at the end of the line along with the rhyme, and thus the couplets close the meaning of the line. Open couplets are couplets in which the meaning is *enjambed*; that is, the meaning runs over the end of the line, rather than being stopped by it. Alexander Pope was one of the foremost poets of the heroic couplet in English literature, and it was to his work that Wheatley looked for inspiration, as she readily admitted. The heroic couplet was the dominant poetic form in the eighteenth century, when Wheatley wrote, and it was a primary means by which poets tried to write poetry that was not personal but rather that expressed immortal and unchanging truths. The heroic couplet fell out of favor in the nineteenth and twentieth centuries as poets sought to express more personal and less universal thoughts and feelings.

HISTORICAL CONTEXT

Wheatley lived and wrote during the Revolutionary period of American history, a period during which ideas about what it means to be a free human being were hotly debated at almost every level of society. English government had accepted the theory that there was an unbreakable social contract between those who ruled and those they governed. The English defined themselves as a free people because in addition to the monarchy, they were ruled by a parliament that was elected by the people. They considered any system of government that did not depend on elections to be tyranny. The American colonists argued that since they did not elect members of parliament, they could not consent to be ruled by it. The English could not concede that they did not have the right to rule the colonies absolutely. The American Revolution was largely fought over this dispute about the meanings of freedom,

liberty, and self-governance and over which body had the power to define those terms.

However, that this free society for which the new American state had fought should harbor slavery was a source of contention right from the beginning. Dr. Benjamin Rush, one of Wheatley's early supporters, is quoted in *The Penguin History of the United States of America* as urging his fellow patriots to remember that "the plant of liberty ... is of so tender a nature that it cannot thrive long in the neighborhood of slavery." He reminded them that the eyes of the world were upon them, and their task was "to preserve an asylum for freedom in this country." Despite the willingness of free white Americans to take up arms to defend and obtain their own liberty, it was England that essentially abolished slavery first, in 1772, nearly a full century before the United States did.

The justification for slavery rested on the question of whether or not blacks of African descent were human beings, and if so, whether they were they the same type of human being as whites or were some inferior subspecies. This argument seems shocking now, but the eighteenth century was the century of scientific exploration and classification, and to white Europeans, blacks seemed so different that they could not help but construct them as fundamentally "other." One reason Wheatley was such a sensation was that most philosophers and scientists believed that blacks were incapable of learning, especially of learning to read and write. Even if they could learn to read and write and calculate, many, including Thomas Jefferson, argued that they were incapable of creating art, especially the arts of poetry and literature.

That the Americans felt it was important in the Declaration of Independence to state that "all men are created equal" is a sign of the inequality that existed in the eighteenth century. Although it was usual for the words "men" and "man" to stand in as synonyms for human beings, in this case, the Founding Fathers really did mean only men, and more specifically, only white men. Women, children, slaves, Native Americans, and, in some states, indentured servants were forbidden to vote. Because the number of delegates for each state to the House of Representatives was calculated by the population, the northern states, which could not abolish slavery without risking losing the southern states, agreed later, in the Constitution, to the "three-fifths compromise," in which five

COMPARE
&
CONTRAST

- **1770s:** Wheatley is required to appear before a panel of eighteen of Boston's most important political and intellectual figures to prove that she is the author of her own poems. At the time, it is thought that Africans are incapable of higher thought, including the creation of literature and art. One reason the Wheatley family cannot raise enough money to publish *Poems on Various Subjects, Religious and Moral* in Boston is that there is general disbelief that a slave can write poetry. The panel agrees to sign the attestation (a statement of authenticity) that prefaces the book; the book's publication becomes evidence that Africans are every bit as human as whites, and thus it is immoral to enslave them. Wheatley becomes a central point of evidence for the abolitionist cause.

  Today: African Americans routinely publish in all genres—fiction, poetry, nonfiction, and children's literature—and the ranks of African American intellectuals increase steadily. African American women have won the Nobel Prize for literature, and female African American poets Maya Angelou and Elizabeth Alexander deliver poems at the inaugurations of presidents William J. Clinton and Barack H. Obama, respectively.

- **1770s:** Out of fear of slave revolts and in an effort to appease the slaveholding states, General George Washington and the Continental Congress forbid the enlistment of black soldiers early in the American Revolutionary War, but as the army becomes desperate for soldiers, first free blacks are allowed, and then any black recruits. The First Rhode Island regiment, an all-black regiment, serves with great distinction. As the war spreads to the South, the British urge slaves to join their cause and use the fear of slave revolts to bully the slave-holding colonies back into the British Empire.

  Today: Integrated by the late 1940s, the United States armed forces is one of the most racially integrated and egalitarian forces in modern society. African Americans serve with distinction at all levels of the military, and General Colin Powell rises through the ranks to become Chairman of the Joint Chiefs of Staff.

- **1770s:** A runaway slave named James Somerset sues in the English courts to prevent being returned to Jamaica, where his owner plans to sell him. Somerset, a trusted assistant to his owner, runs away in 1771 and then is captured and imprisoned on a ship in the river Thames. By the time Granville Sharp, the abolitionist who also championed Phillis Wheatley's cause, obtains a writ of habeas corpus, the ship has already sailed and has to be recalled. Sharp argues that since Somerset has converted to Christianity, he cannot morally be held as a slave, since he is now an equal to any white man in God's eyes. Somerset is declared a free man, and the case in effect ends slavery in England. Thus begins the general trend toward ending slavery that culminates in the American Civil War nearly a century later.

  Today: Not only has slavery been definitively outlawed, the Civil Rights movement of the 1960s and 1970s outlaws legal discrimination against any person due to race. Although social discrimination lags behind legal discrimination, the election of Barack H. Obama to the presidency of the United States demonstrates that the last barrier to political power has been definitively broken for African Americans.

slaves were counted as three people for census and apportionment (number of legislators) purposes. Even as the United States founded itself on the ideals of liberty and equality for all, it declared that certain classes of person were excluded from those ideals.

Deep red foliage in a forest. (Image copyright Giuseppe Parisi, 2010. Used under license from Shutterstock.com)

The Puritan influence in New England and the Quaker influence in Pennsylvania resulted in any number of preachers arguing from the pulpit that the new nation would never win God's blessing and prosper as long as it harbored the sin of the slave trade. These northern states outlawed slavery as they joined the nation. Meanwhile, the Second Continental Congress ruled in 1776 that as an emergency war measure, no more slaves were to be imported into the colonies. When the war ended, the ban continued, and although it would be eighty-seven more years until Lincoln's Emancipation Proclamation finally ended slavery, the importation ban was the beginning of the end of slavery in the United States. Although the progress that was made during this Revolutionary time to define how a democracy based on the ideals of individual liberty should and could work was unprecedented in the history of world governments, it will always be a stain on America's national honor that the intelligent and forward-looking men who founded the nation could not see that the equality they espoused was due to all peoples, not just to themselves.

CRITICAL OVERVIEW

The historical significance of Wheatley's position as the first published African American poet has often overshadowed appreciation of her poetry. As Hilene Flanzbaum noted in "Unprecedented Liberties: Re-reading Phillis Wheatley," published in *MELUS*, the journal of the Society for the Study of the Multi-Ethnic Literatures of the United States, that Wheatley was reading her own poems at all—poems written by a young, black, female slave—in the parlors of Boston and London was regarded as an unlikely feat. "Neither the content nor the quality of these poems was ever at issue," Flanzbaum writes; rather, "merely the fact that she had written them constituted a major event." In her own time, readers were divided about the quality of her poetry. Although prominent thinkers of the eighteenth century, such as Benjamin Rush and Voltaire, saw her work as evidence of the humanity and inherent equality of Africans, others, most notoriously Thomas Jefferson, declared her work "below the dignity of criticism."

Not much changed in the centuries that followed. As Flanzbaum notes in her *MELUS* essay, in the 1930s, critic Benjamin Brawley in *The Negro Genius: A New Appraisal of the Achievement of the Negro in Literature and the Fine Arts* praises Wheatley's significance as a historical figure while at the same time claiming that her actual poetry lacked "intrinsic merit," and Sterling Brown in his anthology *Negro Poetry and Drama* claims that her verses "lack any real emotion." In the 1960s, the black aesthetic movement dismissed Wheatley's work as not inspiring black identity or pride. Flanzbaum quotes Addison Gayle, a prominent scholar in the black aesthetic movement who used Wheatley as an example of black writers who "negated or falsified their racial experience.... She writes as a Negro reacting, not as a Negro." However, more recent scholars, such as Walt Nott, in an essay in *MELUS*, "From 'Uncultivated Barbarian' to 'Poetical Genius': The Public Presence of Phillis Wheatley," argues that because of Wheatley's difficult position as both a slave at the mercy of white society and a person whose work "presented itself as a significant challenge to the assumption of African inferiority," she challenged the underpinnings of slavery. Although it is clear that Wheatley's aesthetic (artistic form) is modeled after the poets she had been taught were great—Milton, Pope, and the classical Greek and Latin poets—and although some have argued that this influence is evidence of the derivative nature of her work, modern scholars have argued that the power of Wheatley's work lies in the manner in which she uses the tropes of these poets' works. These conventions can be seen as the intellectual tools of her oppressors, used to argue against the very oppression from which she suffered. That is, rather than writing derivative poetry that merely mimics the poetic fashions of her day, she uses those fashions, as well as the very act of writing and publishing poetry in the first place, to argue against the claim that Africans could not learn, imagine, or create works of art.

CRITICISM

Charlotte M. Freeman

Freeman is a novelist, freelance writer, and former academic. In this essay, she addresses critiques, including that of Thomas Jefferson, that argue that Wheatley's poetry, including "An Hymn to the Evening," demonstrates merely a formal accomplishment.

It is difficult to overstate the impact that Wheatley and her poetry had on eighteenth-century Boston and London. The eighteenth century was the great age of exploration and scientific classification, and yet race was a confounding factor to the thinkers of the time. When confronted with Africans, whites of the time did not know what to make of them. Scientists and philosophers could not decide whether blacks and whites were both fundamentally human beings, descended from a common ancestor, or whether blacks were, as Henry Louis Gates said in his 2002 Jefferson Lecture in the Humanities, quoting the philosopher David Hume, a "species of men... naturally inferior to the whites." This question of the humanity of blacks was at the core of the abolitionist movement, for if blacks were indeed human beings, as capable of whites of learning, thinking, and becoming Christian, then the slave trade must be abolished, for it would necessarily be fundamentally immoral.

Wheatley landed in the middle of this debate. Purchased as a sickly child who had been kidnapped in West Africa, she showed such intelligence and eagerness to learn that her masters exempted her from the domestic work for which they had purchased her, and they taught her to read and write in English, Latin, and Greek. She must have been adorable, this bright child whom they nursed back to health

> MORE IMPORTANT FOR HER REPUTATION THROUGH THE CENTURIES, HER FATE DEPENDED ENTIRELY ON WRITING THE KIND OF POETRY THAT HER MASTERS WOULD RECOGNIZE AND VALUE, WHICH MEANT NEOCLASSICAL POEMS THAT REFLECTED BACK AT THEM THEIR CONSERVATIVE VALUES OF RESTRAINT, DECORUM, AND CHRISTIAN FAITH."

and who rewarded their interest by becoming the toast of Boston's drawing rooms. For Wheatley, who must have been terrified after her voyage in the bottom of the slave ship, finding herself in a world of comfort, where she was clothed and fed and taught and seemingly loved, must have seemed like waking from a nightmare. But one cannot forget that she was a slave. She was entirely at their mercy. Should they have tired of their protégé, should her gifts have faded over time, they could have sold her at any moment. This would have been disastrous for Wheatley, who, because of her talents, had been exempted from labor and was as a result entirely unprepared to work as a domestic slave, much less as a field slave. Wheatley's fate was absolutely contingent on her ability to write and recite poetry. More important for her reputation through the centuries, her fate depended entirely on writing the kind of poetry that her masters would recognize and value, which meant neoclassical poems that reflected back at them their conservative values of restraint, decorum, and Christian faith.

Wheatley's age, race, and gender caused general disbelief that she had written her own poems. When Susannah Wheatley advertised in the Boston papers to raise a subscription to publish Wheatley's work, she could not raise sufficient funds to publish the book because no one believed that Wheatley had written the poems herself. Subsequently, Wheatley was forced to undergo what Gates called "one of the oddest oral examinations in history." In order to secure publication in England, her London publisher demanded that a quorum of eighteen of Boston's

WHAT DO I READ NEXT?

- In *The Trials of Phillis Wheatley* (2003), Henry Louis Gates examines how Wheatley's poetry and reputation have survived her critics over the centuries. In this book, based on his 2002 Jefferson Lecture in the Humanities for the Library of Congress, Gates gives particular attention to Jefferson's blind spot when it came to Wheatley and the way her slave status blinded him to the merits of her poetry.

- *Hang a Thousand Trees with Ribbons: The Story of Phillis Wheatley* (2005) is a historical young-adult novel by Ann Rinaldi that imagines the life of Wheatley. Although she significantly changes the historical record by making Nathaniel, rather than Mary Wheatley, Phillis's tutor, the book is a lively rendition of what everyday life might have been like for America's first African American poet.

- *The Secret Soldier: The Story of Deborah Sampson* (1990), by Ann McGovern, is a young-adult historical novel set in the same colonial period in which Wheatley lived. Deborah Sampson disguised herself as a man in order to enlist in the Continental army, where she fought for nearly two years before being discovered. By imagining the life of a poor girl, indentured as a young child and denied schooling, McGovern brings to life the everyday details of the colonial world.

- *The Origins of African American Literature, 1680-1865* (2001), by Dickson D. Bruce, Jr., is an academic study that traces the origins of African American literature. Although it is scholarly in tone, this book is not written in academic jargon and provides an excellent overview of the situation.

- *The Collected Works of Phillis Wheatley* (1989) is part of the "Schomburg Library of Nineteenth Century Black Writers" series. Although Wheatley wrote during the eighteenth century, not the nineteenth, this volume collects all of Wheatley's known works in one volume.

- *The Works of Anne Bradstreet* (1981), edited by Adrienne Rich, collects the work of the first female poet published in the American colonies. Bradstreet came to the colonies in 1630, nearly a full century before Wheatley, and was an intellectual and religious leader of the Puritan community. Although much of her poetry is concerned with religious issues, she also writes with great feeling and passion about her children, her husbands, and the consoling power of nature among the hardships of life in the new settlement.

- Kathryn Lasky's *A Voice of Her Own: A Story of Phillis Wheatley, Slave Poet* (2005) is a historical novel about Wheatley's life, written for younger readers. The author draws many parallels between Wheatley's love of freedom and the patriots' cause that was brewing in Boston at the time.

- *Valide* (1986), by Barbara Chase-Riboud, is a novel about an Creole girl sold in to slavery in the Ottoman Empire. It is a realistic view of harem culture and her struggles as she becomes the mother of a future sultan.

- Olaudah Equiano, the author of *The Interesting Narrative and Other Writings*, was a contemporary of Wheatley. He was a free black advocate of abolition in England, and his story is a classic of early abolitionist literature: he was kidnapped from Africa at age ten, served as the slave of an officer in the British Navy, and spent ten years laboring on slave ships before managing to buy his own freedom. A revised paperback edition was published in 2003 by Penguin Classics.

---

most learned men certify that the poems were indeed hers. On October 8, 1772, Wheatley appeared before a group that included John Hancock, Governor Thomas Hutchinson, the Reverend Mather Byles (grandson of Cotton Mather), and fifteen other learned men, most of whom were Harvard graduates and some of whom owned slaves. Wheatley's task was not merely to prove that a person of her station, poor, enslaved, female, and black, had written the poems before them, but it was in a very real sense to prove wrong the greatest philosophers of the age, Hume and Immanuel Kant, each of whom was convinced that blacks were biologically, intellectually, morally, and spiritually inferior to whites and incapable of producing any of the higher arts. Wheatley's task was not only to defend herself but to defend her race and gender as well. She convinced the panel that she had indeed written her own works, and such was the astonishment that a young female African slave could write poetry at all that her reputation was launched, her status sealed as the poetical genius who would serve the abolitionist cause as proof that blacks were not fundamentally inferior to whites.

Critics across the centuries have argued whether Wheatley was indeed the poetical genius that her patrons declared, or whether her poetry is overly religious, empty of emotion, and essentially imitative. Thomas Jefferson, as Gates notes in his 2002 Jefferson Lecture, was particularly harsh on Wheatley. For nearly ten years, abolitionists had been citing her work as evidence of the equality of blacks, and Jefferson's criticism of Wheatley was directed to a friend who had praised her work as such. Jefferson wrote in *Notes on Virginia* that "religion, indeed, has produced a Phillis Wheatley; but it could not produce a poet. The compositions published under her name are below the dignity of criticism." Gates notes that to Jefferson, Wheatley's work is "a product of religion, of mindless repetition and imitation, without being the product of intellect, of reflection." Although Jefferson did free his slaves upon his death, he was a lifelong slaveholder, and he could not bring himself to believe in the equality of the races, which may explain in part the tone of his critique; however, he is not alone across the centuries in criticizing her work as empty of emotion and imitative.

It is important to keep in mind, however, that the poetic tradition in which Wheatley was schooled was neoclassicism. The neoclassicists believed that the moment of poetic perfection had occurred during the golden age of the classical era and was best demonstrated by poets like Virgil and Homer. The proper role of poetry, as they saw it, was to imitate the formal restraint and emotional decorum of the classical poets. In part, they were reacting against the developing romantic

movement, which held that poetry should seek to capture the fleeting intensity of human emotion. The neoclassicists believed that the true task of poetry was to express general and eternal truth, and therefore the task of the poet was to erase the taint of individuality that his or her presence left upon the eternal. In this, Wheatley was very successful. Her poetry perfectly expresses the virtues of the neoclassical movement. It is formal, often written in heroic couplets like those of Pope and Milton, poets she loved. Her subjects are, as in "An Hymn to the Evening," general truths illuminated by religious sentiments, or, as in her many elegies, the lives of exalted men of her time. She was successful in writing exactly the kind of poetry that would most impress her skeptical audiences, and her visit to London in 1773 was a huge success. She met with all the leading abolitionists of the day, impressed both Benjamin Franklin and George Washington, and seemed to have proven by her mere existence that Africans were every bit as capable of creating art as whites were.

Her success, however, did not shield her from the critics like Jefferson, who were unswayed by the fact that Wheatley wrote poetry at all and wanted to argue about the merits of her work. They asked whether it was *good*. Jefferson's criticisms, Gates notes in his Jefferson Lecture series speech, shifted the terms of the argument "from the very *possibility* of her authorship to the quality of her authorship—Jefferson indicted her for a failure of a higher form of authenticity." It is only minority artists, however, who are held to this higher standard of authenticity, and Gates goes on to point out that the history of African American literature is one long struggle to prove not only individual artistic merit but the artistic merit of the race. This is a crushing burden for any artist to carry, and one that would necessarily distort the quality of the work. For Wheatley it was not enough simply to create poetry; she wrote for her very livelihood. Her poetry had to be pleasing to the people who fed and clothed and housed her, the people who could have sold her any time her star began to wane. To then retrospectively critique her poetry, as it has been critiqued throughout the years, for being insufficiently creative or emotive, or even, as many African American critics have rightfully pointed out, for expressing gratitude to her captors for bringing her out of Africa and into, as she saw it, the bright Christian light of white Boston— all these criticisms seem somewhat unfair when one recalls the crucial fact of Wheatley's existence: her total reliance on her masters for support.

Emancipation did not bring Wheatley the sort of freedom one might have hoped. The Wheatleys emancipated her but left her nothing in their wills. There was a second manuscript, a book of poems that she was said to have dedicated to Benjamin Franklin, but her husband sold the pages, and they have been lost to time. She became impoverished, lost each of her three children in infancy, and died unknown and unmourned in a boarding house where she had been working as a domestic servant. Without her patrons, Wheatley had no means of supporting herself as a poet, so it is no surprise that the poetry she wrote during the years of their support was so carefully designed to please them. Perhaps her poems were derivative, formally unsurprising, the poetry of an artist seeking to successfully appropriate a poetic language that would confirm, by its acquisition, that the person writing it was indeed a poet. Considering the unlikeliness of Wheatley's accomplishments, that this poor, young black woman managed to make as much of a life for herself as she did out of sheer intelligence, charm, and wit, it seems unfair to then condemn her for not being a different kind of poet than the one she was. Wheatley learned her lessons well. She learned from Pope and Milton and Virgil and Homer, and she used those skills to write what was widely considered remarkable poetry. She saved her life for many years by doing so, and although she could not make an independent living as a poet, that her poems and her story live on, centuries later, is a testament to her accomplishments.

Source: Charlotte M. Freeman, Critical Essay on "An Hymn to the Evening," in *Poetry for Students*, Gale, Cengage Learning, 2011.

Will Harris

In the following essay, Harris states that Phillis Wheatley is not only the founding figure of African American literature but also a major diasporic writer.

Critics generally agree in considering Phillis Wheatley, the first African American to author and publish a book, as the founding figure of African American literature. In his foreword to the Schomburg series on black women writers, Henry Louis Gates, Jr. goes so far as to acknowledge her as progenitor of African American literature (Gates, "*In Her Own Write*" x)—a label which not only gives her "first" credit, but also suggests that

A country church. The poem discusses living temples for God filled with praise. (Image copyright Jill Battaglia, 2010. Used under license from Shutterstock.com)

her work was in some way a prototype for all "race" literature which followed hers. Although "the overwhelming tendency in Wheatley criticism has been to upbraid her for 'not being black enough'" (Gates, *Trials* 81), a more thorough address of the questions inherent in Gates's assumption about progenitorship places Wheatley's writing at the heart of any definition of an African American canon. If Wheatley's writing can be considered a prototype, what diaspora traces or influences did she distill and reshape? And if, as progenitor, she transmitted a model for African American writing, what was that model? Finally, as progenitor of a body of literature rather than simply a participant in an American strain of poetry, how did this poet possibly influence African American prose writing—a mode of expression which was arguably uncontested in the African American literary canon until the Harlem Renaissance?

Few critics have attempted to account for the uniqueness of Wheatley's contributions to diaspora writing as a key to her foundational

"WHEATLEY'S CONCEPT OF CHRISTIANITY
HAS AN OUTWARD ASPECT AS WELL. HER FAITH
IS NOT JUST A VALIDATION OF HER MORAL
EXISTENCE, BUT ALSO SERVES AS A SUBSTITUTE
AUTHENTICATOR TO THE PLETHORA OF COLONIAL
SOURCES OF AUTHORITY OVER THE SLAVE."

role as African American literary progenitor. Perhaps Katherine Clay Bassard comes closest to explaining Wheatley's landmark role within a diasporic context. Bassard, I believe accurately, suggests that Wheatley's writing represents an evolution in diasporic subjectivity. Bassard's argument does not chart this progression in terms of other African diasporic subjects and commentators. Bassard focuses on the declarative nature of poems such as "An Answer to the Rebus" (1773) as assertions of subjective autonomy. For example, she sees this poem as "a gesture of self-authentication" (31), while viewing Wheatley's adroit negotiation of blackness in poems like "On Being Brought from Africa to America" (1773) as an effort at "cultural mooring" (38–39). Bassard believes that Wheatley perfects this effort in her elegies, through an implied yet absented communal counterpoint (59–70). But as Bassard suggests, Wheatley's pivotal role in diasporic discourse must be understood as a "global" role as well (43). Why was Wheatley's poetry recognized even in England and France as a watershed literary feat? And why was it a focal point for discussion of diasporic literary accomplishment among the likes of Voltaire, John Paul Jones, and François, the Marquis de Barbe-Marbois (Gates, *Trials 33*, 40–41), as well as among diasporic writers such as Ignatius Sancho (Edwards and Dabydeen 27–28)? To fully understand the phenomenon, the "arrival" of Wheatley as African American literary fore-parent must be reconstrued as a consequence of a diasporic phenomenon.

. . . Wheatley's distinctive response to the spirit of her times was to project a reflexively race-conscious presence in her poetry and personal letters. When judged against the western and diaspora literature of her times, this persona stands as a

landmark achievement. The African American and diaspora literary works which followed hers appear to borrow her notion of "blackness"— pervasively understood as a western construction which blacks may simultaneously accept and trope according to contextual demands.

Wheatley's and Hammon's proposed conceptions of slavery, however, are not the only areas of comparison between Wheatley and her diaspora literary predecessor. Wheatley may also have borrowed from Hammon's narrative structure, and translated what she learned into her poetic texts. As mentioned earlier, Hammon apparently took his structural cue from the Indian captivity narratives. Richard Van Der Beets summarizes characteristics Hammon borrows from these narratives: "[1] the salutary effects of captivity, especially in the context of redemptive suffering; [2] the captivity as test, trial, or punishment of God; and, finally and most demonstrably, [3] the captivity as evidence of Divine Providence and God's inscrutable wisdom" (qtd. in F. Foster 181). Wheatley follows a similar pattern in her discussions of her own passage into slavery.

In "To the University of Cambridge" Wheatley focuses on the benefits of her captivity:

> . . . I left my native shore
> The land of errors, and Egyptian gloom:
> Father of mercy, 'twas thy gracious hand
> Brought me in safety from those dark abodes.
> (lines 3–6)

In "On Being Brought from Africa to America," again Wheatley acknowledges Providence's work in bringing her to a saving knowledge of Christ:

> 'Twas mercy brought me from my Pagan
> land,
> Taught my benighted soul to understand
> That there's a god, that there's a Saviour
> too:
> Once I redemption neither sought nor knew.
> (lines 1–4)

Following a poetic technique which shifts attention away from Wheatley's paucity of definitively negative experiences under slavery, she highlights the redemptive captivity in Christ rather than her own purgation through suffering.

Unlike Hammon's narrative, Wheatley's Christ figure replaces the personal captivity experience as the litmus test; the figure evaluates white slave owners rather than the spiritual growth of the suffering captive. For instance, in "To the University of Cambridge" the icon of the suffering Christ (lines 10–20) becomes the scale against which the Cambridge students will ultimately be evaluated ("Improve your privileges while they stay, / Ye pupils, and each hour redeem, that bears / Or good or bad report of you in heav'n" [lines 21–23]). In the passage that follows, the iconic use of Christ allows the humble "Ethiop" to relate the possibility of judgment and punishment upon the haute students, sons of the colonial elite (lines 24–30). In fact, Christ consistently serves as a divine racial leveler in Wheatley's poetry, either by the emulative example of his divine sacrifice (see "To the University of Cambridge" or "On Being Brought from Africa to America," for example), or by the promise of his divine wrath on the inhumane and the haughty (in "To the University of Cambridge" and "Isaiah LXIII. 1–8" [1773]).

The Christ icon, in fact, constitutes a striking adaptation of Hammon's notion of "the captivity as test, trial, or punishment of God." The trial, however, is not so much the slave's challenge as it is that of the enslaving society. Personal or collective judgment is reserved for faults that can be readily associated with slave holders, as observed in poems such as "To the University of Cambridge" (lines 21–30) and "On Recollection" (1772) (lines 25–30). Sometimes her investigation of this theme of slavery as social trial is cloaked in metaphor. For instance, Wheatley suggests an apocalyptic judgment in "Isaiah LXIII. 1–8," but does not clearly identify the slave-holding class as recipients of this judgment. However, we cannot help but consider the implications of a Christ who wages war against "haughty foes" (line 22) in order to execute "man's release" from "the pond'rous load" (line 13), simultaneously exercising both deliverance and "wrath" (line 14). And we cannot help but note the seemingly personal poignancy of the poem's last four lines:

> Against thy Zion though her foes may rage,
> And all their cunning, all their strength engage,
> Yet she serenely on thy bosom lies,
> Smiles at their arts, and all their force defies.
> (lines 26–30)

... In a wider sense, Christianity serves as an important factor in the construction of the black slave narrative/poetic persona. In Hammon's narrative, one's grasp of Christianity can be equated with the maintenance of an ideal moral view and one's humanity, as evidence of "Divine Providence and God's inscrutable wisdom." Hammon can

define himself no longer in terms of his African environment, and his slave experiences constantly subject him to new and changing environments, yet he claims an inner stability and a definition of the world provided by Christ. Wheatley's concept of Christianity has an outward aspect as well. Her faith is not just a validation of her moral existence, but also serves as a substitute authenticator to the plethora of colonial sources of authority over the slave. By embracing Christianity, she embraces a notion of a self outside of "slave" or "woman" or "black" which may also be used to contest colonial ideas about the naturalized construction of blacks as inferior or heathen that were based in colonial interpretations of scripture. Wheatley is not just obeying the call of her faith because Christ said to do so, but obeying Christ rather than spiritually contestable colonial sources which distort the teachings of the Bible.

... To complete our study of Wheatley's possible contribution to the emerging slave narrative, we need only turn to Equiano's text. Equiano, widely recognized as the master of the slave narrative, was a seminal figure in many other ways. He maintained both an informal and literary friendship with Cugoano, and is believed to have had a hand in revising his anti-slavery treatise. Both men apparently exchanged ideas about and borrowed notions from their African literary predecessors (Edwards and Dabydeen 7–8). We may assume both men were familiar with Wheatley's work. It is interesting to note also, that despite evidence of Equiano's revising hand in Cugoano's manuscript, Equiano himself did not publish his own narrative until two years after Cugoano's was published. Equiano apparently had not yet developed a notion of black persona and narrative characterization, since Cugoano's work contains little evidence of it. In fact, Cugoano's work hardly develops a character or slave persona. After a brief rendition of his kidnapping and enslavement, Cugoano shifts from a narrative to a persuasive treatise. If Equiano had by this time developed a notion of a black slave persona, surely he would have recommended it to his friend and literary partner. However, when Equiano does finally publish his narrative, roughly five years after Wheatley's death and two years after his friend's text, he pays Wheatley a curious remembrance. Just as Wheatley had published a sketch of her image on the frontispiece of her book, Equiano became the second slave to do so on a text, thus indirectly acknowledging her as a model. His debt to her may have been more than visual. Both his radical departure from previous slave prose texts through his employment of a persona, and indeed the youth of his persona (Equiano is approximately forty-five years old when he writes his narrative), hint at his indebtedness to the young slave poetess.

Wheatley's creation of an intelligent and vocal slave persona carried certain inherent risks. The development of a critical or questioning discursive stance, offered from the socially inferior position of enslavement or blackness, would necessarily require the hesitation, irony, and signification now firmly associated with the African American phenomenon of "double-consciousness":

> After the Egyptian and Indian, the Greek and Roman, the Teuton and Mongolian, the Negro is a sort of seventh son, born with a veil, and gifted with second-sight in this American world,—a world which yields him no true self-consciousness, but only lets him see himself through the revelation of the other world. It is a peculiar sensation, this double-consciousness, this sense of always looking at one's self through the eyes of others, of measuring one's soul by the tape of a world that looks on in amused contempt and pity. One ever feels his two-ness,—an American, a Negro; two souls, two thoughts, two unreconciled strivings; two warring ideals in one dark body, whose dogged strength alone keeps it from being torn asunder. (Du Bois 3)

"The African American consciousness," by Du Bois's proffered definition, implies both an identification with mainstream culture (American-ness) and with constructed difference within that culture ("African" extraction). Perhaps this literary expression of double consciousness begins with Wheatley, and may well be the source of continuing contestation over her degree of "blackness"—not that she failed to project a black consciousness, but that she may have attenuated hypersensitively that projection to the dominant colonial world.

Wheatley's contributions to the western literary canon can be most fairly evaluated when considered against the backdrop of diaspora literary texts. Although remembered as a poet, she may well have drawn from and contributed to the slave narratives evolving around her. Wheatley's poetic creation of a reflexively race-conscious slave persona may have in fact served as Equiano's model for a consolidated narrative slave persona. Her probable influence on Equiano reverberates in virtually every slave narrative after his, culminating in Douglass's innovative slave narratives/autobiographies. Wheatley's poetics also establish a direct link between the western canon and the diaspora literary tradition. She may have produced the first literary instance of double consciousness and added this inheritance to the African American literary heritage. But the ultimate debut of Wheatley as African American literary progenitor is a historical moment shaped as much by her evolutionary role in diasporic subjectivity as by her direct literary contributions to the American literary canon.

Source: Will Harris, "Phillis Wheatley, Diaspora Subjectivity, and the African American Canon," in *MELUS*, Vol. 33, No. 3, Fall 2008, p. 27.

Mukhtar Ali Isani

In the following excerpt, Isani contends that references to Wheatley can be found in the writings of some of the country's forefathers and that these references in newspapers and magazines of the day contributed to her fame.

The fame of Phillis Wheatley is often measured in terms of references in the writings of such eminent figures as George Washington, Thomas Jefferson and Benjamin Franklin, but these are only a part of the evidence. Recognition among the common populace, as evident in the newspapers and magazines of the time, is also a valid measure. These commonplace and public documents effectively show the reach and the recognition of the poet. While Bostonians and others attested to her creativity within the limited scope of personal correspondence and in a foreword to her book, American newspapers and magazines broadcast news of the poet to far greater numbers and with some frequency. The notices were brief but fairly numerous, representing six colonies. American newspapers focused on Wheatley as American news and reflected some colonial pride; the British magazines often overlooked local significance but offered greater depth of examination. Current events and current sympathies make the focus on the poet somewhat different in colonial America and in the mother country, then engaged in antislavery debate. As the main source of public information, newspapers and magazines contributed to the bulk of Wheatley's contemporaneous fame. This article is based on a page-by-page examination of extant colonial newspapers and magazines falling within the period 1765–1774 and on a selective examination of English publications. [1] Its purpose is to verify known newspaper and magazine notices by personal examination, add new items via a cumulative list, and examine the expanded range of Wheatley notices for its reflection of the poet's contemporaneous fame, still not fully documented. The descriptive essay is based upon this greater breadth of material now available.

American newspaper and magazine notices of the time are brief and those related to Wheatley's work generally do not amount to reviews, but their number is considerable and they are representative of popular opinion in their approach to the poet. The selectivity enforced by the limitations of space in the 18th century newspapers gives further importance to these notices. The survey of American sources for this study lends substance to the inadequately documented contemporaneous and near-contemporaneous suggestions, including those of Margaretta Odell, that Wheatley was famous in her time. [2] Findings in English newspapers and magazines support American findings, besides providing a critical review unobtainable in the more limited American publications. But even a brief notice in America has its significance, for the colonial newspaper was almost universally only four pages long, with little more than a page devoted to news that was not political or commercial. To win recurring attention in these pages is impressive. The Wheatley notices are notable in number and, to a lesser extent, in variety. They show interest in Wheatley both as a person and as a poet. The value of her poetry is recognized, but there is also extraordinary emphasis on her status as a black poet, a slave turned intellectual, and a pious prodigy.

... Wheatley's return to America was widely noted, though again in brief reports. On September 13, the London Packet arrived in Boston. The "List of Notices" will show that even though she came without her book, eight local and regional newspapers announced the poet's return. She was described as the "extraordinary Poetical Genius," "the extraordinary Negro Poetess," and "the celebrated young negro Poetess." Besides the Boston papers, she was mentioned in the newspapers in Portsmouth (New Hampshire), Providence, Hartford, and New Haven. Although triumphal as an event, her return was premature and so did not generate optimal publicity. These reports allude to her fame and brilliance as a poet but unfortunately continue to make no attempt to illustrate or analyze that brilliance or fame. In most American papers, the brevity of the notice limits the paper to assertions of fame.

In mid-September 1773, *Poems on Various Subjects* came off the press in England and British magazines commenced publishing reviews. There are two emphases: the precocious talent of the poet and the shame of slavery as illustrated by her case. The *London Chronicle* advertisement was bombastic when it announced that the work displayed "perhaps one of the greatest instances of pure, unassisted genius, that the world ever produced," [19] but the focus was typical. Almost every reviewer made it a point to note the precociousness of the poet and a number noted, in the words of the book's prefatory "Attestation" by Boston dignitaries, that she had but a few years earlier been brought "an uncultivated Barbarian from Africa." "These poems display no astonishing power of genius," admitted the *London Magazine,* "but when we consider them as productions of a young untutored African, who wrote them after six months casual study of the English language and of writing, we cannot suppress our admiration of talents so vigorous and lively." [20] The *Critical Review* found lines "which would be no discredit to an English poet." [21] As the place of Wheatley's servitude, Boston drew little raise. The antiquary, Richard Gough, of *Gentleman's,* noted "the claims of excellence" and wrote, "Youth, innocence, and piety, united with genius, have not been able to restore her to the condition and character with which she was invested by the Great Author of her being." [22] The *Scots Magazine* also broadcast his opinion. [23] Even the *London Monthly Review,* which had no great expectations of the Negro race, and saw no "endemial marks of solar fife" in the poems, spoke well of the poet and expressed concern that so ingenious a person was still a slave. Lines from the verses to the Earl of Dartmouth attracted the reviewer's attention and suggested irony:

I. young in life, by seeming cruel fate
Was snatch'd from Afric's fancied happy
    seat:
What pangs excruciating must molest,
What sorrow labour in my parents' breast?
Steel'd was that soul, and by no misery
    mov'd,
That from a father seiz'd his babe belov'd:
Such, such my case. And can I then but pray
Others may never feel tyrannic sway?

"The people of Boston," wrote the reviewer, "boast themselves chiefly on their principles of liberty. One such act as the purchase of her freedom, would, in our opinion, have done them more honour than hanging a thousand trees with ribbons and emblems." [24] And-slavery emphasis, humanistic logic, and even persuasive pathos mix in these reviews. Wheatley was both the "rara avis" as well as the humanist's proof of the universal nature of mankind.

The poems illustrating British reviews were obviously chosen with the British reader in mind. None of the elegies, with their American local or regional interest, qualified for reprinting. "On Recollection" was selected again. Likewise, "On Imagination," "Hymn to the Morning" and "Thoughts on the Works of Providence" were appropriate for showing the poet's ability to use abstract thought and themes common in British popular verse. "On Being Brought from Africa to America" was forceful and pious but notable especially for its novel and slavery-related theme. "To Maecenas" was justifiably the choice of four magazines because of its wealth of allusion and evident mastery of the Neo-classic method.

In 1774, Wheatley's ingenuity continued to be publicized in England but the poet was still seen against the background of the anti-slavery concerns and stereotypical views of the time. In a laudatory poem published in the *London Sentimental Magazine*, an admirer's praise of Wheatley was largely swamped by his argument in favor of all Africans. She was proof of the genius of all blacks, so he could ask:

Why stand amaz'd at Afric's muse
Why struck with sacred awe!
One God our genius did infuse;
Our colour's nature's law. [25]

This poem entitled "Wrote after reading some Poems composed by Phillis Wheatley an African Girl" ranks as the earliest contemporaneous poetry on Phillis Wheatley but may be even more notable as a defense of the Negro race. After the peak of 1773, there are very few notices. Clearly there was no unanimity of opinion. When a minor poet, Mary Scott, used Wheatley's *Poems on Various Subjects* as an example of meritorious writing by women, [26] the *Monthly Review* recalled its earlier judgment and again dismissed Wheatley's ingenuity as mere "talent for poetical imitation." [21]

In America, Wheatley remained in the public eye not only through the sale of her book but also through her letter to Samson Occom protesting the condition of the black in America at the hands of "our modern Egyptians" holding a people in bondage. "... In every human Breast," she wrote, "God has implanted a Principle, which we call Love of Freedom; it is impatient of Oppression, and pants for Deliverance; and by the Leave of our modern Egyptians I will assert, that the same Principle lives in us." [28] It was a bold and eloquent statement probably forwarded to the *Connecticut Gazette* by an admiring Occom himself. Its

reprinting in other New England papers "by request" and as "a Specimen of her Ingenuity" makes one wonder about the identity of the requesters. Over a ten-day, period, it appeared in seven more newspapers, the narrow span of dates suggesting that the submission of the letter was the work of one hand. Ten newspapers chose to publish it between mid-March and mid-April, 1774.

Following her manumission and the death of her mistress in March, the sales of her book were of more than literary importance to this ex-slave suddenly forced to subsist on her own. The work was offered in several cities and on different dates and at different prices. "Printed for the Benefit of the Author" was not an idle statement in the advertisements. Some of the variations in price may reflect the judgment of the sales agents appraising the market in troubled times. The year closes with the *Boston Royal American Magazine*'s publication of "To a Gentleman of the Navy" and the gentleman's reply, "The Answer." Joseph Greenleaf's publication of the Wheatley poem is an act of admiration. The Wheatley poem is the lead poem in an issue which commences with a satiric "vision" on British tyranny (entitled "A Dream"). Greenleaf was an American patriot in the mold of Isaiah Thomas, his predecessor at the magazine who had long known of Phillis Wheatley. The editorial introduction to Wheatley's verse, her first magazine publication in America, is reminiscent of the thought in the *British Sentimental Magazine*'s poem in her praise. "By this single instance," declared the American editor, "may be seen the importance of education,—Uncultivated nature is much the same in every part of the globe." This "young Affrican of surprising genius" aroused thoughts of the virtues associated with "the noble savage" though the concept of the black as a "noble savage" was uncommon in America: "It is probable Europe and Affrica would be alike savage or polite in the same circumstances; though, it may be questioned, whether men who have no artificial wants, are capable of becoming so ferocious as those who, by faring sumptuously every day, are reduced to a habit of thinking it necessary to their happiness, to plunder the whole human race." [29] Significantly, "The Answer" by the "Gentleman of the Navy" praised her natural ability, for

... Wheatly is the fair;
That has the art, which art could ne'er
    acquire:
To dress each sentence with seraphic fire.
    [30]

But the year ends also with Wheatley's apprehension of the future without her sponsor and mistress. "The world is a severe Schoolmaster," she wrote to a member of the Countess of Huntingdon's circle, John Thornton, philanthropist and merchant of London. "I attended and find exactly true your thoughts on the behaviour of those who seem'd to respect me while under my mistresses patronage; you said right, for some of those have already put on a reserve...." [31] A new phase was beginning in the poet's life.

But during the phase just concluded, Wheatley had undoubtedly become a celebrity and newspapers and magazines, British and American, had contributed to the bulk of her fame. 42 newspapers and magazines, 27 of which were American, took notice of the poet, generally on more than one occasion. The limited space of the colonial newspaper gives significance even to the usual scanty notices of the time. Interest in the unusual colors most American notices, but one can also read a measure of national pride. British reviews, thanks to the country's magazine experience, have greater literary content and are also noteworthy as social documents, for Wheatley is recognized against the background of the British anti-slavery debate and as illustration of the fact that genius is not limited by the accident of a poet's geographic origin. Wheatley was indeed famous in her time—at least in the initial half of her short two-decade poetic-career.

Source: Mukhtar Ali Isani, "The Contemporaneous Reception of Phillis Wheatley: Newspaper and Magazine Notices during the Years of Fame, 1765–1774," in *Journal of Negro History*, Vol. 85, No. 4, Fall 2000, p. 260.

William J. Scheick

In the following excerpt, Scheick examines how Wheatley used scripture to strengthen her political voice in resisting slavery.

The critical response to the poetry of Phillis Wheatley (c. 1754–1784) often registers disappointment or surprise. Some critics have complained that this African American slave's verse is insecure (Collins 78), imitative (Richmond, *Bid the Vassal* 54–66), and incapacitated (Burke 33, 38)—at its worst the "product of a White mind" (Jamison 414–15) and "the barter of [the poet's] soul" (Richmond, "On 'The Barter'" 127). Others, in contrast, have applauded Wheatley's critique of Anglo-American discourse (Kendrick 222–23), her acknowledgment of her African heritage, and her verification of selfhood (Baker 39–41). Some have observed critiques of slavery in her use of classical tradition and irony

> EMBEDDED WITHIN WHEATLEY'S SURFACE COMPLIANCE WITH AUTHORIZED BIBLICAL AND POETIC TRADITIONS, IS A SECOND VOICE. BY BEING SECOND, THIS VOICE MAY IN A SENSE REMAIN IN BONDAGE TO THE MORE DOMINANT VOICE OF AUTHORITY, BUT IT DOES INDEED SPEAK."

(Shields), especially in her elegies (Levernier, "Style"). And some have specifically discerned various languages of escape in her poetry, each extracted from the traditions of Western culture (Davis; Erkkila; O'Neale). In her poems on religion, death and art, several critics have argued, Wheatley attained a certain freedom. Especially noteworthy is a mode of liberation occasionally evident in her use of "double meaning and ambiguity," both designed for "the close reader of [her] poems" (Matson 119).

Wheatley's use of ambiguity, it is reasonable to suspect, was partially influenced by her exposure to Enlightenment thinking on human rights and abolitionist theory. This exposure came primarily from the pulpit. Insofar as we know, Wheatley attended the New South Congregational Church, where her enslavers worshipped. By 1771, she had become an active member of the Old South Congregational Church in Boston. At that time the clergy, including those with whom Wheatley had contact (Levernier, "Phillis" 23), integrated religious and political concerns in their sermons (Weber 5–13). Also from the pulpit, as well as from her reading and her discussions with others, Wheatley became familiar with select standard eighteenth-century Protestant commentaries on Scripture and, as well, with approved secular applications of biblical passages. Doubtless Wheatley was very attentive to these exegeses, for the King James version of the Bible was among a handful of her favorite books.

Scripture, in fact, profoundly influenced her writings. Sometimes the Bible provided her with a means of undercutting colonial assumptions about race (O'Neale 145). Wheatley's dual exposure to theological and secular applications of Holy Writ accounts for the compatibility of her religious and her political writings (Akers 403–04; Burroughs 61–62). This double exposure encouraged her to relate evangelical Protestantism to both Revolutionary patriotism and romance neoclassicism. These combinations in her writings, Phillip M. Richards's investigations indicate, occupy a liminal space of transformed social position where Wheatley rewrites marginality, exults in spiritual equality, and urges her audience to rethink inherited ideologies.

Wheatley's mingling of evangelicalism and patriotism occasionally included her resistance to slavery. Such a moment occurs in "On the Death of General Wooster" (1977), a Revolutionary-War poem written four years after the poet's manumission. In this elegy, Wheatley forthrightly asks: how can citizens of the emergent American nation expect their freedom to prevail against tyranny "While yet (O deed ungenerous!) they disgrace / And hold in bondage Afric's blameless race?". The sentiment expressed in this poem is also present, albeit much less explicitly, in such earlier verse as "To the Right Honourable William, Earl of Dartmouth" (1773). This poem elliptically associates "wanton Tyranny," which "enslave [s] the [colonial] land," with the "tyrannic" kidnapping experienced by the poet as a child, an experience which fostered her "love of Freedom." Wheatley's attitude toward slavery did not change in the interval between these two poems. What changed was her social status, her emancipation from bondage. In the Wooster elegy she feels free to speak overtly against slavery, in contrast to her covert approach to the subject in her earlier verse. Throughout her career, Wheatley believed that slavery does not "find / Divine acceptance with th' Almighty mind."

In several of her early verses, moreover, Wheatley specifically turns to Scripture to suggest the deity's aversion to slavery. In "On Being Brought from Africa to America," for instance, the direct celebration of her personal delight in Christianity includes a restrained, if resistant, "second voice" subtly speaking through two allusions to Isaiah. As presented by Wheatley's appropriated ministerial voice, these allusions rebuke Christian slave owners (Scheick 137).

This other voice, similarly embedding its unconventional messages in explicit expressions of compliance or gratitude, is evident elsewhere in Wheatley's poetry (McKay and Scheick 73). The establishment of such an alternative voice from within conventional tropes and figures is a feature of resistance literature (Slemon 31). In semiotic terms, this technique may be said to exhibit logonomic conflict—that is, a dialogic encounter between authorized and unauthorized interpretations that implicitly disturbs the status quo (Hodge and Kress 3–12). The detection of logonomic conflict in Wheatley's verse, particularly the emergence of a resistant second voice in contexts in which she makes use of Scripture, enables a better appreciation of both her politics and her artistry. As we will see, Wheatley's deliberate application of biblical matter in her verse often registers underground observations about slavery, observations that she evidently believes are supported by the Bible.

. . . Wheatley's reference to cunning is also pertinent. It likely alludes to Ephesians 4:14: "That we henceforth be no more children . . . carried about with every wind of doctrine, by the sleight of men, and cunning craftiness, whereby they lie in wait to deceive." Possibly, too, the mention of cunning recalls the chief trait of Esau (Genesis 25:27), the man who sold his birthright and who was reputed to be the ancestor of the routed Edomites mentioned at the start of Wheatley's paraphrase (Hastings 203).

"Cunning," however, has another biblical analog. In Exodus this word describes the artistic communication of divine inspiration in "all manner of work, of the engraver, and of the cunning workman" (35:35; cf. 36:8). This sense of special skill and knowledge is not the meaning of the word "cunning" as applied to Zion's foes, who are impiously devious. But if the Isaiah paraphrase (like the Samuel paraphrase) hints at reversals, including the Davidic refunding of defiance in response to Goliath-like forces, then we might reasonably entertain the possibility that Wheatley saw her artistic cunning as a pious antidote for the perverse cunning of those who use Scripture to justify the bondage of her race. Possibly she saw her cunning as divinely sanctioned, scripturally influenced or inspired. She apparently believed that her use of Holy Writ was doubly authorized by select commentaries and the ministerial practice of mingling religion and politics, two sources she encountered in the pew, discussion groups, and books. And from her point of view, this higher cunning would legitimate her pious use of deceptive appearance, her devious use of apparently conventional paraphrase, to implicate Christian slavers as latter-day Philistines and Babylonians. Wheatley would thereby redeem the "arts," invert the stratagems of deception referred to in the last line of her poem, by means of a cunning art subserviently adhering to scriptural exegesis yet also "defiantly" inferring an unorthodox temporal application.

Both paraphrases suggest a connection between divine justice and social justice, specifically spiritual redemption and secular freedom. In forging this connection Wheatley manages her biblically-influenced art as a verbal double-edged sword. She prophetically reminds her readers that the tongue of God's enemies—including Philistine-like and Babylonian-like Christians who enslave—will fatally "fall upon themselves." The clergy of her day put the Bible to political use, but their practice did not license the laity, much less a slave, to make free with Scripture, the paradigmatic double-edged sword. In a significant sense, then, Wheatley arrogates ministerial privilege when she extrapolates an innovative secular message, even if only an intimated admonition, from the scriptural texts prompting her two paraphrases.

This is the piously "defiant" and "cunning" Wheatley who deserves more appreciation as a social critic and as an artist. The double-voicing evident in such works as her verse paraphrases of the Bible is a version of what W. E. B. DuBois would more than a century later identify as African-American "double-consciousness:... two thoughts, two unreconciled strivings, two warring ideals in one dark body, whose dogged strength alone keeps it from being torn asunder" (15). Embedded within Wheatley's surface compliance with authorized biblical and poetic traditions, is a second voice. By being second, this voice may in a sense remain in bondage to the more dominant voice of authority, but it does indeed speak. Empowered by the swordlike Word of God and encroaching upon ministerial privilege, this swordless voice announces an unconventional message in a manner that crosses gender and social boundaries. To hear this restrained, if subtly defiant voice, is to enrich our appreciation of Wheatley's art.

Source: William J. Scheick, "Subjection and Prophecy in Phillis Wheatley's Verse Paraphrases of Scripture," in *College Literature*, Vol. 22, No. 3, October 1995, pp. 122–31.

Christian Examiner and General Review
In the following excerpt, Wheatley's poetry is compared to that of her white contemporaries.

[Phillis Wheatley's poetry] seems to us respectable, though not of a high order. Yet how many of the white writers of this country have enjoyed a transient reputation on much less intrinsic merit! What proportion of the rhymesters, who enrich our newspapers and magazines with their effusions, can write half so well as Phillis Wheatley? She had no assistance. Like one of her favorite authors, "she lisped in numbers, for the numbers came." She seems to have begun to write verses as soon as she had sufficient command of the English language to express her ideas—certainly before she could have known anything of the rules of composition. Accordingly, we find some ill-constructed and harsh and prosaic lines, but not so many by half as in the verses of most of her contemporary American poets. That her lines are full of feeling, no one will deny....(p. 172)

Phillis Wheatley, we think, was a precocious genius, destined very rapidly to acquire a certain degree of excellence, and there to stop for ever. As mediocrity, or even moderate merit in song, is never tolerated, we dare not hope that her works will ever be very popular or generally read; for readers never take into account the disadvantages the writer may have labored under. It is not just that they should; for otherwise the land would be flooded with bad writings, to the exclusion and discouragement of good. It is little consolation to him, who has wasted his time and money in buying and reading a wretched production, to be told that it was written by an apprentice or a woman. We do not mean by this to express any disapprobation of the publication before us, but merely to say that, singular as its merits are, they are not of the kind that will command admiration. Still the work will live—there will always be friends enough of liberty and of the cause of negro improvement not to let it sink into oblivion, and many will desire to possess it as a curiosity. We wish the publisher success, and, if anything we can say shall contribute to it, we shall heartily rejoice. As a friend of the Africans and of mankind at large, we are happy to record our tribute of praise in behalf of one who was an honor and ornament to her race and her kind. (p. 173)

Source: "Phillis Wheatley's 'Poems,'" in *Christian Examiner and General Review*, Vol. 11, No. 2, May 1834, pp. 169–74.

SOURCES

"African Americans in the Revolutionary Period," in *The American Revolution: Lighting Freedom's Flame*, http://www.nps.gov/revwar/about_the_revolution/african_americans.html (accessed February 4, 2010).

Baldick, Chris, "Iamb" and "Neoclassicism," in *The Oxford Dictionary of Literary Terms*, Oxford University Press, 2009, pp. 162, 221–22.

Boyer, Paul S., ed., "Revolution and Constitution, Era of," and "Wheatley, Phillis," in *Oxford Companion to United States History*, Oxford University Press, 2001, pp. 664–65, 827.

Brogan, Hugh, "The War of Revolution: 1775–83," in *The Penguin History of the United States of America*, Penguin, 2001, pp. 179.

Flanzbaum, Hilene, "Unprecedented Liberties: Re-reading Phillis Wheatley," in *MELUS*, Vol. 18, No. 3, 1993, pp. 71–81.

Gates, Henry Louis, Jr., "Mister Jefferson and the Trials of Phillis Wheatley," in *2002 Jefferson Lecturer in the Humanities: Henry Louis Gates, Jr.*, March 22, 2002, http://www.neh.gov/whoweare/gates/lecture.html (accessed February 4, 2010).

Nott, Walt, "From 'Uncultivated Barbarian' to 'Poetical Genius': The Public Presence of Phillis Wheatley," in *MELUS*, Vol. 18, No. 3, 1993, pp. 21–30.

Page, Yolanda Williams, "Phillis Wheatley (1753-1784)," in *Encyclopedia of African American Women Writers*, Vol. 2, Greenwood Press, 2007, pp. 610–13.

Powers, Emma L., "The Newsworthy Somerset Case," in *Colonial Williamsburg: That the Future May Learn from the Past*, 2009, http://research.history.org/Historical_Research/Research_Themes/ThemeEnslave/Somerset.cfm (accessed February 4, 2010).

Preminger, Alex, and T. V. F. Brogan, "Heroic Couplet," "Hymn," "Iambic," and "Neoclassical Poetics," in *The Princeton Encyclopedia of Poetry and Poetics*, Princeton University Press, 1993, pp. 522, 544, 548–49, 825.

Wheatley, Phillis, *Complete Writings*, edited by Vincent Carretta, Penguin Classics, 2001.

FURTHER READING

Blumrosen, Alfred W., and Ruth G. Blumrosen, *Slave Nation: How Slavery United the Colonies and Sparked the American Revolution*, Sourcebooks, 2005.

    The Blumrosens are law professors with backgrounds in civil rights. They argue that the threat that the British abolitionist movement posed to the southern colonies was a powerful inducement for those colonies to agitate for independence.

Carretta, Vincent, *Equiano, the African: Biography of a Self-Made Man*, Penguin, 2007.

    Carretta, a scholar at the W. E. B. Du Bois Institute for African and African-American Research at Harvard University, has done extensive research on Equiano's life story. Although he discovered that Equiano was born in South Carolina and was not kidnapped out of Africa as his narrative declares, Carretta makes a compelling case for Equiano's status as a self-made man.

Clifford, Mary Louise, *From Slavery to Freetown: Black Loyalists after the American Revolution*, McFarland, 2006.

    Clifford traces the little-known story of Virginia and Carolina slaves liberated by the British during the American Revolution. These slaves were first evacuated to Nova Scotia, Canada, and eventually were returned to Africa, where they founded the city of Freetown in Sierra Leone. The little-known tale of this journey and the struggle of these settlers for the rights of self-governance, education, and religious freedom is a fascinating chapter of revolutionary history.

Dungy, Camille T., ed., *Black Nature: Four Centuries of African American Nature Poetry*, University of Georgia Press, 2009.

    Dungy has compiled poetry from four centuries of African American writers in the context of how they approached the natural world. Although nature poetry has always been an important part of the African American aesthetic, it has most often been read as merely a metaphor for political or historical protest issues. Dungy's collection demonstrates the manner in which African American poets have contributed to this important strain of the American poetic tradition.

Haskins, James, *Building a New Land: African-Americans in Colonial America*, Amistad, 2005.

    Haskins's history of the role of African Americans in colonial America is written for young adults and generously illustrated by Kathleen Benson. Topics covered include the role of slaves in the colonies, the rules by which slaves could purchase their freedom and that of their family members, and the struggle to maintain the traditions of the African cultures from whence they came.

Hochschild, Adam, *Bury the Chains: Prophets and Rebels in the Fight to Free an Empire's Slaves*, Houghton Mifflin, 2005.

    Wheatley spent much of her life as a British subject, and it was her visit to England in 1773 that conferred emancipated status upon her. It was the support of British abolitionists that was, in large part, responsible for her success. In this history, Hochschild traces the history of British abolitionism, as well as the rise and fall of slavery in the history of the British Empire.

Waldstreicher, David, *Runaway America: Benjamin Franklin, Slavery, and the American Revolution*, Hill and Wang, 2005.

    Waldstreicher begins with Franklin's history as an indentured servant and a runaway, and he examines the role that slavery played in Franklin's life and career. Like the majority of the founding fathers, Franklin's views on slavery and indentured servitude were contradictory and complicated. Waldstreicher examines the ways in which Franklin was representative of his time and place and what he did to both eliminate and perpetuate the complicated systems of servitude upon which colonial America was founded.

SUGGESTED SEARCH TERMS

Phillis Wheatley

Phillis Wheatley poems

Phillis Wheatley AND Hymn to the Evening

Phillis Wheatley AND Poems on Various Subjects, Religious and Moral

Phillis Wheatley AND poetry

Phillis Wheatley AND slavery

Phillis Wheatley AND abolition

African American AND poetry

African American AND Boston

American Revolution AND slavery

United States Constitution AND slavery

I Am Not One of Those Who Left the Land

ANNA AKHMATOVA

1922

Anna Akhmatova is one of the most important Russian poets of the twentieth century. Her life encompassed some of the most violent and chaotic periods of Russian history, including the years of World War I, the Russian Revolution, the Russian civil war, World War II, and the Stalin years. Her poem "I Am Not One of Those Who Left the Land" speaks of her decision to remain in Russia, despite great hardship, loss, and deprivation, at a time when many artists, writers, and intellectuals fled the country.

"I Am Not One of Those Who Left the Land" appeared in the volume *Anno Domini MCMXXI*, published in 1922. It would be Akhmatova's last book for fourteen years because of governmental suppression of her work. The poem speaks to the pride Akhmatova feels for herself and for those who have chosen to endure the difficult years in Russia. Those who have left the land to live a life of exile elicit her pity and anger.

Akhmatova died in 1966, and in the years since her death, her reputation and stature has increased each year. Many contemporary poets look to her work for inspiration and instruction. "I Am Not One of Those Who Left the Land" appears as "I Am Not with Those Who Abandoned Their Land" in the updated and expanded edition of *The Complete Poems of Anna Akhmatova*, translated by Judith Hemschemeyer, and edited and introduced by Roberta Reeder, published in 2000 by Zephyr Press.

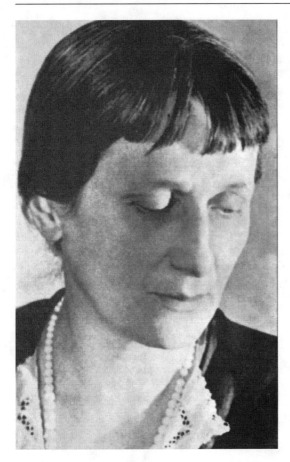

Anna Akhmatova *(© RIA Novosti / Alamy)*

AUTHOR BIOGRAPHY

Anna Andreyevna Gorenko, later known as Anna Akhmatova, was born near Odessa, Russia, on June 23, 1889, to Andrey Gorenko and Inna Erazmovna Stogova. Both of her parents were of aristocratic heritage, and the family was wealthy. When Akhmatova was quite small, her family moved to Tsarkoe Selo, a suburb of St. Petersburg, Russia. There, Akhmatova attended school. However, when she was ten years old, she suffered from a life-threatening illness. Her biographers associate the illness with the beginning of her writing career, as she began producing poetry shortly thereafter.

The Russo-Japanese War (February 1904– September 1905) intruded dramatically in young Akhmatova's life. Her father, a naval engineer, retired from his job after the destruction of the Russian navy by the Japanese. Soon after, her parents separated and Akhmatova moved to Kiev, in what is now the Ukraine. Akhmatova

had lost one sister to tuberculosis several years earlier; in 1905, her sister Inna had to be hospitalized for the same disease, and would also die. By far, however, the most influential event of her life during this time was the worker uprisings across the country that were met brutally by the forces of the tsar.

Akhmatova attended high school in Kiev and graduated in 1907. She took up the study of law at the Kiev College for Women. She also continued to write poetry, an activity her father held in disdain. She changed her name from Gorenko at this time to Akhmatova, to spare her father embarrassment. The name derived from her Tatar great-grandmother.

While in Kiev, Akhmatova was courted by the poet Nikolay Gumilyov. Although she initially rebuffed him, she married him in 1910, and moved back to St. Petersburg. Gumilyov left soon after their marriage for a trip to Ethiopia, and while he was gone, Akhmatova's poetic output increased. She became well known in the St. Petersburg literary circles as her poems were increasingly published by literary journals. She, along with other musicians, artists, and writers, frequented the cabaret known as the Stray Dog to share their works. During this period, she also developed a close friendship with Aleksandr Blok, the leader of the Russian symbolist movement. In spite of this friendship, when Gumilyov returned from his travels in 1911, he, along with Akhmatova and the poet Osip Mandelstam, founded the acmeist movement as a rejection of symbolism. The acmeists believed that poetry should be written in clear language, with concrete imagery.

Akhmatova's first book-length publication was *Evening* (1912), a volume that earned the poet many positive reviews and avid readers. Akhmatova gave birth to a son in 1912. The marriage to Gumilyov, plagued by infidelities, broke down about the same time, and Lev, Akhmatova's son, was raised by his paternal grandparents.

Russia entered World War I in 1914, the same year that Akhmatova published her second book, *Rosary*. The war years were difficult both on the war front and at home. By 1917, the year Akhmatova published *White Flock*, the political situation in Russia was in chaos as the Russian Revolution began. Quickly, the tsar was deposed, and in turn, the subsequent provisional government was overthrown by the Bolsheviks. This event led to civil war, a war that continued until 1921.

Although they had been living apart, Akhmatova and Gumilyov did not divorce until 1918, when Akhmatova wanted to marry again, this time to Vladimir Shileiko. By 1920, however, Akhmatova was once again on her own, having left Shileiko. In spite of the turmoil, Akhmatova's poetic work flourished. She published *Plantain* in 1921 and *Anno Domini MCMXXI* in 1922. "I Am Not One of Those Who Left the Land," which appeared in that volume, was directed at the many members of the Russian intelligentsia who left Russia during the revolution and subsequent civil war.

In August 1921, Akhmatova lost her long-time friend, Blok, and while at his funeral discovered that Gumilyov had been arrested as a counterrevolutionary. She only learned by reading in a newspaper that Gumilyov was executed on September 1, 1921. Akhmatova's ability to publish work in her own country ended, as the government suppressed her work, both because she had been married to Gumilyov and because her work honestly portrayed the conditions of the country, not the ideal country the Communists wanted to portray. Her next book did not appear until 1940.

Although her life was very hard, Akhmatova chose to remain in Russia, the subject of "I Am Not One of Those Who Left the Land." She entered a long-term relationship with Nikolai Punin, an art historian. During the years of repression, she wrote the long poems *Requiem* and *Poem without a Hero*. Akhmatova's friends and admirers memorized her poetry, and Akhmatova destroyed the originals, since she could have been viewed as a traitor to the state and arrested if anyone discovered her work.

Throughout the 1920s, Joseph Stalin worked to consolidate his power, and by the end of the decade, he had become a dictator who ruled harshly through fear and reprisal. Akhmatova's son Lev was arrested in 1935 and was in prison until 1956. In the 1950s and 1960s, Akhmatova was once again permitted to publish her work, and in 1964, she received the Etna Taormina Prize for Poetry in Italy. In 1965, she was awarded an honorary doctorate from Oxford University. She was allowed to travel to accept the awards.

Akhmatova died on March 5, 1966, in Domodedovo, Russia. In the final years of her life, she had become a poet of international renown, although in her own land, she was not recognized with such distinction until the 1980s. By 2000, many critics agreed that Akhmatova was one of the greatest Russian poets.

POEM TEXT

I am not with those who abandoned their land
To the lacerations of the enemy.
I am deaf to their coarse flattery,
I won't give them my songs.

But to me the exile is forever pitiful,   5
Like a prisoner, like someone ill.
Dark is your road, wanderer,
Like wormwood smells the bread of strangers.

But here, in the blinding smoke of the
      conflagration
Destroying what's left of youth,   10
We have not deflected from ourselves
One single stroke.

And we know that in the final accounting
Each hour will be justified. . .
But there is no people on earth more tearless.   15
More simple and more full of pride.

POEM SUMMARY

All of Akhmatova's poems were originally written in Russian. Consequently, English-speaking readers will examine translations of her work, rather than the original poem itself. Translators often make differing decisions concerning word selection, rhyming, and sound. The following summary of "I Am Not One of Those Who Left the Land" is based on Judith Hemschemeyer's translation found in *The Complete Poems of Anna Akhmatova* as "I Am Not with Those Who Abandoned Their Land."

Lines 1–4

The poem is constructed in four regular stanzas of four lines each. While the original Russian may have had regular rhyme and meter schemes, in her translation, Hemschemeyer has chosen to approximate rhymes, such as in lines two and three. The poem maintains a strong, rhythmic pulse even in translation, although it is not in the form of an established meter.

In the first line, the poet separates herself from other artists and poets who have chosen to flee Russia. Hemschemeyer uses the word abandoned rather than left in her poem, casting stronger blame on those who have left than is evident in other translations. Abandonment means leaving without assuming responsibility for those left behind, and it is clear that Akhmatova harbored both resentment and guilt toward those who left.

MEDIA ADAPTATIONS

- *A Film about Anna Akhmatova* is a 2008 film produced by Das Films and distributed by TurnstyleTV. Directed by Helga Landauer, the documentary discusses Akhmatova's poetry and her experiences during the Russian Revolution and civil war.

- *The File of Anna Akhmatova* is a 1990 Russian documentary with subtitles tracing Akhmatova's life and artistic career. It was directed by Semyon Aranovich and released in 2000 by NTSC on DVD.

- *Fear and the Muse: The Story of Anna Akhmatova* is a 2000 documentary film about Akhmatova's life. Released on videotape by Winstars and produced by the New York Center for Visual History, the film is narrated by Christopher Reeve and directed by Jill Janows.

She states that those who left turned their backs on their motherland while foreign forces were slicing her up. The enemy of whom she speaks is the German army; later, the same wording could be applied to those who fought on either side of the civil war.

In line 3, she notes that those who have chosen exile still speak highly of her poetry abroad. She, however, refuses to listen to what they say. In addition, it appears that she is refusing to send them poems as well.

Lines 5–8

In the second stanza, Akhmatova turns to a description of the life of one who has left the country. She pities the exile and comments that although the exile has escaped Russia, he or she is nonetheless imprisoned by his or her exile and made sick by it. Further, the exile is doomed to wander in darkness in foreign lands. Finally, she states that food offered by those who live in foreign lands has the aroma of wormwood. Wormwood is a bitter herb used in the production of

absinthe, an alcoholic beverage considered highly addictive and toxic in Akhmatova's time. Indeed, in 1915, most European countries banned absinthe as a dangerous drug. Nonetheless, absinthe was popular among avant-garde writers and artists. Akhmatova may also be making a biblical allusion through her use of the word wormwood. In Jeremiah 23:15 (*New American Standard Bible*), God castigates the wicked prophets of Jerusalem, and says, "Behold, I am going to feed them wormwood and make them drink poisonous water." In using the term wormwood, she suggests that the exile's life is a bitter, poisonous existence.

Lines 9–12

In the third stanza, Akhmatova turns from her description of the life of the exile to a description of life from where she is speaking. Here, she says, fire and burning fill the land, alluding to a destructive force that makes young people old and destroys the sense of sight. She refers directly to the combined violence of World War I, the Russian Revolution, and the civil war; her images, however, evoke more mythic destruction. Her description is almost biblical, reminiscent of the apocalyptic language of the book of Revelation describing the end of days.

In line 11, she turns to a description of the people who have remained in Russia, a description she carries into the last stanza. Here, in line 11, Akhmatova no longer speaks in first person singular, but shifts to the first person plural "we" form. She reports that she and the others who have remained have not tried to protect themselves in anyway.

Lines 13–16

Akhmatova asserts in the final stanza that the sacrifices of those who have not abandoned their country will not be for naught. She uses another biblical image, that of the final accounting when a person's sins are toted up against him or her. She says that the entire time that they have remained in Russia, bearing the violence and blows, will be "justified." This word has many connotations, and Akhmatova exploits many of them in this simple line. In the first place, the word derives from the same root as the word justice. Thus, the line states that those who stayed will have justice. Secondly, justified means with reason. That is, a justified expense is one for which there is a compelling reason for the expense. Justifiable homicide is a form of murder for which a person is not held responsible, since there is a strong and compelling reason for the murder, such as self-defense. Finally, theologically, the word justified refers to those who are righteous in the sight of God. In this sense, Akhmatova views those who have stayed as having made the virtuous, righteous choice. For their choice, they will someday be rewarded.

Nevertheless, Akhmatova concludes in the final two lines, although those who have stayed are virtuous and righteous, they are also uncomplicated. Their pride derives from the knowledge that they have done the right thing. Moreover, the people who have stayed are without tears, in spite of the extreme difficulties and sacrifices life has given them. Their sacrifices are a source of pride, not self-pity.

THEMES

Exile

In "I Am Not One of Those Who Left the Land," Akhmatova imagines the life of the exile who has left the land. Many of her friends urged her to leave Russia after the 1917 Russian Revolution, and even more strenuously after the Bolsheviks came to power. Many of Akhmatova's friends were arrested and some, such as her former husband Gumilyov, were executed. In addition, soon after the publication of *Anno Domini MCMXXI*, the collection that included "I Am Not One of Those Who Left the Land," the government would not permit her to publish her work. Despite this, she believed that her life was preferable to that of the exile.

A person who is in exile is one who leaves the country of his or her birth, either by choice or by edict. In exile, a person must learn a new language, a new way of acting, develop new friendships, and find a way to earn a living. It is a difficult life. Akhmatova suggests that the exile becomes ill with the struggle of trying to live without his or her homeland. In addition, although the exile is safe in the new country, he or she must endure the company of strangers, breaking strange-smelling bread and tasting the bitterness of separation.

The poem thus opposes Akhmatova's decision to stay in Russia with the decision of many others to leave. For Akhmatova, leaving is a cowardly choice, and the life of an exile is no life at all.

Suffering

Akhmatova's decision to stay in Russia, though she vehemently defends it in "I Am Not One of Those Who Left the Land" and other poems, was nevertheless a decision that brought her much suffering. Nonetheless, in this poem, she writes about suffering as if it is noble. She describes those who have left as essentially cowards. Those who have stayed, however, are willing to sacrifice themselves for the good of the nation. She writes that those who remain in the country do not flinch when they are struck. Indeed, they do not even try to deflect the blows. Thus, it appears that she sees those who stay as martyrs of sorts. They do not betray their country, and they take the blows meant for everyone. This sacrifice, however, is not without honor. She writes that those who stay are both tearless and proud. Indeed, for Akhmatova, the suffering endured by she and the others who remained is virtuous. In the final reckoning, she believes that every moment that they have spent in hardship will be for good purpose. Thus, although the suffering is difficult, it is also cleansing and necessary for the redemption of the country.

Russian History

Akhmatova lived at one of the most difficult and chaotic periods in Russian history. Her poetry reflects the political and social conditions of the time. "I Am Not One of Those Who Left the Land" was written in 1922; by this time, Akhmatova had lived through the Russian Revolution, and the civil war was under way. In addition, her former husband Gumilyov had been executed for treason, simply for some poems he had written.

At this time in Russian history, large numbers of intellectuals, artists, and writers were fleeing the country. Although they had initially supported the revolution, the rise of Stalin and the Bolsheviks dashed their hopes of a democratic government. Regardless, Akhmatova scoffed at their cowardice. Indeed, she understood herself to be a part of Russian history. She believed that in order for a true history to ever be written, there must be witnesses within the country to continue to record and remember events. For this reason, when one reads the poems of Akhmatova, one is also reading an account of Russian history, told in the particular, by one embattled woman.

TOPICS FOR FURTHER STUDY

- With a group of your classmates, research the Stray Dog Cabaret in St. Petersburg, the primary meeting place for members of Akhmatova's literary and artistic circle. In addition, read a selection of poems from poets who performed regularly at the Stray Dog, using a book such as *The Stray Dog Cabaret: A Book of Russian Poems* (2006), translated by Paul Schmidt and introduced by Catherine Ciepiela. Design a stage setting to represent the Stray Dog, and present a poetry reading such as might have occurred in 1917 in St. Petersburg.

- Read the young-adult novel *The Kitchen Boy: A Novel of the Last Tsar* (2004) by Robert Alexander, *The Snow Mountain* (1973) by Catherine Irvine Gavin, and/or *The Midwife of St. Petersburg* (2007) by Linda Lee Chaikin, all stories that focus on the Russian Revolution. In addition, research the history of the Russian Revolution, using the library and the Internet to locate documents, historical texts, and photographs. Use what you have learned to write a short story set in 1922 St. Petersburg.

- Many contemporary poets honor Akhmatova in their work by writing poems about her, dedicated to her, or in her style. Some examples include "Anna" by David Ray, published in the *Iowa Review* in Fall 2008; "Summer Garden" by Laurie Byro, published in the *Literary Review*, Fall 1998; and "For Anna Akhmatova" by Marilyn Hacker, published in *Prairie Schooner* in Fall 2005. Collect as many such poems as you can find by using the library and computer databases. Read the poems carefully and then write a poem to or about Akhmatova. Present a sampling of the poems, including your own, and describe how various writers represent Akhmatova.

- The symbolists, the acmeists, and the futurists were three groups of poets writing in Russia in the years before the rise of Joseph Stalin. Read about the history of each of these groups, as well as finding and reading selected poems from each. Write an essay in which you compare and contrast the three poetic groups.

- With a small group of students create a multimedia presentation of Akhmatova's life and work. Include at least three different types of media, such as music, pictures, video, historic documents, and art, among others. Demonstrate in your presentation how historical events influenced Akhmatova's poetry. To help all team members shoulder equal responsibility for the presentation, use a project management tool such as http://www.teamness.com to help you organize your project and assign all tasks. After completing and presenting your project to the class, write a brief report evaluating the team process with suggestions for how to improve collaborative work in the future.

- Collect as many different translations of the poem "I Am Not One of Those Who Left the Land" as you can find, using the library and the Internet. Compare the translations. What kinds of choices do you see translators making? What do you think is most important in a translation: the way the poem sounds, how closely it follows the original poet's meaning, or how well it works as a poem on its own? Using all of the translations you have found, try to write a version of "I Am Not One of Those Who Left the Land" yourself. Then, write a short essay in which you explore the difficulties of translation.

The narrator of the poem is a person who stands up to fight. (*Image copyright Stavchansky Yakov, 2010. Used under license from Shutterstock.com*)

STYLE

Acmeism

In the years just before the Russian Revolution, St. Petersburg was a hotbed of poetic activity. The symbolists had reached their pinnacle about 1910. This school, loosely related to the French school of poetry by the same name, rebelled against expository poetry and chose instead to focus on the sensations of human life. They concentrated on inner thoughts and private experience. Moreover, the symbolists believed that reality itself was inexpressible; metaphor and image could suggest, rather than tell, the state of the poet's mind and his or her intention in his or her work. As a result, symbolist poetry was often obscure.

By 1910, however, the symbolists were losing their edge. Rebellious in their youth, they became entrenched in their own ideas. As Alexander Kaun writes in *Soviet Poets and Poetry*, "In their preoccupation with the magic of sounds and the mystery of symbols, they drifted farther and farther from reality into foggy narcissism."

Younger poets, in turn, rebelled against their poetic forefathers. Nikolay Gumilyov was the leader of a small group of poets who, in 1911, founded the Guild of Poets, along with Akhmatova and Osip Mandelstam. Their aesthetic goal was to liberate poetry from the fogginess imposed on it by the symbolists. Calling themselves the acmeists, they promoted precise and clear language. Indeed, their goal was to use common speech and employ words with great skill, eliminating the fancifulness of the symbolists.

"I Am Not One of Those Who Left the Land" is a good example of acmeist poetry. Akhmatova is direct in her message: she will not leave the country, and the life of the exile is not a good one. She uses several similes in the poem to describe the exile, but they are clear and straightforward. The use of common language reinforces her contention that the people of whom she speaks are simple people who take pride in their country. She rejects flowery statements and emotions in this poem, preferring instead the sharp sensory image to build the starkness of a world caught up in war. In all, the careful crafting and balance of the four-stanza poem epitomizes the acmeist ideal.

Lyric Poetry

A lyric poem is usually a short poem that emphasizes sound and image. One way to understand the structure of a lyric poem is to contrast it with a narrative poem. A narrative poem tells a story and has dramatic movement, whereas a lyric focuses on a state of being or a brief description. Originally, a lyric was a poem that could be set to music. In contemporary poetry, while the lyric poem has a musical quality, it is not generally set to music.

Because "I Am Not One of Those Who Left the Land" is a translation of a Russian poem, it is difficult to analyze the musical quality of the verse. Critics of Akhmatova's poetry who read the original Russian, however, all note that her poems are quite musical and benefit from being read aloud. It is possible, however, to look at the sensory imagery in this poem. Akhmatova's description of the life of the exile, for example, includes mention of darkness and the smell of bread. In addition, when she turns to describe Russia, the "here" of the poem, she writes of smoke that blinds and massive fires. These terms evoke the senses of sight, sound, smell, and touch. The reader's eye burns from the acrid smoke of battle. In addition, when she writes that those who have stayed have not flinched from being struck, she is using a tactile and kinesthetic image to allow the reader to feel the blow in his or her own body. Likewise, by describing the people who remain in Russia as without tears, Akhmatova appeals both to vision and touch. The lyric form allows Akhmatova to directly touch her reader and convey her message through not only the mind, but also through the senses.

HISTORICAL CONTEXT

The Russian Revolution

The Russian Revolution was a protracted series of events beginning in 1905 that eventually led to the execution of Tsar Nicholas II and the establishment of the Soviet Union.

The Russian Empire historically was ruled by a hereditary ruler known as the tsar or tsarina. Although most European nations had limited the powers of their monarchs by the beginning of the twentieth century, the tsar still wielded nearly absolute power in Russia. Conditions in the country were not good, and they were made worse by the country's participation in the Russo-Japanese War (1904–1905), a war in which the Russian army and navy were unexpectedly and soundly defeated by the Japanese. Peaceful protests against the tsar's government on January 22, 1905, in St. Petersburg met with brutal force from the tsar's troops, who massacred hundreds of peaceful demonstrators. (Imperial Russia continued to use the Julian calendar, known as the "old style," until the adoption of the Gregorian calendar in 1918, known as the "new style." All dates in this entry are in the new style.) Workers across the country engaged in a general strike in response.

Tsar Nicholas finally promised to establish a more representative form of government by instituting the Duma, a legislative parliament with limited power, in October 1905, blunting the revolt. However, in the years following, most of the reforms were rescinded, and there was growing discontent among the populace as the disparity between the rich and the poor grew ever larger.

Meanwhile, the rest of Europe slid into the cataclysm known as World War I in 1914, and Russia joined in on the side of the English and French against Germany and the Austro-Hungarian Empire. Philip E. Mosley, in his 2006 article "Russian Revolution" appearing on the *History Channel* Web site, argues that although the Russians had adequate men to fight the war, they did not have the money to provide the resources to mount a fighting force. Russia, therefore, suffered many casualties among the soldiers, while the people at home endured food shortages and terrible deprivation.

By the winter of 1917, the situation was critical. Sheila Fitzpatrick writes in her book *The Russian Revolution*, "In February 1917, the autocracy collapsed in the face of popular demonstrations." Bread riots broke out in St. Petersburg on March 8. By March 12, the government forces had joined with the revolutionaries. Tsar Nicholas and his family were arrested, and he was forced to abdicate the throne on March 15. The provisional government established by the Duma assumed control of St. Petersburg. However, the Petrograd Soviet of Workers also vied for power. The revolution spread across the country as soviets (revolutionary councils of workers) organized themselves in cities, towns, and the military. The soviets supported full withdrawal from World War I.

Although Russian intellectuals welcomed the revolution and believed that Russia could

COMPARE
&
CONTRAST

- **1920s:** Akhmatova goes from being one of the most popular poets in the Soviet Union to being censured for her work and forbidden to publish.

  Today: Akhmatova is considered to be the greatest woman poet in Russian literature and is revered in her native land.

- **1920s:** Joseph Stalin establishes a brutal dictatorship; he is responsible for the deaths of tens of millions of lives. Those who oppose him are either sent to work camps in Siberia or executed.

  Today: Russia is a federated state under the leadership of a president and prime minister, with a constitution that guarantees certain basic human rights and includes a moratorium on the death penalty.

- **1920s:** Artists and writers in the Soviet Union are severely censured and restricted under Communist rule, where the only acceptable art is "socialist realism." Socialist realism does not depict any flaws in the state, but rather celebrates the socialist state in order to move the hearts and minds of the populace.

  Today: Artists and writers in Russia have much more artistic freedom and are able to create imaginative works on any topic.

- **1920s:** The Russian Revolution of 1917 is quickly followed by the Russian civil war, and subsequently by the rise of Joseph Stalin as absolute dictator of the newly established Soviet Union. He will dictate until his death in 1953.

  Today: The Soviet Union no longer exists, having broken apart in the 1980s. The Communist Party, while still a political force in Russia and the other nations of the former Soviet Union, does not wield total control.

---

accomplish true democracy through the joint rule of the provisional government and the Petrograd Soviet, according to Fitzgerald, their hopes were dashed. In October, members of the Bolshevik (also called the Red) faction of the Soviet executed a successful coup against the provisional government, as well as neutralizing the Menshevik (also known as the White) faction of the Soviet. As Fitzgerald writes, "The Revolution had not brought liberal democracy to Russia. Instead, it had brought anarchy and civil war."

The Russian Civil War

In the months and years following the Bolshevik Revolution of October 1917, the Bolsheviks and Mensheviks continued to struggle to establish complete control. The Bolsheviks managed to withdraw Russia from World War I, and they finally defeated the Mensheviks in 1920. Vladimir Ilich Lenin (1870–1924) became the head of state. In the euphoria of the cessation of civil war, there was a brief but dramatic upsurge in culture and art. Akhmatova's *Anno Domini MCMXXI* was a product of this time.

The aesthetic freedom did not last, however. The Bolsheviks insisted on rigorous aesthetic standards, and they arrested and executed artists whose work seemed critical of the state. It was in this atmosphere that Gumilyov, Akhmatova's first husband and an important poet himself, was arrested and put to the firing squad. Many artists and intellectuals who had remained in Russia despite the hardships and dangers of war now scrambled to find their way out of the country. In his book *New Mecca, New Babylon: Paris and the Russian Exiles*, Robert H. Johnston concurs with estimates that one million people left Russia between 1917 and 1921. Among these, according to Johnston, "could be counted figures prominent in every walk of Russian life and culture."

In 1924, the death of Lenin led to yet another power struggle within the ruling party, later to be known as the Communist Party. Joseph Stalin

Red Square in Moscow *(Image copyright Alexey Fyodorov, 2010. Used under license from Shutterstock.com)*

(1879–1953) defeated all contenders and became a leader with absolute power. He quickly initiated purges to eliminate all opposition to himself in the party and the society. This marked the end of artistic freedom in what was now the Union of Soviet Socialist Republics (USSR), commonly called the Soviet Union. Akhmatova's work, so popular during the revolution and civil war, was viewed negatively. She was banned from publishing between the years 1925 and 1940.

These historical events surround the poems of *Anno Domini MCMXXI.* Akhmatova's choice to stay in the Soviet Union was the single most important influence on her work as a poet, according to her biographers and critics. This is the choice that Akhmatova explores in "I Am Not One of Those Who Left the Land."

CRITICAL OVERVIEW

Akhmatova's poetry, particularly in the years since her death in 1966 and its translation into English, has continued to garner widespread and positive critical acclaim. Indeed, as Richard Eder remarks in the *Los Angeles Times Book Review*, "It is quite reasonable to think of Akhmatova...as the greatest woman poet in the Western World since Sappho."

Few critics have anything negative to say about Akhmatova. For example, while John Simon, writing in the *New Criterion*, does not find Akhmatova's poetry to be as powerful as some have suggested, he does state that in Akhmatova he "see[s] a poet with an original vision and a personal voice who manages to maintain her individual talent within the tradition." Simon also notes that "I Am Not One of Those Who Left the Land" is one of Akhmatova's "finest poems."

Many critics comment on Akhmatova's life circumstances as an influence on her poetry. Majorie Perloff, for example, writing in the journal *Sulfur*, asserts that "Akhmatova let nothing interfere with her work, a work she refused to distinguish from life... neither marriage... nor motherhood... nor the extreme poverty and deprivation that came after the Revolution, nor the censorship of her work under Stalin." Akhmatova's single-minded dedication to her art is a sentiment expressed by many reviewers and literary critics. In addition, many critics note that her choice not to leave Russia after the Russian Revolution played a large role in her development as a poet.

Ervin C. Brody, in a review of *The Complete Poems of Anna Akhmatova* appearing in the *Literary Review*, links "I Am Not One of Those Who Left the Land" to Akhmatova's earlier collection, *Plantain*. He writes, "The most important poem of the collection is devoted to the war, revealing her deep patriotic spirit and rebuking those who wanted to flee the ravaged country." Brody views her later poem as a reaffirmation of "her commitment to remain in Russia in her desperate hour."

Likewise, John Bayley, writing in the *New York Times*, argues that this commitment is at the heart of some of Akhmatova's most profound work. He writes, "Some of her gravest and most emphatic poems repeat her claim to have stood fast, accepted persecution, remained with her people, not sheltered 'under a foreign wing.'" Clearly, Bayley is referring to poems such as "I Am Not One of Those Who Left the Land" in this comment.

Other critics have looked at the aesthetic qualities of Akhmatova's work apart from the historical context. Alexander Kaun, in his book *Soviet Poets and Poetry*, focuses on Akhmatova as a member of the acmeist literary movement. He writes that Akhmatova "achieved poignant effectiveness by using everyday words and phrases, stark in their simplicity and transparency, to convey shades of emotion and tragedy."

Thus, when reading Akhmatova, it is important to consider both the high quality of her poetry as well as the epic events that shaped her destiny. As Maria Rubins summarizes in her essay in *Dictionary of Literary Biography: Russian Writers of the Silver Age*, "For several generations of readers, she has been an iconic representation of noble beauty and catastrophic predicament."

CRITICISM

Diane Andrews Henningfeld

Henningfeld is a professor emerita of English at Adrian College and writes widely on literature. In the following essay, she discusses Akhmatova's "I Am Not One of Those Who Left the Land" as an example of the poetry of witness.

Sometimes people witness horrible events that are too difficult to contain in straightforward narrative: something happens that cannot be shared in literal language, a trauma that refuses to be told in anything other than metaphor, image, and sound. And yet, in order for healing to take place, experiences must be shared. Thus, events of horror and violence often move ordinary people as well as great writers to compose a particular type of poetry known as the poetry of witness. The poetry of witness uses memory to work against forgetting, so that an event is not lost to history. It works for survival and against oppression. As Cassie Premo Steele writes in her book *We Heal From Memory: Sexton, Lorde, Anzaldúa and the Poetry of Witness*, "To witness means to decide to participate—not only with the head but with the heart—in the experience of another, an experience so painful that it must be shared in order to be confronted."

Akhmatova's poetry bears witness to the events that shook Russia in the first half of the twentieth century. That she lived to tell the tale borders on miraculous. Susan Salter Reynolds, writing in the *Los Angeles Times Book Review*, comments on Akhmatova's "instinct for survival." In *Time Asia*, F. Sionil Jose argues that Akhmatova not only survived the cataclysmic events, she grew stronger because of them: "She stayed in Russia all through the terror of the Stalinist years, survived it, ingested it and drew from its torture the indomitable strength that sustained her and her art."

In her poem "I Am Not One of Those Who Left the Land," Akhmatova announces her intention to stay in a land rocked by invasions from without and chaos from within. She witnessed death, burning, destruction, and the end of life as she knew it. On the way to a successful career as a writer, Akhmatova's life was irrevocably changed by World War I, the Russian Revolution, the Russian civil war, and the brutal dictatorship of Joseph Stalin. As Yelena Byelyakova notes, writing in the *Unesco Courier*, many of Akhmatova's circle left the country, but Akhmatova refused to emigrate.

This choice, to remain in Russia, had the most profound effect possible on her life. As a result of her decision, she suffered serious hardship and heartbreak, losing many of her friends, enduring the decades-long imprisonment of her son, and finding herself slip from a position of poetic prominence to near invisibility. Byelyakova writes, "[In] 1923 her work ceased to be published. The official

WHAT DO I READ NEXT?

- *The Complete Persepolis* (2007) by Marjane Satrapi is a memoir in the form of a graphic novel about growing up in revolutionary Iran and Satrapi's ultimate exile from her homeland.

- Julia Alvarez's young-adult novel *Before We Were Free* (2004) is about a girl living under a dictatorship during a revolution in the Dominican Republic.

- *Selected Poems* by Anna Akhmatova, translated by Walter Arndt, first published in 1976, and reprinted in 2009, offers an excellent overview of Akhmatova's finest work.

- Two articles, "The Russian Revolution, February–October 1917" and "The Russian Revolution: Red October and the Bolshevik Coup," written as lectures by Steven Kreis in 2000, are extremely interesting narrative accounts of the events. The articles can be found at http://www.historyguide.org/europe/europe.html on *The History Guide: Lectures on Twentieth Century Europe* Web site.

- *The Pillar of Fire: Selected Poems* (1999; translated by Richard McKane) is a collection of poetry by Nikolay Gumilyov, the founder of the acmeist movement and Akhmatova's first husband.

- Jane Kenyon, a well-known American poet who translated many of Akhmatova's poems, discusses the translation process she followed in her book *A Hundred White Daffodils*, published in 1999.

- George Orwell's *Animal Farm*, first published in 1945, is an allegory, or a story in which characters represent abstract ideas, about the Bolshevik Revolution and Stalin's rise to power.

- *Revolution Is Not a Dinner Party* (2007) by Ying Chang Compestine narrates the story of a young girl living through the Chinese cultural revolution in the 1960s and 1970s.

- Joseph Brodsky's *Collected Poems in English* (2002) includes a wide selection of Akhmatova's work. Brodsky is an exiled Russian poet who, as a young man, was deeply influenced by his friendship with Akhmatova.

---

view was that her lyrics were alien to the new generation of readers produced by the Revolution. Fame was followed by oblivion: for seventeen years her name vanished from literature."

Why, then, did she stay, when her words went unread, and her life was in danger? On the one hand, Akhmatova felt a very close connection to the people and the land of Russia, as evidenced by her poem "I Am Not One of Those Who Left the Land." Ervin Brody argues in the *Literary Review*:

> No matter how terrible her situation had become and how critical her personal traumas, her attachment to her native country was so profound that she refused to leave Russia, and continued to write even if it went unpublished.

For Akhmatova, a life of exile was unthinkable. She associated the life of the exile with sickness and despair. It was unthinkable for her to begin endless wandering or to attempt to make a new home among strangers, in spite of the fact that so many of her friends chose to leave and urged her to do so as well.

In addition, Akhmatova and those poets who remained believed deeply that poetry had power. More than just written words on a page, poetry could change people and change society. Brody notes that to Akhmatova,

> [her] three great contemporaries—Pasternak, Mandelstam, and Tsvetaeva—. . . poetry appeared as a medium of social and spiritual redemption, and their idea of ultimately building a new society was essentially an aesthetic and even mystical process rather than a political one.

Akhmatova believed that she had the ability to help save the people of her country, to give them some way to understand the upheaval, fear, and separation brought about by violence and war. Thus, she believed that as a poet, she must stay to help repair her country. The country needed the poetry she could provide. Akhmatova stated, "I don't know any other country where . . . there is a greater need for [poetry] than here" (quoted by John Simon in his article "Anna Akhmatova," in the *New Criterion*). Simon adds, "She was right. In the large, cold, poor, and often lonely spaces of Russia, poetry came to fill a void."

Finally, she also saw herself as someone who must bear witness to what was happening inside her country. John Bayley, writing in the *New York Times*, argues that Akhmatova understood her decision to stay in Russia as a form of self-sacrifice, at a time when poetry was a "sheer necessity." He notes that while poetry is a pleasant pastime in a country not torn by war and repression, poetry in a country like Russia under Stalin was "the only way to stay living and sane." Bayley continues, "For this reason the poet must never forget, or allow the new barbarism to blot out the past. Akhmatova saw her poetic role as one of remembering and bearing witness."

In sum, Akhmatova stayed for three reasons: she loved her country and its people; she believed that poetry was necessary for healing and redemption; and she knew she must bear witness come what may. Thus, "I Am Not One of Those Who Left the Land" is a kind of manifesto, a public declaration of Akhmatova's policy and aims. In this poem, Akhmatova not only announces her intention to stay in her lacerated land, but also embraces her role as witness to the conflagration, using her head and her heart to work against forgetting.

Source: Diane Andrews Henningfeld, Critical Essay on "I Am Not One of Those Who Left the Land," in *Poetry for Students*, Gale, Cengage Learning, 2011.

John Taylor

In the following essay, Taylor claims that Akhmatova was a link to the Russian literary past for twentieth-century Soviet poets.

She was the "bridge between Not and Was in a wail of torments and rapture." This arresting line, written by the Russian poet Anatoly Naiman (b. 1936), evokes the legendary Anna Akhmatova (1889–66), one of the seminal poets of the twentieth century and the mentor, not only of Naiman, but also of Joseph Brodsky (1940–96), Dmitry Bobyshev (b. 1936), and Evgeny Rein (b. 1935). Beginning in 1959, in Leningrad (now Saint Petersburg), these four aspiring poets—who

> AKHMATOVA'S PRESENCE, LET ALONE HER POEMS (SOME OF WHICH SHE WAS STILL REVISING), GAVE THE FOUR POETS ACCESS TO THE RECENT RUSSIAN LITERARY PAST: THE 'WAS'—THE SILVER AGE—THAT HAD BEEN WALLED OFF BY THE RUSSIAN REVOLUTION."

were friends—sought out the ailing, impoverished, ever transient, and oft publicly discredited Akhmatova, the author of the poetic sequences *Requiem, Poem without a Hero*, and *The Way of All the Earth*. The young men recited their poems to her, helped her out in daily chores, and Naiman served as her secretary from 1962 to her death. Some of the one-to-one friendships in the foursome eventually soured; the reasons are suggested in Rein's poem "In Pavlovsk Park." Let's avoid that topic. "Life is like a letter," he rightly observes in "Signature for a Torn Portrait," "with blotches on the page."

Naiman, Brodsky, Bobyshev, and Rein were writing more or less secretly (their verse circulating in handwritten copies and through private readings), for they rejected the Socialist realism which was promoted—with all too tangible threats for dissenters—by Communist politicians and cultural watchdogs. Brodsky termed Socialist realism "recycled garbage," a quip not to be confused with Akhmatova's famous remark about poets being "born of rubbish." The latter signifies, in Brodsky's gloss (and in regard to Rein):

> . . . everything that a person comes up against, turns away from, to which he pays attention. This rubbish is not only his physical—visual, cognitive, olfactory and acoustic—experience; it is also the experience of everything lived, superfluous, unreceived, taken on faith, forgotten, devoted to, known only by rumor; it is also the experience of what has been read.

In other words: vital, radiant, resonant rubbish. Back then, among the four men's contemporaries, the only Russian poet well known abroad was the politically more ambiguous, poetically more facile, Yevgeny Yevtushenko (b. 1933), who even became the darling of some American politicians and intellectuals. Yevtushenko's case is more complicated than that, but it is important to know that a technically more elaborate, philosophically more ambitious, Russian poetry was being composed at the time by these four men whom Akhmatova had nicknamed her "magic choir." Eventually, translations of poems by Brodsky, who had involuntarily emigrated to the United States in 1972, began appearing, culminating in the *Penguin Selected Poems of 1973*. Brodsky went on to international fame and the 1987 Nobel Prize, while the poetry of his three former sidekicks remained little available in English. This is why the publication of Naiman's *Lions and Acrobats*, a gathering of recent work, as well as Rein's *Selected Poems*, is welcome news. Only missing, alas, is a selection of the work of Bobyshev, who emigrated to the United States in 1979 and teaches at the University of Illinois (Urbana). Samplings are available in *Contemporary Russian Poetry*, *In the Grip of Strange Thoughts*, and *Modern Poetry in Translation* (No. 10, Winter 1996). These men were the "outcasts and custodians of the age," to paraphrase Rein's untitled poem beginning "You walk across a frozen stream in a field lost in snow drifts."

Streams, rivers, and bridges—as metaphors—are common to these poets. Naiman, whose *Remembering Anna Akhmatova* (1989) vividly evokes their formative years, was thinking in his aforementioned poem about how the frail Akhmatova, as a sturdy literary bridge, was the last survivor of the great Russian poets of the first half of the twentieth century. Neither the term "survivor" nor the "Was" of Naiman's poem are to be taken lightly. Most of Akhmatova's literary peers and family had disappeared decades earlier in tragic, violent circumstances. Indeed, "how many ways the poet could meet death," she aptly laments in *Poem without a Hero*. The symbolist Alexander Blok (1880–1921), the "music" of whose verse fascinated her, had long before become discouraged with the Revolution, lost his will to live, fallen ill, and died. Marina Tsvetayeva (1892–1941) had fled the Soviet Union in 1922, then returned in 1939, only to commit suicide. Akhmatova's close friend, Osip Mandelstam (1891–1938), had been arrested, then left to perish in a transit camp. Her first husband, Nikolai Gumilyov, had been executed in 1921; and at about the same time as Mandelstam's death, Akhmatova's son Lev was caught and sent away to a prison, then to the Gulag. These victims constituted a mere handful of the millions who, in Naiman's words, "hung like smoke above labor camp stacks / or [fell] like carrion on long forced marches, / or rotted, crashed to death in hard-labor barges."

With "three hundred women ahead of you," as she phrases it, Akhmatova waited in lines outside jails and camps in the hopes of passing on warm clothing to her son. If the prison guards accepted the package, this meant that the convict inside was still alive. "Can you describe this?" asked a woman who recognized her. "I can," Akhmatova answered, affirming against the starkest odds that poetry can grapple with the most horrific realities. The repartee simultaneously gives birth, it seems to me, to the particular individualism and intricate metaphorical realism that one later finds in the work of her magic choir. In any event, this challenge, cited "instead of a foreword," motivated *Requiem*, of which a new, rhymed version is now provided by Nancy K. Anderson in *The Word That Causes Death's Defeat*. Anderson also offers compelling translations of, and extensive commentaries on, the other two sequences. This is a path-breaking book in what seemed to be a well-traveled forest. Anderson begins with a biography, which includes a sensitive and judicious account of Akhmatova's daily struggles, writing, and political behavior during the regimes of Stalin and Khrushchev. Then, in her translations, she convincingly interprets the "music" of the Russian poems, an important achievement in that Akhmatova contended that a true poet possessed a unique "song." Do not we Americans tend to speak of a poet's "voice," which is something else again? Reading the verse of Akhmatova and her magic choir obliges one to face up to telling differences between two essential "modernisms."

Akhmatova's presence, let alone her poems (some of which she was still revising), gave the four poets access to the recent Russian literary past: the "Was"—the Silver Age—that had been walled off by the Russian Revolution. Moreover, thanks to her vast learning, poetic passion, and sharp ear, the young men had a vital, not just bookish, link to classical European poetry, from Virgil to Petrarch, from Dante to Shakespeare. And because Akhmatova maintained such high standards, her example must have encouraged them to persist in the individual-negating "Not" of the present. Naiman, Rein, and Bobyshev waited for decades before most of their respective oeuvres could be published. Rein seems to evoke this in his lines "life slipped away: forty or fifty years / were needed to conclude / the most vexing of all vexations."

Akhmatova's tutelary role is the immediate meaning of Naiman's bridge metaphor, which crops up again in a poem dedicated to Bobyshev. "How strange," notes Naiman, "to walk half your life over bridges spanning a river." The poet refers to travel after "half a lifetime" spent "nowhere," during which he could cross only the Neva. Now he finds himself on a Hudson River bridge that "is as like as two drops to the first one." "How strange," he repeats, expressing a self-ironic, good-natured bewilderment that recurs often elsewhere. The poet characteristically concludes his poem by meditating on his growing "confusion...at the world not lying, / as [he] just catch[es] the sound of life latching metaphor's lock." Implicitly, the bridge metaphor thus also points to the poet's task of constructing a credible walkway between poetry and life in all its chaotic spontaneity. This is a realism, ever questioning and re-examining its postulates, of the most serious order.

This movement from a central object to existential or metaphysical concerns is typical of Naiman. The metaphorical bridge also spans an "eternal river." Teleology is never far from his thoughts. But even more, he seeks a wisdom superseding his own qualms. His focus on details is precise, but it is rarely a bitter squint, he simultaneously searches for equilibrium, proportion. In fact, Naiman more frequently questions life, not death—what it means to be alive, what it feels like to be alive, a phenomenological enigma that is more difficult to work out in words than it may seem. Attempt to feel yourself feeling, to catch yourself looking, to sense yourself thinking. . . .

Naiman endeavors precisely this when he gazes starward—a favorite pastime. "Whoever has [so] gazed," he posits, "is alive. / Without doubt. No breath-fogged mirror is needed, no proof, / no flutter of eyelids." And yet the poet's initial confidence about his aliveness is, characteristically, called into question by the second strophe: "Still, some sign would be good. A cough. Some such trivial thing. / An answer to whether that's Schumann or Schubert outside, / from the window. That we look at the sky and the one who is looking—/ you or me."

Finally he accepts his initial proposition, which could perhaps be described as "I sense myself gazing, therefore I am." This self-reflexive apperception, reinforcing his belief in his own existence, enables him to deduce stunningly that "optics, not mercury, show / that what came to life was no mere inanimate cosmos."

Other poems (like the engaging "Fuga et vita") similarly enter into, or imply, paradoxes about our experience of time: the future cannot be known; the present moment is fleeting, ungraspable; only the past exists, but in memory, and in fragments perhaps accessible through reminiscence yet otherwise beyond all possibilities of re-experience. Although allusions to Russia's somber past are made in *Lions and Acrobats* (notably in "A Wake for Our Time"), Naiman tends to pursue apolitical themes with philosophical ramifications such as these. A chemical engineer by training, he deftly brings science into his poems as well. This motivates an even greater wonder at existence per se. "Of what is known," he writes, "—a pitiful amount, / [but] no pity is required—it only makes / a handful, but a handful holding all." Our knowledge is scant, but sufficient enough to give us intimations into underlying or overriding unities.

Scientific and philosophical metaphors are crucial to Naiman and Brodsky. Because of his metaphorical propensities, the latter, especially in his English poems, sometimes irritated American critics. In the more circumspect Naiman, the heterogeneous elements going into a metaphor can also be striking. In "Alone on a Hill," an almost childlike question ("What's a tree made of?") leads to this heady answer: ". . . Holes and deep recesses /like a swarming spring of midges hovering in space, / a violinist's bowed designs, figure 8's and passes, / the fiddler like a matador cocooned in swathes of cape."

Like Brodsky, Naiman is fully aware of those "quirky fascinations and nervous flights of feeling," as he puts it in a different context, that define modern man's unstable, anxiety-ridden relationship to nature and his fellow man. His more characteristic tone, however, is one of inquiry and reconciliation. He often renews one's feeling for human fragility, ephemeralness. In "Early Berry-Picking," whose title perhaps nods to Robert Frost (whom Akhmatova met when the American poet visited the Soviet Union in 1962), Naiman writes of "rush[ing] to pick cranberries, head looming over the lunar moss / and together with the falling dew, I let an eyelash drop." Never overbearing, he evokes himself discreetly: we sense him more in the eyelash than in his "rushing." The overall atmosphere is very different in Akhmatova's elegies (not to mention Rein's truculent verse tales), but it is probably not unrelated to Naiman's development that she pioneered an autobiographical poetry that takes off from everyday experience (very grim, in her case) and strives for an unromantic, classically restrained, yet fully empathic and universal, narrative viewpoint. Her approach was not always understood. Even Alexander Solzhenitsyn missed the point. When Akhmatova recited her *Requiem* to him in 1962, shortly before the first Novy mir publication of *One Day in the Life of Ivan Denisovich*, he praised the "beauty" and "sonority" yet told her that "it's a poem about an individual case, about one mother and son.... The duty of a Russian poet is to ... rise above personal grief and speak of the nation's grief." She was doing no less.

Naiman can also be funny, which is remarkable in light of the hardships he himself suffered and eyewitnessed. There's "sense and nonsense mixed" into several pieces, and they counterbalance the darker implications of others. Addressing a series of light-hearted poems to his granddaughter, Sophie, he counsels: "Don't rush to grow up; grownups are dumb; / they don't put their baby teeth out for the fairy to come / but blurt out 'calcium.'" Expectedly, these light verses have a more serious side. Sophie is growing up. And who can forget that "Sophia" is an archetypal figure in Russian literature for "wisdom"?

In contrast, Rein plunges into a half-century of dismal Soviet dailiness with a sort of robust acrimony. Memorable poems recall his camaraderie with Brodsky. The graphic "Ararat" recounts how Brodsky, drinking cognac with Rein in a raucous Armenian restaurant, is suddenly "transfigured": "On his face miraculously appears / all that had been hidden within it: genius / and the future. (...) All around us—an Armenian uproar." A Rabelaisian vitality runs through such verse, which owes as much to Rein's wide reading as to popular songs and an intimacy with urban life. Melancholy, bitterness, erudition, and bits of drollery are refined by sophisticated rhymes and meters. The penultimate poem in the selection is a homage to Rein's deceased pal. Rein first recalls staying with Brodsky long ago, in a "provincial hotel-cum-drinking-den." Disparate historical periods are superposed, before Rein again finds himself with his friend, this time in New York. He asks Brodsky if he will return to Russia. The answer is a resounding "Why should I? No way!" Another flash of memory transports Rein to a Venetian canal, where he asks Brodsky the same question. This time, the author of *A Part of Speech*

> AKHMATOVA BELIEVED THAT HER CHANCE MEETING WITH THE BRITISH DIPLOMAT IN FOUNTAIN HOUSE BROUGHT THE WORLD TO THE BRINK OF NUCLEAR WAR. AND, ALTHOUGH POETS HAVE A TENDENCY TO ATTACH GREAT MEANING TO THE EVENTS IN THEIR LIVES, IN THIS PARTICULAR CASE AKHMATOVA MAY HAVE BEEN AT LEAST PARTIALLY CORRECT."

(1980), *To Urania* (1988) and *So Forth* (1996) says nothing. Remembering the days of Akhmatova's magic circle, Rein can only conclude: ". . . A bell chimed / And told me, Nevermore. You two, you four, I Will never meet again. The night receded. / Venice flowered, decayed, and seemed to drown / In violet darkness, like a painting by Vrubel."

Source: John Taylor, "Poetry Today" in *Antioch Review*, Vol. 64, No. 2, Spring 2006, p. 374.

Lev Lurie

In the following essay, Lurie illustrates Akhmatova's response to the upheavals in Russia through examples of her poetry.

In 1913 Petersburg was like a horseman perched on a cliff, like a Roman on the last day of Pompeii. *Troikas* galloped to the spit of Yelagin Island during White Nights; the Duma raged; at the Mariinsky Theater, Tamara Karsavina danced. But the Great Imperial Era, which began when Peter the Great moved the capital from Moscow to Petersburg, was coming to an end. It was the time of Rasputin, and only a blind person could not see where things were headed....

Culture is always nostalgic—for childhood, for the past, for love, for the Golden Age. In Petersburg at the beginning of the 20th century, a group of poets began to eulogize the city and its imperial past. They sang praises to a city that was, not long ago, during the days of Dostoyevsky, just an ugly assemblage of barracks and rented apartments, in which the residents were anti-nationalistic and cosmopolitan. The poets called themselves acmeists. Their manifesto called for a poetry of clarity, precision and restraint (in contrast to the abstract decadence of the Symbol-ists). Their mentor was a translator of Euripides, a poet and former director of the Tsarskoye Selo *gymnasium*, Innokenty Annensky.

The poets lionized the city just as it was on the verge of collapsing as the center of Peter the Great's State. The acmeist cult anticipated the end of Pushkin's Russia, expressing a nostalgia for life and art during the era of Empire and duels.

Strangely enough, however, those who were the blood heirs of the 19th century traditions—the members of the capital's fading "high society"— did not feel connected to them. They loved the theoretical "Russian style" and the shrines of Mos-cow. Acmeism's adherents were, instead, from the first true generation of Petersburgers—the chil-dren of *raznochintsy* (19th century *intelligentsia* which did not descend from nobility), foreigners and non-Orthodox believers: the artists Alexander Benois and Mstislav Dobuzhinsky, the poets Osip Mandelshtam and Anna Akhmatova.

Anna Akhmatova, who was married to the leader of the acmeists, the poet Nikolai Gumilyov, published her first collection of poems, *Evening*, at 23. Her subsequent publication, in March 1914, of *Rosary*—a "little book of love lyrics," as she called it—made her wildly famous. She became the idol of *kursistkas* (students at women's col-leges), their model for emulation. Painters fell in love with her. There was not a female student in love who did not try on the role of Akhmatova's lyrical heroine—a stylish femme fatale, a heart-breaker. In the 1910s, Akhmatova's heroine was to young women in Russia what Brigitte Bardot was for the French in the 1950s. And only a few suspected, in the words of Osip Mandelshtam, that "her poetry is nearing the point where it will become one of the symbols of Russia's greatness."

After 1918, when the capital was moved back to Moscow, the only thing that remained of the old Petersburg was its architectural ensembles, the Kirov Ballet, the Hermitage, the famous cakes of Nord café…and Anna Akhmatova. Pretension, irony and etiquette protected one from the new reality and helped "preserve the right tone."

Akhmatova, unlike many of her contempo-raries, did not "abandon her country into the destructive hands of the enemy." She did not emigrate, but remained in communist Leningrad.

No, not under an alien sky,
Not protected by alien wings,—
I was with my people then,
There, where my people, unfortunately, were.

Requiem

Remaining led to a life of suffering and per-secution. Her first husband, Nikolai Gumilyov, was shot for participation in a White Guard plot; her third husband, Nikolai Punin died in a labor camp. Her son, the scholar Lev Gumilyov, spent much of his life in Stalin's camps. Akhmatova herself was never arrested.

From the mid-1920s on, Akhmatova's poems were barred from publication. As a result, in the Leningrad of the 1930s, she was the incarnation of silent resistance to totalitarianism—again a model for emulation, the personification of dig-nity. Akhmatova behaved in Stalin's Leningrad the same way she had in Nicholas' Petersburg. She protested the fear and terror which gripped Russia with a voice clearly cracked from personal experience.

The glass doorbell
Lets loose.
Could this really be the day?
Linger at the doorstep,
Wait just a moment,
Don't touch me
For God's sake!

By the Hammer and Sickle they swore
Before your martyr's death:
"For treason we pay in gold,
For songs we pay in lead."

Akhmatova lived through her darkest years— the 1920s, 30s and 40s—in the garden wing of the Sheremetyevsky Palace. She had briefly had an apartment there with her second husband, Vladi-mir Shileiko, then moved in there with her third, common-law, husband Nikolai Punin, the situa-tion made the more difficult by the presence of Punin's ex-wife and family. Akhmatova met and survived the Siege winter of 1941–42 here; she returned here after her evacuation to Tashkent. Today, the building is a museum devoted to her life and work.

Sheremetyevsky Palace, or Fontanka ("Foun-tain") House, as the part of it which runs along the river is known, once belonged to that famous court family. The motto on the Sheremetyevs' coat of arms—*Deus conservat omnia* (God pre-serves all), became the epigraph for Akhmatova's masterwork, "Poem Without a Hero."

Third and Last Dedication

Enough have I been frozen from fear,
Better to summon Bach's *Chaconne*,

And behind it a man will enter.
He will not become a beloved husband,
But together we will accomplish
The twentieth century's unsettling.
I mistakenly took him
For one, mysteriously bestowed upon me,
To share a most bitter fate,
He will visit me at Fountain Palace
Late on a foggy night,
To drink New Years wine.
And he will remember this Epiphany evening,
The maple in the window, the wedding candles
And the poem's mortal flight. . .
But it is not the first lilac branch,
Not a ring, nor the sweetness of prayers,
But death he shall bring.
(*Poem Without a Hero*, January 5, 1956)

The man who did not become Akhmatova's "beloved husband" was the famous English philosopher and literary critic Isaiah Berlin. By "upsetting the Twentieth Century," Akhmatova meant sparking the Cold War. Akhmatova believed that her chance meeting with the British diplomat in Fountain House brought the world to the brink of nuclear war. And, although poets have a tendency to attach great meaning to the events in their lives, in this particular case Akhmatova may have been at least partially correct.

In November 1945, Isaiah Berlin, then a diplomat at the British Embassy, visited Akhmatova at Fountain House. They had not previously met. Akhmatova turned 56 that year, Berlin 36. He spoke Russian fluently, as his parents had emigrated from Petersburg in 1919. An Oxford graduate, Berlin went on to become a professor. When war broke out, he entered the diplomatic service. In 1945, the British Foreign Office sent him to the USSR.

In the autumn of 1945, in a bookstore on Nevsky Prospekt, Berlin was talking to Vladimir Orlov, an Alexander Blok specialist and expert on the "Silver Age" of Russian poetry. Berlin asked about the fate of writers in the city, to which Orlov replied, "You mean Zoshchenko and Akhmatova?"

Berlin could not believe Akhmatova was still alive and Orlov offered to take him to meet her, as she lived right around the corner from where they were talking. "It was as if I had suddenly been invited to meet Miss Christina Rossetti," Berlin later wrote. "I could hardly speak; I mumbled that I should indeed like to meet her."

Orlov took Berlin to Akhmatova's sparsely-furnished apartment. "Anna Andreevna Akhmatova was immensely dignified," Berlin wrote, "with unhurried gestures, a noble head, beautiful, somewhat severe features, and an expression of immense sadness . . . she looked and moved like a tragic queen."

Orlov and Berlin's visit to Akhmatova was, however, soon interrupted by shouts from the building's courtyard: "Isaiah, Isaiah!" It was the journalist Randolph Churchill, son of the British prime minister. Having found out from mutual acquaintances that Berlin had gone to Fountain House to meet Akhmatova, he went to find the place, as he wanted to enlist Berlin's help as a translator. The appearance of Churchill—who was certainly being followed by the Soviet Secret Police (as was, likely, Berlin) broke up the literary meeting and eventually led to rumors in the press that "a foreign delegation has arrived to persuade Akhmatova to leave Russia."

Berlin returned to Akhmatova's apartment later that evening. They talked until morning about literature and mutual friends. She recited for him her still unfinished *Poem Without a Hero* ("even then, I realized I was listening to a work of genius," Berlin wrote) and *Requiem*. Neither work was published in Russia in its entirety until after the end of Soviet rule.

"She spoke of her loneliness and isolation, both personal and cultural," Berlin wrote. "Leningrad after the war was for her nothing but a vast cemetery, the graveyard of her friends: it was like the aftermath of a forest fire—the few charred trees made the desolation still more desolate. . . All poetry and art, to her, was—here she used an expression once used by Mandelshtam—a form of nostalgia, a longing for a universal culture . . . of nature, love, death, despair and martyrdom, of a reality which had no history, nothing outside itself. Again she spoke of pre-revolutionary St. Petersburg as the town in which she was formed, of the long dark night which had covered her thenceforth. She spoke without the slightest trace of self-pity, like a princess in exile, proud, unhappy, unapproachable, in a calm, even voice, at time in words of moving eloquence."

In January, Berlin met with Akhmatova once again. That day Akhmatova presented him with a poem:

Sounds decay into the ether,
And dawn feigned darkness.
In the eternally muted world

Are just two voices: yours and mine.
And from the wind of unseen Ladogas,
Through a ringing not unlike bells,
The night's conversation is transformed
Into the light glitter of rainbows entwined.

It would be another year before the post-WWII split between the wartime allies became an unbridgeable chasm. But the fault lines began showing up in early 1946. The USSR had begun "sovietizing" Eastern Europe, confrontation brewed over the Bosphorus Straits and there were contentious negotiations over war reparations, Berlin, and what would become the Marshall Plan.

A Russian-speaking British diplomat (translation: "spy") meeting with a Russian poet who was in virtual "internal exile," could only be interpreted as interference in the internal affairs of the Soviet Union. Akhmatova's very name had immense political weight in Russia. The former Soviet counterintelligence chief and defector, Oleg Kalugin, alleged that he saw Akhmatova's file when he was deputy head of the Leningrad KGB (the file was never published): she was investigated for "spying" after her meeting with Berlin.

In 1965, traveling to Oxford, where she was awarded an honorary degree, Akhmatova again met with Berlin. At that time, she told him that, the day after he met with her in January 1946, uniformed guards had been posted outside her apartment building and that officers had ceremoniously installed a visible bug in her apartment. Stalin, Akhmatova averred, was personally enraged that "our little nun now receives foreign spies." She went on to say that she felt that the two of them "inadvertently, by the mere fact of [their] meeting, had started the Cold War and thereby changed the history of mankind." Berlin said he did not object to her interpretation, "because she would have felt this as an insult to her tragic image of herself as Cassandra—indeed, to the historico-metaphysical vision which informed so much of her poetry. I remained silent."

Yet Akhmatova was right. Berlin dismissed her interpretation because he saw the Cold War through the prism of geopolitics, as the resident of a western democracy. But, viewed through the prism of Akhmatova's life and existence in Leningrad, her conclusion made complete sense. The *domestic* Cold War, signified by cultural isolationism, the war on "cosmopolitanism," the Leningrad Case and other attendant lunacies of Stalin's last

six years, began shortly after this leading icon of Russian literature "received a foreign spy."

On August 14, 1946, the Central Committee of the Communist Party of the Soviet Union approved a resolution condemning the journals *Zvezda* and *Leningrad* for publishing the works of Akhmatova and Mikhail Zoshchenko. In his report to the Central Committee, Andrey Zhdanov squealed:

> *Anna Akhmatova is one of the representatives of this empty reactionary literary swamp. She belongs to the so-called literary group of acmeists, who emerged from the ranks of the Symbolists, and is one of the standard-bearers of an empty, aristocratic, drawing-room poetry, which is totally alien to Soviet literature. . . .*

> *The thematics of Akhmatova's poetry are personal through and through. The scope of her poetry is wretchedly limited, it is the poetry of a lady foaming at the mouth, constantly dashing from the drawing room to the chapel. Her basic theme is erotic love . . . She is neither a nun, nor a harlot, but really both. . . .*

For Akhmatova, the Cold War was an intimate, profoundly personal tragedy. She was expelled from the Writer's Union, unable to publish once again. In 1949, her son was arrested for a second time, just months after her third husband, Nikolai Punin, was taken away.

Even Stalin's death, on March 5, 1953, did not bring peace. The Central Committee resolution was not rescinded. Punin died in the camps in 1953, and her son was not released until 1956.

> You should have been shown, you tease,
> Beloved of all your friends,
> Happy sinner of Tsarskoye Selo,
> What your life would become.
> How, three-hundredth in line with a parcel,
> You would stand outside Kresty prison
> Your hot tears burning
> Through the New Year's ice.
> There, the prison poplar sways,
> And there is no sound. But how many
> Innocents are dying there. . . .

Requiem, Poem IV

But Akhmatova survived Stalin by more than a decade, mentoring some of the leading poetic lights of the next generation, including Nobel Laureate Joseph Brodsky. Brodsky, whose dignity and independence led him first to exile and then into emigration, inherited his cold disdain for totalitarianism from Akhmatova.

In a touch of historic irony, Anna Akhmatova died 13 years to the day from Stalin's death (a day she and her friends had turned into an annual celebration), on March 5, 1966, in the suburbs of Moscow. Her body was taken to the morgue of the Sklifosovsky Institute—formerly a charity home started by the Sheremetyev family. Over the institute's entrance are inscribed the same words as at Akhmatova's long-time home: *Deus conservat omnia*. In Leningrad, the funeral procession led from the House of Artists in Komarovo, along the Fontanka, stopping at Fountain House.

Twenty-five years later, Leningrad became St. Petersburg once again. The Cold War is now over a decade since gone by, and no monument to Stalin remains in this watery city which he hated. But, on Vosstaniya Street, just off Nevsky Prospekt, there is a monument to Anna Akhmatova. History, it seems, has judged in favor of the defendant.

Source: Lev Lurie, "Anna Akhmatova: The Poet Who Buried Stalin," in *Russian Life*, Vol. 47, No. 3, May/June 2004, pp. 48–55.

Roland Bleiker

In the following essay, Bleiker explains that while Akhmatova was concerned with aesthetic issues, her poetry also had a major political impact.

> Everything has been plundered, betrayed, sold out,
> The wing of black death has flashed,
> Everything has been devoured by starving anguish,
> Why, then, is it so bright?
> **"MCMXXI,"** Anna Akhmatova, June 1921

Poetry is radical critique. It pierces through worn-out metaphors and ruptures tissues of power. It names what had no name before. It slips into memory what was void of voice. It visualizes light that still lingers unseen in the dark. It does so, yes, for poetry disturbs linguistic habits through which we have come to accept the parameters of what is, no matter how unjust and violence prone that demarcated "is" really is. This is why the Russian poet Anna Akhmatova believed that "there is no power more threatening and terrible/Than the prophetic word of the poet."

To be clear: Akhmatova was above all concerned with issues aesthetic, with love and beauty and personal memory. Nothing particularly political, one would think, at least at first sight. And yet, her poems had a tremendous political impact, perhaps precisely because they refused to speak in

> AKHMATOVA BECAME POLITICALLY RELEVANT WHEN SHE SUCCEEDED IN PORTRAYING HER PERSONAL EXPERIENCES AND REACTIONS TO EVENTS IN A LANGUAGE THAT HAD UNIVERSAL APPEAL."

the name of short-term political objectives. Perhaps precisely because they could not be contained within and by the political maneuverings of the day. Having poetically recorded much of her country's troubled experience of the 20th century, Akhmatova became the voice of humanity in a world of turmoil and war. Vision and testimony at once, her poems have remained as radical and politically relevant today as they were at the time of their conception.

Born as Anna Gorenko in the Ukraine in 1889, Akhmatova grew up near St. Petersburg, in cultured and materially well-off circumstances. Her first published poems date back to 1907, and within a few years she was already a leading figure in the artistic world of St. Petersburg. Her poems were in many ways personal testimonies that reflect her reactions to a variety of private and public issues: the coming of age as an aristocrat at the turn of the century, and confrontation with the political events that followed: the First World War, the revolution of 1917, the civil war, the long terror under Stalin, and yet another world war, which she spent in exile in Uzbekistan. By the time she died, in 1966, Akhmatova was internationally recognized as one of the century's most significant poets.

Akhmatova was part of a group of Russian poets, including Alexander Blok, Boris Pasternak, Vladimir Mayakovsky, Osip Mandelstam and Nikolay Gumilyov, who chose to stay in Russia despite protracted periods of terror, fear and poverty. Although none of these poets was a political activist *per se*, the artistic independence of their work was often seen as subversive and thus threatening by the authorities. Gumilyov, who was Akhmatova's first husband, was executed in 1921 for alleged counter-revolutionary behavior, lack of evidence notwithstanding. Mandelstam's fate was similar, though his work was mostly of an apolitical nature. But on one exception, in 1934, he wrote and recited a satirical poem about Stalin, describing the "Kremlin's mountaineer" with his "cockroach whiskers" and "fingers fat as worms." Mandelstam was arrested, interrogated and sent into exile. Having served his sentence he returned to Moscow in 1937, but was soon arrested and deported again. According to Soviet documents he died a couple of years later in unknown circumstances. And so did many other writers at the time. Isaiah Berlin likens Stalin's large-scale purge of intellectuals to the St. Bartholomew massacre. "Russian literature and thought emerged in 1939 like an area devastated by war," he says, "with some splendid buildings still relatively intact, but standing solitary amid stretches of ruined and deserted country."

Akhmatova was one of those few splendid buildings that remained relatively intact. She survived both wars as well as Stalin's purge, but often under very dire material circumstances. And although her work was censored or banned for several extended periods, her poetic voice could not be quelled.

One of the key contributions of Akhmatova's poetry was her break with the ornate and erudite style that characterized the dominant Symbolist poetic movements at the time. Akhmatova's poems, by contrast, were written in a direct and concise way. And this was also the source of her politics.

Akhmatova became politically relevant when she succeeded in portraying her personal experiences and reactions to events in a language that had universal appeal. Consider her way of dealing with issues of gender. Akhmatova wrote at the beginning of the 20th century, at a time when, in her own words, "for a woman to be a poet was absurd." She took on her *nom de plume* of Akhmatova because her father commanded her not to "bring shame upon [the family] name." Several years later, Akhmatova's second husband, Vladimir Shileyko, a distinguished Assyriologist, forbade her to write poetry during the early days of their marriage. She did, indeed, write hardly any poems in the early 1920s, but what she wrote before and afterwards gave voice to emotions and perspectives that had meaning and mattered for many other women. In a poem written in 1917 she remembered how "you forbid singing and smiling." The last stanza:

Thus, a stranger to heaven and earth,
I live and no longer sing,
It's as if you cut off my wandering soul
From both paradise and hell.

Until the advent of Akhmatova's poetry feminine emotions had only rarely been explored in public. Virtually all literary works portrayed love either from the male point of view or through distinct male lenses. By giving voice to several generations of Russian women, Akhmatova demonstrated what would later become one of the key arguments of feminist thought: that the private is political. Consider, for instance, one of those moments when Akhmatova transgressed, or perhaps transposed, her own experiences to take on a different poetic personae, a peasant woman, in "My Husband Whipped Me with His Woven Belt":

My husband whipped me with his woven
    belt,
Folded into two.
All night I've been at the little window
With a taper, waiting for you.

Akhmatova's foray into politics continued when she was confronted with the political and military conflicts that shaped the 20th century. And her perceptions of conflict stood in stark contrast to those of her first husband, Gumilyov, who glorified the onset of the First World War. The latter relished the battlefield as "an opportunity to test his courage." Akhmatova, however, departed radically from the patriotic war fever that engulfed not only Gumilyov but also her country and, indeed, most of Europe. Long before war euphoria gave way to despair and desolation, Akhmatova had already recognized what would lie ahead. She wrote of the terrors of war, of its "black death" and its "starving anguish." It is this ability to anticipate events that Mandelstam recognized in Akhmatova: her tragic fate, the fate of Cassandra, the fate of seeing the future without anyone believing her. Two years before euphoria turned into gloom, she wrote, in a poem entitled "July 1914,"

Fearful times are drawing near. Soon
Fresh graves will be everywhere.
There will be famine, earthquakes, widespread death,
And the eclipse of the sun and the moon.

It is in the process of naming the realities of war that Akhmatova's poetry became not only more political, but also more problematic. Problematic for the political authorities, that is. Problematic because her artistic interpretations of death and suffering would not lend themselves easily to be used as political tools by the regime. "The best war poems of Pasternak and Akhmatova," suggests

Berlin, "were too pure artistically to be considered as possessing adequate direct propaganda value."

Lyric poetry alludes, rather than explains. It shows, rather than argues. And it is this artistic ambiguity that provides poetry with its most potent political force. Akhmatova's poetry was political not in the sense that she rallied for a particular political perspective or cause. Her poetry was political insofar as she documented the atrocities and emotional dimensions of war in a way that clearly diverged from what the political authorities at the time considered the only purpose of art and literature: to help the party educate the masses about communism. Socialist realism was deemed the only possible and correct aesthetic approach to this political project.

Look, by contrast, at another one of Akhmatova's poems about the First World War. Consider its hidden political dimensions. Note, especially, that she seeks to capture the anguish of death without naming an event or a battle or a war, without blaming a general or an army or a country, without endorsing a leader or an ideology or a political agenda. In "And All Day," she merely documents, for example:

And all day, terrified by its own moans,
The crowd churns in agonized grief.
And across the river, on funeral banners,
Sinister skulls laugh.
And this is why I sang and dreamed,
They have ripped my heart in half,
As after a burst of shots, it became still,
And in the courtyards, death patrols.

In the absence of any reference to specific events, this poem about grief and death acquires multiple meanings. It contains elusive and constantly shifting political messages. We cannot even be sure if the poem actually speaks of the tragedy of World War I. Read a few years later, the poem may just as well describe the death patrols that trailed Stalin's purges. We don't really know who the laughing sinister skulls are. Who rips her heart in half. Who shoots. Akhmatova's poem contains a clear but unspecified *j'accuse*. And it is this indirectly accusatory dimension, contained in many of her poems, which alarmed authorities. They were concerned with Akhmatova's striking ability to somehow express things that could not be said openly.

At various moments, the Soviet authorities either banned Akhmatova's poetry or pressured her into pursuing a more acquiescent line. She was among a group of poets that Trotsky declared "irrelevant" to the new Soviet state. In 1925 she was prohibited from publishing altogether by a Communist Party resolution. There were times, as in early 1939, when Stalin would be more tolerant and allow her poems to appear again, just to reverse his policies soon afterwards. By September 1939, for instance, the Central Committee of the Communist Party ordered the withdrawal of her books, for their alleged "allusions to religion and lack of reference to Soviet reality." At other times, pressure was exerted in other ways. In 1933 Akhmatova's son, Lev Gumilyov, was arrested. He was released upon Akhmatova's intervention, just to be arrested again. In 1938 he was sentenced to ten years in a Siberian prison camp, to be released a few years later only to fight the German army. One of the very few moments when Akhmatova acquiesced to the authorities was in the 1950, a few months after her son was arrested again and sentenced to ten years' hard labor. In a series of poems called "In Praise of Peace" she proclaimed that "Where Stalin is, there too are Freedom,/ Peace, and Earth's Grandeur."

Akhmatova's poetic concession was a survival strategy, a desperate attempt to bring about the release of her son. An endeavor that failed. And an endeavor that remained the exception. At virtually all other moments, her poetic urge to "speak truth to power" was far stronger than any pragmatic concern. She was one of those Russian writers who "suffered" from what Mandelstam called "Nightingale Fever," that is, the "inability to stop singing regardless of the consequences," the need to poeticize even in the face of death.

Poetry was unusually important in Russia, where literature took on a more vital force than anywhere else. Or so at least believed Alexander Blok, and many others. Roberta Reeder speaks of a country where "hungry people gathered in cold rooms to read poetry to each other." The reasons for this unusual phenomenon may be as much practical as cultural. Poetry in Russia had for long been a vehicle to express dissident thought, to the point that the voice of leading writers carried enormous political weight. In an authoritarian political system, where censorship entered virtually all domains, literature and art became a surrogate for the annihilated public sphere, a space where political debates could be waged publically, albeit veiled. The ambiguity of poetry further increased its political potential, and so did its form, which lent itself easily to underground distribution. It is thus that "literature and artistic wars became," as Isaiah Berlin expresses it, "the only genuine battlefield of ideas."

The most significant political aspects of poetry, and of Akhmatova's poems in particular, are not necessarily located in their immediate engagement with events of the day. A poem's lasting political contribution lies above all in its function as a critical historical memory. Look at how much Tolstoy, Dostoevsky, Pushkin or Gogol have told the world about social and political life in 19th-century Russia. It is through the voices of Anna Karenina, Count Wronskij, Raskolnikov, Evgenii Onegin or the brothers Karamazov that the values and struggles of an epoch have been conveyed to subsequent generations. Likewise, knowledge about Russia in the 20th century will remain linked to the poetic testimonies of such writers as Akhmatova, Mandelstam, Blok, Mayakovsky, Pasternak and Brodsky.

Akhmatova was well aware of the link between poetry and memory. In a series of astonishing poems called *Requiem,* written between 1935 and 1940, she provided a poetic account of Stalin's terrifying legacy. And although she knew her poems would not reach the Russian people right away—they were first published in 1963 in Munich—she knew that the poetic voice would be stronger than any political leader or institution, no matter how authoritarian: "And if they gag my exhausted mouth/Through which a hundred million scream, // Then may the people remember me/On the eve of my remembrance day."

In their function as memory, just as in their opposition to political dogma, poems never speak in a single voice. They never provide certainty. For it is exactly knowledge without doubt or ambiguity that turns into political dogma. Poems address the inevitable flaws entailed in our attempts to interpret and master the world: the fact that we cannot know without language, and that language always already provides meaning, culturally specific meaning, far beyond our attempts to know. "Never will you discover the bottom of it," says Akhmatova, "and never will its hollow silence/Grow tired of speaking."

Akhmatova's poems continued to speak long after her death. And they spoke and will keep speaking in ways that she did not and could not imagine. Most likely also in ways she would not approve. This is precisely the power of poetic memory. To embark on an undetermined journey, always ready for an open mind, an open heart, an

open soul. To speak, to disturb, to let us not fall into political complacency. It is in "The Cellar of Memory" that Akhmatova discovers that politics goes far beyond the types of agitations and debates presented to us as politics proper. Political insight is above all located in the continuous ability to reveal the unknown, that which cannot even be imagined yet. It is located in the unthought, in "The Cellar of Memory":

I don't often visit memory
And it always surprises me.
When I descend with a lamp to the cellar,
It seems to me—a landslide
Rumbles again on the narrow stairs

Source: Roland Bleiker, "Anna Akhmatova's Search for Political Light," in *Peace Review,* Vol. 13, No. 2, 2001, pp. 181–86.

Joanna Yin

In the following essay, Yin contends that Akhmatova and Emily Dickinson had similar ideas about the origins of their poetry and to whom it should be directed.

While Emily Dickinson's poems were available to few people in the United States during her lifetime, the poems of the Russian poet Anna Akhmatova (1889–1966) were well-known in her country during most of her life, despite frequent attempts by the Communist regime to suppress publication. Akhmatova was born three years after Dickinson's death in Odessa, Russia and soon moved with her family to St. Petersburg, city of the White Nights, where it never gets completely dark around the summer solstice. Although Akhmatova did not know English and there is no evidence that she read Dickinson's poems in translation, these great poets of the nineteenth and twentieth centuries had similar ideas about where their poetry came from and where it should be directed. While both women saw the power to write poems as a divine gift, both used as the matter of their poems the familiar objects and experiences of life. They saw the process of creating poems as active, intense and totally consuming. Juxtaposing three poems by each poet will indicate similar visions of the poet as an inspiring and invigorating voice in her community.

In P454, Dickinson makes it clear that God has given her the ability to create poems, yet it is a skill that she must continually practice and perfect:

It was given to me by the Gods—
When I was a little Girl—
They give us Presents most—you know—
When we are new—and small.

I kept it in my Hand—
I never put it down—
I did not dare to eat—or sleep—
For fear it would be gone—
I heard such words as "Rich"—
When hurrying to school—
From lips at Corners of the Streets—
And wrestled with a smile.
Rich! 'Twas Myself—was rich—
To take the name of Gold—
And Gold to own—in solid Bars—
The difference—made me bold—

This poem is written from the perspective of a grown woman who can play with the sounds of key words from her life: Gods, Girl, Gold, bold. She kept the gift in her "Hand," as a poet would a pen and paper, such treatment gives a physicality to this unnamed gift. She always carries this mysterious ability, for which she chooses to deny herself the physical activities of eating and sleeping. She discerns that the gift makes her, not what she owns, rich—the "difference" between inner and material wealth. The subtle metaphor of alchemy, in the gold at the end of the poem, emphasizes this difference. The speaker takes the name, or the metaphor, of Gold, not the gold itself. In this way she chooses the transformative power of poetry, which can create "Gold." The near rhymes of Girl / small, down / gone, school / smile give way to the final rhyme of Gold / bold. This riddle poem describes the speaker's calling as a poet. Further, it describes the careful, intense and anxious nurture of this gift. This is the last poem in fascicle 21, which contains poems that deal in different ways with transformation.

Akhmatova also sees the ability to create poems as a gift from God and in "The Freshness of Words" urges other poets to remember their obligations to their readers:

For us to lose the freshness of words and
    simplicity of feeling
isn't it the same for a painter to lose—sight,
or an actor—voice and movement,
Or a beautiful woman—beauty?

But don't try to save for yourself
this gift sent by heaven to you:
It is our fate—and we know this ourselves—
to squander it, not hoard it.

Walk along and heal the blind,
in order to know in the heavy hour of doubt,
the gloating mockery of disciples
and the indifference of the crowd

In an illusion to Christ, the speaker states that the poet should not amass wealth but transform blind people into sighted people, who subsequently either ignore or scorn the healing poet. As in Dickinson's poem, the poet creates and bestows worth, which she highlights with dramatic use of the Dickinsonian dash. In 1911, Akhmatova and fellow poets founded the school of Acmeism, which renounced the mystical and vague Symbolist cult of the poet in favor of more moral concerns depicted in the precision of the clear word and the concrete world of everyday reality.

Dickinson strengthens the alchemy metaphor in P448, which I believe is the key poem of fascicle 21, where it appears in the magical number seven position. Here the speaker distills precious substance from the leavings of others:

This was a Poet—It is That
Distills amazing sense
From ordinary Meanings—
And Attar so immense

From the familiar species
That perished by the Door—
We wonder it was not Ourselves
Arrested it—before—

Of Pictures, the Discloser—
The Poet—it is He—
Entitles Us—by Contrast—
To ceaseless Poverty—

Of Portion—so unconscious—
The Robbing—could not harm—
Himself—to Him—a Fortune—
Exterior to Time—

In this poem the speaker is separate from the poet, who is identified as "He." The poet is an interpreter and semiological experimenter who uses the poetic imagination as an alembic to separate things from their old meanings and give them new meanings. The poet takes the old and makes it new yet so natural and vivid that readers wonder why they had not seen in the poet's way before. Repeating the idea of "rich" that appears in "It was given to me by the Gods—," the poet creates wealth from poverty. In this way, the poet represents the ideal recycler, as nobody misses the matter used to transform "ordinary Meanings" and "the familiar species" into something precious. In her grammar and drama of image and statement, Dickinson indeed distills her poems for her readers.

Akhmatova also considers it a moral imperative of the poet to create poetry from other people's leavings. In part 2 of "Creation" (190–91), she declares:

> For me there is no purpose in armies of odes
> and the charm of intricate elegies.
> For me, everything in poetry should be out
>   of place,
> not the way people think it should be
>
> If only you knew from what rubbish
> poetry grows, knowing no shame,
> like a yellow dandelion by the fence,
> like burdock and goosefoot.
>
> An angry shout, fresh smell of tar,
> mysterious mold on the wall . . .
> And a line sounds itself out, ardent, tender,
> to your joy and mine.

This poet transforms weeds and rubbish, anger and strangeness and the most quotidian substances into compelling art that brings joy to the reader as well as the poet herself. In Akhmatova's view, it is the duty of the poet to render such service for her community of readers.

In P1247, the speaker equates poetry and love in a carefully balanced, and dangerously compressed, small poem about the thundering power of poetry:

> To pile like Thunder to it's close
> Then crumble grand away
> While Everything created hid
> This—would be Poetry—
>
> Or love—the two coeval come—
> We both and neither prove—
> Experience either and consume—
> For None see God and live—

In the first line this poem conveys the peril of stormy thunder and the last the terror of facing God, the creator of thunder. At the center the forces of this wild poem change direction as the speaker expands the definition of poetry to include love. It is an act of divinely inspired love to create a poem with a power that can bring the reader to the edge of experience and understanding.

As Akhmatova recalls the creation of some of her poems, she starts "Latest Poem" (192–93) with the power of thunder and ends with the abyss and death:

> One, like an anxious thunderbolt,
> bursts into the house with the breath of life.
> Laughing, it trembles in its throat,
> claps its hands and whirls about.
>
> Another, born in midnight silence,
> sneaks up to me from I don't know where,

stares from the empty mirror
and sternly mutters something.

> And there are some like this: in the middle of
>   the day,
> almost as if they did not see me,
> they flow across the white page,
> like a pure spring into a ravine.
>
> Here's something else: mysteriously it roams
>   around—
> not a sound and not a color, not a color and
>   not a sound,
> it carves, it shifts, it weaves,
> and gives itself alive into my hands.
>
> But this one! . . . It drank my blood to the
>   last drop,
> like that evil girl of my youth—love,
> and, not speaking a word to me,
> made itself silent again.
>
> And I never experienced cruder misfortune.
> It left, and its track led
> up to the very edge of the edge,
> and without it, I am dying.

Akhmatova creates all these poems in danger that ranges from manic high voltage, brooding darkness, pure fluidity, protean vitality, to vampiric allure. As in many of both women's poems, the explosive power of Akhmatova's "Latest Poem" is ordered in quatrains with a rhyme scheme. This particular poem is aabb; perhaps Akhmatova felt that the wild forces of this poem required the discipline of couplets. Like Dickinson, Akhmatova lives for and cannot live without creating poems. The possibilities of transformation that they offer to their readers are worth the dangers of reading them. Each poet offers a community of poems for a community of readers. In her fascicles Dickinson orders about half her poems in ways that often show how each "talks" to and enlivens the others; her fascicle order teaches us to read her corpus in the same way. Readers can bring to all Dickinson poems her passion for poetry as well as her concerns about love, power and death. I believe that Dickinson's concern for creating poetry can illuminate her love poems. For example, we can read "thee" as poetry in "Wild Nights—Wild Nights! / Were I with thee / Wild Nights should be / Our Luxury!" A lifetime mooring in poetry can bring the speaker, "Done with the Compass—/ Done with the Chart!" (P249), joy beyond measure.

Akhmatova gathered poems about poetry, "Secrets of the Craft," at the beginning of her book entitled *Seventh Book*, which contains the second and third poems in this paper. However, many of her poems self-reflexively deal with the creation and function of poetry.

Like Dickinson, she infuses everyday things and words with fresh meaning and emotion. In doing so, she demonstrates how Russians, long a people forced to be innovative with a scarce supply of goods and services, can transform and treasure that which is at hand. By attending to and vivifying the everyday world, Dickinson and Akhmatova dramatize what their readers know. They show how to find true wealth by passionately pursuing that which satisfies the soul. In addition, they demonstrate the bigness that comes from sharing that passion and giving that wealth to other people.

Note: The three poems of Akhmatova are my translations.

Source: Joanna Yin, "Wild Nights and White Nights: Dickinson's Vision of the Poet in Anna Akhmatova" in *Emily Dickinson Journal*, Vol. 5, No. 2, Fall 1996, pp. 55–58.

Richard Eder

In the following review, Eder claims that in the literature of Soviet suffering there are "no pages more powerful than the cycle of poems by Anna Akhmatova in Requiem.*"*

The ship dwindles to the horizon and disappears; it is the watcher on the shore whose heart is shrunk by absence. The sailor, for better or worse, is where he is, life-size.

The night of Stalin's repression has been told in all kinds of ways, most famously by Alexander Solzhenitsyn's books about the prison camps and their inmates. But in the literature of Soviet suffering there may be no pages more powerful than the cycle of poems by Anna Akhmatova entitled *Requiem*.

Nothing inside the prison walls so fiercely expresses deprivation and injustice—with such a large intensity that it stands for an entire order of human loss—as her chronicle of the women who stood, year after year, outside those walls. After the death of both hope and despair, they waited for word of the fate of those within, and for the chance to hand a knitted cap through, or a pair of shoes. Like the mothers of Argentina's Plaza de Mayo, years later, who turned the "disappeared" into a visible presence, the Russian women, by standing outside the city's jails, jailed the entire city:

That was when the ones who smiled
Were the dead, glad to be at rest . . .
And like a useless appendage, Leningrad
Swung from its prisons.

It is quite reasonable to think of Akhmatova, who died in 1966 at age 76, as the greatest woman poet in the Western World since Sappho. In a monumental endeavor, seemingly poised upon the frailest of underpinnings, the tiny Zephyr Press of Somerville, Mass., has brought out the first complete collection of her poems published anywhere in the world.

With original Russian versions and a supple translation that all but turns the facing pages warm to the touch, [*The Complete Poems of Anna Akhmatova*], more than 1,500 pages in length, includes more than 700 poems—some previously unprinted—copious notes, several introductions, prefaces and memoirs, and about 75 photographs and drawings.

Roberta Reeder, who edited the collection and the notes, contributes a monograph placing the poems in their historical and biographical context. Judith Hemschemeyer, the translator, provides additional commentary. Among her perceptive remarks is the point that Akhmatova's poetry, unlike that of many of her contemporaries, nearly always addresses a second person, explicitly or implicitly. The reader receives this burning gaze face to face.

Hemschemeyer's translations are not simply a work but a pilgrimage. A poet, she read a few of Akhmatova's poems in translation about 25 years ago. She then learned Russian so that, with the help of word-by-word literal versions, she could translate them all. "I became convinced that Akhmatova's poems should be translated in their entirety and by a woman, and that I was that person," she writes.

Akhmatova's imperial largeness of spirit is catching, clearly. So is a portion of her art. Hemschemeyer chose a very direct rendering, stressing clarity, intimacy and an unforced syntax over any effort to pursue the original's rhymes and sonorities. But she uses assonance and slant rhyme, and her seeming plain style is governed by a lyrical ear. In truth, her translations are not so much plain as transparent. If I did not know English, I would learn it to read them.

Akhmatova's life and her poetry were brutally cut in two by history. Born to a well-to-do family, living a privileged childhood, she became a glittering figure in the Bohemian literary world of pre-revolutionary St. Petersburg. She was a member of the acmeist circle of poets—Osip Mandelstam, her lifelong brother in poetry and suffering, was another—and her first husband was a poet.

She was a flaming creature. Taking into account her bipolar candle-burning, and the long purgatory she underwent later on, one thinks of Edna St. Vincent Millay turned into Mother Courage. Except that the poetry of her youth, hugely successful, was also incomparably better. She wrote of childhood, of the country-side, of the city, and of all varieties of love from girlish to adult and adulterous.

She had a blinding sense of place and time. She fused the richness of things and passions with a premonition—and later, the memory—of their transience. Thus, an early poem evokes her sumptuous childhood garden together with a stone bust, toppled beside the water: "He has given his face to the waters of the lake / And he's listening to the green rustling. / And bright rainwater washes / His clotted wound . . . / Cold one, white one, wait, / I'll become marble too."

. . . The quick desolation of an early marriage: "The heart's memory of the sun grows faint. / The grass is yellower. / A few early snow-flakes blow in the wind, / Barely, barely . . . / The willow spreads its transparent fan / Against the empty sky. / Perhaps I should not have become / Your wife . . ."

The excitement and insomnia of an affair: "Both sides of the pillow / Are already hot. / Now even the second candle / Is going out, and the cry of the crows / Gets louder and louder. / I haven't slept all night / And now it's too late to think of sleep . . . / How unendurably white / Is the blind on the white window. / Hello."

There was the pride of a woman and a poet in her prime, addressing a no doubt not imaginary lover: "Oh it was a cold day / In Peter's miraculous city. / Like a crimson fire the sunset lay, / And slowly the shadow thickened. / Let him not desire my eyes, / Prophetic and fixed. / He will get a whole lifetime of poems / The prayer of my arrogant lips."

The revolution came, and suddenly poverty gnawed away her life and, worse, her writing went out of favor. Poetry had to be hard and elevating. By 1925, the literary leaders were saying that she should have had the intelligence to be dead.

Hardship and the impossibility of publishing; expulsion from the Writers Union. Worse was to come. The purges of the mid-1930s spared her, but her only son, Lev, was arrested. For a year-and-a-half, she joined the lines outside the Leningrad prison. And, in *Requiem*, she found a voice again: harsh with knowledge, powerful with anger, yet with all the lovely particularity of her youth.

Source: Richard Eder, "The Greatest Woman Poet since Sappho," in *Los Angeles Times Book Review*, March 18, 1990, pp. 3, 7.

SOURCES

Akhmatova, Anna, "I Am Not with Those Who Abandoned Their Land," in *The Complete Poems of Anna Akhmatova*, expanded ed., translated by Judith Hemschemeyer, edited by Roberta Reeder, Zephyr Press, 2000, p. 263.

Bayley, John, "The Sheer Necessity for Poetry," in *New York Times*, May 13, 1990, p. 3.

Brody, Ervin C., "The Poet in the Trenches: *The Complete Poems of Anna Akhmatova*," in *Literary Review*, Vol. 37, No. 4, Summer 1994, pp. 684–704.

Byelyakova, Yelena, "Anna Akhmatova: 'Mother Courage' of Poetry," in *Unesco Courier*, Vol. 43, April 1990, p. 48.

Eder, Richard, "The Greatest Woman Poet Since Sappho," in *Los Angeles Times Book Review*, March 18, 1990, p. 3.

Feinstein, Elaine, *Anna of All the Russias: A Life of Anna Akhmatova*, Alfred A. Knopf, 2006, pp. xvii, 3–80.

Fitzpatrick, Sheila, *The Russian Revolution*, new ed., Oxford University Press, 2008, pp. 40–42.

"Jeremiah 23:15," in *New American Standard Bible*, http://nasb.scripturetext.com/jeremiah/23.htm (accessed March 8, 2010).

Johnston, Robert H., *New Mecca, New Babylon: Paris and the Russian Exiles, 1920–1945*, McGill-Queen's University Press, 1988, pp. 9–12.

Jose, F. Sionil, "We Who Stayed Behind," in *Time Asia*, August 11, 2003, http://www.time.com/time/asia/2003/journey/letters_jose.html (accessed January 7, 2010).

Kaun, Alexander, *Soviet Poets and Poetry*, University of California Press, 1943, reprint, Books for Libraries Press, 1968, pp. 6–9.

Mosely, Philip E., "Russian Revolution," in *History Channel*, 2006, http://www.history.com/encyclopedia.do?articleId=221104 (accessed January 21, 2010).

Perloff, Majorie, Review of *The Complete Poems of Anna Akhmatova*, in *Sulfur*, Vol. 11, No. 27, Fall 1990, pp. 233–37.

Reeder, Roberta, "Mirrors and Masks: The Life and Poetic Works of Anna Akhmatova," in *The Complete*

Poems of Anna Akhmatova, expanded ed., translated by Judith Hemschemeyer, edited by Roberta Reeder, Zephyr Press, 2000, pp. 17–34.

Reynolds, Susan Salter, "Shards of Russian History," in *Los Angeles Times Book Review*, March 21, 1993, pp. 3, 9.

Rubins, Maria, "Anna Andreyevna Akhmatova," in *Dictionary of Literary Biography*, Vol. 295, *Russian Writers of the Silver Age, 1890–1925*, edited by Judith E. Kalb, J. Alexander Ogden, and I. G. Vishnevetsky, Thomson Gale, 2004, pp. 3–20.

Simon, John, "Anna Akhmatova," in *New Criterion*, Vol. 12, No. 9, May 1994, pp. 29–39.

Steele, Cassie Premo, Introduction to *We Heal from Memory: Sexton, Lorde, Anzaldúa and the Poetry of Witness*, Palgrave, 2000, pp. 1–14.

FURTHER READING

Akhmatova, Anna, *My Half-Century: Selected Prose*, Ardis Publishers, 1992.
> A posthumous collection of Akhmatova's prose, the book includes essays, diary entries, historical accounts, and sketches of fellow artists.

Campling, Elizabeth, *The Russian Revolution*, Trafalgar Square Publishing, 1985.
> This young-adult book, part of the "Living through History" series, includes fifteen short biographies of Russians, Americans, and British citizens who witnessed or participated in the Russian Revolution and civil war.

Driver, Sam N., *Anna Akhmatova*, Twayne Publishers, 1972.
> Driver offers an accessible introduction to Akhmatova's work and life, especially suitable for students.

Gerstein, Emma, *Moscow Memoirs: Memories of Anna Akhmatova, Osip Mandelstam, and Literary Russia under Stalin*, Overlook Hardcover, 2004.
> Written by a woman who lived in the Soviet Union from 1903 to 2002, this book provides firsthand accounts of her friends Osip and Nadezhda Mandelstam's circle, including Akhmatova.

Haight, Amanda, *Anna Akhmatova: A Poetic Pilgrimage*, Oxford University Press, 1976.
> Haight's biography of Akhmatova was the first written in English, and it is still considered one of the best sources for an understanding of Akhmatova and her poetry.

Polivanov, Konstantin Patricia Ber, *Anna Akhmatova and Her Circle*, University of Arkansas Press, 1994.
> This book includes memoirs by and about the important poets of the Silver Age of Russian literature.

SUGGESTED SEARCH TERMS

Anna Akhmatova

Anna Andreyevna Gorenko

I Am Not One of Those Who Left the Land

Anna Akhmatova AND I Am Not One of Those Who Left the Land

I Am Not with Those Who Abandoned Their Land

poetry of witness

exile AND Akhmatova

Anno Domini: MCMXXI

Russian Revolution AND Akhmatova

acmeism

Akhmatova AND Russian poetry

I Built My Hut beside a Traveled Road

T'AO CH'IEN

C. 417

"I Built My Hut beside a Traveled Road" is a poem by the Chinese poet T'ao Ch'ien (also called T'ao Yüan-ming). The exact date of composition is unknown. Scholars believe it was written at some point between 403 , when the poet would have been thirty-eight years old, and 417, with the later date being preferred by many. The poem is part of a group of twenty poems collectively called *Drinking Wine*. T'ao prefaced these poems with a note in which he said that he was living in retirement and had developed a habit of drinking wine in the evenings. After he drank the wine, he composed some verse just to amuse himself. He then asked a friend to write them out so they could both enjoy them.

T'ao is considered one of the greatest Chinese poets, and he is also one of the earliest. "I Built My Hut beside a Traveled Road" is one of his best-known poems. In its quiet reflections on a natural scene and its sense of calm detachment, it represents many common themes of this poet who lived on a farm and enjoyed solitude.

The poem was translated into English at least five times during the twentieth century, beginning with the version by Arthur Waley in his *One Hundred and Seventy Chinese Poems* in 1918. Other translators include A. R. Davis, William Acker (under the title "I Built My House near Where Others Dwell"), James Robert Hightower ("I Built My Hut beside a Traveled Road," used in this discussion), and

Painting of Asian chrysanthemums, which a character in the poem is clipping. (*Image copyright JinYoung Lee, 2010. Used under license from Shutterstock.com*)

most recently, David Hinton. Hightower's translation can be found in his book *The Poetry of T'ao Ch'ien*, first published in 1970. It can also be found in *The Columbia Anthology of Traditional Chinese Literature*, edited by Victor H. Mair (1996) and in *The Norton Anthology of World Literature*, second edition (2003). Hinton's translation can be found in his *The Selected Poems of T'ao Ch'ien* (1993). Another translation of the poem appears in *The Columbia Book of Chinese Poetry* (1986), edited by Burton Watson.

AUTHOR BIOGRAPHY

T'ao is also known by his given name, T'ao Yüan-ming. He was born in 365 in the village of Ch'ai-sang in present-day Jiangxi Province, China. The village was near the provincial capital, Hsüan-yang, on the Yangtze river. T'ao's family were minor aristocrats. The poet would have received an excellent education, and in ancient China an educated man was expected

to contribute his talents to public service. This meant working in the government bureaucracy, which T'ao tried on a number of occasions, but the work did not suit his temperament. He first entered government service in 393, but he was not happy in that capacity. T'ao was a man who liked his freedom and did not suffer fools gladly. He disliked having to show deference to his supervisors, whom he regarded as arrogant. After a short time, he resigned from his position and returned to his farm, which appears to have been the only place where he could be happy.

T'ao married, but his wife died in about 395. He remarried soon after her death, and with his second wife he had four sons. Faced with the need to provide for his family, T'ao reentered government service several times. It is likely that he was working in Hsüan-yang from about 395 to 400, after which he briefly returned to his farm before taking up another government position in about 400. The capital was three hundred miles west of his home in Chiang-Ling, and by 401 the poet had resigned from his governmental position and returned to his farm.

Life on the farm was not easy and certainly not prosperous. More than once T'ao's house was destroyed by fire, and when the crops failed, he and his family were poor. He was a recluse in the sense that he wanted nothing to do with the wider world, and he enjoyed quiet periods of reflection in which he wrote his poems. But he was also a sociable man who liked to entertain or visit his friends. On such occasions he would enjoy himself and drink liberal amounts of wine.

In 405, times for T'ao and his family were hard, and he was once again forced to seek a government position. He became a magistrate in P'eng-tse, thirty miles from his home, but he was immediately unhappy there. He refused to pay the expected deference to senior officials; he felt that by doing so he would be compromising his integrity. After less than three months he resigned, and he never again took on any public position. Instead, he remained a farmer. It was during this period of his retirement from public life that he wrote "I Built My Hut beside a Traveled Road."

T'ao wrote a brief autobiography in which he presented himself as a man who had no desire for fame or fortune and who spoke little. He liked to read and drink wine, although many times he could not afford it. He was often hungry because there was not enough food to eat; he wrote poems for his own amusement.

T'ao died in 427. One hundred twenty-five of his poems have survived.

POEM TEXT

I built my hut beside a traveled road
Yet hear no noise of passing carts and horses.
You would like to know how it is done?
With the mind detached, one's place becomes
   remote.
Picking chrysanthemums by the eastern hedge   5
I catch sight of the distant southern hills:
The mountain air is lovely as the sun sets
And flocks of flying birds return together.
In these things is a fundamental truth
I would like to tell, but lack the words.   10

POEM SUMMARY

Lines 1–4

"I Built My Hut beside a Traveled Road" is a poem of ten lines in which the speaker reflects on his current state of mind. He begins by explaining that he built his house at the side of a road that many people use. In the original Chinese, T'ao does not actually use the word road (as the translator acknowledges); the poet means that he built his dwelling not in a solitary spot but where others had their houses, too. In line 2, the poet notes a paradox (a statement which appears to be self-contradictory but is later explained). Although his house is located in a busy area, he does not hear any of the traffic. There must be many travelers making quite a noise as they pass with their horses and carts, but the speaker in the poem says he hears nothing.

In line 3, he directly addresses the reader, asking if he or she would be interested in finding out how such a thing could be. In line 4, he answers his own question. He says that his mind is detached from his surroundings, and he does not notice them. (Some translations use the word heart rather than mind.) It is as if they are far away. What he means is that he is contemplating something else that is more compelling for him, so he does not hear any of the hustle and bustle going on in the road near his house.

Lines 5–8

In line 5, the speaker begins to explain what he is doing that so occupies his mind. He describes a moment that is of particular significance for him. He says he is picking chrysanthemums that grow near the hedge on his property. Then, in line 6, he looks up and sees the mountains far to the south. It is early evening, and he can feel the refreshing mountain air at sunset, described in line 7. In line 8, he also takes note of flocks of birds that are returning home in the direction of the mountain.

Lines 9–10

In the last two lines the speaker reflects once more on his experience. In line 9, he says that the moment he has just described—the picking of the chrysanthemums and the sights of the mountains and the flocks of birds—is full of some deep truth. He states in line 10 that although he would like to explain what this truth is, he cannot find the right words to do so.

THEMES

Introspection

T'ao presents the speaker as being in a serene, detached state of mind in which he can appreciate the beauty of nature and not get distracted by superficial events going on in the human world. It is as if he is distinguishing between what is really important in life and what is not. To do this he gathers his mind into itself and focuses entirely on his experience in the moment without being distracted. The sounds of the human world, as travelers pass by his dwelling, are forgotten, and he is completely absorbed in experiencing the beauty of nature. This state of being, in which the poet is settled within himself, not subject to the cares of the world, resembles the state attained by great spiritual masters in the Eastern religious traditions. These masters are well versed in a kind of steadiness of mind that enables them not to be swept away by the ebb and flow of daily events but always to be aware of the wholeness of nature and their connection to it. T'ao, as a Taoist (Taoism is one of the spiritual traditions of China), must have been well aware of the possibility of attaining such clarity and steadiness of mind.

Nature

The speaker describes one moment in particular when he is able to experience nature in a profound way. This begins in line 5, when he describes the picking of the chrysanthemums by the hedge. One can imagine him savoring the

TOPICS FOR FURTHER STUDY

- Read the poem "Mont Blanc" by Percy Bysshe Shelley, one of the English romantic poets. Shelley wrote this poem after visiting the Swiss Alps. What does the mountain symbolize in Shelley's poem? Write a Web log in which you discuss any similarities or differences between Shelley's mountain symbolism and that employed by T'ao in "I Built My Hut beside a Traveled Road." Encourage your classmates to respond to your discussion with comments and ideas of their own about symbolism in these poems and in poetry in general.

- Write a poem based on a single moment of your experience in nature. How do the sights and sounds of nature that you absorb in that moment make you feel? What thoughts and emotions do you experience? After writing the poem, describe the thought process you used in an essay that accompanies your piece. Illustrate your poem for extra credit.

- Consult *The Ancient Chinese World* by Terry Kleeman and Tracy Barrett (Oxford University Press, 2005), a book about Chinese history for young adults. Using information from this book and other print and online sources, use Glogster or a similar poster maker program to make a poster in which you summarize the main tenets of Confucianism, Taoism, and Buddhism. Explain briefly how they influenced ancient Chinese culture.

- Read the short poem "The Birds Have Vanished into the Sky" by later Chinese poet Li Po (701–762). Write an essay comparing and contrasting it with "I Built My Hut beside a Traveled Road." What elements do the two poems have in common? You can find the poem online at http://www.poetry-chaikhana.com/P/PoLi/birdshavevan.htm.

odor of the flowers; the rest of the world fades away as he experiences that, and only that. His glance up at the mountain as he holds the chrysanthemums then gives him another quite different experience to absorb. The blooms of the chrysanthemums will last only for a very short while, but the mountain endures forever. The two experiences held in a moment together give him a sense both of time and eternity, the transience of nature as well as its permanence. The flying birds and the fresh mountain air also contribute to the speaker's experience of order and beauty in nature.

Beauty, order, and the variety in nature are all part of the truth that the poet states that the speaker senses in line 9, although he does not have the words to express it. Part of that truth also is his own calm, detached mind that can experience those things and sense the connection among all of them. In that heightened moment of experience, perhaps he is aware of the shortness of all life and its aspirations to longevity. The fragility of the flower—like the fragility of human life—is set against the immensity, solidity, and majesty of the mountain, which is itself, perhaps, a reminder of the steadiness of the speaker's mind in moments such as this. That calm mind is in a sense immovable—like the mountain—in its communion with nature, far beyond the reach of the day-to-day human world.

Truth

In the last two lines of the poem, T'ao says that the simple scene he has described, as well as the state of mind with which he contemplates it, embodies a profound truth. He would like to say more about it but cannot find the right words. This may be an expression of the poet's modesty regarding his own abilities, but it hints at something more profound than that. Language itself has limitations; it can only say so much about things, and in a certain way. Many people must have noticed that when they try to explain in words some profound intuition or understanding of life, it will often come out sounding more superficial, less complete, full, and satisfying, than the experience they know they had. Language has failed to capture the complete truth of it. This is partly due to the fact that language has to explain things in sequence, one thing after another, whereas the sort of experience T'ao describes in this poem is often an all-at-once phenomenon. A profound truth is intuitively known in a moment, and to try to convey it in language is impossible. This of course is why poets have recourse to figurative language, such as image and metaphor. The irony of the last line is that the poet may already have done what he says he cannot do: he has created a poem that conveys the truth he felt, but he has done it by using image and metaphor to suggest it rather than spelling it out in analytic language as a philosophical or spiritual idea.

of a genre that would become typical of Chinese poetry through all the ages. The lyric as used by Chinese poets is a personal form; it describes the poet's thoughts, feelings, emotions, and perceptions, the things he has witnessed.

STYLE

Imagery, Metaphor, and Symbolism

The image of the poet picking the chrysanthemums has a particular significance. In T'ao's culture, chrysanthemums were used to make wine, as the poet clearly explains in the seventh of the twenty poems about drinking wine (as arranged by Hightower). The chrysanthemum therefore is not only an image of the beauty of nature and its transience; it is also a symbol for wine and hints at the means the poet often uses to throw off his cares: drinking wine. Chrysanthemum wine was also thought to promote longevity. The mountain, too, is a symbol of long life. When the poet then looks at the mountain that has been there, and will be there, seemingly forever, it reinforces this dimension of meaning. The moment he describes may be fleeting, but because of the symbols the poet chooses, that moment carries with it the hope that life may be long.

Couplets

A couplet is two successive lines of poetry, usually rhymed but not always so. In the translation by Hightower, this poem consists of five unrhymed couplets. Each couplet forms a complete syntactical unit (syntax refers to the arrangement of words to form sentences). Four couplets consist of just one sentence, and there is no punctuation after the first line of the couplet.

In the translation by Hinton, the division of the poem into couplets is particularly noticeable, since he presents the poem as five two-line stanzas. Hinton makes much use of run-on lines, both within and between each couplet. A run-on line (also known as enjambment) is when the syntax and meaning of the line carries over into the following line. The following line must be read as well in order to understand the meaning of the previous line.

Lyric Poetry

The poem belongs to the tradition of Chinese lyric poetry. Indeed, it is one of the first examples

HISTORICAL CONTEXT

The Eastern Chin Dynasty

T'ao lived during a turbulent period in Chinese history that predated his birth in 365 by more than a century. After the collapse of the Han dynasty in 220, China entered a period of instability that lasted four centuries. There were foreign invasions and civil wars, and the period has been compared to the Dark Ages in Europe. From 211 to 265 the Chinese Empire was divided into what were known as the Three Kingdoms; each of the rulers in three different parts of the country claimed the title of emperor. In 265, Ssŭma Yen, known to history as Chin Wu Ti, founded the Chin dynasty. He died in 290, and his successor was unable to maintain the integrity of the empire. There was civil strife, and foreign invaders established themselves in Chinese territory. In 316, Chin Wu Ti's grandson surrendered to non-Chinese forces, and in the years that followed, China was effectively divided into north and south. In the north, the non-Chinese people ruled, but the Chinese continued to rule in the south. A branch of the Ssŭ-ma family ruled in the south from 317 to 420. This was known as the Eastern Chin dynasty, and it coincides with most of T'ao's life. The dynasty established a capital at Chien-yeh (modern Nanking or Nanjing), around the Yangtze river, near where T'ao lived.

Wars and Intrigue

The Eastern Chin dynasty was marked by wars with the northern states, sometimes resulting in success for Eastern Chin, such as the recovery of Szechwan in 347. There was also constant infighting at the imperial court that resulted in several emperors being deposed. It is likely that from 395 to 400, T'ao was in the employment of the central government in Chien-yeh. While there, he would have been a witness to more political turbulence. In 396, the Eastern Chin Emperor was assassinated and his five-year-old son placed on the throne by his family. The boy emperor ruled until 420, and during that period competing factions within the court ensured there would be no

COMPARE
&
CONTRAST

- **300s–400s:** Chinese poems during this period consist of four or five words to a line. The most revered poems in China are the three hundred poems in the *Book of Songs*, also known as *Book of Odes*. These poems, many of which are folk songs, were composed before the time of the great Chinese philosopher Confucius (551–479 BCE), possibly as early as between 1000 to 600 BCE. During the Eastern Chin dynasty, leading poets who precede T'ao are Fu Hsüan (died 278), Lu Chi (261–303), and Yang Fang (died c. 319).

  Today: Fewer people read poetry in China in printed books and magazines than in the previous generation. Traditional publishers are unwilling to take a risk on what may not be a commercially successful endeavor. However, poets in China are freer of government control than they were in the 1970s and 1980s, and Chinese poetry flourishes on the Internet. Some contemporary poets regard the twenty-first century as the most exciting time in Chinese poetry since the communist revolution in 1949 because the Internet facilitates communication between Chinese poets across China and living abroad. Chen Kehua, Lin Yaode, and Chen Feiwen are three poets born after 1960 whose work is well known in China. However, contemporary Chinese poets are little known in the West.

- **300s–400s:** Chien-yeh (modern Nanking or Nanjing), in the Yangtze River delta, becomes the capital city of the Eastern Chin dynasty. It remains the capital for several succeeding dynasties, from approximately 420 to 589. Soon after the Sui dynasty is established in 589, most of Chien-yeh is destroyed, leaving it only as a small town.

  Today: Nanking, now usually spelled Nanjing, is the capital of China's Jiangsu province. It is a large city with 7.4 million residents.

Accessible by water and rail, it is a major transportation artery and important modern manufacturing base. Nanjing is also a center for the high-tech electronics industry, the automobile, petrochemical, and iron and steel industries, and scientific research and education. Since it was a capital city for ten dynasties and the Republic of China over a period of over seventeen hundred years, modern Nanjing is full of historical and cultural monuments and relics that make it a tourist center.

- **300s–400s:** China suffers from division and strife. There are civil wars and wars against foreign invaders. In addition, Buddhism flourishes in China, and Buddhist monks maintain their independence from the state. During the Eastern Chin dynasty they are not required to pay ritual homage to the emperor. Buddhism spreads because it appeals to the masses in a way that Confucianism, the indigenous philosophy of China, does not. It also offers a more philosophical and rational approach to understanding life than is offered by Taoism, China's indigenous popular religion.

  Today: China is a unified country with a strong central government. Since 1949, the country has been ruled by a communist government that has often been unsympathetic to Buddhism. The modern attitude of Chinese authorities toward Buddhism is more tolerant than it was during the 1960s and 1970s. Buddhist institutions are still subject to governmental control, but there is more openness than in former times. In April 2006, China hosts the World Buddhist Forum, the first international religious gathering ever hosted by communist China. There are an estimated one hundred million Buddhists in China.

A character in the poem gazes at a landscape with southern mountains and birds in the evening air.
(Image copyright Christophe Rolland, 2010. Used under license from Shutterstock.com)

stability. In 399, there was a revolt in the eastern territories led by Sun En, and for a while the capital itself, while T'ao was still living there, was under threat from his forces.

When in 400 T'ao took up a position three hundred miles west of the capital under a powerful general, Huan Hsüan, he did not escape the dangerous political and military situation. Huan Hsüan was a threat to the ruling emperor. T'ao did not remain long in the general's employment, and no details are known of the nature of his work or the circumstances of his departure. But it is clear that being involved in government service during this period was not an easy or a safe occupation, which perhaps sheds more light on T'ao's aversion to being involved in public life. In 403, Huan Hsüan conquered the capital city. Marching from the west, he must have passed through the area where T'ao was living.

Huan Hsüan was soon defeated by another powerful general, named Liu Yü. Liu Yü had acquired considerable power in the Eastern Chin dynasty. A series of military successes continued to extend the boundaries of the dynasty. In 405, T'ao worked briefly on the general's staff. Over the next decade or so, the prestige of the ambitious Liu Yü remained high, and in 419 he arranged for the emperor to be killed. He installed a puppet ruler who abdicated within a year, bringing the Eastern Chin dynasty to an end in 420. Shortly after, Liu Yü established the Liu Sung dynasty. This marked the beginning of an era known as the Southern and Northern dynasties, which lasted until 589, when the country finally became unified again. Liu Yü, who became known as Wu, died in 423.

CRITICAL OVERVIEW

T'ao was not highly regarded as a poet during his lifetime, nor for centuries after his death. It was only during the flowering of the arts in the T'ang Dynasty, in the eighth century, that his merits were fully appreciated. Poets of that era, including Tu Fu and Li Po, were great admirers of his work. T'ao was also acknowledged as a poetic master during the Sung Dynasty (960–1280). Since then T'ao's status as one of China's greatest poets has never been challenged. According to translator David Hinton in *The Selected Poems of T'ao Ch'ien*, T'ao was the first poet in the Chinese tradition "to make a poetry of his natural voice and immediate experience, thereby creating the personal lyricism which all major Chinese poets inherited and made their own."

"I Built My Hut beside a Traveled Road" is one of T'ao's most famous poems, as evidenced by the fact that at least five different English translations of it were published during the twentieth century. James Robert Hightower, who translated the poem and included it in his book *The Poetry of T'ao Ch'ien*, writes that it suggests

> the detachment and repose of the Great Recluse who makes his home among men yet remains uncontaminated by the world, whose communion with nature occurs as readily through the chrysanthemums by the eastern hedge as through the distant mountain scenery.

A. R. Davis is another scholar who has translated the poem into English. In *T'ao Yuan-ming: His Works and Their Meaning*, he writes of the twenty drinking poems as a sequence, describing "I Built My Hut beside a Traveled Road" as "The beautiful fifth poem [that] expresses a solemn, still loneliness."

CRITICISM

Bryan Aubrey

Aubrey holds a Ph.D. in English. In this essay, he discusses "I Built My Hut beside a Traveled Road" in terms of Taoism, an ancient Chinese religion.

Standard histories in China dating from the late fifth century classify T'ao as a recluse. By this, it is meant that he shunned the official life at court and in government service, preferring to remain in isolation on his farm. The implication is that T'ao had no use for worldly things, was uninterested in the scramble for power and fame, and preferred to cultivate not only the land he owned but also his inner life.

The reclusive aspect of T'ao's nature can be gleaned from the first few lines of "I Built My Hut beside a Traveled Road," but the term is not quite as simple as might at first appear. T'ao did not build his house in a remote spot, but in a

> HE WOULD LIKE TO EXPRESS THAT TRUTH BUT IS UNABLE TO SUMMON THE RIGHT WORDS. THE POINT HERE IS THAT IS THERE ARE NO WORDS THAT WOULD FULLY CAPTURE THIS MOMENT OF INTUITIVE UNDERSTANDING OF THE PERFECT ORDER INHERENT IN NATURE AND THE SIMULTANEOUS PRESENCE OF TIME AND TIMELESSNESS."

place where other people were gathered. Hightower's translation of the location as being beside a busy road is not a literal rendering of the line, and other translators, including Arthur Waley and William Acker, have made it clear that the line refers to other dwellings nearby. But the point is that T'ao was a man who, at least in how he presents himself in his poems, dwells in his mind and heart apart from others, as if he is always ingathered and detached—in the world but not really of it. He appears often to be lost in his contemplation of things and the reflections on life that such contemplation brings. In the first line of the poem, the word "hut" is also a metaphor for himself, his physical presence in the world. The first few lines of the poem suggest that wherever he goes, whether walking on his farm or dealing with the affairs of the world, he always remains, to a degree, apart and detached.

Such an orientation suggests a spiritual dimension to T'ao's inner life. There were three spiritual or philosophical traditions in China at the time T'ao lived: Confucianism, Taoism, and Buddhism.

Confucianism was a social and ethical doctrine rather than a religious one. It was established in the sixth century BCE by the aristocratic teacher and administrator Confucius. On the evidence of the "Twenty Poems after Drinking Wine" (of which "I Built My Hut beside a Traveled Road" is one), T'ao's attitude to Confucianism is conflicted. Although he respects it, he cannot give it his wholehearted assent. In the last poem of the series, "The Sages Flourished Long Before My Time," he is full of praise for the

WHAT DO I READ NEXT?

- *The New Directions Anthology of Classical Chinese Poetry* (2003), edited by Eliot Weinberger, includes the work of thirty-seven early Chinese poets. *The Book of Odes*, with which T'ao was familiar, is well represented, as is T'ao himself, including "I Built My Hut beside a Traveled Road." Many of the poems are translated by American poets, including William Carlos Williams, Ezra Pound, Kenneth Rexroth, and Gary Snyder. The anthology sheds light on the influence of Chinese poetry on American poets in the twentieth century. It also serves as a study of the art of translation, because the anthology contains different versions of the same poem by various translators.

- *Chinese Poetry: An Anthology of Major Modes and Genres* (1997), edited and translated by poet and scholar Wai-lim Yip, collects 150 poems spanning two thousand years, from the *Book of Songs* (*Book of Odes*) to the poems of the Yuan Dynasty (1260–1368). Each poem appears in both English translation and the original Chinese characters in Yip's own calligraphy. The book includes Yip's translation of "I Built My Hut beside a Traveled Road."

- *The Book of Songs: The Ancient Chinese Classic of Poetry* (1996), translated by Arthur Waley and edited, with additional translations, by Joseph R. Allen, is the oldest collection of poetry in the world, dating back to 600 BCE. These poems were known to T'ao and are the foundational poems of the Chinese poetic tradition.

- *Chinese History Stories: Stories from the Zhou Dynasty* (2009) by Renee Ting is the first volume in the Treasures of China History Stories. For adults and children, this volume tells the story of historical figures and events during the Zhou Dynasty, from 1046 to 221 BCE. Volume 2, *Chinese History Stories: Stories from the Imperial Era*, also by Ting, covers two thousand years of Chinese history from 221 BCE until 1911.

- *The Dynasties of China: A History* (2003) by Bamber Gascoigne covers the period from 1600 BCE to 1911. Gascoigne discusses the Chinese dynasties in a way that illuminates significant individuals and key incidents. The book is lavishly illustrated in color. A postscript surveys China's history in the twentieth century.

- Over three hundred years after the life of T'ao, there was a period during the T'ang dynasty in which several great poets flourished. *Wang Wei, Li Po, Tu Fu, Li Ho, Li Shang-yin: Five T'ang Poets*, translated and introduced by David Young (1990), is an anthology of the work of five of these poets.

- One of the finest of contemporary American poets is Mary Oliver. Like many of the Chinese poets, she often focuses on quiet moments in nature that prompt her to reflect on her feelings and life in general. Oliver's *New and Selected Poems* Volumes 1 and 2 (2005 and 2007 respectively) present a rich selection of her work over many decades.

works of Confucius and regrets that such works are no longer as respected as they were in former times. But in the second poem, he criticizes Confucian doctrine and claims to see little value in it.

In general, Western scholars have seen in T'ao a greater affinity for Taoism than Confucianism.

He never mentions Buddhism directly. Buddhism originated in India in the sixth and fifth centuries BCE and had gained widespread acceptance in China at the time T'ao lived. David Hinton, one of T'ao's most recent translators, notes that T'ao lived close to an important Buddhist monastery and that he visited it more than once. The monastery even tried to recruit him, but T'ao appears to have had no interest in living a strict monastic life.

As far as Taoism is concerned, however, the picture is rather different. Taoism is associated with Lao-Tzu, an older contemporary of Confucius. Its principle text is the *Tao Te Ching*, which is at once a metaphysical treatise, a guide to enlightened being and behavior, and a manual for government. The term Tao is usually translated as the Way. The Tao is the most fundamental aspect of the universe. It is uncreated being, eternally at rest within itself, from which all life emerges. The goal of life, according to this doctrine, is to live in harmony with the Tao, to live according to the Way.

Over the centuries, Taoism developed an emphasis on techniques designed to promote physical longevity and even immortality. According to Trevor Ling, in *A History of Religion East and West*, the Taoists showed a "preoccupation with alchemy, in the search for the elixir of life, and to various kinds of crude rituals and practices of a quasi-magical kind." T'ao had no interest in this. There are many references in his poems to the inevitability of aging and death, and for him, death is the end of the person in every respect. Not only does he reject the possibility of physical immortality, he never considers the concept of the immortality of the soul, which is quite foreign to Chinese religious and philosophical thought.

However, T'ao does appear to have had some affinity with other aspects of Taoism. The Taoists also developed meditative practices aimed at stilling the mind, allowing the practitioner to go beyond the restless thoughts and desires that get in the way of living in harmony with the Way. There are glimmers of this in T'ao's poetry, most obviously in Hinton's translations, but less apparent in Hightower's. In one poem, "Back Home Again Chant," T'ao's celebration of his return to his farm following one of his unhappy short spells in government service, he writes of the joys of being in nature, which is always perfect and in which he discovers a profound, restful mode of being. He states that he will climb a hill and chant in a way that will alter his breathing, which perhaps suggests his awareness of Taoist methods of breath control that aim to establish a state of rest and quietude. (This poem appears in Hightower's translation as "The Return," although it makes no mention of the breath or of chanting, preferring to show the poet climbing a hill and

"whistling," a word also used by A. R. Davis in his translation of the poem.)

In "I Built My Hut beside a Traveled Road" what most links T'ao to the meditative traditions of Taoism (and also to Zen Buddhism) is the final thought the poet expresses. After reporting the moment when he was picking the chrysanthemums, glancing up at the mountain at sunset, and observing the flock of returning birds, he says he is aware of a profound truth in that moment. He would like to express that truth but is unable to summon the right words. The point here is that is there are no words that would fully capture this moment of intuitive understanding of the perfect order inherent in nature and the simultaneous presence of time and timelessness. Both Hinton and Davis, in their translations of this poem, have the poet forgetting the words, which seems very appropriate: as soon as the poet conceptualizes his experience, the words slip away from him and he is back in that state of no-word contemplation of the moment. As the *Tao Te Ching* states, there are no words that can describe the Tao. Any words used to describe it must by definition fall short; the Tao is nameless, beyond language.

The notion that the ultimate truth of life is beyond conceptual language is connected to an essential aspect of T'ao's poetry—once again more noticeable in Hinton's translations than Hightower's—in which the poet emphasizes the importance of not resisting the flow of experience in each moment. To resist what comes his way is to lay down obstacles to the flow of the Tao. Life cannot be captured or explained by rational analysis and concepts because the experience of life demands an immediate awareness and acceptance in the moment.

This Taoist approach to life is also hinted at in the poet's love of wine. One authority on T'ao, William Acker, hypothesized that the poet was an alcoholic who tried but failed to give up drinking, but this seems to be too literal a reading of T'ao's words. Although he no doubt did enjoy the pleasures of good wine, he used references to wine in his poems also as a metaphor for the unrestricted expression of life. To drink wine is to relax the boundaries of the self and allow life to flow more freely, beyond anxious thoughts that serve only to cramp one's experience. As Hightower puts it in connection with the fourteenth of the twenty poems written after drinking wine—a poem that is fulsome in its praise of

wine—"through this convivial drunkenness...
the poet experiences a rapture leading to a kind
of mystical illumination." Hinton further
explains that through drinking wine the poet
attains "that serene clarity of attention...a
state in which the isolation of a mind imposing
distinctions on the world gives way to a sense of
identity with the world." It is this "identity with
the world" that T'ao seems to achieve—without
the aid of wine—in that moment he records in "I
Built My Hut beside a Traveled Road."

Source: Bryan Aubrey, Critical Essay on "I Built My Hut
beside a Traveled Road," in *Poetry for Students*, Gale,
Cengage Learning, 2011.

Eugene Eoyang

*In the following essay, Eoyang claims that "T'ao
Ch'ien's poetry is admired for its simplicity, its
grace, and its naturalness, which is why it he is the
favorite among Chinese poets."*

[1]

By and by, the seasons come and go,
My, my! What a fine morning!
I put on my spring cloak
And set out east for the outskirts.
Mountains are cleansed by lingering clouds;
Sky is veiled by fine mist,
A wind comes up from the south,
Winging over the new sprouts.

[2]

Bank to bank, the stream is wide;
I rinse, then douse myself,
Scene by scene, the distant landscape;
I am happy as I look out.
People have a saying:
"A heart at peace is easy to please."
So, I brandish this cup,
Happy to be by myself.

[3]

Peering into the depths of the stream,
I remember the pure waters of the Yi
There students and scholars worked together,
And, carefree, went home singing.
I love their inner peace,
Awake or asleep, I'd change places,
But, alas, those times are gone—
We can no longer bring them back.

[4]

In the morning and at night
I rest in my house.

"THE SALIENT POINT ABOUT T'AO'S
DEPICTION OF CHANGE IS THAT IT RECOGNIZES
BOTH BUOYANCY AND DECLINE: AND
CHARACTERISTICALLY, HE IS AMBIVALENTLY
HAPPY AND SAD ABOUT CHANGE."

Flowers and herbs are all in place;
Trees and bamboos cast their shadows.
A clear-sounding lute lies on my bed,
And there's half a jug of coarse wine.
Huang and T'ang are gone forever
Sad and alone, here I am.

by T'ao Ch'ien [Tao Qian]

... T'ao Ch'ien's poetry is admired for its
simplicity, its grace, and its naturalness, which is
why he is the favorite among Chinese poets, a
"poet's poet." His philosophy comes closest in
Chinese literature to the perspective of the
Taoist.

Western readers might find T'ao's poetry
glib, even banal. His reclusiveness does appear
to oppose Western notions of responsibility and
public service. But one must remember that there
is an inherent skepticism in Taoism of all ambition as the self-serving, self-aggrandizing piety of
hypocrites or of the self-deluded. Government
was considered the problem, not the solution (a
sentiment of some currency in recent U.S. elections). The Taoist would have applauded the
spirit, if not the exact formulation, of Thomas
Jefferson's dictum: "That government governs
best which governs least."

What is perhaps fascinating about this set of
four poems is (1) how mutability is considered in
very concrete terms, and (2) how immanent is
T'ao's conception of mutability. I submit that
this embodies an irony that any successful poem
on mutability achieves, that, in its very success, it
overcomes the very oppressiveness of time which
it laments. Typical of the practice during that
period, the poems are preceded by a headnote,
which reads: "'The Seasons Come and Go' is a
sequence about an outing in late spring when
spring clothes are made and the weather is
mild. I stroll alone, my shadow my companion,

with joy and sadness in my heart." One may see #2 and #4 as internally contradictory, but Taoists consider "contradictions" as ambivalences rather than as faults in logic.

My translation of the beginning of the first two lines tries to solve a problem of making a familiar trope in Chinese sound natural in English. Chinese like to use reduplicatives (actually, they are merely duplicatives, i.e., doubled phonemes, like "Bully, bully" or more freely, like such rhymed compounds as "hurly-burly," "hocus-pocus," "hugger-mugger," etc.). For generations, the dictionary-mongering, semantically muddled sinologist has, in a misguided attempt at lexical accuracy, rendered each word of the compound individually, rather than rendering the compound. So, we have abominations like: "Luxuriantly, luxuriantly" for *yu-yu,* or "Clearly, clearly" for *ch'ing-ch'ing,* or "Chilly, chilly" for *ch'i-ch'i,* when what is offered in the original are familiar alliterative and assonantal compounds that mean "lush," "clear," and "chill" (although "Chilly, chilly" has the virtue of trying to duplicate the redoubled *ch'i* sounds in *ch'i-ch'i*). The "My, my!" in the second line takes liberties with the original because it puns on the (modern) pronunciation of the duplicative compound *mai-mai* that begins the first line, whereas the *Mu-mu* that begins the second line means "vast" and "wondrous." As it is an interjection proverbially expressing an almost preverbal sigh, I felt that it was appropriate to match it with a conversational interjection in English: it is conversationally natural in the original, in a way that "Vast, vast" or "Wondrous, wondrous" would not have been in English. Some translators make the mistake of rendering interjections with their meaning, which assumes that an enactment of meaning is the same as the meaning itself, like translating the English "Alas!" with "Regret!" James Hightower renders these lines valiantly as "Pell-mell the seasons revolve / Still and calm is this morning." Arthur Waley's version is: "Swiftly the years, beyond recall. / Solemn the stillness of this spring morning."

In a curious bit of serendipity, William Empson focused on the contrast in Waley's use of "Swiftly" in the first line, and of "stillness" in the second line, to illustrate his first type of ambiguity, not knowing that Waley's choice of words was totally fortuitous, unwarranted by the original, which included the duplicative binomes, *mai-mai* ("passing, transpiring") and *mu-mu* ("majestic, profound, beautiful") which,

juxtaposed, lack the contrast the Empson saw between the "swiftness" and "stillness" that Waley had imported into his version. Nevertheless, Empson stumbles on an insight which is, nevertheless, apposite to our concerns with mutability, and not irrelevant to T'ao Ch'ien's original poem:

> I call *swift* and *still* here ambiguous, though each is meant to be referred to one particular time-scale, because between them they put two time-scales into the reader's mind in a single act of apprehension. But these scales, being both present, are in some degree used for each adjective, so that the words are ambiguous in a more direct sense; the years of a man's life seem *swift* even on the small scale, like the mist from the mountains which 'gathers a moment, then scatters'; the *morning* seems still even on a large scale, so that this moment is apocalyptic and a type of heaven.

Although T'ao Ch'ien might not have been quite so analytical or dithyrambic about it, the first two lines do pose, at least implicitly, two kinds of time-frame, or at least two subjective valuations of time. In the first, "By and by, the seasons come and go," there is a sense of the ephemerality of time, of its elusiveness and evanescence; in the second, "My! My! What a beautiful morning!," there is a sense of the immanence of this moment, and of its fullness and its self-sufficiency. *Mu-mu* celebrates the amplitude and the profundity of the moment; *Mai-mai* regrets its passing.

The remarkable feature of T'ao Ch'ien's poems on the passing of the seasons is that there are virtually no abstractions, no conceptualizations of explicit mutability itself, only of its most familiar manifestation, of time passing and of the seasons coming and going. There is a nostalgic *ubi sunt* note sounded in the third stanza, where a moment is recalled from the past. In that will-to-connect with a coveted past is an attempt to annihilate the ravages of time, to negate mutability, but it's an effort made with no heroic pretensions, no sense of self-importance. For a contrast—offered not to be invidious, but merely to highlight the differences—consider Proust's "intimations of immortality": in the familiar madeleine scene, the smell of these orange-flavored cakes recall a forgotten moment in Proust's own childhood. T'ao's "madeleine," on the other hand, thrusts him hundreds of years back—not to the beginnings of his own life, but to an ancient "golden age." T'ao's recollection of an ancient ritual, which is not memory so much as observance and allusion, reminds him of the paltriness of the present, and of his own mundanity. It is not so much that the past eludes him; it's rather that he feels left out of the past, banished from more innocent days when people "carefree, went home singing."

Poems 1 and 3 might also be seen as contradistinctive pairs, the first an immediate experience, the second a lively recollection of a remote, perhaps ultimate experience. The first concentrates on the now; the third focuses on the then. But the translation, to accommodate English grammar, reinforces the "pastness of the past" (T. S. Eliot's phrase); and, in so doing, it undermines its "presence." For in the original Chinese, since there are no tenses comparable to those in Western languages, and as no verbs are declined, the indication of the past here is wholly implicit and contextual. The poem alludes to the actions of the past and "re-enacts" them in what, in narrative, would be "the eternal present." To "remember" (line 2) is not merely to recall, which involves a consciousness of the distance between the past and the present, it is also to call up, which involves the act of making the past present. The lines sandwiched by lines 2 and 7, constituting an entry into and an exit from the past,—"I remember . . ." and "But, alas . . ."—exist in a primordial present, a perennial indicative which is not deadened by any grammatical datedness, nor removed from actuality by resort to the subjunctive.

The contrast between the end of Poem 2— "Happy to be by myself" and Poem 4—"Sad and alone, here I am"—is striking: in the first instance, the poet is enjoying the delights of a spring morning—the weather, the scenery, the freshness of the wind, the scent of new sprouts. If the prospect in the world is at peace, the landscape of the soul is equally serene: "I am happy as I look out." The ability to enjoy life is enhanced by a contentment of the soul: "A heart at peace is easy to please." As with so many nature poems in Chinese, being alone—familiar tropes include a "solitary boat" or a "solitary gull"—is not tantamount to loneliness, in a nature that is nurturing. Self-contentment stems from self-forgetting— one of the few notions that both the Taoists and the Confucians share: "Happy to be by myself" (2:8) is cognate with a line in Poem 3: "And carefree, went home singing" (3:4). The key to being "carefree" is learning to be "self-free."

The poem begins with an intimation of spring, or rejuvenation, not of demise and decline;

it proceeds to a lustration that is playful and spontaneous even while it approaches ritual, reminiscent as it is, of a classic "baptism" in the past. One could be forgiven for forgetting that the season which most naturally calls up mutability is autumn, not spring, when the world is declining, not when it is being renewed. It is spring when people feel most buoyant and most immortal, autumn when they are reminded most of their own mortality. Yet, this annual rebirth, this seasonally new lease on life, is what prompts T'ao Ch'ien with thoughts on the inevitability of change, with the pervasiveness of mutability.

The salient point about T'ao's depiction of change is that it recognizes both buoyancy and decline: and characteristically, he is ambivalently happy and sad about change. It may be argued that rises and falls, ups and downs, are as familiar in Western cosmology as in Chinese: however, what is odd is that the normative Western model should be more often "rise and fall" than "fall and rise" (the demise of Deng Xiaoping prompts the observation that his heroism consisted of three "falls and rises" rather than one "rise and fall"). This preference for the rise-and-fall sequence is by no means without exception: one of the most durable narratives is, of course, the story of the Resurrection, which is the prototypical "fall-and-rise" story, repeated not only by the lives of St. Paul and St. Augustine, but by every "born-again" Christian.

Cognate with this eschatological rise-and-fall bent, this emphasis on a "sense of an ending," is the implicit assumption that earlier times were innocent, in two senses of the word—both less corrupt and sinful as well as less knowledgeable and technologically advanced. The fall from grace, sometimes regarded as "the fortunate fall"—since it signals the advent of the rebellious kind of intelligence: one that privileges invention rather than obedience—suggests a descent into a worldliness that coincides with the rise of technology. But the Taoist would see this innocence not in terms of ignorance and purity; their denigration of the present would not take the form of an indictment against decadence, it would express itself as a remonstrance against a debilitating lack of wisdom. The creature comforts that technological sophistication provides would not be regarded as an advance in civilization so much as a massive disregard for the rest of creation. The wisdom of the ancients was, on the other hand, perfect, providing a perspective that makes the modern not a model of progress, but a manifestation of regress. We are more innocent than our forebears, i.e., less insightful, more adolescent, even if, or often because, our technology is more sophisticated. Our toys may be more advanced, but that does not make us wiser than our forebears.

T'ao's dualism is unbiased, in favor neither of rise-and-fall nor of fall-and-rise, for he laments and celebrates change, concentrating on the explicit renewal in spring as well as on its implicit ephemerality, for both are, for him as for few others, equally salient manifestations of mutability.

Source: Eugene Eoyang, "T'ao Ch'ien's 'The Seasons Come and Go: Four Poems'—A Meditation," in *Chinese Literature: Essays, Articles, Reviews*, Vol. 20, December 1998, pp. 1–9.

Zhang Longxi

In the following excerpt, Zhang explains the challenge of simplicity for Chinese poets such as T'ao Qian (T'ao Ch'ien), stating that the anxiety of articulation affects the meaning of the writing.

If the dialectic movement of the spirit as envisioned and described in Hegel's *Aesthetics* unavoidably leads up to the split of an inward vision and an outward expression, it does not, after all, create the problem of language but merely intensifies it from a philosophical perspective. The examples of Homer, Shakespeare, and Schiller in the previous chapter all remind us that the difficulty of poetic articulation is not just a crisis with modern poets like T.S. Eliot, Mallarmé, and Rilke but a problem that has always inhabited the Western literary tradition, while Lu Ji, a third-century Chinese poet, provides yet another example with his "Rhymeprose on Literature," which clearly shows that the anxiety of articulation is a perennial concern in Chinese poetics as well. Already evident in Lu Ji's poetic essay, a strong sense of the complexity of language and interpretation was later brought to a more conscious level and materialized in Chinese poetry in one way or another. This poetic sensibility, or what I would call the hermeneutic sense in the Chinese tradition, manifests itself in the works of a great poet in fourth-century China, Tao Qian (365–427), also known as Tao Yuanming. His poetry and prose often speak of the difficulty of speaking, and his uniquely plain style embodies a rather sophisticated understanding of the nature of language as well as a subtle use of language to overcome its inherent limitations.

> TO MOST READERS OF HIS TIME, THEN, TAO QIAN'S WRITING MUST HAVE APPEARED RATHER CRUDE AND COLORLESS, MARKED BY ITS RESERVE, RETICENCE, AND ARTLESS SIMPLICITY—SO MUCH SO THAT NONE OF HIS CONTEMPORARIES EVER HELD HIM IN HIGH REGARD AS A POET."

We may recall that Lu Ji characterizes the problem of poetic language as a constant "anxiety that meaning does not match with things, and writing does not convey meaning. And this results not so much from the difficulty of knowing as from the limitation of one's ability." Chinese poetry before and in Tao Qian's time can be seen as largely responding to this problem, trying desperately to counterbalance the incompetence of words by an extremely prodigal use of words. The *fu* or rhymeprose at that time became especially extravagant with elaborate ornaments, and poetry in the so-called Six Dynasties period is notorious for its flamboyant and ornate style. In their effort to overcome the inadequacy of language, poets in Tao Qian's time seemed to have forgotten that the problem, as Lu Ji put it astutely, "results not so much from the difficulty of knowing as from the limitation of one's ability," which could not be solved by piling up words into a sort of verbal monstrosity. Against such a background, the poetry of Tao Qian appeared as a startlingly new phenomenon because it differed from the poetry of his contemporaries precisely in its extreme frugality of words and a style noted for its unadorned simplicity. To the language problem Lu Ji raised, Tao Qian offered a solution that differed so drastically from the one his contemporaries sought, producing a poetry so alien to their ears and minds, that he was not at all taken seriously as a poet in his own time or immediately after. Of course, he has since been celebrated as one of the four or five most important poets in the entire history of China, but unlike the other poets who may be considered his equals in literary excellence—Du Fu (712–770), Li Bai (701-62), or Qu Yuan (c. 340–c. 278 BCE), who were all quickly recognized and honored as poets of great merits—the canonical status of Tao Qian in classical Chinese literature was not firmly established until some five hundred years after his death. "Yuanming's literary fame reached its summit in the Song (960–1279)," as Qian Zhong-shu observes in examining the vicissitudes of Tao Qian's literary fame from the Jin period to the late Tang. The very belatedness in the recognition of the value of Tao Qian's poetry raises a question of immense hermeneutic interest.

In looking at possible patterns of the reception of a new literary work, Hans Robert Jauss observes that the response the first audience may have is likely to be determined by the distance or disparity between the given "horizon of expectations" at the time and the demand a new work makes on the aesthetic sensibility of its audience. In the case of a truly original work that disappoints or refutes the expectations of its audience and challenges their sensibility, the value of the work may take a long time to be recognized and appreciated. "It can thereby happen," says Jauss, "that a virtual significance of the work remains long unrecognized until the 'literary evolution,' through the actualization of a newer form, reaches the horizon that now for the first time allows one to find access to the understanding of the misunderstood older form." The reception of Tao Qian in the history of Chinese literature is a good case in point. The dramatic change in the evaluation of Tao Qian in traditional criticism is significant not only because it tells us something about the mutability of aesthetic taste and judgment but also because it shows, when Tao Qian was finally canonized, what forms of expression were accepted as of paramount value and importance and what stylistic features became part of the familiar horizon of expectations in reading Chinese poetry.

From the very beginning, Tao Qian's plain and simple language poses a problem for readers and critics alike, for its very transparency tends to obscure its value and significance. When Yan Yanzhi (384–456), himself a poet much admired at the time for his elaborate style, composed a eulogy on Tao Qian, he praised Tao's moral virtues but practically ignored his literary merits, only mentioning that in his writings Tao "intended to get to the point." To be sure, this was meant as a commendation, for Yan Yanzhi was alluding to Confucius' remark on the proper use of language; "So far as words can get to the point, that is enough." In doing so, however, he tacitly dismissed Tao Qian's writing for lacking

the elaborate embellishment and rhetorical fireworks he and his contemporaries so highly valued in poetry. To most readers of his time, then, Tao Qian's writing must have appeared rather crude and colorless, marked by its reserve, reticence, and artless simplicity—so much so that none of his contemporaries ever held him in high regard as a poet. This may account for the rather peculiar negligence of two important works of criticism written within one hundred years after his death, Liu Xie's (465?–522) *Wenxin dixolong* (The Literary Mind or the Carving of Dragons) and Zhong Rong's (459–518) *Shi pin* (Ranking of Poetry), for both fail to do him justice: the former does not mention Tao Qian at all, whereas the latter classifies him as belonging to the "middle rank," that is, as being of only secondary importance, though it honors him as "the paragon of all hermit poets, past and present." In all likelihood, Tao Qian was simply out of tune with his time, for he neither wrote the kind of wooden "metaphysical poetry" (*xuanyan shi*) which was the literary fashion when he was young nor followed the ornate style that became increasingly the predominant mode of writing for his contemporaries. "He was all alone," as Kang-i Sun Chang observes, "for he lived in a period of transition, and was judged by a set of poetic criteria directly opposed to his own literary taste." It was the verdict of earlier critics that Tao Qian gave at best a lackluster performance in writing and that his language was too simple and flat to be really poetic. Even Du Fu, the great poet of the High Tang period, despite his deep respect for Tao, still found it difficult to appreciate his insipidly "dry" language:

> Old Tao Qian who shunned the world
> May not have attained the *tao* thereby,
> Reading his poems, I feel it a pity;
> His language is so seared and dry.

The question is, why would Tao Qian use a "seared and dry" language that many poets considered inadequate for poetic expression? Why would he choose to write in a sort of zero degree style when flowery language was the accepted norm of his time? When we read his poetry and prose, it soon becomes clear that Tao Qian was never bent on following the trend of his time—in life as well as in writing poetry. For more than fifteen hundred years, he has been justly famous for his moral integrity, and people love the story of Tao Qian's refusing to humble himself before his superiors and protesting. "How can I bow to a country boor just for five pecks of rice!" With these proud words he quit the minor official post he had held and, like an ancestral Candide, withdrew to tend his own garden and live a farmer's life. There was a certain stubbornness and a great deal of courage in Tao Qian that made him a solitary traveler on the path he chose, and the same unyielding, independent spirit made him what he was both as a man and as a poet. *Le style est l'homme* may be a deceptive cliché, but in the case of Tao Qian, there is a close relationship between his style of living, and style of writing, for both are the result of a well-thought-out choice, and both have simplicity as the definitive feature. Traditional criticism has exalted Tao Qian's moral integrity as a man and the edifying effect of his poetry, but it has largely failed to notice that the same principled adherence to what he believed to be true in nature and life has also determined his use of language. Though somewhat oversimplified, Zhong Rong's capsule characterization, "the paragon of all hermit poets, past and present," does mark out the most salient features of Tao's poetry and personality: his aversion to the insincerity and pretentiousness of officialdom, his awareness of the perils lurking at every corner of a political career, his appreciation of the simple joys of his home and his garden, his love of nature, and the purity of spirit revealed in the purity of his language. Nevertheless, many critics have overlooked his search for stylistic features that could express the simplicity he held so dear in a form that was congenial in it. Artificial ornaments are incompatible with natural spontaneity as he understood it, and that sense of incompatibility was the essential cause of his refusal to adopt the flowery style of contemporary writing. That he thus shunned all artificiality may also explain why so few of his imitators could succeed in achieving the effect of his style, since they tried to imitate the idealized simplicity of a farmer's life, while Tao Qian *lived* such a life. His life and personality are so closely interwoven into the text of his poetry that to understand his poetry and its stylistic features is also to understand his life as presented in his poetry, and in this sense it becomes possible to read his works as a sort of poetic autobiography. His poetry is an *autobiography* in the sense that in most of his poems, the poet becomes the subject of his own writing, which speaks about his life in the fields and comments on the meaning of such a life. But more importantly, his autobiography is *poetic*

because Qian, that self-alienation, a momentary separation from his true nature, is his fall into "the net of dust," his brief entanglement in officialdom, which he now admits to be a mistake and contrasts with the purity of his private life, unsoiled by dust of any kind. The regret of a momentary *faux pas,* the recantation of his briefly held official post, indeed appears again and again as one of the central themes in Tao Qian's writing from poems on nature and farming to his well-known rhymeprose, "Returning Home."

Given his love of the purity and freedom in nature, the stylistic simplicity of Tao Qian's poetry becomes thematically significant, as it implies his acceptance of life in the "fields and gardens," his preference for the "pure air" in his "bare rooms," and his rejection of the pomposity and formality of officialdom. His sketch of the village scene is remarkably new and fresh, for the picture of a dog barking in a deep lane and a cock crowing on top of a mulberry tree, with its simple vocabulary and natural rhythm, virtually cannot be found in earlier poetry. A few folk songs in the ancient *Book of Poetry* may be comparable, but the language of those songs was archaic even in Tao Qian's time and could not have the same refreshing effect as his simple diction. Of course, as Owen reminds us, Tao Qian's simple language is never simple, for his words always point away from themselves, and simplicity as a stylistic feature is not something that comes naturally without the poets' conscious effort. To write poetry at all necessarily involves composition and arrangement of materials taken from the poet's life experiences, and the complexity of Tao Qian's style is recognized by many scholars. In a discussion of Tao Qian's use of allusion, for example, James Hightower shows how Tao's poetry "can be as mannered, erudite, and allusion-laden as that of any Six Dynasties poet." It seems that most of Tao Qian's contemporaries failed to recognize this complexity, and in Tao's works we often find intimations of a sense of loneliness, his desire for a fit audience, frequently expressed as a wish to find *zhiyin* or "the one who knows the sound." Frustrated in his effort to fulfill this wish, the poet imaginatively travels back in time to converse with men of his own caliber in past history.

Source: Zhang Longxi, "The Use of Silence," in *The Tao and the Logos: Literary Hermeneutics, East and West*, edited by Stanley Fish and Fredric Jameson, Duke University Press, 1992, pp. 110–18.

James Robert Hightower

In the following excerpt, Hightower seeks to explain the less popular "fu" form poems written by T'ao Ch'ien.

T'ao Ch'ien is famous as the greatest lyric poet of China before the T'ang dynasty, and his poems have frequently been translated. With the exception of "The Return," his rare compositions in the *fu* form are less well known than his lyrics, and justly so. My purpose in offering new translations of T'ao Ch'ien's three *fu* is to show how in each of them he was writing in a well-established tradition, and to point out the nature of his achievement in "The Return," where, by subverting the tradition to his own ends, he made a conventional form the vehicle for intensely personal expression.

The only one of these *fu* which is dated is "The Return," written when T'ao Ch'ien was thirty and at the full maturity of his poetic power. The other two are almost certainly earlier; at least they are avowedly written as poetic exercises, variations on established themes, and should be approached by way of the conventions they accept and exploit. Of these two *fu*, "Stilling the Passions" is more nearly a stereotype, and it deals with a theme which does not elsewhere appear in T'ao's poetry. The "Lament for Gentlemen Born out of Their Time" is equally conventional, but is a topic which he treated frequently in his lyrics and which was apparently more congenial. I shall take them up in order, reserving for last "The Return." T'ao's preface to "Stilling the Passions" defines the nature of his poem and names two of his models:

> First of all Chang Heng wrote a *fu*. "On Stabilizing the Passions," and Ts'ai Yung one "On Quieting the Passions." They avoided inflated language, aiming chiefly at simplicity. Their compositions begin by giving free expression to their fancies but end on a note of quiet, serving admirably to restrain the undisciplined

> and passionate nature: they truly further the ends of salutary warning. Since their time, writers in every generation have been inspired to elaborate on the theme, and in the leisure of my retirement I have taken up my brush to write in my turn. Granted that my literary skill idea of those original authors.

... So far I have yet to quote an integral specimen of a *fu* on this subject, but already its wholly conventional nature should be apparent. As one reads T'ao Ch'ien's version, the impression of *déjà vue* grows with each couplet. It is perhaps going too far to imagine that every line had its prototype in the original complete texts of those *fu* which time has mercifully destroyed or left in hackneyed fragments, but surely T'ao Ch'ien was not striving for originality in his version.

Stilling the Passions

Ah, the precious rare and lovely form
She stands out unique in all the age.
Though hers is a beauty that would over-
  throw a city
She intends to be known for her virtue.
In purity she rivals her sounding pendant
  jades
In fragrance she vies with the hidden orchid.
She disowns tender feelings among the
  vulgar
And carries her principles among the high
  clouds.
She grieves that the morning sun declines to
  evening
That human life is a continual striving.
All alike die within a hundred years

How few our joys, the sorrows how many!
She raises the red curtain and sits straight,
Lightly playing the clear-sounding either to
  express her
feelings.
She plays a lovely melody with her slender
  fingers,
As her white sleeves sweep and sway in time.
A swift glance from her lovely sparkling
  eyes—
Uncertain whether to speak or smile.

The melody is half played through
And the sun is sinking at the western
  window
The sad autumn mode echoes through the
  woods
And white clouds cling to the mountain.
She glances up at Heaven's road,
She looks down and tightens the strings.

In spirit and behavior she is charming,
Her attitudes are altogether lovely.

I am moved as she quickens the clear notes'
    tempo
And wish to speak with her, knee to knee.
I would go in person to exchange vows,
But I fear to transgress against the rites.
I would wait for the phoenix to convey my
    proposal
But I worry that another will anticipate me.
In uncertainty of mind and discomposure
My soul in an instant is nine times
    transported.

I would like to be the collar of your dress
And breathe the lingering, fragrance of your
    flower-adorned hair.
But at night you take your silken dress off—
How hateful autumn nights that never end.

I would like to be the girdle of your skirt
And bind the modest slender body
But as weather changes, cool or warm
The old is cast aside, the new put on.

I would like to be the gloss on your hair
As you brush out the dark locks over sloping
    shoulders.
But all too often lovely women wash their
    hair
And it is left dry when the water leaves.

I would like to be your penciled eyebrow
To move gracefully with your eyes as you
    glance around.
But rouge and powder must be fresh applied
And it is destroyed as you make up your face
    anew.

I would like to be the reed that makes your
    mat.
On which you rest your tender body until
    fall
But then a robe of fur will take its place:
A year will pass before, the mat is used again.

I would like to be the silk that makes your
    slipper
To press your white foot wherever you go.
But there is a time for walking and a time for
    rest
The shoes alas are thrown beside your bed.

I would like to be your daytime shadow
To cleave to your body always, to go east or
    west.
But tall trees make so much shade
At times, I fear, we could not be together.

I would like to be your nighttime candle

To shine on your jade-like face in your room
But with the spreading rays of the rising
    sun
My light at once goes out, my brilliance
    eclipsed.

I would like to be the bamboo that makes
    your fan
To dispense a cooling breeze from your ten-
    der hand.
But mornings when the white dew falls
I must look at your sleeve from afar.

I would like to be the wood of the *wu-t'ung*
    tree
To make the singing lute you hold on your
    knees
But music, like joy, when most intense turns
    sad
And in the end I am pushed aside as you play
    no more.
Put to the test my wishes are all frustrated
And I feel only the desolation of a bitter
    heart.
Overcome with sadness, and no one to con-
    fide in,
I idly walk to the southern wood.
I rest where the dew still hangs on the
    magnolia
And take shelter under the lingering shad-
    ows of the
green pines.
On the chance I should see her as I walk
I am torn in my breast between hope and
    fear.
To the end all is desolate, no one appears
Left alone with restless thoughts, vainly
    seeking.
Smoothing my light lapel I return to the
    path
Continually sighing as I watch the setting
    sun.
With steps uncertain, destination forgotten
Dejected in hearing, face filled with grief.
Leaves leave the branch and flutter down
The air is biting as cold comes on.
The sun disappears bearing its rays
The moon adorns the cloud fringes with
    light.
With sad cries the solitary bird flies home,
Seeking its mate an animal passes and does
    not return.
I am sorry that the present year is in its
    decline
I regret that this year draws to a close.

Hoping to follow her in my nighttime dream,
My soul is agitated and finds no rest;
Like a boatman who has lost his oar,
Like a cliff-scaler who finds no handhold.

Just now
The winter constellations shine at my window
The north wind blows chill.
I am agitated and unable to sleep,
Obsessed by a host of fancies.
I rise and tie my sash to await the
    morning,
Deep frost glistens on the white steps.
The cock folds his wings and has yet to crow
While from afar floats the shrill sad note of a
    flute.
At first a harmony of delicate strains,
At last it becomes penetrating and sad.

I imagine that it is she playing there
Conveying her love by the passing cloud—
The passing cloud departs with never a
    word,
It is swift in its passing by.
Vain it is to grieve myself with longing,
In the end the way is blocked by mountains
    and crossed
by rivers.
I welcome the fresh wind that blows my ties
    away
And consign my weakness of will to the
    receding waves.
I repudiate the meeting in the Man-ts'ao
    poem
And sing the old song of the Shao-nan.
I level all cares and cling to integrity,
Lodge my aspirations at the world's end.

This *fu* of T'ao Ch'ien's is not the last of the series, but there is no point in adding more to the list. Now it is, or should be, a general principle of criticism that an adequate reading of a poem must be based on an understanding of the poet's intent in writing the poem. It has been argued that since the private mental states of the poet are beyond the reach of the critic, all he has to go by is what he finds in the poem he is immediately concerned with, which must be read and judged as something unique. Whatever the theory, good critical practice has never so limited itself. For there are a number of clues to the poet's intent. Sometimes, especially in Chinese poetry, the poet provides a preface to his poem in which he states quite explicitly what he is proposing to do. An intimate knowledge of the poet's life will often suggest attitudes and concerns relevant to understanding

a given poem, though such information is usually lacking for Chinese poets. A poet's own statement of his theory of the nature and function of poetry is a valuable guide to his practice. But the most generally available of all these adventitious aids is a knowledge of the poetic tradition in which a poet is writing, and both the genre he is using and the subject of his poem should be viewed in the light of tradition.

I do not propose here to trace the history of the *fu*, a sufficiently complex subject in itself, but shall point out a few features of the form as developed by the Later Han and Six Dynasties periods. Huang-fu Mi (215–282) said, "The *fu* takes its themes from natural objects, whose aspects and properties are elaborated to the point where no one can add anything more." This formula accords well enough with actual practice, and applies both to the descriptive *fu* and, by extension, to the lyric *fu* with which we are presently concerned. Logically such a definition should exclude the possibility of two *fu* on the same subject, for one exhaustive treatment hardly leaves room for a second. However, Ssu-ma Hsiang-ju early established the precedent of taking up a theme already celebrated in a *fu* with the avowed intention of outdoing the first effort. With the growth of the popularity of the *fu* this practice was practically the only excuse for writing *fu* at all, as writers became hard put to find new subjects. By early Six Dynasties times not only were the categories exhausted, it was not easy to think of a suitable individual bird, insect, tree, flower, or household utensil that had not been elaborately described in at least one *fu*. Thus as time went on nearly every possible *fu* subject came to be treated in a whole series of *fu*, each member of a series representing a poet's deliberate attempt to incorporate everything his predecessors had written on the subject. This generalization is subject to the usual reservations, but it does apply as a marked tendency that affected the nature of the *fu* form. One result was the production of stereotypes: the development of a subject in any series follows an established sequence, and successive *fu* on that subject differ chiefly in length, the later ones being the longer. In extreme cases even the vocabulary available to the writer of a *fu* on an established theme was to a large degree limited to what his predecessors had used, so that the form is marked by clichés.

At the same time that the *fu* was becoming a stereotyped treatment of a conventional subject, its metrical structure, at one time quite free, was being reduced to a pattern allowing little more variation than the strict *shih* form. From its occasional use as a rhetorical ornament, parallelism became more and more rigid until it was the invariant basis for the construction of each couplet. These various factors combined to make the *fu* little more than an exercise in versification. It was at once a measure of a poet's erudition and an index of his skill if he could write a *fu* to order.

Source: James Robert Hightower, "The Fu of T'ao Ch'ien," in *Harvard Journal of Asiatic Studies*, Vol. 17, No. 1–2, June 1954, pp. 169–230.

SOURCES

"China Hosts First Buddhist Forum," in *BBC News*, April 13, 2006, http://news.bbc.co.uk/2/hi/4905140.stm (accessed January 4, 2010).

Davis, A. R., *T'ao Yüan-ming: His Works and Their Meaning*, Vol. I, Cambridge University Press, 1983, p. 105.

"General Introduction of Nanjing," in *Nanjing.gov.cn*, http://english.nanjing.gov.cn/gk/200812/t20081214_256642.htm (accessed December 31, 2009).

Hightower, James Robert, *The Poetry of T'ao Ch'ien*, Clarendon Press, 1970, pp. 130–32, 145.

Hinton, David, *The Selected Poems of T'ao Ch'ien*, Copper Canyon Press, 1993, pp. 5, 7, 52.

Hucker, Charles O., *China's Imperial Past: An Introduction to Chinese History and Culture*, Stanford University Press, 1975.

Lao Tze, *Tao Te Ching*, translated with an introduction by D. C. Lau, Penguin, 1972.

Latourette, Kenneth Scott, *The Chinese: Their History and Culture*, 4th ed., Macmillan, 1972.

Lea, Richard, "A New Cultural Revolution," in *Guardian* (London, England), January 16, 2008, http://www.guardian.co.uk/books/2008/jan/16/fiction.richardlea (accessed December 31, 2009).

Ling, Trevor, *A History of Religion East and West: An Introduction and Interpretation*, St. Martin's, 1968, p. 105.

T'ao Ch'ien, *T'ao the Hermit: Sixty Poems by T'ao Ch'ien (365–427)*, translated by William Acker, Thames and Hudson, 1952, p. 66.

Waley, Arthur, *One Hundred and Seventy Chinese Poems*, Constable, 1947, p. 76.

Yeh, Michelle, "Anxiety and Liberation: Notes on the Recent Chinese Poetry Scene," in *World Literature Today*, July 1, 2007.

FURTHER READING

Hightower, James Robert, "T'ao Ch'ien's 'Drinking Wine' Poems," in *Wen-lin: Studies in the Chinese Humanities*, edited by Chow Tse-Tsung, University of Wisconsin Press, 1968, pp. 3–44.

> This is a detailed study of the twenty poems T'ao grouped together as having been composed after drinking wine.

Li, Po, and Tu Fu, *Li Po and Tu Fu*, translated by Arthur Cooper, Penguin, 1973.

> A selection from two of China's most renowned poets from the T'ang dynasty, 618–907, this collection includes a guide to Chinese pronunciation and an introduction to the times in which the poets lived and the background to T'ang poetry.

Michael, Franz, *China Through the Ages: History of a Civilization*, Westview Press, 1986.

> This book surveys Chinese history from its beginnings to the 1980s. It is particularly useful for its coverage of China's social, political, and intellectual movements, as well as its art and literature.

Zong-qi-Cai, *How to Read Chinese Poetry*, Columbia University Press, 2007.

> This guide to Chinese poetry from ancient to modern times is divided into six sections and includes more than 140 poems in many different genres. The poems are presented in Chinese and English. Themes, cultural context, and poetic conventions are among the topics discussed in each chapter.

SUGGESTED SEARCH TERMS

T'ao Ch'ien

T'ao Ch'ien AND poems

T'ao Ch'ien AND Chinese poetry

Chinese AND wine AND poetry

Eastern AND Chin AND dynasty

Taoism

Confucianism

The Idea of Ancestry

ETHERIDGE KNIGHT
1968

Etheridge Knight wrote "The Idea of Ancestry" while he was serving a prison term for theft. The poem was first published in 1968 in a collection of works, *Poems from Prison*, that were all completed during his incarceration. In "The Idea of Ancestry," Knight contemplates how much he misses his family as he stares at their photographs taped to his prison wall.

"The Idea of Ancestry" is considered by literary critics to be one of Knight's more powerful pieces. The poem is filled with the poet's feelings about his family as well as his frustration with his addiction to drugs. The drugs, as much as the prison walls, have kept him separated from his family. The theft he committed was to gain access to money to buy more drugs. Even when he was not in prison, his addiction to drugs created invisible walls that prevented him from fully engaging with the members of his family. In this poem, as he stares at the photographs of his family, he also stares into himself, examining how he has come to this point in his life.

Knight wrote many more poems, but "The Idea of Ancestry" is one of the most often anthologized. This poem is an example of his mastery of creating verbal images that help him to explore his emotions.

AUTHOR BIOGRAPHY

Knight, the second oldest of seven children, was born to Etheridge and Belzora Knight in Corinth, Mississippi, on April 19, 1931. His family was very poor, and when Knight was in the eighth grade he dropped out of school. It did not take long for Knight to realize that without a high school diploma, his chances of making a decent salary were limited to low-paying jobs, such as shining shoes. Knight spent a lot of time in bars and pool halls, where he was introduced to a poetic form similar to rapping, called toasting. It was through this form of storytelling that Knight was introduced to poetry.

Later, to earn a better living, Knight enlisted in the army and was eventually sent to Korea, where he worked as a medic. Four years later, in 1951, Knight was granted a medical discharge from the army. To ease the pain of his injury, Knight had been given pain-killing drugs to which he became addicted. In 1960, desperate for drug money, Knight stole a purse from an elderly woman and received a sentence of ten to twenty-five years to be served in the Indiana State Prison.

Knight served eight years of his prison term from 1960 to 1968. During that time, his interest in poetry was rekindled. He honed his skills, and by the time he was released from jail, he had written enough poems to fill a book. His first collection was called *Poems from Prison* and was published in 1968. "The Idea of Ancestry" was included in this collection. In 1970, several of Knight's poems were included in a collection called *Black Voices from Prison* that included writings of other prisoners.

Poems from Prison proved to be successful, and Knight was invited to teach a poetry class at the University of Pittsburgh in 1968 and 1969. In 1969, the University of Hartford offered Knight a writer-in-residence position, as did Lincoln University in 1972. These experiences, as well as Knight's association with the Black Arts movement, deepened Knight's understanding of poetry and led to his second collection, *Belly Song and Other Poems* (1973). This book was nominated for both the Pulitzer Prize and the National Book Award. His work also won him a National Endowment for the Arts grant (1972) and a Guggenheim fellowship (1974), which offered financial assistance to further his studies.

Knight published *Born of a Woman: New and Selected Poems* in 1980. A compilation of all Knight's work, *The Essential Etheridge Knight*, was published in 1986.

The poet Sonia Sanchez, who helped convince authorities to release Knight before his full prison term was served, married Knight in 1968. Their marriage lasted two years. In 1972, Knight married Mary McNally. The couple had two children but separated in 1977. Knight pursued a degree in poetry and criminal justice and earned a bachelor's degree from Martin Center University in 1990. He died of lung cancer on March 10, 1991, in Indianapolis, Indiana.

POEM TEXT

1

Taped to the wall of my cell are 47 pictures: 47 black
faces: my father, mother, grandmothers (1 dead), grandfathers (both dead), brothers, sisters, uncles, aunts,
cousins (1st & 2nd), nieces, and nephews. They stare
across the space at me sprawling on my bunk. I know   5
their dark eyes, they know mine. I know their style,
they know mine. I am all of them, they are all of me;
they are farmers, I am a thief, I am me, they are thee.

I have at one time or another been in love with my mother,
1 grandmother, 2 sisters, 2 aunts (1 went to the asylum),   10
and 5 cousins. I am now in love with a 7-yr-old niece
(she sends me letters written in large block print, and
her picture is the only one that smiles at me).

I have the same name as 1 grandfather, 3 cousins, 3 nephews,
and 1 uncle. The uncle disappeared when he was 15, just took   15
off and caught a freight (they say). He's discussed each year
when the family has a reunion, he causes uneasiness in
the clan, he is an empty space. My father's mother, who is 93
and who keeps the Family Bible with everbody's birth dates
(and death dates) in it, always mentions him. There is no   20
place in her Bible for "whereabouts unknown."

2

Each fall the graves of my grandfathers call me,
    the brown
hills and red gullies of mississippi send out their
    electric
messages, galvanizing my genes. Last yr / like a
    salmon quitting
the cold ocean-leaping and bucking up his
    birthstream / I   25
hitchhiked my way from LA with 16 caps in my
    pocket and a
monkey on my back. And I almost kicked it
    with the kinfolks.
I walked barefooted in my grandmother's
    backyard / I smelled the
old
land and the woods / I sipped cornwhiskey
    from fruit jars with the   30
men /
I flirted with the women / I had a ball till the
    caps ran out
and my habit came down. That night I looked
    at my grandmother
and split / my guts were screaming for junk /
    but I was almost
contented / I had almost caught up with me.   35
(The next day in Memphis I cracked a croaker's
    crib for a fix.)

This yr there is a gray stone wall damming
    my stream, and when
the falling leaves stir my genes, I pace my cell or
    flop on my bunk
and stare at 47 black faces across the space. I
    am all of them,
they are all of me, I am me, they are thee, and
    I have no children   40
to float in the space between.

POEM SUMMARY

Part 1

Stanza 1 of "The Idea of Ancestry" begins with the image of photographs on the wall of the speaker's prison cell. All the pictures are of black people, the speaker informs the reader. There are almost fifty of them. The speaker then vaguely identifies the people in the photos. They are members of his immediate and extended family. Included in the collection of pictures are his grandparents, his parents, his siblings and their offspring, his parents's sisters and brothers and their children. Most of the people in the pictures are still alive, but a few of them have passed on.

As the speaker looks at these photographs, he feels they are looking back at him. They see

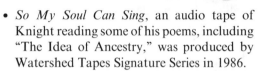

MEDIA
ADAPTATIONS

- *So My Soul Can Sing*, an audio tape of Knight reading some of his poems, including "The Idea of Ancestry," was produced by Watershed Tapes Signature Series in 1986.

him lying on the bed in his prison cell. The speaker feels that he knows these people well and that they know him too, even though they are separated by time and space. They share physical traits, such as the color of their eyes. He remembers their different personalities, and he is sure that they remember his. He knows them so well that he feels he is them and that they are him. Some things about them, however, are different from him. The speaker insinuates that they live off the land, tilling the soil and raising their own food, while he has been designated a criminal who steals from others.

In stanza 2, the speaker expounds on his relationships with and emotion for the people in his family. He mentions his love for the women in his family: his mother and grandmother, aunts, and sisters. He adds that his most current love, however, is for one of his nieces. She is seven years old and often corresponds with him through the mail. Of all the photographs he has taped to his wall, the image of his niece is the only one that is portrayed with a smile. Readers could interpret this smile as reflecting the niece's youth and, therefore, her innocence. One might ask if the other people in the photographs are not smiling because they are not pleased with the speaker being in jail, whereas the young niece loves the speaker unconditionally.

The speaker mentions, in stanza 3, that he shares his first name with his grandfather as well as a few cousins, nephews, and an uncle. In other words, not only does he share physical and personality traits with members of his family, he also has another bond, the passing on of the same name. He then offers more information about the uncle who shares his name. This man, possibly similar to the speaker, disappeared from the family as a youth. The young man hopped trains to travel to places unknown. The family has not heard from him since, it is implied. He has left them with no knowledge of where he is or how he is doing. All he has offered them is a hole in their genealogy. Whenever the family gets together, though, they talk about him, as if possibly trying to fill in the gaps. His absence makes the family members feel unstable. This musing could be the speaker reflecting on the instability that he himself might also cause the family.

On the other more stable side is the speaker's paternal grandmother, who faithfully records the family's history in the family Bible. His grandmother always talks about this missing uncle, the speaker says. He might also be wondering, and maybe hoping, that his grandmother also talks about him when the family gathers. The grandmother, who keeps track of everyone's birth dates and death dates in the Bible, does not seem to be bothered by the fact that no one knows where the missing uncle might be, what he is doing, or even whether he is still alive. Readers might infer that the grandmother keeps this missing uncle alive by talking about him.

Part 2

The second part of "The Idea of Ancestry" reads differently from the first. For one, the setting changes. In the first part, the speaker is in his prison cell and focuses mostly on what he is viewing there—the photographs that are taped to his wall. The pace of the poem is leisurely as the speaker thinks about his family. In the second part of the poem, although the speaker continues to ruminate about his relatives, he does so from a different perspective. Instead of being present in his cell, the speaker mentally drifts into the past as if he has stepped away from the present and is physically visiting his family. He is remembering the psychological pull that he feels when he knows it is time for a family reunion. The speaker relates the tugging on his heart to the instinctual pull a salmon feels when it is time to return to the waters in which the fish was born. The need to go home and visit his people is so deep that the speaker feels it might even be genetic.

The pace of the poem quickens, as emphasized by the slashes the poet uses, breaking up the lines of the poem. It is also in this second part of the poem that the speaker talks about his drug use. In his need to see his family, he has faced the challenge of hitchhiking from California to Mississippi. This is an almost 2,000-mile journey. To sustain his habit, he has stuffed his pocket with drugs. He refers to his addiction with the old saying of having a monkey on one's back. This means the speaker knows that his addiction is a problem.

In the remaining part of the stanza 1 of the poem's second part, the speaker explains that he almost kicked his habit. He credits having been around his family as the reason he was almost successful. He felt good being back home, taking his shoes off, and feeling like he was one of them again. The smell of the land and the memories of what it felt like being in his grandmother's garden help him remember what it was like to be a child again. When he shares drinks with his uncles and flirts with his aunts, he recalls the more pleasant times of his young adulthood, before his addiction, which has since pulled him away.

The speaker is happy back home until he runs out of drugs and becomes once again aware of how badly his body and mind crave them. The drugs have changed him. Where once his family was all he needed to make him happy, now he is dependent on the drugs. He must ingest drugs in order to remember how to be happy. Once he realizes he is in the throes of the drugs, he has to leave not only to find more drugs but also because he cannot stand to let his grandmother see him this way. When he looks at her he senses that she can see the truth about him—who he once was and who he has become. As he is leaving his family again, he realizes that his reunion with them almost made him happy. His family almost made him forget about his drug habit. They almost gave him enough support for him to come back to himself, ridding himself of the metaphorical monkey. But "almost" was not enough. He runs away. His addiction forces him back into his life of crime. He breaks into a doctor's office and steals the drugs his body is demanding.

In the last stanza of the poem, the speaker returns to his present time in the prison cell. The pace of the poem slows down as the slashes he used before are now missing. The speaker begins by comparing where he was last year (at the family reunion) to the present year, when he is in jail. He is now held back by the gray walls, like salmon are sometimes held back from returning to their spawning grounds by man-made dams. When the speaker is stirred by memories and a longing to go home, he is stopped by the walls of his cell. He stares at the photographs to remind himself of his family. He sees them across the space of his cell, which could be likened to the space between his prison and his home. He repeats the idea that he mentioned in the beginning of the poem as he looks at the pictures of all his relatives. Even though he is separated from them, he sees himself in them. He also sees them in himself. The last line of the poem is possibly filled with sadness as he laments that he has no children to bridge the gap between himself and his missing family members. This could also be interpreted to mean that his limb of the family tree stops with him, for he has no progeny. There will be no one looking back beyond him through time, along his line of ancestry.

THEMES

Separation

The speaker in "The Idea of Ancestry" is incarcerated. This means he is separated from society, his family, and his normal life. He has been enclosed and secured by the gray walls that surround him. He can no longer do what he wants to do, which is, according to the focus of this poem, to go home and visit his family.

The theme of separation is presented by the space that the speaker mentions in the poem. There is the space between him, where he lies on his bed, and the photographs that hang on the wall. There is also space between him in the prison and his family, which gathers in Mississippi in the summer to celebrate a reunion.

The speaker also mentions psychological distances. Even when he was with his family during the last reunion he attended, he felt there was a space of separation. The drugs he was using kept him from fully enjoying his family and being fully present with them. The drugs were a distraction, always demanding that he have them on hand and consume them. When they were gone, he had to leave his family in search of them. Even when he took them, he still could not quite reach the state of contentment that he was looking for. He was imprisoned by the drugs much as he is imprisoned by the gray walls. Just as the prison walls are like dams that stop migrating fish from returning home, the drugs keep his inner river of emotions and well-being from flowing. The drugs separate him from himself.

Loneliness

From the theme of separation in this poem comes the theme of loneliness. Being separated from his family is obviously not something the speaker of this poem enjoys. He has taped pictures of his family on the wall of his cell to help him imagine his family around him, and he apparently enjoys looking at them. While he stares into their faces he feels comfort because the pictures give him a sense of belonging, but he also feels loneliness. He wishes he could be with them.

The speaker also expresses his loneliness in the last lines of the poem. Here he mentions that he has no children. He has no one to look after and consequently no one to look after him. Although Knight did eventually conceive children, he wrote this poem before that time. Therefore, as he sits in his cell and ponders his own ancestral line from his grandfathers down to the present time, he has to stop when he reaches himself. No one will carry on his name. No one will look back and claim him as their father. His branch of the family tree will bear no more fruit. He alone holds his position.

Family

Family is very important to the speaker of this poem. He explores what family means to him both when he is with them and when he is away. He studies photographs of his family so he can spot his resemblance to them. He wants to know where he came from. He also needs to know that someone in the outside world really knows who he is, not so much on an intellectual level but on a biological level. The speaker feels reassured in that he and his family are connected genetically. They share not only names but similar characteristics in their eyes, hair, and faces.

Family is a unit that cannot be broken apart even if the members disappear. The speaker's uncle, for instance, a man with whom he shares a name, has not been seen for a long time. No one knows where he is, but his name remains imprinted in the family Bible. This reassures the speaker. Even though he can no longer return home because he has been incarcerated, he holds onto the sense that he will not be forgotten by his family. Even though he has no children of his own, he has a young niece who remembers him. She loves him enough to write letters to him and send him a picture in which she smiles at him. The autumn urge to return home

TOPICS FOR FURTHER STUDY

- Knight was born in Corinth, Mississippi. Research the town of Corinth through the Internet as well as books at your library and provide a profile of the town. How many people live in this town? How does the current population differ from when Knight was born there? Where in the state is Corinth located? What businesses support the town's economy? Describe the landscape and weather. What is the town's history? Imagine that your class is interested in moving there as you present your findings to them in a travel-type brochure. Be prepared to answer their questions.

- Write a poem about your ancestors. Try to follow a similar pattern as presented in Knight's poem. You might look through photo albums as you list members of your family. What feelings do these photographs evoke? In the second part of your poem, recall a significant reunion you might have recently attended. List some of the things you did. To end the poem, return to the photo album and summarize your feelings.

- Research prison population statistics. The U.S. Justice Department papers are a good place to start. You might also search on the Internet for newspaper articles about the topic. How many people are currently in prison? How does the U.S. prison popula-tion compare with those in other countries? What are the percentages of various ethnicities in prison? Also provide statistics for the types of crimes that have sent people to jail. Create computerized graphs and charts to present your findings to your class.

- Create a Web site that compares the Harlem Renaissance with the Black Arts movement. List some of the major contributors to each group. How did these movements differ? How were they similar? What were some of the major themes explored by each group of artists? Offer details about the political and social environment during these two time periods. Include short biographies and bibliographies of the artists in both groups. Then share the Web site with your class.

- Read Gwendolyn Brooks's poem "We Real Cool," which is available online and in *The Essential Gwendolyn Brooks* (2005). This poem sounds like the poet had written it to Knight or to a teenager like him. Ask seven classmates to join you in reciting Brooks's poem, each of you taking a single sentence. For dramatic effect, insert a long pause before reading the last line. Use background music to emphasize the rhythm. At the end of your presentation, ask the rest of the class what they think Brooks is really trying to say.

---

will always be with him no matter where he goes. That urge is spurned by the love of family.

Lineage

The title of Knight's poem accentuates another theme, that of ancestry or lineage. Although lineage is related to the theme of family, it differs in some ways. Lineage represents a long, unbroken history. When one knows one's great grandparents and beyond, one appreciates and understands where one has come from.

In the African American community, the idea of ancestry or lineage is a sensitive topic for some. Many African Americans were stolen or sold into slavery from their homeland. Many have no idea where they came from. Not only might they not know in which country their ancestors were born, they might not even know their lineage after it was established in America. Parents were often separated from their children and wives separated from husbands if they were slaves. So lineage might only be traceable from the end of slavery.

The narrator of the poem is in prison. *(Image copyright Dan Bannister, 2010. Used under license from Shutterstock.com)*

In "The Idea of Ancestry," the speaker does not mention great-grandparents. He goes back only as far as his grandfathers and grand-mothers. Though deeper lineage could be implied by using the terms grandfathers or grandmothers to mean all ancestors, one could also conclude that the speaker is able to claim knowledge of his relatives only from his grand-parents forward. But even with this relatively short lineage, it is obvious that the speaker is emotionally drawn to it. His ancestors call to him. His connection to his lineage is what pulls him back home.

STYLE

Reading Pace and Punctuation

The reading pace, as accentuated by punctua-tion, of "The Idea of Ancestry" changes dramat-ically in various stanzas. The first three stanzas as well as the last one use normal markings that are found in most prose sentences. One reads the lines as if one were reading an essay or a story,

moving from one sentence to the next, stopping briefly at punctuation marks such as commas, then stopping a little longer after a period or at the end of a line.

However, something changes as the reader comes to the beginning of the second section, which starts with the fourth stanza. Here the author adds slash marks to punctuate the lines. These slash marks were typical of Knight's poetry. He often used them to signify how one was to read his poems out loud. One of Knight's strengths as a poet was as a performer, or a reader, of his works. He used punctuation marks to guide his recitation as well as to help others who wanted to read his poems out loud. The slash mark was his particular favorite. In the second part of this poem, where Knight wants the pace to pick up, he uses slash marks to emphasize this. It is in this part of the poem that the images become harsher. The quicker pace enhances this roughness. It is here that the speaker tells the reader about his drug addiction and how it negatively affected his relationship with his family. The slash marks also help to intensify the irrationality that his drugs were causing, suggesting a twisting of his emotions. He wants to be with his family, for example, but the drugs were pulling him away.

In the last stanza, the slash marks disappear. The speaker returns to the present moment, back in the prison cell. He returns to looking at the pictures on the wall and contemplating them. The pace of reading slows down, and the punctuation returns to normal markings, suggesting that the poem be read like one would read any other poem.

Images

Knight peppers his poem with strong images, or words that conjure mental pictures. The images enhance the emotional content of the poem. By using these picture-like phrases, the poet offers the reader a broader landscape through which to interpret and more fully understand the feelings the poet is attempting to express. The phrase "a picture is worth a thousand words" might help readers comprehend how this poetic device works.

Examples of images that Knight uses in this poem can be found in the beginning of the second part of the poem. Here, Knight refers to the burial places of his forebears, for instance, stating that these cemetery plots of his grandparents are calling him home. This image refers to the speaker's heritage. In using the cemetery image, however, readers can imagine not only the physical grounds filled with tombstones or the grandfathers that the speaker mentions but also all the great grandfathers who have been buried down the speaker's entire line of ancestry. Everyone who has preceded the speaker's birth, in other words, call him back to his home, to his family. Through the image of the cemetery, the author stirs the emotions of sorrow at the death of his ancestors and appreciation and love for those who still remain.

Enhancing the picture of the cemetery and his forefathers calling him home, the speaker creates the image of migrating fish who return home without rationally comprehending why they are doing so. The speaker's urge to return home, the poem suggests, works on the speaker in the same way. The fish have no choice but to return to the place they were born, and neither does the speaker. Without the image of the fish, readers would not have as full an understanding of how strongly the speaker feels this instinct.

The speaker assumes his readers will be aware of how some fish overcome all obstacles to reunite with the place where they were spawned. By using this image of migrating fish, he does not have to expound on how he too is compelled to overcome every barrier to get home. The image implies these feelings with fewer words and more emotional impact.

HISTORICAL CONTEXT

Black Arts Movement

The Black Arts movement is often placed in the decade between 1960 and 1970. The time frame coincides with the civil rights movement as well as an increased awareness of what it meant to be black in the United States during this period. The Black Arts movement incorporates the literature that was written by a specific group of African Americans during this period. Politics and an exploration of black culture were common themes. Prominent Black Arts movement authors include Amiri Baraka (formerly known as LeRoi Jones), Gwendolyn Brooks, Nikki Giovanni, Lorraine Hansberry, Ntozake Shange, and Etheridge Knight.

The literature of the Black Arts movement tended away from protest as practiced by those involved in the civil rights movement and toward the concept of empowerment. Often the Black Arts movement is referred to as the artistic branch of the Black Power movement, whose emphasis was on racial pride. African Americans, according to this movement, should be proud of their African heritage rather than trying to emulate white people.

During the Black Arts movement publishing houses, magazines, and theater groups were founded and run by African Americans. These black-run organizations promoted literature and journalism that dealt with issues facing the black community. Literature was written by black authors for black audiences, something that had rarely been done before.

Toasts

Knight began his poetic experience with an African American form referred to as the toast. Toasts are a narrative form of poetry made popular in the twentieth century. They preceded and probably influenced contemporary hip-hop music.

COMPARE
&
CONTRAST

- **1960s:** The War on Drugs is initiated by President Richard Nixon, who declares in front of the U.S. Congress that drug use is causing a serious threat to the United States.

  Today: As the War on Drugs continues, the U.S. government funds programs and works closely with Mexican, Colombian, and Afghani officials in an effort to decrease the amount of illegal drugs that enter the United States each year.

- **1960s:** The Black Arts movement is initiated in reaction to the murder of Malcolm X. The movement brings an awareness of African American literature to the general public readership.

  Today: African American literature is produced by major publishing houses and is taught in colleges through black studies programs and in general literature classes.

- **1960s:** Teens and older black men perform toasts on street corners and in pool halls in many urban areas. This form of improvisational poetry relates the adventures of stock characters and is often punctuated with sexual innuendo.

  Today: Teens and other young adults perform rap poetry both informally on street corners in urban settings and as mass-produced recorded music. The words of the poems are generated from the performers' experiences and can be filled with sexual and sometimes violent references.

Toasts are often improvised, or made up on the spot. They come from the African oral tradition of unrehearsed storytelling. The stories upon which toasts are based have a long history behind them, having been retold many times from the perspectives of different poets. A semi-mythical main character often lies at the center of the toast, with the poet/narrator recounting this character's adventures by adding new and more profound exaggerations of the character's feats. Some of the more popular toasts are based on characters known as Stack-olee, Signifying Monkey, and Shine. Toasts were often performed in prisons, bars, and pool halls and on street corners in black communities.

Black Power Movement

As the movement for civil rights continued into the 1960s, some African Americans grew frustrated with the nonviolent themes that Dr. Martin Luther King Jr. professed. Black activists believed King sacrificed too much in his fight for liberties for black people, such as the right to vote, the right for better schools, and the end of segregation. Black people who followed King were being beaten and imprisoned for their peaceful acts of civil disobedience and their protest marches. Some activists, such as Stokely Carmichael, who headed the Student Nonviolent Coordinating Committee, began altering their belief in nonviolence so their voices would better be heard. Carmichael advocated that African Americans stop asking for their civil rights and start acting on the rights that were already theirs as legal citizens of the United States. Inspired by the words of Malcolm X, Carmichael promoted the concept of black power. Blacks need not try to assimilate into the white culture by trying to look like white people and act like them. Rather, he said, blacks should be proud of their ancestry, their dark skin, and their African American culture.

Huey P. Newton and Bobby Seale were even more aggressive than Carmichael in the movement for black power. They formed a group called the Black Panther Party. Members of this group were often seen in public carrying guns, which they felt were necessary to defend

The poem discusses a family Bible and entries of family members' names. *(Image copyright Suzanne Tucker, 2010. Used under license from Shutterstock.com)*

themselves against racism. Several gun battles between the Black Panthers and city police occurred as the movement grew in intensity, especially after King was assassinated.

From the black power movement, many positive changes occurred. An emphasis on a new definition of what it meant to be black in the United States rose to the surface. On a personal level, for some, hairdos changed from chemically treating hair to make it straight to allowing the natural curls to remain, creating what came to be called the Afro style. Tight braids called cornrows as well as long twisted curls called dreadlocks also became popular. In addition, African clothing, such as dashikis—brightly colored shirts made of African prints—became fashionable. Some African Americans changed their names, taking on traditional African names. On a larger scale, African Americans came together to create and to support black businesses. Activists also turned to politics. In 1972, the first National Black Political Convention was held in Gary, Indiana. The goal was to work together to get more blacks elected to public office.

Malcolm X and Langston Hughes

After the deaths of Malcolm X and Langston Hughes, Knight wrote poems dedicated to each man. In his poem "For Malcolm, a Year After," Knight expresses his anger over Malcolm X's murder. In "For Langston Hughes," Knight is saddened by the loss of Hughes, to whom Knight refers as a man who created dreams for black people.

Like Knight, Malcolm X (1925–1965) spent time in prison. While serving his term, Malcolm (who was born Malcolm Little) educated himself by reading all the books he was allowed, including an entire dictionary. During his time in jail, Malcolm also converted to Islam. Upon his release, Malcolm eventually became a prominent leader in the American Muslim group called the Nation of Islam. Due to his eloquence in giving speeches and his charismatic appeal, he helped to take the Nation of Islam from a small, mostly unknown faction to a nationally recognized and influential organization, especially throughout the black community. Tensions rose, however, when Malcolm's popularity increased, threatening others in the Nation of Islam leadership. Tensions increased further after Malcolm returned from a pilgrimage to Mecca, making it known that his former ideas of complete separation from all white people had mellowed. This put him at odds with other leaders of the Nation of Islam, in particular Elijah Muhammad, the official head of the group.

Malcolm X was one of the first in the black community to promulgate the need for all African Americans to be proud of their heritage. He was assassinated while giving a speech on February 21, 1965. Three men from the Nation of Islam were found guilty of the crime. It was in response to his murder that the Black Arts movement was inaugurated.

Langston Hughes (1902–1967) was a black poet, novelist, and playwright. He belonged to what was called the Harlem Renaissance, a group of black artists who preceded the artists of the Black Arts movement by several decades. After graduating from Lincoln University, Hughes moved to Harlem, where he spent the rest of his adult life.

The topic of much of Hughes's writing was the lives of ordinary, working-class black people. Ahead of his time, he also promoted the idea that black people should be conscious of their heritage and culture and proud of their race.

CRITICAL OVERVIEW

"The Idea of Ancestry" has been published two of the poet's collections, *Poems from Prison* (1968) and *The Essential Etheridge Knight* (1986), which was honored with the 1987 American Book Award. The poem has also been included in many anthologies. In a review of *The Essential Etheridge Knight*, Raymond R. Patterson, writing for the *American Book Review*, states that this collection of poems will "show that Knight's place in an Afro-American literary tradition cannot be described simply." This is because Knight's poetry is difficult to define. For example, writes Patterson, Knight's "themes of family and black identity addressed in 'The Idea of Ancestry'" are contradicted in some of Knight's other poems. Patterson does not find this disconcerting but is merely pointing out the poet's depth.

Sanford Pinsker published an interview with Knight in *Black American Literature Forum*. As a way of introducing the poet, Pinsker writes: "Etheridge Knight is the kind of poet who gives poetry a good name." Pinsker praises Knight's first collection, referring to it as "still the hardest-hitting, funniest, and wisest example of the [prison poem] genre." Pinsker appreciates the natural language of Knight's poems, emphasizing "that aesthetic which keeps its faith with the language men actually speak and the raw power of their stories."

Jean Anaporte-Easton, reviewing Knight's poetry for *Callaloo*, finds that "one of the main supports" of Knight's poetics is this: "When the poet speaks from his own specific experience as honestly as possible . . . he becomes most universal, most understandable, not only to those who share his background and experience, but to others."

Writing in *Hollins Critic*, Howard Nelson describes "The Idea of Ancestry" as "a field of emotions grounded in concrete situations and images." Nelson adds, "The idea may remain unparaphrasable, but when Knight has finished his poem it has become a solid, subtle, moving thing."

Writing for *Black American Literature Forum*, Patricia Liggins Hill finds that Knight's poetry functions "as a liberating force. Since slavery has been a crucial reality in Black history, much of Knight's poetry focuses on a modern kind of enslavement, imprisonment, and searches for and discovers ways in which a person can be free while incarcerated." Reflecting on "The Idea of Ancestry," Liggins states that "the prosaic quality of the first section of the poem is striking. For the most part, it takes on the narrative qualities of an autobiography and flows with long, rolling, sonorous lines controlled by the breath of the poet."

CRITICISM

Joyce Hart

Hart is a published writer and creative writing teacher. In this essay, she examines the different types of spaces that Knight portrays in his poem "The Idea of Ancestry."

"The Idea of Ancestry" consists of a lot of spaces. Some of the spaces represent freedom. Others cause pain. There are places in this poem

WHAT DO I READ NEXT?

- *Belly Song and Other Poems* (1973) was Knight's second collection of poems. Howard Nelson, writing for *Hollins Critic*, claims that this book of poems has the perfect title. The poems contained in this collection, Nelson writes, represent two of Knight's strengths as a writer: "powerful feeling, which centers in the belly, the gut; and music, a vital, full-breathed music that demonstrates steadily that the poet is in touch with old, elemental sources of poetic energy."

- Bill Aguado and Richard Newirth worked with teenagers through the WriterCorps to put together the collection *Paint Me Like I Am: Teen Poems* (2003). In this book, teens explore the challenges they face, such as racial issues in a multicultural world, drug abuse, and the development of a strong self-awareness. Critics found this book to contain open and honest emotional expressions.

- *The Essential Etheridge Knight* (1986) is a collection of Knight's best poems from his first three books as well as some poems that had not been previously published. Knight won the 1987 American Book Award for this collection.

- For an introduction to some of the artists of the Black Arts movement, read Gloria House's *A Different Image: The Legacy of Broadside Press* (2004). This anthology includes works by Gwendolyn Brooks, Sonia Sanchez, Knight, and others.

- Useni Eugene Perkins's *Poetry from the Masters: The Black Arts Movement* (2008) provides young-adult readers with a background of the artists involved in this movement. The book offers brief biographies as well as a discussion of each author's work and how that work influenced the literary world.

- Langston Hughes had a strong effect on many of the poets and authors involved in the Black Arts movement. In *The Collected Poems of Langston Hughes* (1995), the publishers have put together the first collection of the poet's work. The poems are listed chronologically, providing the reader with a historical view of the poet's development.

- Gwendolyn Brooks was a prominent author from the Black Arts movement. She became the first African American to win the Pulitzer Prize. The prize was awarded in 1950 for her second collection of poems, *Annie Allen*. She also won the National Book Foundation Medal for Distinguished Contribution to American Letters in 1994. To gain an appreciation for her work, read her *Selected Poems* published by Perennial Classics in 1999.

- A 1966 young-adult novel that explores cultural and spiritual identity, *The Fixer*, by Bernard Malamud, is based loosely on the life of a turn-of-the-twentieth century Russian Jew, who while a prisoner, uses the time to reconsider his Jewishness.

---

in which the speaker openly mentions these spaces and the emotions they create inside of him. In other parts of the poem, the uneasiness, or sometimes the pleasure, of these spaces is only hinted at. But when readers keep the context of the poem in mind and explore the poem more closely, the tension of these spaces becomes most apparent. At times, readers will see wide spaces

that seem to go on indefinitely. At other points in this poem, they will read about spaces that appear to be very narrow and confining. The spaces are sometimes physical. There are also psychological spaces that can only be felt. Sometimes the speaker focuses on the objects that lay beyond the spaces. At other times, the emphasis is on the space itself. Whether expanding or

WHETHER EXPANDING OR CONTRACTING, VISIBLE OR HIDDEN, THE SPACES REPRESENTED IN KNIGHT'S POEM ARE ESSENTIAL TO ITS EMOTIONAL DEPTH."

contracting, visible or hidden, the spaces represented in Knight's poem are essential to its emotional depth.

Patricia Liggins Hill, in her essay "'The Violent Space': The Function of the New Black Aesthetic in Etheridge Knight's Prison Poetry," even states that Knight himself becomes what she terms "the violent space." She argues that the spaces are both literal, as in his cell, and figurative, as in his sense of ancestry and the separation he feels from his relatives—the violent space. Hill's interpretation of the spaces suggests that "'time' and 'space' have traveled full circle in the poem—back to the present condition of the poet in his cell."

In the first line of "The Idea of Ancestry," the speaker defines the space in which he is living by pointing out that he is in a cell. He is a prisoner, spending most of the hours of his day in a small, confined space. In addition to being narrow and confined, this space offers no privacy. It is open for inspection any time a guard or fellow prisoner happens to walk by. So the speaker cannot fully claim any of this space as his although it is now his home. And for the duration of this poem, except when the speaker travels through his memories and imagination, this prison space provides the setting of his poem.

Readers can better imagine the tiny space that the speaker has been sentenced to by listening to the details that the poem provides. First, one knows that the space inside the cell is divided. On one side of the cell is the speaker's bed. One can assume that this bed is no wider than a single mattress. Though the speaker mentions that he spreads his body across this bed, the size of the mattress cannot provide much space for the full extension of his arms and legs. Like the space of the cell that contains it, the bed is necessarily narrow and therefore limited. In other words, this is definitely not a motel room

with a queen-sized bed. A prison cell provides only the minimum comforts and space.

Across the cell from the bed, the speaker describes a gray concrete wall. Readers might not know the exact size but are told that the wall is big enough to hold the forty-seven photographs that the speaker has placed there. In some ways, this display of photographs provides a sense of expanded space. The pictures offer a warm, open place, almost like a window, through which the speaker emotionally escapes his cell's confinement. It is also upon these photographs that he projects his thoughts and emotions. But the wall is also cold and hard and represents the speaker's lack of freedom. The wall surrounds the speaker and defines the narrow space in which he lives. Thus, the wall with its photographic exhibit both symbolizes expansion and creates the speaker's confinement. Although the wall offers space for the speaker to explore his memories, it also keeps the figurative waters—the stream the speaker refers to as his symbolic mode of travel—dammed up and stagnant. The space on the wall offers the speaker a place to dream about his relatives but disallows him the space through which he might travel to go home and physically reunite with his family.

As the speaker lies on his bed, he stares at the family photographs from across the space between his bed and the wall. This space in between is both narrow and indefinitely wide, depending on how one looks at it. The physical space between the speaker and the wall of family pictures could probably be traversed in no more than a few steps. But the psychological space between the speaker and what the photographs represent—his mother, siblings, aunts, uncles, and cousins—is almost insurmountable. The speaker lives in a different world from his family members. He implies that they are decent folks, making honest livings. He describes himself, on the other hand, as a criminal. In comparison to the small space in which he lives, the space where his family lives seems limitless. Their space is sprawled out upon the hills and gullies of Mississippi. His space is contracted, and this is so not merely in a physical sense.

The speaker's psychological space also differs from that of his relatives. His is polluted and constricted both by his crimes and by his dependence on drugs. As he examines his family through the pictures on his wall, he recalls his last visit home. Reflecting on these memories, he realizes that even when he was near enough to physically embrace his family members, he was not really close to them. Even when the physical space between them was all but negligible, a psychological space kept him at a distance. He might have laughed with them, danced with them, drunk with them, but he could not truly be with them. The drugs that his mind and body craved had created an impenetrable psychological space between them. Though he tried to bridge that space by touching them and enjoying his presence among them, his addiction kept pulling him away. He was dependent on feeding his habit, and when he ran out of drugs, his addiction once again intervening. The speaker confesses that his addiction to drugs had even created a space inside of him. Just as he could not bridge the space between himself and his family, he could not close the gap between who he remembered he used to be, free of his addiction, and who he had become through his drug habit.

Many of these spaces in the speaker's life made him uneasy. The spaces also made his family uncomfortable. Space can be defined in many different ways. In some instances, space can represent the unknown, which can be unsettling to many people. The speaker emphasizes this point in the case of the missing uncle who shared the speaker's name. This man had been away from the family for most of his life. He left his family as a youth and never returned. No one knew anything about this uncle's adult life. They did not know who he had become but only had memories of him up to the age of fifteen. They did not even know if he was still alive. This was disturbing for them: they could not emotionally release him since he was part of the family, but they did not know him well enough to fully embrace him. The speaker focuses on this uncle for a reason. One might conclude that the speaker felt that he, in many ways, resembled this missing uncle. When the speaker recalls his return to his family for the previous year's reunion, he mentions that he almost was able to reintroduce himself to his real self. This implies that he also was almost able to reintroduce himself to his family. But if the speaker does not know who he is, then his family cannot know him. They might remember him from his youth, but like the missing uncle, he is all but unrecognizable in his adult wardrobe. The passing years have changed him, but more than that, the drugs have altered him, making him unpredictable and therefore unknown. This is where the uneasiness

seeps in. Unlike the missing uncle, the speaker appeared at the previous year's reunion. But even though there was no physical space between the speaker and his family, his relatives did not recognize who he had become, creating psychological distance.

In the second part of the poem, the speaker talks about the time before he was incarcerated and the space that this freedom allowed him. He was able to travel across the country to visit his family, to eat with them and laugh with them. But that wide-open space contracted when the speaker's sense of freedom went too far. Even his freedom had boundaries, and he dared to cross them. He stole money from people and broke into their homes in order to feed his addiction. So his space was further confined, and he was sent to jail.

Now when he feels his grandfathers calling to him to come home, the speaker cannot follow his instincts and return to Mississippi to see them. He cannot reunite with the family he craves. He can only visit them through the photographs that hang on the wall across the space of his cell. Readers can sense his longing to walk away from that narrow space. But all the speaker can do is pace back and forth, his feet measuring the confined space in which he is stuck. As he paces, he continues to stare at those familiar faces. The more he thinks about his family, the more he begins to see more spaces. This is the space that Hill spoke of when she referred to "the violent space"—"a vastness of space" that he cannot reach across to be with his family or contribute to the ancestry. With the final lines of the poem, the speaker tries to merge with his ancestors. If he cannot be with them, he can at least convince himself that the space between him and them does not exist. He tries to persuade himself that no miles exist between him and them because they are all one and the same. But then he stumbles upon a new space. This space is very sad because it appears even wider than any space before it. He sees this space as infinite emptiness because it is about the future, which belongs to children, and he has none. If one were to imagine a drawing of a family tree, the growth of the speaker's limb would be stunted. It does not extend beyond him. He is alone on that limb. Beyond it lies only empty space.

Source: Joyce Hart, Critical Essay on "The Idea of Ancestry," in *Poetry for Students*, Gale, Cengage Learning, 2011.

David Seelow

In the following excerpt, Seelow describes how Knight establishes the boundary between the prison and the world in "The Idea of Ancestry."

In turning to black poet Etheridge Knight, the themes of grief, fatherhood, and fierceness are radically transformed. Grief is a given in Knight's world. The reality of imprisonment necessitates separation from loved ones. Bly's desire to return men to the forest is nothing but a romantic daydream to the prisoner, and the cell is hardly a domestic image. The central fact of Knight's (1986) poetry is enclosure:

> Taped to the wall of my cell are 47 pictures:
> 47 black
> faces: my father, mother, grandmothers (1
> dead), grand-
> fathers (both dead), brothers, sisters, uncles,
> aunts,
> cousins (1st & 2nd), nieces and nephews.
> They stare
> across the space at me sprawling on my
> bunk. I know
> their dark eyes, they know mine. I know
> their style,
> they know mine. I am all of them, they are
> all of me;
> they are farmers, I am a thief, I am me, they
> are thee.

"The Idea of Ancestry" establishes the boundary between the prison and the world. What sustains the poet is family, which for Knight is extended and even tribal. Further, he shares his name and identity with eight relatives. The "I" is always communal, and, paradoxically, the poet is never, even in prison, isolated. The entire family, therefore, is enclosed.

The family exists in the larger prison of American society, and the walls of the larger prison, as Knight states, are those of racism. The poet speaks, then, for an ancestral heritage. Nonetheless, he calls the above poem "The Idea of Ancestry." Why? The counterpoint lyric clarifies the title's harsh irony:

> This yr there is a gray stone wall damming
> my stream, and when
> the falling leaves stir my genes, I pace my cell
> or flop on my bunk
> and stare at 47 black faces across the space. I
> am all of them,
> they are all of me, I am me, they are thee,
> and I have no sons
> to float in the space between.

This lyric evokes the pain of imprisonment, but without pity. He simply calls attention to the reality of familial separation and its impact on the black man. The poet will bear no children, a situation repeating the reality of slavery and its forced separation of the father from his family. Etheridge is cut off from the future, and consequently, the past, making ancestry only an idea.

Source: David Seelow, "Loud Men: The Poetic Visions of Robert Bly, Ice Cube, and Etheridge Knight," in *Journal of Men's Studies: A Scholarly Journal about Men and Masculinities*, Vol. 6, No. 2, Winter 1998, pp. 149–68.

Jean Anaporte-Easton

In the following excerpt, Easton claims that Knight's contributions to American poetry lie in his clear, direct language that is comprehensible to people who are not critics.

While collecting material for a volume of statements on poetry by the late poet, Etheridge Knight, I ran across a transcript of a substantial interview that Charles H. Rowell had conducted with Knight sometime between mid 1973 and late 1975. When I telephoned Rowell to find where his interview had been published, I discovered instead that, for the past twenty-five years, the interview had been lost. Lost, that is, to Rowell. Apparently, shortly after Rowell transcribed the interview, he sent a copy to Knight requesting some revisions. Knight never made the revisions, but he kept the interview among his papers until he sold them to the Ward M. Canaday Center at the University of Toledo. Since Knight tried to earn a living from his poetry, and since his identity was crucially connected with his being a poet, why, so early in his career, did he put aside the opportunity for attention that publication would have attracted? The answer lies perhaps in the note Rowell penned to Knight at the end of the manuscript: "My tape broke before I was able to get this part of the interview. Please complete this and make it sound like the conclusion to the entire interview." Rowell is, in other words, simply asking Knight to write a conclusion to the interview.

All writers sitting down to a blank page experience a moment in which the blank page reflects their own emptiness—a fear of having nothing to say or of being inadequate to the task of saying it. But Knight's frequent references to emptiness and fear in his poetry, other writings, and this interview indicate a larger struggle. In fact Louis McKee organized an entire interview

> KNIGHT'S CONTRIBUTIONS TO AMERICAN POETRY LIE IN HIS ENDURING 'POPULISM' AS HE CALLED IT. HIS LANGUAGE IS CLEAR AND DIRECT, UNDERSTANDABLE TO PEOPLE WHO ARE NOT WRITERS AND CRITICS."

with Knight and the poet Elizabeth McKim around Knight's resistance to writing a brief introduction to the poem, "The Idea of Ancestry," for Steven Berg's book, *Singular Voices*. Knight offered two answers: having to write something felt like an assignment and sitting down to write felt like being back in prison.

Though Knight tells later interviewers he wrote more outside of prison, he tells Rowell that it is no easier to write in the outside world "because in all the real senses I am still in prison." Ironically, much of Knight's finished writing seems to have taken place while he was in prison or during stays in jail or rehabilitation centers. Furthermore, it was in prison that he first defined himself as a poet. From the poems available to us now, over half of those Knight published, and the majority of his best poems, were written by 1973. He had been out of prison only five years and had spent at least a year of that time in jail and drug and alcohol rehab programs. Just as a prison with ribbon wire and chainlink fences might be easier to deal with than the invisible prison of cultural assumptions and values, so might it be easier to confront and cope with the finite emptiness of solitary confinement than an infinite interior emptiness.

As an adolescent in Kentucky, Knight ran away from home repeatedly, and at seventeen forged his parents' signature to enlist for Korea. Sometime between leaving Korea and returning to Indianapolis, Indiana, where his family had moved, he became addicted to heroin. His twenties were spent on the streets, doing and dealing drugs, pimping, and stealing until his arrest and conviction for armed robbery in 1960. Such was his rage that prison officials labeled him an incorrigible and transferred him from the Indiana State Reformatory to the Indiana State Prison in Michigan City. He was so

angry, he told Art Powers, that he had no memory of his first few months at the prison. But then, realizing prison could destroy him, he pulled himself together, read voraciously, and committed himself to poetry.

His first poem, a tribute to Dinah Washington, was published in Hoyt Fuller's *Negro Digest* in 1965. Poets no less prestigious than Gwendolyn Brooks and Dudley Randall visited him at Michigan City. His first book, *Poems from Prison*, was published by Randall's Broadside Press in 1968, while Knight was still in prison. He corresponded with Haki Madhubuti and Sonia Sanchez, poets active in the Black Arts Movement, and married Sanchez in 1969 upon his release. He left prison already a major spokesman for the Black Aesthetic, along with Amiri Baraka, Clarence Major, and Haki Madhubuti.

Outside the prison walls, success carried Knight forward faster than he was able to move without losing his balance. As he confesses in his April 5, 1970, letter to Dudley Randall, he was using heroin again by about August 1969. Knight's sense of failure in this letter is so thorough and his personal losses so great that, in spite of his optimism each time he returned to a rehab center or hospital, he may have lost confidence that he really could change. Nevertheless, while he dropped in and out of jails and hospitals, honors accumulated.

. . . In talking to Rowell about his identity as a poet, Knight's stance is one of frankness. But his frankness is disarming as well as open. He tells Rowell that he's drinking at the moment and that he's aware of the consequences, but then he says it's no easier to write outside prison because "in all the real senses, I am still in prison." The implication is that, despite drinking, he is writing as much as he did in prison and that he is imprisoned more by racism than by his addiction. In the last months of his life, however, he acknowledges that he wrote more in prison: While in the joint he had worked at his desk seven or eight hours a day—sometimes by the light of a fish tank. Once outside, it had been harder to sit at a desk; there had been the distractions of getting and traveling to gigs; and as the years went by, he had written less and less. Knight's consistently dichotomous description of himself as a poet reflects that reality. On the back of his first book, he writes, "I died in 1960 from a prison sentence and poetry brought me back to life." Yet he tells Rowell, "If I don't poet, then I am a thief because that is what I was doing before I was poeting." The use of the present tense during a time when he was giving readings, holding posts as a visiting writer, and publishing books is a red flag. His options are always two extremes—death or poetry, thief or poet—and they always co-exist in the present. He writes in an unfinished poem, "Junky's Song," "I am not one, I am not whole; / A war, me against my / self / (and THEM against me too) /. . . ." The outside world might be a prison, but Knight imprisons himself as well.

Like many of us, when he feels in control, as when he offers Healy advice or includes him in a book, he is confident; but when he feels threatened, as in the fight with McAnally, he tightens up. In prison, whether he believed in his role or not, he was regarded as the spokesman for the African-American inmates. Prison is also where he was first recognized as a poet. He wrote a column for the prison newspaper; he wrote letters for illiterate inmates; he told toasts; and, if prodded, he showed his poems. Powers claims Knight was regarded among friends as an "arrogant sonofabitch," although Powers found him to have the gentle, easy-going heart of a poet. Powers can't resist adding, nonetheless, that Knight could be "mean and petty at times, out of sorts with everyone and everything around him . . ." (117). Whatever the men may have thought, Knight apparently felt no pressure to win their approval. Young prisoners wrote him letters attacking his politics and he replied with more of the same, no equivocation. Regardless of the pain, prison may have been the place where Knight experienced most clearly who he was (see also McCullough, 4).

Knight told the interviewer Ron Price that his "major metaphor" was prison (168). Through his last reading, Knight continued to include the early poems about his prison experience and at least one prison joke. He frequently referred to prison in his conversation. Prison stood for emptiness and aloneness. Yet Knight writes in letters from the Bridgeport jail descriptions of the jail sounds at night and of a convict called "Country"—legendary in the way that Hard Rock was legendary—with a poignancy that approaches romanticization.

If Knight's major metaphor was prison, his metaphor for art was freedom (Price). Freedom stood for love, for reaching out, being at the center of life. Yet whenever Knight reached

freedom, he let go. A previously unpublished poem, "I Am a Tree, My Lovers Fly to and from Me," expresses both emptiness and fear. As in "Belly Song," the individual lover faced with his beloved falls back into the state of aloneness which love could assuage. The pain of that aloneness is also an alienation from himself, and we are back at "Junky's Song": "A war, me against my / self / . . ." Instead of wholeness there was the "hole" of solitary confinement or the emptiness of looking within triggered by physical freedom. The love of self that he speaks of to Healy and Randall is something he appears never really to have learned. Lacking that love or too vulnerable to counter the pain, Knight may not have been able to, as he exhorts Healy, "write, write, write, write," letting the truths about who he was "spill" through the typewriter.

Knight's contributions to American poetry lie in his enduring "populism" as he called it. His language is clear and direct, understandable to people who are not writers and critics. He improvised on blues, folk rhythms and folk narratives to explore his own experiences and contemporary lore (Tracy 9–10 and Hill). To the subject matter and language of American poetry, he added the prison experience and street slang. The strength of his best poems comes from the humility with which he told the truths about his life. His humility and his loving inclusion of whomever attended his readings enabled people who had never shared his experiences to recognize themselves. In his times of confidence, he knew that we all shared these truths—we all lie; we all desire and fear love; we are all incomplete, longing for the freedom of wholeness yet sometimes lacking the courage to reach.

Source: Jean Anaporte-Easton, "Etheridge Knight: Poet and Prisoner: An Introduction," in *Callaloo*, Vol. 19, No. 4, Autumn 1996, pp. 941–46.

Myles Raymond Hurd

In the following excerpt, Hurd states that Walt Whitman's influence on Knight's style is most evident in "The Idea of Ancestry," his best-known and most frequently anthologized work.

This "double eye," which evidences Walt Whitman's strong influence on Knight's style, is most prominent in "The Idea of Ancestry," the black Southerner's best-known and most frequently anthologized work. Often hailed as "one of the best poems that [have] been written about the Afro-American conception of family history and human interconnection," it underlines Knight's discovery of a "particularly effective combination of the vocabulary of the drug culture, of black slang, and of concrete images to make the idea of ancestry come alive" (Lumpkin 204). Moreover, in identifying it as the "best poem of Black cultural history" (24), Paul Mariah reminds us of a deeper dimension of its impact. Indeed, Patricia Liggins Hill observes that the "form of the poem as well as the idea of ancestry in the poem also represents the problem of ancestral lineage for the Black race as whole. Many Blacks, such as Knight himself, can...trace their ancestral lineage back [only] two or three generations because of the conditions of Black slavery which were imposed on them" (118); analyzing Knight's effort from this broad historical purview, Agnes Stein, in *The Uses of Poetry*, "regards this poem as especially important for those such as Blacks 'whose history as a group has been denied within a larger culture'" (Hill 118). Yet, its meaning is in no sense restricted to a race-specific identification because in Knight's lines readers of various ethnological stripes can easily recognize descriptions of similar relatives from their own genealogies. In "The Idea of Ancestry" the yoked perspective of familial history and racial heritage allows Knight to focus on photographs of his Corinthian other relatives to establish a bond of intimacy between himself and them as he draws on a black prison argot to enhance his Whitmanesque technique. The three stanzas composing the poem's first section register a strong emotional charge for his multiracial readership in that they highlight the urgency of his need to "claim kin" with blood-related men and women he cannot speak or shake hands with because of the restrictions of his prison cell:

> Taped to the wall of my cell are 47 pictures: 47 black
> faces: my father, mother, grandmothers (1 dead), grand-
> fathers (both dead), brothers, sisters, uncles, aunts,
> cousins (1st and 2nd), nieces, and nephews. They stare
> across the space at me sprawling on my bunk. I know
> their dark eyes, they know mine. I know their style,
> they know mine. I am all of them, they are all of me;

> REFERENCES TO BURIAL SITES, EGG-LAYING SALMON, BARE FEET, A PHYSICIAN DESCRIBED AS A 'CROAKER,' AND A GLANCE AT A GRANDMOTHER IN THE SHADOW OF DARKNESS HINT AT A FIXITY OF DISTANCE ARGUING AGAINST THE POSSIBILITY OF A FUTURE COMMUNION."

> they are farmers, I am a thief, I am me, they are thee.

> I have at one time or another been in love with my mother,
> 1 grandmother, 2 sisters, 2 aunts (1 went to the asylum),
> and 5 cousins, I am now in love with a 7-year-old niece
> (she sends me letters written in large block print, and
> her picture is the only one that smiles at me).

> I have the same name as 1 grandfather, 3 cousins, 3 nephews,
> and 1 uncle, The uncle disappeared when he was 15, just took
> off and caught a freight (they say). He's discussed each year
> when the family has a reunion, he causes uneasiness in
> the clan, he is an empty space, My father's mother, who is 93
> and who keeps the Family Bible with everybody's birth dates
> (and death dates) in it, always mentions him, There is no
> place in her Bible for "whereabouts unknown."

Aware that the "soothing, sweet-flowing rhythms in Part I reflect the poet's reminiscences about his relationships with his relatives—memories that are filled with warmth, gentleness, regret and nostalgia" (Hill 117), readers also note that the poetic situation is one with which they can easily identify. In cataloging the men and women in the photos, Knight alludes to the similarities between himself and them, bonds manifesting themselves as male and distaff links between himself and his family's oldest members, mentally ill closet "skeletons," namesakes, cousins in the same age bracket, and a favorite niece. As we follow the branches of this Corinth-based family tree, we see that the controlling images of love and distance dominate the lines. Whereas the poet sets himself apart from his family's economic background—"they are farmers/I am a thief" (line 8)—he imagistically places himself within their midst in the reunion that the forty-seven pictures symbolically create: "I am all of them, they are all of me" (line 8).

Even in his self-classification as his family's incorrigible miscreant (and potential outcast), he never obliterates the connection with all these relations, including the uncle whose name still appears in the homestead Bible though his whereabouts remain unknown. Thus, Knight establishes another bond between himself and his African-American roots through a "black sheep"/"lost sheep" association. The first stanza's repetition of "know" accentuates the poet's spiritual communion with the other members of his clan, and "taped"—the poem's first word—directs our attention to adhesiveness, an important element of distanced love. Additionally, when Knight refers to the mostly unsmiling faces of his ancestors and mentions the "large block print" (line 12) characterizing his niece's penmanship, we concentrate on the image of his cell, an image sharpening the reality of his incarceration. And the mixture of words and numerals within the lines further emphasizes his estrangement from these Alcorn County blacks because of his heavy prison sentence.

In the poem's second section Knight enumerates contrasts between the past and the present as he shifts from a predominantly spatial to a largely temporal modality:

> Each fall the graves of my grandfathers call me, the brown
> hills and red gullies of Mississippi send out their electric
> messages, galvanizing my genes. Last yr /
> like a salmon quitting
> the cold ocean—leaping and bucking up his birthstream / I
> hitchhiked my way from LA with 16 caps in my pocket and a
> monkey on my back. And I almost kicked it with the kinfolks.
> I walked barefooted in my grandmother's backyard/I smelled the old
> land and the woods / I sipped cornwhiskey from fruit jars with the men

> I flirted with the women/I had a ball till the caps ran out
> and my habit came down. That night I looked at my grandmother
> and split/my guts were screaming for junk/ but I was almost
> contented/I had almost caught up with me.
> (The next day in Memphis I cracked a croaker's crib for a fix.)

> This yr there is a gray stone wall damming my stream, and when
> the falling leaves stir my genes, I pace my cell or flop on my bunk
> and stare at 47 black faces across the space, I am all of them,
> they are all of me, I am me, they are thee, and I have no children
> to float in the space between. (12–13)

Besides illustrating Knight's trademark virgules and frequent alliteration, these lines conjoin different patterns of imagery to underscore his geographical and spiritual remove from the blood-related environists of "the brown hills and red gullies of Mississippi" (lines 22–23). Significantly, one group of images is (perhaps unconsciously) associated with death and ties in with the poet's description of his literary creativity as a resurrection; the images simultaneously suggest that his separation from his family will be either of long term or permanent. References to burial sites, egg-laying salmon, bare feet, a physician described as a "croaker," and a glance at a grandmother in the shadow of darkness hint at a fixity of distance arguing against the possibility of a future communion. Moreover, in describing his arrival at a past Corinth family reunion by hitchhiking from California, Knight stresses the force calling him not to his grandfathers, but to their graves, which, in black folkloric terms, are said to sink when "drawing" an ill relative to his (or her) final resting place.

Juxtaposed against these death-related images is a second cluster emphasizing Knight's recollected sentient awareness of the persons and objects around him in his Southern stomping grounds. He smells the old land and woods, sips whiskey from mason jars, listens to the conversation of other Knight men, walks without shoes in his grandmother's backyard, and touches accommodating, unspoken-for women.

A third set of images, steeped in the language of the drug subculture, polarizes the two other clusters by pointing to the difference between what Knight was and what he has become. The sixteen cocaine-filled plastic vials that he brings with him from Los Angeles testify to his having a serious addiction, and his joy at the recalled family gathering is brought up short "when the caps ran out" (line 30) and his "guts" subsequently "were screaming for junk" (line 32). And nearness to forebears gives way to distance from them as he breaks into a Memphis doctor's home the next day for more illegal drugs or money to buy them. In the poem's final stanza the "gray stone wall damming [Knight's] stream" (line 35) emerges as both a time marker and a spatial divider. Locked up in the prison, the poet is unable to heed the beckoning to his hometown when autumn leaves once again fall.

Source: Myles Raymond Hurd, "The Corinth Connection in Etheridge Knight's 'The Idea of Ancestry,'" in *Notes on Mississippi Writers*, Vol. 25, No. 1, January 1993, pp. 1–9.

Jim Dempsey

In the following article, Etheridge Knight is remembered as a man of immense complexity who had a way of taking what many would consider the negative elements of our society and creating in them a sense of humanity, but not sentimentality, and never exonerating them.

America lost a poet Sunday when Etheridge Knight died in Indianapolis, and Worcester, which he knew, will feel a little of the sadness and sense of loss that comes with his death.

Being a successful poet in America rarely includes financial success, so it shouldn't be a surprise that even though Knight was a nationally known, award-winning poet whose works were widely anthologized, he died poor. His last home was "the Triple Nickel," a building of subsidized apartments in Indianapolis occupied mostly by the elderly. The nickname comes from its address—555 Massachusetts Ave.

Knight had been sick for a while. In November 1988, he was struck by a hit-and-run driver in Philadelphia. He was treated at the veterans hospital in Indianapolis, and not long after, cancer was discovered.

TRIBUTE FOR KNIGHT

In January, poets from all over the country held a tribute for Knight in Indianapolis to raise money for the ailing poet. Knight used to earn his living from poetry readings and workshops but, weakened by the cancer, he had done fewer

and fewer readings over the last two years. The tribute was "the biggest single literary event in memory around here," said *Indianapolis Star* columnist Dan Carpenter.

Knight came to Worcester in 1976 at the invitation of Worcester poet Fran Quinn. That was the first of many trips to this city, and the beginning of an association that lasted until a couple of years ago when he gave his last reading here.

Knight once wrote, "I died in Korea from a shrapnel wound and narcotics resurrected me. I died in 1960 from a prison sentence, and poetry brought me back to life." He wrote his first book, *Poems From Prison*, in an Indiana state prison while serving time for armed robbery. After his release in 1968 he published more books, won various awards including the Shelley Poetry Prize and the American Book Award, and served as poet-in-residence at several universities.

IMMENSELY COMPLEX

Knight seems to have been a man of immense complexity. On the one hand there was the heroin addiction, on the other his great talent. He could be disarmingly warm, but extremely hard to live with. "He was a great guy but he could drive you crazy," said Assumption College English Professor Michael True. "You never knew what was going to happen."

Quinn, who now splits his time between Worcester and Butler University in Indianapolis, where he teaches poetry, last spoke to Knight about three weeks ago. "He talked about his life, his poetry," Quinn said. "I was trying to get some of the facts straight. The problem with Etheridge is that there are as many rumors as there are facts about him."

Yesterday's obituary in the *Indianapolis Star* gives Knight's age as 61, but Quinn says the poet was really 59. The discrepancy, Quinn said, comes from Knight's lying about his age when he joined the Army.

"He was a stunning performer," Quinn said. "He memorized the poems, so he wasn't always looking down and they were delivered straight out. And it wasn't poetry that avoided the world. The problems you felt, he wrote about.

NEVER EXONERATED HIMSELF

"He also introduced many people to the prison scene. He had a way of taking what many would consider the negative elements of our society—prisoners—and creating a sense of humanity, but not sentimentally, and never exonerating them. He never exonerated himself. I remember once an interviewer asking him if the Korean War was to blame for his addiction. He said no. There were a lot of people shooting up in Korea, he said, but they didn't all come back and keep doing it. He didn't blame the war. He didn't blame."

One of Knight's missions was to bring poets together, and everywhere he went he tried to set up what he called the Free Peoples Poetry Workshop. The Worcester group met at Circe's, a bar on Franklin Street that is now the site of a Japanese restaurant. It was a strange place for a poetry group. The poets, declaiming their poetry and arguing about philosophy and technique in the back of the room, drew curious stares from the patrons at the bar.

"Etheridge figured that if a man is on the way to the men's room with a full kidney, and you can make him stop with a poem, you've got a good poem," Quinn said. "He started many of these groups, and every one produced somebody who won a major award."

Christopher Gilbert ran the Worcester group for five years, and went on to win the Walt Whitman Award and the Robert Frost Award. "Etheridge was a troubador, a nomad, restless," Gilbert said. "He started our group and then said to us, "OK, you take over," and he was gone.

A VERY WARM MAN

"At one time he lived in Worcester briefly, and I found him to be a warm man, very warm. His poems speak to you directly. Even though they might be handling big ideas, they are written in the language of the streets and they are accessible on first reading. They sing to you."

Michael True's favorite Knight poem is "He Sees Through Stone." "It's a prison poem about an older prisoner who watches the young men come in, and who softly teaches them how to survive in the cruelty and oppression," True said. "He has a kind of wisdom that grows out of suffering."

Warmth, survival, wisdom, suffering. Words about Knight's poems, words about his life.

Source: Jim Dempsey, "From Suffering Grew Wisdom: Winning Poet Will Be Missed," in *Telegram & Gazette* (Worcester, MA), March 13, 1991, p. A1.

> AS A BLACK POET HE STANDS IN A LIVING TRADITION OF TOAST-TELLERS, RHYMERS, AND SINGERS."

Howard Nelson

In the following excerpt, American poet and critic Nelson provides a thematic and stylistic analysis of Knight's poems.

... In the work of most poets there are certain words or images that recur regularly, in some cases obsessively. Not surprisingly in a poet who spent years in prison, one of Knight's persistent images is stone. It represents not just physical walls and imprisonment, of course; more importantly it stands for emotional barriers, insensitivity, the dead weight in the spirit that needs to be pushed away or penetrated or transformed in order for caring energies to flow again.

There are two kinds of stone in the poem: the stone walls of the prison, and the stone wall each person sets up himself. Knight picks up the slang metaphor "eats" and elaborates its suggestions: the "black cats" "circle," "flash white teeth," "snarl," have "shining muscles." But all this fierceness is a pose, a mask, ultimately another kind of stone wall erected in the name of defense. The old man leaning in the sun against actual stone is not impressed by the posturing. He understands and penetrates it: "he smiles/he knows"—knows the vulnerability that lives behind it. And somehow, the poem suggests, he is consequently a reassuring force, an outer presence who is also an inner presence, a kind of steady witness and companion to the hidden life the self lives within walls within walls.

... While doing eight years (1960–68) in Indiana State Prison on a drug-related armed robbery charge, Etheridge Knight turned to poetry. Within the bleakness of steel bars and concrete walls, the frustration, immobility, rage, fear, and loneliness of prison life, and the long stretches of prison time, Knight twisted the space and created poems of remarkable force and clarity. This work was published in 1968, while Knight was still incarcerated, by Dudley

Randall's Broadside Press as a chapbook titled simply, *Poems from Prison*. This slender book was one of several important additions to the tradition of prison writing to come out of the sixties. (Another, overlapping contribution was an anthology Knight edited, published by Pathfinder Press, called *Black Voices from Prison*, which contained in addition to Knight's poems a number of valuable prose pieces, by himself and others.) Beyond that, *Poems from Prison* was, as Gwendolyn Brooks said in her extremely concise and penetrating preface, "a major announcement." In terms of poetry, both in the context of the black poetic explosion of those years and of American poetry as a whole, an important new voice was making itself known. It was poetry that came out of painful experience, but instead of any shrillness or self-pity, there was a boldness, a solidness, that suggested deep reservoirs of strength.

In 1973 Broadside brought out a second collection by Knight, *Belly Song*. The title was well-chosen, because it identified precisely the two outstanding qualities of Knight's art: powerful feeling, which centers in the belly, the gut; and music, a vital, full-breathed music that demonstrates steadily that the poet is in touch with old, elemental sources of poetic energy.

Now Houghton Mifflin has brought out *Born of a Woman*, which brings together virtually all of the poems from the earlier books and a good deal of more recent material. It isn't a thick book for nearly twenty years' work, and it is no doubt uneven. But it contains a number of poems—"The Idea of Ancestry,""The Violent Space,""For Freckle-Faced Gerald,""As You Leave Me," and "Ilu, the Talking Drum" would certainly be among them—which should become permanent entries in the ledger of American poetry, should "lodge themselves in a place where they will be hard to get rid of." As a total volume, too, *Born of a Woman* is a moving and life-enhancing book, recording the motions of a spirit that is torn and frayed but resilient and persistently loving. Through the qualities of life it contains and the qualities of its art, it describes a victory over desolation, against the odds.

. . . What keeps us alive? In or out of prison, one answer is other people. "We must love one another or die," as Auden put it. Knight has always been sure to acknowledge this. In the preface to the *Black Voices from Prison*, anthology, he acknowledged "Gwendolyn Brooks,

Sonia Sanchez, Dudley Randall, and Don L. Lee: black poets whose love and words cracked these walls." In *Born of a Woman*, he gives a list that has grown to over forty people he feels indebted to.

In a way, Knight's poetry itself is another form of acknowledgment. People, relationships between and among people, are his compelling theme; it is present in nearly all his work in one form or another. I want to follow this thread in talking about Knight's poetry.

Another strong group is the poems that deal with family. Some of these take a sort of ritual form—words spoken for important events, such as a birth ("On the Birth of a Black/Baby/Boy") or an escape from death ("Another Poem for Me—after Recovering from an O.D."). There are straight-forward elegies, such as "The Bones of My Father," and anecdotes, as in the warm, low-key "Talking in the Woods with Karl Amorelli." Also within this group are two poems which, rightfully, have usually been among those representing Knight in anthologies: "The Idea of Ancestry" and "The Violent Space."

"The Idea of Ancestry" is a poem about what it means to belong to a family—not just a nuclear family, but a large weaving of people that spreads out to include several branches and generations—and what it feels like to be isolated from it. The poem is in two parts. It begins with the poet lying on his prison bunk gazing at the forty-seven photographs of relatives he has taped to his wall. Looking at them, he gives a series of small catalogues of connectedness: "I know/their dark eyes, they know mine. I know their style, they know mine. . ./I have at one time or another been in love with my mother, / 1 grandmother, 2 sisters, 2 aunts (I went to the asylum). . ./I have the same name as 1 grandfather, 3 cousins, 3 nephews,/and 1 uncle. . . ." The pictures and his thoughts make him feel part of a vital human flow—the ongoing, complex, living thing a family that has a sense of itself can be—but at the same time sharpens his loneliness. This is particularly so because the uncle at the end of the last list, it turns out, has long since vanished: "disappeared when he was 15, just took/off and caught a freight (they say)." He is at once a part of the family and "an empty space." Year after year he has been discussed by the family, especially by the ninety-three-year-old matriarch of the clan who is the keeper of the family Bible and the symbol of family roots and tradition. "There is no/ place in her Bible for 'where-abouts unknown.'" The uncle's absence is a presence when the family gathers, and the poet, alone in his cell, ripped out of the fabric by a prison sentence, is haunted by the feeling that he has more in common with his uncle than a name.

The second section of the poem is a flashback to a family reunion which took place a year earlier. Both parts of the poem are set in fall, the season when the poet's yearning to get back to the family is always strongest—appropriate because of Thanksgiving as well as more subtle mortal reasons. With his characteristic vivid conciseness, Knight describes the longing to get back among family and family places—as basic as the instinctual drive of a migrating salmon—and the pleasure and ease of finally being on home ground again. But this time too he was pulled away from the family, in this case by a narcotics habit which forced him to leave and in turn led to his imprisonment. Then the poem returns to the present and the cell with its silent "47 black faces." The poet's thoughts have made him very restless: he paces, flops down on his bed—torn by his double sense of connectedness and isolation. He repeats a sort of invocation of the lone individual to the family spirit, spoken earlier as well—"I am all of them,/they are all of me, I am me, they are thee"—, then closes with another specter of loneliness and the breakdown of his life-lines within the family: ". . .and I have no children/ to float in the space between." In these last two statements the poem follows its fundamental curve, away from abstract formulation of an "idea of ancestry" into definition in terms of a field of emotions grounded in concrete situations and images. The idea may remain unparaphrasable, but when Knight has finished his poem it has become a solid, subtle, moving thing.

. . . In the years since his release from prison Etheridge Knight has earned his living principally by giving poetry readings. He is an excellent reader. His deep, resonant voice is a gift. He is sensitive to the rhythms and inflections of poetry and "ordinary" speech, and he is sensitive to his audiences and knows how to reach them. As a black poet he stands in a living tradition of toast-tellers, rhymers, and singers. He believes that poetry is most fully itself when it is spoken aloud to other people; and as I've said, his poem

have an immediacy and music that lend themselves to that kind of presentation. So I suppose he has all the qualifications to be called an oral poet. But the term is not a very precise or useful one, and too often it is used to put poems in a category without granting them full status as poems.

Source: Howard Nelson, "Belly Songs: The Poetry of Etheridge Knight," in *Hollins Critic*, Vol. 18, No. 5, December 1981, pp. 1–11.

Patricia Liggins Hill

In the following excerpt, Hill claims that Knight's poem "The Idea of Ancestry" is an example of black cultural history—that the form of the poem, as well as the idea of ancestry, represents the problem of ancestral lineage for African Americans as a whole.

In the poem "The Idea of Ancestry," which Paul Mariah has hailed as "the best poem of Black cultural history," Knight himself becomes "the violent space." In the first section of the poem, which flows in a Whitmanesque style, the poet is spatially defined in his prison cell:

Taped to the wall of my cell are 47 pictures:
     47 black
faces: my father, mother, grandmothers
     (1 dead), grand
fathers (both dead), brothers, sisters, uncles,
     aunts,
cousins (1st & 2nd), nieces, and nephews.
     They stare
across the space at me sprawling on my
     bunk. I know
their dark eyes, they know mine. I know
     their style,
they know mine. I am all of them, they are
     all of me;
they are farmers, I am a thief, I am me, they
     are thee.

I have at one time or another been in love
     with my mother,
1 grandmother, 2 sisters, 2 aunts (1 went to
     the asylum),
and 5 cousins. I am now in love with a 7 yr
     old niece
(she sends me letters written in large block
     print, and
her picture is the only one that smiles at me).

I have the same name as 1 grandfather,
     3 cousins, 3 nephews,

and 1 uncle. The uncle disappeared when he
    was 15, just took
off and caught a freight (they say). He's
    discussed each year
when the family has a reunion, he causes
    uneasiness in
the clan, he is an empty space. My father's
    mother, who is 93
and who keeps the Family Bible with every-
    body's birth dates
(and death dates) in it, always mentions him.
    There is
no place in her Bible for "whereabouts
    unknown."

The poet is conscious of the fact that all of
his ancestors, except for his smiling, seven-year-
old niece, stare at him across the space. He
shares the same name as one grandfather, three
cousins, three nephews, and one uncle. The uncle
is an empty space in the family, just as the poet is.
And yet in spite of the poet's being an empty
space, he takes a Whitmanesque stance in the
poem: He stands at the center of his universe,
his ancestry, and sings, "I am all of them, they
are all of me." But he realizes his separation from
his ancestry as well: "they are farmers, I am a
thief, I am me, they are thee."

The prosaic quality of the first section of the
poem is striking. For the most part, it takes on
the narrative qualities of an autobiography and
flows with long, rolling, sonorous lines controlled by the breath of the poet; declarative
statements; story-like details; and specific references to people, places, and actions. The soothing, sweet-flowing rhythms in Part I reflect the
poet's reminiscences about his relationships with
his relatives—memories that are filled with
warmth, gentleness, regret, and nostalgia.

In Part II, the pace quickens. The thoughts
recollected by examining the pictures of his relatives on his cell wall (in Part I) lead the poet
gradually to a retelling of his personal ritual of
suffering: . . .

"Each Fall," the poet enacts the ritual of
return to the home of his ancestry. From this
mythic sense of time, the poet switches to direct
references and specific definitions of time: "Last
yr . . . That night. . . . " The experience is relived,
but with qualification: " . . . I had almost caught
up with me." The rhythms in Part II explode
with violence. Separations are made: "That
night I looked at my grandmother/ and split/
my guts were screaming for junk. . . . " The

slashes, which are absent in Part I of the poem,
crowd several activities into one sentence: "I
walked barefooted in my grandmother's back-
yard/ I smelled the old/land and woods/I sipped
cornwhiskey from fruit jars with the men/I
flirted with the women/I had a ball till the caps
ran out/and my habit came down." Words col-
lide at the slashes to build up the tension evident
in the countercurrents of the poet's life: "birth-
stream/I hitchhiked," "backyard/I smelled,"
"woods/I sipped cornwhiskey," "men/I flirted
with the women," "junk/but I was almost/con-
tented." The crackling sounds explode with
meaning: The poet uses such terms as "croaker"
(doctor) and "crib" (house) for their harsh alliterative impact.

In the last fines of the final stanza, the quick-
ened pace exhausted, the drama rests:

> This yr there is a grave stone wall damming
>   my stream,
> and when
> the falling leaves stir my genes, I pace my cell
>   or flop on
> my bunk
> and stare at 47 black faces across the space.
>   I am all of them,
> they are all of me, I am me, they are thee,
>   and I have no sons
> to float in the space between.

"Time" and "space" have traveled full circle
in the poem—back to the present condition of
the poet in his cell. But whereas the space
between the poet and the pictures described in
the first stanza is chiefly the distance between his
bunk and the wall where the pictures hang, the
last notation of space in the poem involves the
galvanization of the poet's genes—his sense of
ancestry. He has no sons to hold his ritualistic
space within the family. No sons of his are
marked in the family Bible. This is a quiet time
of despair for the poet: "they are farmers, I am a
thief." Now, he is "the violent space," an entity
separate from his ancestry. He is different: At
this moment in the time and space of the poem,
he has no physical linkage to his history, his
family. And, unfortunately, because he is imprisoned, he can do nothing at present about the
situation. The spatial/temporal movement of
the poem is carried along by the tide of his
music: from the very concrete reality of a prison
cell, to a ritual revitalization of a sense of ancestry through a returning home, to this year when
there will be no re-enactment of the ritual and no

one to move for him: "I have no sons/to float in the space between." With this line the poem reaches an abrupt halt. The reader then becomes aware of the vastness of space, "the violent space," which follows the line.

The form of the poem as well as the idea of ancestry in the poem also represents the problem of ancestral lineage for the Black race as a whole. Many Blacks, such as Knight himself, can only trace their ancestral lineage back two or three generations because of the conditions of Black slavery which were imposed on them. In this context, Agnes Stein, in *The Uses of Poetry*, regards this poem as especially important for those such as Blacks "whose history as a group has been denied within a larger culture."

Source: Patricia Liggins Hill, "'The Violent Space': The Function of the New Black Aesthetic in Etheridge Knight's Prison Poetry," in *Black American Literature Forum*, Vol. 14, No. 3, Fall 1980, pp. 115–21.

SOURCES

"The African American Toast Tradition," in *Louisiana's Living Traditions*, http://www.louisianafolklife.org/LT/Articles_Essays/creole_art_toast_tradition.html (accessed January 6, 2007).

Anaporte-Easton, Jean, "Etheridge Knight: Poet and Prisoner," in *Callaloo*, Vol. 19, No. 4, Autumn 1996, pp. 941–46.

"A Brief Guide to the Black Arts Movement," in *Poets*, http://www.english.illinois.edu/Maps/blackarts/historical.html (accessed January 2, 2007).

Hill, Patricia Liggins, "'The Violent Space': The Function of the New Black Aesthetic in Etheridge Knight's Prison Poetry," in *Black American Literature Forum*, Vol. 14, No. 3, Autumn 1980, pp. 115–21.

Joseph, Peniel E., *Waiting 'til the Midnight Hour: A Narrative History of Black Power in America*, Holt Paperbacks, 2007.

Knight, Etheridge, "The Idea of Ancestry," in *The Essential Etheridge Knight*, University of Pittsburgh Press, 1986, pp. 12–13.

Leach, Laurie F., *Langston Hughes: A Biography*, Greenwood Press, 2004.

Malcolm X, with Alex Haley, *The Autobiography of Malcolm X: As Told to Alex Haley*, Ballantine Books, 1987.

Nelson, Howard, "Belly Songs: The Poetry of Etheridge Knight," in *Hollins Critic*, Vol. 18, No. 5, December 1981, pp. 1–11.

Patterson, Raymond R., Review of *The Essential Etheridge Knight*, in *American Book Review*, Vol. 9, No. 4, September/October 1987, p. 1.

Pinsker, Sanford, "A Conversation with Etheridge Knight," in *Black American Literature Forum*, Vol. 18, No. 1, Spring 1984, pp. 11–14.

"Timeline: America's War on Drugs," in *National Public Radio*, April 2, 2007, http://www.npr.org/templates/story/story.php?storyId=9252490 (accessed January 2, 2010).

Zinn, Howard, *A People's History of the United States: 1492–Present*, HarperCollins, 2003, pp. 407–562.

FURTHER READING

Bly, Robert, *American Poetry: Wildness and Domesticity*, Harper & Row, 1990.
    In this collection of essays, the poet Bly ponders some interesting questions about the direction poetry in the United States has taken over three decades. He discusses poetry from the Beats to the Black Arts movement and then moves forward to contemporary times. Among other things, he ponders how poetry is influenced by politics and the intellect, with a special emphasis on what he calls the wildness, or inward contemplation.

Charters, Ann, ed., *The Portable Sixties Reader*, Penguin Books, 2003.
    Charters provides a journey through the turbulent 1960s by exploring the political, environment, social, and literary revolutions that were occurring. With themes such as women's rights, civil rights, antiwar movement, and black power, she explores some of the most creative voices of this era. Knight's influence as well as that of Nikki Giovanni, James Baldwin, and others are identified and examined.

Cullum, Linda, ed., *Contemporary American Ethnic Poets: Lives, Works, Sources*, Greenwood Press, 2004.
    Cullum presents written biographies and discussions of poets' works in this collection. Cullum also offers information on African American authors including Knight as well as prominent American authors with Native American, Hispanic, Middle Eastern, Asian, and Eastern European backgrounds.

Pettis, Joyce, *African American Poets: Lives, Works, and Sources*, Greenwood Press, 2002.
    Covering some of the most important African American poets of the twentieth century, this book contains short biographies bibliographies for such writers as Maya Angelou, Amiri Baraka, Lucille Clifton, Rita Dove, Langston Hughes, Ishmael Reed, and Jean Toomer.

Pinsker, Sanford, *Conversations with Contemporary American Writers: Saul Bellow, I. B. Singer, Joyce Carol Oates, David Madden, Barry Beckham, Josephine Miles, Gerald Stern, Stephen Dunn, Etheridge Knight, Marilynne Robinson, William Stafford*, Rodopi, 1985.

Having authors talk about their own work provides insight into the themes they write about. Pinsker has chosen fiction writers as well as poets in this collection of interviews, providing readers with a personal exploration of the authors' accomplishments.

Robson, David, *The Black Arts Movement*, Lucent Books, 2008.

In this book, written for young-adult readers, Robson explains what the Black Arts movement was all about, who the major contributors were, and why the movement was so influential.

SUGGESTED SEARCH TERMS

Etheridge Knight bio

Etheridge Knight poems

Knight AND The Idea of Ancestry

Knight AND The Essential Etheridge Knight

Knight AND poems

Knight AND Poems from Prison

Black Arts movement

Knight and Prison Poets

Moon Rondeau

CARL SANDBURG

1963

"Moon Rondeau" was published in 1963 by Carl Sandburg in a collection of poetry titled *Honey and Salt*. This was one of his later works; he had already been named the People's Poet, and he focused on his favorite themes in the collection. "Moon Rondeau" is a lyrical love story about nature and people, a longing for the ethereal, and an illustration of the moon in ordinary yet lovely language.

Sandburg wrote nearly twenty poems with the word "moon" in the title and many more about evening skies, stars, fogs, and other celestial and atmospheric themes. The moon usually represents the inspiration of light to darkness, hope, and longing, though in "Red Moon," for example, it suggests violence. In "Moon Rondeau," the moon represents love and constancy.

A rondeau is a strict poetic form that uses fifteen lines of rhyming refrains in which the first line or the first words of the first line are repeated. In his usual habit of breaking rhyming rules and giving his poetry a free verse structure, Sandburg does not use this form for "Moon Rondeau." Perhaps he chooses to use the word "rondeau" in his title to reinforce the need to repeat the act of professing one's love for another or to compare love to the constancy of the moon that repeats its appearance every night. The roundness of the moon can represent eternal love, a circle unbroken, with no beginning and no end.

Carl Sandburg (*The Library of Congress*)

AUTHOR BIOGRAPHY

Sandburg was born on January 6, 1878, to poor Swedish immigrants in Galesburg, Illinois. They had seven children, and Sandburg's father worked as a blacksmith for the local railroad. Sandburg had to quit school in the eighth grade to help support the family with odd jobs such as stacking wood, collecting eggs, and shining shoes while helping care for five younger siblings. He developed a strong work ethic, and as he got older, he continued to help by washing dishes, helping a tinsmith, working in a barbershop, and being a painter's assistant. It was during these formative years of his life that his thoughts on poverty and materialism, love for the common person, and ambitions to help people were formed.

He left home at the age of eighteen to experience life on the road, determined to be a hobo and a poet. It was a dire existence, catching illegal rides on boxcars, stopping to earn a few cents for a meal, and then back on the hard metal front-row seat watching panoramic views of the Midwest. He developed a true love for the down-on-their-luck men he met as he traveled, and much of his poetry is written about people who struggle in poverty in the cities and countryside in the Midwest.

When the Spanish-American War erupted, he enlisted, and he served in Puerto Rico for six months. Returning to Galesburg, he attended Lombard College and began to put his poetry in writing. He never graduated, but he did receive accolades from professors for his poetry. He began working as a writer for newspapers and magazines, proffering his ideas for social reform. While in Milwaukee, working as the editor of the *Social-Democratic Herald* newspaper, he met Lillian (Paula) Steichen. They were instantly compatible, especially in ideology, agreeing on the necessity for social and labor reform. They married in 1908 and moved back to his beloved Illinois, where he began working for the *Chicago Daily News*. In 1916, his *Chicago Poems* was published: a collection filled with poetry that lovingly railed against the dirty, dark underbelly of the city. In 1917, a riot broke out in the city between blacks and whites after an altercation at a segregated swimming area. Sandburg was asked to cover the incident, and his articles were collected as The Chicago Race Riots, published by Harcourt and Brace the same year. Surprising many, it portrayed the black population of the city as the recipients of injustice.

Sandburg was a prolific poet, and he became increasingly popular. *Cornhuskers* was published in 1918, followed by *Smoke and Steel* in 1920 and *Slabs of the Sunburnt West* in 1922. He used the vernacular of the common person and often portrayed people in the bleakest of conditions, while he also wrote poems painting idyllic portraits of the prairie. He wrote collections for children, including *Rootabaga Stories*, published in 1922, which he loved to read to his two daughters. *American Songbag* showed his love for the American folk song and ballad and included poems to be sung. He performed these works himself, accompanied on the banjo.

Aside from his poetry, Sandburg is most remembered for his biographies of the life of President Abraham Lincoln. As a fellow Illinoisan and champion of the downtrodden, he felt a kinship and reverence for the man who dared to challenge social mores nearly a hundred years earlier. His four-volume *Abraham Lincoln: The War Years* won the Pulitzer Prize for History in 1940.

The Sandburg family moved to Flat Rock, North Carolina in 1951 to a farm named Connemara. Paula wanted the family to enjoy country life for the first time, and she became a prize-winning goat breeder. Sandburg was still traveling in the beginning but soon began to enjoy his respite on the farm. In *Carl Sandburg: A Biography*, Penelope Niven recounts that "at home at Connemara, Sandburg loved to work in the bright sunlight, often taking a chair out to the wide shelf of rock up the hill just behind his house."

He was awarded his second Pulitzer Prize, this time for poetry, in 1951 for his *Collected Poems*. "Moon Rondeau" was published in 1963 in the collection *Salt and Honey*, which appeared shortly after he was named the Poet Laureate of Illinois in 1962. He fell out of favor with critics in his later years as the simplicity and humorous tone of his work became unfashionable. He died at the age of 89 in Flat Rock, North Carolina, on July 22, 1967.

POEM SUMMARY

Stanza 1

The first line of the poem "Moon Rondeau" begins with quotation marks, indicating that the voice that is speaking is not that of the poet. There seem to be two people discussing their future, a future of love. Love is depicted as a door that they will open. This poetic device, in which one thing is likened to another thing, is a metaphor. (If the poet had said that love is *like* a door, the device would have been called a simile.) It is a declarative sentence that requires action. Sandburg suggests that love is something that is done, not passively possessed. It is not clear who the lovers are or whether they are old or young, married or single, simply that they agree to love one another. Line 2 explains that they are standing outside under the moon and are expressing their love for each other. In literature, the moon is often a symbol of love, and many oaths are made to it. The moon is often present in the lines of Shakespeare's lovers; for example, there is a lively exchange regarding the moon between Kate and Petruchio in *The Taming of the Shrew*, a comedic play about a difficult courtship that ends in true love. Line 3 describes the scene as being evening, and the imagery appeals to the sense of smell: musty leaf mold is mentioned. The first impression, therefore, is of late fall and dying foliage. However, the next two lines give clues that this is not true. These lines reveal that the smell of new roses and beginnings of potatoes abound, brought in by the wind. It is a

MEDIA ADAPTATIONS

- *Sandburg Out Loud* is an audiobook of poems narrated by celebrities and produced by August House (2006).
- *The Poems of Carl Sandburg*, an audiocassette published by Audio Literature in 1996, is narrated by Carl Reiner and Elliot Gould.

time of beginnings, of new growth, of spring. Leaf mold is used to fertilize plants, and spring is the symbolic season of love. The noted Victorian poet Alfred Lord Tennyson proclaims in "Locksley Hall" that in the spring, a young man's thoughts are of love. In that poem, the speaker tells of unrequited love while looking up into the night sky. Even in the earliest medieval manuscripts of English literature, the moon and the time of spring are powerful forces in the promotion of love. In Geoffrey Chaucer's *Troilus and Criseyde*, the young lovers are subject to the powers of the moon, the season of spring, and the influence of those forces on human actions. It is not clear where Sandburg's poem takes place, but because most of his poetry is written about the Midwest, it must occur somewhere in the American heartland, where the smell of leaf mold would be familiar during spring planting.

Stanza 2

The first line of stanza 2 gives an indication of what time of night the poem takes place. It is late, probably after midnight, a magical time when dreaming and wishing are active and the cares and practicalities of the day are over. It is a romantic time, a time when emotions are keen and thoughts of love are evoked. The second line describes the couple looking longingly at the moon for hours as its mystical powers overtake them. They begin to see shapes in it as they stare dreamily, like a child watching clouds turning into puppies, balloons, or monsters. They see it as a silvery button; one says that it is a copper coin. A lover' game begins, and creative minds, inspired by the moment, call out more names. They think of a wafer (a thin, round piece of metal) made of bronze. The next offering, in the third line of the stanza, is that of a gold plaque, an award, again pleasing and inspirational. Next, an even higher honor is imagined: a royal crown. However, it is one that has disappeared, which may suggest wistfulness or, on a more literal level, may suggest that dawn is near. In the last line of the stanza, one last submission is offered: the moon is a brassy hat dripping and melting away into a deep watery blue.

Stanza 3

Stanza 3 is again a quotation from the lovers. They declare that the moon belongs to people like them: lovers. To them, it is placed in the night sky only for people in love, and more importantly, it is their personal property. It cannot be claimed by the earth, the sun, or the stars; it exists to revolve around them. There is no one else in the world but them, they think, and everything evolves to please them—thoughts that lovers often believe.

THEMES

Love

"Moon Rondeau" is essentially about love. It is the first word of the poem, and the poem describes two lovers looking at the heavens and dreaming about their future together. The scene is a starry night when the couple is stargazing and declaring their love beneath the moon.

Ambiguity

There is a sense of ambiguity about the lovers in the poem. Are they young or old? Are they new to love or have they been together for a long time? Although they are allowed to speak to the reader, nothing is revealed about them, as if to say that it does not matter; all lovers must fall under a romantic spell beneath the moon.

Travel

In this poem, love is presented as a door that the lovers will open. They will travel through it to find their destinies together. This night is a beginning. The poem suggests a romantic sense of adventure and excitement at what lies ahead of the two, as they speak of their love.

Nature

Many lovers have pledged their love on an early spring evening beneath the moon. Roses, potatoes, and even the smell of leaf mold describe the evening setting and evoke the natural world. The wind brings a sensory element to the poem with the smells of nature on a moonlit evening.

Imagination

The lovers create lavish, fanciful images of the moon in comparisons meant to delight one another. They have nothing better to do than stay awake all night and watch the moon as it wanes, describing it as a coin, a crown, a button, a dripping hat.

Innocence

Whether the lovers are young or old, there is an innocence about them. They believe that the moon is hung above them simply for them and others who feel love as strongly as they do. They own the world and the heavens, and the rest of people lost without love in the world are merely renters.

Mysticism

Poetry and all forms of literature have used the moon as a mystical force that calls forth love. It exerts a supernatural force over people's emotions and often makes them behave in ways they might not under the ordinary noonday sun. In the same way, the setting of the evening has a softening effect upon lovers; it is secret and intimate, and it also has an otherworldly effect on the human heart.

Hope

Most of Sandburg's works are filled with hope, and if there is darkness, there is redemption, or at least a moral. "Moon Rondeau" is no different. The message is conveyed that dreams will be fulfilled and love will prevail. The lovers believe that the world is at their fingertips.

Rural Life

This poem depicts a setting of rural life, perhaps on a farm. Leaf mold is used in spring planting to mulch and fertilize new crops, but within the poem its main purpose is to evoke a memory by its smell. Roses and potatoes are beginning to grow, most likely in a nearby field. The image of the moon is always enhanced by an evening sky free of city lights. Its details are described here in simple, though fanciful terms, also indicative of a rural life.

TOPICS FOR FURTHER STUDY

- What season do you think the poem "Moon Rondeau" is set in? What clues can you get from the descriptions of the potatoes and roses, the smell of the fertilizer? What season do you think is the best season for lovers, and how does this compare with the poem? Write a paper and explain your answer based on the clues from the poem. Include at least three reasons from different disciplines (such as science, literature, cultural beliefs, history, or art) and write at least one paragraph on each.

- Construct a piece of artwork to complement the poem. It can be a sculpture, painting, or any other form. It can be a literal representation or more abstract. Include several elements of the poem, not just the moon. Interpret your creation for the class.

- Write a musical composition to accompany the poem and sing or play the song for the class. If you sing, you do not have to include all the sections of the poem; select those easiest to put to music. You may accompany yourself or have someone else accompany you, or you may sing a capella. You may present an instrumental composition only, but be sure it matches the tone and theme of the poem. The composition should be at least one to two minutes long.

- Make a slide show on the computer (such as a PowerPoint presentation) to represent the poem as you read it. Have each picture correlate to what is being narrated at the time it appears. If you are unable to produce a voice-over, read the poem aloud in class as the slide show is being presented. Add background music as well, if you like.

- Write a children's bedtime story using the themes and words from the poem. The theme of love is very important, and the image of the moon should be integral to the story. Illustrate your story and read it aloud to the class. It should be at least eight to ten pages long.

- *Thirteen Moons on Turtle's Back* by Joseph Bruchac (1997) is a young-adult book of poems and illustrations of the Native American legends of the cycles and seasons of the moon represented by the scales on the back of a turtle's shell. Compare and contrast three poems, preferably set during the spring, from the selection with the poem "Moon Rondeau" preferably during the spring. Draw correlations between the images, themes, styles, characters, and moods of the poems.

STYLE

Free Verse

Sandburg is renowned for his use of free verse. This poem is completely unrhymed, and yet it is written in a rhythmically pleasing way. It lends itself to a feeling of romanticism, and he uses the poem's structure to convey his themes in a pleasing and convincing manner. There is no apparent form, only a free-flowing cascade of words that evoke images, emotions, and romance.

There is some uncertainty as to why Sandburg titled this poem "Moon Rondeau." It is certainly not in the style of a rondeau, which is a French poetry form that has fifteen lines with two repeating rhymes, nor does it fit the musical form of French verse, although that version does have thirteen lines, as "Moon Rondeau" does; that verse style must have two repeating rhymes, and the first line of the poem is generally repeated more than once. It is possible that Sandburg had the musical form in mind and preferred to use his free verse style of poetry that does not rhyme or

The poem talks about lovers opening a door. (Image copyright Martina I. Meyer, 2010. Used under license from Shutterstock.com)

conform to any type of meter. Because many of his poems are humorous, perhaps he is making a pun on the rondo style of music, (which is instrumental only), since that is pronounced the same as "rondeau." Much of Sandburg's poetry is meant to be sung, and he traveled across the country, performing his poems and accompanying himself of the banjo. His collection *American Songbag* is full of such song-poems. Another possibility is that he is making a pun on the roundness of the moon—a rondo can be sung as a round, a children's song that is sung in a never-ending, circular fashion. Sandburg wrote many poems and songs for children.

Figurative Language

The first line of stanza 1 uses dialogue (a conversation between people), as indicated by the use of quotation marks. It is not the voice of the poet, but that of the characters in the poem: the two lovers.

A metaphor is used as they declare love to be a door through which they will embark upon their future. The next line is the voice of the poet narrating the story and using assonance, or the repetition of vowel sounds. The letter *o* is used repeatedly in this line, though it is not always pronounced the same. In these first two lines, the poem has taken on a romantic, lyrical, and ethereal tone with the use of figurative language, the characters of love, and the setting of a romantically moonlit night. Sandburg enlists the reader's senses in the next lines, enticing the reader with the lush smells and images of early spring at night. Leaf mold and the reference to potatoes inspire visions of planting crops, and the smell of roses— the flower of love—wafts gently in on the wind.

In the second stanza, it is revealed that the lovers have stayed out late, and they begin to make up names for the moon. The names they assign are more metaphors: the comparisons of things that

COMPARE
&
CONTRAST

- **1963:** Carl Sandburg has been married to Lillian Steichen for sixty years. In "Moon Rondeau," he writes about love that seems endless and as everlasting as the moon; at this stage of their lives together, their love has come full circle as Carl has little time left on the earth. The divorce rate in America in 1963 is around 10 percent, and probably much less for couples married as long as the Sandburgs have been.

  Today: The divorce rate in the United States is at an all-time high of around 50 percent. Love is still a constant theme in poetry, music, and other media, but love as a lifelong relationship is rarely depicted.

- **1963:** The "real-life" love interest of "Moon Rondeau," Paula Steichen, lives at the farm described in the poem. She stays home and raises her three daughters. About the same time, Betty Friedan releases *The Feminine Mystique*, which influences the American workforce by suggesting that women no longer need to stay at home with children and housework but might be more fulfilled working outside the home.

  Today: Most married women do not need a book to tell them that they will be working outside the home. The mainstream American economy is based on a two-income family. For most women, staying home with children is not possible, and day care establishments exist in abundance. Few women today have time to raise three children, grow potatoes, cultivate rose and delphinium gardens, and raise goats as Steichen did.

- **1963:** Carl Sandburg, dubbed the People's Poet, writes free verse poems about nature and love, including "Moon Rondeau."

  Today: W. S. Merlin wins the Pulitzer Prize for Poetry in 2009 writing poetry about nature and love. His free verse style, with no punctuation, is reminiscent of Sandburg's work. In "Late Spring," love is found using the same metaphor Sandburg uses in "Moon Rondeau": the opening of a door. Merlin's winning collection *The Shadow of Sirius* evokes meaningful images of the moon and the brightest of stars.

are generally unalike to show unusual likenesses. The third, fourth, and fifth lines of stanza 2 are filled with the glimmering imagery of shiny coins, silvery buttons, gold medals, crowns lost in a shipwreck, and brassy, dripping waters.

The last stanza, of just three lines, is again a dialogue between the lovers. It is a bold statement that they make as they feel unchained from the fetters of the world, an ambitious and romantic notion that they and other lovers are the ones alone who possess the moon. There is also an allusion here to the notion, dating back to ancient Greek culture and before, that proposed that celestial objects ruled the actions of people. Throughout literature, the moon has been seen to have a powerful hold over the emotions of lovers.

HISTORICAL CONTEXT

The post-World War II era ushered in a time period unparalleled in American history. The United States and its allies had been victorious in World War II. People around the world celebrated as the Axis powers were defeated and the devastation of Europe ended, though it was after the death of millions. Men came home from war and a huge new generation of babies were born, who were later called baby boomers. Peace was short lived, with the cold war era bringing the Korean War in 1950 and then the Vietnam War. The American economy was strong, however, and people bought cars, homes, and the latest must-have trend: the television. The suburbs grew as families

Two lovers in the moonlight (Image copyright red-feniks, 2010. Used under license from Shutterstock.com)

moved out of the cities and out of traditional multigenerational households to developments of cookie-cutter homes, built close enough to the city to allow workers to commute in their new automobiles. Teenagers bought phonographs to play a new sound that erupted in their generation, rock and roll. The Beatles' first album was released in England in 1963, the same year as the publication of "Moon Rondeau." In the South, the civil rights movement was growing. Also in 1963, President John F. Kennedy was assassinated.

It was a time of upheaval, and young artists strove to be nonconformists. From flower children to peace signs and sit-ins, antiwar demonstrations, abstract art, free thought, and free love—by the 1960s, popular culture seemed dominated by young people and revolution. In the 1950s, the Beat Poets were on the cutting edge of literature and poetry; they wrote about themes of political and social antiestablishment and formerly taboo subjects, such as sexual morals and drug use. The avant-garde influence, characterized by unorthodox or experimental expression, was prevalent in much of the arts. Its influence continued into the 1960s and reappeared in San Francisco through poets like Allen Ginsberg, Bob Kaufman, Richard

Brautigan, and Philip Whalen. E. E. Cummings, Allen Ginsberg, Martin Luther King, Jr., Timothy Leary, Norman Mailer, Harper Lee, and Kurt Vonnegut were some of the major voices of the decade.

Carl Sandburg's poetry fell out of fashion in mainstream American literature during the 1960s. Becoming known as the People's Poet in 1940, he wrote on simple, uplifting themes, using the voice of the common man, in a style that was no longer in vogue in the 1960s. Rebellion, antiestablishment feelings, and complex avant-garde thinking stood in stark contrast to Sandburg's lyrical and optimistic themes of classic love and agrarianism in "Moon Rondeau." Students were required to read his work, but it is doubtful that many were his fans in the 1960s. It was only much later, around the turn of the twenty-first century, that there was a resurgence of interest in his work. Simple, free verse using the language of the common person has been reborn in forms of literature like slam poetry and music like rap. Like Sandburg's *Chicago Poems*, such free verse is a sound of the struggles of the down-and-out on the streets of the city. Poetry that is sung with an emphasis on rhythm is being written and performed in a contemporary fashion. It may not sound much like Sandburg, with its street slang and hip-hop sound, but it is.

CRITICAL OVERVIEW

Penelope Niven writes in *Carl Sandburg: A Biography* that *Honey and Salt*, the collection in which "Moon Rondeau" appeared, was generally well reviewed. However, some of Sandburg's contemporaries wondered what happened to the voice of protest that had been evident in his *Chicago Poems* and *Smoke and Steel*. Where, they wondered, was the Sandburg who talked about labor and poverty and difficult social issues?

North Callahan in *Carl Sandburg: His Life and Works* tells the story of the elderly Sandburg and his mindset at the time of writing "Moon Rondeau." "When they brought him his guitar, he strummed the chords and asked them if they wanted to hear 'Red Iron Ore.' Then he admitted he might have forgotten the words. Instead he asked, 'How about when the curtains of the sky are pinned back by the stars and the beautiful moon swept the sky?'" The poet no longer wished to champion the causes of the poor or eulogize

heroic presidents. "Moon Rondeau" was about love, the night sky, and the beautiful moon.

The sheer volume of Sandburg's work covers the lifetime of a man. His younger years represent the young man's cries against the injustices of the city and his aging years depict a man wanting to spend time looking at the moon and stars at home with his family. Richard Crowder, in his essay "Sandburg's Chromatic Vision in *Honey and Salt*" in *The Vision of This Land* explains, "The first poem of *Chicago Poems*, records the details of a brawny metropolis; over seven hundred fifty pages later, the last poem in *Honey and Salt* celebrates the evolutionary rise and triumph of The Family of Man." Sandburg's words in his last book came from where his heart was—at Connemara, with the pastures and flower gardens and his daughters, his grandchildren, and Paula.

CRITICISM

Cynthia Gower

Gower is a novelist, playwright, and freelance writer. In this essay, she explains that "Moon Rondeau," one of the last of Sandburg's poems, stands distinctly apart from his former poetry as an ethereal depiction of love that uses the imagery of the evening moon.

Carl Sandburg was known as the People's Poet. He wrote creatively and imaginatively in everyday language that appealed to the common person. He took on the cause of the downtrodden and wove redemption and hope into every verse. He took to the road to meet everyday people and sang his poems to them. He wrote voluminously about poor people, African Americans, cities, labor unions, race riots, and the dance halls known as honky-tonks. He was loved by an entire generation of Americans.

"Moon Rondeau" is about the steadfastness of love, set in the ethereal light of the moon. Sandburg was eighty-five when he wrote this poem, having received the Pulitzer Prize for his *Collected Poems* just a few years previously. "Moon Rondeau," unlike Sandburg's earlier work, is an ethereal poem about everlasting love, inspired by the love he shared with his wife, Lillian (Paula) Steichen. The dirty industrialism of his **Chicago Poems** is absent from this poem, and his devastating pictures of the poor and hopeless are years in the past. Visions of racial prejudice and abusive big business are gone. In "Moon Rondeau" Sandburg, is an

- *Not Everyday an Aurora Borealis for Your Birthday: A Love Poem* (1999) is one of Sandburg's many beloved children's books. It is beautifully illustrated by Anita Lobel.

- *Never Kick a Slipper at the Moon* is another of Sandburg's poems for children featuring the moon (1988). Illustrated by Rosanne Litsinger, it is a favorite bedtime book.

- *Du Fu: A Life in Poetry*, a collection of works by the eighth-century Chinese poet, is similar to Sandburg's work in its simple style and themes of nature and love, especially "Full Moon." It was translated by David Young in 2008.

- *Always the Young Strangers* is Sandburg's 1953 autobiography starting with the day of his birth, retelling his days as a hobo, reporter, writer, and Pulitzer Prize winner.

- *Carl Sandburg: A Biography* (1991), by Penelope Niven, is the most comprehensive overview of Carl Sandburg's life, work, and criticism.

- *The Love Song of J. Alfred Prufrock* (1917), by T. S. Eliot, is one of the most famous poems of this contemporary of Sandburg. This masterpiece is quite different from Sandburg's work. It is driven, not lyrical, terse and not easily understood, yet still in a standardized rhyming style.

older, wiser, less aggressive poet who delights in retelling his story of love.

The rural scene lends itself to love, as well as the smells of new growth and roses. It is interesting to note that Sandburg used the words "potatoes" and "roses" as pet names for family members. The wind joins the lovers, and they share an intimate, playful, imaginative conversation.

The lovers have stayed up late at night, and it is suggested that dawn is near. All things are possible when considered at this mystical time of night, and a sense of privacy is pervasive. Anyone

coming upon them or even reading their words must surely intrude.

The colors and shimmers ascribed to the moon create an otherworldly theater as a backdrop for the lovers. Their feelings about the prospects of love are optimistic, like the idealistic view of the young. They proclaim that the moon belongs to them alone. The poet, however, is old; the freshness of the love he describes gives the impression that his own lifelong love is both new and eternal. Penelope Niven, in *Carl Sandburg: A Biography*, quotes Sandburg as saying, "At the root of love—romantic, patriotic, platonic, family love, love for life—was passion."

At the time he wrote "Moon Rondeau," literature had taken on the moniker "postmodernist," one into which Sandburg did not fit. There is not a definite date for the onset of this movement, but it appeared after World War II and was greatly influenced by the generation of Beat Poets in the 1950s who chronicled the rebellions of the disaffected youth of the time. Unlike Sandburg's writing, the poetry was not in the language of everyday people, but in a style in which the reader must strive to decode the fragmented symbols and images to come up with a transcendental truth. Themes were not absolute, like the symbol of love in "Moon Rondeau," but were subject to multiple and esoteric interpretations. Optimism was no longer the order of the day. Pessimism and dark irony became popular, and postmodernism peaked with the publication of Heller's *Catch 22*, a story filled with satire, irony and hopelessness. The lovers' happy declarations of the permanence and fidelity of love in "Moon Rondeau" seem something of an anachronism in comparison to the plight of the young pilot in *Catch 22* published just two years before.

The lovers are persuaded that they can do anything together. Together they can open the door to love. Their commitment to each other is as constant as the presence of the moon. They are confident they can possess the moon—that they *do* in fact possess it. Many people consider their worth to be the sum total of what they own, but these lovers own something otherworldly and ethereal, like love. The moon is compared to precious and solid things: silver, gold, brass, copper, bronze; however, its value is greater to them than any material good. Its worth cannot be bought, and its value is greater than jewels. The moon is something that is eternal, like the love they have for each other. Love is something they must do, that they must achieve together, not just a feeling. Even the shape of the moon, the roundness and infinity of its circle (like the symbolism of a wedding ring), portrays the perpetual nature of true love.

The love between the poet and "Paula," as Sandburg nicknamed Lillian, lasted sixty years. She adored his poetry and loved his singing. William A. Sutton retells the comment of family friend, Lilla Perry, in *Carl Sandburg Remembered*, stating, "When Carl sings, Paula can forgive him anything." When Paula was asked the secret of the success of their marriage, according to Niven in *Carl Sandburg: A Biography*, she answered: "He always wanted me to do what I wanted to do and I always wanted him to do what he wanted." He constantly praised her, she reported, in whatever she did. He said that he sat down to the best dinner on earth every night, and obviously ate plenty. He said he was making up for all those days he had spent as a hobo. Paula told him jokingly that he had always been a bum, which greatly pleased him—he said that he had decided when he left home as a young man that he could not decide whether to be a poet or a bum. He loved to sit out on a flat rock in the back yard for hours and stare and write, write and stare. Paula was a proficient gardener, especially of flowers; she made a landscape of inspiration. There were masses of rose beds and delphiniums and hollyhocks. She earned a good living as a breeder of goats, studying the genetics of breeding and raising champion varieties. He was prolific in his admiration for her and the living she made, although by that time he was quite famous. He said that she must not need him at all. She needed his words, though, and he wrote dozen of love poems dedicated to her. As young people, they had the same ideals for political reform and for making America free and equal in all opportunities. They both had a love for writing, and many of her early letters to him ask for new poems to read.

Paula was an early feminist, keeping her maiden name, Steichen, throughout her life. Her love for him and his success forced her into the role of homemaker and mother as children came along, but it seemed to fit her; she raised three daughters and helped raise two grandchildren. He wrote to her constantly while out on the road. After they moved to the farm in North Carolina, he seemed to miss home more and resent the constant demands that public performances and speaking engagements made on him.

Eventually, he did stay home most of the time, and that is when he began to write *Honey and Salt*, in which "Moon Rondeau" appears. He said that life was full of honey and salt, and with enough honey you could not taste the salt. As he aged, his heart weakened and he became forgetful. Paula was careful to overlook it and change the subject. Finally, when he struggled to breathe and had to stay in bed, Paula waited on him faithfully. Even in death his thoughts were of her. His last word, according to Niven, was "Paula."

Source: Cynthia Gower, Critical Essay on "Moon Rondeau," in *Poetry for Students*, Gale, Cengage Learning, 2011.

Will Manley

In the following review, Manley explains that the great irony of Sandburg's literary life is that his best books, the "Rootabaga" titles, were in fact written for children and, thus, remain largely unread by most serious literary critics.

Writers are like clothing: they go in and out of style almost whimsically. Particularly hard hit lately is the American icon Carl Sandburg. He has become as outdated as the farmer's overalls that he used to wear to his folksinging concerts. In the hip-hop 1990s, everything about Sandburg seems rather old-fashioned—his folk songs, his 1930s-style socialism, his white patch of hair parted meticulously off center, his dusty bow tie, and most of all, his homespun, apple-pie smile. Great artists, writers, and musicians are supposed to be intense and tortured souls with drinking problems and manic-depressive personalities. Sandburg is simply too placid to be considered a genius.

His mid-century reputation as an American literary giant was based largely upon the strength of two widely disseminated poems. The first, "Fog" ("The fog comes on little cat's feet"), can be found in almost every elementary-school poetry collection; and the second, "Chicago" ("Hog Butcher for the World"), is widely anthologized in high-school literature texts.

These two little poems, however, form too frail a foundation to support Sandburg's voluminous output of verbiage, and therein lies his problem with contemporary critics and readers. Although Sandburg is primarily known as a poet, his prose works are particularly expansive. His biography of Lincoln, for example, ranges over six volumes, and his autobiography is two volumes. His only serious stab at fiction, a rambling wreck of a novel entitled *Remembrance Rock*, is a tiresome compilation of more than 600 largely unreadable pages that cover the entire history of America from Plymouth Rock to World War II. Looking at Sandburg's entire oeuvre, his more sympathetic critics use such adjectives as undisciplined; less-sympathetic sorts pick a different word: mediocre.

Even his poetry has been seen more and more as a cheap imitation of the authentic and original nineteenth-century American wordsmith, Walt Whitman (who, ironically, is in the news today because he had the great fortune of having his *Leaves Of Grass* become one of the notorious gifts that President Clinton bestowed upon Monica Lewinsky, which proves how frivolously literary reputations are restored and strengthened). William Wilson and Judy Jones, in their popular book of American cultural history, *An Incomplete Education,* list Sandburg as one of four twentieth-century poets "not to touch with a ten-foot strophe" and claim that he "almost certainly liked ketchup on his eggs."

Even in the best of times, Sandburg has always had his fair share of critics. Rival poet Robert Frost labeled him a "fraud," and during the McCarthy years, any number of conservatives attacked Sandburg for his left-wing political positions. His once-sacred biography of Lincoln, which actually started out as an instructive children's book, has been attacked for being "mythological," a nice euphemism for "inaccurate."

The great irony of Sandburg's literary life is that his best books, the "Rootabaga" titles, were in fact written for children and, thus, remain largely unread by most serious literary critics. A further irony is that many serious critics of children's literature have not read them. There's a catch-22 quality to this point. The children's experts do not know Sandburg because he was primarily an adult author who merely dabbled in children's fiction, and dabblers, no matter how well they dabble, do not get serious attention because they are not part of the children's literature establishment. As a consequence, Sandburg's children's books are poorly known to most children's librarians and almost completely unknown to children.

Personally, I would have never found the *Rootabaga Stories* if I had not moved to Galesburg, Illinois, in 1979 to become the director of the public library there. Galesburg, a charming little community nestled peacefully in the western Illinois prairie, is the birthplace and hometown of Carl Sandburg. It's a place that he wrote about affectionately in *Always the Young Strangers.* One day, while poking around in the library's local archives, I came across a very old edition of *Rootabaga* (it was published in 1922) with quaint pen-and-ink illustrations by Maud and Miska Petersham. At the time, my boys were quite young, and David, who was with me, asked, "Dad, what's a rootabaga?" David was only eight and still under the wonderful illusion that I knew everything because I was a librarian. "I think," I said, "that it's some kind of a vegetable—a root shaped like a little bag."

"Oh," he responded, "who would want to read a book about a stupid vegetable?" He made a good point, and I hastily put the book down as though it were an actual rutabaga that I had rejected in the produce section of the supermarket, unimpressed by its rough texture and irregular shape. Several weeks later, however, still curious about the taste of this book with the strange title, I stopped by the archives and picked it up anew. This time I took it home and read it to David.

Neither of us had ever been so entertained by a work of fiction. One bite of the rootabaga took us to a magical place filled with fun and enchantment. The book combined many of the ingredients of the best children's stories: a fantasy setting that was nevertheless recognizably and comfortably familiar (in this case, midwestern); unique characters with comical names and troublesome conundrums; a twisting, turning plot line; wistful drawings; and singsong sentences replete with repetitive word play, quizzical questions, ridiculous rhymes, and apt alliteration. Best of all, there was precious little moralizing in the book and no top-heavy message to weigh it down and take out the fun.

In fact, the language in the *Rootabaga Stories* is so playful that there is an almost-effortless poetic quality to it ("It is a misty, moisty evening and everything is mystical in the moonshine"). If Sandburg had only been so relaxed, unrestrained, and whimsical with his "real" poetry, he would be remembered for far more than "Fog" and "Chicago," and I think, deep down inside, Sandburg would agree. Near the end of his long life when he was asked about his literary legacy, he answered, "I am not sure but when the rest of my work fades out there will be two or three *Rootabaga* stories standing."

Source: Will Manley, "The Taste of Rootabaga," in *Booklist*, Vol. 95, No. 17, May 1, 1999, p. 1562.

Eleanor Graham Vance

In the following essay, Vance, an admirer of Sandburg, recalls a conversation with him about free-verse poetry, in which Sandburg stated that rhyming was too confining and its strict demands were stifling to ideas.

The first time I saw Carl Sandburg, he didn't see me. I was simply an admiring member of his audience as he read and sang and played the guitar at a program at Northwestern University in 1931 when I was working for my master's degree. His hair, not as white as nowadays, even then had fallen into the way of hanging down picturesquely over his forehead. (I am not sure that he held his words so long in his mouth at that time. Later, it seemed to me that he turned them lovingly on his tongue and refused to let them go until he had fully savored them.)

The next time must have been the autumn of 1937. I had been to the Writers' Conference at Bread Loaf, Vermont, that summer, and there I had heard Robert Frost make his famous statement about free verse. Perhaps he made it at other times and in other places, too, but it was all new to me that night. Frost had been talking and reading for an hour to a spellbound audience in a big barn of a building with a hard rain pelting on the roof. During the question period afterward, someone asked: "Mr. Frost, do you ever write free verse?" and Frost gave his famous answer: "I would no more think of writing free verse than of playing tennis without a net."

In the intervening years, I have heard this riposte quoted many times, but I have never heard anyone mention Sandburg's equally interesting rejoinder.

In the autumn after that Bread Loaf summer, I was invited to the Pennsylvania College for Women (now Chatham College) on an evening when Sandburg was to entertain. Frost's remark had evidently already been repeated to him, for at one point he said: "One of our foremost poets has said that he would no more think of writing free verse than of playing tennis without a net, but I would have him know that I have not only played tennis without a net but have used the stars for tennis balls."

Later that evening I had an opportunity to talk to Sandburg. In the receiving line everyone mentioned his poems, but I happened to speak of my enthusiasm for his *Rootabaga Stories* with that wonderful beginning about the house where the chimney sat on top of the roof to let the smoke out, the doorknobs opened the doors, the windows were always either open or shut, and everything was the same as it always was. Maybe Sandburg had a special feeling in his heart for *Rootabaga Stories,* for soon we were deep in conversation about writing in general, and I even had the temerity to argue with him on the subject of free verse.

"If you write in rhyme," said Sandburg, "you can't say what you want to. When you come to the end of the line, instead of saying what you started out to say, you have to say what will rhyme."

I argued that poets for several centuries had been willing to accept the challenge of saying what they wanted to say *and* making it rhyme. I have learned since that writers like or dislike rhyme for exactly the same reasons. Those who dislike it feel as Sandburg did that it is too confining, that its strict demands are stifling, to ideas. Those who like it say that, on the other hand, those very demands open up new vistas and shed light on the idea that was not there before—that searching for a rhyme or rephrasing in order to make a rhyme is *in itself* stimulating to ideas. I really didn't mean to argue for one or the other, but rather to defend both. Why should anyone, writer or reader, limit himself to rhymed verse or to free verse? Why not enjoy some of both? I can understand that a writer might feel impelled toward one or the other as a form of *expression,* but why condemn the other? Dog lovers need not be cat haters.

The last time I met the poet was in 1945 when I was working in the research department of Colonial Williamsburg, and Sandburg came there to visit.

"If you stay here long enough," my boss had told me when I took the job, "you will meet everyone you've ever known since you were in kindergarten, because sooner or later everybody comes to Williamsburg." It seemed to be true.

Sandburg enjoyed the restored colonial town with the gusto of a small boy. He even had his picture taken in the stocks. When he was brought to the research department I didn't expect him to remember me, but he said he did. "Oh yes," he explained to his amused listeners, "I met this young lady in Pennsylvania. She fell out of her Conestoga wagon and I came by on horseback and picked her up." I was slightly startled by this account, but I later wondered if the poet improvised on a humorous impulse to remind us that Pennsylvania had "history" as well as Virginia.

The real reason for his visit to Williamsburg that year was that he had been invited to give the Phi Beta Kappa poem at the College of William and Mary. He shared the platform that night with the well known scholar and critic, Chauncey B. Tinker, and the poet seemed bored or sleepy during Professor Tinker's address. The next day I was invited to be one of a small group to take Sandburg to Jamestown. On the way someone remarked jokingly that Mr. Sandburg might not care for a project like Colonial Williamsburg, the purpose of which is to preserve the past, because he had written, "The past is a bucket of ashes."

"Well, I'll revise that right now," said Sandburg with a grin. "I'll make it, 'The past is Chauncey B. Tinker.'"

Sandburg was seeing Jamestown for the first time, and the rest of us were seeing Sandburg see Jamestown. In those days, there was little at the site of our country's first permanent English settlement to mar the natural beauty. The ruins of the ivy-covered church tower, the graveyard, the statues of Pocahontas and John Smith looking out over the peaceful sweep of the broad James River, and the remains of the foundations of some seventeenth-century houses served only to make the scene impressive and add to the sense of history we were feeling.

There is a plaque on a wall of the Jamestown church in memory of the Indians who brought corn to the settlers "during the starving time." Those of us who worked in seventeenth-century writings had read a great deal about "the starving time," but the words were evidently new to the poet, and he spoke them with deep feeling and then whipped out a little notebook and wrote them down. I was always looking for a Sandburg poem in which they would appear, but if he used the phrase I never saw it. Seeing what an impression it made on him may have had something to do with *my* using it in the poem I later wrote about Jamestown.

Source: Eleanor Graham Vance, "Glimpses of Carl Sandburg," in *North American Review*, Vol. 252, No. 2, March 1967, pp. 9–10.

Guy Owen

In the following review, Owen contends that the aging poet has lost little of his lyrical drive.

Sandburg's publishers have chosen to celebrate his eighty-fifth birthday by issuing a new volume of his poetry. *Honey and Salt* contains seventy-seven new poems (most of them affirming the "honey" side of life); for an octogenarian to continue to produce at this rate is remarkable in itself. Perhaps the critic should no more carp at these poems than at Frost's last uneven collection, *In the Clearing*; one should merely be grateful for a handful of gems, though one must read through unrewarding and repetitive work to discover them. At any rate, the reader finds here the kind of poems he has come to expect from Sandburg. They often lack the power and freshness of his *Chicago Poems*, but the aging poet has lost little of his lyrical drive. Here are poems about skyscrapers and workers, about love and death, and the minutely observed beauties of nature. The long poems tend to become diffuse; they seem to come much too easily. Moreover, the love poems risk cuteness or sentimentality. The most successful poems, in my opinion, are the short, stark ones, often written in slangy folkspeech: "Buyers and Sellers" and "Fifty-Fifty." For example, here is all of "Pass, Friend":

The doors of the morning must open.
The keys of the night are not thrown away.

I who have loved morning know its doors.
I who have loved night know its keys.

In addition there are the fresh and lovely lyrics which embody Sandburg's own distinctive voice: "Bird Footprint," "Early Copper" and "Impossible Iambics." *Honey and Salt* will add little to Sandburg's reputation, but there are nearly a dozen poems here that we would not wish to lose.

Source: Guy Owen, Review of *Honey and Salt*, in *Books Abroad*, Vol. 38, No. 2, Spring 1964, p. 193.

Daniel Fuchs

In the following review, Fuchs debates the idea of Sandburg's appeal as a "national poet," since he is both ignored and adored by critics and readers.

For decades Carl Sandburg has had the ambiguous distinction of being "America's favorite poet," as the front of the book jacket says, or even better, "our national Poet," as it says on the back. (The late Robert Frost seems to have taken over the title in the last decade.) When we consider the self-satisfaction and dynamism of our middle-class culture vis-a-vis the obscure poet whose first impulse is to conceive of this culture as a problem, a threat or a nightmare, we can see why Sandburg is both adored and ignored. Adored by schoolteacher, high-school student, Harry Golden, politician, literate worker, self-made entrepreneur; by anyone who likes to be congratulated on living out the American Dream; by anyone who wants his

> SANDBURG'S POETRY HAS BEEN ECLIPSED
> BY THE TENDENCY OF THE SERIOUS READER TO
> TAKE POETRY AS A KIND OF SALVATION."

poetry clear, wholesome, "positive," bardic; by anyone who turns from the spectacle of much of modern poetry as an imaginary garden with real turds in it. Ignored, by and large, by the little reviews, the poets, by the readers of Eliot, Pound, Stevens, Tate, Lowell, by anyone who sees his views as a form of strenuous revision.

I have no quarrel with much of the current critical judgment of Sandburg. He *has* for a long time been repeating himself in a way which cannot be confused with a fresh exploration of new themes, his work *does* reflect a failure of intelligence, a lack of the critical faculty which blinds him to his own excesses and binds him to a sentimentality about "the people" who are as indifferent to the situations from which poetry comes as are the "millionaires" he used to write about. And what of Sandburg's oafish dismissal of the intellectual life, that somehow Eastern phenomenon. What do the New Critics—to take a group Sandburg has explicitly accused—*want* in their concern with the integrity of a work of art if not the integrity of the individual consciousness? It is, of course, precisely his inability to focus convincingly on the individual life as it is lived away from the mass which makes Sandburg inimical to a time which has more and more considered the merits of a private vision. Lowell, Roethke, Hall, Snodgrass have succeeded in creating a personal poetry. Some of the best poems of recent years have been about the poet's genealogy, his parents, his wives, his child. Yet in the middle of an often confessional, therapeutic lyricism, Adrienne Rich has lamented the loss of the big, flaunty manner of the by now classic modernists. It is not only Eliot, Pound and Stevens who are to be credited for the height of this great argument, this engagement with the reality of the culture which they inhabited, but too and in a way it would be salutary to recall. Sandburg too was part of the modernist revitalization of language, though where the others negotiated from a hypothetical East of the mind, he expressed what was thought to be a wise ignorance, a new intelligential West.

For all his Populist sympathies, it is primarily as a poet of Chicago that Sandburg must be considered. What did Chicago mean in literature? What new reality did it embody? Most obviously and most importantly it was not the East, it was not New England, it was not a tradition of moral strenuousness, a literature built around moral crisis, the growth or failure of consciousness. For the Chicago writers the mystery was not consciousness but force, a reality which would not exclude the impersonal, the amoral, the magnetic. Edwin Arlington Robinson felt this in a somewhat different way and as a New Englander he suffered a deep pessimism. What was different about the Midwest was the creation of an arresting poetry of the brute, an expression of an arbitrary, material world which did not separate wonder from fear. Sandburg's "Chicago" is an example. He himself considered it a paradoxical subject for poetry, but in that paradox resided its appeal. Dreiser's Chicago of *Sister Carrie* is another instance. Sandburg is often compared to Masters and Lindsay in point of Populist sentiment, but a comparison with the novelist is apt for reasons which are equally engaging. Both Dreiser and Sandburg were shocked into consciousness by the existence of the city. Where for the Eastern writer the city was primarily a place to live, a scene, a logical if sometimes sinister extension of the culture, for the Midwestern writer it was more apt to be taken as the foremost manifestation of the inequality of wealth, the indifference to the individual, the radical dislocation from prairie life. But if the city was a wicked arbitrary force it was also the embodiment of a collective energy which was a force within the force, at least for Sandburg. In both writers there is the feeling that man does not live so much as he is lived by something. Sandburg is a prairie Dionysus come to town, a celebrant of the libido everywhere present in the making of a city. By no means is all of his affirmation unwarranted. "Prayers of Steel," for example, remains a fine rhapsody. Yet Sandburg never went much beyond seeing will and desire as collective, whereas Dreiser's virtue was to conceive of these in terms of character itself. (In Dreiser the city is even more of a monolith, unrelieved as it is by the prairie and farm. Were Chick Lorimer a Dreiser character there could be no doubt as to where she had gone.)

In his confusion of the one and the many, his spiritual world with his real one. Sandburg exhibits what is often taken to be the cardinal Whitman characteristic, the reduction of the individual to a mystical, prophetic sense of merging. But Whitman was far from making this the central idea of his poetry, being aware of the "me Myself" as different from the "they" ("Song of Myself"). The most obvious, and crucial, distinction between Whitman and Sandburg is that Whitman's poetry, for all of its absorption in the mass, presents us with an arduous delineation of the self as it relates obliquely as well as directly to that mass. Whitman dramatizes the relation of self to culture in a way which is often dissonant and problematic. Who is Whitman? What is he? that both Sandburg and Ginsburg commend him? Sandburg much more than Whitman, is the too apparent paradigm of Tocqueville's democratic poet, the recorder of the minute and clear on the one hand, and the extremely vague and general on the other. He is at his best when the two are integrated (as distinguished from placed side by side) as in the well-known "Limited."

> I am riding on a limited express, one of the crack trains of the nation.
> Hurding across the prairie into blue haze and dark air go fifteen all-steel coaches holding a thousand people.
> (All the coaches shall be scrap and rust and all the men and women laughing in the diners and sleepers shall pass to ashes.)
> I ask a man in the smoker where he is going and he answers: "Omaha."

The pun in the title—a crack train, finite existence—indicates a tension between energy and particularity over against stasis and eternal obliteration of distinction. The final line is typical of Sandburg's humor, as the actuality of "Omaha" rings strangely, beautifully in the context of the poet's larger considerations. (Omaha is now hog butcher for the world—one of the many changes that have taken place in the Second City.)

Death, for Sandburg has always been the last court of egalitarian appeals, a too comfortable metaphor for the triumph of democracy. Does Sandburg feel any differently about the ominous subject? *Honey and Salt* is full of allusions to evening sunsets, old river towns, many lost anchors, the tall gates beyond, clocks, gongs, "the final Announcement from the Black Void." But the Unknowable has been and remains too great a temptation for predictable abstracting tendencies in Sandburg's. In "Mummy," a poem less effective than the early "Southern Pacific," Death emerges again as "the grand democrat."

In "God Is No Gentleman" we learn that God wears overalls. And in "Timesweep," the longest poem in the volume, Sandburg tells the elephant and the flea etc., concluding that "There is only one man in the world/and his name is All Men." Also on the negative side are the familiar, arbitrary similes, the predictable, random catalogues of sundries, the stale moralizing, the lazy language. Then there are some competent poems which are an imitation of somewhat better predecessors. "City Number" is the pastel description of a busy city dawn which he has done admirably through the years. "Two Fish" is a descriptive poem which might have been included in the *Imagist Anthology*. "Early Copper" is vintage Sandburg, a fine, homey, love poem to the prairie. Is it any wonder that Sandburg's latest volume(s) strike one immediately as literary history?

It would be ungrateful not to be thankful for the distinction of a number of the early poems, and the love that went into the making of that encyclopedia-poem, *The People, Yes*. Sandburg's poetry has been eclipsed by the tendency of the serious reader to take poetry as a kind of salvation. But need one be a major figure in American letters to be read and appreciated? We have become opulent in our literature and are for the first time in a position where we need not resent secondary figures for not being major.

Source: Daniel Fuchs, Review of *Honey and Salt*, in *Chicago Review*, Vol. 16, No. 2, Summer 1963, pp. 119–22.

Michael Yatron

In the following essay, Yatron contends that students who do not like poetry would be well served to start by reading Sandburg.

Carl Sandburg, who wrote simple poetry for simple people and who recently hushed the halls of Congress, is a good poet for the high school English teacher, faced with indifferent students, to begin his poetic chore with. Sandburg devoted his life to translating into poetry the idiom of the people, by whom he meant the majority of native-born and naturalized Americans, who built post-Civil War America with the strength of their hands, the sweat of their brows, and the obstinacy of their spirit into the present-day Colossus. Sandburg was not sure he was writing poetry, but he was sure that what he said had to be meaningful to the average truck driver on Chicago's Wabash Avenue, whose intelligence "the Dark Spirits," Sandburg's epithet for esoteric poets and critics, treated with contempt. The success of Sandburg's communication with the masses has been measured by a study, made by a librarian, which revealed that one hundred readers of his poetry were very much like the characters of his poems. In other words, truck drivers, clerks, salespeople, ditchdiggers, laundry workers, waiters—toiling America—has constituted Sandburg's readership.

Sandburg's popular appeal can be extended to the classroom, precisely because his diction and content are not likely to arouse the antagonism of antipoetic students. If anything, he offers the thrill of recognition to the student, particularly since the America Sandburg chants of is an America that, despite jet airplanes and television sets, still exists and conforms to the students' own experience.

It will help considerably if the teacher can read like a divinely inspired madman, like Plato's Ion reciting Homer, or like bardic Sandburg himself, pulling all the stops of his organ voice. Poetry is not prose; it has always belonged with the lyre and the grape, and its appeal is sensual and emotional rather than intellectual. So the teacher need not feel self-conscious; his wildest chantings are likely to seem mild to adolescents conditioned to the gyrations and caterwauling of Rock and Roll.

In addition to recognizable sound, Sandburg presents a model of non-conformity and humanitarianism and, it is here, in my opinion, that his true worth for the student lies. In our age of the supremacy of the state and the rationalization of industry the individual has been reduced to a cipher. The Myrmidons of Hitler, Stalin, and Tojo and the American "organization man" are symptomatic of the antlike society toward which twentieth century man is gravitating. And with the pressure of population, the necessity for food and automated production, Huxley's and Orwell's automaton societies are becoming realities daily.

Not that there is anything new about such societies; they are simply the old Oriental despotisms equipped with modern technologies. But there is still time to stem the pell-mell, lemming-like flight from freedom.

The first requirement for freedom is the recognition that the state is not the master of the individual, but his servant. This requirement of freedom is met by the individual's having a voice in the ultimate power of the state, the power to go to war. In this connection Sandburg's voice has always been the voice of a free man. He has written many anti-war poems, pointing out that wars are often made by despots and fought by and suffered by the people. The following lines are typical:

A million young workmen straight
and strong lay stiff on the grass and
roads.
A million are now under the soil and
their rotting flesh will in years
feed roots of roots of blood-red
roses.
—"A Million Young Workmen"

Sandburg himself served as a common soldier in the Spanish American War, attended West Point briefly as a "veteran," turned violently pacifistic during World War I, and rejected pacifism in World War II. This completion of the circle shows that Sandburg was not stupidly consistent, and its value for our conformist students lies in sowing the seed in their minds that there is nothing sacred about militarism and rascality, albeit they may wear the cloak of patriotism.

Sandburg was equally scathing as regards big business, which too often has maximized profits while minimizing humanity. He wrote many variations of the following lines:

What is the story of railroads, of oil,
steel, copper, aluminum, tire?
Of the utilities of light, heat, power,
transport?
What are the balances of price and
shame?
Who took hold of the wilderness and
changed it?
Who paid the coast in blood and
struggle?
What will the grave and considerate
historian loving humanity and hating
no one dead or alive have to
write of wolves and people?
—*The People, Yes*

Today our euphemism for greed in industry is "administered prices," while greed in the higher echelons of labor is explained in terms of conspicuous consumption, that labor leaders cannot sit down as equals with corporation executives unless they too have Brooks Brothers' suits and Cadillacs; or else it is blatantly stated that the American labor movement is not an ideological one. Where is our bedeviled teenager who sees the many discrepancies between moralistic theory and cynical practices to get his idealism from, if not from the poet? He is not supposed to get it from his teachers since they are charged to keep their opinions to themselves.

RACIAL VIEWS

In the area of racial relationships, Sandburg is without prejudice. Hungarians with accordions ("Happiness"), Greeks shoveling gravel ("Near Keokuk"), Italians working with pick and shovel ("The Shovel Man"), and Jews selling fish ("Fish Crier") are presented sympathetically. And what is more to Sandburg's credit is that his tolerance is extended to Asiatics. "My prayers go . . . for the Russian people. If they are merely 'Asiatic hordes,' then I'm a barrel-house bum," he stated. For a man born in the isolationist Middle West, whose mind was formed during the period when the spectre of "the yellow peril" was publicized often, this sanity is reasonableness itself.

The strength of Sandburg's convictions can be inferred from the fact that two of his closest friends of many years' standing, Theodore Dreiser and Edgar Lee Masters, were violent anti-Semites. Dreiser had had unfortunate relationships with various publishers of Jewish extraction and he was thoroughly convinced that sharp dealing was peculiar to the Jews. Masters' legal skirmishes with real estate men and money lenders of Jewish extraction and his disgust with New York publishers and critics bred prejudice in him. And it must be remembered that Masters had Sandburg's ear and sought to get his first book of poems published for him. Yet Sandburg refused to concede to his friends' bigotry. On the contrary he was proud to broadcast during World War II that Barney Ross "the battling Jew who held three prize-ring championships enlisted in the Marines over-age. . . ."

Quite consistently, Sandburg was a champion of the Negro. At the close of World War I, some white boys of Chicago stoned a colored youth on a raft with the result that he was drowned. A race riot ensued and Sandburg was sent by the Chicago *Daily News* to report the situation. Out of this reportage grew a book, *The Chicago Race Riots*, which clearly revealed Sandburg's belief that "a man's a man for a' that."

OTHER VIEWS

Another ugly thing that Sandburg saw growing in American society is class stratification. It began its cancerous growth in his youth, but it has proliferated most since World War II. Veblen noted it, some fifty years ago, and recently Vance Packard has chronicled it in *The Status Seekers*. We see it all around us in terms of suburban homes, swimming pools, two cars and more, prestige schools and universities, foreign travel, in clothing, and in a hundred and one expressions of imagined superiority. Again it is our poet who is a democrat. Sandburg is not ashamed of unpressed and patched pants, of unshined and worn shoes, of long hair. He detests expensive night clubs and dress suits, and, I suppose, fin-tailed automobiles. Material things and glossy appearances may have their place in brightening life, but they are not the end-all and be-all of existence which our middle class society has made them. And they are certainly not worth the never-ending wage slavery and bill-paying which their possession entails. Our poet in ignoring materialism again provides youth with a needed alternate possibility to the drive for success.

Sandburg is a fine example for the youth who suspects that a mess of pottage isn't worth a soul and a life. Sandburg rode freight trains, washed dishes, worked in a construction camp, threshed wheat, learned the painter's trade, enlisted in the Army, was a college student, a hobo, a wandering minstrel, a newspaperman, a militant Socialist, a poet, and a man of letters. He was a man trying to find himself but always moving in the direction of his true self. And his trials and errors are healthier than the diseased certainty of the Princeton seniors who know what income they require, what corporation they will work for, what pension plan they will benefit most by, before they are graduated from college and have lived a single day as an adult.

Another area where our student may profit from Sandburg's voice is the area of work. Our middle class society is making many forms of work ignoble. It is sending most of its children to college, and soon there will be nothing but white collars: school teachers, dentists, doctors, lawyers, journalists, engineers, publicity men, advertising executives, entertainers, salesmen, corporation presidents, vice-presidents, and executive trainees. Vance Packard calls it the diploma elite. Would that it were a true intellectual elite and not a dullard elite which receives a high school diploma for attendance, and often a college degree just as automatically. At any rate Sandburg sings praises of honest toil; he calls work a privilege. And he does not think a diploma makes a man. He realizes that many folk with homely virtues and skills are far superior to both lettered and unlettered blockheads, and their society healthier and stabler than a parasitic one where men prey on men.

Sandburg, then, has a basic content which can be summed up in the word Man and which can nourish the mind of the young in the best traditions of Western Civilization. The next question to be raised is, Is what Sandburg writes poetry, and, if so, how good is it?

Sandburg, as I have stated earlier, was not sure that he was writing poetry. He was trying to communicate to an audience which was not sophisticated verbally, to whom the connotations of words are very closely related to their denotations, to whom literary allusion and subtle metaphor are meaningless. He has been an exponent of Wordsworth's "man talking to men." But this use of a *lingua communis* carries with it its own trap, as Coleridge pointed out. The language of prose and the language of metrical composition are two different entities. Thus Sandburg's work quite often degenerates into a pedestrian prosaism summed up by the word "talk." Accordingly, he has been accused, justifiably in this writer's opinion, of being diffuse, clownish, and vulgar.

Such criticism, however, is by no means the final word. It is rather a matter of taste, and stems from people who have been weaned on measured meters, rhymes, striking metaphors, and word music. In other words, I am well aware that my personal preferences or prejudices may create in me a blind spot toward Sandburg's type of expression.

There is no blind spot, however, in my feeling that Sandburg has many limitations. His is not a lyric gift; he neither sings nor can he give expression to deep human emotions. He is not a philosophical poet, nor a dramatic one—rather he is a poet descriptive of the surface, whose eye and ear are keen and who reproduces America as no one else has. He is, as I have stated, a good beginning for the anti-poetic—no mean contribution. He can attract to poetry many of our youth who would normally be repulsed by other poets who seem to say nothing in antiquated and dull language. And once Sandburg has been the initial magnet, and he has given the student the thrill of recognition and of understanding, the next step is to teach the mechanics of traditional poetry and lead the student to the rich veins of English, and ultimately, world poetry.

Source: Michael Yatron, "Carl Sandburg: The Poet as Nonconformist," in *English Journal*, Vol. 48, No. 9, December 1959, pp. 524–39.

Louis Untermeyer

In the following essay, Untermeyer extols the combination of strength, delicacy, and passion in the verses of Chicago Poems *and* Cornhuskers.

I can begin this chapter on Carl Sandburg in no better way than by admitting the worst thing that most of his adverse critics charge against him—his brutality. And, without hastening to soften this admission, I would like to quote a short passage from a volume to which I have already referred. In Synge's preface to his *Poems and Translations* (published in 1911) he wrote, "In these days poetry is usually a flower of evil or good; but it is the timber that wears most surely, and there is no timber that has not strong roots among the clay and worms. . . . Even if we grant that exalted poetry can be kept successful by itself, the strong things of life are needed in poetry also, to show that what is exalted or tender is not made by feeble blood. It may almost be said that before verse can be human again, it must learn to be brutal."

John Masefield was the first in England to respond to this rousing prophecy and, with half a dozen racy narratives, he took a generation of readers out of the humid atmosphere of libraries and literary hot-houses. He took them out into the coarse sunlight and the rude air. He brought back to verse that blend of beauty and brutality which is poetry's most human and enduring quality. He rediscovered that rich and almost vulgar vividness that is the life-blood of Chaucer and Shakespeare, of Burns and Rabelais, of Horace and Heine and Villon, and all those who were not only great artists but great humanists. At a time when people were fumbling about, grasping tentatively at every banal or bizarre novelty in a search for strange things to thrill them, Masefield showed them that they themselves were stranger, wilder and far more thrilling than anything in the world or out of it. He brought a new glamor to

> THERE IS AN AFFILIATED SIDE OF SANDBURG'S POWER THAT MOST OF HIS CRITICS HAVE OVERLOOKED, AND THAT IS HIS ABILITY TO MAKE LANGUAGE LIVE, TO MAKE THE WORDS ON THE PRINTED PAGE SING, DANCE, BLEED, RAGE, AND SUFFER WITH THE AROUSED READER."

poetry; or rather, he brought back the oldest glamor, the splendid illusion of a raw and vigorous reality.

And so Sandburg. With a more uncovered directness and even less fictional disguise, he goes straight to his theme. Turn to the first poem in the volume *Chicago Poems* (Henry Holt & Co., 1916) and observe this uplifted coarseness, this almost animal exultation that is none the less an exaltation.

"Chicago"

Hog Butcher for the World,
Tool Maker, Stacker of Wheat,
Player with Railroads and the Nation's
Freight Handler;
Stormy, husky, brawling,
City of the Big Shoulders:
They tell me you are wicked and I believe them, for I have seen your painted women under the gas lamps luring the farm boys.
And they tell me you are crooked and I answer: Yes, it is true I have seen the gunman kill and go free to kill again.
And they tell me you are brutal and my reply is: On the faces of women and children I have seen the marks of wanton hunger.
And having answered so I turn once more to those who sneer at this my city, and I give them back the sneer and say to them:
Come and show me another city with lifted head singing so proud to be alive and coarse and strong and cunning.
Flinging magnetic curses amid the toil of piling job on job, here is a tall bold slugger set vivid against the little soft cities;

Fierce as a dog with tongue lapping for action, cunning as a savage pitted against the wilderness,
Bareheaded,
Shoveling,
Wrecking,
Planning,
Building, breaking, rebuilding;
Under the smoke, dust all over his mouth, laughing with white teeth,
Under the terrible burden of destiny laughing as a young man laughs,
Laughing even as an ignorant fighter laughs who has never lost a battle,
Bragging and laughing that under his wrist is the pulse, and under his ribs the heart of the people,
Laughing!
Laughing the stormy, husky, brawling laughter of Youth, half-naked, sweating, proud to be Hog Butcher, Tool Maker, Stacker of Wheat, Player with Railroads and Freight Handler to the Nation.

Here is a picture of a city and a man. It is brilliant, bold and, for all its loud vigor, visionary. Throughout the book, the poet is strangely like his city. There is the mixture of a gigantic, youthful personality and an older, alien will to mount. This blend of impulses shows even stronger in other sections of the volumes. In "Fogs and Fires" and the more definitely socialistic poems, we see Sandburg's inheritance of Swedish mysticism fused with an American, I might almost say a practical idealism; stubbornness turned to a storm of protest.

There is an affiliated side of Sandburg's power that most of his critics have overlooked, and that is his ability to make language live, to make the words on the printed page sing, dance, bleed, rage, and suffer with the aroused reader. This creative use of proper names and slang, the interlarding of cheapness and nobility which is Sandburg's highly personal idiom, would have given great joy to Whitman. That old barbarian was doubtless dreaming of possible followers when he said that the *Leaves of Grass*, with its crude vigor, was a sort of enlarged sketch-piece, "a passageway to something, rather than a thing in itself concluded," a language experiment. In that unfinished sketch for a projected lecture (*An American Primer*) he seemed to be praying for future Sandburgs when he wrote:

"A perfect user of words uses things—they exude in power and beauty from him—miracles from his hands, miracles from his mouth—lilies, clouds, sunshine, women, poured copiously—things, whirled like chain-shot rocks, defiance, compulsion, houses, iron, locomotives, the oak, the pine, the keen eye, the hairy breast, the Texan ranger, the Boston truckman, the woman that arouses a man, the man that arouses a woman.

Words are magic…limber, lasting, fierce words. Do you suppose the liberties and the brawn of These States have to do only with delicate lady-words? with gloved gentleman-words?

What is the fitness—what the strange charm of aboriginal names?—Monongahela—it rolls with venison richness upon the palate.

American writers will show far more freedom in the use of names. Ten thousand common, idiomatic words are growing, or are today already grown, out of which vast numbers could be used by American writers, with meaning and effect—words that would be welcomed by the nation, being of the national blood."

Turn now, while still on a consideration of words, raciness, and brutality in language, to what is to many the most offensive piece of writing in the volume. It is called "To a Contemporary Bunkshooter" and it begins:

You come along…tearing your shirt…
    yelling about Jesus.

Where do you get that stuff?

What do you know about Jesus?

Jesus had a way of talking soft and outside
    of a few bankers and higher-ups
among the con men of Jerusalem everybody
    liked to have this Jesus around
because he never made any fake passes and
    everything he said went and he
helped the sick and gave the people hope.

You come along squirting words at us, shak-
    ing your fist and calling us all dam
fools so fierce the froth slobbers over your
    lips…always blabbing we're all
going to hell straight off and you know all
    about it.

I've read Jesus' words. I know what he said.
    You don't throw any scare into me.
I've got your number. I know how much you
    know about Jesus.

He never came near clean people or dirty
    people but they felt cleaner because he

came along. It was your crowd of bankers
    and business men and lawyers hired
the sluggers and murderers who put Jesus
    out of the running.

I say the same bunch backing you nailed the
    nails into the hands of this Jesus of
Nazareth. He had lined up against him the
    same crooks and strong-arm men now
lined up with you paying your way.

Here we have an angry opponent of Billy Sunday answering that frothing evangelist in his own sweet mixture of slang, vilification and religious ecstasy. It is not only a tremendous protest at the falsification of Jesus but a passionate praise of the real martyr. And, incidentally, it is a startling experiment in the use of words. It seems almost a direct answer to Whitman's insistence that before the coming poets could become powerful, they would have to learn the use of hard and powerful words; the greatest artists are, he affirmed, always simple and direct, never merely "polite or obscure." He loved violence in language. "The appetite of the people of These States, in talk, in popular speeches and writings, is for unhemmed latitude, coarseness, directness, live epithets, expletives, words of opprobrium, resistance.—This I understand because I have the taste myself as largely as any one. I have pleasure in the use, on fit occasion, of 'traitor,' 'coward,' 'liar,' 'shyster,' 'skulk,' 'dough-face,' 'trickster,' 'backslider,' 'thief,' 'impotent,' 'lick-spittle.'"

There are, of course, times when, in the midst of rugged beauties, Sandburg exalts not beauty but mere ruggedness. He often becomes vociferous about "big stuff," "red guts," and the things which, on the printed page, are never strong but are only the stereotypes of strength. Sometimes he is so in love with the physical quality of Strength itself that one hears his adjectives creak in a straining effort to achieve it. See, for instance, such merely showy affairs as "Killers," "Fight," and one or two others. They put one in mind of a professional strong man in the glare of the footlights, of virility in front of a mirror, of an epithet exhibiting its muscle.

But, if any one imagines that Sandburg excels only in verse that is stentorian and heavy-fisted, let him turn to the page that immediately follows the title-poem. A greater contrast is inconceivable. This is the delicate and almost silent poem:

"SKETCH"

The shadows of the ships
Rock on the crest
In the low blue lustre
Of the tardy and the soft introlling tide.
A long brown bar at the dip of the sky
Puts an arm of sand in the span of salt.
The lucid and endless wrinkles
Draw in, lapse and withdraw.
Wavelets crumble and white spent bubbles
Wash on the floor of the beach.
Rocking on the crest
In the low blue lustre
Are the shadows of the ships.

or, two pages further on, witness this:

"LOST"

Desolate and lone
All night long on the lake
Where fog trails and mist creeps,
The whistle of a boat
Calls and cries unendingly,
Like some lost child
In tears and trouble
Hunting the harbor's breast
And the harbor's eyes.

Here we see what I think is Sandburg's finest artistic quality—the sharp and sympathetic gift of the etcher with his firm, clean-cut and always suggestive line. And the passion against injustice, against the economic horrors that stamp out beauty and kill even the hunger for it, cries equally through these more delicately-drawn pieces. Read, for utter poignance, "Graceland," "Anna Imroth," "Mill-Doors," "Onion Days," "Masses." Or this even more wearied and pathetic poem:

"HALSTED STREET CAR"

Come, you cartoonists,
Hang on a strap with me here
At seven o'clock in the morning
On a Halsted street car.
Take your pencils
And draw these faces.
Try with your pencils for these crooked faces,
That pig-sticker in one corner—his mouth.
That overall factory girl—her loose cheeks.
Find for your pencils
A way to mark your memory
Of tired empty faces.
After their night's sleep,
In the moist dawn
And cool daybreak,

Faces
Tired of wishes,
Empty of dreams.

Here again, as in "They Will Say," "Fish Crier," "Fog" and a dozen others, one sees how Sandburg evokes background and actors, a story or sorrow, with the fewest possible strokes and with a sympathy that none of our poets can surpass. His hate, a strengthening and challenging force, would distort and overbalance the effect of his work, were it not exceeded by the fiercer virility of his love. No writer in America is so hard and soft-speaking; beneath the brutality, he is possibly the tenderest of living poets. Read, as an instance, the poem on page 89:

"MURMURINGS IN A FIELD HOSPITAL"

[*They picked him up in the grass where he had lain two days in the rain with a piece of shrapnel in his lungs.*]
Come to me only with playthings now. . .
A picture of a singing woman with blue eyes
Standing at a fence of hollyhocks, poppies
    and sunflowers. . .
Or an old man I remember sitting with children telling stories
Of days that never happened anywhere in
    the world. . .
No more iron cold and real to handle,
Shaped for a drive straight ahead.
Bring me only beautiful useless things.
Only old home things touched at sunset in
    the quiet. . .
And at the window one day in summer
Yellow of the new crock of butter
Stood against the red of new climbing roses. . .
And the world was all playthings.

It is this delicate touch, this exquisite poignancy that makes Sandburg's harsher commentaries doubly important. His anger at conditions and his hate of cruelty proceed from an intense understanding of men's thwarted desires and dreams. This lavish but never sentimental pity shines out of all his work. It glows through poems like "Fellow Citizens," "Population Drifts," "The Harbor" and burns through the half-material, half-mystic "Choices," "Limited" (a sadness edged with irony) and the unforgettable, stern pathos of

"A FENCE"

Now the stone house on the lake front is
    finished and the workmen are beginning
the fence.

The palings are made of iron bars with steel
  points that can stab the life out of
any man who falls on them.

As a fence, it is a masterpiece, and will shut
  off the rabble and all vagabonds and
hungry men and all wandering children
  looking for a place to play.

Passing through the bars and over the steel
  points will go nothing except Death
and the Rain and Tomorrow.

Throughout the volume one is continually surprised to see so personal a twin picture; a double exposure, I might say, of a man and a city. In spite of a few affectations of idiom and twisted lines which lead up the same literary blind-alley that Ezra Pound has chosen as his habitat, *Chicago Poems* is a fresh proof of how our poetry has grown more vigorous and, at the same time, more visionary. It is made of rough timber; it has "strong roots in the clay and worms."

In the new volume, *Cornhuskers* (Henry Holt & Co., 1918), there is the same animal and spiritual blend, the same uplifted vulgarity; but here it is far more coordinated and restrained. The gain in power is evident with the very first poem, a magnificent panoramic vision of the prairie that begins:

I was born on the prairie and the milk of its
  wheat, the red of its clover, the eyes
of its women, gave me a song and a slogan.

Here the water went down, the icebergs slid
  with gravel, the gaps and the valleys
hissed, and the black loam came, and the
  yellow sandy loam.

Here between the sheds of the Rocky Mountains and the Appalachians, here now
a morning star fixes a fire sign over the timber
  claims and cow pastures, the corn
belt, the cattle ranches.

Here the gray geese go five hundred miles
  and back with a wind under their
wings, honking the cry for a new home.

Here I know I will hanker after nothing so
  much as one more sunrise or a sky
moon of fire doubled to a river moon of water.

The prairie sings to me in the forenoon and I
  know in the night I rest easy in the
prairie arms, on the prairie heart!

. . .

After the sunburn of the day
handling a pitchfork at a hayrack,

after the eggs and biscuit and coffee,
the pearl-gray haystacks
in the gloaming
are cool prayers
to the harvest hands.

. . .

In the city among the walls the overland
  passenger train is chocked and the
pistons hiss and the wheels curse.

On the prairie the overland flits on phantom
  wheels and the sky and the soil
between them muffle the pistons and cheer
  the wheels.

. . .

I am here when the cities are gone.
I am here before the cities come.
I nourished the lonely men on horses.
I will keep the laughing men who ride iron.
I am dust of men.

These are the sonorous, opening lines of the volume, a wider and more confident rhythm than Sandburg has yet attempted. The entire collection is similarly strengthened; there is a greater depth and dignity in the later poems, the accent is less vociferous, more vitalizing. Observe the unusual, athletic beauty of "Manitoba Childe Roland," "Always the Mob," "The Four Brothers" and this muscular

"PRAYERS OF STEEL"

Lay me on an anvil, O God.
Beat me and hammer me into a crowbar.
Let me pry loose old walls.
Let me lift and loosen old foundations.
Lay me on an anvil, O God.
Beat me and hammer me into a steel spike.
Drive me into the girders that hold a
  skyscraper together.
Take red-hot rivets and fasten me into the
  central girders.
Let me be the great nail holding a skyscraper
  through blue nights into white stars.

In this volume Sandburg again shows how responsive he is to the limber and idiomatic phrases that are the blood and bones of our speech. His language lives almost as fervidly as the life from which it is taken. Yet here his intensity is seldom raucous. What could be quieter and yet more positive than the calm irony in "Knucks," the pioneer-celebrating "Leather Leggings," the suggestive force in "Interior," the solemn simplicity of "Grass," the epigrammatic brevity of

"SOUTHERN PACIFIC"

Huntington sleeps in a house six feet long.
Huntington dreams of railroads he built and
  owned.
Huntington dreams of ten thousand men
  saying: Yes, sir.
Blithery sleeps in a house six feet long.
Blithery dreams of rails and ties he laid.
Blithery dreams of saying to Huntington:
  Yes, sir.
Huntington,
Blithery, sleep in houses six feet long.

Similarly notable are the modern rendering of the tablet writing of the fourth millennium BCE in "Bilbea," the faithful picture of a small town in "Band Concert," the suggestive "Memoir of a Proud Boy," the strange requiem note in

"COOL TOMBS"

When Abraham Lincoln was shoveled into
  the tombs, he forgot the copperheads
and the assassin... in the dust, in the cool
  tombs.

And Ulysses Grant lost all thought of con
  men and Wall Street, cash and
collateral turned ashes... in the dust, in the
  cool tombs.

Pocahontas' body, lovely as a poplar, sweet
  as a red haw in November or a
pawpaw in May, did she wonder? does she
  remember?... in the dust, in the cool
tombs?

Take any streetful of people buying clothes
  and groceries, cheering a hero or
throwing confetti and blowing tin horns...
  tell me if the lovers are losers... tell
me if any get more than the lovers... in the
  dust... in the cool tombs.

This fresh blend of proper names and slang, which would so have delighted Whitman, is Sandburg's most characteristic idiom and is used with excellent effect in *Cornhuskers*. And it is this mingling that enriches his heritage of mingled blood. Beneath the slang one is aware of the mystic. The poet has learned to give his penetrative *patois* a cosmic significance; he gives us Swedenborg in terms of State Street. This peculiar mysticism looks out of "Caboose Thoughts," "Wilderness," "Localities," "Old Timers," "Potato Blossom Songs and Jigs." There is a more extended and musical spirituality here than was contained in the earlier volume; a quality that is no less dynamic but far more lyric. There have been few rhymed

poems that blend sweetness and sonority more skillfully than some of the lyrics in the sections "Haunts" and "Persons Half Known." Notice the subtle flow of "Laughing Corn," the tympanic syllables in "Drumnotes," and the almost feminine grace of this poem from the latter division, a tribute to a singer who died as she had begun to sing:

"ADELAIDE CRAPSEY"

Among the bumble-bees in red-top hay, a
  freckled field of brown-eyed Susans
dripping yellow leaves in July,
I read your heart in a book.

And your mouth of blue pansy—I know
  somewhere I have seen it rain-shattered.

And I have seen a woman with her head
  flung between her naked knees, and her
head held there listening to the sea, the great
  naked sea shouldering a load of salt.

And the blue pansy mouth sang to the sea:
Mother of God, I'm so little a thing,
Let me sing longer,
Only a little longer.
And the sea shouldered its salt in long gray
  combers hauling new shapes on the
beach sand.

And here is an example of a mood that Sandburg mirrors so skillfully, a cloudy loveliness reflected in the hazy outlines of the free-rhythmed, unrhymed lyric:

"RIVER ROADS"

Let the crows go by hawking their caw and
  caw.
They have been swimming in midnights of
  coal mines somewhere.
Let 'em hawk their caw and caw.
Let the woodpecker drum and drum on a
  hickory stump.
He has been swimming in red and blue pools
  somewhere hundreds of years
And the blue has gone to his wings and the
  red has gone to his head.
Let his red head drum and drum.
Let the dark pools hod the birds in a looking-
  glass.
And if the pool wishes, let it shiver to the
  blur of many wings, old swimmers
from old places.
Let the redwing streak a line of vermilion on
  the green wood lines.
And the mist along the river fix its purple in lines
  of a woman's shawl on lazy shoulders.

Here, in the work of Sandburg, is another phase of the new and definitely American spirit in our poetry. Here, in spite of its moments of delicacy, is no trace of delicate languors, of passion extracted from songs or life that is gleaned in a library. This is something carved out of earth, showing the dirt and the yellow clay; there are great gaps and boulders here, steaming ditches and the deep-chested laughter of workers quarreling, forgetting, building. As of *Leaves of Grass*, it can be said that he "who touches this book touches a man"—and there is nothing arts-and-crafty about him. Brutal, tender, full of anger and pity, his lines run light as a child's pleasure or stumble along with the heavy grace of a hunky; common as sunlight or talk on Third Avenue of a Saturday. Rough-hewn and stolid; perhaps a bit too conscious of its biceps; too proud of the way its thumping feet trample down quiet places. But going on, on... gladly, doggedly; with a kind of large and casual ecstasy. One thinks of a dark sea with its tides tossing and shouting. Or the streets of a crowd-filled city when a great wind runs through them.

Source: Louis Untermeyer, "Carl Sandburg," in *The New Era in American Poetry*, Henry Holt, 1919, pp. 95–109.

SOURCES

Callahan, North, *Carl Sandburg: His Life and Works*, Pennsylvania State University Press, 1987, p. 186.

Crowder, Richard, "Sandburg's Chromatic Vision in *Honey and Salt*," in *The Vision of This Land*, edited by John Halwas and Dennis Reader, Western Illinois University Press, 1976, p. 94.

Niven, Penelope, *Carl Sandburg: A Biography*, Charles Scribner's Sons, 1991, pp. 614–701.

Sutton, William, "Part 1: The Perry Friendship," in *Carl Sandburg Remembered*, Scarecrow Press, 1979, p. 10.

FURTHER READING

Currey, J. Seymour, *Chicago: Its History and Its Builders*, S. J. Clarke, 1912.

Written just prior to Sandburg's publication of *Chicago Poems*, this illustrated book examines the Chicago World's Fair, infrastructure, sanitation, the elevated train system, and other aspects of Chicago life in the early twentieth century. It is a great resource for gaining an understanding of the Chicago Sandburg was describing.

Sandburg, Carl, *Abraham Lincoln: The Illustrated Edition: The Prairie Years and The War Years*, edited by Edward C. Goodman, introduction by Alan Axelrod, Sterling, 2007.

This abridged and illustrated edition of Sandburg's original six-volume work allows for visualization of Lincoln's life as well as the words Sandburg so lovingly crafted.

———, *Rootabaga Stories*, illustrated by Maud and Miska Petersham, Applewood Books, 1998.

Originally published in 1922, this is a highly entertaining reprint of Sandburg's children's anthology of fantasy stories that was considered by some critics to be his finest work.

Steichen, Paula, *Carl Sandburg Home: Official National Park Handbook*, United States National Park Service, Division of Publications, 1982.

This three part handbook created for the National Park site at Sandburg's home in Flat Rock, North Carolina, was written by his granddaughter, Paula Steichen (named after her grandmother). It contains three parts, one on life at Connemara, a biographical essay of her grandfather, and finally, tourist information and reference materials about Sandburg and the homesite.

SUGGESTED SEARCH TERMS

Carl Sandburg

Sandburg AND Moon Rondeau

Sandburg AND Honey and Salt

Sandburg AND rondeau

Sandburg AND People's Poet

Carl Sandburg poems

Carl Sandburg AND awards

Carl Sandburg AND historic site association

Prayer to the Masks

LÉOPOLD SÉDAR SENGHOR

1945

Over the course of his long career as a writer, philosopher, and statesman, the Senegalese poet Léopold Sédar Senghor inspired countless young writers throughout the French-speaking world. Along with Aimé Cesaire and Léon Damas, he founded the *négritude* movement, which argued that the black people of colonial Africa and the Caribbean should take pride in their African roots and find in their native traditions an inspiration for a new literature and a new way of life. Senghor put these ideas into practice in his wide field of activity. He wrote voluminously as a poet and as a philosopher of the new culture and politics of African independence from colonial rule. In the political arena, he was one of the major architects of independence for his own country, Senegal, and for French West Africa more generally. He served as president of Senegal for two decades.

"Prayer to the Masks" is typical of Senghor's writing throughout his long career, although it comes from his first collection, *Songs of the Shadow*, published in 1945. It exhibits clearly the features that characterized his poetic writing: the use of African themes and settings, the highly rhythmic long lines reminiscent of the Bible and Walt Whitman, the evocations of music and song, and the contrast of the vitality of a mythic (and future) Africa with the present of both Europe and Africa under colonialism. It is the poem of a young man seeking to connect with the past; he senses that this connection will inspire him to struggle through the damaged life of the present to forge a better future for himself and his people.

Léopold Sédar Senghor (*The Library of Congress*)

AUTHOR BIOGRAPHY

Senghor was born in Joal, a village in Central Senegal, in 1906. His father was a successful merchant dealing with the French in goods for the export trade. After one year of elementary education in Joal, he was sent to a missionary school in Ngasobil and later a Catholic high school in Dakar, where he was educated in the French language and French culture. Although he originally wanted to enter the priesthood, Senghor was sent on scholarship to France in 1928, where he pursued the study of literature at the Lycée Louis le Grand and the Sorbonne. In the preparatory class at the lycée (school), Senghor befriended his classmate Georges Pompidou, who later became president of France. Senghor earned the License-és-lettres (equivalent to a bachelor's degree), the Diplôme d'études supérieures (equivalent to a master's degree), and the agrégation (similar to a doctorate). He was the first African from the French colonies to earn the agrégation.

The 1920s and 1930s were decades of developing political and cultural consciousness on the part of American, Caribbean, and African-born blacks. Relatively large urban communities of blacks developed in cities such as New York and Paris, and previously separate groups—African Americans, Caribbean-Creoles, and Africans from French colonies such as Senegal—began to encounter one another, form friendships and organizations, and collaborate in cultural and literary publications. Their response was a literary and cultural movement, affirming the unique value of blackness and the black cultures of Africa and the Americas, under the banner of négritude. The founding figures were Senghor, Aimé Césaire, and Léon Damas, all of whom were students in the early 1930s in Paris and contributors to a series of reviews and journals. The term négritude itself was coined by Césaire in his book-length poem *Notes on a Return to the Native Land*. In 1947 and 1948, Damas and Senghor published anthologies that further gave shape to the literary movement.

Senghor served in the French army during World War II and was confined for several months in a German prisoner-of-war camp. After the war, he was actively involved in Senegalese and African politics. In 1945 he published *Chants d'ombre* (Songs of Shadow), which contains "Prayer to the Masks." The poems in this volume, written before the war, express his feelings for Africa, thoughts on racism, and his fears about his native land's future. The translation used here is from the 1991 edition, *The Collected Poetry*, translated by Melvin Dixon.

He served in the cabinet of the French prime minister Edgar Faure in 1955 as secretary of state. In 1960, he was closely involved in attempts to form a multistate federation of West African states, and in that same year, he was elected president of the newly independent Republic of Senegal. While president, Senghor wrote critical and political prose, in addition to multiple award-winning volumes of poetry, including an acclaimed collection of essays on socialism, *On African Socialism*, written in 1964. He served as president until 1980, when he voluntarily stepped down from office, the first African president to do so. In 1984, he was appointed to the prestigious Académie Francaise for his literary and humanistic achievements. Senghor died at age 95 in 2002.

POEM SUMMARY

Lines 1–4

The poem begins with an address to an object or spirit. Here, as the title indicates, this address is a prayer to the masks, which appear in the poem both as works of African art and as more general spirits of African culture, society, and history. The poet lists the colors of the masks as black, red, and black and white, suggesting the masks are symbols of race and skin color. In the third line, Senghor suggests that these masks are also spirits of nature, linked to the winds that blow from the four directions of north, south, east, and west. As spirits that blow, they also may be related to the poet's breath and poetic inspiration. As the fourth line indicates, he greets them with silence, as if listening to what the mask-spirits will whisper to him on the wind.

Lines 5–9

The poet introduces his family's guardian animal, the lion, symbol of aristocratic virtue and courage. Traditionally, these animals were thought to be the first ancestor and the protector of the family line. In mentioning his lion-headed ancestor, Senghor alludes to the name of his father, Diogoye, which in his native Serer language means lion. In ceremonies in which masks would be used, the family might be represented by a lion mask. Senghor further reinforces the implications of long tradition and patriarchal power. The lion guards the ground that is forbidden to women and to passing things, in favor of values, memories, and customs that stretch back into mythic antiquity.

Lines 10–14

These lines develop a complex relationship between the faces of the ancestors, the poet's face, and the masks. Line 10 speaks of the masks as idealized representations of previously living faces. The masks eliminate the mobile features and signs of age in the faces of the living ancestors, but in doing so they outlive their death. In turn, they are able to give shape to the face of the poet bent over the page and writing his prayer to the masks. He appeals to them to listen to him, for he is the living image of those masks to whom he is writing a prayer.

Lines 15–17

These lines contrast the glorious past of Africa, when vast black-ruled empires spanned the continent, and the present, in which the peoples of Africa have been subjugated by the imperial conquests of European nations. The daughter of royalty symbolizes the nobility of traditional Africa, and her death represents both the general suffering and decline of traditional African culture and the loss of political power of blacks to rule

themselves. However, the relationship to Europe is not presented solely in a negative way. The image of the umbilical cord suggests that the European conquest has nourished a new Africa soon to be born, but one that will eventually have to sever its ties with its European "mother" if it is to live and grow.

Lines 18 and 19

The masks are called to witness the sad history of modern Africa, and they look on, god-like with their changeless faces. However, Senghor also suggests that the traditional customs and values have apparently not been able to respond to the great changes that history has brought about. The poem implicitly comes to a question and a turning point: Do the masks represent a valuable long view from which the present can be seen in its proper perspective, or are they merely relics of a past that have nothing to say to those who are exploited and suffering in the present?

Lines 20 and 21

The poet prays to the magic spirits of the masks to help speed the rebirth suggested by the image of the umbilical cord connecting Africa to Europe in line 17. Implicitly, reviving the ancestral spirits of the masks will help sever the ties of dependence. In turn, a reborn African creativity can help Europe to a more life-affirming use of its material and scientific wealth, just as brown yeast is necessary for making bread from white flour.

Lines 22–27

These lines further develop the idea that Africa will provide the life impulse to a Europe that is oriented toward mechanical values, materialist gain, and war. It is the rhythm of African music and dance that can change the thud of machines into something better. A reborn Africa will lend its youthful energy to a senile Europe, bringing joy and hope where there has been isolation, exhaustion, despair, and death through thirty years of war and depression.

Lines 28 and 29

Senghor refers to the exploitation of Africa for its raw materials and to European conceptions of black Africans as merely a source of cheap labor and economic profit. Looking back to the figures of death and rebirth in the previous lines, he ironically notes how the Europeans view the black African as a fearful image of death.

TOPICS FOR FURTHER STUDY

- Create a presentation about how Senghor depicts the past, present, and future in his poem. How does the present relate to the traditional African past? What role will tradition play in the future of Africa? Design a computerized slide show to use with your discussion that visually depicts what Senegal looked like in the past, the present, and a possible future.

- Senghor was a central participant in the négritude movement, a literary and cultural movement that asserted pride in being black and in the traditions of Africa and of the African peoples brought to the Americas as slaves. Other important participants included the Martiniquean poet Aimé Césaire and the Guyanese poet Léon Gontran Damas. In what ways might the idea of Africa and African roots be different for Senghor, who grew up in a small village in Senegal, and the "New World" négritude poets, who had never been to Africa when they began writing? Start a Wiki to discuss your findings with other students using examples from the poetry of the other poets as evidence of the differences.

- Senghor was educated in French schools and universities, and he wrote in French, yet he also uses French, the language of the colonizer, to criticize colonialism and to assert the value of African traditions, history, and beliefs. What sorts of problems do you think his literary use of French might have posed for Senghor in writing his poems? What did he gain by writing in French? Would it have been better for him to have written his poetry in Serer, his native language? What does Senghor bring to French literature and language from an African perspective? How does Senghor's use of the French language relate to his vision of future relations between Africa and Europe? Find and compare several translations of "Prayer to the Masks." Create a list of translation differences and explain how they affect the interpretation of the poem.

- Research the role of the mask in African history in the young-adult book *The Art of African Masks: Exploring Cultural Traditions* by Carol Finley (1998). Senghor puts at the center of his work a form of African art and spirituality, the mask. Paul Laurence Dunbar wrote the poem "We Wear the Mask" in 1896 in *Lyrics of Lowly Life*. Compare how the mask functions in that work with the role of the masks in Senghor's poem. Design a mask that would be representative of each poem and label the elements of each of them to explain your response.

- The African American scholar and writer W. E. B. Du Bois argued that being both a highly educated American citizen and a man subject to American racial prejudice caused him to possess a "double consciousness" typical of the experience of blacks in America. He was compelled to think of himself both as a legally equal citizen of the United States and as a socially stigmatized black man, to live his life as a man aware of his superior education and accomplishments and as a man viewed by many of his fellow citizens as inferior because of his race. In what ways does Senghor's poem, which negotiates a relationship between his pride in his "négritude," his aspirations for African independence, and his French education, exhibit a similar double consciousness? How do the particular circumstances of Africa and French colonialism differ from the American racism and legacy of slavery to which Du Bois was responding? Record your thoughts in an essay.

Lines 30 and 31

Rather than allowing their humanity to be reduced to the economic value of the agricultural goods listed in line 28, the African of the future will have a different, creative relationship to the soil and the natural world. Like the participants in a traditional ceremony in which masks are used, these new Africans absorb the powers of the natural spirits through the rhythm of dance, music, and poetry.

THEMES

Ancestry

The figure of the mask is Senghor's central image in the poem of the traditional past and the ancestors for whom it was a living reality. He uses the word "mask" as a kind of incantation to call up the ancestral spirits who in the present, implicitly, are hidden and hard to hear. The silence to which the poet refers suggests the need to greet the ancestors with attention and respectful awe. He also notes that the masks are the way that he can access the "breath of [his] fathers," that is, the living spirit of the ancestors who will inspire the poet to his song. His own face, he writes, resembles the face of the masks, because the masks bear the idealized features of the real faces of his ancestors. The latter part of the poem admits that the ancestral past is in danger of being lost to the forces of modernity, which have come to Africa in the form of the colonial conquests of the French, British, Dutch, and Belgians. The princess of line 16 refers to the aristocratic past of the African empires, and in line 18 the eyes of the masks suggest both the god-like tranquility of the ancestors and their inability to do more than witness the sufferings of the present. The poem as a whole wrestles with the question of whether the appeal to the ancestral spirits will be able to help the African overcome the present state of subjugation and hopelessness.

This ancestral past includes a sacred aspect. Senghor refers to the protected ground of the lion-headed ancestor, a sacred space in which the poet can link himself to the line of "fathers" leading all the way back to the mythic first ancestor, the lion. In the last line, it is the soil itself that transmits its power to the feet of the dancer and by implication, too, to the metrical feet of the poet in writing his poem.

African Culture

Africa appears in the poem in a dual light. It is the suffering victim of oppression, economic exploitation, and violence, wrenched from its traditional beliefs and ways of life and forced to serve a foreign master. At the same time, though, it is an irrepressible source of life, creativity, and positive relationship with the natural world. Europe, too, is ambivalently presented. It is a cruel mother on which modern Africa is dependent, yet whose embrace is crushing rather than sustaining. In the questions that make up lines 22–27, the world of Europe appears to be the bleak ground of mechanized industry and war, a space of death, hopelessness, and oblivion. At present, Africa depends on Europe, and Europe exploits the labor and natural riches of Africa. However, what Europeans see disdainfully as the African's closeness to nature and the land, seemingly a lack of higher spirituality, the African knows to be a profound spirituality and artistic creativity, as symbolized in the final line by the dance.

Colonial Africa, 1870-1960

Senghor projects a future overcoming of Africa's subordinate position, through which not only the colonized people of Africa but also the European colonizer stands to benefit. The central image in which this theme is developed is that of bringing the brown yeast of African culture to the white flour of European civilization to make bread that is higher and more nourishing than either element taken separately. Similarly, lines 26–27 suggest that Africa can become a revitalizing force for European societies that have grown cold, weary, and decadent. It is by embracing the life-affirming aspects of African culture that European culture can refresh itself.

STYLE

Apostrophe

Senghor often uses a figure of speech called apostrophe which means a direct address to an object, a place, an abstraction or ideal, or an immaterial entity such as a god or spirit. In "Prayer to the Masks," the narrator is speaking directly to the masks, which in turn are figures of the ancestors and repositories of mythic powers. Apostrophe is characteristically used to imply the power of the poet's word or voice to wake hidden powers in

Lion masks. In the poem, the author's family is represented by a lion. (© *JJM Stock Photography | Panama | Alamy*)

nature or to bring the dead to life. Thus, in the latter half of "Prayer to the Masks," Senghor begs the masks to join with him in pushing forward the rebirth of Africa, but at the same time implies that it is his poetic cry that can force the cooperation of the masks.

Rhythmic Repetition and Musicality

Senghor uses a strongly cadenced verse, with the rhythm marked by frequent and strongly accented repetitions. Indeed, several of his later poems carry subtitles indicating musical accompaniment by "jazz orchestra with trumpet solo"; by such traditional African instruments as the khalam, tama, gorong, talmblatt, and mbalakh; or by such combinations as flutes and balafong or organs and a tom-tom. In the first three lines of "Prayer to the Masks," the word mask is used six times; this repetition is typical of Senghor's chant-like use of rhythm. The final line, with its evocation of dancing feet beating the ground, is another example of the rhythmic character of the poem itself, a dance of the words across the page.

Use of Analogy

Through his use of analogy, the poet sets in resonance the human and natural worlds, and the historical present with the mythic past. Thus, in the third line, the mask becomes a map that in turn relates to the territory across which the wind blows. The figure of the lion refers at the same time to the father's name, to the mythic lion who was said to be the first ancestor of the family line, to the mask that represents the ancestor's spirit, and to the noble qualities that have communicated themselves through the blood. The flour and yeast in line 21 both refer to the colors associated with Europeans and Africans (white flour and brown yeast) and suggest a future cooperation that will be nourishing to everyone. The image of the natural resources and crops in line 28 brings together the features of the hair and skin of the African with the typical products of his labor.

Contrasts and Oppositions

A steady alternation of opposed lines is a key device in "Prayer to the Masks" and many other poems by Senghor. In the first half of "Prayer to the Masks," for example, Senghor contrasts the ephemeral (not permanent) or trivial subjects that he associates with women to the serious, eternal ground connected with the lion, the spirit of the fathers. The latter half contrasts Africa, as a dying princess, with Europe, as the mother from which a new Africa will have to separate itself. Similarly, the vitality and life-giving creativity of a future Africa is opposed to the mechanical, death-seeking hopelessness of Europe. The final lines reverse the valuations of black man by the European. If the European sees the African as an exploitable extension of material goods such as cotton, coffee, and oil, the African knows himself to stand in a creative, joyful, artistic, and religious relationship to the natural riches of Africa.

Literary Heritage

Senegal's literary and artistic traditions are connected to the rich heritage of the great African empires of the precolonial past, to Islamic culture, and to the oral cultures of the several groups of people that occupy its different regions. In his poetry, Senghor refers to the rituals and beliefs associated with masks and other forms of traditional art, to the dance, and to troubadour storytelling accompanied by a wide variety of instruments and drums. However, the legacy of colonialism also strongly marked this native heritage with the influence of French language and culture. The French colonial administrations placed a particular emphasis on the educational system as a way of spreading the French language and civilization into its colonial territories. Thus, when Senghor entered the French schools, he would have been taught the history of a country he had never visited, and he would have been taught that Africans were inferior and had no proper culture of their own. This division of his cultural heritage between the native land and language of his childhood and the adopted language and learning of his later life would become a central issue for Senghor in his poetry, politics, and thought. While he was a student of French and classical literature in Paris in the early thirties, he sought to regain contact with the African culture from which he had been cut off, and he studied ethnography (the study of human cultures) and African languages. His entry into political life, which would eventually lead him to the presidency of independent Senegal, was as an investigator and speaker on educational policy, especially about the problem of how best to balance French and native culture in the education of French-African colonial subjects.

HISTORICAL CONTEXT

French Colonialism in Africa

French colonial settlement in Africa dates back to the seventeenth century, when the French were involved in the slave trade both on the African side and in the Caribbean. The trade reached its heights in the middle decades of the eighteenth century and then fell off rapidly with the French Revolution, the wars that rocked Europe in the late eighteenth century, the successful slave revolts in Haiti and elsewhere, and the efforts of humanitarians and enlightenment intellectuals to abolish this ugly denial of human freedom.

A second wave of colonization occurred in the second half of the nineteenth century, with the scramble of the European powers to conquer the territories of Africa, Asia, and Latin America for European colonial empires. The colonized areas were seen as sources of cheap raw materials, cut-rate labor, and new markets for expanding industrial societies. At the same time, new ideologies began to emerge that "scientifically" justified imperial conquest on grounds of natural and unchangeable differences of intelligence between the races. French colonialism wavered between two contradictory sets of values. Convinced of the universal value and legitimacy of French civilization, based on the enlightenment principles that animated the French Revolution, France aggressively sought to "assimilate" the native populations of the colonies. The French language, culture, and history were taught, and the rights and institutions of French politics were extended to the colonized peoples. At the same time, though, both "scientific" racism and modern ethnography, with its emphasis on the specificity and organic unity of individual cultures, tended to undermine that universalist outlook.

Senghor's personal experience in many ways exemplifies the rather contradictory ways in which these two opposed ideas of how French and native African cultures were related. On the one hand, he was allowed access to the French educational system, in which he excelled, gaining a measure of prestige and respect even within the ordinary channels of French society. He mastered the French language and academic curriculum and eventually earned the equivalent of a Ph.D. in Classics and Literature, going on to teach for a time in a high school outside of Paris. However, at the same time, as an African born outside the "French" enclaves of Senegal, he had to argue several times for special exceptions to be made

COMPARE
&
CONTRAST

- **1945:** Senegal has been a colony of France since 1895, but after World War II, it is given both a rural and urban seat in the French parliament. Senghor wins the rural seat, which he holds until he forms his own political party, the Senegalese Democratic Bloc.

  Today: Senegal is governed as a multiparty parliamentary republic, although recent elections have been marred by boycotts and record low voter turnout.

- **1945:** The négritude movement, which emphasized the international desire of blacks to be free from French colonialism, gains strength in the aftermath of World War II. Senghor is one of the main literary voices in the movement.

  Today: The négritude movement still exists, more informally, in any artistic form that expresses black identity.

- **1945:** At the end of World War II, only three African countries are independent. Mohandas Gandhi's quest for self-rule in India is responsible for the beginning of independence movements in Africa. Senegal is one of the first wave of colonies to gain independence in 1960. By 1977, nearly all of Africa is made up of independent nations.

  Today: Despite gaining independence decades ago, economic dependence and political instability have hindered development of the continent. Senegal is one of a few nations that is economically stable.

---

to allow him to continue on to higher stages of his education. The more recent, racist ideas about what level and what kind of education was right for the African had led to obstacles to an African's assimilation through education in the French system.

Vichy France and World War II

With the outbreak of World War II, men from all over the French empire, including black Africans such as Senghor, were called up or volunteered to fight for France against the threat posed by Hitler's German army. The French army, however, was quickly defeated, and on July 14, 1940, the Nazis entered Paris. The government fled south to the resort of Vichy; and on July 17, the World War I war hero Marshall Pétain called an armistice that split France between the northern two-thirds under German occupation and a southern piece under the nominally French, but actually collaborationist, Vichy government. Following the Allied invasion of North Africa in November 1942, the Nazis moved in to occupy the rest of France, ending even the thin pretense that the Vichy government was anything but an instrument of the occupiers. After the D-Day invasion and after the German army was pushed back across the Rhine, the liberation of France became the true turning point of the war. Paris was liberated on August 25, 1944, and the leader of the free French forces, General Charles de Gaulle, began the task of rebuilding France's government at home and in the colonies.

Decolonization and Independence

After World War II, there were stirrings throughout the colonized world for independence. Several factors contributed to this movement. For one thing, the German and Japanese occupations had demonstrated the vulnerability of France and other colonial powers. For another, those nations attempted to revive the old colonial hierarchy, despite the courageous sacrifices of many natives during the war. Similarly, partisan struggles in which communist parties had gained great prestige and the victory of Mao Zedong's revolutionary army in China helped inspire similar guerrilla movements. The successful struggle for independence from British colonialism in India,

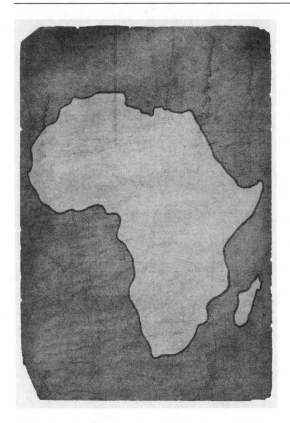

Africa *(Image copyright Alena Yar, 2010. Used under license from Shutterstock.com)*

led by Gandhi and Jawaharlal Nehru, further fueled the sense of colonized peoples that their long-suppressed hopes for self-rule might soon come to fruition. Outright warfare broke out in Vietnam shortly after the war, leading to the defeat of the French army at Dien Bien Phu in May 1954. Anti-French riots occurred in Madagascar, Tunisia, and Morocco, and most decisively, in November of 1954 an insurrection broke out in Algeria. This conflict would lead to the engagement of half a million French soldiers and nearly provoke civil war in France itself. In 1958, in order to stave off a coup attempt by the French army in Algeria, General de Gaulle returned to power and introduced a new constitution. Among the features of the constitution was a referendum of the colonial member states of the French empire allowing them to ratify the constitution or to vote no and effectively choose immediate independence. Of the African states, only Guinea chose to vote against the constitution; it paid a high price when the French

immediately withdrew its resources, expertise, and administrative structure from the newly founded country. The other states sought to form an African federation that would move toward independence but on friendly terms with France. The Federation failed to take shape, but Senghor's skillful political work and his efforts in finding a third, more moderate road to decolonization allowed Senegal to become independent, with French support, in 1961. Senghor was elected as the first president and governed for the next two decades.

CRITICAL OVERVIEW

Critics have tended to discuss "Prayer to the Masks" along two lines. It is seen as an assertion of the value of African traditions and the African past, including Senghor's own childhood experience; it has also been discussed as Senghor's most hopeful vision of Africa's potential contribution to a new synthetic, global culture that will supersede colonial domination. Dorothy S. Blair maintains in an overview of Senghor's career in *Senegalese Literature: A Critical History* that "Prayer to the Masks" "expresses the poet's deep concern for Europe's fate in the years of tension leading up to the Second World War." Blair further points out that "with the two continents linked by an umbilical cord, he is acutely aware that Europe's downfall must be accompanied by that of Africa, 'in the death-throes of a piteous princess.'"

The poem's assertions of the African's spontaneous joyfulness and attunement to the rhythm of the land and nature, qualities that Senghor opposes to the coldness and despair of the European, are seen as early expressions of the négritude philosophy that would achieve its greatest influence after World War II. Robert W. July states in the *New York Times Book Review*, "One cannot fail to respond to . . . the thudding rhythm" of "Prayer to the Masks." The more hopeful tone of the poem connects it with other works in *Chants d'ombre* (Shadow Songs) and contrasts with the somber note of the next volume, *Hosties noires* (Black Hosts, or Black Victims), collections in which many of the poems date from the same period as those in the earlier volume.

CRITICISM

Tyrus Miller

Miller has taught comparative literature and English and published a book titled Late Modernism: Politics, Fiction, and the Arts between the World Wars. *In the following essay, Miller considers the problem of an African writer educated in France who wishes to address African themes in his writing, including "Prayer to the Masks."*

"Prayer to the Masks" appeared in Senghor's first book, *Chants d'Ombre* (Shadow Songs), which collected his poems written during the 1930s and early 1940s. These poems reveal the influence of Senghor's original displacement from his homeland to study in France, and their tone goes back and forth between a melancholic view of Europe as it descended toward war and fascism (a political system in which the state is all-powerful) and an often nostalgic image of the Africa of Senghor's childhood. However, Senghor's evocation of African traditions, customs, beliefs, and settings should not be seen merely as the nostalgic fantasy of an expatriate poet for his homeland. Behind Senghor's poetic Africa lies a much more comprehensive program of cultural, educational, and political ideas, the ideal of négritude that he would pursue with other black poets of the Caribbean and African colonies. Senghor's early poetry, "Prayer to the Masks" included, explores the predicament of the colonial intellectual, trained in the language and culture of the colonizer, who seeks to turn a sense of cultural alienation into a perspective from which to look on the homeland with new eyes.

Within this broader cultural predicament, moreover, lies a more focused artistic problem for the French-African poet: how to relate his acquired artistic medium of expression, the poem written in the French language and European verse forms, to the African content he seeks to express. Senghor addresses this artistic challenge by referring his poem to the traditional African art form of the mask. The African masks, as the object of his "prayer" and the native counterpart of his French poetry, serve as an ideal image in the poem, for they allow Senghor to claim that his poetry is not something foreign and artificial, a break with the traditions of Africa, but an extension of those traditions into new forms. In a sense, his poem claims to be another type of mask, a mask made wholly of words but performing the same function as the more typical mask carved from wood or ivory. Senghor suggests that it is the spirit that

> SENGHOR SUGGESTS THAT IT IS THE SPIRIT THAT OCCUPIES THE ARTWORK, AND NOT THE MATERIAL FROM WHICH IT IS MADE, THAT INVESTS IT WITH ITS POWER."

occupies the artwork, and not the material from which it is made, that invests it with its power. The test of the carved object and of the shaped words of a poem is their fidelity to the ancestors, the source of their sacred energies. Similarly, in his conclusion to the poem, Senghor rejects the colonialist's image of the black African as "men of cotton, of coffee, of oil." Just as with the traditional and modern works of art, for Senghor it is not the materials but the spirit that dwells in them that shows the true value of these men. The vital forces they manifest in the dance, their musical and rhythmic relation to their land, are the genuine measure of their worth, not the narrowly economic standard of profits and payments.

Although the image of the mask in the poem is comprehensible without any deeper knowledge of African thinking about masks, this background of belief, which Senghor could assume in at least his African readers, enriches the symbolism still further. Masks are utilized in a few specific contexts, such as initiations, funerals, or the beginnings and endings of seasonal agricultural labor. They tend to be connected primarily with rural, agrarian (farming) peoples and places, such as Senghor's native village, Joal. Ceremonies involving masks are means by which these rural communities call up and display for themselves the events of the mythic past, such as the founding of a family line, the settlement of an area, or the defeat of an enemy. By representing and repeating the mythic event in the framework of the present, the masks function to bind the community to its past and to allow its present representatives to draw strength and legitimacy from that past. Masks also serve to channel spiritual forces, coming out of the world of the ancestors and the mythic past into the work of daily life. In this function, they play a dual role, that of trapping energies from the spirit world and that of protecting living humans from the powers of the ghosts, spirits, and demons that surround

WHAT DO I READ NEXT?

- Senghor's *On African Socialism* (1964) collects three important essays outlining his vision of nationhood and the special nature of African societies on the road to national development and socialism. These works are considered classics of modern African political philosophy.

- *Ujamaa: Essays on Socialism* (1968), by the Tanzanian leader Julius Nyerere, is a useful point of comparison to Senghor's political thought.

- Janet G. Vaillant's biography of Senghor, *Black, French, and African: A Life of Léopold Sédar Senghor* (1990), offers extensive context for Senghor's education, political activities, and friendships with writers and statesmen. It is clearly and accessibly written.

- Aimé Césaire's *Notebook of a Return to the Native Land* (2001) is a book-length poem, partially in prose and partially in verse, that recounts the homecoming to Martinique of this poet, a friend of Senghor and a comrade in the négritude movement. Symbolically, it enacts the rebirth of the black poet beyond the partial, damaged self-images he had taken over from both black and white perceptions of him.

- *The Negritude Poets: An Anthology of Translations from the French* (1975), edited by Ellen Conroy Kennedy, presents a wide selection of poets from Africa, the Caribbean, and the French-speaking island nations of the Indian Ocean, Madagascar and Mauritius, who were inspired by the négritude movement. The volume provides a useful context for the founding poets—Senghor, Césaire, and Damas—and shows the wide influence of their example and ideas.

- Franz Fanon's *Black Skins, White Masks* (1952) is a brilliant and influential exploration of the problem of personal identity in a racially divided, colonial society. Written while Fanon was studying psychiatry in Paris after World War II, this book gives a very powerful, poetic account of his confrontation with French racism, but it also explores his own false self-conceptions as a French-educated colonial subject from Martinique. The similarities and differences between Senghor's and Fanon's experiences as students in Paris are instructive. A new edition, more accessible to today's readers, was translated from the French by Richard Philcox and published in 2008.

- *Léopold Sédar Senghor: The Collected Poetry*, translated and with an introduction by Melvin Dixon, was published in 1998. It provides an abundance of poems from Senghor's entire writing career.

- The young-adult best-seller *Sugar Street* (1957) is the last book in Nobel Prize-winning author Naguib Mahfouz's Cairo trilogy. Set in Egypt during and after World War II, it chronicles the political and social aspects of the lives of two generations as Africa changes rapidly. It was translated into English in 1992.

---

them. The mask, as it is used in the ritual, allows a dancer to impersonate the spirit and be invested with the spirit's power, but also to trick the spiritual beings and be able to control and manipulate them. In sum, masks play a crucial role in helping those societies that use them to maintain a delicate balance between the world of the living and the world of the ancestors, between present and past, between life and death. To fail to recall the ancestors and their glorious deeds would be to lose touch with the life-giving wellsprings of tradition, yet to grant the dead too much power over the living would be dangerous as well.

Although in his poem Senghor generally celebrates the African traditions represented by the masks, this background helps the reader to better understand how this celebration is qualified and ambivalent in ways similar to the cautious attitude toward the dead expressed by the dual function of the mask. Senghor writes a poem about masks in which he creates an analogy between his poem and the traditional mask and a bond between himself and the mythic "lion-headed" ancestor of his father's family line. Clearly, in this respect, Senghor seeks to recall and reactivate the spiritual powers of the ancestors, the dead, the mythic and magical traditions of African ritual. More difficult to perceive, however, is the other, protective face of his poem-prayer. This aspect can be seen in Senghor's *difference* from the traditions and ritual art forms that he appears to be celebrating. His poem, one might say, is a mask that mimics the African past and its ritual forms rather than the undiminished presence and power of that traditional past. After all, Senghor has chosen to write a poem (and a poem in French at that!) rather than actually carve a mask. His poem is printed on the two-dimensional flatness of paper rather than etched into the rugged graininess of the wood. It is meant to be read, whether aloud or silently, so that although its lines may conjure up the feeling and sense of a ritual, they are not literally chanted on a ceremonial occasion, such as a funeral or seeding of the ground. The drummed and danced rhythms to which his poem alludes are never physically sounded in the poem, however much its metrical accents allow a reader to imagine them. Senghor's poem thus calls upon the strength of the ancestral spirits for its inspiration, but it purposefully weakens the power of these spiritual forces over the poet by reducing them to paper, ink, and words.

Senghor's poetic mask however, may be turned not only toward the African past, but also toward the French colonial present. In other words, in writing his poetry, Senghor not only mimics the traditional mask of African ceremony, seeking to tap and control its energies, but also adopts the prestigious mask of the French writer and intellectual. This act of masking allows him to show that the cultural power of the French intellectual is not a "natural" result of some essential Frenchness but rather a role for which they and he have been trained to perform. It also enables him to draw upon the formidable power of the colonizer's culture while maintaining his separate identity intact and hidden behind the countenance his writing displays in public. In a manner of speaking, Senghor tricks the powerful French "spirit" (or its representatives in the university, the colonial administration, and the government) into acting benevolently toward him.

In composing his poem-prayer, then, Senghor is metaphorically donning a kind of paper mask to mimic the carved and ornamented masks of traditional ritual. As a French-African poet, he captures something of the power of African tradition and of French cultural prestige while not being totally absorbed into either. He needs the ancestral spirits to inspire him, and he fulfills his obligation to them in recalling them in the artistic place of his poem. However, it is not from the village society and according to the standards of traditional African values that he, the French-educated poet living in Paris, is seeking recognition. Rather, those who will grant him recognition are urban, literate French speakers, men and women reading him in large cities such as Paris, Dakar, Tangiers, and New York. To succeed as a poet, he must be African, but not too African; French, but French with a difference. He must manage the difficult act of expressing a local content and feeling, rooted in his rural Senegalese childhood, in a cosmopolitan form learned through his French education and residency in Paris.

This complex relationship of resemblance and difference is captured most explicitly in the difficult tenth through fourteenth lines. The simplified features of the masks are mirrored by the concentrated expression of the poet's own face as he performs his own form of artistic worship, the ritual of sitting down to write poetry. The poet's relation to the ancestral spirits of the mask is not, however, simply a reflection. It is rather a *translation*, a difficult and risky movement between artistic media, between the Serer language and the French language, and between the cultural idiom of villages such as Joal and the European cosmopolitan dialect spoken by Parisian intellectuals.

Senghor's poem expresses the wish that this translation of the past into the present might be possible rather than fully convincing the poet or his readers that it is. It is in this sense that it is properly called a prayer. Its attitude is forward-looking, seeking a better, brighter future and pointing to itself as anticipating a time when African energies and French forms might work in cooperation. At present, however, Senghor acknowledges that Africa is suffering the loss of its traditions, while the painful and traumatic process of rebirth, which will convulse both Africa and Europe, has not yet occurred. Africa remains bound by the umbilical cord of dependency to Europe, in a state of latency and infancy, unable to separate itself, speak, move, and grow.

African mask *(Image copyright Fedor Selivanov, 2010. Used under license from Shutterstock.com)*

Ultimately, Senghor offers his "Prayer to the Masks" as a token of hope, as a single example of all that might be brought to life out of the two cultures that have shaped his life, through their exchanges, cooperative efforts, and mutual translations. However, he also recognizes that this wishful dream at present remains unfulfilled for both him and his people, and that, like other dreams deferred and opportunities lost, it might still fail because of historical realities. It is thus not with complacency but with an urgency haunted by the presence of danger that Senghor asks the questions in lines 22–27, suggesting the contributions that Africa can make to the world. His poem uses all the power that Senghor can muster from both cultures to answer: it is our task to try.

Source: Tyrus Miller, Critical Essay on "Prayer to the Masks," in *Poetry for Students*, Gale, Cengage Learning, 2011.

Chris Semansky

Semansky is a widely published poet, fiction writer, and critic and has taught literature and writing. In this essay, he argues that the locale of "Prayer to the Masks" is Senghor's Parisian apartment, a lodging transformed through writing the poem.

Perhaps one of the first questions occurring to readers contemplating "Prayer to the Masks" by Léopold Sédar Senghor is where the poem occurs, more specifically, what is indicated by the sixth line's "this place." A possible answer is Senghor's apartment in Paris. This theory comes from "In Memoriam," the first poem in Senghor's first poetry collection, *Shadow Songs* (1945), the volume also containing "Prayer to the Masks." "In Memoriam" portrays the exiled black African Senghor anxiously considering venturing out of his Paris apartment on a Sunday that also happens to be All Saints' Day, a doubly sacred occasion. The poet is in the process of summoning the courage necessary to walk down and into the Parisian streets, meet those solemn faces and blue eyes, those people who are at once brothers and historical enemies. Senghor writes that his apartment is filled with masks upon whom the poet calls to help explain history and customs.

"In Memoriam" is an earlier, and one might say, a more immature poem than "Prayer to the Masks" since "In Memoriam" shows the poet asking for *personal* help, entreating the ancestors to guard his dreams and embolden him enough to join the Parisians outside. "Prayer to the Masks," on the other hand, has Senghor calling on the masks/ancestors to save *the world*, specifically from the incursions of Europe. As a result of this progress from self-centeredness toward altruism, a theory might be proposed: the longer Senghor remained apart from his homeland, the more religiously mature he became.

Whereas "In Memoriam" shows the poet gazing down upon the roofs and streets of Paris, "Prayer to the Masks" allows readers—those pedestrians strolling along lines of words instead of boulevards of buildings—to look back and up into the poet's apartment, likely a small space, probably a room serving as both living space and study. Looking up, the pedestrian is able to see only the masks on the walls, but upon entering the building, the poet's room might look this way: on each of the four walls hangs a mask representing one of the four cardinal points. On a table or desk is an image of the ancestor to which the poem refers, perhaps a statue or a mask like the others.

Throughout Africa, masks are multifunctional, one of their functions being to breathe life into myths that attempt to explain the origins of daily customs. As happens in many African ceremonies, the poet calls upon the masks, and the lion-like ancestor in particular, to reinvigorate the time and space of white-dominated Africa and restore the meaning of human existence—if not to its pristine state, then to a state reinvigorated through imagining the pristine. When Senghor calls upon the four masks or points, through which a spirit or wind blows, to save a dying Africa and animate a dead Europe, his invocation can be imagined as a call to hot African winds—called ghibilis, samiels, and simooms—to warm a Europe grown chilly with civilization. But the appeal to the masks can also be interpreted as the private ritual of a writer in exile calling upon his four masks to inspire him with the spirit of homeland, to breathe inspiration into the ritual of his writing—a ceremony that is often dear to exiles. The poet calls upon the African masks because in them ancestors and homeland are fused. Ancestors buried in the land decay into and become part of the ancestral land from which the masks are presumably made (whether they be made of wood, clay, or metal). The masks carry with them the air of home and ancestors, which the poet will inhale. For those less inclined to believing in spirits, the masks can be imagined as in possession of an odor rich with the remembered smell of ancestral land, an emanation the poet inhales as inspiration. In sum, the transformation of the buried dead into ancestral masks can be seen as a poetic idea that blows beyond the borders of a page of poetry, advancing outward into the world.

Senghor's invocation to the masks can also be seen in the light of African initiation ceremonies in which a masked priest, representing a spirit, initiates an inexperienced youth into adulthood. On the one hand, the poet, separate from the mask, can be said to be the young person, yearning for the ability to harness the magic of words; on the other hand, the poet is the priest, initiating readers, especially Western readers, into the mystery of words and poetry. Senghor also depicts himself as split between African and European identities, sometimes torn between them and sometimes trying to reconcile them or be a part of both worlds. Indeed, such characterizations correspond with what is written about Senghor's life.

Masks are also charms to ward off evil, like a crucifix or bulb of garlic to protect against vampires. The poet calls upon the masks (as protector spirits or ancestors) to guard his lodgings from laughter and his African brethren from the suffering caused by European invasions and colonizations. In addition, the poet calls upon the masks to transform his poem into a charm to protect the people of Africa from the harm caused by Europe. (The image of the two continents being tied together at the navel could suggest Europe as Africa's parent, but it is more likely that Europe is to be understood as Africa's child, since Africa is usually considered home to humanity's ancestors.) This type of mask is often worn by dancers to harness invisible spirits for the protection of society. Because such spirits are powerful, laying hold of them can be dangerous, and so the mask must also protect its wearer from being overwhelmed when channeling the spirits' power into the community. Although Senghor does not specifically call upon his masks to protect him in the same way as he does in "In Memoriam," the masks, or at least, the specific ancestor he references, are thought to be already protecting his room from being mocked and profaned.

That ancestor, described as having a lion's head, has multiple meanings. Senghor's father's name is Basile Diogoye Senghor, Diogoye meaning "the lion" in Senghor's native Serer language (both people and language are known as *Serer*, pronounced "seer-ear"). In addition to this paternal connection to the lion-headed ancestor, there is the rich cultural symbology associated with lions, with meanings differing little between Africa and Europe. For example, among the Bambara, a people dwelling in and just south of Senegal, the lion symbolizes divine knowledge and occupies a rank in the Bambara traditional social hierarchy only one step below that of priest-sage. The lion, then, can be viewed as a set of identities: ancestor, source of divine knowledge, protector against frivolousness, guardian of the sacredness of Senghor's study, and inspiration. The characterization is of a serious parental god for whom divine knowledge is no laughing matter. These masks/ancestors/gods are *grounded* and serious, not frivolous mischief-makers like some gods of other traditions. Although they are grounded, these ancestors are still idealized; they are eternally unchanging, and their faces are described as smooth and unwrinkled. These are dead ancestors resurrected and elevated into godlike beings, who in turn transform the poet into a priest.

The origin of gods is thought by some to have been a transformation of dead ancestors, thought of as remaining to guard the living. Senghor builds on this transformation by symbolically elevating the status of his room or study into a sanctuary, his desk into an altar, himself (as poet) into priest, and the poem ("Prayer to the Masks") he is writing into a sacred document or prayer. Typical of prayer, Senghor's "Prayer to the Masks" is an entreaty to the masks/ancestors/gods to save Africa from Europe and grant Africa the role of leavening the "white flour" of Western civilization, inspiring it to rise to new heights by, paradoxically, bringing it back to earth, back to expressions of joy, rhythm, and dance, back to poem, psalm, and prayer. In the same way that Senghor recognizes that "white flour" must be leavened by black African influence, "Prayer to the Masks" shows how empty, white paper can be transformed by black ink into poem, prayer, psalm, and possibly scripture.

Source: Chris Semansky, Critical Essay on "Prayer to the Masks," in *Poetry for Students*, Gale, Cengage Learning, 2011.

SOURCES

Bâ, Sylvia Washington, *The Concept of Negritude in the Poetry of Léopold Sédar Senghor*, Princeton University Press, 1973.

Blair, Dorothy S., "After Independence, the First Twenty Years: New Themes, New Names," in *Senegalese Literature: A Critical History*, Twayne's World Author Series, Twayne Publishers, 1984, pp. 45–141.

Hymans, Jacques Louis, *Léopold Sédar Senghor: An Intellectual Biography*, Edinburgh University Press, 1971.

July, Robert W., "Rolling Rhythms," in *New York Times Book Review*, October 25, 1964, p. 54.

"Léopold Sédar Senghor, "Senegal's First President, Succumbs at 95," in *Jet*, Vol. 101, No. 4, January 14, 2002, p. 17.

"Negritude Movement," in *Black Past.org*, http://www.blackpast.org/?q = gah/negritude-movement (accessed February 25, 2010).

Sartre, Jean-Paul, "Orphée Noir," in *Situations III*, Gallimard, 1949, pp. 229–86.

"Senegal," in *CIA: World Factbook*, https://www.cia.gov/library/publications/the-world-factbook/geos/sg.html (accessed February 25, 2010).

"Senegal—Country History and Economic Development," in *Encyclopedia of the Nations*, http://www.nationsencyclopedia.com/economies/Africa/Senegal-COUNTRY-HISTORY-AND-ECONOMIC-DEVELOPMENT.html (accessed February 25, 2010).

Senghor, Léopold Sédar, *The Foundations of "Africanité" or "Négritude" and "Arabité,"* translated by Mercer Cook, Presence Africaine, 1971.

————, *Léopold Sédar Senghor: The Collected Poetry*, translated and with an introduction by Melvin Dixon, University of Virginia Press, 1991, pp. 13–14.

————, *Selected Poems/Poésies Choisies*, translated by Craig Williamson, Rex Collings, 1976.

Spleth, Janice, *Léopold Sédar Senghor*, Twayne's World Authors Series, Twayne Publishers, 1985.

FURTHER READING

Balonze, John, ed., *Street Children in Senegal*, translated by Shannon Delaney, GYAN France, 2006.
    This book is a collection of essays that together describe the horrific living conditions for some of the children of Senegal.

Castaldi, Francesca, *Choreographies of African Identities: Negritude, Dance, and the National Ballet of Senegal*, University of Illinois Press, 2006.
    Castaldi examines the works of both the American ballet and the Senegalese national ballet as expressions of the performing arts legacy of Africa and the idea of négritude.

Harney, Elizabeth, *In Senghor's Shadow: Art, Politics, and the Avante-Garde in Senegal, 1960-1995*, edited by Nicholas Thomas, Duke University Press, 2004.
    Harney examines Senghor's contributions to art and culture during his presidency of Senegal. She explains his funding and desire to attach an artistic national identity to postcolonial Senegal. The volume contains many color illustrations from a wide range of the arts.

Sartre, Jean-Paul, "Orphée Noir," in *Situations III*, Gallimard, 1949, pp. 229-86.
    This essay was Sartre's controversial introduction to Senghor's 1948 anthology of négritude poets.

SUGGESTED SEARCH TERMS

Léopold Sédar Senghor

Léopold Sédar Senghor poems

Léopold Sédar Senghor biography

Léopold Sédar Senghor AND Prayer to the Masks

negritude

Senghor AND negritude

Senghor AND Senegal

African colonialism

imperialism in Africa

Prodigy

CHARLES SIMIC
1980

Charles Simic's poem "Prodigy" blends together the elements of a game and a war. Much of the poem is seen through the eyes of a child. Not everything this child has witnessed is pleasant; in fact, the child has seen much that most children are not forced to live through.

On a positive note, the narrator of this poem recalls the joys of his youth. He spends a lot of time playing chess, a game he loves. Outside his house, however, and sometimes right on the other side of his windows, a war is raging in his country. The narrator remembers how his house shakes when heavy tanks pass by on the streets. He also recalls the noise of military planes hammering the skies. He cannot recall, however, the most horrific images, such as men hanging dead from telephone poles. He knows that someone told him he saw such things, but he refuses to call up these images. He would rather think about the professor who taught him all he knows about chess. He does not want to remember feeling afraid and belittled by the soldiers and their guns. He would rather think about mastering his favorite game.

"Prodigy" is one of Simic's more popular poems. The writing style is simple and easy to understand. Although Simic leaves the reader with many unanswered questions, he provides enough hints that readers can infer the hidden meanings. The poem was first published in 1980 in Simic's award-winning collection *Classic Ballroom Dances*.

Charles Simic *(Brendan Smialowski / Getty Images)*

AUTHOR BIOGRAPHY

Simic was born on May 9, 1938, in Belgrade, Yugoslavia (now called Serbia). He grew up there during World War II. In the midst of the war, his father, an engineer, immigrated to Italy to find work. Later, his father was able to flee to the United States. Simic's father was separated from his family for ten years. During that time, Simic's mother attempted to leave Belgrade several times, but the communist government would not allow it. After one attempt, she and her sons were turned back and spent two weeks in jail. Eventually, they did leave and spent one year in Paris before obtaining visas to continue on to the United States. While in France, Simic learned to speak English.

Ten years after the war ended, when Simic was sixteen, his family was reunited. They lived one year in New York City then moved to Oak Park, Illinois, a suburb of Chicago. Simic attended Oak Park High School, the same school that novelist and short story writer Ernest Hemingway graduated from more than forty years earlier. It was in high school that Simic

began writing poetry. In 1961, Simic attended classes at the University of Chicago before being drafted into the U.S. Army. When he was discharged from service in 1966, Simic moved back to New York City, where he earned a bachelor's degree in Russian from New York University. A year later, in 1967, Simic published his first collection of poems, *What the Grass Says*.

In 1978, Simic's book *Charon's Cosmology* (1977) was a finalist for the National Book Award for Poetry. In 1980, Simic's collection *Classic Ballroom Dances*, in which his poem "Prodigy" was first published, won the di Castagnola Award and the Harriet Monroe Poetry Award. In 1990, Simic was honored with the Pulitzer Prize for poetry for his collection *The World Doesn't End* (1989). Simic also won the 2005 Griffin Poetry Prize, an international award, for his *Selected Poems: 1963–2003*, which was published in 2004, and his collection *Jackstraws* (1999) was named a Notable Book of the Year by the *New York Times*.

In 2007, the Library of Congress appointed Simic the fifteenth Poet Laureate Consultant in Poetry. As a professor at the University of New Hampshire, Simic has taught creative writing and literature for thirty-four years. In 2007, Simic won the coveted Wallace Stevens Award from the Academy of American Poets for lifelong excellence in poetry.

Simic has published twenty poetry collections, five books of essays, and the memoir *A Fly in the Soup* (2000). He is married to Helen Dubin, a fashion designer. The couple has two children, a son and a daughter. As of 2010, Simic lives with Helen in the countryside outside of Strafford, New Hampshire.

POEM SUMMARY

Stanza 1

Simic opens his poem "Prodigy" with a line that describes in seven words an image of his childhood. The speaker declares, in those few words, that much of his time as a child was spent playing chess. Based on the title of the poem, one can deduce that the speaker was considered advanced in his skills of chess, ahead of other children in his age group.

Simic is often praised for the images he uses in his poems. Stanza 1 is a good example of how

MEDIA ADAPTATIONS

- Simic reads the poem "Prodigy" in a video recording on YouTube (http://www.youtube.com/watch?v = pXK9f4-PdTU).

his images allow him to say so much more than the few words he uses. For example, the image of a child leaning over a chessboard offers one layer of meaning. When the speaker implies that when he was a child he spent most of his time in that position, the image takes on deeper meaning. This is not an ordinary child playing an ordinary game. This is a child who is obsessed with the game—one who wants to learn the game's strategy and memorize the complicated moves. Children who demonstrate mastery of chess are often gifted.

Stanza 2

Stanza 2 of Simic's poem consists of only one line. With this line, he makes it clear that as a child not only took pleasure in learning the different moves, he also loved the words that were associated with the game.

The word that the speaker emphasizes in stanza 2 denotes a special portion of a chess game—the period close to the end. In chess, this portion of the game represents more than just a completion. At the end of a game of chess, there are usually fewer pieces left on the board. It is a time when the lowly pawn, the least powerful piece of the game, becomes more important. The chances of a pawn bringing down a king increase because if the pawn reaches his opponent's end of the board without being captured, it could be promoted to a queen, knight, rook, or bishop—all of which have much greater chances of bringing about a checkmate, or the fall of the king.

Perhaps the child thinks of himself as a pawn, especially in light of the information the speaker provides in the next lines. There is a war going on around him, somewhat similar, figuratively speaking, to what is happening on the chessboard. This child who loves to play chess has no weapons to protect himself. He has little or no power to save

his mother and brother from possible military threats. In mentioning the end of the game of chess, the speaker might be dreaming of himself as a pawn and wishing that he could make it to the end of the chessboard so he too could be promoted. He might wish for a magical transformation of himself into someone who is stronger.

Stanza 3

Stanza 3 is also a single line, one that also provides a stunning image. Here the speaker identifies the manner in which some of his cousins react to him. The image suggests that the speaker, as a child, has trouble communicating with his cousins. They are concerned for him.

Readers might wonder if the cousins' concern comes from the fact that all the child wants to do is to play chess. There could, however, be other reasons for the cousins to worry. Does the child not want to play with them? Does the child not want to talk to them? With this new line, the poet creates ambiguity. He presents a complete sentence, but he does not offer any explanations. Readers are left with an image but without the story that might surround it. Simic is known for creating images that make his readers ponder what else might be going on. It is up to the reader to fill in the blanks.

Stanza 4

Not until stanza 4 is the reader given a sense of the setting of this poem. In line 1 of this stanza, the reader learns that the young boy lives in a small house. This at first sounds commonplace. Many children are raised in small houses. Also, this small house could be anywhere. Not until the next line does the speaker provide a hint as to where this stanza is headed. In line 2 of stanza 4, the speaker mentions a cemetery. The house is located very close to where people are buried. With this, the speaker introduces the concept of death and fear. To a child, a cemetery can be a very fearful place. To live close to one can be unsettling. For the speaker to use the cemetery to place the house in its setting means that the cemetery was either very prominent on a physical level or very important on a psychological level. Either way, when the speaker thinks about the small house in which he lived, the first thing that he associates it with is the place where people are buried.

These suggestions of death and fear are enhanced in the final two lines of stanza 4. Here the speaker brings even more startling images into the poem. First there is heavy military machinery rumbling down the streets in front of the child's house—a fearful image of tanks passing by, equipped with canon-like weaponry attached to their fronts. Next, the speaker tells of the military aircraft that blast through the skies overhead. Though he does not mention the bombs that these planes are dropping, the speaker does state that these aircraft and tanks are so heavy and so loud that they rattle the boy's house. It does not take much effort to realize that the boy must also be rattled, though the speaker does not mention this.

Stanza 5

In stanza 5, the speaker changes the tone of the poem. He averts his eyes from the streets outside his house and turns them back to the chessboard. The speaker changes the topic from war to the man who is teaching him how to play chess. The speaker also offers that on a professional level, this man teaches astronomy.

Symbolically, the speaker might be relating this professor's knowledge of the stars to the war planes that are flying overhead. This teacher might be helping the young boy to take his mind off the threat of war by talking about the nighttime skies. The professor looks to the skies not to see bombs falling out of planes but to see the stars. The stars are distant. In focusing on them, maybe the man and the boy are able to transport themselves away from their fears.

Stanza 6

Like stanzas 2 and 3, this stanza also consists of only one line. The space around this line makes it stand out visually. It is as if this line were surrounded by silence. That silence could in turn be related to sadness. In this line the speaker confirms that he was living his childhood in the midst of World War II.

If readers are aware of the poet's background, they will know that as a child he lived in Yugoslavia. They will also know that the war machinery surrounding the child's house was probably that of German dictator Adolf Hitler's Nazi army. Merely by mentioning the date, therefore, the poet has said much more than a simple six-word sentence.

Stanza 7

After rousing the reader by implying the horrors of war, the speaker tones down the emotion of the poem. Once again, he returns the reader's focus to the chessboard. He describes the chess pieces, which are showing signs of age, battered from playing war games on the chessboard. A parallel might be drawn between those chipped chess pieces and the wounded and weary soldiers the child probably sees outside his windows.

The speaker mentions that the black pieces in particular have lost most of their paint, making one wonder if it is difficult to distinguish the white set from the black. The implication is that the black pieces are white underneath. The poet might be suggesting that there is little difference between the two sides of the war raging outside. When uniforms are discarded, one cannot tell what side a soldier is on. Underneath their national colors, all soldiers are the same. They are all human beings.

Stanza 8

After discussing the black set of chess pieces in the previous stanza, the speaker turns his attention to the white set. The white set has no king. One cannot play chess without the king, as the king is the figure that defines a win or a loss. So the white set needs something to stand in for the missing king. The speaker does not tell the reader what is used to replace the king. There is no image of the substitute that stands in the king's place.

Readers are therefore left on their own to create a vision of the replacement king. This is somewhat difficult to do without first thinking of the empty space left by the missing king. The poet might have done this on purpose, wanting the empty space to surround whatever image the reader conjures up. The reason the poet does this is not clear, unless one supposes that the poet wants to present a sense of the white set lacking leadership or a feeling of loss. One interpretation might be that the poet is using the white set to represent his country of Yugoslavia, and the missing king stands for the overthrow of his country's government by the Germans.

Stanza 9

Stanza 9 presents a morbid scene. The ruthlessness of the war seeps into the poem more rigorously in this stanza. The speaker recounts, without emphasizing any emotional reaction, that he recalls someone telling him what he witnessed. Notice that the speaker does not recall the actual experience of seeing men hanging but remembers only that someone told him he saw this awful scene. The speaker infers, through this statement, that he has blocked this horrid memory. It is not clear whether the boy is too young when this incident takes place and therefore truly forgets it or whether the image is so unspeakable that as an adult the speaker does not want to recall the image.

Stanza 9 contrasts sharply with the previous stanza. This is so not only because stanza 8 depicts a mellow scene at the chessboard while stanza 9 provides an image of death but also because the speaker remembers specific details about chipped paint in one stanza but has no recollection of the hung bodies in the other. Assuming that both scenes take place in a similar time, one can deduce that the murder scene in stanza 9 is too emotional for the child to process. One will also notice, however, that the poet presents the details of stanza 9 in a similar manner to the way he offers the details in the eighth. There are no emotional phrases or expressions in either of them. In a rational tone, the poet merely states the facts in both stanzas.

Stanza 10

In stanza 10, the speaker hints at a possible reason he does not retain memories of the brutalities of the war. His mother often covered his eyes. This he does remember. No one had to tell him that his mother protected him in this way. He remembers his mother hiding him inside her coat, offering him a protective cover inside of which he might feel more secure.

In stanza 10, readers can sense the mother's love for her son. She is necessarily forced to walk the streets, possibly to gather food and other needed supplies. She had no other choice but to take her son with her. But she tries to keep him in the world of childhood by covering his eyes to what is going on in the adult world of war.

Stanza 11

In the final stanza of Simic's poem, the speaker returns to the game of chess. He subtly relates himself to stories of previous chess masters who were blindfolded just as he is by his mother. There is an obvious difference, however. The speaker, as a child, is blindfolded for emotional protection, whereas the chess masters covered

their eyes to prove their outstanding ability to play a game without seeing the board.

One possible reason for the poet to end in this way may be to show that even though the game of chess is based on elements of war, the two are very different. Both war and chess involve competition and strategy, but chess does not result in pain and death. The greatest of the chess masters can compete in several so-called chess wars at one time. The implication might be that chess masters are smarter than the people who created wars.

THEMES

War

The theme of war runs through Simic's poem "Prodigy" in two different ways. The first is through the game of chess. The references to war are subtle when the speaker brings up the topic of chess. If readers are familiar with the game, they will know that the game is based on war-like strategies. Those less familiar with the game, however, might miss the allusions to war.

Even if readers do not play chess, they will find more obvious examples of the war theme. First there is the mention of military planes and tanks that the speaker remembers seeing as a young boy. Simic's homeland of Yugoslavia, where he lived as a child, was invaded and then occupied by the German army. The mention of the tanks and planes alludes to this German occupation. When the speaker states that the setting of the poem (or of his memories of playing chess as a child) was in 1944, the element of war is confirmed. In 1944, World War II was still being waged in Europe. If these comments are not enough to convince readers that war is a theme, the speaker mentions some of the atrocities that occurred, such as the hanging of bodies from telephone poles.

Fear

Though Simic's emotional expressions are very subtle, they are present in this poem. One of the easiest to notice is fear. As the speaker describes himself as a young boy seeing military vehicles rumbling past his house, he describes how the windows shake. Readers can insinuate from this description that the child also is shaking. One has to search for this emotion, but it does not take too much effort to assume that the noise of

TOPICS FOR FURTHER STUDY

- Simic was born in Belgrade, Yugoslavia (now Serbia). Research the history of Belgrade from the early 1900s through the present time. Create a Web site for your findings. Create pages to post on your site, dividing your information into categories such as history, politics, economy, and culture of Belgrade. How has the city changed over the years? Provide photographs to illustrate your site. Also link your site to other sites that were most helpful or informative for your project. Give the address of your Web site to your classmates and invite them to visit it.

- Do an Internet search for Kim Ung-Young, who has been listed as having the highest IQ. He was a child prodigy and took some college-level classes at the age of four. Gather information about Kim Ung-Young. When was he born? What are some of his accomplishments? What was his favorite subject in school? Use an online poster maker program, such as Glogster to make a poster showing copyrightable photographs of him and a timeline of important dates in his life. Present the poster to your class as you give a short speech about him. Be prepared to answer questions at the end of your presentation.

- Define the surrealist movement in the visual arts and literature. How does this movement differ from others such as dada and modernism? Who were the major contributors? Read other poems by Simic as well as literary analyses of his work. How does Simic's work fit into this movement? Provide examples in the essay you write and read it to your class.

- Write a poem using the game of chess as a metaphor. You need to be familiar with the strategies of chess either from playing the game or from reading about it. Think about how chess might be compared to life or to war. How might the game teach you a lesson? Who might be compared to the pawns, the knights, or the bishops? In a democracy, who might be comparable to the queen or the king? Try to mimic Simic's minimalist style, using as few words as you can. Then read your poem to your class.

- Use Daniel King's book for young-adults, *Chess: From First Moves to Checkmate*, to become familiar with the pieces of a chess game. By using common objects found around your house, create a set of your own. Be creative in choosing the items you will use. Just make sure that the most dominant pieces are used for the most important pieces of the chess set, such as the king and queen. Make the pawns the smallest. Show the set to your teacher and challenge him or her to a game.

---

the planes overhead (as well as the bombs that must have been falling) and the size and significance of the huge military tanks filling the narrow streets must have been frightening for a child. The tanks were so big (and the bombs so loud) that they shook the child's house. Although the poet does not write that he was frightened by these sounds, he allows the shaking house to speak for him.

Simic also alludes to fear when he pictures his mother hiding him under her coat. The mother is obviously fearful of what is going on around her. She is also concerned about her son. She does not want her child to remember the horrors of war, and she does not want him to be fearful. By the act of trying to protect him, however, she demonstrates her fear. Again, the poet does not write about his own fears in this poem, but most children sense their parents' emotions. If someone suddenly pushes a child under his or her coat, the child might not see what is going on, but the act of being pushed into the darkness might itself be a frightening experience.

In the poem, Simic describes bending over a chessboard as a boy. (*Image copyright Sakala, 2010. Used under license from Shutterstock.com*)

Memories

Most of Simic's poem is described through memory. The speaker remembers a time when his life was a mixture of both exciting experiences and dreadful ones. Some of the memories are recalled in fine detail, and others are remembered only through another person telling the speaker that certain events happened.

Some of the memories of the child in this poem are exaggerated. For instance, the speaker could not have really grown up leaning over a board game. The exaggeration is used to stress the potency of his memory of growing up playing chess. It is obvious that chess was very important to the speaker not only for the pleasure of learning the game but also because it distracted him from the war that was being fought in front of his eyes. The memory of playing chess is also much more pleasant than the images of death that he recalls seeing through the windows of his house.

Some of the memories in this poem are understated. This could be due to the horror of the events and the speaker's attempts to forget them, especially as a child. Alternatively, this could be Simic's way of making the memories seem even more haunting. For instance, when he talks about his mother putting blindfolds on him, the poet describes this memory in a tone similar to his description of the chess pieces that he played with. He merely states this memory of his mother as a fact, as if this were not something unusual for a mother to do to her child. Although Simic understates this memory with little emotional content, most readers will add their own reactions. Rather than divulging his emotional memories in words, the poet uses understatement to encourage his readers to feel these memories for themselves. The point of the poem is to put these memories down on paper, possibly to remember them but certainly to share them with his readers.

STYLE

Minimalism

The term "minimalism" in relation to literary works refers to a style of writing in which the author uses as few words as possible. Generally in a minimalist work, only the barest of details are presented. Often these details at first seem to imply the ordinary events of a day. Emotional and other descriptive phrases are usually understated or not stated at all. The major points, rather than being written out, are implied in minimalist works, leaving the reader the responsibility of figuring them out on their own.

However, it is the responsibility of the minimalist writer to provide hints to the reader that more meaning lies hidden behind the minimal details that are given. An example of how Simic does this is by his informing the reader, in a simple statement, that the particulars of his poem occurred in 1944. He never uses the word war. However, war is implied in his use of this date. Simic merely mentions the date as if that year were like any other year. Careful readers will associate the year with the horrific circumstances of World War II. Simic only trips the reader's memory and then invites the reader to discover the hidden emotions and meaning.

Imagery

Being an author of few words, Simic takes advantage of images to help convey deeper meaning in his poems. "Prodigy" begins with a powerful image. Through this image, readers can envision a young boy sitting at a chess table, possibly spending hours studying the board and the pieces on it. Through this image, readers can begin to guess at what kind of a boy this was. Chances are he was quiet, intelligent, studious, observant, and dedicated to this game. If this image is correct, then the boy probably rarely went outside, rarely played the games that other children normally played. The interpretations of this image could continue as the reader envisions personality traits for this young boy. However, all Simic did was to offer a picture through a few simple words.

Another powerful image is that of the young boy being blindfolded by his mother. At first, a reader might find this image disturbing. Then the author adds an image that clarifies that the boy's face is not covered with a piece of material that is knotted at the back of his head. Rather, the mother ducks the boy inside her coat, which makes the boy blind. In the image of the boy inside his mother's coat, readers can better sense the emotions that are involved in the blinding. The mother is scared, and she does not want her son to see what is happening on the war-torn

streets. Readers might imagine the mother cowering to soldiers or running away from the sight of dead bodies. Through these images that the poet has created, readers' imaginations fill in the emotional gaps.

HISTORICAL CONTEXT

History of Yugoslavia

The country of Yugoslavia was created at the end of World War I. The formation was an intellectual and political one and occurred after the fall of the Austro-Hungarian and Ottoman Empires, which had previously held rule over this part of the Balkan peninsula. At first, this new union was called the Kingdom of Serbs, Croats, and Slovenes. Serbia, with its major city of Belgrade, was the most dominant in the union. Later, the nations of Vojvodina and Montenegro were added to this union.

Political uprisings threatened the kingdom. These were caused mostly by the Croats, who resented being controlled by the government in Belgrade, which was located in Serbian territory. Fearing separatist activities, King Alexander I banned all political groups and divided the kingdom into nine districts, providing each with some sense of local administration. He hoped this would ease the threatening surge of those who wanted to dissolve the union. The king, in 1929, also changed the name of the union to Yugoslavia, which translates to "the land of southern Slavs." Alexander's attempts at a more heavy-handed rule, however, upset the Croatians even more. In addition, the countries of Germany, Italy, and Russia also disagreed with the union of these countries as well as Alexander's dictator-style rule. They all had their own ideas of what they hoped to gain from the Balkans. As the pressure mounted, the king visited France in October 1934, and he was assassinated by a Bulgarian named Vlado Chernozemski. Chernozemski was a member of a revolutionary group that sought the secession of Macedonia from Yugoslavia. Upon his death, Alexander's eleven-year-old son, Peter II, became king, but he was too young to rule. So his cousin, Prince Paul, assumed authority through a regency council.

In 1941, army general Dusan Simovic, supported by the governments of Nazi Germany and fascist Italy, launched a military coup, which

COMPARE
&
CONTRAST

- **1940s:** German dictator Adolph Hitler orders his Nazi army to take over other European countries.

  1980s: Insurgents fight against a military-controlled government in El Salvador.

  Today: The forces of the Taliban attempt to control the democratic government of Afghanistan.

- **1940s:** Russian chess players, including Mikhail Botvinnik, dominate the international chess championships.

  1980s: Garry Kasparov, a Russian, becomes the youngest world champion in chess at age 22.

  Today: Viswanathan Anand, born in India, dominates the first decade of the twenty-

first century, winning world chess championships and becoming the oldest (in his thirties) to do so.

- **1940s:** Child prodigy Ruth Duskin is seven years old and a member of the radio/television program called Quiz Kid. Six years later, Duskin publishes her first book at age thirteen.

  1980s: Child prodigy Derek Trucks, at the age of ten, tours with his famous father, Butch (of the Allman Brothers Band), having mastered the guitar.

  Today: Child prodigy Sho Timothy Yano graduates from Loyola University at age twelve. He is eighteen when he earns his doctorate in molecular genetics and cell biology.

---

resulted in Prince Paul's exile. Alexander's successor, Peter II, was only seventeen years old but was put into power. Taking advantage of these unstable conditions, German leader Adolf Hitler tried to pressure Yugoslavia to join the political powers referred to as the Axis, which included Germany, Italy, Japan, and Bulgaria. Though the official powers in Belgrade were willing to work out a compromise with these foreign powers, the people of Yugoslavia were strongly against the Nazi influence. In retaliation, Germany invaded Yugoslavia and bombed Belgrade and other major cities. Yugoslavia was completely occupied by outside forces by April and then dismantled, with each of the Axis powers taking their share. Germany ruled Belgrade. Hundreds of thousands of Yugoslavians were imprisoned, murdered, or exiled.

The National Liberation Army was established by the Serbian resistance under the leadership of Josip Broz Tito. In cooperation with the National Liberation Army, the Allied Forces, made up of United Kingdom, United States, and Soviet Union nations, invaded Yugoslavia, and Serbia was liberated from Nazi rule in 1944.

However, Tito, a committed communist, continued his governance of Yugoslavia for almost forty more years. Upon his death in 1980, the separatist movement regained strength. Slobodan Milosevic eventually took power in Serbia and demanded direct rule over the country from Belgrade. As Milosevic favored Serbs over other ethnic groups, tensions grew worse. In 1997, armed resistance emerged. As civil war raged on, the United Nations became involved as the organization set up a military presence in Kosovo in 1999. This led to the dissolution of Yugoslavia in 2003, as a new constitution for a new state union was created. Serbia and Montenegro became the Republic of Serbia in 2006. In 2008, Kosovo declared independence, although Serbia has not officially recognized this. The status of the former group of nations that once made up Yugoslavia continues to be unsettled.

The Game of Chess and World Masters
The game of chess has been traced back to ancient times, possibly as far back as 100 CE. Although the modern game of chess, as most people who

live in Western cultures recognize it, differs a lot from the ancient form, the first chess games were probably played in what is now northern India and in what was once called Persia, in modern-day Iran. European countries have records of the game that date back to 1000 CE.

Chess is played on a checkered board, with two players controlling sixteen pieces each. Each set of pieces is usually differentiated by the colors white and black. The pieces of each set are a king, queen, two rooks, two knights, two bishops, and eight pawns. The game is somewhat war-like, as the object of the game is to capture the king. The pawns are the least powerful but carry their weight much as foot soldiers would do in a real-life battle.

Competition for chess players usually begins with games with friends or family. Then it intensifies, depending on how serious a player is. There are chess clubs in schools and community centers. One can find competitive players online, too. There are also state-level competitions and national ones. The top layer of competition is found in world championships. The first official world chess champion was Wilhelm Steinitz, who won the title in 1886.

Since the 1940s, Russian chess players have dominated the competition. Until the Soviet Union dissolved, only one person who was not Russian held the title of World Champion. That one non-Russian champion was American Bobby Fischer, who claimed the title from 1972 until 1975. Russian chess masters included Mikhail Botvinnik (1948–1954, 1958, and 1961.) Boris Spassky was the victor from 1969 until 1972. More recently, the Russian chess players remained the ones to beat, with Garry Kasparov and Veselin Topalov holding the titles until 2007. Then in September 2007, a new country, India, was represented by Viswanathan Anand, who claimed the title until 2010, when Magnus Carlsen came on the scene. Carlsen is from Norway and has been referred to as a child prodigy.

Carlsen played his first chess tournament when he was eight years old. At the age of thirteen, Carlsen won the title of Grandmaster, the third youngest person to do so. At eighteen, he played a game in the Nanjing Pearl Spring Tournament that has been deemed one of the greatest games ever played. In 2010, Carlsen was the youngest chess player in history to be ranked number one in the world when he defeated Russian player Vladimir Kramnik in the World Chess Championship. Carlsen was only nineteen at the time.

In the poem, the white king is missing. (Image copyright Shutterstock Images LLC, 2010. Used under license from Shuttestock.com)

CRITICAL OVERVIEW

"Prodigy" has been published in several collections because of its simple yet powerful form. As *Poetry* magazine's Steven Cramer explains in his review of Simic's *Selected Poems 1963–1983*, "Prodigy" is one of Simic's finest. Poems like this "bear the scars of historical witness," Cramer writes. He adds that Simic's "memories of growing up in war-torn Belgrade provide an experiential groundwork for the primeval violences in his work." Cramer concludes with praise for Simic's writing, stating that "future readers will return to Simic's mythic well for enchantment and instruction."

In an article for the *Texas Observer*, Yvonne Georgina Puig writes, "Applied in admiration or disdain, 'accessible' is among the truest claims to be made for the poetry of Charles Simic." Puig continues: "At their best, Simic's poems are observant meditations on the unseen and overlooked. . . . His poems are accessible not because they're prosaic or simple, but because they make the mundane compelling."

Many critics of Simic stress the accessibility or simplicity of his poems. William Corbett, writing for *Poets and Writers*, describes Simic's style in this way: "He continues to write in sentences and prefers an everyday language, words that know hard use and give good value." In speaking directly about Simic's poem "Prodigy," Virginia Stuart, writing online for the *University of New Hampshire Magazine*, uses some of the images of the poem to describe Simic's strengths as a poet. Stuart writes: "In short, the prodigy has become not a master of chess, but a master of words—words he can use to transport readers, fight a modern-day tyrant, or galvanize young writers."

In a review of Simic's *Selected Poems: 1963–1983* for the publication *Erato*, a critic notes that "in all of his work Simic confronts the mystery which lies behind the world's plainness. He gives an almost romantic life to what we are too busy or jaded to notice." In a review for *World Literature Today* of Simic's *The Voice at 3:00 A.M.: Selected Late and New Poems*, Fred Dings writes: "When so much contemporary poetry seems to sprawl in loquacious and prosaic free verse, Simic's succinct, powerful, revelatory expressions... remind us why the best poetry is an essential art."

Diana Engelmann, writing for the *Antioch Review*, notes Simic's bilingual and bicultural background and how these elements influence his work. She writes, "A Simic poem may begin with a corner musician's tune in New York, and then move to the street's end where a gypsy fortune-teller whispers some odd lines resembling old Slavic proverbs, and we suddenly discover that the same street ends in a different country and in a different time."

Langdon Hammer, writing for *American Scholar*, observes that Simic is "one of America's most honored poets." Hammer makes reference to Simic's dual Eastern European and American influences when he says that Simic "is typically seen as a surrealist, carrying forward a European tradition of an oblique, bemused way of looking at the world that probes the strangeness of daily life in brief fables and anecdotes. This is a fair characterization, but his jazzy meanderings and smoky riffs are also intensely American."

CRITICISM

Joyce Hart

Hart is a published writer and creative writing teacher. In this essay, she explores the various insinuations Simic makes about the life of a gifted child in "Prodigy."

In his poem "Prodigy," Simic alludes to the qualities involved in being a prodigy, though he never mentions the word directly in the text of his poem. The poet merely uses this word in his title. Readers might therefore question why the poet chose this word as the title. What aspects of being a prodigy does the poet emphasize in the text? Why was it important for the poet to use this title? What might be inferred from the word *prodigy* when analyzing the meaning of the poem?

First, readers should understand what the word *prodigy* means. A prodigy is a child with a special gift or intelligence. The child in this poem is shown to be gifted. He plays chess for long hours. He spends most of his childhood studying the game. Chess is a difficult game to understand, let alone to master. This boy, one can assume, dreams of mastering this complicated game. One can also assume that this is an unusual child. An adult teaches him how to play chess and talks to the boy about chess masters. The teacher expounds on the masters' feats, such as playing blindfolded and competing in multiple games simultaneously. The teacher, one could imagine, inspires the boy to study hard so that he too might one day become a master.

This child spends so much time studying the game of chess that his cousins think that he is strange. They worry about him. He does not act like them or like other children they know. He is different from them, which could mean that he is probably often left alone. When he is not leaning over the chessboard, he probably is studying books about chess. He is so absorbed in the game of chess that he even loves the words that are associated with the game. His life, in many ways, is probably spent lost in thoughts of chess. As a prodigy, he is especially good at the game. He has special skills that help him to understand chess in ways that other children cannot quite grasp. Maybe that is why his cousins worry about him. They do not understand the boy's complete satisfaction in playing and studying this game, which probably looks to them like any other board game they play from time to time. These other children might ask themselves

WHAT
DO I READ
NEXT?

- Simic's Pulitzer Prize-winning collection *The World Doesn't End: Prose Poems* (1989) provides a comprehensive overview of this poet's style. Some of these poems touch on the absurd. Others make readers laugh. Most of them present the unexpected. All of these poems are written in a lyrical and uncomplicated prose style. They are easy to read but, typical of Simic's poems, not always so easy to understand.

- Simic also is known for his books of essays. In *The Renegade: Writings on Poetry and a Few Other Things* (2009), Simic comments on some of his own poetry and offers his views of some of his fellow poets, such as Robert Creeley, Donald Hall, Christopher Marlowe, and W. G. Sebald.

- In *A Fly in the Soup: Memoirs* (2000), Simic offers his readers memories of his early years in Yugoslavia and then in the United States. This memoir covers such topics as the bombing of Belgrade, his experiences while he was in the army, some of his favorite foods, and his philosophical ideas.

- Donald Hall was the U.S. Poet laureate who preceded Simic. Hall's 2006 collection

White Apples and the Taste of Stone: Selected Poems, 1946–2006 gives a comprehensive overview of his life's work. In these poems, Hall speaks of his love of the New Hampshire landscape, his experiences as a child growing up in the suburbs, and his development into middle age. His writing style is simple and descriptive and easy to comprehend.

- Betsy Franco has collected works by teenage boys in *You Hear Me? Poems and Writing by Teenage Boys* (2000). This young-adult anthology contains poems and essays about the joys and the pains of coming of age. Some of the emotions that run through these pieces include love, anger, jealousy, and fear as the authors search for a strong sense of self.

- In *War and the Pity of War* (1998), compiled by Neil Philip, readers will gain access to poems about war written by authors from all over the world, including China, India, Japan, African nations, and Europe. The origins of these poems span from ancient Persia to twentieth-century Bosnia. Some of these poems focus on the glory of war while others express the horror and pain that war can cause.

---

what is so intriguing about chess that it captures the boy's full attention and interest. They, unlike the boy, are not prodigies. Their intellects are still forming. They are childlike in every way, unlike this prodigy. Like some adults much older than he, this child is driven to the point of mastery.

Because he is a prodigy, the child in this poem stands out in contrast to his cousins. He has an intellect far ahead of his age and therefore ahead of his peers. Not only is he better at chess than his cousins, he is probably better than most adults. He knows how to look at the chessboard and see multiple, complicated moves. To win this game and to master it requires him to see not

only what he will do seven, eight, or more moves ahead of where he is but must also be able to anticipate where his opponent will move. The feats a chess prodigy is capable of are in no way ordinary.

Nonetheless, as extraordinary as this child might be in the world of chess, he is still a young boy. He has no special advantages over his young cousins when it comes to the world outside his house. Though the game of chess is warlike in its strategies, this child prodigy has no adult understanding of the war that is being waged outside the windows. On one side of his life, this young boy has been assigned a special tutor to teach him how to master the game of

"FURTHERMORE, THE POEM SUGGESTS THAT THE GIFTEDNESS OF THE CHILD, THOUGH IT MADE HIM EXTREMELY COMPETENT IN THE GAME OF CHESS, COULD NOT SAVE HIM FROM THE TORMENT OF THE WAR THAT CONSUMED HIS WORLD."

chess. When it comes to the miseries of war, however, he is purposefully kept in the dark. Thus begins the poet's comparison and contrast between the chess and war, with this child prodigy caught somewhere in between.

With chess, the boy is treated as an adult. All doors are opened to him. He can learn as much about the game as he can absorb. The object of the game is to bring down the king. In the process, bishops, rooks, knights, pawns, and sometimes even the queen are sacrificed. The boy learns to be victorious in his journey to capture the king and therefore to win the game. He learns to use his chess soldiers to surround the king, offering the opponent's monarch no mercy and no chance to escape. To win at chess, one cannot afford to have compassion for the opposition.

In the real world, though, the elements of war are not so simple. Although the goals might be similar—capturing the king or the country that is being attacked—the players in real wars are not made of plastic or wood. In real wars, human life is at stake. Blood is shed. Screams of pain are heard from the wounded. Fear for one's own safety can become so powerful that it can become debilitating. To protect this child prodigy in real life, his mother tries to keep the war a secret. She shields his eyes so he cannot see. There is no mention of a tutor to teach the child what is going on in his country. Instead, his mother covers the boy's eyes when he is outside, and then when they are home, she attempts to keep her son's mind focused on chess.

Keeping the boy unaware of the war is impossible, of course. He feels the house shake when tanks rumble by on the street. He hears the rattling of the windows. Children are naturally curious, so one can assume that the boy runs to the window when he feels the tanks roar through his town. He hears the sounds and sees the presence of the military aircraft. If the planes are dropping bombs, the boy could not be unaware of them. So despite the mother's efforts, the boy is not kept completely in the dark. The mother attempts to shelter her son from the atrocities of war, but she cannot be completely successful. Even if the boy does not understand the specifics of the war or the politics behind why it is being fought, he can hear the loud sounds of destruction. He can see the fear on his mother's face, hear it in her tone of voice, and sense it in her attempts to hide him.

This is the dilemma of being a child prodigy, the poem suggests. Here is a child with a mind capable of understanding adult-level complexities, at least in the game of chess. He is a young boy who is treated as an adult in his studies of the chess game. This child has the ability to compute complicated mathematical possibilities. His advanced intellect allows him to visualize abstract patterns and apply them in his efforts to master the game. But here, too, is a boy whose emotional development lags far behind his rational faculties. He is a youth who lacks experience in the real world. He does not comprehend why people kill one another and then display the dead bodies on telephone poles. None of this makes sense to him. With chess, his mind is fully open. But with the atrocities of war, he must close his mind in order to maintain his sanity. Though he remembers his mother hiding him, the speaker declares in this poem, this child cannot remember seeing the bodies hanging on the poles.

Why did Simic use the word *prodigy* as title but not use this word in the text of his poem? Readers can only guess. Maybe the author wanted only to hint at the special gifts that this child possessed. Maybe he wanted readers to keep in mind that although this child was extremely competent in intellectual ways, he was nonetheless very young and therefore emotionally vulnerable. Or maybe Simic wanted to emphasize the divide between intellect and emotion by creating a disconnect between the title and the text of the poem. On one hand there is a gifted child, a prodigy, the title informs the readers. On the other hand, the poem describes the painful memories of the war. There are the clear-cut, carefully planned, rational moves on the chessboard. There is the emotional devastation of people suffering. Furthermore, the poem suggests that the giftedness of the child, though it made him extremely competent in the game of chess, could not save him from the torment of the war that consumed his world. Prodigy is not an all-encompassing gift, the poem suggests. Prodigy can be very narrow in its scope.

Source: Joyce Hart, Critical Essay on "Prodigy," in *Poetry for Students*, Gale, Cengage Learning, 2011.

Jeffrey Thomas

In the following article, Thomas offers insight into Simic's career and the place of poetry in the contemporary United States.

Charles Simic, the new poet laureate of the United States, did not begin learning English until he was 15 and moved to New York City, then Chicago, after a traumatic childhood in the former Yugoslavia.

"The big, big influence on my life was being born in Yugoslavia in 1938. And then, in 1941, the war started and I was there during the war, and then in the years after the war under communism. The war years in Yugoslavia were pure hell," Simic told USINFO in an interview August 9.

In 1953, Simic, his mother and brother were able to travel to Paris, where they stayed for a year. Then they moved on to the United States to join Simic's father. "If you came to New York in 1954, it was incredible. Europe was still gray; there were still ruins. New York was just dazzling. When I was a little kid in Yugoslavia I loved jazz, I loved movies, so this was paradise," Simic said.

Later, as a youth in Chicago, he wanted to be a painter. "I started writing in high school and then I met people who were writers and poets. We would talk about poetry, read poetry. I started publishing my first poems in 1959 in the *Chicago Review*—a pretty good magazine. So five years after I entered the United States, I published my first poem."

An immigrant learning English in his teens "doesn't take it for granted," Simic said. "One notices things about language, one notices things about American culture and other things that I imagine a native-born would not see."

Although he published his first book of poems in 1967, Simic did not really take himself seriously as a writer until a few years later. "The first time I realized my poetry meant something

was in 1970. I was living in New York City, working. I worked at a photography magazine. I started getting letters out of the blue from colleges and universities asking me whether I would come and teach creative writing and literature. I had planned to spend the rest of my life in New York City working at different jobs, but to my surprise these offers kept coming."

In 1971, Simic took a teaching job at California State College at Hayward. In 1973, he moved to the University of New Hampshire, where he taught until his recent retirement.

His appointment as the 15th poet laureate was announced by the Library of Congress August 2. On the same day, the Academy of American Poets awarded him the $100,000 Wallace Stevens Award for "outstanding and proven mastery in the art of poetry."

"The range of Charles Simic's imagination is evident in his stunning and unusual imagery. He handles language with the skill of a master craftsman, yet his poems are easily accessible, often meditative and surprising. He has given us a rich body of highly organized poetry with shades of darkness and flashes of ironic humor," said Librarian of Congress James H. Billington in making the appointment.

The position of "poet laureate consultant in poetry" at the Library of Congress, modeled on its British equivalent, was created in 1986. It was held in the past by such notable poets as Robert Penn Warren, Richard Wilbur, W.S. Merwin, Mark Strand, Rita Dove and the Russian-born Nobel Prize laureate, Joseph Brodsky. From 1937 to 1986, the position existed under two separate titles.

According to the Library of Congress, the poet laureate "seeks to raise the national consciousness to the greater appreciation of the reading and writing of poetry." But in Simic's words, the position "is pretty much what you make of it." He will give a speech at the library's National Book Festival September 29 and a poetry reading October 17.

Simic rejects the notion that the poet has any role other than "to write good poems." Every time he is asked about the role of the poet, he thinks of the communists and their "cultural policy."

"They always had duties and roles for writers and poets. Poetry presents poetry. Any poet is an individual voice. If he is a good poet or she is a good poet, the whole question is of trying to do what you do well—the integrity that comes with the work that you do," he said.

The audience for poetry in the United States today is "terrific," Simic said, and has been so since the so-called "Beat" poets of the 1950s and early 1960s. "Poetry readings became really, really popular everywhere, so that there isn't a college, university or community center in this country that doesn't have a poetry series. People are used to going to poetry readings. The audiences are huge."

Simic sees himself as writing in the New England tradition of Emily Dickinson, Robert Frost and Wallace Stevens, and feels "at home philosophically with New England writers like Nathaniel Hawthorne or Ralph Waldo Emerson or Thoreau—all the grumpy ones."

He has won many awards, including a Pulitzer Prize and the "genius award" from the Mac-Arthur Foundation.

He also has won major awards for his numerous translations of French, Serbian, Croatian, Macedonian and Slovenian poetry, and is currently revising and expanding an anthology of Serbian poetry, for which he won an award from the Academy of American Poets in 1993.

For someone unfamiliar with his work, Simic suggested a selection of his later poems, *The Voice at 3:00 AM* (2003), as the best place to start.

He recommends "Prodigy," a poem set in Belgrade, Serbia, during World War II. He remains especially fond of this poem, he told USINFO.

Source: Jeffrey Thomas, "New U.S. Poet Laureate Charles Simic Immigrated as a Teen," in *U.S. Federal News*, August 10, 2007.

Belinda McKeon

In the following essay, McKeon contemplates the ways in which Simic's sense of the world influences his work.

"Son," the poet Charles Simic's mother would greet him when he visited her in the Chicago nursing home where she spent the last years of her life, "You still write poetry?" He laughs as he remembers. "And I'd say, 'Yes, mother', and she'd shake her head and say, 'my poor boy . . . .' She always thought that I would get into trouble. She thought that I had a big mouth."

Though grounded in an earlier world of experience, Helen Simic's anxiety was understandable. The Belgrade into which her son was

> 'I'M NOT A STICKLER FOR TRUTH,' HE SAYS.
> 'TO ME, LYING IN POETRY IS MUCH MORE FUN. I'M
> AGAINST LYING IN LIFE, IN PRINCIPLE, IN ANY
> OTHER ACTIVITY EXCEPT POETRY.'"

born in 1938 was on the brink of a war which would ravage both it and its inhabitants; his earliest memory is of a night in 1941, when Nazi forces launched a series of bombings that claimed thousands—some estimate up to 17,000—lives. Simic himself, on that morning, was a toddler thrown from his cot by the force of a bomb striking outside his home. Walking through the ruined city afterwards, he would not look at the Germans standing on the street corners—his mother forbade it. He would not see the bodies of Serbs hanged on the main square—his mother pulled her coat over his eyes, shielding him from the sight. Saying little and looking less; such were the keys to survival in a dangerous time. For his mother, they would remain crucial even after 1954, when she got herself and her children out of Belgrade, moving first to Paris and eventually following her husband to the new life he had begun in the United States.

But the prospect of getting into trouble caused less worry to the young Simic, despite his mother's warnings. To him and his friends, the occupied city was a playground of shattered houses and soldier games, and one in which parents were much too preoccupied to enforce any rules. "They were years of violence, but they were extremely interesting to someone growing up in the city, in the heart of the city," he explains. "And we loved it. I mean, when I was a kid, we thought it was great."

More than half a [century] later, Simic is still immersed in adventure, still playing games, but this time in and with language itself; though neither starkly experimental or narratively obscure, his poetry toys with currents of menace, darkness and fear as easily as it draws life from the moments of good in the world, from the simple objects in which we find hope, or humour, or both at once. "What is beautiful," he writes in

"The Altar," from his 2001 collection, *Night Picnic*, "is found accidentally, and not sought after / What is beautiful is easily lost." The rare beauty of Simic's poetic voice was evident even with the publication, in 1967, of his first collection, *What the Grass Says*, with its loving, intricate knowledge of the concrete elements of a life. In the 15 collections since then, that beauty has grown, if anything, rarer still, enriched by sadness, foreboding, defiance, realisation. Simic's poems know the world, in both its blackness and its light, its heaviness and its gentle mundanity, and the determined precision of his gaze has won him both the Pulitzer Prize and the PEN Award for translation. Another major accolade brought him to Dublin last month; he was this year's international winner of the $40,000 Griffin Poetry Prize, which was honoured with an evening of readings by Simic and other Griffin poets at the Dublin Writers Festival.

Asked about the difference that a prize like the Griffin can make to a poet's career, Simic is characteristically deadpan. It makes a change, he says, from being a loser. "I've been, previously, in similar situations," he says. "I've been all dressed up in a suit, and been a loser. And one of the hardest things about losing is not losing itself, but that you have to spend the next two hours and days after accepting condolences, from people saying, 'I'm so sorry you lost.' Or, 'I was praying for you.' And you say, 'It's ok, it's fine, don't worry, I'm a big boy.'" He laughs. "Yeah. So I was happy I didn't have to do that again."

Simic laughs a lot, lightly, quietly, often self-deprecatingly. His accent is a mealy mixture of New York (where he lived in his 20s), New Hampshire (where he currently teaches) and old Belgrade. He takes some things very seriously, and some things less so, including himself—he doesn't mind conducting an interview in his hotel room, beside his rumpled bed, because everywhere else is too noisy, or jamming open the hotel window with one of his own books, because the humidity, even this early, is becoming too much.

He doesn't mind admitting that, although he considers himself to have retained something from his Eastern European background—"humour, cynicism, a tragic view of life mixed with farce, mixed with comedy"—the poets of that tradition have rejected him as a stranger, and he doesn't fight against the tone of resignation, or maybe even

sadness, that slips into his voice as he describes this rejection. "They regard me as a foreigner," he says, "They don't think my poetry has anything to do with them. So, you know. There's nothing there for me. I mean, they translate my work, and they're happy to have someone in America ... but during the nationalist days, I read it again and again, 'he's a complete foreigner,' said in a very pejorative way. An alien. That was their view."

Simic looks towards the U.S. now, and has done for many years, he says. As a 20 year-old arriving in New York in the late 1950s, he found himself drawn slowly into the literary scene—the parties after readings where "you would see from a distance the famous names, Lowell, Berryman," the little magazines, "awfully produced, mimeographed and cheap-looking but extremely exciting"—yet resisted the notion of being part of a school or movement.

Such resistance was not easy; he was faced with the fervent efforts of contemporaries and commentators to pin him down, along with Mark Strand and Charles Wright, as a neo-surrealist, or a deep image poet. "I suppose they had to call us something," he says. "But we wanted to keep our independence. I mean, because the generation before us exhausted themselves in polemic, fighting with issues, for us, just being a little bit detached from that, you could see interesting things that you could appropriate, here and there."

What Simic was least interested in appropriating, at this stage, was the deeply self-referential style of poetry associated with Lowell and Berryman, among others; the poem which tells directly of the life was not the poem he strove to create. And, though they were giants in the literary scene of the time, Lowell and Berryman meant, he says frankly, "nothing" to him. He may have been helped in this reaction by the vehemence of older writers in Chicago, where he spent his teenage years before coming to New York. "I remember when I was a young fellow in Chicago and someone gave me a copy of Lowell's *Life Studies*, and the novelist Nelson Algren, who despised East Coast writers, and just the East Coast, said, 'what are you reading there?,' and took the book out of my pocket. And he said, 'Charles, don't read that shit. You're a kid off the boat. Read Whitman. Read Carl Sandburg. Don't read these Boston, these Ivy League phonies. ...'" He laughs at the memory, and then comes upon another. "It was very much a

Chicago thing. You know, when I decided to move to New York, my friends were all in a panic. That I would become one of those typical East establishment types, in tweeds, smoking a pipe, drinking scotch and soda.... I told them, don't worry."

Still, for all his independence from the dominant schools, the autobiographical impulse found its way into his work. Not in the naked manner of *Life Studies*, but subtly, unmistakably. It's there in poems like "Prodigy," where the poet writes of a summer witnessing "men hung from telephone poles," or, in "Against Whatever It Is That's Encroaching," where a small boy comes home "to a room almost dark" as "the grown-ups raise their glasses to him," looking as if they might either "cry or sing," in an echo of that night in Simic's old childhood when the grown-ups told him that the war was over (and when he complained, in reply, that there would be no more fun).

"You know how it is," Simic says with another laugh. "If one does live a life, it's going to intrude at some point. And there was a book, my fourth I think, *Charon's Cosmology*, where I just sort of rediscovered my life as a second World War child. Good stories, interesting things would just crop up. You know, a night of drinking and you tell your friends about your early life, and you remember something, and it leads to something else...."

But Simic never bound himself rigidly to the memories that resurfaced; that sense of play so endemic to his poetry was there from the start. "I'm not a stickler for truth," he says. "To me, lying in poetry is much more fun. I'm against lying in life, in principle, in any other activity except poetry. So a poem may start with some autobiographical material, but you know, if, along the way, a more interesting fictional conclusion or turn proposes itself, I'm very happy to leave myself behind. To wave to little Charlie, and then go on and make something up."

Reality, however, has always been at the core of Simic's work, even of his most arguably surrealist work. "The world as it exists has always been very important to me," he says, laughing as if at the notion that anything else could be centrally important to a poet. "I'm all for the imagination, but there's a part of me, an equal part, that believes in a kind of hard realism. I'm not interested in nonsense, in not communicating. No matter how daring, how

seemingly obscure and complicated an image, I will only use it if I can smell in it some meaning lurking, or something happening. That can take the reader someplace."

The key, he says, is to get back to reality with a fresh perspective. "Because all we have is reality, finally. I mean, the imagination, as imaginative as you can be, it's not inexhaustible. It tends to be the same old film, played over and over. You need reality to make the imagination do interesting things, to renew itself. Take the reality out of the equation and you simply repeat yourself."

The reality facing any American poet right now, he agrees, is a harsh one, and not an easy one to confront without losing artistic integrity. "We are living in a kind of reality that is...unreal. Reality is actually a great enemy of the present administration and of the official Washington. Nobody wants to hear about reality. And it's very difficult to describe, that sense of displacement, that sense of being bewildered in a world in which one is living." Remembering the flood of political poems which came with the Vietnam war, he is reluctant to rush toward the subject in his own work, but it forces its way through; his own horror at the return of "a love of war, an idea that war is noble" is something that he finds difficult to keep out of his writing. Recently, he has written a poem about the flag-draped coffins of American soldiers returning from Iraq at the dead of night, delivered to their parents houses when nobody can see them, when nobody can photograph the truth. But the truth can become a poem.

"Always in the background of my poems is that sense of the world," he says. "When I was a kid, when I came to this country and faced the possibility of being drafted, and then my sons did, and my brother was in Vietnam...it just never ends." Nor, thankfully, does the impulse to write. "This year," he says, and the realisation transforms his face as he puts it into words, "it will be 50 years since I started writing poetry. It's just an ongoing obsession, preoccupation in my life. And that's why I write. Because I cannot imagine myself without this inner life, this mental life, this constant worry. This poetry."

Source: Belinda McKeon, "Making the Truth into Poetry," in *Irish Times*, July 23, 2005, p. 11.

Daniel Morris

In the following excerpt, Morris discusses "Prodigy" as a poem of "traumatic displacement."

...Simic begins a poem entitled "Prodigy" (1977) by stating: "I grew up bent over / a chess-board. / I loved the word endgame" (*Selected Poems* 1–3). In "Prodigy," Simic reports how in Belgrade in 1944, he learned to play chess from a retired professor of astronomy when "Planes and tanks / shook [the] windowpanes" (7–8). Simic also recalls playing chess with an incomplete set of broken pieces: "the paint had almost chipped off / the black pieces" and "The white King was missing / and had to be substituted for" (13–16). At the end of the poem, Simic extends the memory of playing chess amidst the war bombings into a narrative about traumatic displacement. He combines the image of the blind chess player with a story about his mother shielding his eyes as a man is hanged from a telephone pole:

> I remember my mother blindfolding me a
>   lot. She had a way of tucking my
> head suddenly under her overcoat.
>
> In chess, too, the professor told me, the
>   masters play blindfolded, the
> great ones on several boards at the same
>   time. (20–27)

Simic represents chess as a metaphor for metaphor, a scene of instruction in how creativity may enable the child to resist trauma through displacement. Describing chess as his initiation into poetic vision, Simic suggests how the writer, by interpreting art as a theater of play, may, indirectly, act out and work through experiences that were beyond his control as a child. By remembering how he learned chess from the blind master, Simic claims that poetic insight is contingent upon experiential deprivation. Shielded by his mother from directly witnessing terrible events such as a hanging, Simic imagines the past in his mind's eye. In the poet Alan Shapiro's terms, he "transform [s] into pleasure experiences that otherwise would terrify or repel" (184). Playing chess while blindfolded in "Prodigy" is comparable to the classic image of the blind singer found in Homer, Sophocles, and Milton, as well as in the African-American blues tradition, much admired by Simic, in the figures of Blind Lemon Jefferson, Ray Charles, and Stevie Wonder.

Source: Daniel Morris, "Responsible Viewing: Charles Simic's Dime-Store Alchemy: The Art of Joseph Cornell," in *Papers on Language & Literature*, Fall 1998, p. 337.

> AS YOU GET OLDER, THE SUBJECT OF A POEM IS ASTONISHMENT AT WHAT IS BEFORE YOU. IT'S ALMOST A RELIGIOUS EXPERIENCE, ONE OF STANDING APART AND SEEING YOURSELF IN AWE BEFORE THE WORLD."

Molly McQuade

In the following excerpt, Simic discusses his life growing up as a young immigrant in New York City.

In his new book of poetry, a Pulitzer Prize winner returns to the New York City of his youth.

Charles Simic is Yugoslav and American, skeptic and believer, a poet convinced, as he once wrote, that "writing is always a rough translation from wordlessness into words." Poetry "attracts me because it makes trouble for thinkers," he has declared. "Poetry is an orphan of silence. The words never quite equal the experience behind them. We are always at the beginning, eternal apprentices, thrown back again and again into that condition."

... "I came to New York in August of 1958, and it was amazingly simple," Simic recalls. "I would work at some place for a few months, and quit. I'd live the life of a bohemian. Then I'd realize I was running out of money, and I'd get a haircut—and a new job. I had all sorts of office jobs. I got to be pretty good at bookkeeping. I went to school at NYU; it took me 10 years to get a B.A. at night. All that seemed perfectly fine. It was great to be in New York and have a job and buy records and go to movies and jazz clubs. All those street scenes, sights, made a tremendous impression on my mind—I have an endless anthology of them.

"I was aware, in writing *The Book of Gods and Devils*, of an almost pagan impulse," he continues. "Pagans would invent gods or demons for any place where people had intense experiences. A big city is a home of multiple gods, not just the obvious religions. There are things one worships and things one is afraid of. I have a certain pessimism about history that is very Balkan; I'm suspicious of attempts to idealize human beings. We are not noble savages, not kind, good, wholesome. But I don't think the demons are very strong in the book; there is a lot of humor and there are a lot of gods."

What he calls "the shock, the newness" of New York helped make Simic what he is. So did his solitude there. As his poem "The Immortal" tells it, "You had your own heartbeat to listen to./ You were perfectly alone and anonymous./ It would have taken months for anyone/ To begin to miss you."

He elaborates, sitting at the dining room table of his house in Strafford, N.H. "You're lonely, you're figuring out everything from scratch. You're broke. I used to spend evenings on long walks, looking at store windows, watching people. But it was a great feeling. I drifted in the most pleasant fashion. It was a time of purity. Cities are places of sphinxes, enigmas. Even though you may think about them for the rest of your life, you'll never come to the bottom. You're the sum of everything you don't understand."

A tall, pale, exuberant and excitable man, Simic has lived with his wife, Helen, for many years in the New Hampshire woods and admits happily to his "peasant" heritage, but his relish for things urban is vigorously evident when he says, "You could smell a certain high lunacy in New York. And there's always been an element of the grotesque in my work; much in *The Book of Gods and Devils* seems totally surrealist. Yet it's based on the most factual stuff imaginable." Moreover, he argues, he is "a realist and a surrealist, always drawn between the two." By way of example, he invokes "The Fourteenth Street Poem," set in "a long block/ Favored by doomsday prophets," and where an obstreperous bag lady holds court. It is "real," but to a heightened degree.

"There is a story to this lady which I couldn't tell," he confides in a rumblingly resonant voice. Simic does not just talk—he groans, whoops and whispers, offering heavily accented phrases that twist and slide with American slang.

"The first time I saw her, I was crossing Washington Square Park late one night. This woman comes up to me, of uncertain age, with flying hair, an older version of the homeless person. And she says to me, 'I'm Venus, the goddess of love. If you don't give me a dollar, I'm gonna curse you, and you'll be unhappy in love.'" Simic laughs ringingly and uproariously

at the absurdity of his predicament. "So I said to her, 'Beat it!' And I told myself, 'I'm cursed. There's nothing I can do.'

"A couple of months went by. I was at Barnes & Noble. It's late afternoon, I'm getting some book, I look up and there she is! So I just sort of blurt out, 'You're Venus, the goddess of love!' And she says [and Simic assumes sotto voce], 'How did you know?'"

Being a raw youth in echt New York thus had its charm. "I was ignorant, and I'm glad now that I was," Simic says. "A lot of it came from being an immigrant and having really, really low expectations."

He regards his early life and world wanderings with a certain dark glee: "My travel agents were Hitler and Stalin. They were the reason I ended up in the United States." Born in Yugoslavia in 1938, he survived the World War II bombing of Belgrade, where his family lived and his father worked as a telephone engineer for a branch office of Western Electric. In 1944 his father was captured by the Germans, who examined the blueprints in his suitcase—intended for installing phone service in mountain villages—and judged them highly suspicious. "It looked pretty bad for him—it looked like they were going to shoot him. But he was liberated by the Americans and went to Trieste." Simic and his mother made several attempts to cross the Yugoslav border into Austria; in 1953 they were finally permitted to immigrate legally. Before joining the elder Simic in the U.S., where he was again working as an engineer, they spent a year or so in Paris.

Simic, precociously on the outs with adult authorities, found himself in trouble with French schoolmasters. "I knew I was doomed. I was gonna pump gas on some turnpike outside of Paris." But in 1954 the family was reunited, and he landed in New York "speechless with excitement." The Simics soon proceeded to Chicago, where his father had been transferred; he went to the same Oak Park high school that had claimed Ernest Hemingway as a student. "When I finished high school, I was so happy! All my sins had been absolved." A great, guttural laugh shakes him.

"I don't feel in any way Yugoslavian," insists Simic, who has visited the Eastern Bloc before and since its democratization. "Sometimes this comes to me with some regret. But the first literature I knew was American literature. Most of the important things in my life happened to me in this country. There's no question that many of my outlooks are completely Slavic: Hitler and Stalin fought over my soul, my destiny. Yet I'm never classified among the exiled writers. I really could not go back now. I see thing differently. And the language you write in, you have to hear."

Simic was a painter first, not a poet. In his essay collection *Wonderful Words, Silent Truth*, published this year by the University of Michigan Press in its Poets on Poetry series, he writes, "One day, two of my friends confessed that they wrote poetry. I asked them to show it to me. I wasn't impressed with what I saw. I went home and wrote some poems myself in order to demonstrate to them how it's supposed to be done. At first, the act of writing and the initial impression were exhilarating. Then, to my astonishment, I realized that my poems were as stupid as theirs were. I couldn't figure it out... [but] in the process of writing, I discovered a part of myself, an imagination and a need to articulate certain things, that I could not afterwards forget."

His first published poems appeared in the winter 1959 issue of the *Chicago Review*. Simic enthusiastically accepted many influences—Edgar Lee Masters, Vachel Lindsay, Ezra Pound, Walt Whitman, Hart Crane. But while serving in the U.S. Army in 1962, he destroyed his work to date and started over again. As he explained in a 1972 interview, "When confronted with the life I was leading at the time, [the poems] struck me as no more than literary vomit.... Life and its intensity had conquered."

The struggle that followed was difficult and prolonged. The results led Simic to join "a generation of writers who are committed to experimentalism, so much so that I'm struck by the timidity and predictability of a lot of writing today. I read books and get mad. In American poetry at the moment, 75% of American experience is invisible." Simic's first book, *What the Grass Says*, was published by Kayak Press in 1967. "It had a tremendous circulation—something like 27 reviews," and was followed by *Somewhere Among Us a Stone Is Taking Notes*, also a Kayak release.

His success meant that Simic, by then married in New York, received invitations from universities to teach. "Incredible! How could that be? But little by little I realized that working two days a week is better than five." He is now a professor of English at the University of New Hampshire. "I could live and die in a good library," he has written. Yet, "I'm suspicious of the pedantry that kind of learning is prone to." He confesses to a horror of abstractions and the intellectuals that go with them—too many of the latter, he feels, have disgraced themselves as collaborators in corrupt regimes of one kind or another to retain much credibility as a class.

Poems from Simic's first two books, along with new ones, were published by George Braziller in *Dismantling the Silence* in 1971. Braziller was Simic's main publisher for 15 years by his count, issuing six books that included his *Selected Poems* (1985). Simic has also translated more than half a dozen volumes of poetry, among these the work of Ivan Lalic, Vasko Popa ("an enormous influence on me") and Tomaz Salamun. "In order to do a translation, you have to be a kind of a shaman—you have to pretend, for a moment, that you're somebody else. You realize that the other person is very different from you—disgustingly different. That's fascinating."

In 1986 Harcourt Brace Jovanovich became Simic's publisher. "I had a good friend at HBJ, Drenka Willen, who was interested in me. George [Braziller] had always been very nice. But then you sort of say, would I be happy someplace else?" He decided he could indeed after receiving a Pulitzer Prize for Poetry this year for *The World Doesn't End*, a collection of prose poems.

"*The World Doesn't End* happened without too much deliberation," Simic maintains, marveling at winning the Pulitzer "lottery." What did the prose poem form offer him that poetry had not? "A lyric impulse is an impulse in which everything stands still," he replies. "It's like a song that repeats. Nothing ever happens in a lyric poem. It's a great acknowledgment of the present moment. In a prose sentence, however, things do happen. A prose poem is a dialectic between the two. You write in sentences, and tell a story, but the piece is like a poem because it circles back on itself.

"Books of poems—it takes a long time for the writer to really understand what's inside them," he admits. "It's like being in a period of your life." Simic reflects on the version of himself that appears in *The Book of Gods and Devils*. "It's amusing to see oneself at that distance. It isn't personal anymore. As you get older, the subject of a poem is astonishment at what is before you. It's almost a religious experience, one of standing apart and seeing yourself in awe before the world."

Source: Molly McQuade, "Charles Simic: In His New Book of Poetry, a Pulitzer Prize Winner Returns to the New York City of His Youth," in *Publishers Weekly*, Vol. 237, No. 44, November 2, 1990, pp. 56–57.

Kenneth Funsten

In the following review, Funsten suggests that Simic's earlier poetry was more startling and evocative than his later work.

> At night some understand what the grass
> says.
> The grass knows a word or two.
> It is not much. It repeats the same word
> Again and again, but not too loudly...

The best poems by Charles Simic harbor an enigmatic simplicity, contain an evasive weight to them. Influenced by riddles, parables and nursery rhymes, Simic populates the folk world of his poems with simple objects and puzzling omens. His poems have the atmosphere of a Bruegel feast day, without any of the people.

Born in Yugoslavia in 1938, Charles Simic spent his childhood watching Europe turn into rubble. "it's always evening / In an occupied country. / Hour before the curfew. / A small provincial city. / The houses all dark. / The storefronts gutted."

In 1949, he emigrated to America, eventually working as an editorial assistant at *Aperture*, a photography magazine.

The fact is significant. For Simic's best poems share a quality with good photographs, the unceasing attention to objects in an effort to see them anew. At his best, it is the intensity of Simic's imagination as it attempts to animate the objects and renew itself that interests us. For example, in "Fork":

> This strange thing must have crept
> Right out of hell.
> It resembles a bird's foot
> Worn around the cannibal's neck.
> As you hold it in your hand,
> As you stab with it into a piece of meat,
> It is possible to imagine the rest of the bird:
> Its head which like your fist
> Is large, bald, beakless and blind.

Specifics, such as the fork, give the poet's surrealism the focus it needs. His catalogues of imagination improvise the souls of our most everyday objects, bringing them back to life and light as if from the world of our dreams.

His first two books, *What the Grass Says* and *Somewhere Among Us a Stone Is Taking Notes*, were published and championed by George Hitchcock's Kayak Press in the late '60s, and then combined with new poems into Simic's first Braziller volume, *Dismantling the Silence* (1971).

Here, *Selected Poems* gives us some of his best work, including the famous "Bestiary for the Fingers of My Right Hand."

When Simic's metaphors are good, the disparate things they yoke together are both contradictory and strangely appropriate. His achievement in these early poems is maintaining that tension of the suspense between known and unknown, object and spirit.

But, of course, a poet cannot perform the same trick *ad infinitum*—even if it is his best. So, in his later books, Simic's task has been to branch out, to grow into the tree his acorn promised.

Simic's third book from Braziller was *Charon's Cosmology*. There is less zip, more speculation on death, more pessimism here. Many poems, like "The Prisoner," seem derivative of an earlier self:

> It's been so long. He has trouble
> Deciding what else is there.
> And all along the suspicion
> That we do not exist.

But *Classic Ballroom Dances* (1980) announced the rebirth of a sort of classic Simic, lean, mystical, authentic again. Many of the poems are about the poet's childhood in war-torn Yugoslavia.

The last 20 or so pieces in this *Selected* volume are from Simic's 1982 book, *Austerities*. Less dark, both literally and figuratively lighter, these are mostly too cute, too pat. Bordering on self-parody, many poems indulge what Auden called "the Dada giggle": "Pascal's own / Prize abyssologist / In marriage. / On her knees / Still scrubbing / The marble stairs / Of a Russian countess."

The tired symbols are recycled again—gravediggers, their spades, mirrors, bones, utensils. But they are no longer unnerving.

So what is the verdict? Has Simic's achievement amounted to automatic, clever writing that must forever sacrifice its future breadth and seriousness to remain its present self? Is this poet finally ensnared in his own cleverness? This collection of *Selected Poems* might make it appear so.

Source: Kenneth Funsten, Review of *Selected Poems: 1963–1983*, in *Los Angeles Times Book Review*, March 16, 1986, p. 9.

SOURCES

"Charles Simic: Online Resources," in *Library of Congress*, http://www.loc.gov/rr/program/bib/charlessimic/ (accessed January 18, 2010).

Corbett, William, "Charles Simic," in *Poets and Writers*, Vol. 24, No. 3, 1996, pp. 30–35.

Cramer, Steven, Review of *Selected Poems: 1963–1983* and *The Book of Gods and Devils*, in *Poetry*, Vol. 159, No. 4, January 1992, pp. 227–34.

Dings, Fred, Review of *The Voice at 3:00 A.M.: Selected Late and New Poems*, in *World Literature Today*, Vol. 79, No. 1, January/April 2005, p. 90.

Engelmann, Diana, "'Speaking in Tongues': Exile and Internal Translation in the Poetry of Charles Simic," in *Antioch Review*, Vol. 62, No. 1, Winter 2004, pp. 44–47.

Hammer, Langdon, "Invisible Things," in *American Scholar*, Vol. 74, No. 2, Spring 2005, pp. 49–50.

Harrell, Eben, "A Bold Opening for Chess Player Magnus Carlsen," in *Time*, Vol. 175, No. 1, January 11, 2010, p. 42.

———, "Magnus Carlsen: The 19-Year-Old King of Chess," in *Time*, December 25, 2009.

Mazower, Mark, *The Balkans: A Short History*, Modern Library, 2000.

Puig, Yvonne Georgina, "Easy Access," in *Texas Observer*, Vol. 101, No. 6, March 20, 2009, p. 28.

Simic, Charles, "Prodigy," in *Charles Simic, Selected Early Poems*, George Braziller, 1999.

"Somewhere among Us," in *Erato*, No. 1, Summer 1986.

Stuart, Virginia, "Poetic Justice," in *University of New Hampshire Magazine*, Fall 2007, http://unhmagazine.unh.edu/f07/poetic_pf.html (accessed January 18, 2010).

FURTHER READING

Hulse, Michael, *Charles Simic in Conversation with Michael Hulse*, Between the Lines, 2002.
    In this interview with Hulse, Simic talks about his childhood, the drastic changes in his life after moving to the United States, his early interest in painting and music, and his early writing.

McGowen, Tom, *World War II*, F. Watts, 1993.
    McGowen covers the invasion of Yugoslavia by Hitler's army in this brief study of the major events of World War II. The book includes overviews of the biggest battles of this war and the resultant political changes that occurred in the affected countries.

Popescu, Julian, *Yugoslavia*, Main Line Books, 1991.
    This book introduces young-adult readers to the history, geography, economy, and culture of the largest Balkan country in southeastern Europe.

Shenk, David, *The Immortal Game: A History of Chess*, Doubleday, 2006.
    Shenk offers an easy-to-understand, nontechnical background of the game of chess in this book. Covering the fifth century roots of this game as well as some of the greatest chess masters, Shenk provides an extensive history of the game.

Silber, Laura, and Allan Little, *Yugoslavia: Death of a Nation*, Penguin, 1997.
    Through a series of recorded interviews with politicians, soldiers, and regular citizens who experienced the bloody destruction of Yugoslavia, readers are given first-hand accounts of the civil war that took place in this country.

SUGGESTED SEARCH TERMS

Charles Simic

Charles Simic AND prose poems

Charles Simic biography

Charles Simic interview

Simic AND Prodigy

Simic AND Pulitzer Prize

Simic AND poems

Charles Simic AND Classic Ballroom Dances

Simic AND Yugoslavia

Self in 1958

ANNE SEXTON
1966

Anne Sexton's poem "Self in 1958" was first drafted in 1958 and then revised in 1965. It was published in her Pulitzer Prize-winning collection, *Live or Die*. The book, which was published in 1966, was Sexton's fourth collection and was written at the height of her poetic prowess. Sexton was one of the foremost poets of the confessional movement, a style of poetry popular in the United States from the 1950s to the 1970s. Poems in the confessional movement were characterized by free verse and deeply personal themes and content. "Self in 1958" is no exception, and it stands as a shining example of confessional poetry penned by one of the movement's leading writers. The poem explores the feeling of being a doll, that is, of conforming to the expectations of society rather than to one's individuality. This theme can also be read as remarkably feminist; in it, the speaker feels trapped by her body, one she deems to be made of plaster and not at all under her control. In this way, both the speaker's body and her surroundings (described in the poem as a stereotypical dollhouse) become a sort of prison. Although written in free verse, "Self in 1958" is composed of four ten-line stanzas. This structure underscores the rigid world that the speaker, the doll, inhabits.

AUTHOR BIOGRAPHY

Sexton was born Anne Gray Harvey on November 9, 1928, in Newton, Massachusetts. Her mother,

Anne Sexton (The Library of Congress)

Mary Gray Staples, was a failed writer, and her father, Ralph Harvey, was a salesman and textile manufacturer. They enjoyed an upper-middle-class lifestyle, but the family was dysfunctional. Sexton's father was an alcoholic, and some biographers have hinted that Sexton may have been sexually abused by one or both of her parents. Sexton was a poor student, though she did enjoy writing poetry and acting. She attended Garland Junior College from 1947 to 1948 but eloped at the age of nineteen with Alfred M. Sexton II. He was a salesman who also served as a soldier in the Korean War. Sexton was often unfaithful to her husband while he was away, but the couple did not divorce until 1974. They had two daughters, Linda and Joyce. Before the birth of her children, Sexton worked briefly as a fashion model.

Sexton struggled with depression through much of her life, and this was compounded by the death of her favorite aunt in 1954 and a severe bout of postpartum depression following the birth of her second child in 1955. After making several failed suicide attempts around this time, Sexton was briefly committed to a mental hospital. Her therapist urged her to begin writing in order to deal with her depression. By 1957, Sexton had joined numerous Boston-based writing groups, through which she met and was influenced by such leading confessional poets as Sylvia Plath, Robert Lowell, and Maxine Kumin. Her first collection, *To Bedlam and Part Way Back*, was published to positive reviews in 1960. Both of Sexton's parents died in 1959, spurring another bout of depression and affairs. Alfred also became abusive toward his wife at this time, likely due to his own frustrations with her growing celebrity.

Sexton's next collection, *All My Pretty Ones*, was published in 1962. *Selected Poems* followed two years later. In 1966, she published *Live or Die*, the collection in which "Self in 1958" first appeared. The volume garnered Sexton a Pulitzer Prize in 1967. By then, Sexton was receiving invitations to speak at universities and had been honored with a Guggenheim fellowship, along with numerous other grants and small honors. Her next collection, *Love Poems*, published in 1969, forever secured Sexton's reputation as a leading confessional poet. The 1972 volume *Transformations*, however, presents a collection of prose poems that are markedly more feminist than confessional.

Despite her success, Sexton continued to struggle with depression, affairs, suicide attempts, and a growing dependence on alcohol. Her poems published during the early 1970s, *The Book of Folly* (1972) and *The Death Notebooks* (1974) became more religious and personal but were not as popular as her previous works. During the early 1970s, she was also a lecturer and later a professor in creative writing at Boston University. She was also named Crawshaw Professor of Literature at Colgate University in 1972. Sexton initiated divorce proceedings in 1973, and her personal struggles continued to worsen. On October 4, 1974, Sexton committed suicide, suffocating herself with carbon monoxide in the garage of her home in Boston. That year, she had written the collection *The Awful Rowing toward God*, which was published posthumously in 1975. *45 Mercy Street* followed in 1976, and *Words for Dr. Y: Uncollected Poems with Three Stories* was released in 1978. Her poetic output culminated in *The Complete Poems*, which was published in 1981.

Although Sexton was predominantly a poet, she did write in other genres as well. She teamed with friend and fellow poet Maxine Kumin to author the children's books *Eggs of Things* and *More Eggs of Things*, released in 1963 and 1964, respectively. Her 1969 play, *Mercy Street*, was also well received. Her essays and other prose can be found in the 1985 *No Evil Star: Selected Essays, Interviews, and Prose*.

POEM SUMMARY

Stanza 1

Comprising ten lines (as do all of the stanzas in the poem), the first stanza of "Self in 1958" opens with a question as to the nature of reality. The speaker then goes on to indicate that she is a doll made out of plaster. Her eyes are set into holes in the plaster and they see nothing, neither the world around her nor the light as it changes. She is glazed and has a smile painted on. Her eyes are blue, like metal, and have lids attached, causing them to appear as if they close and open. Here, the speaker again sets forth a question. She wonders whether she has been bought from a (now defunct) high-end department store called I. Magnin. Because of the way that name is written, however, with a period, it at first appears that the speaker is wondering at the nature of identity and struggling with how to define it.

She has black hair that is fine, like an angel's. It adorns her like padding and exists only to be combed. Her legs are made of nylon, her arms are shiny and radiant. The speaker is dressed in store-bought clothes, clothes that have been marketed to entice the consumer (perhaps the doll's owner) to purchase them. This latter detail about the marketability of the doll's clothes may be seen as social commentary regarding the nature of consumer culture.

Stanza 2

The doll resides, as one might expect, in a dollhouse. Whereas stanza 1 lists the doll's attributes, the stanza 2 lists those of the house. It contains four chairs and a fake table. The roof is level. The door to the house is enormous, and although the speaker says that the door is large, she says that numerous people have arrived at a place like this, one she describes as tiny and constricting. The bed in the house is made of iron. Next, in parentheses, the speaker states that life expands and that it sets its sights. On what, exactly, life sets its sights is not explained or even hinted at. The floor in the house is made out of cardboard. The windows open and they face a city that belongs to someone else (again, who that someone else might be is not explained). In both instances, this lack of

explanation emphasizes the speaker's dispossession and lack of control—her powerlessness, so to speak. The windows reveal the city and little else.

Stanza 3

Another mysterious someone moves the speaker, the doll, about. This someone could be God or society or any other invisible motivational force that comes from without rather than within. This someone places the speaker squarely in her modern dollhouse kitchen. The speaker then wonders whether the phrase about the modernity of her kitchen was coined by Mrs. Rombauer. This is an allusion to Irma S. Rombauer, author of the famed cookbook *The Joy of Cooking*, which was first published in 1931 and remained in print as of 2010. The book was once a household staple. The mysterious someone plays with the doll as a child would, making noises and playing out imaginary scenarios. The speaker is trapped by the noise they make as they play with her.

Someone places the doll upon a level bed. Here, because the speaker ascribes the bed to someone outside herself, it is unclear whether this is the iron bed referred to earlier or some other bed. Either way, the speaker's disassociation from the bed, from all of her surroundings, is remarkable. This intense disassociation can be seen in the statement that immediately follows: The speaker notes that the someone who plays with her thinks that she is herself. She questions this someone's body heat or perhaps their loving feelings and finds that they are not friendly or welcome. She says the person forces open her mouth to make her drink gin or eat old bread. The way this observation is written, though, one could instead read it to mean that the someone attempts to drink and eat from the doll's mouth. Even the gin and the bread belong to someone outside of the doll.

Stanza 4

Stanza 4 begins as stanza 1 did, with the speaker wondering about reality and its definition. She comments that she is a manufactured doll, one who should be cheerful and keep the house in order, opening it and filling it with a wholesomeness that is nonetheless dysfunctional. In doing so, she should hide all hints of her decay and unhappiness. She wonders what reality could be to one who must live in such a manner. The speaker would rather weep and remain connected to her mother, who was a wall at some point. This seemingly nonsensical statement refers to the doll's assertion that she is made of plaster. She would rather remain a part of the plaster wall from which she was presumably formed. The speaker would do all of this if she could recall how to do so. She would also do this if she had any tears to cry.

THEMES

Imprisonment

The theme of imprisonment can be seen throughout "Self in 1958." It is first apparent in the speaker's description of herself as a doll made of plaster. She does not move of her own free will, but can only be posed. Her grin is immovable, painted on, and she is unable to cry or speak or change expression. She is a store-bought product who cannot even comb her hair. It exists to be combed, but not by her. The speaker is literally imprisoned in her doll body. Her house is also a prison. It contains the requisite qualities of a house (a table, chairs, a roof, a bed, a door), but none of the qualities of a home. The house, no matter its size, is described as a small and crushingly limited place. The windows look out onto an alien city that the speaker is unable to identify with.

The speaker is also a prisoner of the whims of the someone else who moves her and plays with her, plopping her down in the modern kitchen, crushing her with the noises they make as they do so. The doll has no freedom; she is placed in a bed and accosted by affection. When the speaker states that the someone thinks that she is herself, she speaks of another form of imprisonment, that of perception. The speaker is slave to the other's impressions of her. The speaker cannot even feed herself and is force-fed bread and gin. In the last stanza of the poem, the speaker once more emphasizes her emotional imprisonment. She is expected to smile, and a smile is painted onto her; she may not show her sadness, and is unable to. She wants to cry but cannot. She wishes to return to the plaster wall from which she was made, but she cannot. The speaker is powerless in all ways, lacking freedom of movement, freedom of surroundings, and freedom of feeling.

Isolation

One of the lesser themes in the poem is that of isolation. The only other person present in the poem aside from the speaker is a nameless someone wholly divorced from the speaker; that is, the speaker has no connection to the nearly invisible force that moves her and force-feeds her and assaults her with warmth. Certainly, "Self in 1958" is a lonely poem. The speaker is also isolated from her body; she speaks of it as if it is a foreign object— and it is. The speaker is a stranger not only in her own body but also in her house. It is filled with objects that have no emotional connection to the speaker. They are described in only the most utilitarian of terms, specifically regarding the materials from which they are made. When the bed is mentioned a second time, it is described as literally belonging to someone else. Even the city that the dollhouse windows reveal is unfamiliar to the doll. The speaker is as isolated from herself and her surroundings as she is imprisoned by them.

Suburban Life

Though the poem's critique of suburban life is not immediately apparent, several reviewers have noted that "Self in 1958" is a scathing criticism of suburban life and the role of the homemaker. Given this interpretation, the doll is the perfect embodiment of the 1960s housewife. She is always smiling, adorned with the latest style of clothing. Certainly, the description of a perfect, beautiful woman as a doll is not alien to the modern reader. Suburbs are sometimes termed "bedroom communities"—where city workers live and sleep—and are made up mainly of private residences, like the house in the poem. The speaker's world is wholly limited to the house in which she lives. The materialism of suburban life is also evident in the description of the house; it is merely the sum of its parts, a list of furnishings and the materials from which they are made. The house is the doll's entire world, and despite the large front door, it is a small, constricted place, a place in which, as the speaker points out, several have found

TOPICS FOR FURTHER STUDY

- Use the Internet to research other poets in the confessional movement. Choose three and create a Web log (blog) on their lives and work that includes visual representations and excerpts of poems. Be sure to cite your sources. Invite your classmates to comment on your blog entries.

- One contemporary of Sexton's was Sylvia Plath, a confessional poet who also took her own life. Read Plath's poetry and compare it with Sexton's in an essay. How is her work similar or different from Sexton's? Can you draw any direct comparisons between their work or their lives? Report your findings in an essay.

- Because "Self in 1958" and much of Sexton's later work was predominantly feminist in tone, research the feminist movement during the 1960s. Pick one prominent feminist leader from that time and present a brief PowerPoint report on the life and work of your chosen subject.

- Read *Impulse*, Ellen Hopkins's verse novel for young adults. The book portrays three teens who have been hospitalized in the same psychiatric facility after attempting suicide and their roads to recovery as they explain why they felt compelled to end their lives. As the patients meet and come to support one another, the verse novel takes on a more prose-like form. In a book group, discuss how the book's unique form affected the story and your reaction to it.

- Research suicide statistics from the 1970s and those from the 2000s. Be sure to look at how statistics break down demographically between different sexes and races. Try looking at studies from the U.S. Census Bureau or contacting your local librarian for additional resources. Create a chart that illustrates your findings.

- Create an artistic piece, using any medium you choose, in which you depict the doll and dollhouse described in Sexton's poem.

themselves. The narrowness of suburban life can also be seen when the speaker states that the city outside of her windows is foreign to her.

The modern kitchen with its up-to-date electric appliances is also a clear reference to suburban life (both in the 1960s and today). The speaker's allusion to the author of *The Joy of Cooking* accomplishes this effect as well. This famous cookbook was once a household staple. If one reads "Self in 1958" as a homemaker's lament, the someone who plays with her can be either the speaker's husband or her children (or both). The speaker is trapped by the noise the make, by their imprisoning her in the house and, particularly, in the kitchen. She is trapped by their love and their demands. As the matriarch, she is expected to embody the sunnier aspects of femininity and therefore is unable to cry. She is expected to cheerfully take on the role of a perfect caretaker, to puts others before herself despite any possible harm to herself.

Conformity

In many ways, suburban life embodies conformity. Suburbs are often made up of nearly identical houses on neatly laid out blocks, each filled with nearly identical furnishings and a modern kitchen. Perhaps, each is filled with its doll (that is, the homemaker). This reading (understanding or interpretation) of the poem also implies that the speaker's description of being force-fed is more accurately read as her being forced to nourish the children and husband in her care. The modern kitchen and the allusion to the standard cookbook are also evidence of conformity. Certainly "Self in 1958" portrays conformity as a prison, an unhappy one that does not even allow its prisoners to express their own unhappiness. The doll's appearance and house, her entire life, are the embodiment of conformity. Thus, both she and her surroundings are reduced to little more than objects.

The narrator of the poem mentions an "all-electric kitchen." (*Image copyright Jo Chambers, 2010. Used under license from Shutterstock.com*)

STYLE

Rhyme

"Self in 1958" is written in free verse, which means that it has no discernible pattern of rhythm or rhyme. However, that does not mean that it lacks rhythm or rhyme. In the first stanza, lines 2, 5, and 10 rhyme. Line 8 is a slant rhyme related to these lines as well. A slant rhyme occurs when a word does not rhyme exactly with its pair (or pairs), but contains a similar sound. In this case, that sound is a long *o*. Another slant rhyme also occurs in this stanza, between lines 3 and 7. In the second stanza, lines 14, 18, and 20 rhyme. In the third stanza, rhymes are found in lines 23, 26, and 30. Slant rhymes appear in lines 22 and 29. In the poem's final verse, rhymes appear in lines 33, 35, and 40. An additional slant rhyme is evident in this stanza

as well, occurring in lines 34 and 38. Notably, all of the last lines in each stanza end with an exact rhyme. This pattern reinforces the poem's sense of insularity, or narrow focus.

Repetition

Another stylistic effect in "Self in 1958" that reinforces the poem's sense of isolation and insularity is the use of repetition. The third and fourth stanzas of the poem contain the most straightforward examples of repetition. In the third stanza, lines 21, 24, and 27 end with the word *me*. This is an interesting repetition: It seems that the speaker is vainly attempting to assert her identity and individuality in the stanza in which it is most compromised. This is the stanza in which the doll is plopped into the kitchen and onto the bed, assaulted by the love of those around her, and force-fed.

In the second and third stanzas, the dollhouse bed is mentioned. In this case, the repetition changes the bed's meaning. It is first mentioned as being made of iron (like the bars of a prison). In its second mention, it is an object upon which she is placed, an object that belongs to someone else. Repetition also underscores the importance of various statements, signs, or symbols. This is the case when the speaker questions reality in the poem's first line and again in the first line of the final stanza. Although they are not technically a repetition, the rhymes ending lines 5 and 10 are homonyms, words that sound exactly the same but have different meanings.

HISTORICAL CONTEXT

Confessional Poetry

Sexton's poetry was written at the height of the confessional movement. It features the personal and autobiographical elements characteristic of the confessional style. Maxine Kumin, another confessional poet was perhaps Sexton's greatest influence, and also a personal friend and occasional coauthor. Other important confessional writers who influenced Sexton were Robert Lowell and Sylvia Plath. The timeline of Sexton's writing career also mirrored that of the rise and fall of the confessional movement. She began writing in the 1950s, when the style was first developing, and began publishing in the 1960s, when the style was at its peak. Sexton's career reached its own peak in the

COMPARE
&
CONTRAST

- **1960s:** Suburbs in the United States begin to form after the end of World War II, and by the 1960s they are a popular place of residence for middle-class nuclear families.

   Today: Although suburbs are still exceedingly common, some reverse migration to cities has occurred. This is due in part to the increasing cost of fuel, as suburbanites rely upon cars and other motor vehicles to travel to and from the city. It is also a result of the aging of the baby boom generation, whose children are grown and who now long for more social stimulation.

- **1960s:** In 1960, about 37.7 percent of women participate in the labor force. By 1965, 39.2 percent did so. The vast remainder are homemakers.

   Today: As of 2007, 82.2 percent of women participate in the labor force.

- **1960s:** Second-wave feminism, focusing on equal rights in society, is in full swing as women fight to be allowed into the workplace and for wage parity (that is, being paid equally to men). They also advocate for sexual equality.

   Today: Since third-wave feminism came to the fore in the 1990s, it is sometimes said that the movement has not had a definable character. Critics feel that the movement has historically focused on middle-class Caucasian women and point out that nonwhite women or women in lower income brackets have been overlooked.

1960s, as can be seen in her Pulitzer Prize-winning collection, *Live or Die*, which was published in 1966.

Confessional poetry evolved from the modernist style popular during the early twentieth century. The modernists challenged the rigid verse forms that once dominated and defined poetry. Modernism was also one of the first movements to highlight and defend the individual person. Confessional poetry merely extended and deepened both trends. In addition to the focus on personal topics, confessional poetry was marked by an awareness of Freudian and Jungian psychology, and it used signs and symbols to represent deeper emotional truths. The doll and dollhouse in "Self in 1958" present an example of this technique. Still, many readers make the mistake of referring to the poem's speaker as the poet himself or herself. This is misleading and often simply an error, as confessional poetry is not solely defined by personal confession. It is more accurate to say that the movement tried to create a poetic self, or persona, one that is spoken of as "I."

Furthermore, although modernism was founded in Europe, the confessional movement was founded in the United States, and it is a major milestone in the history of distinctly American verse forms. Modernism was also a more universal movement; its influence can be seen in architecture, the visual and performing arts, philosophy, and psychology. The confessional movement is mostly limited to writing, especially poetry. Although confessional poetry began to fall out of favor in the late 1970s, its influence can still be found in modern poetry, particularly in the use of free verse and the creations of the poetic self.

1950s Culture and the American Suburb

Following the end of World War II, the American landscape underwent a cultural and social change dominated by the growing popularity of suburbs. American society was once largely urban or rural. Urban residences were typically apartments where multiple families lived close together. Rural communities were typically defined by houses set miles apart and surrounded by vast quantities of land. In both cases, it was not uncommon for multiple generations of the same family to live in the same household. The suburb, however, featured single-

The poem references Irma Rombauer, coauthor of the popular 1950s cookbook The Joy of Cooking, *seen here (right) with her daughter and coauthor Marion.* (© Bettman / Corbis)

family homes that were built close to one another and were entirely self-sufficient. The establishment of the suburb historically occurred due to a surge in population and the increasing reliability of motorized transportation (cars and trains). This new style of community also represented a cultural backlash of sorts. During World War II, women had taken on many jobs that had previously been held by men, and they enjoyed more freedom than they had before. After the war, though, women were once again relegated to the home. America during the 1950s and early 1960s upheld the values of home and family. The culture was saturated with images of the nuclear family: a single-family house in the suburbs, a car, a dog, a green lawn, and a white picket fence, all inhabited by a cheerful homemaker, her gainfully employed husband, and their children. This ideal became the new American dream, one perhaps best illustrated in the television show *Leave it Beaver* (1957-1963).

However, this happy ideal was not without its downsides. The ideal itself was dictated by a strict conformity. Women's identities and purposes were defined largely by their marital status. They had little opportunity for a life outside the household. If women did work outside of the home, they earned significantly less than their male equivalents. This lifestyle and its limitations are largely what Sexton rails against in "Self in 1958." She was not alone in her dissatisfaction. By the late 1960s, the feminist movement was again in full swing as it advocated for women's equality in society and the workplace. This dissatisfaction was not limited to feminism alone. The 1950s culture of repression and conformity was being challenged in all levels of society. For example, student movements questioned government authority, and the civil rights movement fought against segregation.

CRITICAL OVERVIEW

Critical reaction to "Self in 1958" has been mostly positive, with critics comparing it to the work of such famed poets as Edna St. Vincent Millay and Sylvia Plath. *Live or Die*, the collection in which the poem first appeared, has also been hailed as Sexton's best work. According to Diana Hume George in *Oedipus Anne: The Poetry of Anne Sexton*, "Sexton comes to happy resolutions repeatedly in her work, from poem to poem, volume to volume. *Live or Die* is structured in just such a pleasing, simple shape: after a struggle with destruction, it ends with the affirmation of life." Certainly, it would seem that "Self in 1958" tends more toward the destructive side of the collection than the affirmative. Another comment about the collection that applies to "Self in 1958" is offered by Gail Pool in the *New Boston Review*. She states that "many of the successful poems in *Live or Die*...depend upon the creation of concrete scenes." Arguably, the vast majority of "Self in 1958" is devoted to describing the doll and her house. Robert Phillips, discussing the poem in *The Confessional Poets*, writes that "'Self in 1958' is a strong portrayal of deadened sensibilities." Philips also observes that *Live or Die* "continues the poet's search for reconciliations, her obsession with the limits of the body and its failures to be equal to the demands of the spirit."

CRITICISM

Leah Tieger

Tieger is a freelance writer and editor. In the following essay on "Self in 1958," she presents a brief discussion of the poem's form as well as an overview of various critical interpretations and readings of it.

Anne Sexton's "Self in 1958" is a descriptive poem. It describes the speaker as a doll and details that doll's appearance. It describes the doll's house and her living situation within it. It describes how the doll is manipulated in those surroundings and the speaker's emotional and mental state therein. The poem portrays a small, miniaturized world, and it conveys a sense of insularity and circularity through its rhyme scheme and repetition. For instance, the question of reality is posed at the beginning of the first stanza, and again at the beginning of the last stanza. The word *me*, appearing three times in the third stanza, is also telling. The speaker tries desperately to insert herself into the verse in which she is most obliterated. This is the stanza, after all, in which the doll is force-fed and placed in the kitchen and on the bed. It is the stanza in which she has the least control, the least individuality. The final stanza addresses the speaker's frustrated desire to cry: the doll can only speak to her emotional state and reiterate it in a futile attempt to truly feel it. Although the poem's rhyme scheme is predominantly erratic and changing, each stanza nevertheless ends with an exact rhyme. This tactic lends a self-reflexive sense not only to the poem as a whole but to each stanza individually.

However, as introspective as "Self in 1958" may at first appear, the poem is in fact very much a part of the cultural and literary *zeitgeist*—that is, the climate of its moment. The moment, in this case, is both the height of the confessional poetry movement and the growing backlash against the suburb and (most importantly) against the restrictive roles women were required to play in it. In *Health and the Modern Home*, Jo Gill remarks on the poem's dual role as both a cultural critique and its position as a representative work of confessional verse. Gill writes that it can be interpreted "as figuring both the modern woman and the confessional poet—relentlessly cutting herself open, displaying her inner demons for the edification of some anonymous audience." "Self in 1958," then, is deceptive in its seemingly apparent circularity. Even its title contributes to this deception. In fact, as Gill points out, the poem was originally titled "The Lady Lives in a Doll House" (though it was never published under this heading).

In discussing the poem, Gill also quotes Sexton's lecture notes, which further reveal "Self in 1958," to be a cultural critique. Sexton says of the poem: "We have me stopped as the perfect housewife, as the advertised woman in the perfect little ticky tacky suburb." The poem's second verse perhaps exemplifies this best, as it describes the little dollhouse and the alien city outside its windows, it is the third verse, with its modern kitchen and *Joy of Cooking* allusion, that truly capture the claustrophobia of the American housewife. Gill observes that in the poem, "Sexton's speaker/doll demurs from...[her role] and questions the ideal. She is placed in the kitchen against her own volition and uncertain how to perform once she is there, hence the repeated questions, exclamations, and parenthetical dashes."

Another reading of the poem offered by Gill is that of womanhood as a medical condition, and a threatening one at that: "Femininity in this poem

WHAT DO I READ NEXT?

- Some critics have pointed out that the lyrical poet Edna St. Vincent Millay (who wrote predominantly during the 1920s and 1930s) had a profound influence on Sexton's verse. Artemis Michailidou, writing in the *Feminist Review*, finds that in particular, "Self in 1958" can be compared to Millay's poem "The Plaid Dress." Decide for yourself by reading the poem in Millay's 1939 collection *Huntsman, What Quarry?*

- Sylvia Plath, Sexton's contemporary and one of the best-known confessional poets, wrote *The Bell Jar* under the pseudonym Victoria Lucas in 1963. The book was republished under her actual name two years later. The novel portrays a young woman's struggles with depression and suicidal tendencies. Though not on the surface a book intended for young-adult readers, the *The Bell Jar* has remained popular among teens for several decades.

- For more insight into suburbs and their history, read *The New Suburban History*, edited by Kevin M. Kruse and Thomas J. Sugrue. The book, part of the "Historical Studies of Urban America" series, was published in 2006. The volume presents ten essays that challenge stereotypical views of American suburbia. The essays also explore changing American politics, culture, and values through the development and changing nature of the suburbs.

- Whereas becoming a homemaker was once a given for married women (an assumption that Sexton laments in "Self in 1958"), it has since become a lifestyle choice. A contemporary debate regarding this choice can be found in Leslie Morgan Steiner's 2007 volume *Mommy Wars: Stay-at-Home and Career Moms Face Off on Their Choices, Their Lives, Their Families.*

- *Feminism: The Essential Historical Writings*, edited by Miriam Schneir, was published in 1994. The volume is an anthology of noteworthy feminist essays, literature, and criticism. The selections date back to the American Revolution and continue into the early twentieth century. These landmark writings will present readers with a more detailed and thorough knowledge of the ideals underlying Sexton's more feminist themes.

- A whimsical informative look at the history of dolls and dollhouses is *Dollhouse & Miniature Dolls, 1840-1990*, by Marcie Tubbs, Bob Tubbs, and Dian Zillner. Published in 2009, this guide contains more than five hundred color photographs and presents more than fifteen hundred dolls made from various materials, as well as their accompanying period houses. The book also takes an international approach, covering doll manufacturers worldwide.

- A close friend and peer of Sexton's, Maxine Kumin was not only an accomplished confessional poet but also an occasional coauthor with Sexton. An overview of her work can be found in *Selected Poems: 1960-1990* (1998).

- In *The Sixties: Years of Hope, Days of Rage* (1993), Todd Gitlin presents a chronicle of the vast political and cultural changes that took place over the decade (many of which are reflected in the anxiety apparent in Sexton's poem). In the book, Gitlin includes both personal recollections and academic information.

- Pat Mora's *My Own True Name: New and Selected Poems for Young Adults* was published in 2000. The collection is somewhat confessional, as it traces the author's questioning of her Mexican American heritage culture as it relates to her identity. Young readers of similar heritage will find the collection to be a fascinating read, and the book's more universal themes, such as that of motherhood, will also appeal to a more varied audience.

- For a look at Sexton's prose, read *No Evil Star: Selected Essays, Interviews, and Prose*. Posthumously published in 1985, the collection will give students of Sexton a greater understanding of her life and views on literature and society.

is medicalised or pathologised . . . and it is dangerous." Here, the speaker's description of herself as a
doll made out of plaster takes on a dual meaning,
as plaster is also used as a medical tool. In this
view, the female body, given its biological functions, is quite literally uncontrollable. In compen-
sation, the female role of homemaker is made
entirely rigid, utterly controlled. The dollhouse is
a mass-produced product, as is the doll herself. The
doll's body in the first verse is made of plaster. In
the fourth verse, it is described only as a manufactured material. Discussing this detail in the *Feminist Review*, Artemis Michailidou remarks of the
speaker that "the only versions of herself she is
familiar with are artificial, and there is no actual
difference in the move from the plaster to the
synthetic." She adds that "both versions suggest
the ease with which the speaker's identity is forged
and molded by the requirements of those" around
her. Furthermore, "both descriptions imply that
the speaker is no longer able to make" her own
identity "part of the equation."

In *Anne Sexton: Telling the Tale*, Gary Blankenburg comments on the poet's work as a general
critique of the American lifestyle. He observes that
although "her writing resists overt political commentary, she is very much aware of the unique
character of our century, of the leveling of standards and the rampant destruction of individual
identity at the roots of mass society." He then goes
on to note that "this awareness is reflected in 'Self in
1958.'" This "destruction of individual identity" can
also be seen in terms of the public and the private,
and the ceaseless blurring of the boundaries
between the two. Tensions between the public and
the private abound in the poem, particularly
through Sexton's mention of the dollhouse windows. The windows look out onto a city, providing
the doll's only view, and the city belongs to someone else. It is hers to see, but not hers to participate
in. In the poem's final stanza, the requirement that
the doll should open the doors of her house without
betraying the turmoil within her heart also portrays
a strange blurring of the public and the private.

This latter reading of the poem is best
explained by Deborah Nelson in *Pursuing Privacy
in Cold War America*. She claims that for "Sexton,
like most women of her generation, the home was
not a private place at all. However, because it
offered little opportunity for adult communication,
for public or political discussion, it was not really
public in any significant way just as it was not
private in any meaningful way." Nelson also finds

that "Self in 1958" exemplifies "this paradox of
mass-produced privacy." In fact, Nelson takes her
interpretation one step further, bringing us back to
the notion that "Self in 1958" is a poem of its
moment in both theme (feminism/social critique)
and style (confessional). She declares that the "cor-
relation between the physical architecture of the
house—its absence of personal privacy—and the
psychic structure of women—their loss of personal
identity—governs confessional poetry as well." Nelson then explains that "the loss of personal identity,
which derived from a loss of privacy, gave birth to
an autobiographical mode of writing that appeared
to construct the personality of the poet obsessively
while eschewing [discarding] any notion of privacy." Given this reading, one can conflate (combine) both the doll and the poet (Sexton herself), as
both are forced to create a manufactured "I." The
former does so as homemaker and the latter as
poem maker.

Source: Leah Tieger, Critical Essay on "Self in 1958," in
Poetry for Students, Gale, Cengage Learning, 2011.

Cheryl Vossekuil

*In the following essay, Vossekuil considers the poems
of* Live or Die *and concludes that Sexton chooses life
in the volume that includes "Self in 1958."*

Contrary to critical perceptions of Anne Sexton as a death poet, her first three collections—*To
Bedlam and Part Way Back* (1960), *All My Pretty
Ones* (1962), and *Live or Die* (1966)—show her to
be life-affirming, struggling with the temptation of
death, but choosing life—at least for a time. All
three collections are written in the voice of a single
personate—a female who is wife and mother as
well as poet, and who questions much in her life,
immediately disclosing her dissatisfaction with her
current life, a half-life of stasis and inactivity. She
sees her life as a prison, and herself as a being for
whom fulfillment and growth are an ever-receding
dream. Despite the elusiveness of this dream, however, through the first three books, she persistently
searches for a life conducive to growth. For Sexton, however, growth is a process that inevitably
leads to and is present in death as well as in life,
and so the poet must choose between the two.
Either involved life or death offers escape from
the static condition she sees as poisoned, and
after careful consideration, by the end of *Live or
Die*, Sexton's choice is to live.

Throughout the first three collections, Sexton
argues that she must escape from her current life.
In "Cripples and Other Stories" she reveals her

The poem references a doll's house and table with four chairs. (Image copyright Douglas Freer, 2010. Used under license from Shutterstock.com)

feelings of ugliness and her repulsion at her life, as well as her inability to disguise those feelings: "My cheeks blossomed with maggots. / I picked at them like pearls. / I covered them with pancake. / I wound my hair in curls." The perception of decay just under the surface, barely hidden from view, is indicative of the persona's entrapment between life and death; like a snake shedding its skin, she must "strip away a dead self"—her poisoned self. A quotation from Saul Bellow serves as an epigraph to *Live or Die*: "Live or die, but don't prison everything...." As Sexton explains, "Saul Bellow had given me a message about my whole life. That I didn't want to poison the world, that I didn't want to be the killer; I wanted to be the one who gave birth, who encouraged things to grow and to flower, not the poisoner." Sexton's determination not to poison becomes the resolve to escape the "menacing flat accent of life-in-death."

The stasis that Sexton loathes is well-illustrated in poems such as "The Farmer's Wife" (*Bedlam* 19). The persona has little life of her own—and that life is a passive one; she is described as "her husband's habit, as he urges her toward sex, saying, "honey bunch let's go." "Honey bunch," a pet name as easily used for a child as for a lover, intimates that he treats her as less than an equal: one cannot grow in such a relationship. Additionally, Sexton's use of "habit" here is studied. Nunlike, the farmer's wife wears her role like a habit; she is almost asexual, for though she participates physically in the love act with her husband, she is mentally chaste. The only knowledge one has of this woman is in her responses to and relationships with others, as the title suggests; she is trapped in her life as a reflected image. There is a sense, however, that animosity is building and that the passive wife might act "as her young years bungle past." The persona recognizes her life of stasis, represented by the sexual act without fruition, so that a potentially life-giving act becomes a life-denying act: after all, it is simply a habit. She wishes her husband "cripple" or "dead" to complete the life-denying concept; he is already dead emotionally.

> MOVEMENT, GROWTH, AND FREEDOM ARE THE OPPOSITE OF A STATIC, POISONED LIFE; THE MANY IMAGES THAT DETAIL MOVEMENT FORESHADOW AND REINFORCE SEXTON'S STRONG ATTRACTION TO LIFE."

Or she wishes him "poet"; poetry for Sexton is a life-affirming act. In an interview with Barbara Kevles, Sexton observed that "Suicide is, after all, the opposite of the poem."

Sexton regularly explores the theme of poetry as life. The inability to act or to grasp the fullness of life is described in "For the Year of the Insane" (*Live*): "My body is useless. / It lies, curled like a dog on the carpet. / It has given up." Here, the nonmovement of the body indicates the lethargy of the entire person, who exists only on a basic physiological level. As automatic as breathing, even the words used within this state of torpor are routine, rote: "the 'Hail Mary' and the 'full of grace.'" Too late, the speaker realizes that she has entered "the year without words." A poet unable to use her words is essentially dead, but if she is still living physiologically, there is a conflict, because she is dead creatively: this is an intolerable situation. Sexton aligns herself, in this state of living-nonliving, with "people who stand at the open window like objects waiting to topple" ("The House," *Pretty*). Standing is, figuratively, inactivity, and the coupling of standing with waiting alludes to an eventual crisis. The poet often describes such arrested movement, as in "The Operation" (*Pretty*): "I wait like a kennel of dogs / jumping against their fence." These lines elicit the restlessness (and possibly the kindling aggression) of the trapped animal and the understanding of motion without gain, as well as a mounting sense of tension.

Concurrent realities of life as death are clear in "The Double Image" (*Bedlam*), in which the persona is split into two personalities she cannot unite—one of substance, the other a mirrored reflection. Since the mirrored image is a reflected one, and is consequently dependent upon the other for its existence, it only partially represents reality. This notion is reminiscent of Socrates' "Parable of the Cave," in which he discusses

reflections cast on the cave wall by a fire, concluding that to the observers of these reflections, "the [apparent] truth would be nothing but the shadows of the images." One sees a "shadow" in the mirror, not one's true self. She who is reflected exists independently of her mirror-image, and not vice-versa. Therefore, the mirror imperfectly portrays life because it captures only a part of reality. The persona is stymied between the two images— reality and doppelganger—as between life and death: "And this was the cave of the mirror, / that double woman who stares / at herself, as if she were petrified / in time."

... This vision of preserved, if petrified, life— life that Sexton struggles to escape—occurs throughout her poetry. Because much of the landscape within the poems is the landscape of institutions, one notes there the duality of life and death: the lack of freedom in institutions limits the inmates' lives to half-lives. Sexton refers to the mental institution as a "hierarchy of death" ("Flee on Your Donkey," *Live*) and to the inmates as the "moving dead" ("You, Doctor Martin,"*Bedlam*). Having surrendered their identities, the broken people are counted at the "frozen gates of dinner," one by one, like sheep. Frozen in their incarceration, the inmates cannot grow.

In addition to the prison that is external, Sexton reveals the internal prison of her own mind and body in "Wanting to Die" (*Live*); "[death] waits for me, year after year, / to so delicately undo an old wound, / to empty my breath from its bad prison." One of the ways in which the persona escapes this self-described imprisonment is through medication, drugs. The imagery of pills and needles represents both release and avoidance in Sexton's poetry. While the drugs provide comfort, in the form of calm or sleep, they also numb, so that a sleeping pill becomes "a splendid pearl [which] floats me out of myself" ("Lullaby" [*Bedlam*]). The very title "Lullaby" connotes something soothing, and the juxtaposition of sleeping pill and lullaby conjures an elemental sense of comfort—the mother who rocks her child to sleep. And indeed, "the pills are a mother, but better" ("The Addict,"- *Live*). Additionally, the proliferation of white images suggests a purity, a return to the state of loved daughter and a life of possibility, but the images also elicit the elusiveness of a dream: only in a dream is such singularity of color possible.

Despite her reliance on these medications, despite their capacity to keep her "on a diet from death," the persona realizes the danger inherent in her "addiction": "I like them more than I like me.../ It's a kind of marriage / It's a kind of war / where I plant bombs inside / of myself" ("The Addict,"*Live*). Furthermore, the poet's ambivalence toward the drugs is evident as she praises them as "eight chemical kisses," yet admits she is slowly killing herself. In numbing her, the pills are also a kind of poison: they prevent her from fully experiencing life.

Because the poet knows that she cannot continue much longer on her present course before the "bombs" she has planted explode, she recognizes the need to change. Or, to follow the plentiful Christian symbolism, an escape from sin— salvation—is warranted. "With Mercy for the Greedy" (*Pretty*) declares "I was born / doing reference work in sin, and born / confessing it."

Another Christian image Sexton uses is the garden. The poet wills a return to the garden, that is, innocence, so that things would only grow, not die, for the concept of death began with the first sin: the death of innocence. In "Little Girl, My String, Bean, My Lovely Woman" (*Live*), Sexton maintains that her prepubescent daughter, "at eleven / (almost twelve), is like a garden." In her gardenlike state Sexton's daughter remains untainted, yet a change—represented here as "high noon"—is imminent. At high noon the persona's daughter is nearly at the zenith of her life, both as adult and as woman who has the possibility of new life within her; she is the very embodiment of growth: "The summer has seized you, / I think even of the orchard next door, / where the berries are done / and the apples are beginning to swell." Despite the fruition, however, growth will continue: she has only begun to ripen. The poet also seems to be in awe of having given life to this child, finding hope and affirmation in the thought:

> If I could have watched you grow
> as a magical mother might,
> if I could have seen through my
> magical transparent belly,
> there would have been such ripening within:
> your embryo,...
> a world of its own....

Because growth in the form of continuance comes through children, the persona feels reborn as she watches her children grow. As her daughters live, so too will she.

However, growth inevitably leads to, and is present in, death as well as life. The process of dying begins at the moment of conception, for "death too is in the egg" ("The Operation,"*Pretty*),

and death "was in the womb all along" ("Menstruation at Forty,"*Live*). Therefore, the processes of life and death are interchangeable. Juhasz describes Sexton's view of life as a continuum:

> One is born with one's death inside oneself, like an egg, or a baby. Through the process of living one transforms oneself into one's own death, through a process of hardening, stiffening, freezing. Each birth only hastens the process, so one grows from baby to child to daughter to mother: in the last act of birth, a mother gives birth to her own death, a death baby.... I give birth to my own death. I am my mother's baby; I am my mother's death; I am my mother; I am my baby; I am my death.

Growth that leads to death is present in another form as well: cancer. In several poems Sexton portrays this growth that leads not to fruition, but to death. She speaks of her mother in the poem "The Operation" (*Pretty*): "[Cancer] grew in her as simply as a child would grow, / as simply as she housed me once, fat and female.... [an] embryo of evil." Whereas here cancer is represented as a naturally growing malevolent thing—a "death baby," a twin to the poet—in a later poem written about John Holmes, her first writing instructor ("Somewhere in Africa,"*Live*), Sexton describes cancer with language and imagery that border on lushness in detailing growth: "cancer blossomed in your throat, / rooted like bougainvillea into your gray backbone,.../ The thick petals, the exotic reds, the purples and whites...." The cancer finally causes Holmes to blossom through death into a state of rebirth, of innocence, as he is welcomed by a female who is the very embodiment of fertility, of the earth mother, of Eve: "a woman naked to the waist / moist with palm oil and sweat, a woman of some virtue / and wild breasts, her limbs excellent, unbruised and chaste."

In addition to the growth of cancer that leads to death, growth comes out of death itself. After death the body continues to grow, in that the nails and hair seem to lengthen, and mold, decay, and the growth of bacteria set in. "The Moss of His Skin" (*Bedlam*), a dramatic monologue in the persona of a young girl entombed, by ancient custom, with her dead father, presents this process: "daddy was there, /...his hair growing / like a field or a shawl. / I lay by the moss / of his skin until / it grew strange...." "The father's body begins to decay, and so gestates anew in the womb-like interior of the tomb. Were the body in the ground, it would give life through its decomposition, returning nutrients to the soil.

While some growth through death—life that comes out of death—is physical in nature, the poet also implies repeatedly that the dead have a consciousness, and so continue to live after death, albeit in a diminished capacity. In "Letter Written During a January Northeaster" (*Pretty*), Sexton writes: "It is snowing, grotesquely snowing, / upon the small faces of the dead. . . . / The dead turn over casually, / thinking . . . / Good! No visitors today." As she argues the choice between life and death, Sexton makes a strong case for her belief in life and movement after death, perhaps revealing why the choice is a difficult one—both offer possibilities for growth.

In addition to showing growth through theme, the poet uses imagery to detail movement. Movement, growth, and freedom are the opposite of a static, poisoned life; the many images that detail movement foreshadow and reinforce Sexton's strong attraction to life. Representing escape and control—a seeming paradox—bird imagery is used often through these first three books. The persona admires the birds' ease of movement, appreciating their sense of freedom, strength, volition, and power: "I planned such plans of flight, . . . / I planned by growth and my womanhood / as one choreographs a dance" ("Those Times," *Live*). The poet remembers herself during childhood as she dreams of her adult life. Only during dreams, it happens, will innocence and control occur for her now, as in childhood she could fly only in dreams; even so, the poet must try to regain her sense of innocence, her zeal for life.

The movement that leads out of the stasis in the persona's life is represented in much other imagery as well. That movement is detailed through fish, for example, as they move through water, the life force, though there is also the understanding that water kills things by drowning. Other symbols of growth—trees, for example, which grow though standing still—and much plant and animal imagery are prominent and plentiful in the poetry. One of the most interesting sets of images is the bells that mark progression of time and life-passages as they are tolled at christenings, marriages, and deaths; yet Sexton also uses the bells to represent life that is in stasis—motion without gain: "And this is the way they ring / the bells at Bedlam . . . / and this is always my bell responding / to my hand that responds to the lady / who points at me, E flat . . ." ("Ringing the Bells," *Bedlam*). Here the persona functions perfunctorily as the extension of a bell, meekly submissive to the director of the bell choir.

The movement and growth that lead the persona out of stasis, then; must result in a choice of either life or death. As "Live," the final poem in the collection *Live or Die*, makes clear, Sexton's choice is against death. Just as prisoners leave their cells either by returning to the mainstream of life or by dying, so too the poet must make a choice that allows her to escape from the poisoned state. Robert Boyers observes, "Miss Sexton's propensities are similarly violent and suicidal [to Plath's], but she convinces herself, and her reader, that she has something to live for. We are grateful to Miss Sexton as we can be to few poets, for she has distinctly enlarged and enhanced the possibilities of endurance in that air of lost connections which so many of us inhabit." Appropriately, "Live" ends Sexton's first three books, emphasizing her positive choice:

> Today life opened inside me like an egg
> and there inside
> after considerable digging
> I found the answer. . . .
> I say 'Live, Live' because of the sun,
> the dream, the excitable gift.

Clearly affirming life, the poet discovers that the potential for growth (the sun as an "egg"), or for hope (daily possibility of renewal), is reason enough to keep living. It is possible to change. Boyers finds "Live" to be:

> a triumph of determination and insight, a final resolution of irreconcilabilities that had threatened to remain perpetually suspended and apart. Miss Sexton's affirmation represents a rebirth of astounding proportions, a veritable reconstruction of her self-image in the face of a corrupt and corrupting universe.

Sexton herself insists that she consciously chose to keep living; as she finished writing *Live or Die* she came to realize—when unable to kill a litter of puppies—that "I could let me live, too, that after all I wasn't a killer, that the poison just didn't take."

Sexton chooses to examine life fully, in all its contradictions and restrictions, and then to embrace it fully. It is all too easy to misinterpret her early, clear-sighted and yet unflinching examination of life as a decision against life. However, in the epigraph to *The Awful Rowing toward God* (1975), Sexton quotes Thoreau: "There are two ways to victory—to strive bravely, or to yield" (417). And, in these early poems Sexton undeniably chooses "to strive bravely," to embrace life. Her explicit hope for growth, her belief in life-cycles, will admit to no other choice. In contrast to those who maintain that Sexton is an unwavering death poet, her early poetry dearly shows that she chooses life, albeit after much struggling and soul-searching. Although she will prove to be only "part way back," she *did* embrace life for a time. As Boyers observes: "Miss Sexton's decision to live, with her eyes open, and the responsibilities for human values planted firmly on her competent shoulders, is a major statement of our poetry." Anne Sexton, for a while at least, proved herself without a doubt to be a life-affirming poet.

Source: Cheryl Vossekuil, "Embracing Life: Anne Sexton's Early Poems," in *Critical Essays on Anne Sexton*, edited by Linda Wagner-Martin, G.K. Hall, 1989, pp. 120–26.

Greg Johnson

In the following excerpt, Johnson argues that Sexton searches for her identity throughout her poetic work.

I

> When we must deal with problems, we instinctively resist trying the way that leads through obscurity and darkness. We wish to hear only of unequivocal results, and completely forget that these results can only be brought about when we have ventured into and emerged again from darkness....—*Carl Jung, The Stages of Life*

At the heart of Anne Sexton's poetry is a search for identity, and her well-known infatuation with death—the cause of her rather notorious fame, and the apparent reason her work is often dismissed as beneath serious considerations—has little to do with this search; in her best work, in fact, it is most often an annoying irrelevancy, however potent it seems in its occasional command of the poet's psyche. Quite simply, Sexton's poetry is a poetry of life, and if her work is "confessional" at times, or even most of the time, this does not mean that the poet's confessions (the word itself is misleading) necessarily describe experiences ridden with guilt or pain. This is where Sexton's poetry diverges so dramatically from that of Sylvia Plath, of whom she is frequently seen as a kind of epigonic follower. Plath mythologizes death with great power and succinctness, and places herself at the center of a myth whose message is "blackness—blackness and silence"; her vision is brutally nihilistic, and she embraces it willingly. Plath's struggle is that of the mythmaker—primarily artistic rather than personal, since the personal self is mercilessly pared away in her poetry (as are all other selves) in deference to the controlling myth. Anne Sexton, on the other hand, speaks longingly and lovingly of a world of health, of childlike wholeness—a world

> YET THERE ARE MANY ELEMENTS WHICH FORM A CONSTANT, HOPEFUL STRAND IN THE FABRIC OF SEXTON'S CONTINUED PAIN: HUMOR AND TENDERNESS, THE RECOGNITION OF MADNESS AS A WASTE OF TIME, A CAUSTIC, DISAPPROVING ATTITUDE TOWARD SUICIDE, AND A REMARKABLE DEVELOPMENT OF THE POET'S ARTISTIC POWERS."

toward which she struggles valiantly and against insuperable odds. To understand her poetry as a record of this struggle, and as a testament to its value and importance, is to appreciate its special relevance to the contemporary world, a world of increasing disjunction between personal and social selves and one whose chaotic, literally "maddening" effect on the individual mind Anne Sexton manages to convey with that blend of craft and vulnerability that is her special magic.

Unlike Plath, and certainly unlike Robert Lowell—with whom her name is also frequently and pointlessly linked—Sexton is a Primitive, an extraordinarily intense artist who confronts her experience with unsettling directness, largely innocent of "tradition" and privately developing an idiom exactly suited to that experience. As Louis Simpson remarked after the publication of her first book, "This then is a phenomenon ... to remind us, when we have forgotten in the weariness of literature, that poetry can happen." The reader's sense of the direct and seemingly spontaneous quality of Sexton's earliest volumes—*To Bedlam and Partway Back* (1960), *All My Pretty Ones* (1902) and *Live or Die* (1966)—can partially be explained by noting that she first began writing poetry, at the age of twenty-eight, as a form of personal therapy, a way of formalizing past traumas and of coping with an increasing sense of disorientation in her conventional role of suburban wife and mother. Her emotional instability, including her suicidal impulses, contributed to the immediacy, rawness and power of much of the poetry. This kind of therapy no doubt helped the poet in her personal life, but what is heroin in Sexton's case, and particularly relevant to her readers, is the earnestness and scrupulosity with which she mastered her craft, developed her highly original voice, and set about the task of communicating her experience to others. That Anne Sexton herself later succumbed to the "weariness of literature"—her later work, on the whole, is distinctly inferior to her early poetry, and verges at times on self-parody-and finally to her own destructive impulses, does not diminish the value and irresistible power of her finest achievements, which speak to us in a voice by turns inspired and beleaguered, joyful and aggrieved, lost in the confusions of self but found, ultimately, in her masterful articulation of her experience as a whole, a complex experience which serves as a painfully truthful mirror of the age.

IV

...With two accomplished volumes behind her, with a blossoming career and innumerable devoted readers, she summoned the courage to bluntly question the value of living—to decide whether, in fact, the pain of life does not outweigh its rewards. In "The Black Art" she insisted: "A woman who writes feels too much, / those trances and portents!" Her decision to explore fully those excessive feelings, to relate her mysterious "trances and portents" to her central concerns of identity, poetry and survival, helped her toward. *Live or Die* (1966), winner of a Pulitzer Prize and the finest achievement of her career. The volume's title represents an ultimatum; the poems themselves, arranged in chronological order and reading, as Sexton herself noted, like a "fever chart," show the poet moving toward a stark confrontation with her suicidal impulses and with her "portent" that life as a whole—not only for her, but perhaps for everyone—is simply not worthwhile. And yet, as one astute reviewer, Thomas P. McDonnell, noted at the time *Live or Die* was first published, Sexton gives us more than "impulses": "(this) is not a poetry of spasmodic revelation or of occasional incident transformed from similitude to artifact: in its continuing wholeness one perceives the suggestion of a journey." It was a journey, as *Live or Die* makes clear, upon whose outcome rested her life itself, and one she approaches with great courage and her developed artistic powers.

Carl Jung, discussing the obstacles to personal growth, notes that venturing into "obscurity and darkness" is absolutely essential in the quest for a new stage of development, a higher individuation of self. For Anne Sexton, there were two kinds of "darkness"—her madness, which represented personal defeat; and that agonizing uncertainty about

her life and her identity which could only be eased through poetry and whose resolution—even if temporary—could represent significant progress toward mental stability and a secure sense of self. In *Live or Die,* Sexton has greatly matured as woman and as poet: she does not glorify madness, setting herself apart from the rest of humanity, but rather perceives it as an ignoble escape and, most of all, as a colossal waste of time. The most fearsome "obscurity and darkness," Jung suggests, lies in a sane, ego-centered approach toward personal problems, not in a surrender to the chaotic promptings of the id. In her third volume Sexton recognizes this truth, and the recognition helps produce some of her finest poetry.

In her long, moving description of yet another confinement in a mental institution, "Flee on Your Donkey," the poet betrays little of her former fascination with madness; now the asylum is "the scene of the disordered senses," a place where she has wasted some of her best years:

> Six years of such small preoccupations!
> Six years of shuttling in and out of this place!
> O my hunger! My hunger!
> I could have gone around the world twice
> or had new children—all boys.
> It was a long trip with little days in it
> and no new places.

She now sees that her doctor represented a kind of crutch, someone who "promised me another world / to tell me who / I was." The poem concludes that madness is merely "the fool's disease," a way of "allowing myself the wasted life," and the poet finally exhorts herself: "Anne, Anne, / flee on your donkey, I flee this sad hotel ... "

Sexton, refusing the descent into madness, must now attempt to deal rationally with her nearly irresistible impulse toward suicide. Many poems *Live or Die* deal explicitly with this subject: "To Lose the Earth," "Wanting to Die," "Suicide Note," and "Sylvia's Death," a poem about the suicide of Sylvia Plath. "The Addict" describes the part of Sexton that is a "death monger": "I'm an expert on making the trip / and now they say I'm an addict." What has not been remarked about these poems, however, is that their imagery, tone, and often their explicit argument speak against suicide; Sexton is not flirting with death but attempting to exorcize personal demons, to understand her impulses and thereby transcend them. In "Wanting to Die" she addresses an unnamed "you"—perhaps the rational, questioning part of the poet's own psyche—and her voice seems rueful, melancholy. The poem's first stanza is one of the finest Sexton ever wrote:

Since you ask, most days I cannot remember.
I walk in my clothing, unmarked by that
    voyage.
Then the almost unnameable lust returns.

Here the desire for suicide is a "lust," and therefore love—as the poem's final line claims—can only represent an "infection." Sexton emphasizes not only this perversity in the suicidal impulse but also its blatant irrationality: "suicides have a special language. / Like carpenters they want to know which tools. / They never ask why build." Summoning up her own former persona, the glamorous witch of her earlier volumes, Sexton realizes that she had "possessed the enemy," had "taken on his craft, his magic," but that this represented an erroneous course, a capitulation to destructive forces. In "Suicide Note" she admits that "I am only a coward crying me me me" and in "Sylvia's Death," despite her acknowledged envy of Plath ("I know at the news of your death / a terrible taste for it"), Sexton emphasizes Plath's defeat. She gained nothing through her suicide, Sexton implies, since death is nothing but an "old belonging," and she finally refers to Plath's diminishment, her new identity as a mere "blonde thing" who has relinquished her own "special language" and received nothing in return.

In "Wanting to Die," Sexton notes that her own body, her essential physical sell is only a "bad prison" that should be emptied of breath, of life. Through poetry she sought liberation from this cruel and unnecessary prison, a liberation that could come only through a compassionate acceptance of her own flawed but redeemable self. Thus her emphasis in *Live or Die* is not upon "confession," with its implication of guilt, but upon compassion for herself and for all those who have influenced her personal existence. Seeking out the origin of her illness in childhood traumas and inadequate relationships with her parents, she is not interested in assigning blame but in bringing to light the dismal facts themselves; there is a new, strong impulse to face past realities and to assess their impact on the present. If this produced only a partial liberation, at least it represented an earned freedom that could directly affect the poet's life— acting as a form of therapy—and intensify the honesty of her art as well.

"They put me in the Closet," Emily Dickinson wrote, "because they liked me 'still'"—but the poem focuses upon her elders' inability to imprison the poet's spirit (defined as inhering in her poetic faculties) even in childhood. Anne Sexton is far less confident than this; she lacks Dickinson's firm sense of mission, she frequently distrusts her own creative excitement, and she cannot conceive of her identity—even in its aspect of poetic creativity—as having sufficient strength to withstand external constraints. Her typical reaction to her own analogous experiences is one of fear. "Imitations of Drowning," for instance, includes this bleak reminiscence: "I was shut up in that closet, until, biting the door, / they dragged me out, dribbling urine on the shore." The poem concludes: "in the end it's fear that drowns you." In her superb long poem, "Those Times . . . " she elaborates upon the sufferings of her childhood:

I was locked in my room all day behind
    a gate,
a prison cell.
I was the exile
who sat all day in a knot.

Although this situation may recall that of Plath's "Daddy," in which the poet recalls living under her father's domination like a foot trapped inside a black shoe, "poor and white, / Barely daring to breathe or Achoo," Sexton's poem lacks vindictiveness or even anger; it simply tells what happened.

The poem's description brilliantly conveys her early terror and helplessness:

The closet is where I rehearsed my life,
all day among shoes,
away from the glare of the bulb in the
    ceiling,
away from the bed and the heavy table
and the same terrible rose repeating on the
    walls.

Locked in her bedroom, the child retreats into an even smaller cell, her closet, but one whose conditions she could control. There she "rehearsed" her life, as if unconsciously attempting to ignore the distorting influences of her present experience. When her stern, punishing mother "came to force me to undress"—the phrase contains an unmistakable suggestion of rape—Sexton says that she "lay there silently, / hoarding my small dignity." Certain phrases recur throughout the poem, testifying to the child's ignorance: "I did not question it," "I did not ask," "I did not know." The poem is remarkable for its withholding of judgment: it creates sympathy for the mother as well as for the suffering child. As so often in Sexton's work, the true villain seems to be life itself, whose tragic process insists upon the movement away from innocence toward unending pain, and its resulting tragic awareness.

Live or Die is Sexton's first volume, after all, which simply arranges the poems in chronological order, as if surrendering to the flux of experience, its chequered pattern of elation and despair. Yet there are many elements which form a constant, hopeful strand in the fabric of Sexton's continued pain: humor and tenderness, the recognition of madness as a waste of time, a caustic, disapproving attitude toward suicide, and a remarkable development of the poet's artistic powers. The volume frequently celebrates personal relationships, and it exalts the artist's autonomy and necessary solitude. The poem "Live," which Sexton chose to conclude the volume, represents a new, mature attitude, a recognition of these positive elements as a possible starting point for a new stage of personal development. It ends with a positive, infectious excitement:

> The poison just didn't take.
> So I won't hang around in my hospital shift,
> repeating The Black Mass and all of it.
> I say Live, Live because of the sun,
> the dream, the excitable gift.

Source: Greg Johnson, "The Achievement of Anne Sexton," in *Hollins Critic*, Vol. 21, No. 3, June 1984, pp. 1–13.

Thomas P. McDonnell

In the following review of Live or Die, *McDonnell argues that Sexton's confessional, personal poetry is suggestive of a journey.*

Anne Sexton's latest book of poems, *Live or Die* (Houghton. $4), presents a good opportunity to look at her achievement in three published volumes. It is by now a rather worn observation to say that her poetry is not only personal but clearly the autobiography of the psyche itself. (Poetry has come around again, since the excesses of 19th-century romanticism, to recognizing something like the existence of the soul.) It is the kind of poetry frequently written by Robert Lowell, W. D. Snodgrass and Jon Silkin, and by Sylvia Plath in her last tragic years. And it is a kind of poetry that seems much in favor today, chiefly because it has been so long denied as legitimate matter for poetry by the art-as-dissociation critics.

Anne Sexton's poetry, however, is not a poetry of spasmodic revelation or of occasional incident transformed from similitude to artifact: in its continuing wholeness one perceives the suggestion of a journey. The journey is not a calculated one, marked with clear directions along the

> IN THIS AGE OF DEHUMANIZATION, ANNE SEXTON'S IS A NECESSARY KIND OF POETRY TO HAVE ON THE RECORD."

way, ("... here are no signs to tell the way"), but a journey in and out of the various dark. The poems are fragments of light that illuminate not so much the general landscape as parts of the immediate terrain—and that only now and then.

In the first poem of her first book, *To Bedlam and Part Way Back* (Houghton, 1960), Anne Sexton said: "Late August, / I speed through the antiseptic tunnel / where the moving dead still talk / of pushing their bones against the thrust of cure," in that immediate terrain where she is "queen of this summer hotel / or the laughing bee on a stalk / of death." Of course, "bones" has all but become a poetic cliché in modern verse and "thrust" a sociological one. Nevertheless, Anne Sexton very early wrote a kind of poetry in which you were not always sure whether the center was in motion and the periphery still, or the periphery in motion and the center still—with a stillness not of tranquility but, ineffably, at the point of fear itself.

"Kind Sir," she says in a poem addressed to Thoreau, "lost and of your same kind, / I have turned around twice with my eyes sealed / and the woods were white and my night mind / saw such strange happenings, untold and unreal. / And opening my eyes, I am afraid of course / to look—this inward look that society scorns—/ Still, I search in these woods and find nothing worse / than myself, caught between the grapes and the thorns." But not all the early poems—remarkable poems, really—have "this inward look that society scorns." Anne Sexton looks outward, too, "up there" to the gulls "godding the whole blue world"; and she listens ("Oh, la la la") to the music that swims back to her:

> The night I came I danced a circle
> and was not afraid.
> Mister?

Not afraid, but still there is that implication—perhaps supplication—in "Mister?" at the end: thus in and out of the shadows of the still journey again.

What is at once perfectly clear about Anne Sexton's verse is that it so stunningly reveals the poetry of psychic disturbance in all its frightful fluctuations between terror and clarity—and the poetry is in both the terror and the clarity. A young Catholic girl, some years ago, wrote a book of poems called *Songs of a Psychotic,* which was both more naive and more innocent than the knowledgeable but dark world of Anne Sexton. Where the younger poet was indeed all but otherworldly, Anne Sexton is a poet and woman intensely of this world. It was evident, even in *To Bedlam and Part Way Back,* that we were witness to a dimension of poetry unique in English literature, a poetry uniquely ours in this post-Freudian era.

Such poetry exists, surely, in "Her Kind," "Ringing the Bells," "A Story for Rose on the Midnight Flight to Boston" and "For John, Who Begs Me Not to Enquire Further," which is a poetic statement on the book's epigraph by Schopenhauer, and which also introduces Part Two of the *Bedlam* poems. (Anne Sexton's epigraphs to the several volumes, by the way, are extremely pertinent to the revelation of the poems.) Too, in these poems of the first volume, we begin to recognize certain tensions that later inform—though in larger freedoms of organization—the stark yet delicate impact of Anne Sexton's poetry.

In the last poem in *To Bedlam and Part Way Back,* "The Division of Parts," autobiography becomes poetic catharsis on that Good Friday when "In Boston, the devout / work their cold knees / toward that sweet martyrdom / that Christ planned." But "It does not please / my yankee bones to watch / where the dying is done / in its ugly hours." Still, "Such dangerous angels walk through Lent. / Their walls creak *Anne! Convert! Convert!*" At last, though, the poet herself resigns to the non-miraculous grace of reality: "And Lent will keep its hurt / for someone else. Christ knows enough / staunch guys have hitched on him in trouble, / thinking his sticks were badges to wear."

In *All My Pretty Ones* (Houghton, 1962), Anne Sexton reaches into the full power of the autobiographical poem, at once, with "The Truth the Dead Know," on the death by cancer of her mother, at 57, and of her father by heart attack, at 59, only three months later. The book's title poem begins: "Father, this year's jinx rides us apart" —a line that comes much too close, perhaps, to the rub-off from Robert Lowell's obvious influence on Anne Sexton. But the whole poem manages to recover itself in the working out of her own

authentic idiom. Disconcertingly, though, the poem ends: "Whether you are pretty or not, I outlive you, / bend down my strange face to yours and forgive you." Here, unfortunately, the reader cannot get close enough to the personal anguish of the poet to disabuse himself of the notion that to forgive the dead is the ultimate condescension of the living.

The journey into autobiography continues in "The Operation"—surely one of the remarkable poems of its kind in English—and in "The Abortion" ("*Somebody who should have been born / is gone*"). This is followed by "With Mercy for the Greedy," with the epigraph, "For my friend, Ruth, who urges me to make an appointment for the Sacrament of Confession." The poem itself carries the journey farther: "Concerning your letter in which you ask / me to call a priest and in which you ask / me to wear The Cross that you enclose"; and the reader—at least this reader—says to himself: Oh, no, don't ask this of the poet, don't proselytize at this point of her genuine anguish, which is all confessional, anyway; and who are we to say whether it is sacramental in the formal sense or not, or even in the most understanding empathy of friendship, to press more upon the poet than is actually necessary? But the poet herself answers this best in the last stanza of the poem:

> My friend, my friend, I was born
> doing reference work in sin, and born
> confessing it. This is what poems are:
> with mercy
> for the greedy,
> they are the tongue's wrangle,
> the world's pottage, the rat's star.

Poem follows remarkable poem: "For God While Sleeping," "In the Deep Museum," "Water," "Letter Written on a Ferry While Crossing Long Island Sound," each like a flash of light on the landscape of Anne Sexton's journey in and out of the dark. And not all dark at that, because in "From the Garden" Anne Sexton has written one of the loveliest poems of love that we have in contemporary American poetry, and one of the most beautifully dark ones ("Though I was bony you found me fair") in "Love Song for K. Owyne."

Not so incidentally, by the way, Anne Sexton is a strikingly beautiful woman, as anyone can see from the photo on the back dust jacket of her latest volume, *Live or Die.* The fact is that press agents and movie makers do not know what authentic glamour is, chiefly because they don't know what a woman is; and Anne Sexton is one of the few women writing poetry in the United States today of whom it is possible to say that her womanness is totally at one with her poems—and never more so than when she partially and poetically, in "Consorting With Angels," denies it: "I was tired of being a woman, . . . / I'm no more a woman / than Christ was a man." But if a woman alone, in the physiological sense, could have written a poem like "Menstruation at Forty," then also a woman alone, in the fullest possible sense, could have written so exquisite a poem as "Little Girl, My String Bean, My Lovely Woman."

Now, in *Live or Die*, Anne Sexton is writing in a more powerful and a freer mode of poetic expression than that already, and almost at once, achieved in her two previous volumes. Her poems have a marvelously wrought discipline of free form in, say, "Flee on Your Donkey," as well as the discipline of strict form in "Cripples and Other Stories," notably so here, and in the elegy to a fellow New England poet in seven a-b-a-b quatrains with the concluding couplet:

> John Holmes, cut from a single tree,
> lie heavy in her hold
> and go down that river with the ivory,
> the copra and the gold.

Sometimes, though rarely (as in "Those Times"), Anne Sexton's confessions become almost too much the poetry of the couch. Still, even here of course, it is a perfectly valid kind of poetry and surely in keeping with the journey backward as well as with the one that probes both the present and the future tense: of the woman who "did not know the woman I would be / nor that blood would bloom in me / each month like an exotic flower." Too, the poem "Too Lose the Earth" seems to me about as Freudian as a poem can get, even in these days when the couch has become a rack of pain rather than a bed of pleasure. In the poem on Sylvia Plath's suicide, "Sylvia's Death," one can almost read the terrible anguish of people who know not too little of themselves but perhaps too much.

Anne Sexton is a deeply religious poet in the existential sense of that depleted term. For her, the religious experience has nothing whatever to do with the ordinary comforts of piety: it daily involves one's struggle to survive, to somehow come to terms with the terrible mystery of existence and at last to find a measure of salvation in the life one has to live. For example, "For the Year of the Insane" is no idle prayer in poetry but the poetry of prayer itself. In following immediately upon

"Protestant Easter," it perfectly reveals the modality from rote to authentic supplication.

The journey in and out of the dark continues in "Crossing the Atlantic," a passage in "steel staterooms where night goes on forever":

> Being inside them is, I think,
> the way one would dig into a planet
> and forget the word *light*.

But the journey always comes home again, from "Walking in Paris," to dialing a telephone number in Boston, and indeed walking again down Marlborough Street. The later poems in *Live or Die*—all dated 1965, and the last two, 1966—are powerful "meditations" of the kind the saints might reveal if they were poets (in the technical sense) as well as humanists caught in the terrors of the modern world; and I think it is folly to pretend that our world is no different, say, from the mystical age of the 17th century. These remarkable poems could have been written by no one not thoroughly a child of this century:

> . . . I am not what I expected.
> Not an Eichmann.
> The poison just didn't take.
> So I won't hang around in my
> hospital shift,
> repeating The Black Mass and all of it.
> I say *Live, Live* because of the sun,
> the dream, the excitable gift.

If the excitable gift is life itself, it is also life transformed by art as personal catharsis. In this age of dehumanization, Anne Sexton's is a necessary kind of poetry to have on the record. We need the poetry of a woman who couldn't drown the eight Dalmatians in the pails of water set aside for them. Anne Sexton is a woman and poet who "kept right on going on, / a sort of human statement," in that long and intricate journey where the dark is neither all nor forever.

Source: Thomas P. McDonnell, "Light in a Dark Journey," in *America*, Vol. 116, May 13, 1967, pp. 729–31.

SOURCES

"America's Families and Living Arrangements: 2007," in *U.S. Census Bureau*, September 2009, http://www.census.gov/prod/2009pubs/p20-561.pdf (accessed December 31, 2009).

Blankenburg, Gary, "Anne Sexton: The Voice of Illness," in *Anne Sexton: Telling the Tale*, edited by Steven E. Colburn, University of Michigan Press, 1988, pp. 103–254.

Coleman, Margaret, "Homemaker as Worker in the United States," in *Challenge: The Magazine of Economic Affairs*, November/December 1998.

Farber, David, *The Age of Great Dreams: America in the 1960s*, Hill and Wang, 1994.

Freedman, Estelle, *No Turning Back: The History of Feminism and the Future of Women*, Ballantine, 2003.

George, Diana Hume, *Oedipus Anne: The Poetry of Anne Sexton*, University of Illinois Press, 1987.

Gill, Jo, "Anne Sexton's Poetics of the Suburbs," in *Health and the Modern Home*, edited by Mark Jackson, Routledge, 2007, pp. 63–80.

Lerner, Laurence, "What Is Confessional Poetry?," in *Critical Quarterly*, Vol. 29, No. 2, pp. 46–66.

Michailidou, Artemis, "Gender, Body, and Feminine Performance: Edna St. Vincent Millay's Impact on Anne Sexton," in *Feminist Review*, No. 78, 2004, pp. 117–40.

Middlebrook, Diane Wood, "Anne Sexton," in *Dictionary of Literary Biography*, Vol. 169, *American Poets since World War II*, edited by Joseph Conte, Gale Research, 1996, pp. 244–52.

———, *Anne Sexton: A Biography*, Vintage, 1992.

Nelson, Deborah, "Penetrating Privacy: Confessional Poetry, *Griswold v. Connecticut*, and Containment Ideology," in *Pursuing Privacy in Cold War America*, Columbia University Press, 2002, pp. 74–111.

Phillips, Robert, "Anne Sexton: The Blooming Mouth and the Bleeding Rose," in *The Confessional Poets*, Southern Illinois University Press, 1973, pp. 73–91.

Pool, Gail, "Anne Sexton: Poetry and Witchcraft," in *New Boston Review*, Spring 1978, pp. 3–4.

Sexton, Anne, "Self in 1958," in *The Complete Poems: Anne Sexton*, edited by Maxine Kumin, Mariner Books, 1999, pp. 155–56.

Teaford, Jon C., *The American Suburb: The Basics*, Routledge, 2007.

Wagner-Martin, Linda, "Anne Sexton's Life," in *Modern American Poetry*, http://www.english.illinois.edu/maps/poets/s_z/sexton/sexton_life.htm (accessed January 4, 2010), originally published in *American National Biography Online*, Oxford University Press, February 2000, http://www.anb.org/articles/16/16-01490.html (accessed January 4, 2010).

Wills, Charles A., *America in the 1950s*, Chelsea House, 2005.

FURTHER READING

Duany, Andres, Elizabeth Plater-Zyberk, and Jeff Speck, *Suburban Nation: The Rise of Sprawl and the Decline of the American Dream*, North Point Press, 2001.

> This critique of the American suburb, written by a group of architects, explores how suburban design and planning has undermined social structures, particularly an essential sense of community.

Farber, David, and Beth Bailey, *The Columbia Guide to America in the 1960s*, Columbia University Press, 2003.

> This extensive and comprehensive work presents a history, chronology, and almanac of the 1960s. It explains the cultural and social change that swept the decade and discusses popular culture of the day as well.

Lowell, Robert, *Collected Poems*, edited by David Gewanter, Farrar, Straus and Giroux, 2007.

> Robert Lowell was one of the leading confessional poets of the day; he was a contemporary of Sexton's who influenced her poetry. This volume presents a fine introduction to Lowell's body of work.

Sexton, Anne, *Live or Die*, Houghton Mifflin, 1966.

> Sexton's most successful collection, *Live or Die* contains not only "Self in 1958" but some of the author's best poems. The volume garnered Sexton her only Pulitzer Prize in 1967.

SUGGESTED SEARCH TERMS

"Self in 1958"

Anne Sexton

Anne Sexton poems

"Self in 1958" AND Anne Sexton

Anne Sexton AND confessional poetry

Anne Sexton AND feminism

Anne Sexton biography

Anne Sexton awards

Anne Sexton AND "Live or Die"

Snow-Bound

JOHN GREENLEAF WHITTIER
1866

Subtitled "A Winter Idyl," John Greenleaf Whittier's *Snow-Bound* is a long poem in which the poet recounts an event from his childhood, when a New England snowstorm left Whittier and his family confined to the home and surrounding grounds at his birthplace in Haverhill, Massachusetts, for several days. The poem was originally published as a single volume in 1866 and soon achieved both popular and critical success. As a narrative poem, *Snow-Bound* tells a story in verse and develops a number of characters, including Whittier's family and the boarders in the home. The work is considered Whittier's masterpiece. In it, Whittier recalls the homestead of his childhood and the isolation the residents of the home endured as a result of the storm. Being so cut off from one's neighbors and community was not without danger in the early nineteenth century, but the threats of freezing and starvation are countered in the poem by warmth of the fire and as well as the warmth of the family's affection and the sense of comfort derived from their spirituality. As the poem was published just after the end of the American Civil War (1861–1865), its sense of nostalgia for a simple, peaceful rural life certainly played a role in its appeal to a people reeling from the turmoil of war.

Snow-Bound was reprinted in a 1916 edition by Houghton Mifflin, titled *Snow-Bound, Among the Hills, Songs of Labor, and Other Poems.* More recently, Fredonia Books published *Snow-Bound and Other Autobiographic Poems* in 2003.

John Greenleaf Whittier

AUTHOR BIOGRAPHY

Whittier was born to Quaker parents on a seventeenth-century homestead near Haverhill, Massachusetts, on December 17, 1807. When he was nineteen years old, Whittier entered the newly opened Haverhill Academy, and he studied there for about a year; he was unable to afford to stay longer. In 1829, Whittier was offered an editorial position at a political newspaper called the *American Manufacturer* in Boston. Abolitionist and journalist William Lloyd Garrison helped him secure the position, and Garrison's influence would continue to steer the course of Whittier's life. Later, Whittier also worked as an editor at the *New England Review* in Hartford, Connecticut. While living in Hartford, Whittier published his first volume of tales and poems, *Legends of New England*, in 1831. He returned to the homestead in Haverhill later that year due to poor health. In March of 1833, Garrison asked Whittier for his help in advancing the cause of abolitionism. A few months later, in June, Whittier published a pamphlet that supported abolitionist aims and attacked a group known as the Colonization Society, which proposed ending slavery by sending slaves and free

Africans in America to Africa. That same year Whittier became affiliated with the American Anti-Slavery Society. Two years later, he was elected to a seat in the state legislature and served one term. He continued to write abolitionist poetry and served as the editor of the *Essex Gazette*. After selling the family farm in 1836, Whittier, his mother, and his sister moved to Amesbury, Massachusetts. In the decade that followed, Whittier regularly published volumes of poetry, along with prose sketches and even a novel. He wrote throughout the Civil War and continued to speak out as an abolitionist, although his poetry became increasingly less political. Whittier's sister Elizabeth died just prior to the war's end, in 1864. To Whittier, it was a devastating blow. In the poem Whittier wrote after the end of the war, *Snow-Bound*, published in 1866, Elizabeth's death is mourned. Themes of death and darkness in the poem are countered with a sense of hopefulness. The poem was immediately successful. He lived until 1876 in the house in Amesbury and then moved to Danvers, Massachusetts. Whittier continued to write until his death on September 7, 1892, in Hampton Falls, New Hampshire, where he spent many of his summers.

POEM TEXT

> The sun that brief December day
> Rose cheerless over hills of gray,
> And, darkly circled, gave at noon
> A sadder light than waning moon.
> Slow tracing down the thickening sky   5
> Its mute and ominous prophecy,
> A portent seeming less than threat,
> It sank from sight before it set.
> A chill no coat, however stout,
> Of homespun stuff could quite shut out,   10
> A hard, dull bitterness of cold,
> That checked, mid-vein, the circling race
> Of life-blood in the sharpened face,
> The coming of the snow-storm told.
> The wind blew east; we heard the roar   15
> Of Ocean on his wintry shore,
> And felt the strong pulse throbbing there
> Beat with low rhythm our inland air.
> Meanwhile we did our nightly chores,—
> Brought in the wood from out of doors,   20
> Littered the stalls, and from the mows
> Raked down the herd's-grass for the cows;
> Heard the horse whinnying for his corn;
> And, sharply clashing horn on horn,
> Impatient down the stanchion rows   25
> The cattle shake their walnut bows;
> While, peering from his early perch

Upon the scaffold's pole of birch,
The cock his crested helmet bent
And down his querulous challenge sent.   30
Unwarmed by any sunset light
The gray day darkened into night,
A night made hoary with the swarm
And whirl-dance of the blinding storm,
As zigzag, wavering to and fro   35
Crossed and recrossed the wingèd snow:
And ere the early bedtime came
The white drift piled the window-frame,
And through the glass the clothes-line posts
Looked in like tall and sheeted ghosts.   40

So all night long the storm roared on:
The morning broke without a sun;
In tiny spherule traced with lines
Of Nature's geometric signs,
In starry flake, and pellicle   45
All day the hoary meteor fell;
And, when the second morning shone,
We looked upon a world unknown,
On nothing we could call our own.
Around the glistening wonder bent   50
The blue walls of the firmament,
No cloud above, no earth below,—
A universe of sky and snow!
The old familiar sights of ours
Took marvellous shapes; strange domes
          and towers   55
Rose up where sty or corn-crib stood,
Or garden-wall or belt of wood;
A smooth white mound the brush-pile showed,
A fenceless drift what once was road;
The bridle-post an old man sat   60
With loose-flung coat and high cocked hat;
The well-curb had a Chinese roof;
And even the long sweep, high aloof,
In its slant splendor, seemed to tell
Of Pisa's leaning miracle.   65

A prompt, decisive man, no breath
Our father wasted: "Boys, a path!"
Well pleased, (for when did farmer boy
Count such a summons less than joy?)
Our buskins on our feet we drew;   70
With mittened hands, and caps drawn low,
To guard our necks and ears from snow,
We cut the solid whiteness through;
And, where the drift was deepest, made
A tunnel walled and overlaid   75
With dazzling crystal: we had read
Of rare Aladdin's wondrous cave,
And to our own his name we gave,
With many a wish the luck were ours
To test his lamp's supernal powers.   80
We reached the barn with merry din,
And roused the prisoned brutes within.
The old horse thrust his long head out,
And grave with wonder gazed about;
The cock his lusty greeting said,   85
And forth his speckled harem led;
The oxen lashed their tails, and hooked,

And mild reproach of hunger looked;
The hornèd patriarch of the sheep,
Like Egypt's Amun roused from sleep,   90
Shook his sage head with gesture mute,
And emphasized with stamp of foot.

All day the gusty north-wind bore
The loosening drift its breath before;
Low circling round its southern zone,   95
The sun through dazzling snow-mist shone.
No church-bell lent its Christian tone
To the savage air, no social smoke
Curled over woods of snow-hung oak.
A solitude made more intense   100
By dreary-voicèd elements,
The shrieking of the mindless wind,
The moaning tree-boughs swaying blind,
And on the glass the unmeaning beat
Of ghostly finger-tips of sleet.   105
Beyond the circle of our hearth
No welcome sound of toil or mirth
Unbound the spell, and testified
Of human life and thought outside.
We minded that the sharpest ear   110
The buried brooklet could not hear,
The music of whose liquid lip
Had been to us companionship,
And, in our lonely life, had grown
To have an almost human tone.   115

As night drew on, and, from the crest
Of wooded knolls that ridged the west,
The sun, a snow-blown traveller, sank
From sight beneath the smothering bank,
We piled with care our nightly stack   120
Of wood against the chimney-back,—
The oaken log, green, huge, and thick,
And on its top the stout back-stick;
The knotty forestick laid apart,
And filled between with curious art   125
The ragged brush; then, hovering near,
We watched the first red blaze appear,
Heard the sharp crackle, caught the gleam
On whitewashed wall and sagging beam,
Until the old, rude-furnished room   130
Burst, flower-like, into rosy bloom;
While radiant with a mimic flame
Outside the sparkling drift became,
And through the bare-boughed lilac-tree
Our own warm hearth seemed blazing free.   135
The crane and pendent trammels showed,
The Turks' heads on the andirons glowed;
While childish fancy, prompt to tell
The meaning of the miracle,
Whispered the old rhyme: "*Under the tree*   140
When fire outdoors burns merrily,
There the witches are making tea."

The moon above the eastern wood
Shone at its full; the hill-range stood
Transfigured in the silver flood,   145
Its blown snows flashing cold and keen,
Dead white, save where some sharp ravine
Took shadow, or the sombre green

Of hemlocks turned to pitchy black
Against the whiteness of their back. 150
For such a world and such a night
Most fitting that unwarming light,
Which only seemed where'er it fell
To make the coldness visible.

Shut in from all the world without, 155
We sat the clean-winged hearth about,
Content to let the north-wind roar
In baffled rage at pane and door,
While the red logs before us beat
The frost-line back with tropic heat; 160
And ever, when a louder blast
Shook beam and rafter as it passed,
The merrier up its roaring draught
The great throat of the chimney laughed,
The house-dog on his paws outspread 165
Laid to the fire his drowsy head,
The cat's dark silhouette on the wall
A couchant tiger's seemed to fall;
And, for the winter fireside meet,
Between the andirons' straddling feet, 170
The mug of cider simmered slow,
The apples sputtered in a row,
And, close at hand, the basket stood
With nuts from brown October's wood.

What matter how the night behaved? 175
What matter how the north-wind raved?
Blow high, blow low, not all its snow
Could quench our hearth-fire's ruddy glow.
O Time and Change!—with hair as gray
As was my sire's that winter day, 180
How strange it seems, with so much gone
Of life and love, to still live on!
Ah, brother! only I and thou
Are left of all that circle now,—
The dear home faces whereupon 185
That fitful firelight paled and shone.
Henceforward, listen as we will,
The voices of that hearth are still;
Look where we may, the wide earth o'er,
Those lighted faces smile no more. 190
We tread the paths their feet have worn,
We sit beneath their orchard trees,
We hear, like them, the hum of bees
And rustle of the bladed corn;
We turn the pages that they read, 195
Their written words we linger o'er,
But in the sun they cast no shade,
No voice is heard, no sign is made,
No step is on the conscious floor!
Yet Love will dream and Faith will trust 200
(Since He who knows our need is just)
That somehow, somewhere, meet we must.
Alas for him who never sees
The stars shine through his cypress-trees!
Who, hopeless, lays his dead away, 205
Nor looks to see the breaking day
Across the mournful marbles play!
Who hath not learned, in hours of faith,
The truth to flesh and sense unknown,

That Life is ever lord of Death, 210
And Love can never lose its own!

We sped the time with stories old,
Wrought puzzles out, and riddles told,
Or stammered from our school-book lore
"The chief of Gambia's golden shore." 215
How often since, when all the land
Was clay in Slavery's shaping hand,
As if a far-blown trumpet stirred
The languorous, sin-sick air, I heard
"Does not the voice of reason cry, 220
Claim the first right which Nature gave,
From the red scourge of bondage fly
Nor deign to live a burdened slave!"
Our father rode again his ride
On Memphremagog's wooded side; 225
Sat down again to moose and samp
In trapper's hut and Indian camp;
Lived o'er the old idyllic ease
Beneath St. François' hemlock trees;
Again for him the moonlight shone 230
On Norman cap and bodiced zone;
Again he heard the violin play
Which led the village dance away
And mingled in its merry whirl
The grandam and the laughing girl. 235
Or, nearer home, our steps he led
Where Salisbury's level marshes spread
Mile-wide as flies the laden bee;
Where merry mowers, hale and strong,
Swept, scythe on scythe, their swaths along 240
The low green prairies of the sea.
We shared the fishing off Boar's Head,
And round the rocky Isles of Shoals
The hake-broil on the driftwood coals;
The chowder on the sand-beach made, 245
Dipped by the hungry, steaming hot,
With spoons of clam-shell from the pot.
We heard the tales of witchcraft old,
And dream and sign and marvel told
To sleepy listeners as they lay 250
Stretched idly on the salted hay,
Adrift along the winding shores,
When favoring breezes deigned to blow
The square sail of the gundalow,
And idle lay the useless oars. 255

Our mother, while she turned her wheel
Or run the new-knit stocking-heel,
Told how the Indian hordes came down
At midnight on Concheco town,
And how her own great-uncle bore 260
His cruel scalp-mark to fourscore
Recalling, in her fitting phrase,
So rich and picturesque and free
(The common unrhymed poetry)
Of simple life and country ways, 265
The story of her early days,—
She made us welcome to her home;
Old hearths grew wide to give us room;
We stole with her a frightened look
At the gray wizard's conjuring-book, 270

The fame whereof went far and wide
Through all the simple country-side;
We heard the hawks at twilight play,
The boat-horn on Piscataqua,
The loon's weird laughter far away;   275
We fished her little trout-brook, knew
What flowers in wood and meadow grew,
What sunny hillsides autumn-brown
She climbed to shake the ripe nuts down,
Saw where in sheltered cove and bay   280
The ducks' black squadron anchored lay,
And heard the wildgeese calling loud
Beneath the gray November cloud.
Then, haply, with a look more grave,
And soberer tone, some tale she gave   285
From painful Sewel's ancient tome,
Beloved in every Quaker home,
Of faith fire-winged by martyrdom,
Or Chalkley's Journal, old and quaint,—
Gentlest of skippers, rare sea-saint!—   290
Who, when the dreary calms prevailed,
And water-butt and bread-cask failed,
And cruel, hungry eyes pursued
His portly presence mad for food,
With dark hints muttered under breath   295
Of casting lots for life or death,
Offered, if Heaven withheld supplies,
To be himself the sacrifice.
Then, suddenly, as if to save
The good man from his living grave,   300
A ripple on the water grew,
A school of porpoise flashed in view.
"Take, eat," he said, "and be content;
These fishes in my stead are sent
By Him who gave the tangled ram   305
To spare the child of Abraham."

Our uncle, innocent of books,
Was rich in lore of fields and brooks,
The ancient teachers never dumb
Of Nature's unhoused lyceum.   310
In moons and tides and weather wise,
He read the clouds as prophecies,
And foul or fair could well divine,
By many an occult hint and sign,
Holding the cunning-warded keys   315
To all the woodcraft mysteries;
Himself to Nature's heart so near
That all her voices in his ear
Of beast or bird had meanings clear,
Like Apollonius of old,   320
Who knew the tales the sparrows told,
Or Hermes, who interpreted
What the sage cranes of Nilus said;
A simple, guileless, childlike man,
Content to live where life began;   325
Strong only on his native grounds,
The little world of sights and sounds
Whose girdle was the parish bounds,
Whereof his fondly partial pride
The common features magnified,   330
As Surrey hills to mountains grew
In White of Selborne's loving view,—

He told how teal and loon he shot,
And how the eagle's eggs he got,
The feats on pond and river done,   335
The prodigies of rod and gun;
Till, warming with the tales he told,
Forgotten was the outside cold,
The bitter wind unheeded blew,
From ripening corn the pigeons flew,   340
The partridge drummed i' the wood, the mink
Went fishing down the river-brink.
In fields with bean or clover gay,
The woodchuck, like a hermit gray,
Peered from the doorway of his cell;   345
The muskrat plied the mason's trade,
And tier by tier his mud-walls laid;
And from the shagbark overhead
The grizzled squirrel dropped his shell.

Next, the dear aunt, whose smile of cheer   350
And voice in dreams I see and hear,—
The sweetest woman ever Fate
Perverse denied a household mate,
Who, lonely, homeless, not the less
Found peace in love's unselfishness,   355
And welcome wheresoe'er she went,
A calm and gracious element,
Whose presence seemed the sweet income
And womanly atmosphere of home,—
Called up her girlhood memories,   360
The huskings and the apple-bees,
The sleigh-rides and the summer sails,
Weaving through all the poor details
And homespun warp of circumstance
A golden woof-thread of romance.   365
For well she kept her genial mood
And simple faith of maidenhood;
Before her still a cloud-land lay,
The mirage loomed across her way;
The morning dew, that dried so soon   370
With others, glistened at her noon;
Through years of toil and soil and care,
From glossy tress to thin gray hair,
All unprofaned she held apart
The virgin fancies of the heart.   375
Be shame to him of woman born
Who had for such but thought of scorn.

There, too, our elder sister plied
Her evening task the stand beside;
A full, rich nature, free to trust,   380
Truthful and almost sternly just,
Impulsive, earnest, prompt to act,
And make her generous thought a fact,
Keeping with many a light disguise
The secret of self-sacrifice.   385
O heart sore-tried! thou hast the best
That Heaven itself could give thee,—rest,
Rest from all bitter thoughts and things!
How many a poor one's blessing went
With thee beneath the low green tent   390
Whose curtain never outward swings!

As one who held herself a part
Of all she saw, and let her heart

Against the household bosom lean,
Upon the motley-braided mat   395
Our youngest and our dearest sat,
Lifting her large, sweet, asking eyes,
Now bathed within the fadeless green
And holy peace of Paradise.
Oh, looking from some heavenly hill,   400
Or from the shade of saintly palms,
Or silver reach of river calms,
Do those large eyes behold me still?
With me one little year ago:—
The chill weight of the winter snow   405
For months upon her grave has lain;
And now, when summer south-winds blow
And brier and harebell bloom again,
I tread the pleasant paths we trod,
I see the violet-sprinkled sod,   410
Whereon she leaned, too frail and weak
The hillside flowers she loved to seek,
Yet following me where'er I went
With dark eyes full of love's content.
The birds are glad; the brier-rose fills   415
The air with sweetness; all the hills
Stretch green to June's unclouded sky;
But still I wait with ear and eye
For something gone which should be nigh,
A loss in all familiar things,   420
In flower that blooms, and bird that sings.
And yet, dear heart! remembering thee,
Am I not richer than of old?
Safe in thy immortality,
What change can reach the wealth I hold?   425
What chance can mar the pearl and gold
Thy love hath left in trust with me?
And while in life's late afternoon,
Where cool and long the shadows grow,
I walk to meet the night that soon   430
Shall shape and shadow overflow,
I cannot feel that thou art far,
Since near at need the angels are;
And when the sunset gates unbar,
Shall I not see thee waiting stand,   435
And, white against the evening star,
The welcome of thy beckoning hand?
Brisk wielder of the birch and rule,
The master of the district school
Held at the fire his favored place;   440
Its warm glow lit a laughing face
Fresh-hued and fair, where scarce appeared
The uncertain prophecy of beard.
He teased the mitten-blinded cat,
Played cross-pins on my uncle's hat,   445
Sang songs, and told us what befalls
In classic Dartmouth's college halls.
Born the wild Northern hills among,
From whence his yeoman father wrung
By patient toil subsistence scant,   450
Not competence and yet not want,
He early gained the power to pay
His cheerful, self-reliant way;
Could doff at ease his scholar's gown
To peddle wares from town to town;   455

Or through the long vacation's reach
In lonely lowland districts teach,
Where all the droll experience found
At stranger hearths in boarding round,
The moonlit skater's keen delight,   460
The sleigh-drive through the frosty night,
The rustic party, with its rough
Accompaniment of blind-man's-buff,
And whirling plate, and forfeits paid,
His winter task a pastime made.   465
Happy the snow-locked homes wherein
He tuned his merry violin,
Or played the athlete in the barn,
Or held the good dame's winding yarn,
Or mirth-provoking versions told   470
Of classic legends rare and old,
Wherein the scenes of Greece and Rome
Had all the commonplace of home,
And little seemed at best the odds
'Twixt Yankee pedlers and old gods;   475
Where Pindus-born Arachthus took
The guise of any grist-mill brook,
And dread Olympus at his will
Became a huckleberry hill.
A careless boy that night he seemed;   480
But at his desk he had the look
And air of one who wisely schemed,
And hostage from the future took
In trainèd thought and lore of book.
Large-brained, clear-eyed,—of such as he   485
Shall Freedom's young apostles be,
Who, following in War's bloody trail,
Shall every lingering wrong assail;
All chains from limb and spirit strike,
Uplift the black and white alike;   490
Scatter before their swift advance
The darkness and the ignorance,
The pride, the lust, the squalid sloth,
Which nurtured Treason's monstrous growth,
Made murder pastime, and the hell   495
Of prison-torture possible;
The cruel lie of caste refute,
Old forms remould, and substitute
For Slavery's lash the freeman's will,
For blind routine, wise-handed skill;   500
A school-house plant on every hill,
Stretching in radiate nerve-lines thence
The quick wires of intelligence;
Till North and South together brought
Shall own the same electric thought,   505
In peace a common flag salute,
And, side by side in labor's free
And unresentful rivalry,
Harvest the fields wherein they fought.

Another guest that winter night   510
Flashed back from lustrous eyes the light.
Unmarked by time, and yet not young,
The honeyed music of her tongue
And words of meekness scarcely told
A nature passionate and bold,   515
Strong, self-concentred, spurning guide,

Its milder features dwarfed beside
Her unbent will's majestic pride.
She sat among us, at the best,
A not unfeared, half-welcome guest,   520
Rebuking with her cultured phrase
Our homeliness of words and ways.
A certain pard-like, treacherous grace
Swayed the lithe limbs and drooped the lash,
Lent the white teeth their dazzling flash;   525
And under low brows, black with night,
Rayed out at times a dangerous light;
The sharp heat-lightnings of her face
Presaging ill to him whom Fate
Condemned to share her love or hate.   530
A woman tropical, intense
In thought and act, in soul and sense,
She blended in a like degree
The vixen and the devotee,
Revealing with each freak or feint   535
The temper of Petruchio's Kate,
The raptures of Siena's saint.
Her tapering hand and rounded wrist
Had facile power to form a fist;
The warm, dark languish of her eyes   540
Was never safe from wrath's surprise.
Brows saintly calm and lips devout
Knew every change of scowl and pout;
And the sweet voice had notes more high
And shrill for social battle-cry.   545
Since then what old cathedral town
Has missed her pilgrim staff and gown,
What convent-gate has held its lock
Against the challenge of her knock!
Through Smyrna's plague-hushed thoroughfares,   550
Up sea-set Malta's rocky stairs,
Gray olive slopes of hills that hem
Thy tombs and shrines, Jerusalem,
Or startling on her desert throne
The crazy Queen of Lebanon   555
With claims fantastic as her own,
Her tireless feet have held their way;
And still, unrestful, bowed, and gray,
She watches under Eastern skies,
With hope each day renewed and fresh,   560
The Lord's quick coming in the flesh,
Whereof she dreams and prophesies!
Where'er her troubled path may be,
The Lord's sweet pity with her go!
The outward wayward life we see,   565
The hidden springs we may not know.
Nor is it given us to discern
What threads the fatal sisters spun,
Through what ancestral years has run
The sorrow with the woman born,   570
What forged her cruel chain of moods,
What set her feet in solitudes,
And held the love within her mute,
What mingled madness in the blood,
A lifelong discord and annoy,   575
Water of tears with oil of joy,
And hid within the folded bud
Perversities of flower and fruit.

It is not ours to separate
The tangled skein of will and fate,   580
To show what metes and bounds should stand
Upon the soul's debatable land,
And between choice and Providence
Divide the circle of events;
But He who knows our frame is just,   585
Merciful and compassionate,
And full of sweet assurances
And hope for all the language is,
That He remembereth we are dust!

At last the great logs, crumbling low,   590
Sent out a dull and duller glow,
The bull's-eye watch that hung in view,
Ticking its weary circuit through,
Pointed with mutely-warning sign
Its black hand to the hour of nine.   595
That sign the pleasant circle broke:
My uncle ceased his pipe to smoke,
Knocked from its bowl the refuse gray,
And laid it tenderly away,
Then roused himself to safely cover   600
The dull red brand with ashes over.
And while, with care, our mother laid
The work aside, her steps she stayed
One moment, seeking to express
Her grateful sense of happiness   605
For food and shelter, warmth and health,
And love's contentment more than wealth,
With simple wishes (not the weak,
Vain prayers which no fulfilment seek,
But such as warm the generous heart,   610
O'er-prompt to do with Heaven its part)
That none might lack, that bitter night,
For bread and clothing, warmth and light.

Within our beds awhile we heard
The wind that round the gables roared,   615
With now and then a ruder shock,
Which made our very bedsteads rock.
We heard the loosened clapboards tost,
The board-nails snapping in the frost;
And on us, through the unplastered wall,   620
Felt the lightsifted snow-flakes fall;
But sleep stole on, as sleep will do
When hearts are light and life is new;
Faint and more faint the murmurs grew,
Till in the summer-land of dreams   625
They softened to the sound of streams,
Low stir of leaves, and dip of oars,
And lapsing waves on quiet shores.

Next morn we wakened with the shout
Of merry voices high and clear;   630
And saw the teamsters drawing near
To break the drifted highways out.
Down the long hillside treading slow
We saw the half-buried oxen go,
Shaking the snow from heads uptost,   635
Their straining nostrils white with frost.
Before our door the straggling train
Drew up, an added team to gain.
The elders threshed their hands a-cold,

Passed, with the cider-mug, their jokes 640
From lip to lip; the younger folks
Down the loose snow-banks, wrestling, rolled,
Then toiled again the cavalcade
O'er windy hill, through clogged ravine,
And woodland paths that wound between 645
Low drooping pine-boughs winter-weighed.
From every barn a team afoot,
At every house a new recruit,
Where, drawn by Nature's subtlest law,
Haply the watchful young men saw 650
Sweet doorway pictures of the curls
And curious eyes of merry girls,
Lifting their hands in mock defence
Against the snow-balls' compliments,
And reading in each missive tost 655
The charm which Eden never lost.

We heard once more the sleigh-bells' sound;
And, following where the teamsters led,
The wise old Doctor went his round,
Just pausing at our door to say 660
In the brief autocratic way
Of one who, prompt at Duty's call,
Was free to urge her claim on all,
That some poor neighbor sick abed
At night our mother's aid would need. 665
For, one in generous thought and deed,
What mattered in the sufferer's sight
The Quaker matron's inward light,
The Doctor's mail of Calvin's creed?
All hearts confess the saints elect 670
Who, twain in faith, in love agree,
And melt not in an acid sect
The Christian pearl of charity!

So days went on: a week had passed
Since the great world was heard from last. 675
The Almanac we studied o'er,
Read and reread our little store
Of books and pamphlets, scarce a score;
One harmless novel, mostly hid
From younger eyes, a book forbid, 680
And poetry, (or good or bad,
A single book was all we had,)
Where Ellwood's meek, drab-skirted Muse,
A stranger to the heathen Nine,
Sang, with a somewhat nasal whine, 685
The wars of David and the Jews.
At last the floundering carrier bore
The village paper to our door.
Lo! broadening outward as we read,
To warmer zones the horizon spread; 690
In panoramic length unrolled
We saw the marvel that it told.
Before us passed the painted Creeks,
And daft McGregor on his raids
In Costa Rica's everglades. 695
And up Taygetus winding slow
Rode Ypsilanti's Mainote Greeks,
A Turk's head at each saddle bow!
Welcome to us its week-old news,

Its corner for the rustic Muse, 700
Its monthly gauge of snow and rain,
Its record, mingling in a breath
The wedding bell and dirge of death:
Jest, anecdote, and love-lorn tale,
The latest culprit sent to jail; 705
Its hue and cry of stolen and lost,
Its vendue sales and goods at cost,
And traffic calling loud for gain.
We felt the stir of hall and street,
The pulse of life that round us beat; 710
The chill embargo of the snow
Was melted in the genial glow;
Wide swung again our ice-locked door,
And all the world was ours once more!

Clasp, Angel of the backward look 715
And folded wings of ashen gray
And voice of echoes far away,
The brazen covers of thy book;
The weird palimpsest old and vast,
Wherein thou hid'st the spectral past; 720
Where, closely mingling, pale and glow
The characters of joy and woe;
The monographs of outlived years,
Or smile-illumed or dim with tears,
Green hills of life that slope to death, 725
And haunts of home, whose vistaed trees
Shade off to mournful cypresses
With the white amaranths underneath.
Even while I look, I can but heed
The restless sands' incessant fall, 730
Importunate hours that hours succeed,
Each clamorous with its own sharp need,
And duty keeping pace with all.
Shut down and clasp the heavy lids;
I hear again the voice that bids 735
The dreamer leave his dream midway
For larger hopes and graver fears:
Life greatens in these later years,
The century's aloe flowers to-day!

Yet, haply, in some lull of life, 740
Some Truce of God which breaks the strife,
The worldling's eyes shall gather dew,
Dreaming in throngful city ways
Of winter joys his boyhood knew;
And dear and early friends—the few 745
Who yet remain—shall pause to view
These Flemish pictures of old days;
Sit with me by the homestead hearth,
And stretch the hands of memory forth
To warm them at the wood-fire's blaze! 750
And thanks untraced to lips unknown
Shall greet me like the odors blown
From unseen meadows newly mown,
Or lilies floating in some pond,
Wood-fringed, the wayside gaze beyond; 755
The traveller owns the grateful sense
Of sweetness near, he knows not whence,
And, pausing, takes with forehead bare
The benediction of the air.

POEM SUMMARY

Whittier's *Snow-Bound* consists of 759 lines. These lines are divided into stanzas (groups of lines of poetry that divide verse in the same way that paragraphs divide prose). Different editions of *Snow-Bound* reflect subtle differences in the grouping of lines into stanzas, resulting in differences in the number of stanzas the poem has. In this summary, the stanzas discussed are based on the stanzaic divisions in the 1916 edition of the poem published by Houghton Mifflin, in the collection *Snow-Bound, Among the Hills, Songs of Labor, and Other Poems*, edited by Horace Scudder. (The collection was originally published in 1878.) Scudder's edition of the poem contains twenty-four stanzas.

Stanza 1

In the first stanza, Whittier reveals the signs of an impending snow storm. He lists such details as the weakness of the sun, the shortness of the day, the biting cold, and the growing strength of the wind blowing from the east, off the ocean.

Stanza 2

Next, Whittier, speaking in first person plural (that is, referring to himself and a group of thus far unnamed others as "we"), describes the chores that are accomplished that evening. Firewood is brought in, and the farm animals are fed and bedded down for the night. Night descends as the snow begins to fall. The poet recalls how even before he goes to bed, the snow has begun to pile up on the window frames and to make the posts from the clothes appear like ghosts, already shrouded as they were in snow.

Stanza 3

In the next stanza, Whittier describes how the storm rages on all night, and the next morning begins without a glimmer of the sun. Little of this day is described. Whittier does state that the snow showers continued all that day. The following morning, the world is unrecognizable. The poet and his companions can see nothing when they look outside except snow and blue sky. The once-familiar sights visible from the house are transformed by the thick blanket of snow into strange shapes.

Stanza 4

Whittier's father asks for his sons' help in clearing a path through the snow to the barn. The boys eagerly comply and bundle up to go outside.

MEDIA ADAPTATIONS

- Whittier's *Snow-Bound* is available as an MP3 download from the compilation *Winter: A Season in Verse*, released in 2009 by Portable Poetry. The poem is read by Gideon Warner.

Digging a path, sometimes a tunnel, the boys reach the barn and rouse the hungry animals.

Stanza 5

The landscape described in the next stanza is one in which silence and isolation reign. Whittier notes the absence of the sound of church bells and the sight of chimney smoke in the air. The only sounds are those of the wind making the tree branches groan and the sleet hammering on the window panes. No signs of human life are visible beyond the confines of the home and property.

Stanza 6

As the sun sets, the inhabitants of the Whittier home pile the firewood for the night near the chimney stack. A fire is started in the fireplace, and the gloomy mood is transformed as the fire gives off a rosy glow. The snow drifts visible through the window and beyond the bare limbs of a lilac tree sparkle with the reflection of the flames. Through this image, the warmth and comfort of the hearth expands to encompass the natural world beyond the home.

Stanza 7

The warmth described in the previous stanza is contrasted with the cold silvery world of the moonlit hills beyond the Whittier property. The images convey a sense of danger, as when the image of the deathly white snow is followed by one of jagged ravines and pitch-dark tree shadows. The cold, unwelcoming world outside the home is made even bleaker by the contrast provided by the cozy glow of the fire discussed in the sixth stanza.

Stanza 8

In this stanza, Whittier sets the stage for the next phase of the poem, in which his family and the other boarders in the Whittier home settle in by the fire. Mugs of cider simmer on the grate, and apples and nuts are roasted in the fire, serving as a source of emotional comfort and providing physical sustenance. Additionally, the fire draws the people in the home to the central gathering place of the hearth, emphasizing the solidifying of familial and communal bonds that the storm generates and that the fire encourages.

Stanza 9

Whittier ruminates on the contrasts between the storm outside and the cozy gathering in front of the fire. He calls attention to the fact that the events that took place in the poem occurred long ago. Whittier additionally reveals that of the circle gathered in front of the fire that he has just described, only he and his brother (Matthew) still remain. Here it is made clear that Whittier and Matthew, the two still living, are the "we" Whittier has been referring to. The remainder of this stanza laments the deaths of family members, people with whom the poet still feels very much connected. He feels the presence of his deceased loved ones as he sits in the orchard, walks through the cornfield, or thumbs through the pages of a book. Whittier affirms his faith in God and in the fact that one day he will be reunited with his departed family members.

Stanza 10

Returning from his present grief to the past, Whittier describes how the people gathered around the fire embark on an evening of storytelling. In the next several stanzas, Whittier offers brief portraits of the individuals in the home. First, Whittier recalls the stories told by his father (John Whittier), who speaks of his travels in Canada and his childhood in the American Northeast. Providing geographic references with names such as Memphremagog (a lake situated between Vermont and Quebec, Canada) and the Salisbury marshes (near the Merrimack River in Massachusetts), Whittier captures his father's tales of a rugged childhood spent outdoors, hunting, camping, and fishing.

Stanza 11

Next, Whittier's mother (Abigail Hussey Whittier) spins wool into yarn on a spinning wheel and knits stockings while she narrates tales of her childhood, in which early North American settlements were troubled by encounters with Native Americans. Her geographic references include the town of Cochecho and the Piscataqua River in New Hampshire. Whittier describes the way his mother's storytelling invites the listeners to experience events as she did, to feel as though they too could hear the odd call of the loon or know the woodland flowers. Whittier's mother transitions from descriptions of her youth to religious stories pertaining to the Whittier family's Quakerism.

Stanza 12

Whittier introduces his uncle (Moses Whittier, the brother of Whittier's father) in the next stanza. Describing his uncle as unschooled, Whittier explains the richness of his uncle's knowledge of the natural world. As Whittier's uncle and father are brothers, the uncle's memories are similar to those recounted earlier by Whittier's father. As the uncle describes the landscape and woodland creatures, his listeners forget the cold wind blowing outside their own door.

Stanza 13

Whittier devotes the next stanza to his unmarried aunt (Mercy Hussey, the sister of Whittier's mother). Describing her as lonely, Whittier also characterizes his aunt as peaceful and pleasant. She recalls episodes from her childhood, sleighing in the winter, sailing in the summer. The ordinary details of her life, Whittier comments, are interwoven with a sense of idealism and nostalgia.

Stanza 14

The next stanza pertains to Whittier's older sister (Mary). The first several lines of this stanza are devoted to Whittier's loving description of his sister's character. He finds her to be truthful and steadfast, as well as impulsive. The ending lines of the stanza lament Mary's death, and reveal Whittier's faith in an afterlife in which his sister is free from the bitterness and toil of life.

Stanza 15

Another sister, the youngest (Elizabeth), is described in the next stanza. She sits on a mat by the fire, taking in all the events of the household. Whittier reveals that she is now deceased. He wonders if his sister is watching him, and he recalls how recently, just a year ago, they had been together. The pain of Elizabeth's death is evident, as Whittier recalls activities he and Elizabeth once shared, such as walking among the springtime flowers. He transitions from the use of "we," which had included his brother, to "I" as he expresses his personal grief over Elizabeth's death. Whittier chastises himself for grieving, observing that the wealth of memories of his sister has left him richer than he has ever been. He senses that his sister remains near to him and that he will once again see her, upon his own death.

Stanza 16

Having reported in detail the stories and characteristics of his family members, Whittier now turns to the other people boarding in the Whittier home at the time of the great snowfall. The first is a schoolmaster, who has been identified as George Haskell, according to the editor, Scudder. Whittier depicts the schoolmaster as young and playful. The stories he tells are markedly different from those of the other adults. The schoolmaster recounts his days as a student at Dartmouth College in New Hampshire. The reader is told of the schoolmaster's yeoman father (a yeoman is a man who holds a small estate), and how he farmed his land and in doing so earned an honest living. Whittier emphasizes the schoolmaster's sense of self-reliance and optimism. As the stanza continues, Whittier uses the schoolmaster's youth, energy, and earnestness to turn to a discussion of war and slavery, stating that the nation now needs men like the schoolmaster to repair the wrongs that still exist despite the fact that the war has ended and the slaves have been freed.

Stanza 17

Another guest that evening is Harriet Livermore. Whittier mentions her by name in a brief introduction he wrote for *Snow-Bound*, and in the poem he describes her as a guest who is not entirely welcome. Livermore is described by Whittier in his introduction as outspoken, fervently devout, and sharp-tongued. In the poem, Whittier depicts her in terms of contrasts. She seems not young, but not old, and her sweet voice is contrasted with her passionate, willful nature. She is compared to the aggressively assertive figure of Kate in Shakespeare's play *The Taming of the Shrew*, and also with St. Catherine of Siena, who Scudder informs was known for her visions and her vow of silence.

Stanza 18

The fire is beginning to die out, and the clock shows that it is nearly nine o'clock at night. The people gathered by the fire are beginning to ready themselves for bed, dampening the fire for the evening. Whittier's mother lays down her needlework and says a prayer expressing the family's thankfulness for all they have.

Stanza 19

Now in bed, Whittier and the rest of the inhabitants of the home listen to the wind outside, knowing that the storm still rages on. Yet all are able to sleep well, as they are safe and warm, and renewed by the companionship they have shared.

Stanza 20

In the morning the group is awakened by shouts from the teamsters, who are driving a team of oxen through the snow to clear a path for horse-drawn carts. The adults in the group enthusiastically greet the teamsters, sharing steaming mugs of cider with them. Whittier imagines people beginning to emerge from their homes, and youngsters engaging each other in snowball fights.

Stanza 21

The sound of sleigh bells alert the Whittier home to the approach of the doctor, who asks for Whittier's mother's help in tending to a sick neighbor. As she prepares to leave, Whittier comments on the Christian spirit that motivates his mother and the doctor to help others in need.

Stanza 22

Whittier notes the passage of time, observing that a week has now passed. He talks about the many books they have read and re-read to pass the time. Whittier recalls how the group rejoiced when the village paper was finally delivered. The paper provides reports of current events, and it also contains a poetry section, weather reports, wedding and death announcements, and a crime report. The paper inspires in the Whittiers and their boarders an enthusiasm for their community and a sense of relief that their isolation from it has ended. The paper is significant for one other reason. It provides an indication of the time period to which Whittier refers in the poem. Whittier mentions the Scotsman Gregor McGregor. As Scudder states in his notes to the poem, McGregor attempted to establish a colony in Costa Rica in 1822. This fixes Whittier's age at the time of the snowstorm at fifteen years old.

Stanza 23

In this stanza, Whittier implores what he describes as the angel of the storm to close and clasp shut the stormy book of the past. He speaks of that time as one in which joy and sorrow were mingled. Whittier is keenly aware of the passage of time; he alludes to the notion of the sands of an hourglass, falling relentlessly.

Stanza 24

In the final stanza, Whittier expresses his gratitude for the ability to look back on his childhood and on the memories such as those he has recounted in *Snow-Bound*. He likens his poem to the Flemish school of painting, which focuses on capturing images of domestic life. In the last lines of the poem, Whittier envisions future readers who will embrace the poem and its view of the past.

THEMES

Family

The sense of community Whittier exposes in *Snow-Bound* begins with the notion of family and expands outward to include family friends, such as the schoolmaster, as well as boarders who may not inspire affection but are nevertheless included in the warm circle by the fire. As the poem progresses, the sense of community expands to include the surrounding area and its inhabitants, such as the teamsters who arrive to plow the roads and the doctor who needs Mrs. Whittier's help. Once the village paper arrives, Whittier's sense of community is broadened even further, as he includes details about global events. At the heart of these ever-expanding circles is the family—his family. The family members who appear in the poem include Whittier's brother (Matthew), his sisters (Mary and Elizabeth), his mother and father, his uncle (Moses Whittier), and his aunt (Mercy Hussey). Aside from Matthew, who is the only family member still alive when Whittier writes his poem, Whittier offers loving portrayals of each family member. Their stories signal to the reader personalities and interests. Whittier's father eagerly tells tales of woodland rides and village dances, and his mother cannot be idle, her hands busy with yarn as she speaks. Her story opens with tales of encounters with Native Americans, moves to a peaceful recollection of her childhood, and ends with a religious discussion. Moses, brother to Whittier's father, describes a similar past of hunting, fishing, and exploring the woods. Mercy, sister to Whittier's mother, offers details of activities she enjoyed as a child, such as sleighing and sailing. Whittier interjects details about each individual as well: his aunt is sweet and lonely, and his uncle, though uneducated, possesses a vast amount of knowledge about the land and wildlife. His mother is deeply religious and industrious, and his father is somewhat adventurous. Whittier's siblings tell no tales themselves, but Matthew is by Whittier's side as they perform their chores at the beginning of the poem, and Mary

and Elizabeth are described in glowing terms, and their deaths deeply mourned.

In this intensely personal poem, Whittier does more than include his family members as characters in his story. Through them, he reveals the importance of these family bonds to his own sense of self. As a child enduring the snowstorm with his family, he received from these ties a sense of security and warmth. He describes how he rested easily during the storm after hearing everyone's shared stories; his heart is light and peaceful. As an adult, with most of his family now dead, Whittier longs for the comfort and companionship he shared with his family.

Faith

The Whittiers were Quakers. Quakers are members of a religious group known as the Society of Friends. They are Christians and believe that God reveals himself to individuals directly, and they reject conventional forms of worship. Quakerism and Christian religious beliefs appear with some regularity in *Snow-Bound*. Whittier's mother specifically references works by Quaker writers. Whittier additionally affirms his faith in the notion of an afterlife when he discusses the deaths of his sisters. He believes they are in heaven and at peace, and he believes that he will be reunited with them upon his own death. Whittier returns repeatedly in the poem to the ideas of death and the passage of time, and just as repeatedly he turns to his faith to comfort himself when painful feelings and dark thoughts overtake him. At the end of stanza 17, in which Harriet Livermore's religious views on salvation are presented, Whittier asserts that God is just and will judge people fairly and mercifully. Christianity is also brought up in another context, when the doctor visits the Whittiers and asks for Mrs. Whittier's help with an ailing neighbor. Whittier comments on both his mother's Quakerism and the beliefs of the Calvinist doctor (Calvinism is a branch of Protestantism), maintaining that it is out of a sense of Christian charity that the two are inspired to help those in need.

New England

Whittier writes about a specifically New England past in *Snow-Bound*. Having lived so much of his life in the Haverhill, Massachusetts, homestead described in the poem, Whittier's sense of the history of the place as a Northeastern one is strong. The rural of life on a New England farm in the early nineteenth century is one in which family and community ties must be strong out of necessity. The region is lovingly portrayed by

TOPICS FOR FURTHER STUDY

- Using sources such as *How to Be a Perfect Stranger: A Guide to Etiquette in Other People's Religious Ceremonies*, edited by Arthur J. Magida and published in 1996, research the religious practices of Quakers and compare them to the religious practices of another religion of your choosing. Do the religions make use of any similar traditions? Do they honor important life events in different ways? What ceremonies are considered significant in these religions? Write a comparative essay and share it with the class orally or via a Web log (blog).

- Whittier and several other poets, including William Cullen Bryant and Henry Longfellow, are often labeled the Fireside Poets or the Schoolroom Poets. Research this group. Why are they so described? Who are the other poets in their group? In what ways are the works of the other poets in this classification like or unlike Whittier's *Snow-Bound*? Compile your findings into a written report or on a Web page viewable by your classmates. Be sure to cite all your sources, including both print and electronic sources.

- Whittier was an active abolitionist, and in discussing the schoolmaster in *Snow-Bound*, he briefly touches on the issue of slavery. Research the American abolitionist movement in the nineteenth century. Who were the prominent leaders? Consider what role Whittier played in the movement. To what extent did he use his poetry as a means toward achieving abolitionist goals? Create a timeline poster by hand or by using an online program such as Glogster in which you highlight significant dates in the abolitionist movement.

- A number of African American poets were contemporaries of Whittier's. Research the African American poets of the mid-nineteenth century, and select one, such as James Madison Bell, Charlotte Grimke, or another, and write a biographical essay in which you discuss the life and works of the poet you selected. Be sure to include some discussion of the themes and forms employed by the poet.

- In lines 693 through 698 of *Snow-Bound*, Whittier mentions several items of national and global news that appear in his village paper. Using the notes that are appended to the version of *Snow-Bound* edited by Horace Scudder, research these historical events. Create your own newspaper—it may be either a print or a Web publication—in which you report on these happenings.

- According to the January 1866 issue of the *North American Review*, James Fenimore Cooper's *Stories of the Woods, or Adventures of Leatherstocking*, published in 1865, was one of the outstanding children's books of the year. (Library of America published these stories as *The Leatherstocking Tales*, Volume 1, in 1985.) In Cooper's stories, which were published the same year as Whittier's *Snow-Bound* and were intended for a young audience, the American frontier is mythologized, just as the American Northeast is idealized in Whittier's poem. Read a selection from Cooper's work and compare it with Whittier's poem. Which of the works do you think would have been more appealing to young adult readers in 1866? Are there similarities in the ways the authors approach their treatment of the American landscape, and the place of settlers and farmers in it? Discuss your findings in a reading group on an Internet social network program established by your teacher.

Whittier as he draws attention to the farm life, the physical landscape, and the proximity of the ocean. Interspersed with his own descriptions of the area are the reminiscences of his family and friends, who recall in their own ways their New England pasts. Whittier's father and uncle both recall a boyhood spent outdoors, hunting, fishing, and exploring. Whittier's mother speaks of the region's

A snowbound cottage *(Image copyright Richard Semik, 2010. Used under license from Shutterstock.com)*

conflicted history with Native Americans, and she provides a loving account of a childhood lived in the country. His plain-speaking aunt similarly has fond memories of her New England youth. Many of these descriptions specifically name numerous locations in the Maine, New Hampshire, and Massachusetts areas. The schoolmaster's story involves tales of his college days at Dartmouth, a college in rural New Hampshire. The schoolmaster also describes in detail his life in various small towns throughout the region. In the characters' recollections and in his own, Whittier describes a region full of natural beauty, in which people are in tune with the land and with each other.

STYLE

Narrative Poem

Whittier's *Snow-Bound* is a narrative poem. A narrative poem is one in which the poet tells a story. Whittier recounts the events that occurred when a snowstorm cut his family off from the rest

of the world. Within this story, Whittier includes his own summaries of the stories told by others, as the family and friends in the home gather in front of the fire. These other individuals are treated in Whittier's poem the way characters are treated in a story; they are integral players in the narrative Whittier is sharing. Their habits, mannerisms, and the stories they tell suggest to the reader details about their personal characteristics. During the course of the poem, Whittier informs the reader that the events of the poem took place when he was a child. He is now an older man, looking back on the past to express his narrative.

Idyl

Whittier indicates in the subtitle of his poem that is an idyl, "A Winter Idyl." Also known as a pastoral poem, an idyl (also spelled "idyll") is a poem in which rural living is described in nostalgic, idealized terms. Although the realities of the storm are conveyed, Whittier focuses less on the danger posed by the snowstorm than on the familial warmth and intimacy generated by the family's being snowbound. This idealized view of the past is consistent with the trend of romanticism in poetry during the nineteenth century. Romanticism was a movement in both art and literature that prized individual experience, imagination, and emotion over rigid rules and strict rationality. This does not mean that Whittier's poem lacks a sense of realism. Throughout the poem, the details he provides offer the reader a vivid picture of both the snow-covered countryside and the home's cozy interior. Yet the poet's longing for a time long past, and for the people who populated his personal history, does color his recounting of the snowstorm in a wash of nostalgic idealism. Additionally, as is typical of romantic verse, *Snow-Bound* explores Whittier's emotional responses to the story he is telling, rather than simply presenting the facts of the event.

Metrical Structure and Rhyme Scheme

Idyls, or pastorals, are typically written in metered verse. Meter is a pattern of unaccented and accented syllables within a line of poetry. In *Snow-Bound*, the lines of verse are composed of a pattern in which an unaccented syllable is followed by an accented one. Each pair of unaccented and accented syllables is called an iamb. Each line of the poem contains four iambs; therefore, the meter of the poem is described as iambic tetrameter.

Whittier divides his poem into stanzas. A stanza is a division of poetry into a series of related lines. Whittier determines the length of his stanzas not by number of lines, as is sometimes the case in formal verse, but rather thematically and chronologically. As Whittier makes his way around the fire, for example, telling the reader about the family and friends gathered and sharing their stories, he typically begins a new stanza with each change in storyteller. The poem is further structured as a series of rhymed couplets. A rhymed couplet is two lines of verse in which the last two syllables of each line rhyme. The metrical structure and rhyme scheme Whittier employs suit the storytelling mode of the poem. The use of the iamb conveys a sense of natural, conversational rhythm. Whittier's use of rhymed couplets imparts to the poem a pleasant, lyrical tone that encourages the reader to read the poem aloud. It is a story meant to be shared, just as the speakers in the poem share their own stories.

HISTORICAL CONTEXT

The Civil War

Whittier's *Snow-Bound* was written in 1865, in the final year of the American Civil War, which began in 1861. While the issue of slavery was inexorably tied to the war, it was not the only factor contributing to the conflict between the Northern and Southern states. To some degree, the war was also precipitated by the disagreement between the federal government and the Southern states concerning the balance of power between state government and federal government. The Southern states demanded more power than the federal government deemed appropriate. By 1860, Southern leaders contemplated the notion of withdrawing, or seceding, from the United States. South Carolina became the first of the Southern states to secede, in December of 1860. Following South Carolina's lead, Mississippi, Florida, Georgia, and Louisiana seceded in January 1861. The seceded states elected Jefferson Davis as the president of what they called the Confederate States of America. The newly elected U.S. president, Abraham Lincoln, ordered the use of force by Union (Northern) troops after the Confederate troops attacked Fort Sumter, a military fort off the coast of South Carolina. This marked the beginning of the Civil War. In the aftermath of the attack, Virginia, Arkansas, North Carolina, and Tennessee also joined the Confederacy. By the end of the war, hundreds of thousands of people had died. During the course of the war, Lincoln took the first steps toward the abolition of slavery, signing the Emancipation Proclamation in 1863, which freed slaves in the Confederacy. The war ended in 1865 when the Confederate general Robert E. Lee surrendered.

Nineteenth-Century American Quakerism

In *Snow-Bound*, Whittier makes several mentions of Quakerism. In particular, he speaks of his mother's references to the Quaker historian William Sewel, who in 1799 published *The History of the Rise, Increase, and Progress of the Christian People Called the Quakers*. Also referenced is English Quaker Thomas Chalkley, who published his *Journal of the Life, Travels, and Christian Experiences of Thomas Chalkley* in 1749. Whittier's mother describes a story taken from Chalkley's work in which the seafaring author found himself at sea, starving. As Whittier's mother interprets the tale, God sent to the starving Chalkley porpoises to catch and eat. Whittier also discusses in more general terms his faith in God and in the notion of an afterlife. David Hackett Fischer, in a chapter on American Quakers in the 1989 *Albion's Seed: Four British Folkways in America*, outlines some of the

COMPARE
&
CONTRAST

- **1820s:** American poetry is influenced by the European romantic movement, with its emphasis on individual experience and natural themes. American romantic poets publishing in the 1820s include William Cullen Bryant and Edgar Allan Poe.

  1860s: Poetry is influenced by the impact of the Civil War on the American psyche. Following the violence and turmoil, poets such as John Greenleaf Whittier look to a more peaceful past for comfort. The continued influence of European romanticism encourages the nostalgic idealization of the past. Additionally, poets such as Walt Whitman and Emily Dickinson explore free verse, poetry lacking the formal structures—such as meter and rhyme scheme—of traditional verse forms.

  Today: Contemporary poetry encompasses a variety of forms. Free verse poetry remains immensely popular and is exemplified in the works of poets such as John Ashbery and Louise Erdrich. New formalism is a type of contemporary poetry in which traditional forms and structures are embraced, as in the work of Dana Gioia and Jane Kenyon.

- **1820s:** American Quakers, who established communities in colonial America in the seventeenth century, experience a schism based on two distinct viewpoints of their faith. Elias Hicks and a group of followers splinter from the Orthodox Quakers, affirming that the notion of the inner light (one's personal experience of the divine), rather than scripture, should be the primary authority of one's personal faith.

  1860s: As pacifists with comparatively liberal views regarding equality, Quaker abolitionists actively campaign to eradicate slavery and to help escaping slaves during the Civil War and freed slaves in the aftermath of the war. John Greenleaf Whittier is a well-known Quaker abolitionist.

  Today: Quakers practice their religion worldwide, with the largest percentages living in Africa and North America. In the United States, according to the Quaker Information Center's count of practicing adult Quakers, there were more than 86,000 Quakers in 2007.

- **1820s:** Decades before the Civil War, the United States is torn regarding the issue of slavery. The topic is debated in terms of the American economy as well as morality. Antislavery groups exist in both the North and the South. Dorothy Schneider and Carl J. Schneider point out in the 2007 *Slavery in America* that "in the 1820s, the slave states actually had more antislavery societies than the free states."

  1860s: Slavery has become one of the issues that divides the Northern and Southern states. Abolitionists continue to fight for the elimination of slavery from the United States. In 1863, President Abraham Lincoln signs the Emancipation Proclamation, freeing slaves in most of the Confederacy. In 1865, the Thirteenth Amendment to the Constitution is ratified, abolishing slavery throughout the United States. Racial tensions continue to plague the nation as newly freed slaves attempt to assimilate into an often hostile society.

  Today: The issue of race relations still plagues Americans, despite the 2008 election of the first African American U.S. president, Barack Obama. A 2009 Gallup poll shows that a year after Obama's election, 41 percent of Americans believe that race relations have improved since Obama's election, compared to the 70 percent who, the previous year, expected race relations to improve following the election.

---

basic beliefs of American Quakers. Speaking of the Quakers in early America, Fischer explains that in general their belief system was derived from the New Testament of the Bible, and formal doctrines and creeds were rejected. Rather, they believed in an "inner light," which was "an emanation of

The narrator of the poem describes cows in the snow. *(Image copyright Mark Grenier, 2010. Used under license from Shutterstock.com)*

divine goodness and virtue passed from Jesus into every human soul." Salvation was possible for every person who sought out this light through introspection; faith for the early American Quakers was based on a personal experience with God. Unlike other Protestant sects, such as the Calvinists, Quakers believed that everyone could be saved (that is, rewarded with an eternal life in heaven), not just those predetermined by God. Although Quakers rejected a formal church structure led by preachers deemed authorities on matters of faith and whose job it was to interpret and explain the teachings of God, they did rely on an organized structure of meetings where they could come together to worship. Leaders of these meetings counseled and offered support rather than dictated religious strictures. The emphasis of Quakerism in nineteenth-century America was on family, community, and morality. Despite some splintering off of various groups in the 1800s, largely for issues dealing with the particulars of Quaker doctrine, the core ideals of Quakerism— particularly the notion of the inner light and of a

personal, experiential conception of faith— remained unchanged from the early beliefs Fischer delineates.

CRITICAL OVERVIEW

A number of critics, including Elizabeth Gray Vining in her 1974 *Mr. Whittier*, have observed that Whittier's *Snow-Bound* enjoyed immediate success upon its 1866 publication. Robert Penn Warren, in the 1971 *John Greenleaf Whittier's Poetry: An Appraisal and a Selection*, similarly comments on the immense popularity of the first edition of the work. Critics today lavish praise on the poem. Vining describes it as "a perfect example of its type, the idyl or pastoral." She goes on to examine the poem's structure and Whittier's character studies. Warren similarly approaches the poem by way of its structure and characters, finding that despite the work's "nostalgic appeal" to a generation reared in the northeastern countryside, it also employs "a firm realism in the drawing of character." Warren's analysis is characteristic of the modern critic's desire to assess the poem in ways that transcend a view of it as quaint and nostalgic. John B. Pickard, in a contribution to *Critical Essays on John Greenleaf Whittier*, published in 1980 and edited by Jayne K. Kribbs, takes this approach as well, maintaining that the work possesses "a genuine literary value far beyond local or historical interest." Pickard studies the unity Whittier achieves in the poem by using a series of contrasts to support the poem's "theme of love and immortality struggling against pain and death." In *Snow-Bound*, some critics maintain, the apparent peacefulness is not as perfect as it seems.

Critics such as Marilyn C. Wesley and Gregory E. Jordan focus on the female guest in the poem, whom Whittier identifies as Harriet Livermore. Jordan, in an article for the winter 1995 issue of the journal *ANQ*, studies Whittier's juxtaposition of Livermore with St. Catherine of Siena. Explaining that St. Catherine is associated with the extinguishing of fires, Jordan contends that "Harriet's coldness threatens to extinguish the hearth of love and the Holy Spirit that animates the Whittier family." Wesley, in the 1999 *Secret Journeys: The Trope of Women's Travel in American Literature*, asserts that Whittier's portrayal of Livermore is an ambiguous one. Wesley states: "Whittier's treatment of the historic Harriet Livermore in *Snow-Bound* reveals the complexity of both masculine identity and of feminine representation in the male literature of the day." Offering a detailed assessment of Whittier's depiction of Livermore, and contrasting this characterization with that of Whittier's sister Mary, Wesley finds that Whittier's simultaneous fascination with and disapproval of Livermore is evident in the fact that such a volatile, aggressive woman is drawn into the family circle and allowed to partake in the Whittier's peaceful domesticity. Explorations of the historic figures in the poem, such as Livermore, provide modern critics with new opportunities for the investigations of the poem's subtleties.

CRITICISM

Catherine Dominic

Dominic is a novelist and a freelance writer and editor. In the following essay, she contends that Snow-Bound *exhibits characteristics of the poetic form of the elegy. In studying the elegiac components, Dominic demonstrates the significance of the act of grieving to the poem.*

In *Snow-Bound*, Whittier gives a fresh voice to a past that haunts him, rekindling the strong ties of family, friends, and faith that he remembers from his childhood. He provides the opportunity for the deceased to once again, in memory, have their say. In this way, Whittier honors the dead in his poem. References to the deaths of his loved ones are numerous, and the deep sense of loss Whittier felt as a result is expressed repeatedly. Some critics have discussed the attention Whittier gives to the passage of time and to the inevitability of death in *Snow-Bound*, yet these analyses often stress the way Whittier balances these dark elements with affirmations of hopefulness, salvation, and the permanence of familial bonds. Death may be one of the themes of the poem, but the poem itself is an act of grieving. As such, it may be regarded as an elegy. An elegy is a poem in which the death of an individual or a group is mourned. Elegies may take a variety of forms, but they typically feature expressions of sorrow, praise for the dead, and finally, consolation. In David Kennedy's 2007 study of the elegy, *Elegy*, the critic, citing a 1995 work by Peter Sacks (*The English Elegy: Studies in the Genre from Spenser to Yeats*) also lists the use of the pastoral context and images of resurrection as typical conventions of the elegy. Kennedy, in tracing the development of the elegy, stresses the ways in which it came to be associated with an individual expression of emotion, and with death in particular, as opposed to loss in general. Kennedy additionally observes that the genre of "pastoral elegy...examines change and loss against continuity." In *Snow-Bound*, Whittier employs the conventions of the elegy, including the expression of grief, the exaltation of the virtues of the dead, and the consolation derived from the hope of resurrection, within the pastoral, or idyl, form. Whittier explicitly draws attention to this form in the poem's subtitle: "A Winter Idyl." Studying the elegiac characteristics of *Snow-Bound* offers the reader more than just another label—elegy, pastoral, narrative verse—to affix to Whittier's poem. Such an examination brings to the foreground the grief that is as much at the heart of the poem as Whittier's treatment of the themes of family, faith, and the Northeastern American spirit.

WHAT DO I READ NEXT?

- Editor W. F. Jolliff introduces and compiles Whittier's poetry in *The Poetry of John Greenleaf Whittier: A Reader's Edition*, published by Friends United Press in 2000. Throughout the collection Jolliff prefaces individual poems with pertinent items of historical or thematic interest. A general introduction to Whittier and his works is provided as well.

- George Arms's *The Fields Were Green*, published in 1953 by Stanford University Press, is a collection of poetry by the Schoolroom Poets. Arms includes an overview of the poets and poetry of this group in his introduction.

- *African American Poetry of the Nineteenth Century: An Anthology*, edited by Joan R. Sherman and published in 1992 by the University of Illinois Press, offers a selection of poetry from well-known and obscure poets who wrote during Whittier's lifetime, often about similar themes, such as slavery, faith, and family.

- *Robert Merry's Museum* was a periodical published in the nineteenth century and written for younger readers. It was published from 1841 to 1872 and included children's stories and letters from children to the editors, including Samuel Goodrich, who founded the

magazine. The informative letters provide a glimpse into the daily lives of young Americans during the years leading up to, including, and directly following the Civil War. Numerous volumes of the work are available through Google Books and can be found by using the search term "Robert Merry's Museum." Students of Whittier's *Snow-Bound* will be provided with valuable historical anecdotes regarding the activities and interests of young people during this turbulent time in American history.

- Hal S. Barron's *Those Who Stayed Behind: Rural Society in Nineteenth-Century New England*, published by Cambridge University Press in 2008, explores the social and economic challenges faced by rural communities in New England during the nineteenth century.

- In *The Transformation of American Quakerism: Orthodox Friends, 1800–1907*, published by First Midland Books in 1992, Thomas D. Hamm traces the history and development of the Quaker religion in nineteenth-century America. Important figures are discussed, as is the major split experienced by the religion when Elias Hicks and his followers split from the group of Orthodox Quakers in the 1820s.

The first several stanzas of the poem tell of the approach of the storm, the preparations made, and the first night and day of the storm itself. The opening stanza in particular contains a number of words or images that set a somber tone for the poem. The day is short and dark, and the sun moves feebly through the course of the day, offering a gloomy light. The cold is deep and biting. The subsequent stanzas delineate the progress of the storm and the chores accomplished in anticipation of it.

Not until line 179 does Whittier arrive at the subject of his family. As the family prepares to settle in by the fire with food and drink, Whittier

mourns the passage of time. He begins this section in general terms, explaining first that his hair is now as gray as his father's hair was during the events he is relating. His wail to the forces of time and to change, at first obscure, now is clarified as the reader understands that the Whittier telling the story is now an old man himself. (He was fifty-nine when the poem was published in 1866.) Whittier observes how unsettling it is to still go on living when so much he has loved, so much of the life he cherished, is now gone. At line 183, Whittier offers at last the reason for his anguish when he, addressing his brother, states that of the circle that gathered in front of the fire during the snowstorm

> IN *SNOW-BOUND*, WHITTIER EMPLOYS THE CONVENTIONS OF THE ELEGY, INCLUDING THE EXPRESSION OF GRIEF, THE EXALTATION OF THE VIRTUES OF THE DEAD, AND THE CONSOLATION DERIVED FROM THE HOPE OF RESURRECTION, WITHIN THE PASTORAL, OR IDYL, FORM."

he is recalling, only he and his brother remain; the rest have died. The "we" Whittier has referred to in the poem is now understood to be Whittier and his brother. He has not yet explained who the other members of that circle are.

Having spent a number of stanzas describing the storm itself and what was done outside—Whittier and his brother, for example, cleared a path to the barn and fed the animals—Whittier turns to the family inside the home, and when he does so, the story of the storm continues. At the same time, his elegy truly begins. When he recalls the dead throughout the poem, Whittier uses a combination of lament (a mourning of loss) and exaltation of the dead (praise of their character), followed by a consolation (the attempt to soothe his grief, most often with an expression of faith). Whittier's lament for his family members is the first elegiac element to appear within the idyl. Whittier notes that no matter how hard he and his brother listen for the voices of the others, they will hear nothing. From lines 185 through 199, Whittier mourns the loss of his loved ones by describing the Whittier homestead in terms of absence. He will no longer hear the voices of his loved ones chatting in front of the fire, nor will he see their smiling faces. He may walk the paths he once walked with his departed family members, and he may sit in the orchard, listening to the murmur of the bees and the sound of the wind in the cornfields. He may read the books they once read, or read what they themselves wrote. Yet they can no longer cast a shadow or speak a word, Whittier states. In the way Whittier captures his sense of loss, by cataloging the activities he once shared with this family and then by discussing the absence of their physical presence—their footsteps, their voices, even the

ability to cast a shadow—Whittier is demonstrating that his memory of his family is insufficient. His longing for their companionship, for their substantial presence rather than their immaterial memory, is evident, as is his grief.

Turning to his faith in God for consolation, Whittier assures himself that one day, somewhere, he will meet his loved ones again. Imagining the pain of burying one's dead without this faith in an afterlife with them, Whittier reassures himself of the enduring power of love. Assuaging his grief in this manner, Whittier resumes his story, describing the tales told by the fire, first his father's and then his mother's. Following the stories offered by his aunt and his uncle, Whittier arrives at his older sister, Mary. He speaks of her nature, rather than of anything he recalls of that night specifically. Exhibiting the characteristics of an elegy through their praise of the dead, lines 380 through 385 pay homage to Whittier's sister Mary. Whittier describes Mary as trusting and honest, eager and earnest, and possessing a generous, self-sacrificing nature. Whittier follows the exaltation of Mary's character with another, now recurring element of the elegiac form, the lament and the consolation. In lines 386 through 391, Whittier grieves the loss of his sister, a woman, he observes, who blessed the lives of others. Once again Whittier consoles himself with his faith in an afterlife in which Mary may be at rest and have respite from the bitterness of life.

Next Whittier turns to his younger sister, Elizabeth. After acknowledging his belief that she now resides in heaven, Whittier embarks upon the longest lament *Snow-Bound* conveys. From lines 403 through 421, Whittier expresses a deep and abiding sense of loss. He wonders if Elizabeth is watching him from her place in heaven. The pain of her death is fresh; she died in 1864, a year before Whittier wrote *Snow-Bound*. Having described her grave in winter, Whittier goes on to recall the activities he shared with his sister when she was alive. In painting such a vivid picture in which the sweetness of the air, the bloom of the flowers, and the song of the birds is recalled, the emptiness he now feels in traversing the walks he shared with Elizabeth is especially poignant and tragic. The elegiac consolation that follows is as prolonged as the lament itself. Whittier reminds himself of how enriched he is by the memories he retains of his sister. Describing her as safe now in her immortal resting place, Whittier considers his own death. He envisions himself at sunset (a metaphor for the

The characters in the poem gather around the fire while snow bound. (*Image copyright Bob Cheung, 2010. Used under license from Shutterstock.com*)

final days of his life) walking toward his sister, whose hand is outstretched toward him, welcoming him.

For several stanzas, Whittier sets aside his mourning and returns to the tale of the snowstorm, recounting the arrival of the ox carts to plow a road, and the delivery of the village paper, which reconnects the family with the rest of the world. As the period of isolation forced by the snowstorm draws to a close, Whittier turns one last time to elegiac forms, combining lament and consolation in the penultimate stanza of the poem. He speaks of the inevitable forward march of time as well as the ghosts of the pasts. Here is the continuity the pastoral elegy offers as a counterweight to loss and death. The stanza repeatedly juxtaposes loss and death with the certainty of time's progress and life, as when he speaks of verdant hills representing life that slope inevitably toward death, or of the sorrowful cypress trees (cypress is a common Christian symbol for death, mourning, and immortality)

that are contrasted with the white amaranth growing beneath them (white amaranth is life-giving in the sense that the seeds, leaves, and blossoms are edible). Whittier's final expression of consolation occurs in the final stanza of the poem, when he considers the notion that *Snow-Bound* might offer comfort to future readers.

Whether or not Whittier's poem is viewed as an elegy or as a poem containing elegiac elements, the repeated use of the elegiac constructs of lament and consolation suggest the centrality of grieving to the poem's overall meaning. The past, while remembered fondly, is not treated purely in nostalgic terms. It is as much as source of sorrow as of comfort to Whittier. In particular, the death of Elizabeth, the freshest in Whittier's mind as he composed the poem, is of major importance. The lament is long and anguished, and the consolation that follows involves thoughts of Whittier's own death. The other sections of lament in the poem are followed by consolations that focus on Whittier's acceptance of death and sense of peace in knowing that his loved ones are at rest. The pain of Elizabeth's death is so great, however, that Whittier can only console himself by envisioning the day that he will be reunited with his sister when he himself dies. The presence of the elegiac element in Whittier's poem enriches its meaning and balances its more lighthearted components, leaving the reader with the sensation of having truly shared in the another's experience, with all the joy and sorrow that entails.

Source: Catherine Dominic, Critical Essay on *Snow-Bound*, in *Poetry for Students*, Gale, Cengage Learning, 2011.

James E. Rocks

In the following excerpt, Rocks considers the context of Whittier's life at the time he composed Snow-Bound.

When John Greenleaf Whittier's younger sister Elizabeth, the companion of his mature years, died on 3 September 1864, he suffered a loss no less severe than if a wife of many years had died. More sociable than her shy brother, Elizabeth had been at the center of his life, the person whose support had helped nurture a public career of considerable success and fame and a private domestic life of exceptional warmth and security. Writing to his wide circle of friends, particularly to Gail Hamilton, Grace Greenwood, and Lydia Maria Child, he expressed the profound depression that her death had induced, but also his acceptance of the will of God that had determined the course of his sister's illness and death. To Annie Fields, his publisher's wife and among his closest women friends, he wrote: "I find it difficult even now to understand and realize all I have lost. But I sorrow without repining, and with a feeling of calm submission to the Will which I am sure is best."

While acceptance of the divine ways distinguishes Whittier's letters to his consoling friends, Elizabeth's death brought about a major transition in his life. One consequence of this change was a temporary failure with language; the glib pen that had composed dozens of poems on national, political, and social topics was unable to express this personal loss. To Theodore Tilton, a New York journalist who supported abolition and women's rights, Whittier expressed his speechlessness in a terse, poetic line: "I cannot now write anything worthy of her memory." Responding to his friends' condolences was painful but necessary; expressing the meaning of his sister's life as his companion and

> *SNOW-BOUND* DESERVES TO BE REREAD FOR THE WEALTH OF ITS CONNECTIONS TO THE IMPORTANT DISCUSSIONS OF THE TIME ON FAMILY AND HOME."

the domestic order and tranquility which she, like their parents before her, had sustained for him was far more difficult. Within a year the Civil War concluded, and one of his last, and best, anti-slavery poems "Laus Deo" put some finality on a lifetime of combatting slavery. And by October 1865 he finished the work that was "worthy of her memory." Published in February 1866, *Snow-Bound* became Whittier's most popular and famous—and his best—work, one of the important autobiographical writings of the nineteenth century. It was, as Robert Penn Warren has aptly called it, a "summarizing poem," because in it Whittier discovered the power of language again—the very weapon against the destructive, frightening natural world that his solitary family employs in the charmed circle around the hearth—and because the poem articulated the domestic and gender ideology of Whittier's time to an audience ready to be healed after the schism of the Civil War and responsive to a philosophy that linked home, hearth, and heaven into one vision of a unified past and future.

Readings of *Snow-Bound* have generally not placed the poem in the context of Whittier's whole life—why the poem came to be at a critical time in his personal life, his public career, and the post-Civil War period of anticipated reconciliation and the reuniting of the "house divided." Studies have recognized the complexity of his personality and the interrelationship of his work and his times and, more recently, his advocacy of women in the literary marketplace, but they have not examined sufficiently the domestic and gender ideological issues that give the poem its considerable relevance as a coalescence of the discourses on domestic economy during the first half of the nineteenth century. *Snow-Bound* deserves to be reread for the wealth of its connections to the important discussions of the time on family and home. Whittier's definition of the masculine and the feminine in the poem reveals his long-held beliefs about his own gender identity, at a time when male writers often felt insecure about their masculinity in a commercial world, and discloses his traditional values regarding the family and women's role, which was defined in the writings of, among others, Catharine Beecher and her sister Harriet Beecher Stowe, as that of the dominant moral authority of society. While his portrayal of women in *Snow-Bound* does partake of the sentimental tradition of the time, his views in that poem, as well as in his letters, transcend the purely patriarchal and reflect his strong Quaker principle of human rights.

In an essay on the Scottish poet William Burleigh in the 9 September 1847 issue of the *National Era,* the anti-slavery paper of which he was for fifteen years a contributing editor and in which most of his literary works appeared until the founding of the *Atlantic Monthly* in 1857, Whittier described a poetic country very like the one he would create in *Snow-Bound.* The charm of the poetry of Scotland, he wrote, was "its simplicity, and genuine, affected sympathy with the common joys and sorrows of daily life. It is a hometaught, household melody." He also lamented that the poetry of home, nature, and the affections was lacking in America; there were no songs of American domestic life, "no Yankee pastorals." By the time Whittier accomplished in *Snow-Bound* his call for a native form of the antique genre, there were already major examples of the pastoral, but by the mid-1860s the genre was rather played out (except of course for Whitman), and much of the appeal of *Snow-Bound* was its backward glance to a simpler world, to a time prior to the social and political upheaval of the 1830s to 1860s. Whittier's readers had always valued him for what James Russell Lowell, in the *North American Review* of January 1864, called his "intense home-feeling." Later, in a review of *Snow-Bound,* Lowell expressed the effect of the poem's nostalgia on a sentimental audience: "It describes scenes and manners which the rapid changes of our national habits will soon have made as remote from us as if they were foreign or ancient." Lowell was correct in his assessment of the poem's appeal, but his future verb tense was mistaken; by the time of the publication of Whittier's major poem, those rapid social changes had already made the scenes and manners of the world of Whittier's boyhood farm remote and quaint for many of his readers.

In *Snow-Bound* Whittier returned to his youthful past for two immediate, compelling, yet contradictory reasons. He wanted his niece Lizzie to know the family portrait, and he needed the money that a longer poem about the rural past could earn. But there were also other reasons, perhaps not so easily identified, that inspired his "winter idyl." Creating this poem would bring further healing to the recovery from his loss of Elizabeth and, unaware as he might have been of another consequence, it would contribute in a small way to the public appeals for national reconciliation after the Civil War. And most importantly *Snow-Bound* would characterize a domestic ideology of home and hearth that dated as it might have seemed to some readers in Whittier's time, was, however, a representation of the principal values that had defined the American family in the nineteenth century. Whittier's desire to recreate his home life served both his own practical and emotional needs and those of a nation seeking order once again; for Whittier the time could not have been more favorable.

On the flyleaf of a first edition of *Snow-Bound,* Whittier wrote some lines in 1888 expressing the faith and peace of his old age (he would die within two years). Thinking of the time when he composed his pastoral, he wrote about his sorrow then: "Lone and weary life seemed when / First these pictures of the pen / Grew upon my page." The general dispiritedness and lack of confidence in his poetic ability, exacerbated by and contributing to his chronic ill health, are reflected in the letters he wrote, primarily to James T. Fields, during the several months (August to October 1865) while he was composing and revising the poem. Because Whittier tended to be self-effacing in his correspondence—and particularly so to other writers and his publisher—he refers to his manuscript only as "tolerably good" or "pretty good." To Lucy Larcom, a close friend of Elizabeth and one of his "pupils" among the women authors he knew, Whittier wrote in a postscript to a letter in January 1866, a month before the poem's publication: "I'm not without my misgivings about it." On the other hand, reading proofs of it in December 1865, he wrote Fields that he agreed with him and his wife Annie that the poem was "good"; furthermore, he took a particular interest in its physical make-up, engravings, and date of publication (a December distribution would make it a timely gift-book, he suggested), and fussed over some last-minute revisions. His anxieties were groundless: within two months of the February publication, *Snow-Bound* had sold 10,000 copies and by mid-summer 20,000 copies. Ultimately Whittier earned $10,000 from this one volume; its success provided him economic security and reaffirmed his poetic reputation.

Source: James E. Rocks, "Whittier's *Snow-Bound*: The Circle of Our Hearth and the Discourse on Domesticity," in *Studies in the American Renaissance 1993*, edited by Joel Myerson, University of Virginia Press, 1993, pp. 339–53.

Helen L. Drew

In the following essay, Drew argues that the school teacher in Snow-Bound *was based on George Haskell, not Joshua Coffin, as has often been assumed.*

The decision of a careful editor in favor of Joshua Coffin as the schoolmaster in Whittier's *Snow-Bound* makes it pertinent to review the evidence for Coffin and that in favor of Dr. George Haskell. There may be added to the evidence a fact not hitherto noticed in connection with it, and whatever weight lies in a tradition existing in Rockford, Illinois, the community to which Haskell migrated, that *he* was the schoolmaster.

For the Riverside Edition of his poems in 1888, Whittier in his note to the poem "To My Old Schoolmaster" named Joshua Coffin as the man there celebrated, while in his note to *Snow-Bound* he left the schoolmaster of that story unnamed. The two poems do not refer to the same year of Whittier's life. Joshua Coffin is spoken of in "To My Old Schoolmaster" as having taught Whittier his ABC's; the district schoolmaster in *Snow-Bound*, if we can trust the poem to be true to fact, was his teacher when he was old enough to share in the work of shovelling the path to the barn. The statement in S. T. Pickard's biography: "Some years afterward, in 1821, Coffin was again a teacher in that district, and he spent many of his evenings at the Whittier homestead, a most welcome guest," would seem to make it possible that Coffin could have been the prototype for both portraits. But it seems probable that if he had been, Whittier would have said so in his note to *Snow-Bound*, especially when he maintained connection with Coffin through their work for the antislavery cause. In his note for "To My Old Schoolmaster" he calls Coffin "my worthy friend" and in the poem says:

> As remembering thee, I blend
> Olden teacher, present friend.

We have also the testimony of Pickard, a biographer who knew Whittier, that the poet later remembered the name of the schoolmaster he had portrayed in *Snow-Bound* to have been Haskell. He says:

> Until near the end of Mr. Whittier's life, he could not recall the name of this teacher whose portrait is so carefully sketched, but he was sure he came from Maine. At length, he remembered that his name was Haskell, and from this clue it has been ascertained that he was George Haskell, and that he came from Waterford, Maine.

The fact that has not been brought to bear upon the matter is that S. T. Pickard was a nephew of Joshua Coffin's. Certainly he would not be establishing the claim of George Haskell if he were not sure that the honor did not belong to his uncle.

Source: Helen L. Drew, "The Schoolmaster in *Snow-Bound*," in *American Literature*, Vol. 9, No. 2, May 1937, pp. 243–44.

Nathaniel L. Sayles

In the following essay, Sayles explains the allusion to the game of crosspins used by Whittier in his poem.

> Played cross-pins on my uncle's hat....

When, a short time ago, Professor S. F. Davidson of Indiana University asked his class in American Literature to explain a number of allusions in Whittier's *Snow-Bound*, I was somewhat surprised to learn that no one was acquainted with the game "cross-pins." A search in the *New English Dictionary*, through biographies of Whittier, and through notes on the poem had failed to reveal any explanation. The general opinion seemed to be that the game was a form of jack-straws. But not for me.

Fourteen years ago in Meadville, Pennsylvania, every small boy played cross-pins. We would borrow our mother's straight pins and play for hours at a time on someone's hat. The hat was placed on a flat surface with the brim down and the crown dented slightly so that there was a little circular depression at the center. One of us would place a pin in the middle of the depression, and another would lay his on the edge of the crown with the point toward the center. Taking care not to hit the pin, the latter would thump sharply the rim of the crown and make the pin fly into the center of the hat. If he could thump his pin so that any part of it lay across his opponent's, he won that pin. Then it was the opponent's turn to thump.

We all carried hat-bands and coat-lapels full of pins to school, and whenever two of us could get together, we took a whirl at this game of chance. Although Mr. Hoyle would have had us always use a hat, we sometimes had to substitute a cap. Only very small boys played, for, as I remember, at eight years I was sufficiently grown up to leave off cross-pins for marbles.

Source: Nathaniel L. Sayles, "A Note on Whittier's *Snow-Bound*," in *American Literature*, Vol. 6, No. 3, November 1934, pp. 336–37.

James Russell Lowell

In the following review, Lowell praises Snow-Bound *for its "spiritual picturesqueness" as well as its historical importance, although he is critical of Whittier's "carelessness in accents and rhymes."*

We are again indebted to Mr. Whittier, as we have been so often before, for a very real and a very refined pleasure. The little volume before us [*Snow-Bound: A Winter Idyl*] has all his most characteristic merits. It is true to Nature and in local coloring, pure in sentiment, quietly deep in feeling, and full of those simple touches which show the poetic eye and the trained hand. Here is a New England interior glorified with something of that inward light which is apt to be rather warmer in the poet than the Quaker, but which, blending the qualities of both in Mr. Whittier, produces that kind of spiritual picturesqueness which gives so peculiar a charm to his verse. There is in this poem a warmth of affectionate memory and religious faith as touching as it is uncommon, and which would be altogether delightful if it did not remind us that the poet was growing old. Not that there is any other mark of senescence than the ripened sweetness of a life both publicly and privately well spent. There is fire enough, but it glows more equably and shines on sweeter scenes than in the poet's earlier verse. It is as if a brand from the camp-fire had kindled these logs on the old homestead's hearth, whose flickering benediction touches tremulously those dear heads of long ago that are now transfigured with a holier light. The father, the mother, the uncle, the schoolmaster, the uncanny guest, are all painted in warm and natural colors, with perfect truth of detail and yet with all the tenderness of memory. Of the family group the poet is the last on earth, and there is something deeply touching in the pathetic sincerity of the affection which has outlived them all, looking back to before the parting, and forward to the assured reunion.

But aside from its poetic and personal interest, and the pleasure it must give to every one who loves pictures from the life, *Snow-Bound* has something of historical interest. It describes scenes and manners which the rapid changes of our national habits will soon have made as remote from us as if they were foreign or ancient. Already, alas! even in farm-houses, backlog and forestick are obsolescent words, and close-mouthed stoves chill the spirit while they bake the flesh with their grim and undemonstrative hospitality. Already are the railroads displacing the companionable cheer of crackling walnut with the dogged self-complacency

and sullen virtue of anthracite. Even where wood survives, he is too often shut in the dreary madhouse cell of an air-tight, round which one can no more fancy a social mug of flip circling than round a coffin. Let us be thankful that we can sit in Mr. Whittier's chimney-corner and believe that the blaze he has kindled for us shall still warm and cheer, when a wood fire is as faint a tradition in New as in Old England.

We have before had occasion to protest against Mr. Whittier's carelessness in accents and rhymes, as in pronouncing "lýceum," and joining in unhallowed matrimony such sounds as *awn* and *orn, ents* and *ence*. We would not have the Muse emulate the unidiomatic preciseness of a Normal schoolmistress, but we cannot help thinking that, if Mr. Whittier writes thus on principle, as we begin to suspect, he errs in forgetting that thought so refined as his can be fitly matched only with an equal refinement of expression, and loses something of its charm when cheated of it. We hope he will, at least, never mount Pegásus, or water him in Helícon, and that he will leave Múseum to the more vulgar sphere and obtuser sensibilities of Barnum. Where Nature has sent genius, she has a right to expect that it shall be treated with a certain elegance of hospitality.

Source: James Russell Lowell, Review *of Snow-Bound*, in *North American Review*, Vol. 102, No. 211, April 1866, pp. 631–32.

SOURCES

Bacon, Margaret Hope, "The Middle Years of American Quakerism: 1775–1875," and "The Abolition of Slavery," in *The Quiet Rebels: The Story of the Quakers in America*, 1985, New Society Publishers, pp. 70–93, 94–121.

"Biographical Sketch," in *Snow-Bound, The Tent on the Beach, and Other Poems by John Greenleaf Whittier*, Houghton Mifflin, 1896, pp. v–viii.

"A Brief Guide to New Formalism," in *Poets.org*, http://www.poets.org/viewmedia.php/prmMID/5667 (accessed January 20, 2010).

"Children's Books of the Year," in *North American Review*, January 1866, pp. 236–49.

"Distribution of Quakers in the World," in *Quaker Information Center: A Gateway to Quakerism*, http://www.quakerinfo.org/resources/worldstats.html (accessed January 20, 2010).

"A Divided Nation: Causes of the Civil War," in *World Book Encyclopedia and Learning Resources*, http://www.worldbook.com/wb/Students?content_spotlight/civil_war (accessed January 20, 2010).

Fischer, David Hackett, "North Midlands to the Delaware: The Friends' Migration, 1675–1725," in *Albion's Seed: Four British Folkways in America*, Oxford University Press, 1989, pp. 419–604.

Jordan, Gregory E., "Wind and Fire: St. Catherine of Siena and the North Wind in John Greenleaf Whittier's *Snow-Bound*," in *ANQ*, Vol. 8, No. 1, Winter 1995, pp. 18–21.

Kennedy, David, "Form without Frontiers," and "What Was Elegy?," in *Elegy*, Routledge, 2007, pp. 1–9, 10–34.

Pickard, John B., "Imagistic and Structural Unity in *Snow-Bound*," in *Critical Essays on John Greenleaf Whittier*, edited by Jayne K. Kribbs, G. K. Hall, 1980, pp. 130–36.

Saad, Lydia, "U.S. Waiting for Race Relations to Improve under Obama," in *Gallup: Politics*, November 9, 2009, http://www.gallup.com/poll/124181/u.s.-waiting-race-relations-improve-obama.aspx (accessed January 21, 2010).

Schneider, Dorothy, and Carl J. Schneider, "The Argument over Slavery: 1637–1877," "The End of Slavery: 1861–1877," and "Reconstruction: 1865–1877," in *Slavery in America*, Facts on File, 2007, pp. 248–86, 318–45, 346–94.

Scudder, Horace Elisha, ed., "Notes and Queries," in *Snow-Bound, Among the Hills, Songs of Labor, and Other Poems*, Houghton Mifflin, 1878, reprint, 1916, pp. 94–107.

"Secession," in *World Book Encyclopedia and Learning Resources*, http://www.worldbook.com/wb/Students?content_spotlight/civil_war/secession (accessed January 20, 2010).

Vining, Elizabeth Gray, "*Snow-Bound*," in *Mr. Whittier*, Viking, 1974, pp. 132–38.

von Frank, Albert J., "John Greenleaf Whittier," in *Dictionary of Literary Biography*, Vol. 243, *The American Renaissance in New England, Fourth Series*, edited by Wesley T. Mott, The Gale Group, 2001, pp. 360–71.

Warren, Robert Penn, "John Greenleaf Whittier: Poetry as Experience," in *John Greenleaf Whittier's Poetry: An Appraisal and a Selection*, University of Minnesota Press, 1971, pp. 3–61.

Webber, F. R., and Ralph Adams Cram, "A Glossary of the More Common Symbols," in *Church Symbolism*, J. H. Jansen, 1927, pp. 357–94.

Wesley, Marilyn C., "The Not Unfeared, Half-welcome Guest: The Woman Traveler in John Greenleaf Whittier's *Snow-Bound*," in *Secret Journeys: The Trope of Women's Travel in American Literature*, State University of New York, 1999, pp. 3–20.

"What Do Quakers Believe?," in *Quaker Information Center: A Gateway to Quakerism*, http://www.quakerinfo.org/quakerism/beliefs.html (accessed January 20, 2010).

Whittier, John Greenleaf, "Introduction to *Snow-Bound*," in *Snow-Bound, Among the Hills, Songs of Labor, and Other Poems*, edited by Horace Elisha Scudder, Houghton Mifflin, 1878, reprint, 1916, pp. 94–95.

———, *Snow-Bound*, in *Snow-Bound, Among the Hills, Songs of Labor, and Other Poems*, edited by Horace Elisha Scudder, Houghton Mifflin, 1878, reprint, 1916, pp. 3–23.

FURTHER READING

Colbert, C. C., *The Other Civil War: American Women in the Nineteenth Century*, Hill and Wang, 1984.
    Colbert examines the social and economic impact of the Civil War on American women.

Cooper, Wilmer, A., *A Living Faith: An Historical and Comparative Study of Quaker Beliefs*, Friends United Press, 1990.
    Cooper offers a detailed discussion of the theology of Quakerism prefaced by an overview of the history of the faith.

Kete, Mary Louise, *Sentimental Collaborations: Mourning and Middle-class Identity in Nineteenth-Century America*, Duke University Press, 2000.
    Kete surveys the treatment of death and mourning in the poetry and literature of nineteenth-centuryAmerica. The work includes an examination of the relationship between personal grief, literary sentimentality, and political agendas, such as abolitionism.

Pickard, Samuel Thomas, *Life and Letters of John Greenleaf Whittier*, Vols. 1 and 2, Bibliolife, 2008.
    Originally published in 1894, Pickard's biography and collected correspondence offers a comprehensive assessment of Whittier's life and works.

SUGGESTED SEARCH TERMS

Snow-Bound AND Whittier

John Greenleaf Whittier

John Greenleaf Whittier poems

John Greenleaf Whittier biography

Whittier AND pastoral

Whittier AND schoolroom poets

Whittier AND Quakerism

Whittier AND abolitionism

Whittier AND Snow-Bound

Song to the Men of England

PERCY BYSSHE SHELLEY

1819

While Percy Bysshe Shelley is often thought of today primarily as a poet, he is also an important figure in the history of the democratization of western Europe and of the development of socialism. He formed a theory of nonviolent resistance to oppression and was acknowledged as an inspiration by Gandhi. Shelley developed his political ideas in poetic form. His early work *Queen Mab* was perhaps his most influential, becoming known as the bible of the Chartists (a movement for democratic reform in England in the 1830s), but the Peterloo Massacre in 1819, in which a crowd of working class men, women, and children demanding the broadening of the right to vote were attacked by the British army, inspired Shelley to produced a torrent of political poems and pamphlets calling for political revolution. Among them was his 1819 poem "Song to the Men of England," which can be found in most larger collections of Shelley's verse, for instance, the standard textbook *English Romantic Writers*.

Shelley is recognized as one of the great poets of the second generation of romantics in the early nineteenth century, alongside John Keats and George Gordon, Lord Byron. Poems like "Ozymandias" and "To a Skylark" single him out as among the greatest lyric poets in English from any period. He also produced longer works of great psychological and literary depth such as *Prometheus Unbound* and *The Witch of Atlas* that are comparable to the work of John Milton or T. S. Eliot. However, relatively little of Shelley's work

Percy Bysshe Shelley (The Library of Congress)

was published in his own lifetime, and, given the very rich manuscript sources of Shelley's writings that survive, not all of his extant poetry has yet been published.

AUTHOR BIOGRAPHY

Shelley was born to aristocratic parents in Sussex, England, on August 4, 1792. His grandfather was a baronet whose title was eventually inherited by Shelley's son, Percy Florence, whose mother was Shelley's second wife, Mary. Shelley had a conventional education, beginning at home with tutors and continuing at Eton (a prestigious boys' boarding school). Shelley was literarily precocious, publishing a book of poetry and a novel (*Zastrozzi*) while still at Eton. In 1810 he began to study at University College, Oxford, but was expelled in less than a year for publishing *The Necessity of Atheism*, espousing the then radical position of disbelief in any god whatsoever. This also caused a breach with his father, who cut Shelley off from most of the family wealth. He eloped with Harriet Westbrook with whom he had several children. In 1811 Shelley visited Ireland and spoke and wrote in favor of Irish independence, which brought him to the attention of British legal authorities.

In 1814 Shelley abandoned his wife and children and entered the politically radical circle of William Godwin. He moved to the continent with Godwin's daughter Mary, frequently traveling with Lord Byron. Shelley was not able to wed Mary until 1816 when his first wife killed herself. Taking up residence in Switzerland, Shelley wrote "Mont Blanc," a romantic meditation on history and existence, while Mary wrote the famous novel *Frankenstein, or the Modern Prometheus*. Moving to Italy, Shelley then wrote *Prometheus Unbound*, a recreation of a lost play by the ancient Greek dramatist Aeschylus.

In 1819, Shelley heard about the Peterloo Massacre in Manchester, England, in which a group of several thousand workers gathered together to demand the right to vote in parliamentary elections but were attacked by government troops, who killed about a dozen people and wounded over five hundred more. Shelley was outraged by this blow to the cause of political reform and wrote a string of poems and other writings criticizing the British government, including *The Mask of Anarchy*, the sonnet "England in 1819," and "Song to the Men of England," as well as the pamphlet *The Philosophical View of Reform*. Shelley remained in Italy because it would have been politically dangerous for him to return to England. In 1822, he wrote *Adonais*, a meditation on the death of John Keats, whose work as a poet Shelley alone among the leading romantics fully appreciated. Shelley himself died on July 8, 1822, in a boating accident off the coast of Tuscany. It has sometimes been suggested that Shelley was assassinated by British agents, but this seems unlikely. His body was cremated (except his heart, which Mary Shelley preserved as a keepsake), and his ashes are buried in the Protestant Cemetery in Rome. University College, Oxford, which once expelled him, now houses a monument to Shelley's genius.

POEM SUMMARY

In "Song to the Men of England" Shelley presents in simple language, using simple metaphors, literary devices, and much repetition in the manner of a popular song, the case for significant social reform based on equality and the overthrow of the British class system, which is presented as having become destructive of the lower classes, that is, the greater mass of society. He asks the men of England why they collaborate in their own oppression and destruction and do not instead simply refuse to obey and enforce the laws and social structures that oppress them. If they do not change, he warns, they will end in the grave.

The use of the word *song* in the title reflects Shelley's intention that the piece become a popular song as part of the political movement for reform, although it remained unpublished in his lifetime and was never set to music. The remainder of the title takes the form of an address, as if Shelley were writing a letter to the men of England at large. The use of *men* is quite intended. Although Shelley's mother-in-law, Mary Wollstonecraft, had already envisioned political and social equality for women including the right to vote in her *A Vindication of the Rights of Women*, and Shelley may ultimately have agreed with her, in the circumstances of 1819 he was satisfied with the more practical project of gaining voting rights for all men.

Stanza 1

In the very first sentence of the poem Shelley accuses the aristocratic class of attacking the common people of England. This is a reference to the Peterloo Massacre in which the British army attacked a group of workers in Manchester who had gathered together to publicly demand the right to vote. The purpose of the attack was indeed to preserve the class structure of English society in which all political power was concentrated in a small landowning aristocracy. Aristocratic rule is characterized as a tyranny, meaning that its rule is illegitimate because it does not represent the interests of the English population as a whole or even a majority of it. As he does throughout the poem, Shelley rhetorically questions the working class about why they continue to farm for the landowners and work in the factories (mostly textile mills in 1819) of the wealthy industrialists who seem bent on their destruction and oppression.

Stanza 2

In the second stanza Shelley again asks the workers why they spend their whole lives working to enrich aristocrats. The landlords and factory workers are now likened to drones, male bees who eat the honey provided by the worker bees, but who do nothing productive themselves. The drones ungratefully take everything the workers make and demand more, even their blood. This is another reference to the deaths in the Peterloo Massacre.

Stanza 3

Shelley now extends the bee metaphor. The men of England are addressed as worker bees. The drones are described as taking by force what the workers make. This means the force of law because workers must either pay their rent on farmland or accept their wages as payment, but the law is backed up by the threat of physical force, either by the police or, if the aristocrats feel threatened enough as at Peterloo, by the army. The aristocratic drones themselves, Shelley says, lack any weapons of their own. In fact, the threat of force against English workers from the police or army is only possible with the consent of the working class. In the first instance, of course, workers manufacture the weapons that are used against them, but, more pointedly, workers make up the personnel of the police and the army. If they refused to enforce the class structure and the rule of the landed gentry, the aristocrats would be powerless to do it themselves. Shelley is anticipating the socialist slogan "a bayonet is a weapon with a worker on both ends," meaning that it is possible for aristocrats to control and exploit the workers only because the workers themselves comply with the system. It is important to remember that physical punishment was frequently exercised by factory owners: workers who committed workplace infractions or simply worked too slowly could be and were whipped by supervisors.

Stanza 4

Shelley rhetorically asks the men of England if they have adequate living conditions, expecting the answer that they do not. With the slump in wages and rising food prices after the industrial boom of the Napoleonic Wars, with the long hours required of factory workers, and with no benefits that modern workers enjoy such as vacations, days off, or medical care, workers felt pushed to the edge, under threat of malnutrition and starvation. Even farm workers did not enjoy any benefit from high food prices because they were paid by being allowed to keep part of their crop, rarely more than was necessary for them to feed their own families and use as seed corn. Shelley reminds workers that in addition to being so poorly compensated for their work, they must live in fear, another reference to the threat of coercive violence from the government as at Peterloo.

Stanza 5

In this stanza Shelley makes his most sophisticated division of the laboring classes, referring to farm workers, miners, industrial workers in the textile mills, and workers servicing the factories and shipyards that supported the armed forces. Shelley does not now ask but rather tells them that they all have in common the fact that their work and the wealth it creates does not benefit themselves but others, namely the aristocratic classes.

Stanza 6

Shelley for the first time calls on the men of England to act to change their conditions. They should continue to work, but not let the aristocratic classes rob them of the wealth their labor creates. Although this could certainly be read in a highly socialistic manner, as, for example, calling for the workers' control of factories, such sophisticated economic ideas did not exist in 1819. More likely he is simply calling for social reforms aimed at creating equality, such as the crowds at Peterloo wanted, which would lead to a more fair distribution of wealth and a legal regime that would favor the interests of the greatest number of people rather than the narrow interests of those already wealthy and powerful.

Stanza 7

Shelley now chides the men of England, suggesting that they are too cowardly to face their oppressors and ought therefore to hide themselves away in their hovels far from the mansions of the rich rather than face oppression by the very weapons they have made. Shelley's tone is ironic. He is actually calling on the men to do precisely the opposite, to stand up for their rights against oppression and tyranny.

Stanza 8

Finally, Shelley suggests that the alternative to political reform is death, a metaphor for the unabated oppression of the men of England if they do not act in their own interests. The men of England are presented using the characteristic tools of their professions to make their own tombs.

THEMES

Utopianism

The ancient Roman author Virgil wrote a short Epic poem in four books about life in the countryside known as the *Georgics*. The first book concerns the land itself, the second farming and horticulture, the third animal husbandry, and the fourth

TOPICS FOR FURTHER STUDY

- Read the speeches collected in *Che Guevera Talks to Young People*, translated by Mary-Alice Waters and published in 2000, in which Che Guevera calls on the youth of Cuba and the world to live revolutionary lives. What themes do the speeches have in common with Shelley's "Song to the Men of England"? How do both authors develop these themes? How do they differ in their style and in the content of their message? Write a paper exploring these two calls to revolution.

- Write a song about your reaction to an event in American history that has similarities to the Peterloo Massacre, such as the Kent State shootings, the Stonewall riots, or the Selma voting rights march. Record your song using the Garageband computer program or sing the song to your class if you feel comfortable doing so.

- Create a PowerPoint presentation comparing various nonviolent resistance moments such as Gandhi's campaign to liberate India, the American civil rights movement, the Tiananmen Square movement, and the present campaigns for civil rights in Iran and Tibet.

- Write an imaginary letter from Gandhi to Shelley discussing his practical application of the poet's ideas.

- Read the *Autobiography of Malcolm X* and Shelley's 1819 works including *A Philosophical View of Reform* and "Song to the Men of England." Write a paper comparing the attitudes of both authors regarding civil rights reform.

beekeeping. Virgil's description of life within the bee hive is a satirical allegory of his own contemporary society. Virgil describes the bee hive as a sort of utopia that mankind ought to emulate. For instance, he says that the bees live without sexual desire, because he believes that they reproduce by shutting up drops of nectar in the wax cells of the hive that spontaneously generate into young bees.

All of the bees work together without compulsion and equally share the honey and shelters (hives) that they build. The only difficulty the bees face is when they produce drones who lead the hive into swarms that fight each other as in war, leaving vast number of bees dead. The drone whose swarm eventually wins rules over all and is revealed to be superior to ordinary bees, in contrast to his defeated foes who are exposed as robbers and bandits. This has nothing to do with the behavior of real bees but is a comment on the civil wars that plagued the Roman world in Virgil's lifetime and on the new imperial system of government under his patron the Emperor Augustus.

Shelley had a fine classical education, so Virgil was at the heart of his intellectual world. Shelley would naturally assume that many readers of his poems would know Virgil as well, since reading Latin rather than learning English was the basis of any formal education in the nineteenth century: a grammar school was originally understood to be a Latin grammar school. Learning Latin almost invariably meant reading Virgil as the first author. Shelley undoubtedly found in the egalitarian society of Virgil's bees a basis for his beliefs in social equality and class leveling. This forms a background for the whole of "To the Men of England," but especially for the second and third stanzas, where the English aristocratic classes that Shelley denounces as oppressors are characterized as drones. These drones are not real male bees, which play hardly any role in actual bee society, but the self-aggrandizing warlords of the *Georgics*.

In the second stanza, Shelley presents what he sees as the new realities on industrial society, in which the aristocrats live as parasites on the workers, consuming everything the workers produce and giving them nothing in return. By hyperbole Shelley makes them even drink the workers' blood. For Shelley these are the drones who no longer make war on one another at the cost of the lives of their followers but who now have become worse, stealing the lives and property of their dependents. The third stanza is addressed to the workers of England as bees. Shelley asks them why they are content to forge the weapons that the drones, who have no force of their own, use to despoil the fruits of their labor. This is alluding to the idea that if the workers stopped cooperating with the aristocrats, in particular by serving in the army that was used as a tool to oppress the populace at the Peterloo massacre in 1819, then the oppression of the lower classes would not be possible. Shelley builds these two stanzas on Virgil's metaphor of the beehive, his utopian model.

Agriculture

1819 is the second or third generation of the English industrial revolution, the great driver of social change that brought the inequalities and ruptures of tradition that Shelley complains about in "To the Men of England." Shelley alludes to this fact with his repeated mention of weaving, since the most important part of industrial work at that time was tending automatic steam-powered spinning and weaving machinery. However, for the most part Shelley talks about farm workers, which still in 1819 constituted most of the people living in England. Most farmers were tenants of aristocratic landlords, working in a system relatively unchanged from medieval feudalism. They worked a plot of land and kept the grain they harvested, paying a portion of it to their landlord.

This relationship was fundamentally changed by the Corn Laws passed by the British parliament in 1815. These laws reduced the relationship between tenants and landlords to the simple economic exchange of paying rent. The traditional rights of tenant farmers were completely stripped away, as were the duties of the landlord. For instance, tenants had traditionally had the right to glean the small amount of corn (meaning what is usually called wheat in American usage) left in the field after the harvest, but under the new laws, this grain was denied them, and any attempt to take it amounted to criminal trespass. Since it was hardly worth the time of the landlord to collect this grain, it was simply left to rot in the fields over the winter, even if in bad years (and there were many difficult years during the economic depression following the Napoleonic Wars) it could make a real difference in the very survival of the tenants. This arbitrary termination of traditional rights was received as an outrage in liberal circles. John Keats, also writing in 1819, protested against the Corn Laws in his *Ode to a Nightingale* with the image of the Biblical heroine Ruth, who in modern Britain would not be able to glean as she does at the beginning of her story. The same laws are also behind Shelley's outrage over the recharacterization of the traditional relationship between landlords and tenants, so that the landlords become drones eating the corn that is rightfully the tenants and even drinking their very blood, that is, denying them life.

A poor English farmer plowing a field. The poem contrasts the poor ploughman with the wealthy lord.
(SSPL / Getty Images)

STYLE

Romanticism

Romanticism was a school of thought, art, and literature that developed in the late-eighteenth century, especially in England and Germany. It was marked by an idealized view of the past, of nature, and of human nature and an attempt to reconcile this view with the plain realities of the present. It was a reaction against the Enlightenment of the early-eighteenth century, which discounted idealism. Romantic poetry was deeply influenced by contemporary German philosophy. The most important romantic poets were Johann Wolfgang von Goethe in Germany and first by William Wordsworth, Samuel Taylor Coleridge, and William Blake in England and then, in the second generation, Shelley and his contemporaries John Keats and Lord Byron.

Romanticism viewed history on the model of German idealist philosophy, especially as developed by Georg Wilhelm Friedrich Hegel, which attempted to impose logical order on the world as a whole. In this view, history unfolded on the model of the syllogistic (relating to a formal deductive philosophical argument) logic of the ancient Greek philosopher Aristotle. One historical era exists as a thesis, gives rise to an antithesis, and is resolved into a new era by reconciling the two into a synthesis. The romantics considered tradition or antiquity, or some admittedly idealized version of the past, as a ground in which human life existed in an ideal state. This was a society that was integrated in the sense that every individual was connected by ideal, beneficial relationships with other human beings, defined by a state, a religion, and a culture that nourished and supported the individual.

The modern world, the world of 1819, stood in contrast to this traditional ideal in two ways. On the one hand, the modern world lacked integration. The individual was alienated from his fellow men because the traditions that once tied communities together—shared beliefs and customs—were being destroyed. The relationship of the individual to the larger culture became the experience of oppression, both in the industrial workplace and economy, and in regard to the distant, impersonal state, but on the other hand, modernity also had a beneficial aspect. The industrial economy produced new wealth (something completely unknown in the traditional world) that could have, if properly managed, enriched society as a whole. Science also allowed modern man to directly perceive truths about the physical and social worlds in a way that was never possible before, even as this analysis distanced the observer from participating in them. Romanticism aimed at the reconciliation of the thesis of tradition with the antithesis of modernity to create a new synthesis that would combine the virtues (and only the virtues) of both. The romantic project failed in never being able to achieve this synthesis.

Indeed, it was never clear how a romantic synthesis could possibly be achieved. Romantic poetry is often about the failure of the romantic project. Shelley, alone of the English romantics, became convinced that political and social revolution was the only hope of reaching the new synthesis. It is rare for any romantic work to give an outline of the whole romantic project. Shelley's "Song to the Men of England" portrays the worst aspects of the modern antithesis and suggest how the synthesis may begin. Shelley describes the breakdown of traditional feudal ties, in which the rich and powerful are supposed to help the weak. Now instead they use their power to oppress and exploit their dependents. Shelley calls for this social order to be transformed or else human civilization will become a graveyard.

Poetics

Despite the politically revolutionary tone of "Song to the Men of England," the form of the poem is highly conventional. It consists of eight stanzas, each of four lines. Each line is composed of four iambic feet (the smallest units of verse, consisting of an unstressed followed by a stressed syllable). There are a large, but not unusual, proportion of substitutions of other feet for the iambs, as well as resolutions (counting two very weak unstressed syllables as one) based on colloquial speech. Intended as a popular song, a sort of political hymn, the structure of the meter is highly conversational rather than formal. The beginning of each stanza takes on the form of a march. Each stanza has a simple AABB rhyme scheme where the first and second line rhyme, as do the third and fourth.

HISTORICAL CONTEXT

Peterloo Massacre

In the last months of 1819, Shelley produced a flurry of politically radical poems and pamphlets, including "Song to the Men of England," "England in 1819," "The Mask of Anarchy," and *A Philosophical View of Reform*. These poems came in response to a specific event, the Peterloo Massacre of August 16, which began with a political meeting in the city of Manchester motivated by deteriorating social conditions in England. Since the end of the Napoleonic Wars in 1815, wages for industrial work had fallen by as much as two-thirds and, because of the Corn Laws of 1815, which forbade the importation of grain, food prices had steadily risen. Workers felt completely helpless, at the mercy of both their employers and the government.

Workers were not represented in Parliament because only landowners were allowed to vote; also, parliamentary district boundaries had not been redrawn since the middle ages, in spite of the large numbers of people moving from the country into towns for factory work. An industrial area like Lancashire (the county containing Manchester) with nearly a million inhabitants had only two members of Parliament, the same as some rural counties that had as few as a single voter (these were called rotten boroughs). The solution favored by workers and many businessmen was to reform the parliamentary election procedures and give all adult men the right to vote, but most politicians, government officials, and landowners considered this position to be radical and certain to lead to the kind of bloody revolution that had troubled France after 1789. Accordingly, when a crowd of sixty thousand or more workers gathered to hear radical speakers in St. Peter's field in Manchester, arrest warrants on charges of sedition (encouraging resistance to lawful authority) were issued for the speakers and given to regular army troops to carry out. In the process of making the arrests, a unit of cavalry charged into the crowd, killed eleven people, and wounded as many as six hundred more. One of the dead was a two-year-old child, and another was a pregnant woman. Thanks to the relatively recent institution of daily civic newspapers, the massacre was widely and immediately reported throughout the country (the government was unable to react swiftly enough to stop publication). It was called the Peterloo Massacre in mockery of the army's recent victory over Napoleon at Waterloo.

COMPARE
&
CONTRAST

- **1810s:** In Great Britain, only wealthy land-owners are allowed to vote for members of Parliament. The votes of 154 men control half of the seats in Parliament.

  Today: Every citizen at least eighteen years old can vote in English parliamentary elections.

- **1810s:** Great Britain has an enormous national debt as a result of the Napoleonic Wars against France, owed almost exclusively to wealth British landowners and paid by taxes that disproportionately fall on the working poor.

  Today: Great Britain again has a large national debt from the 2009 banking crisis, mostly owed to Saudi Arabia, China, and other foreign governments.

- **1810s:** The British economy is in the process of becoming fully industrialized.

  Today: The British economy is post-industrial, de-emphasizing industrial production in favor an information-based economy.

- **1810s:** Freedom of speech is severely curtailed by the British government. No dissent is tolerated, making it impossible for Shelley to publish any of his writings about the Peterloo Massacre in his lifetime.

  Today: Freedom of speech in Great Britain faces new threats from antiquated libel laws and the demands of religious minorities that criticism of their beliefs be removed from the public sphere.

The government response was to support the local magistrates and military commanders responsible and to further curtail civil liberties because of an increased fear of revolution. Reformers redoubled their efforts to expand the franchise as the only peaceful way of changing the government. Shelley was outraged by Peterloo, as were many other Englishmen, but his writings in reaction were not published because of new censorship laws. While "The Mask of Anarchy" came out in a pirated edition in 1832, it and the other two poems were not formally published until 1839 by Mary Shelley (and even then they were edited to remove politically sensitive portions). The poems were not included in critical editions until the 1960s. His pamphlet on reform did not come out until 1920 when it was published by a descendent who had inherited the manuscript.

Chartism

One legacy of the Peterloo massacre was the Chartist movement. This was a demand by workers beginning in 1832 that the government accept the Great Charter, a document that called for universal male suffrage (the right to vote). While this movement occasionally had violent clashes with the police or army, for the most part it proceeded by peaceful means, including strikes and the offering of petitions in 1839 and 1848 urging Parliament to pass the Charter. The petitions had as many as three million signatures. In an age before mass market advertising, poetry played an important part in creating popular support for the Charter, and Shelley was the most important poet to the Chartists. Shelley's early poem "Queen Mab," which laid down an outline for social reform, was considered the "Chartist bible" while much of Shelley's radical verse was frequently reprinted and explicated for its political message in Chartist newspapers. "Song to the Men of England," because of its form as a popular song as well as its message, was widely used as source material by Chartist poets. Although the Chartist movement failed in securing universal suffrage at an early date, voting rights were gradually broadened throughout the nineteenth century, though it was not given to all adult men regardless of property holdings or income until 1918.

The drawing room of an aristocratic Englishman. The poem contrasts the obscenely wealthy aristocracy with the workers who support them. *(Central Press | Hulton Archive | Getty Images)*

CRITICAL OVERVIEW

The main problems that have concerned scholars in connection with Shelley's "Song to the Men of England" relate to the characterization of the poem and even to the authenticity of the text that we have and the attribution of the poem to Shelley. The poem is relatively rare among Shelley's works in having not survived in an original manuscript copy written in the poet's own hand. It was first published in the 1839 edition of Shelley's poems edited and overseen by his widow, Mary Shelley. She explained that this poem was one of the radical poems Shelley wrote in 1819 in reaction to the Peterloo Massacre, but some scholars consider this information secondhand and therefore doubtful.

Writing in 1845, the pioneering communist Friedrich Engels (quoted by Timothy Morton in

the introduction to the *Cambridge Companion to Shelley*) writes of Shelley's and Byron's works, and Shelley's radical 1819 poems in particular, that they "find most of their readers in the proletariat; the bourgeoisie owns only castrated editions, family editions, expurgated in accordance with the hypocritical morality of today." In the same work, Morton recalls that even early in the 1990s, he was not allowed to present a show on Shelley's 1819 poems on the British Broadcasting Corporation (BBC) because the aristocratically educated editors there refused to acknowledge that Shelley had written them. He explains, "Some circles have still not forgiven Percy Shelley for having been a class traitor." At the same time, some critics want to cover over Shelley's radicalism by simply denying it, producing an effete and innocuous lyricist whose work is pure poetry in several senses. This idea is most famously expressed by Matthew Arnold in his *Essays in Criticism*. Arnold characterizes Shelley as "a beautiful *and ineffectual* angel, beating in the void his luminous wings in vain."

This tendency to ignore the political side of Shelley's work began with Mary Shelley. Hers is the family edition to which Engels refers. Neil Fraistat in his article in *Shelley: Poet and Legislator of the World*, shows how Mary Shelley, as much for economic as personal reasons, wanted to cultivate a version of her husband's poetry that would shock no one. Michael Henry Scrivener in his *Radical Shelley* points out that one can see where Mary expurgated the most inflammatory elements from many of the 1819 poems compared with Shelley's own handwritten versions. Scrivener believes she did this precisely so that her husband's memory could be accepted by a middle class audience. Because no manuscript of "Song to the Men of England" survives, it is impossible to say what she might have deleted from the poem.

During the 1960s in the United States, Shelley's radicalism was purposely used by instructors to convince students that he should be read as a fellow hippie. Leo Hamalian and James V. Hatch in an article in *College English* in 1971 describe converting a class on Shelley into "the Happening" (a sort of staged-reality performance art) by telling the students they will hear a lecture on Shelley from one of his descendants and then importing an actress who

> declares that if Shelley were alive today he would surely belong to the SDS or one of the radical student groups. In proof, she reads "Men of England" and passes out, as he would have done, leftist and atheist propaganda.

When the professor attempted to restore the class to a conventional lecture, the actress was to lead the students in shouting him down and use slogans from the radical poems to exclude any but a political identity for Shelley.

CRITICISM

Bradley A. Skeen

Skeen is a classics professor. In this essay, he discusses Shelley's poetical contribution to the political doctrine of nonviolent resistance in "Song to the Men of England."

For all of Shelley's calls for revolutionary political change, it is interesting that the practical part of his political philosophy promoted nonviolence rather than violence as the means of change. Shelley

> NEVERTHELESS, WHAT SHELLEY HAD ENVISIONED, GANDHI BROUGHT TO PASS AS A REALITY, ALBEIT IN A CAUSE SHELLEY HAD SCARCELY IMAGINED."

was well aware of what had happened in the French Revolution. That momentous historical upheaval from the previous generation dominated the thought of Shelley and his contemporaries about political change. The ideals of that movement closely matched the reforms Shelley wanted: economic and political equality of all classes or, if not complete equality, at least a fair distribution of freedom and wealth. However, starting with the execution of the French king as a political criminal, the revolution became tainted with blood. The actual emphasis of the revolution shifted from reform to the execution of ideologically unsound individuals, so that, far from achieving liberty, the revolution degenerated into the Terror of Robespierre, a far worse tyranny than the former government of the king and aristocrats. This culminated in the new monarchy of Napoleon, who projected violence and bloodshed on a continental scale, to a level never seen before, for which Shelley denounced him in "Written on Hearing the News of the Death of Napoleon" (1821). Rejecting France as a model, Shelley wanted to see Great Britain be governed in approximately the same manner as the contemporary United States, a republic with at least equality of opportunity, but he wanted no violent revolution to achieve that goal.

Rejecting violence as a failed means of achieving reform, Shelley was left with nonviolence. The kernel of the doctrine of nonviolent resistance to tyranny is present in the teachings of Jesus described in the New Testament. Although Shelley was an atheist and thought that Jesus' teachings had been misused by the Church and the aristocracy to justify their oppression of the masses throughout the centuries, he held Jesus himself in great respect as a political reformer. Besides the example Christianity offers of the political power to persuade and move followers contained in the narratives of the execution of Jesus himself and of

WHAT DO I READ NEXT?

- William Gibson and Bruce Sterling's 1991 science fiction novel *The Difference Engine* imagines that Charles Babbage actually built his analytical computer in 1822 so that the information revolution started by computers in the 1960s and still continuing today instead took place at the same time as the industrial revolution, resulting in an alternate history. In this world, the authors have Shelley become a political revolutionary and criminal, urging workers to destroy the new machines.

- John Keats's *Collected Poems* edited by Jack Stillinger in 1991 presents the work of Shelley's contemporary Keats, whose career Shelley fostered, and who perhaps surpassed Shelley in the greatness of his poetry.

- The 2006 biography *Gandhi* by Primo Levi and Amy Pastan gives an account of Gandhi's life and philosophy of nonviolence aimed at a young-adult audience.

- Twayne's "English Author" series volume *Percy Bysshe Shelley*, updated in 1990 by Donald Reiman, one of the leading Shelley scholars in

the world, gives a biographical, critical, and historical overview of Shelley and his work.

- *The Complete Poetry of Percy Bysshe Shelley*, edited by Donald Reiman and Neil Fraistat, aims to publish of all of Shelley's poetry, including works that so far have existed only in manuscript, beginning with his school exercises. A detailed line by line commentary on critical and literary matters is included for each poem. This is one of the most extensive publication projects for any English poet. So far two volumes have been published in 2000 and 2004, covering the period through 1813.

- The 2005 *Percy Bysshe Shelley, A Biography: Exile of Unfulfilled Renown, 1816-1822* concentrates on Shelley's years of self-imposed exile in Italy.

- Harold Bloom's 1959 study, *Shelley's Mythmaking* is largely responsible for rehabilitating Shelley's modern reputation as a poetic genius, though it does not deal with his political thought and writing.

---

other martyrs by tyrants, the New Testament has an interesting encapsulation of the doctrines of modern movements of nonviolent resistance. When an aristocrat in the Roman Empire struck a slave or person from the lower orders with his hand, he would do so with the back of his left hand. Following the advice that Jesus gives on such an occasion, "But I say unto you, That ye resist not evil: but whosoever shall smite thee on thy right cheek, turn to him the other also" (Matthew 5:39), would invite the aristocrat to strike again but force him to do so with the right hand, a violation of social taboos concerning left and right. This kind of nonviolent resistance put the victim in control of the situation and shamed the aristocrat. This is how the doctrine of nonviolent resistance operated in the nineteenth and twentieth centuries, but on a larger scale. The perpetrators of violence in opposition to

reform are meant to feel shame at injuring or killing people who offer no violence in return and indeed do nothing whatsoever to resist violence directed against themselves. Once they are shamed, the oppressors are meant to re-evaluate their policy of oppressing the resistors.

Shelley was the first figure to develop a modern doctrine of pursuing political reform through nonviolence. In "Song to the Men of England" Shelley calls for reform and points out the tyranny of the aristocratic ruling class as he sees it. He demonstrates that it is based on the power of the aristocrats to use violence against their subjects in the reference to drinking their blood and the repeated references to weapons. He suggests that the only weapons the aristocrats have are those made by the workers and particularly that the people bearing those weapons on behalf of the aristocrats, the police and army, are themselves workers. Without the cooperation of these workers, the aristocrats would be powerless, and he advises that this cooperation be withdrawn. This is the nonviolent tool of noncooperation. Shelley does not suggest at any point that violent revolution is a possibility. He does, however, suggest that the workers would be better off bearing the arms they manufacture in their own defense, and one could read a full-blown doctrine of violence into that statement if one wanted to. It seems unlikely, however, that this is what Shelley intended in light of other and more definite statements of nonviolence he makes in works written in that same fall of 1819. This statement is out of place in "Song to the Men of England" and is better explained as a remnant of less radical thought or as a concession to popular sensibility insofar as Shelley intended the piece to be a popular song. If the iron discipline and purity of purpose necessary to give up one's life gladly is lacking, resistance is better than submission.

Shelley takes up nonviolence more explicitly in another 1819 poem, "The Mask of Anarchy." In that poem Shelley describes the social order of his day as a world turned upside down, in which the people who were supposedly given power to protect the poor instead abuse their power to become oppressors. The title of king, which stands for security and peace, is a mask covering over a world descended into the violence of anarchy. He means that a law and government that can sustain itself only by acts of violence like the Peterloo Massacre is no law or government at all. Accordingly, tyranny is not to be met with violence but, paradoxically, with nonviolence. Those who would resist tyranny must let the tyrant kill them without making the slightest effort to resist, and then the shamefulness of the tyrant's own actions will destroy him.

A Philosophical View of Reform is a political pamphlet Shelley wrote in 1819. As an essay, it presents his ideas in a more straightforward way than his poems of that period. He states that the French Revolution failed because the French people, accustomed to violence by their oppressors, did not know any other way to respond when the opportunity came. Shelley wrote:

> The oppressed, having been rendered brutal, ignorant, servile and bloody by slavery, having had the intellectual thirst, excited in them by the process of civilization, satiated from fountains of literature poisoned by the spirit and the form of monarchy, arose to take a dreadful revenge on their oppres-

sors. Their desire to wreak vengeance, to this extent, in itself a mistake, a crime, a calamity, arose from the same source as their other miseries and errors.

For Shelley, the French Revolution failed in its response to tyranny because the revolutionaries could not free themselves from the tyrannical mode of thought.

Shelley wanted to see universal suffrage, tax reform, and the redistribution of wealth and would have been willing for the current government, corrupt as it was but recognizing that things could not go on as they were, to gradually bring these reforms to pass. However, he considered it all too likely that this would never happen. Peterloo had taught him that any attempt to organize reform outside of the government would be met with violence from the government. He explains in *A Philosophical View of Reform* that "misery and extermination would fill the country from one end to another." Shelley is very blunt about how this violence, when it comes, is to be met. He wrote:

> If circumstances had collected a considerable number as at Manchester on the memorable 16th of August, if the tyrants command the troops to fire upon them or cut them down unless they disperse, [the patriot] will exhort them peaceably to defy the danger, and to expect without resistance the onset of the cavalry, and wait with folded arms the event of the fire of the artillery and receive with unshrinking bosoms the bayonets of the charging battalions.

The reader might be tempted to take this as some sort of metaphor, but Shelley means just what he says. Although Shelley does not go into detail, this is exactly how many soldiers experienced battle in the early nineteenth century, and much of his immediate audience would have been well aware of this fact. At the Battle of Waterloo in 1815, many British regiments had indeed done nothing throughout the course of the battle except stand in place for ten or more hours and not move when French artillery shot at them. Some units had as many as half of their men killed or wounded in this way but did not break. It is this kind of discipline that Shelley calls upon the champions of reform to emulate. If men will spend their lives in this way, Shelley asks, just to win a victory, will they not do it to win their liberty? Shelley believes that British soldiers would not long endure the situation of having to slaughter their unarmed and unresisting fellow citizens and would eventually mutiny rather than obey such orders. After that, the existing government and its basis in force would vanish, and reform could proceed unhindered. In 1831, indeed, during political riots in Bristol, the British commander charged with restoring order refused to have his troop fire on unarmed civilians, even though he was court-martialed for it. Political change probably could have been brought about in England by the nonviolent means Shelley describes, but the Chartists that controlled the reform movement in the 1830s and 1840s never had a sufficiently disciplined following to carry out such a plan.

If Shelley's own countrymen could follow his program for reform, others could as well. Shelley exercised a powerful influence on later movements of nonviolent resistance, especially that led by Mohandas Gandhi for the liberation of India from British rule in the first half of the twentieth century. While Gandhi was in law school in London in 1888, he was introduced to the leadership circle of the British vegetarian movement. Despite its name, this political movement was concerned with far more than doing away with eating meat. It aimed at the elimination of violence from society in general, including the end of the death penalty and the promotion of pacifism, including the doctrine of nonviolence. Gandhi was deeply impressed by Henry Salt's 1886 pamphlet, *A Plea for Vegetarianism*, which in turn drew from Shelley liberally. Shelley had remained at the forefront of English radical thought, and Salt drew from the poet's work in his depiction of a new society based on social justice. Unfamiliar with *A Philosophical View of Reform*, because it had not been published during the period of his intellectual formation, Gandhi was deeply influenced by "The Mask of Anarchy." In later years Gandhi quoted from Shelley in his writings and speeches, especially those aimed at British audiences. He found especially effective the depiction of nonviolent resistors standing still like the trees of the forest as they are hacked down by a tyrant's soldiers in "The Mask of Anarchy," echoing Shelley's practical advice to English reformers in *A Philosophical View of Reform*. However, Gandhi did not utilize Shelley as widely as one might expect and never cited "To the Men of England," despite the suitability of its popular message to his cause. This is often thought to be because the ascetic (practicing self-denial as a measure of spiritual discipline) Gandhi objected to Shelley generally because of the latter's doctrine of free love. Nevertheless, what Shelley had envisioned, Gandhi brought to pass as a reality, albeit in a cause Shelley had scarcely imagined.

> THE POEM MIGHT HAVE BEEN TITLED 'CHALLENGE TO THE MPS OF ENGLAND': THE SEQUENCE OF QUESTIONS IN THE FIRST 16 LINES CONVEYS CRITICAL DISMAY AT, AS WELL AS SYMPATHY FOR, THE OPPRESSED CONDITION OF ITS AUDIENCE."

Source: Bradley Skeen, Critical Essay on "Song to the Men of England," in *Poetry for Students*, Gale, Cengage Learning, 2011.

William Keach

In the following excerpt, Keach considers what leftist radicals "have made and can still make" of poems such as "Song to the Men of England."

The task of reclaiming Shelley's poetry for the revolutionary left, most notably undertaken by Paul Foot in his book *Red Shelley*, inevitably raises difficulties and complications which I would like to address. I worried about some of these difficulties and complications several years ago in a 1985 review essay that considered Foot's *Red Shelley* together with Michael Scrivener's *Radical Shelley* and Paul Dawson's *The Unacknowledged Legislator*. My judgement then was that, while Foot's desire to claim Shelley for the real socialist left was deeply important, his book did not address some of the difficult questions of Shelley's political writing as convincingly as Scrivener's and Dawson's had done. My perspective today has shifted substantially from what it was in 1985, when I had just finished an avowedly formalist study of Shelley's style and was still a member of a social democratic group called the Democratic Socialists of America. I have come to have a much stronger commitment to the political tradition from which Foot's work on Shelley springs, and I see strengths in *Red Shelley* that I had not seen or had not been able fully to realise before. However, I still think that the questions posed by Scrivener in his case for an anarchist and utopian Shelley, and by Dawson in his case for a reformist Shelley, need to be confronted.

It is not that Foot himself is unaware of these questions. I was struck, rereading *Red Shelley*, by his acknowledgment of Shelley's doubts and uncertainties and contradictions. I was also struck by the perspective of 'reform or revolution' announced in the title of Foot's sixth chapter and rooted in his understanding of Rosa Luxemburg's great argument that revolutionaries make the best fighters for reforms because they see them as coming from below and contributing to a fundamental transformation of society. I was struck by how effectively Foot used this perspective to relate the tactical changes in Shelley's political writings to their overarching drive. Still, Foot's declared purpose, 'to pass on Shelley's political enthusiasms to today's socialists, radicals and feminists, in the hope that their commitment will be strengthened and enriched by Shelley, as mine has been', means that he often moves very quickly past doubts, difficulties and contradictions. There is something to be gained, I think, politically as well as critically, from slowing down and staying with the hard points, with things that do not fit, or that fit only uneasily, with the 'enthusiasms' that Foot so engagingly transmits.

What I propose to do here involves a double agenda. On the one hand, I want to keep alive the main points at issue in recent scholarly assessments of Shelley's politics: the implications of his epistemological idealism and scepticism; the problem of Shelley's audiences, of his writing for 'a select class of readers' more often than 'for the people'; the consequences of his class position for, among other things, the social and cultural circumstances of his Italian self exile; the question of Shelley's practical relation to political organisation and action, including his relation to armed resistance and struggle. On the other hand, I want to give the views of Shelley's readers on the militant left their own independent validity and interest, whether they correspond to what Shelley scholars take to be his 'actual' politics or not. That is, I am concerned with what leftist radicals have made and can still make of Shelley's writing.

Ultimately, of course, I would like to see the doubleness of this agenda dissolve. To say this may be to 'talk utopia,' as Maddalo says in chiding Julian or perhaps to entertain an ideal of intellectual work that is more Gramscian than Shelleyan. But Julian, not Maddalo, has the last, grimly antiutopian word. And what Gramsci and Shelley share is a concern with a revolutionary social transformation in which the seemingly ineluctable division between intellectuals and 'the people' disappears. More concretely and practically, I want

to look at some of the poems Shelley would probably have included in the volume of 'popular songs wholly political' he thought of publishing in 1819 and ask this question: what doubts, uncertainties and complications might people encounter who have been inspired by Paul Foot to read Shelley?

Among other things, doing so will allow me to focus on the little volume of Shelley's 1819 political poems, together with *A Philosophical View of Reform* and a wonderful introduction by Foot, published in 1992 by *Redwords*. Everyone who works on Shelley's poetry, including Mary Shelley, talks about this projected volume, but now it is a reality called Shelley's Revolutionary Year. It stands in the great tradition of cheap editions of Shelley brought out by radicals who lay claim to him as one of their own.

Even the typographical error on the excellently designed front cover, the subtitle is The Peterloo Writtings of the Poet Shelley, a mistake that Redwords was, of course, truly embarrassed by probably has its analogues in some of the Chartist and 19th century socialist editions of Shelley's poems. The reading texts of the three poems from the volume that I want to look at are as good as those in any available edition of Shelley, I hasten to add (though, as you might expect, there is no scholarly apparatus). So imagine that someone buys Shelley's *Revolutionary Year* and reads 'Song to the Men of England' on the basis of Foot's claim that it is one of the poems which 'are direct and deliberate appeals to the masses to rise up and trample their oppressors.' In line 24 the poem is explicit and unflinching in its call for armed insurrection: 'Forge arms in your defence to bear.' It is also, as Scrivener says, unique among radical texts of its day in its 'uncompromising view on labour alienation.' An understanding of economic exploitation that generates alienation for workers and surplus value for 'the lords who lay ye low' is unmistakably articulated in the poem, through diction, imagery and cadences to which a very broad range of readers could and can respond.

However, the tone of the poem, the mode in which Shelley addresses the Men of England, might well present a problem. (I am responding particularly here to a very good article in the 1978 *Keats-Shelley Journal* by Richard Hendrix called 'The Necessity of Response: How Shelley's Radical Poetry Works.') The poem might have been titled 'Challenge to the MPs of England': the sequence of questions in the first 16 lines conveys critical dismay at, as well as sympathy for, the oppressed condition of its audience. That Shelley's 'appeal' to the oppressed here primarily takes the form of critical challenge becomes even clearer in the shift to declarative and imperative rhetoric in stanzas five and six. But the real difficulty comes in the final two stanzas:

> Shrink to your cellars, holes, and cells;
> In halls ye deck another dwells.
> Why shake the chains ye wrought? Ye see
> The steel ye tempered glance on ye.
> With plough and spade, and hoe and loom,
> Trace your grave, and build your tomb,
> And weave your winding-sheet, till fair
> England be your sepulchre.

Bernard Shaw tells us that Mr G W Foote (no relation), President of the National Secular Society, recited this poem before a large audience of 'working men who took Shelley quite seriously' at the Hall of Science in St Luke's parish, east London, on the occasion of the 1892 Shelley centenary. There were, says Shaw, 'thunders of applause.' My students have tended to respond differently to this poem with respect and admiration for Shelley's poetic analysis of economic oppression, but also with puzzlement about how to take the last two stanzas. It is surprising to me that the Shelley critics who have commented in any detail on this passage have not themselves been more puzzled. Kenneth Cameron acknowledges that 'the conclusion is at first puzzling':

> Shelley, after urging the workers to arise and take back the wealth they have created, defending themselves by armed force, here seemingly tells them to retreat. The mood, however, is sardonic, the motive that of shaming the workers into action, implying that unless they act, they will become lethargic.

And Cameron leaves it at that, without any further comment on what we or Shelley's immediate audience among the oppressed are to make of being shamed into action. The only detailed analysis of these lines that I am familiar with is Stephen Behrendt's in *Shelley and His Audiences*. 'Shelley concludes,' Behrendt writes, 'in a disturbing tone of bitter irony.' The poem's 'argument,' he says, is 'sceptical':

> [T]his poem comes as close as Shelley ever comes to sanctioning violence as a last resort, and I believe that the reversal in both sense and tone in the final two stanzas suggests that he did not consider the 'men of England' actually capable of so decisive an assertion.... The poem's conclusion is

a variation on the reverse definition. Having presumably raised the audience's ire in the opening stanzas... Shelley's final lines are a calculated challenge to the audience to reject their subhuman images... and to assume their full status as human beings. The deluded masses fall into the habit of nursing their oppressors, literally 'giving them all they have,' rather than risk the destabilising trauma of resisting this unjust arrangement.

What I find striking, and also disturbing, about Behrendt's reading is its emphasis on the complicated sceptical irony of Shelley's tone. If you think he has over-read the last two stanzas I don't think he has, though I disagree with some of his interpretive inflections then I would like to hear a simpler and more straightforward reading that accounts plausibly for what Shelley says to his readers in these lines.

I can imagine why Mr G W Foote's audience in 1892 gave 'thunders of applause' to the poem's call, challenging as it is, for workers to defend themselves by force against economic exploitation and alienation. But I cannot imagine why that audience, or any of us reading Shelley's poem now, would give 'thunders of applause' to a sardonic request that workers do what Marx and Engels said the capitalist bosses do, dig their own graves. Bracing defiance, perhaps even wincing appreciation for a dose of necessary medicine but 'thunders of applause'? Behrendt's commentary begins to get at the political and poetic difficulties here, and those of us who believe that Shelley is powerfully on the side of the working class need to do more to meet his elaboration of Shelley's challenge.

Source: William Keach, "Rise Like Lions? Shelley and the Revolutionary Left," in *International Socialism*, Vol. 75, July 1997, pp. 91–104.

Seymour Reiter

In the following excerpt, Reiter briefly analyzes the structure of Shelley's poem, demonstrating how it reinforces the thematic concern of the poem: that having so many men work for the benefit of the few is morally wrong.

Song to the Men of England

In the autumn of 1819 Shelley wrote other poems to give heart to those facing the oppression of Government. It looked as though revolution must issue. "Song to the Men of England," meant to inflame, would have caused the prosecution of any publisher and so lay unpublished for twenty years.

The "Song" begins: Why do the men of England submit to the lords, "these stingless drones?" [The drone, stingless, makes no honey; in like manner the lords, having only the weapons the people make, live on the labors of the people. The image, familiar enough to most Englishmen in an age when people lived nearer to the country than most of us do today, has an antecedent in Plato's *Republic*, 552C: "Shall we, then, say of him that as the drone springs up in the cell, a pest of the hive, so such a man grows up in his home, a pest of the state?"] Three stanzas of rhetorical questioning concretely proclaim the wrongness of the many wearing themselves out for the few. There are anger and irony in the fourth stanza. The fifth stanza hammers away, exposing the people's loss; and the sixth, with powerful inverted repetition, calls upon the people to claim the wealth their labor creates and to make good that claim with armed force. If they do not, they deserve the contemptuous tone in the alternative that the seventh stanza without pausing for transition presents, and they deserve the powerful irony in the sadness of the closing stanza.

Less well known than "Song to the Men of England," undeservedly, is the acidly satirical "Similes for Two Political Characters of 1819," also not published until 1839. A manuscript version bears the heading "To S—th and C—gh," Sidmouth and Castlereagh. The language, rhythms, and images are like those that make Thomas Hardy now admired. I give the third stanza:

> As a shark and dog-fish wait
> Under an Atlantic isle,
> For the negro-ship, whose freight
> Is the theme of their debate,
> Wrinkling their red gills the while—
>
> Are ye . . .

It would have been foolhardy for a publisher to issue that satire in face of the libel laws of the time.

Source: Seymour Reiter, "'Song to the Men of England,'" in *A Study of Shelley's Poetry*, University of New Mexico Press, 1967, pp. 212–13.

Desmond King-Hele

In the following excerpt, King-Hele presents the historical context of England in 1819 and traces the growth of Shelley's political thought, culminating in the writing of "Song to the Men of England."

> THOUGH PROFESSEDLY PARTISAN, SHELLEY NEVER LAPSES INTO HYSTERIA, AND HE COMFORTABLY SUCCEEDS IN PERFORMING THE TASK HE SETS HIMSELF—TO PUT ON RECORD IN VERSE, DOGGEREL EVEN AT TIMES, HIS FAITH IN GRADUAL REFORM."

1

In the spring and early summer of 1819 Shelley had been occupied with high poetic themes, Acts II and III of *Prometheus Unbound* and *The Cenci*. On finishing the latter his mood changed, and during the autumn he cast a critical eye on the homeland he so often wanted to return to, her system of government, her people's wrongs, and the hardening of the arteries in her leading poet, Wordsworth.

England in 1819, four years after the most exhausting war she had known, was still trying to jog along within the eighteenth-century pattern which events and inventions had rendered obsolete. The Prince Regent's nine years as head of the State had so signally failed to endear him to his people that he hardly ever dared show his face in public. His Prime Minister was the tactful and easy-going Lord Liverpool, who was halfway through his fifteen-year spell as Premier. The chief members of his Tory Cabinet were Castlereagh, Foreign Secretary and leader of the House of Commons, Eldon the Lord Chancellor, Lord Sidmouth the Home Secretary and Wellington, who was Master-General of the Ordnance. The government's home policy was one of studied inaction, punctuated by occasional repressive measures to scotch popular risings. Potentially the most dangerous of the risings had been the Luddite riots provoked by the trade depression in 1812. The inadequate 'police' forces at the disposal of the Lords Lieutenant of the counties chiefly affected—Nottingham, Yorkshire and Lancashire—had crumbled in face of these spontaneous protests from the industrial proletariat. Though the Luddites had these counties at their mercy, the government was in little danger since there was no revolutionary leader to co-ordinate the rioters and widen their local and limited aims. If a real threat had arisen in 1812 it would probably have been ignored until too late, for Perceval's murder in May had led to a lengthy ministerial crisis, and the government, when it did at last come into being, was too engrossed by the war to worry about home affairs.

When the disturbances broke out again in 1817 the war was over and the government, more alive to the danger, replied by suspending Habeas Corpus, and, later, by passing the six 'Gag' Acts. In 1819 this policy seemed to be leading the nation to the brink of revolution. But by 1821 trade was recovering and, without the spur of hunger, popular discontent slackened. At the same time open agitation for Parliamentary reform was growing, for in peace-time reformers were no longer automatically classed as traitors or Jacobins. The reformers were still a small minority, however, and the government, by ignoring the rights of the industrial population, was able to preserve the *status quo* for ten years more. Only severe pressure from outside would make a comfortable and privileged society like the House of Commons sign its own death-warrant, and in Shelley's lifetime that pressure had not built up. Behind the façade of stability the cogent forces of change were remoulding the face of England. The new factories proclaimed that Britain led the world in mechanization. The jerry-built slums beginning to spring up around them warned the world not to follow her example too eagerly, and set that industrial urban pattern which is one of the most familiar and least admired legacies of the nineteenth century. In contrast to the slums and social injustice are the literary and artistic glories of the period, and these latter will no doubt impress posterity more, just as the pyramids of Egypt and the Greek thinkers come to mind before the slaves who toiled around them. Those living at the time could not take this retrospective view, and it is no accident that the long line of English reformers is at its richest during the thirty years of Shelley's life. The list includes names as diverse as Godwin and Grey, Cobbett and Bentham, Mary Wollstonecraft and Elizabeth Fry, Fox and Robert Owen, Tom Paine and William Wilberforce. Their germinal ideas, which bore most fruit after 1830, are responsible for a large part of the better conditions we take for granted to-day. Shelley had always been an ally of the reformers, and in 1819, having left the heat and smoke of the conflict, he was ready to analyse the political situation in England more coolly.

His last and longest sortie into the 'great sandy desert of Politics' is an unfinished essay of some fifty pages, *A Philosophical View of Reform.*

He begins by reviewing notable systems of government, from the Roman Empire onwards. He looks at them with a strong liberal bias, assuming that creative activity will be stifled whenever a tyrannic government is in league with a strong acquiescent Church, and that the arts begin to flourish whenever political freedom revives. Though despotism seemed on the wane all over Europe, Shelley saw most hope for the future in America, a land with no king, no hereditary aristocracy, and no established Church.

Shelley devotes much of his essay to reform in England, then, he believed, at a crisis in her destiny. Parliament, he argues, no longer represented the English people, because the unfranchised poor had multiplied and the link which once united aristocracy and people, distrust of the monarch, had been broken. As the King's power declined, the landed aristocracy had grown into a despotic oligarchy, keeping their position not by force but by the fraudulent device of credit, public and private. By means of credit notes the rich can enjoy the advantages of wealth they don't possess. When they use this privilege they produce, in the political cant of the day, 'an increase in the national industry': that is, they condemn the workman to a sixteen-hour day and foment the evil of child labour—'the vigorous promise of the coming generation blighted by premature exertion.' Shelley's tirade against paper-money and his neglect of other causes of industrial distress serve to remind us that he was an approving reader of the *Political Register,* which he received regularly. Politically, in 1819, he stood halfway between Cobbett and the Whigs.

To remedy the abuses, Shelley proposes to pay off the national debt, to disband the standing army, to abolish sinecures (while respecting the rights of existing holders), to make all religions equal in the eye of the law and abolish tithes, to make justice cheap, certain and speedy, and, of course, to reform Parliament. There need be no insurrection, he says, if Parliament is wise enough to reform itself: the rotten boroughs should be disfranchised and their rights transferred to unrepresented cities, with the ultimate aim of equalizing the population in each constituency at about 40,000; Parliament should be elected every three years; the franchise should be gradually extended, first to include all small property owners, then to adult male suffrage, and finally to universal adult suffrage, the logical end of the process, but an end which England was not yet ready for.

Most of Shelley's proposals are now accepted as commonplace. Only the most radical one, paying off the national debt by orderly confiscation of lands, calls for any explanation. The national debt was incurred, he contends, in two unjust wars undertaken by the privileged classes to protect their own interests. Their property was already mortgaged: 'let the mortgagee foreclose.' Shelley goes on to distinguish between what we now call earned and unearned income, and restricts his capital levy to those who enjoy the latter. Some, he says, would lose a third, some a quarter of their wealth.

The Marxist picture of a dictatorship decaying spontaneously into free associations would never have seemed practical to Shelley, who, though at times loath to accept human nature as it is, was realistic enough to assume that privileged groups fight hard to preserve their status. He was most anxious, too, that the forces of privilege should be ousted without bloodshed. The outcome of the French Revolution had confirmed him in his conviction that ill-won power corrupts, and that a *coup d' état* leads the insurgents into habits of violence and mistrust, which jeopardize the new régime and stultify the benefits expected of it. To avoid this ruinous national rake's progress Shelley calls for passive resistance and non-co-operation. Some martyrs there would be, at first; but English soldiers would not for long consent to slaughter their unresisting countrymen. The non-co-operation should take such forms as refusing to pay taxes, and showering the House of Commons with petitions.

A Philosophical View of Reform, the last and best of Shelley's political utterances, falls naturally into place beside its predecessors. Having learnt from *Queen Mab* that poetry's heightened language was unsuitable for political dialectic, he was, in subsequent poems, usually content to glorify freedom in the abstract, relying on the incantation of the verse to edge readers towards his own camp. His practical schemes for political and social reform he put into a series of prose essays, which grew in wisdom with the years. Even the 1812 pamphlets seem temperate and responsible, almost over-cautiously so, when compared with say the *Letter to the Bishop of Llandoff* which Wordsworth wrote when he was 23. The ingenuous moments which mar the early pamphlets are eliminated in the more realistic *Proposal for Putting Reform to the Vote* of 1817. The *Philosophical View of Reform*, unfinished though it is, marks the final advance.

. . . Insistently in the *Philosophical View of Reform* Shelley advocates a limited step forward if the full reform arouses a frenzy of opposition in the diehards. He thus foreshadows the piecemeal growth of the reforms later in the century. Since 1900 reform has continued in the spirit though not according to the letter of his plan. His proposal to deprive landowners of a part of their property, for example, has come to apply, more stringently than he suggested, in the system of recurrent death-duties. He might not approve of this more drastic system: for when he made his proposal he was excited by the flagrantly unjust division of wealth between the landowners—'no class had ever enjoyed such riches as the landed gentry of England' in his day—and the needy poor, whom he saw during their worst winters, 1811–12 and 1816–17. Remembering those winters, he looked on England in 1819 as dry tinder wanting only the spark of a financial crisis to flare into insurrection. In fact, as we have seen, economic conditions were on the mend (though there was no reason to foresee it in 1819), and the government staved off the inevitable for over ten years. When the inevitable came, the long years of agitation had left their mark even on the diehards, with the result that the ship of State was able to weather the squalls and reach the reasonably safe anchorage of the first Reform Bill in 1832. Shelley's hopes of avoiding a bloody revolution were thus realized, by the very means he had proposed.

2

On 16 August 1819, while Shelley was putting the finishing touches to *The Cenci,* a meeting in St. Peter's Field, Manchester, was due to be addressed by the radical orator Henry Hunt. Some 50,000 people, many of them carrying banners, had gathered in orderly groups to hear him. The local magistrates became alarmed at the size of the crowd, and ordered the troops under their command to arrest Hunt. In the ensuing *mêlée* 11 of the crowd were killed and about 400 injured. When Shelley heard of the 'Peterloo Massacre' early in September, he confessed to a 'torrent of indignation . . . boiling in my veins,', and this frenzied language truly reflected his feelings. By the end of the month he had distilled his indignation into a poem of some 400 lines, "The Mask of Anarchy." As in *The Cenci,* he avoids elaborate metaphor: there are no glaucous sea-woods or purple chasms to perplex the oppressed poor who, he hoped, would read the poem. Instead the language is simple, unpolished sometimes, direct and vigorous, and the story is easy to follow. The most obscure feature of the poem is its title;

mask be read as *masque,* not a disguise, and *anarchy* as *misrule,* not lack of rule.

Though the sting of the topical allusions has faded, the first five stanzas are still compelling:

As I lay asleep in Italy
There came a voice from over the Sea,
And with great power it forth led me
To walk in the visions of Poesy.

I met Murder on the way—
He had a mask like Castlereagh—
Very smooth he looked, yet grim;
Seven bloodhounds followed him:
All were fat; and well they might
Be in admirable plight,
For one by one, and two by two,
He tossed them human hearts to chew
Which from his wide cloak he drew.

Next came Fraud, and he had on,
Like Eldon, an ermined gown;
His big tears, for he wept well,
Turned to mill-stones as they fell.

And the little children, who
Round his feet played to and fro,
Thinking every tear a gem,
Had their brains knocked out by them.
338. 1–21

To-day, when Castlereagh's skilful handling of foreign affairs looms larger than his acquiescence in his government's home policy, it is perhaps worth recalling how deeply he was hated in the country. Castlereagh was the only one of the Cabinet 'Big Five' in the Commons, and he never shirked responsibility when introducing the government's unpopular repressive measures in the House. The cheers and boos which greeted his funeral procession in 1822 may make us squirm now; but they do show that Shelley was merely accepting the popular view, not being specially vindictive. Against Eldon, on the other hand, Shelley did have a personal grudge. It was only a year since Eldon had finally deprived him of his right to bring up Ianthe and Charles. So Shelley naturally stresses the Chancellor's duties as guardian of wards in Chancery, while making capital too out of Eldon's habit of weeping on the Bench.

Last in the poem's 'ghastly masquerade,' symbolizing England's repressive laws, came Anarchy:

He rode
On a white horse, splashed with blood;
He was pale even to the lips,
Like Death in the Apocalypse.
And he wore a kingly crown;
And in his grasp a sceptre shone;

On his brow this mark I saw—
'I AM GOD, AND KING, AND LAW!'
338. 30–7

Accompanied by uniformed 'hired murderers,' among them the butchers of Peterloo, he trampled down the populace in the provinces and rode with pomp into London 'to meet his pensioned Parliament.' Then Hope, a 'maniac maid,' lay down in the street before his cavalcade. A misty light promptly appeared, and, while the bystanders are still watching it, Anarchy and his crew have been annihilated, and Hope has began to speak:

'Men of England, heirs of Glory,
Heroes of unwritten story,
Nurslings of one mighty Mother,
Hopes of her, and one another;

'Rise like Lions after slumber
In unvanquishable number,
Shake your chains to earth like dew
Which in sleep had fallen on you—
Ye are many—they are few.'
341. 147–55

In Shelley's eyes every man of England who opposed the existing régime wore a halo, and from the other side of the Alps those haloes shone brightly enough to blot out venial faults. These heirs of glory are next reminded of the slavery they know too well:

'Tis to work and have such pay
As just keeps life from day to day
In your limbs, as in a cell
For the tyrants' use to dwell....

'Tis to hunger for such diet
As the rich man in his riot
Casts to the fat dogs that lie
Suffeiting beneath his eye.
341. 160–3, 172–5

In contrast is what Shelley hopes to see when Freedom reigns:

For the labourer ... bread
And a comely table spread
From his daily labour come
In a neat and happy home.
342. 217–20

And how is the change to be brought about? Not by violent revolt, but, as the parable of Anarchy and Hope has hinted, by passive resistance. A 'vast assembly' should gather and make a solemn declaration of rights. If the oppressors intervene, as they did at Manchester, the people's course is clear:

With folded arms and steady eyes,
And little fear, and less surprise,

Look upon them as they slay
Till their rage has died away.

Then they will return with shame
To the place from which they came,
And the blood thus shed will speak
In hot blushes on their cheek.
344. 344–51

The language is as simple and passionate as that of Blake's songs, and seems the more sincere for being so artless. Shelley ends by reiterating the catchy verse

Rise like Lions after slumber
In unvanquishable number....
344. 368–9,

scarcely the best slogan for promoting the stoic virtues of passive resistance.

"The Mask of Anarchy" is one of the best polemical poems of its kind. Though professedly partisan, Shelley never lapses into hysteria, and he comfortably succeeds in performing the task he sets himself—to put on record in verse, doggerel even at times, his faith in gradual reform. Though his own reaction to social injustice was to fight, he knew that the passions aroused by fighting were often worse than the evils the fight aimed to remove. In his treatment of the class war he was a pacifist, confident that a clash between social classes could best be brought to a happy end if those who were in the right sacrificed some potential advantage with a generous gesture, in the hope that the other side would be shamed into doing the same. The *Philosophical View of Reform* is full of the spirit of conciliation, and "The Mask of Anarchy" is best looked upon as a companion-piece to the prose essay, or rather as a prologue, since it was written first. "The Mask of Anarchy" did not have to lie dormant as long as the essay, but it was not published in Shelley's lifetime, nor in the *Posthumous Poems* of 1824. Soon after finishing it Shelley sent it to Leigh Hunt for his *Examiner*. But Hunt, who had already been imprisoned once for seditious libel, was too wary to invite another prosecution. He kept the poem by him until 1832, when he published it as a pamphlet, in time for it to be quoted by political speakers during the struggle for the Reform Bill. And a hundred years later the poem was chanted by hunger-marchers in Toronto.

When, as in the autumn of 1819, Shelley allowed himself to be lured again into the tangled thicket of politics, the exuberance which had animated the Irish evangelist of 1812 tended to bubble up inside him, and the surplus not absorbed by the more serious writings would expend itself in lively squibs. The best of the 1819 crop is the "Song to the Men of England" (which George Orwell parodied in the first chapter of *Animal Farm* with the song 'Beasts of England'):

Men of England, wherefore plough
For the lords who lay ye low?
Wherefore weave with toil and care
The rich robes your tyrants wear?...
572. 1–4

Another spirited piece of treason is his revised version of the National Anthem:

God prosper, speed, and save,
God raise from England's grave
Her murdered Queen!
Pave with swift victory
The steps of Liberty,
Whom Britons own to be
Immortal Queen....
574. 1–7

Returning from hope to reality, Shelley catalogued the country's ills in a powerful and untidy sonnet, "England in 1819." The sestet comes before the octet, and the punctuation is so bad that I have been driven to alter it. Despite these flaws, or perhaps because of them, the poem usually pleases those who like to admire the non-Romantic facets of Romantic poets:

An old, mad, blind, despised, and dying
king;
Princes, the dregs of their dull race, who
flow
Through public scorn,—mud from a muddy
spring;
Rulers who neither see, nor feel, nor know,
But leech-like to their fainting country cling,
Till they drop, blind in blood, without a
blow;
A people starved and stabbed in the untilled
field;
An army, which liberticide and prey
Makes as a two-edged sword to all who
wield;
Golden and sanguine laws which tempt and
slay;
Religion   Christless,   Godless—a   book
sealed;
A Senate,—Time's worst statute unrepealed;—
Are graves, from which a glorious Phantom
may
Burst, to illumine our tempestuous day.
574

The rude vigour of the first twelve lines contrasts well with the abstract, diffident final couplet.

It is as if a phalanx of English aristocrats with their well-fed families and retainers—something like the Peers' chorus in *Iolanthe* augmented—were set beside a handful of scraggy reformers anxiously peering into the distant haze, which may hide a 'glorious Phantom.' The ironic stress on *may* makes the contrast the more poignant.

Source: Desmond King-Hele, "England in 1819," in *Shelley: The Man and the Poet*, Thomas Yoseloff, 1960, pp. 139–50.

SOURCES

Alexander, Meena, "Shelley's India: Territory and Text, Some Problems of Decolonialization," in *Shelley: Poet and Legislator of the World*, edited by Betty T. Bennett and Stuart Curran, Johns Hopkins University Press, 1996, pp. 169–78.

Arnold, Matthew, "Shelley," in *Essays in Criticism: Second Series*, MacMillan, 1888, pp. 205–52, http://books.google.com/books?id=eaMwAAAAYAAJ&source=gbs_navlinks_s (accessed December 13, 2009).

Bennett, Andrew J., "The Politics of Gleaning in Keats's 'Ode to a Nightingale' and 'To Autumn,'" in *Keats-Shelley Journal*, Vol. 39, 1990, pp. 34–38.

Fraistat, Neil, "Shelley Left and Right: The Rhetorics of the Early Textual Editions," in *Shelley: Poet and Legislator of the World*, edited by Betty T. Bennett and Stuart Curran, Johns Hopkins University Press, 1996, pp. 105–13.

Hamalian, Leo, and James V. Hatch, "How to Turn the Hip Generation on to Shelley and Keats," in *College English*, Vol. 33, 1971, pp. 324–32.

Keegan, John, *The Face of Battle*, Penguin, 1976, pp. 160–62.

Morton, Timothy, ed., "Introduction," in *The Cambridge Companion to Shelley*, Cambridge University Press, 2006, pp. 1–13.

Royle, Edward, *Chartism*, 3rd ed., Longman, 1996.

Scrivener, Michael Henry, *Radical Shelley: The Philosophical Anarchism and Utopian Thought of Percy Bysshe Shelley*, Princeton University Press, 1982, pp. 227–30.

Shaaban, Bouthaina, "Shelley and the Chartists," in *Shelley: Poet and Legislator of the World*, edited by Betty T. Bennett and Stuart Curran, Johns Hopkins University Press, 1996, pp. 114–25.

Shelley, Percy Bysshe, *A Philosophical View of Reform*, Oxford University Press, 1920, http://books.google.com/books?id=SfgNAAAAIAAJ&dq=label:"Schlager"&lr=&source=gbs_navlinks_s (accessed December 19, 2009).

———, *Shelley's Poetry and Prose: A Norton Critical Edition*, 2nd ed., edited by Donald H. Reiman and Neil Fraistat, W. W. Norton, 2002.

———, "Song to the Men of England," in *English Romantic Writers*, edited by David Perkins, Harcourt Brace Jovanovich, 1967, p. 1019.

Virgil, *Georgics*, in *The Works of Virgil*, translated by John Dryden, Ellerton and Byworth, 1807, pp. 167–87, http://books.google.com/books?id=5SAOAAAAYAAJ&source=gbs_navlinks_s (accessed December 15, 2009).

Weber, Thomas, *Gandhi as Disciple and Mentor*, Cambridge University Press, 2004, pp. 26–30.

FURTHER READING

Carlyle, Thomas, *The French Revolution: A History*, 2 Vols., Everyman's Library, 1906.
Originally published in 1837, this is one of the first large studies of the French Revolution written in English. It makes a link between personal heroic action and history very much in keeping with Shelley's romanticism.

Hay, Daisy, *Young Romantics: The Tangled Lives of English Poetry's Greatest Generation*, Farrar, Straus and Giroux, 2010.
This book written by a Cambridge Ph.D. talks about the unorthodox lifestyles, individuality, and political radicalism of a group that included Percy and Mary Shelley, Leigh Hunt, Lord Byron, John Keats, musician Vincent Novello, artists Benjamin Haydon and Joseph Severn, and others. It is both a personal and professional perspective on the English romantics.

Ingpen, Roger, ed., *The Letters of Percy Bysshe Shelley*, 2 Vols., Sir Isaac Pitman & Sons, 1909–1912.
This is a collection of Shelley's correspondence with family, publishers, and other poets.

Young, Art, *Shelley and Nonviolence*, Mouton, 1975.
Young explains Shelley's nonviolent philosophy with reference to Gandhi's movement in action, though without necessarily establishing secure links between the two at every point.

SUGGESTED SEARCH TERMS

Percy Bysshe Shelley

Percy Bysshe Shelley AND Song to the Men of England

Percy Bysshe Shelley poems

Percy Bysshe Shelley biography

Song to the Men of England

Romanticism

Peterloo AND massacre

Peterloo AND Shelley

Shelley AND Gandhi

To Autumn

JOHN KEATS

1820

"To Autumn" is a poem by the English romantic poet John Keats. It was written in 1819 and published the following year in his collection *Lamia, Isabella, The Eve of St. Agnes, and Other Poems.* Keats was living in Winchester in the county of Hampshire in southern England at the time that he wrote the poem. Every day he walked for an hour before dinner. On Sunday, September 19, 1819, he walked along the Itchin River and across the meadows in fine weather. Two days later, he wrote a letter to his friend Joshua Reynolds, in which he described the genesis of "To Autumn":

> How beautiful the season is now—How fine the air. A temperate sharpness about it. . . . I never lik'd stubble fields so much as now—Aye better than the chilly green of the spring. Somehow a stubble plain looks warm—in the same way that some pictures look warm—this struck me so much in my sunday's walk that I composed upon it.

"To Autumn" is the last of the six great odes Keats wrote in 1819, and it has always been recognized as one of his finest poems. Reviewers have regarded it as one of the most perfect poems in English literature. It is notable for its serene appreciation of the autumn season, the sense of acceptance it conveys of the passage of time and the seasons, and the way in which it presents and reconciles opposites. "To Autumn" can be found in most editions of Keats's poems.

John Keats (The Library of Congress)

AUTHOR BIOGRAPHY

Keats was born on October 31, 1795, in London, England. His father died after falling from his horse when Keats was only eight, and his mother died six years later in 1810. In 1811, when Keats was fifteen, he was taken out of school by his guardian, Richard Abbey, and apprenticed to an apothecary. Four years later, Keats entered Guy's Hospital in London to continue his medical studies. He qualified as an apothecary in 1816 but had no interest in becoming a surgeon. Instead, he decided to dedicate his life to writing poetry. He had already met the poet and journalist Leigh Hunt, and Hunt introduced him to other literary men, including William Hazlitt, Charles Lamb, and Percy Bysshe Shelley. In 1816, Keats wrote his first major poem, a sonnet titled "On First Looking into Chapman's Homer," which was published in 1817 in his first volume of poetry. Later that year he wrote his long poem *Endymion* and began an epic poem, *Hyperion*, modeled on John Milton's *Paradise Lost*.

The year 1818 was a tumultuous one for Keats. *Endymion* was published but received hostile reviews in the literary press. Keats's older brother George married and emigrated to the United States, where he lost all his money in a bad business venture in Kentucky. Keats's younger brother Tom contracted tuberculosis, and Keats nursed him until his death in December. Caring for his brother aggravated Keats's own bad health, which had begun when he caught a severe cold on a walking tour in Scotland in the summer and was so feverish he had to return home. Keats also met and fell in love with eighteen-year-old Fanny Brawne. They became engaged the next year and lived next door to each other in Hampstead, London.

In 1819, Keats wrote most of the poems that would make him famous, including *The Eve of St. Agnes*, "La Belle Dame Sans Merci,""Ode to a Nightingale,""Ode on a Grecian Urn,"*Lamia*, and "To Autumn." These poems were published in his third book in 1820. Keats also recast his unfinished epic *Hyperion* into *The Fall of Hyperion*. However, in October, only a month after writing "To Autumn," he became seriously ill with tuberculosis, a tendency to which seemed to run in the family. In 1820, his health rapidly worsened. In September, he left England for Italy, hoping that the warmer climate would improve his health. He stayed in Rome but did not recover. Keats died on February 23, 1821, and was buried in the Protestant Cemetery in Rome.

POEM TEXT

I

Season of mists and mellow fruitfulness,
Close bosom-friend of the maturing sun;
Conspiring with him how to load and bless
With fruit the vines that round the thatch-eves run;
To bend with apples the moss'd cottage-trees,   5
And fill all fruit with ripeness to the core;
To swell the gourd, and plump the hazel shells
With a sweet kernel; to set budding more,
And still more, later flowers for the bees,
Until they think warm days will never cease,   10
For Summer has o'er-brimm'd their clammy cells.

II

Who hath not seen thee oft amid thy store?
Sometimes whoever seeks abroad may find

Thee sitting careless on a granary floor,
Thy hair soft-lifted by the winnowing wind;   15
Or on a half-reap'd furrow sound asleep,
Drows'd with the fume of poppies, while thy
      hook
Spares the next swath and all its twined flowers:
And sometimes like a gleaner thou dost keep
Steady thy laden head across a brook;   20
Or by a cyder-press, with patient look,
Thou watchest the last oozings hours by hours.

III

Where are the songs of Spring? Ay, where are
      they?
Think not of them, thou hast thy music too,—
While barred clouds bloom the soft-dying day,   25
And touch the stubble-plains with rosy hue;
Then in a wailful choir the small gnats mourn
Among the river sallows, borne aloft
Or sinking as the light wind lives or dies;
And full-grown lambs loud bleat from
      hilly bourn;   30
Hedge-crickets sing; and now with treble soft
The red-breast whistles from a garden-croft;
And gathering swallows twitter in the skies.

POEM SUMMARY

Stanza 1

"To Autumn" consists of three stanzas of eleven lines each. Stanza 1 begins with a general description of the characteristics of autumn. Autumn is a time when nature's processes of growth come to fruition. Everything has reached a mature stage of growth, yet growth still continues. Beginning in line 2 and continuing throughout the stanza, the season of autumn is presented as being in league with the sun to bring about this state of ripeness in nature. The vines that cling to the eaves of the cottages' thatched roofs are flowering. Trees are weighed down with apples, and all the fruit is ripe (line 6). In line 7, the poet gives more examples of ripeness, using verbs that convey images of growth and fullness as applied to gourds and hazelnuts. Flowers continue to bloom (lines 8–9), providing a seemingly endless supply for the bees to gather nectar or pollen. In lines 10–11, the bees are presented as being so full of what they gather from the flowers that they think the heat of summer will never end.

MEDIA ADAPTATIONS

- *John Keats*, an audio CD in the Great Poets series, was released by Naxos AudioBooks in 2007.
- *Poetry of Keats*, read by Sir Ralph Richardson, was released on audio cassette by Caedmon in 1996.

Stanza 2

In stanza 2, the poet addresses autumn directly. Autumn is personified as a woman, perhaps a kind of goddess figure, as shown by the use of the word *thee* to address her. In lines 12 and 13, the poet says that she can often be seen by anyone who cares to look. The emphasis in this stanza is not on growth but on harvesting. Autumn is presented in four different guises. First (lines 14–15), she might be found sitting on the floor of a granary (a storehouse for grain), her hair just fluttering a little in the breeze. Then perhaps (lines 16–17) this female autumn figure might be found asleep, pushed into slumber by the odor of poppies, in a furrow of a partially harvested field of grain. As autumn sleeps, the poet imagines a brief moment while the harvesting stops (line 18). In line 19, autumn is presented in a third guise, this time as a gleaner stepping across a brook with a load on her head. A gleaner is a person who picks up grain that has been left in the field by harvesters. In lines 21 and 22, autumn is seen in yet another guise. She watches in a state of repose a cider press as it creates cider from pulped apples.

Stanza 3

Stanza 3 continues for the first two lines the direct address to autumn. The first line has a note of regret, as the vanished sounds of spring are twice recalled, but in line 2 the poet states that the passing of spring is not something to be regretted. Autumn has its own sounds that are, it is implied, of equal value and beauty. The remainder of the stanza evokes these sounds of autumn. First, in line 3, the poet refers to a gentle autumn sunset in which the stubble on the harvested fields takes on a reddish color. At that time of day, the sound of gnats can be heard, like a choir singing a melancholy song. Coming from the sallow trees by the river, the sound of the gnats is heard in the gentle breeze as it rises and falls (lines 28–29). A sallow tree is a kind of willow tree with broad leaves. In lines 30 and 31, the poet refers to more sounds that can be heard in autumn: the bleating of lambs and the singing of the crickets in the hedges. Finally, completing the variety of natural sounds, the poet evokes the songs of the robin with its red breast and the swallows that call as they gather in the sky ready to migrate for the winter.

THEMES

Nature

The poem, especially in the first stanza, creates the impression of the fullness of the natural world. At this point in autumn, nature is full and complete. The earth and the sun combine to create abundance. Everything is ripe. Indeed, nature is almost weighed down by its own fullness. The vines that run around the thatched roofs of the cottages are loaded with fruit; the apple trees are so full of apples that the branches are bending under the weight. The fullness presented is not a static condition; everything is still growing and filling out, as is emphasized by the description of the gourd and hazelnut in stanza 1, line 7. The flowers are still budding, and the sense of a never-ending fullness is conveyed by the repetition of the word *more* in stanza 1, lines 8 and 9. The word is used to describe the flowers but applies to all of nature's processes that are presented in the first stanza of the poem. Nature is so full that even the bees can hardly keep up with their work.

The pattern of imagery in this first stanza ensures that all of nature, from great to small, is included in this fullness. The poem begins rather like a cinematic long shot of a misty autumnal scene, and this is followed by the expansive image of the sun. Following this is what might be referred to as a medium shot of vines growing around the eaves of thatched cottages and orchards full of apple trees. Then the images of nature become smaller and smaller, as if nature is being revealed in a series of close-ups. From the apple trees, the reader is taken to gourds and hazelnuts, flowers and bees, and finally to the overfilled cells of bees, a detailed image that completes the picture of nature's fullness in all its manifestations.

Opposites

In stanza 1, the emphasis is on action and movement in nature, but in stanza 2, while movement still continues, it is balanced by moments of stillness and inaction. This is conveyed through the personification of autumn as a female figure, who is shown in various attitudes of repose: sitting on the granary floor, asleep in the fields, and watching the cider press. There is still activity going on, but beside it there is rest; the two opposites are somehow reconciled. This is part of a wider set of opposites that are reconciled in the poem. Whereas stanza 1 emphasizes fullness and continued growth, stanza 3 focuses on another aspect of autumn. Although the beauty of the sounds of autumn are celebrated, there is also an awareness that nature's cycle is beginning to shift and move on; the other side of fullness is emptiness and death, the qualities of winter. The reference in the last line to the swallows gathering in order to migrate is a sign that winter is approaching. The two direct references to death in this stanza—the dying day and the dying down of the light wind—are also gentle hints about what is to come. The same is true of the reference in line 5 to the mournful wailing of the gnats. This may be part of the pleasing music of autumn that the poet announces in line 2 but is also a subtle reference to loss and death that puts in mind the wider reality of nature's processes. If there is life there is also death, not only of all the natural phenomena mentioned in the poem, but of human life, too.

Natural Cycles

Throughout the poem there is a feeling of relaxed acceptance of nature's processes. This is apparent even in line 1, where the word *mellow* suggests not only the pleasing flavor resulting from the ripeness of the fruit but also the relaxed frame of mind of the speaker. The poet just watches, observes, and accepts everything that nature does; he does not argue, regret, or speculate. Indeed, at the beginning of stanza 3, the poet takes it upon himself to cheer up the personified figure of autumn by telling her not to regret the absence of the sounds of spring because she, autumn, has her own sounds that are of equal value. In this way, the poet lays out his own acceptance of life and death. Everything in nature may be impermanent, but that is no cause for distress or protest: just as there is a time for growth, there is a time for decay.

TOPICS FOR FURTHER STUDY

- Write an essay in which you compare and contrast "To Autumn" with either "Ode to a Nightingale" or "Ode on a Grecian Urn." Do the poems have themes and imagery in common? How do they differ in mood, atmosphere, and formal structure?

- Using for your research *The Romantics: English Literature in Its Historical, Cultural, and Social Contexts* by Neil King, one of five volumes in the young-adult "Backgrounds to English Literature" series published by Chelsea House in 2002, or other print and online sources, give a class presentation in which you explain why "To Autumn" should be considered a romantic movement poem. What characteristics does it have that classifies it as romantic? Use PowerPoint or a similar program to present your main ideas.

- Write a short poem about autumn or any of the seasons. For preparation, you might want to take a walk, like the one Keats took on that Sunday in September 1819 that led to him writing the poem "To Autumn." Note what you see and use it as a basis for the poem.

- Visit http://www.npg.org.uk/home.php, the Web site of London's National Portrait Gallery, and do a search on John Keats. The search will produce a number of portraits of Keats. Two are by Joseph Severn, who accompanied Keats to Rome and tended him until his death. Other artists include Henry Meyer, Charles Armitage Brown, and William Hilton. Look at all the portraits, and then select two or three that you like best. Write a paragraph or two in which you describe Keats's appearance in each portrait. What clothes does he wear? How would you describe his face and hair? What is the expression on his face? What is in the background? Are the portraits realistic or romanticized? Does Keats look similar in each portrait or different? How is he different? Which portrait do you like best, and why?

STYLE

Ode

"To Autumn" is an ode. An ode is an elaborate lyric poem with a formal structure consisting of several stanzas. It is dignified in tone and language and usually treats a serious topic. The first two lines of Keats's ode illustrates the kind of formal, elegant diction that is typical of the ode form. (Diction refers to the language of the poem and the type of words and phrases used.) The elaborate way in which autumn is addressed in these first two lines is an example of periphrasis, in which indirect phrases are used to describe an ordinary object, an abstraction, or a simple action in a roundabout way. Periphrasis was common in eighteenth century English poetry, and Keats is following in this tradition.

The ode was first developed in classical literature by the Greek poet Pindar and the Roman poet Horace. In English literature, odes either follow the pattern of Pindar or Horace or of a third category, the irregular ode. An example of the latter is Wordsworth's "Ode: Intimations of Immortality." Most of Keats's odes, including "To Autumn" are Horatian in form, in which all of the stanzas follow the same structure. The eleven-line stanza and its rhyming pattern in "To Autumn" is Keats's own invention.

Rhyme and Meter

The rhyme scheme varies only slightly. In stanza 1, line 1 rhymes with line 3, line 2 with line 4, line 5 with lines 9 and 10, line 6 with line 8, and line 7 with 11. This rhyme scheme might be represented as follows: *abab cde dcce.* In stanzas 2 and 3, there is a slight alteration. The fifth line rhymes with eighth line, while the sixth line rhymes with ninth and tenth lines. This rhyme scheme might be represented as follows: *abab cde dcce.*

The poem describes apples on "the moss'd cottage-trees" and "all fruit with ripeness to the core."
(Image copyright Vphoto, 2010. Used under license from Shutterstock.com)

The meter (pattern of stressed syllables) is predominantly iambic pentameter. An iamb is a poetic foot (unit of meter) consisting of two syllables, the first unstressed and the second stressed. It is the most common foot in English poetry. A pentameter consists of five feet. Lines 4, 7, and 26 are examples of regular iambic pentameter. However, Keats varies the meter on many occasions. He makes frequent use of spondees. A spondee is a foot in which both syllables are stressed. The third foot of line 10 in stanza 1 is a spondee that emphasizes the warmth of summer. The fact that the first syllable of that foot is stressed makes it stand out against the expected iambic rhythm, in which the first syllable of the foot is always unstressed. Spondees also occur in stanza 2 (lines 16 and 18) and frequently in stanza 3: the last foot of line 27 (the gnats), line 29 (the wind), line 30 (third foot), line 31 (first foot), and line 32 (second foot). Keats also employs trochaic feet. A trochaic foot is an inverted iamb: it consists of a stressed syllable followed by an unstressed one. The most common place for this inversion is at the beginning of a line. Examples occur in stanza 1, line 1; stanza 2, lines 17, 18, and 20; and stanza 3, line 23.

Apostrophe

Apostrophe is a figure of speech in which an absent person or a personified object is directly addressed. The title of the poem, "To Autumn," illustrates this figure of speech, which is employed throughout stanza 2 and continued in the first two lines of stanza 3. Keats also uses apostrophe in one of his other famous odes, "Ode on a Grecian Urn."

Personification

Personification is a figure of speech in which an object or an abstraction is given human qualities. Personification was a common figure of speech in eighteenth century English poetry, and Keats continues that tradition in stanza 2 of the poem, in which he personifies autumn as a female figure going about her tasks, sometimes resting from weariness.

Imagery

The imagery in the poem is drawn from nature, such as fruit, flowers, bees, and birds. The images appeal primarily to the sense of sight, as the poet creates a series of pictures of autumn. The last stanza, however, contains as many auditory (related to the sense of hearing) as visual images as the poet describes the variety of natural sounds that are heard in autumn. In stanza 2, there is a notable olfactory (related to the sense of smell) image in line 17, referring to the poppies.

HISTORICAL CONTEXT

The English Romantic Movement

The romantic movement in English literature began in the last decade of the eighteenth century, when William Wordsworth (1770–1850), Samuel Taylor Coleridge (1772–1834), and William Blake (1757–1827) began to publish their poetry. Keats belongs to the second generation of romantic poets and was the youngest of the six major figures. He was a contemporary of Percy Bysshe Shelley (1792–1822) and Lord Byron (1788–1824).

One of the seminal works of the emerging movement was Wordsworth and Coleridge's *Lyrical Ballads*, published in 1798, in which Wordsworth rejected the formal poetic diction of the eighteenth century and wrote in a language that was closer to the way ordinary people spoke. Wordsworth is also known for his love of nature, particularly the area in northwest England known as the Lake District, where he lived almost all of his life. Keats did not discover the poetry of Wordsworth until 1816, and he quickly judged him England's greatest living poet. Wordsworth was to have a great influence on Keats's poetic development.

Keats was a typical romantic in that he valued imagination over reason, feeling over thought. Along with Wordsworth and Blake, he believed that the imagination provided a more complete understanding of truth than could be gained by the unaided rational mind. In one of his letters he wrote, "What the imagination seizes as Beauty must be truth" (a thought he would also express in his "Ode on a Grecian Urn"), and he longed for "a Life of Sensations rather than of Thoughts." Also typical of romanticism was Keats's interest in dreams as a way of exploring aspects of human consciousness beyond the everyday waking mind. His poem "The Eve of St. Agnes" is an example of this.

Many of the romantics expressed their response to nature through the form of the lyric poem, including the ode, and in this Keats was also typical of his time. Wordsworth, Coleridge, and Shelley all wrote odes. Shelley's "Ode to the West Wind" is one of the most famous.

Keats and Shelley were personally acquainted, but they kept their distance from each other. They met in December 1816, and Shelley, having read some of Keats's poems, advised him not to publish them—advice that Keats did not take. After Keats died Shelley wrote an elegy, *Adonais*, in his memory. Byron did not know Keats personally, but he did express a dislike of Keats's poetry, although he modified his judgment after Keats's death, praising Keats's unfinished epic poem, *Hyperion*.

The Peterloo Massacre

In the 1810s England was in a period of economic distress. Life for the working classes was particularly hard. Wages were falling, unemployment was high, and there was growing agitation for political reform. In the summer of 1819, public protest meetings were held in the English cities of Leeds, Stockport, and Birmingham, as well as in Glasgow, Scotland. On August 16, a huge crowd of between sixty and eighty thousand people gathered in St. Peter's Fields, Manchester, to call for political reform, including universal suffrage. Barely had the meeting started when orders were given for the militia to arrest one of the leaders of the reform movement, Henry Hunt, known as "Orator" Hunt. In the ensuing cavalry charge, fifteen people were killed, and between four hundred and seven hundred were injured. The incident quickly became known as the Peterloo Massacre and produced shock and outrage throughout the country.

Several of the English romantic poets reacted strongly to the massacre. Living in Italy at the time, Percy Bysshe Shelley, who was always on the side of reform, expected a revolution to break out shortly. He wrote a poem, "The Mask of Anarchy," in which he encouraged the masses to rise up against their oppressors. Lord Byron, who was also living in exile in Italy, expressed a similar view about the imminence of a revolution. However, no revolution occurred. The British government responded swiftly to the Peterloo Massacre by passing repressive laws later that year aimed at stifling the reform movement. These laws were known as the Six Acts. Political reform would

COMPARE
&
CONTRAST

- **1810s:** Britain emerges victorious in the Napoleonic Wars following the victory at the Battle of Waterloo in 1815. In this battle, Britain and its ally Prussia defeat France under Emperor Napoleon I. Victory does not bring prosperity, however, and Britain endures hard economic times for the remainder of the decade.

  Today: Britain joins the U.S.-led invasion of Iraq in 2003 and withdraws its combat forces six years later, in April 2009. Britain also endures, along with much of the rest of the world, a severe economic recession beginning in 2008.

- **1810s:** The most popular poets in England are Lord Byron and Sir Walter Scott. Byron's personal magnetism and scandalous life make him the most famous poet in Europe, while Scott's

  verse narratives such as *The Lady of the Lake* (1810) are perennial favorites.

  Today: In an online British Broadcasting Corporation (BBC) poll taken to mark National Poetry Day, T. S. Eliot is voted Britain's favorite poet. The only living poet to make the top ten is Rastafarian performance poet Benjamin Zephaniah. Keats places ninth.

- **1810s:** Romanticism is a growing movement in literature, art, and music in Europe, especially England and Germany.

  Today: Literature is dominated by the movement known as postmodernism. Most poets do not write formal verse such as odes but prefer the flexibility of free verse.

---

have to wait more than a decade, until the Great Reform Act of 1832.

Keats, who is not thought of as a political poet, nonetheless followed political events quite closely and had decided opinions about the state of the country. He was in the huge supportive crowd that greeted Orator Hunt when he reached London on September 13 to await trial. Keats expressed his thoughts about the matter as part of a long letter he wrote to his brother George over ten days in late September, which was exactly the time during which he wrote "To Autumn." He believed that in spite of the current repression, there was hope that liberty would triumph.

CRITICAL OVERVIEW

"To Autumn" has always been regarded as one of Keats's finest poems. When books about Keats's work began appearing in the late-nineteenth century, the poem was often singled out for praise. In *Keats: A Study* (1880), the first book-length critical

study, F. M. Owen refers to the "autumnal glory which had touched the poet" when he wrote "To Autumn." In 1886, poet and critic A. C. Swinburne declared that Keats's odes are "unequalled and unrivalled." He selected "To Autumn" and "Ode on a Grecian Urn" as "perhaps the two nearest to absolute perfection, to the triumphant achievement accomplishment of the very utmost beauty possible to human words." Swinburne's comment was echoed by poet Robert Bridges in his book *A Critical Introduction to the Poems of John Keats* (1896), in which he places "To Autumn" as the finest of Keats's odes, declaring, "I do not know that any sort of fault can be found in it."

The assessments by Swinburne and Bridges set the tone for much twentieth-century criticism of the poem. M. R. Ridley, for example, in *Keats' Craftsmanship: A Study in Poetic Development*, first published in 1933, describes it as "the most serenely flawless poem in our language." In an influential collection published in 1963, Walter Jackson Bate acknowledges that the ode "is one of the most nearly perfect poems in English," and he points out that it brings together many of Keats's typical

Sheep grazing on English hillside with autumn colors (*Image copyright Kevin Eaves, 2010. Used under license from Shutterstock.com*)

concerns and reconciles them, such as presenting a union between process and stasis, movement and stillness. In *John Keats: His Life and Writings* (first published 1966), Douglas Bush builds on Bate's reading and refines it. He argues that "To Autumn" is not quite the "poem of untroubled serenity" that many have taken it to be. Even while the poet celebrates, in the first two stanzas, the fullness inherent in autumn, there is "the overshadowing fact of impermanence. The summer has done its work and is departing; and if autumn comes, winter cannot be far behind." These "melancholy implications" are more fully developed in the final stanza in which "every item carries an elegiac note." The final result Keats achieves is "the power to see and accept life as it is, a perpetual process of ripening, decay, and death."

In an unusual reading, Dorothy van Ghent in *Keats: The Myth of the Hero* analyzes the poem in terms of the archetypal quest myth of the hero. The hero is the lyric voice of the speaker of the poem who attends "as celebrant on the epiphany of the earth-goddess and her withdrawal to the underworld." She explains that the poem contains all the elements of a fertility ritual, including the harvest, a goddess, and a priest (the poet). For another prominent critic, Helen Vendler, in *The Odes of John Keats* (1983), the ode arises not from a sense of fullness about the season leading to celebration but the opposite, a sense of deprivation, which is apparent in the stubble fields. Keats saw the stubble fields on the walk that inspired the poem. Vendler argues that Keats, on seeing those fields, "wished to fill up the empty canvas of the landscape, to replenish its denuded volume, to repopulate its boundaries." So he fills the scene with a succession of images to convey nature's fullness rather than its emptiness.

In his biography *Keats* (1997), Andrew Motion writes that the poem "seems easily to balance forces of life and death, and to combine a sense of natural growth with individual effort." He also takes into account more recent readings of the poem that emphasize the social context of the poem. This was a time of working-class unrest and government repression in England, and Keats's use of the word *gleaner* is significant. Gleaning had been made illegal in 1881, and Motion points out that Keats's use of the image of a gleaner "refers to his sympathy for the denied and the dispossessed."

CRITICISM

Bryan Aubrey

Aubrey holds a Ph.D. in English. In this essay, he considers "To Autumn" in terms of the ideas about poetry and creativity that Keats discussed in his letters.

Readers since Keats's day have been struck by the serenity and sense of acceptance that pervades the ode "To Autumn." In this respect it differs from two of the great odes Keats wrote just a few months earlier. In "Ode to a Nightingale," for example, the poet is a distressed figure who finds solace in a momentary loss of self stimulated by the song of the nightingale. The ode has some of the luxurious imagery of nature (although in springtime) that is also found in "To Autumn," but it ends on a note of loss and doubt; the poet cannot permanently lose himself in nature as he does in the later poem. He questions the nature of the self and of reality. Like the nightingale ode, "Ode on a Grecian Urn" also alludes to the sorrows inherent in earthly life. The poem celebrates the figures on the urn precisely because they are beyond the world of process and change. The trees depicted will never shed their leaves; spring will never depart. The life depicted on the urn is frozen in a moment of passionate desire that can never fade. It is this vision of the eternal sensual moment that makes the urn a comfort, says the poet, to humans throughout the ages, who must deal with the realities of change, decay, suffering, and loss.

There is none of this need for escape or comfort in "To Autumn." There is no contrast or opposition between eternity and change; there is no flight from earthly reality followed by an anguished return. "To Autumn" strikes a note of acceptance from the beginning and does not waver. The poet not only contemplates but also relishes and celebrates the natural process, including the cycle of the seasons. There is no sense in which the poet's self is struggling to understand or to escape from life. He observes the scene untroubled and undisturbed. The only question he asks (in the first line of stanza 3) is a rhetorical one, to which he already knows the answer. He says that no one should regret the passing of the songs of spring because autumn has its own sounds that are of equal beauty. Keats answers his own question not by a process of intellectual reasoning, of which he was always suspicious, but

POETRY FOR KEATS EMERGES
SPONTANEOUSLY FROM A WELL OF STILLNESS,
AND THE ENTIRE PROCESS RESEMBLES A
NATURALLY RECURRING EVENT."

through a kind of intuitive understanding, felt in the blood rather than reasoned in the mind.

It is this sense of serene acceptance of whatever life brings that makes this ode the perfect example of what Keats described as "negative capability." This is part of a definition of the state of mind that Keats believed the poet should cultivate. He described it in a letter he wrote to his brothers George and Tom in late December 1817. He mentions a discussion he had just had with a friend that had led him to a new understanding of the nature of poetic creativity:

> [S]everal things dovetailed in my mind, & at once it struck me, what quality went to form a Man of Achievement especially in Literature & which Shakespeare possessed so enormously—I mean *Negative Capability*, that is when man is capable of being in uncertainties, Mysteries, doubts, without any irritable reaching after fact & reason— Coleridge, for instance, would let go by a fine isolated verisimilitude caught from the Penetralium of mystery, from being incapable of remaining content with half knowledge. This pursued through Volumes would perhaps take us no further than this, that with a great poet the sense of Beauty overcomes every other consideration, or rather obliterates all consideration.

This passage, along with many others in Keats's letters, has become famous as an ideal to which the poet might aspire. Keats means that the poet should not allow the constant, restless questioning of the mind to dominate his awareness, because the mind is more likely to obscure truth than to reveal it. The poet should pay no attention to it but instead be more present in each moment with his whole being, open to whatever experience is presenting itself to him. When a person can lay the mind aside, the beauty inherent in all things may reveal itself. Keats pokes a little fun at Samuel Taylor Coleridge, his older contemporary, a man of enormous intellect who followed his mind wherever it insisted on leading him and whose poetic

WHAT
DO I READ
NEXT?

- Keats's "Ode to a Nightingale" is one of his great odes. It was written in May 1819, only a few months before "To Autumn." The poem was stimulated by the delight Keats took in the song of a nightingale that he listened to as he sat in the garden outside Charles Brown's house in Hampstead, London, where he was living at the time. One morning Keats sat for several hours in the garden under a plum tree and wrote the poem. It can be found in any edition of Keats's poetry, including *Complete Poems and Selected Letters of John Keats*, with an introduction by Edward Hirsch (2001).

- William Wordsworth's majestic "Ode: Intimations of Immortality from Recollections of Early Childhood" completed in 1804 and published in 1807, is one of the greatest odes in the English language. Keats knew it well, and it was very influential on his thinking. The ode can be found in any collection of Wordsworth's poems, including *William Wordsworth: The Major Works, including the Prelude* (2007) edited by Stephen Gill.

- *Poetry and Politics in the Cockney School: Keats, Shelley, Hunt and their Circle* by Jeffrey Hunt (2004) is a detailed look at the circle of writers who gathered around the journalist, minor poet, and radical Leigh Hunt. These include the second generation of English romantics, not only Shelley, Keats, and Byron but also the essayist William Hazlitt and others. Jeffrey Hunt draws out their relationships and gives a fascinating picture of

how this literary group operated and the principles it represented.

- *John Keats* by Stephen Hebron (2002) is a biography of Keats for young adults. It is well illustrated, with paintings, drawings, and etchings that bring the romantic period to life. Hebron gives a compelling portrait of Keats's short, tragic, but inspiring life.

- *Art & Nature: An Illustrated Anthology of Nature Poetry* (1992) by Kate Ferrell is a lavishly illustrated volume. It contains almost two hundred nature poems, organized by season, and is illustrated with photographs of artwork from the Metropolitan Museum of Art.

- *From Totems to Hip-Hop: A Multicultural Anthology of Poetry Across the Americas 1900–2002*, edited by the poet and novelist by Ishmael Reed (2002), is an anthology that spans over a hundred years of American poetry. Poets of all races are represented, including Sylvia Plath, Yusef Komunyakaa, Thulani Davis, Bob Holman, Jayne Cortez, Diane Glancy, Garrett Hongo, Charles Simic, Al Young, Nellie Wong, Gertrude Stein, Ai, and Tupac Shakur. The anthology shows how poetry has changed over the last century and even more so since Keats wrote his formally structured ode "To Autumn." The anthology also includes poetic manifestos and commentaries that can be compared with Keats's own beliefs about poetry as expressed in many of his letters.

---

genius flamed out before he was thirty. Keats referred to his friend Charles Wentworth Dilke in terms similar to those he used about Coleridge. At almost exactly the time he wrote "To Autumn," he wrote to his brother George and his wife that "Dilke will never come at a truth as long as he lives; because he is always trying at it."

Keats wrote often about how he would lose himself in contemplation of whatever came his way.

In November 1817, he wrote to his friend Benjamin Bailey that "if a Sparrow come before my Window I take part in its existence and pick about the Gravel." It is this sense of the poet's self standing aside in order to allow the fullest possible experience of life in all its manifestations that is so apparent in "To Autumn." The questing self has retreated before the beauty of the perceived moment and the larger natural process of which it is a part.

It is perhaps this absence of the self that enables the poet to sense the stillness that underlies the ongoing process of autumn. Underlying the movement of the season is a state of rest. These two states, activity and rest, coexist in an easy equilibrium. This is presented in the second stanza. The personified figure of autumn is shown sitting (not working) on a granary floor, asleep in a field as the reaping is momentarily suspended, and as a gleaner carefully balancing a load on her head as she steps across a brook. The last image all by itself suggests a balance between activity and stasis, and as such it is typical of Keats's poetry. He was frequently inspired in his work by sculpture and painting that showed human figures caught in a moment of repose yet also contained great dynamism (potential for physical energy, movement, or change).

The second stanza of "To Autumn" shows that although Keats has often been thought of as a poet of the richness of sensual experience—and he is that—he is also a poet of silence and stillness. For Keats, a kind of inner silence was not an idea but a direct experience. He often appears to have slipped into a quiet state of mind in which the boundaries of the self relaxed, and he uses various phrases in his poetry to describe this (in "Ode to Psyche" for example). It was clearly an experience he valued greatly. Sometimes he called it idleness or indolence, but he gave those terms a positive meaning, associating them with creativity. Poetry emerges from those moments of relaxed quietness.

In one of his early poems, "Sleep and Poetry," he personifies poetry as a figure of great power half-sleeping on its own arm, which is another image, as in "To Autumn," of the coexistence of rest and dynamism. Seen in this light, stanza 2 of "To Autumn" becomes a metaphor of the creative process, one that adheres to some fundamental principle in life as a whole. Poetry for Keats emerges spontaneously from a well of stillness, and the entire process resembles a naturally recurring event. Keats expressed this idea in a letter he wrote to his friend and publisher John Taylor on February 27, 1818: "the rise, the progress, the setting of imagery should like the Sun come natural. . . . If Poetry comes not as naturally as the Leaves to a tree it had better not come at all." So it was with "To Autumn," a poem that appears to have been written quickly and easily, although as M. R. Ridley pointed out in *Keats' Craftsmanship: A Study in Poetic Development*, a preserved earlier draft of the poem shows that stanza 2 gave Keats some difficulties. Once he had solved them the poem emerged in the form it is read today. Given the turmoil of Keats's life at the time, in which he was beset by financial, emotional, and health problems, the serenity of this ode seems like a minor miracle. It was to be the last major poem he wrote. Seventeen months later, John Keats was dead.

Source: Bryan Aubrey, Critical Essay on "To Autumn," in *Poetry for Students*, Gale, Cengage Learning, 2011.

Arnd Bohm

In the following essay, Bohm asserts that "To Autumn" should be read in the political context of 1819.

The suggestion that Keats drew on James Thomson when composing the closing line of "To Autumn" has not aroused any consternation (Vendler 322). The situations are similar, and Keats echoes the crucial verb twitter: "And gathering swallows twitter in the skie" (361). Thomson had described the "swallow-people":

> rejoicing once
> Ere to their wintry slumbers they retire,
> In clusters clung beneath the mouldering bank,
> And where, unpierced by frost, the cavern sweats:
> Or rather, into warmer climes conveyed.
> With other kindred birds of season, there
> They twitter cheerful, till the vernal months
> Invite them welcome back—for thronging now
> Innumerous wings are in commotion all.

The discussion of Keats's reception of Thomson's Autumn has been directed by the assumption that both poets were linked primarily through the imagery and vocabulary of nature and that both poems dealt simply with nature. However, with growing awareness of Keats's social consciousness, especially troubled in the wake of the Peterloo Massacre, the language of "To Autumn," resonates with ever-clearer political overtones. For example, when set into the political context, the verb conspiring in the third line makes an explicit reference to the political climate of 1819, as Nicholas Roe has shown (254–57).

A word in the poem that has gone unexplored for its political implications is gathering in the last line. On one level, the adjective can be read as a straightforward description of what swallows and other birds do at that time of year, as Helen Vendler does: "the swallows (in the most gently touched of these phrases) are 'gathering' in a mutual cluster—whether for their night-wheeling

A thatched English cottage in autumn (*Image copyright Gary Andrews, 2010. Used under license from Shutterstock.com*)

or for their migration is deliberately left unspecified, but the steady onward progress of the season in the poem urges us to think of winter" (452–53). But when it is set in the historical context, the gathering also makes us think of the politics of public assemblies, so violently contested in 1819. First there were the events in Manchester, which pitted a lawful assembly against an increasingly repressive government (Chandler 15–21; Thompson 681–93). The entry of Henry Hunt into London on 13 September 1819 reinforced the right of free English people to assemble in public and to demonstrate their convictions. Keats happened to be in London and reported on the spectacle in a letter:

> You will hear by the papers of the proceedings at Manchester and Hunt's triumphal entry into London—It would take me a whole day and a quire of paper to give you any thing like detail. I will merely mention that it is calculated that 30,000 people were in the streets waiting for him—The whole distance from the Angel Islington to the Crown and anchor was lined with Multitudes. (Letters 2: 194–95)

Although English law recognized neither an unrestricted right of free assembly nor an explicit right of voluntary association, there was a widespread conviction that such rights did exist and had done so since Anglo-Saxon times. The constellation of facts, institutions, and historical myths that sustained belief in the "ancient constitution" offered reassurance that the people were the ultimate source of political power. A patriotic poet such as Thomson could wax eloquent in describing an England where free men joined together for the common good:

> Then gathering men their natural powers
>   combined,
> And formed a public; to the general good
> Submitting, aiming, and conducting all.
> For this the patriot-council met, the full,
> The free, and fairly represented whole;
> For this they planned the holy guardian
>   laws,
> Distinguished orders, animated arts,
> And, with joint force Oppression chaining,
>   set
> Imperial Justice at the helm, yet still
> To them accountable: nor slavish dreamed
> That toiling millions must resign their weal
> And all the honey of their search to such
> As for themselves alone themselves have
>   raised.

Gathering, grammatically identical with the present participle of Keats's "gathering swallows," here initiates a series of actions that becomes unstoppable progress to liberty and prosperity. If in September 1819 Keats turned his mind to Thomson's *Autumn*, as the "twittering swallows" indicate, then, by the same token, he would have recalled Thomson's vision of an England where justice and liberty prevailed (Griffin 74–97; Ridley).

When read in isolation as a poem about one season, "To Autumn" appears to end on a somewhat desolate note, anticipating the bleakness of winter without even the optimism of cyclical progress. However, Thomson explicitly reminds readers that the swallows return in the spring; the onset of winter is a phase, not an end. The "swallow-people" twitter cheerfully as they participate in the natural process. In the same vein, the interpolated vision of how liberty had been established in England through the actions of "gathering men" stressed that history was a process. Thomson was confident that if liberty were threatened, the same forces that had first freed people could and would act again in the present and future. The restoration of liberty, like the return of spring, would take its natural course.

However cloying Thomson's sentimentalism might seem to a jaded observer today, in the gloom of 1819 it was a bulwark against despair. The echo of gathering suggests that Keats let himself be persuaded that the autumn of political oppression and social injustice would be followed by a spring of liberation and the government by "the patriot-council, the full, / The free, and fairly represented whole." If it was natural for the swallows to assemble without hindrance, then surely the people of England could do likewise, without being trampled and killed as they had been in Manchester.

Source: Arnd Bohm, "The Politics of Gathering in Thomson's *Autumn* and Keats's 'To Autumn,'" in *ANQ*, Vol. 20, No. 2, Spring 2007, pp. 30–32.

Thomas Dilworth

In the following essay, Dilworth discusses Keats's use of the word "barred" as a descriptor for clouds.

I have always wondered why in line 24 of Keats's "To Autumn" the clouds at sunset are "barred." Keats writes that Autumn has its own songs, "While barred clouds bloom the soft-dying day, / and touch the stubble-plains with rosy hue" (lines 24–25). The adjective "barred" implies that the clouds are long and thin like horizontal bars. It is, however, an odd modifier for clouds and, as

merely descriptive, seems underemployed. This is especially so considering that Keats took some trouble over the image, "barred clouds bloom" being a manuscript replacement for "a gold cloud gilds." In a poem of such tactile and kinesthetic imagery, "barred" seems to have more than visual force. Bars obstruct, curtail movement, may be grasped and held. Furthermore, they verbally correspond with the "cells" of bees in line 11, which "Summer has o'er-brimm'd" with honey. Cells in a honeycomb are not prison cells, of course, but the word is the same, and the sameness is augmented by the bee cells being "clammy." The connotation of discomfort increases possible association with prison cells, which are conventionally, if not clammy (though dungeon cells are), uncomfortable. Windows in prison cells are barred. If "barred clouds" do evoke imprisonment, they symbolically mean one or both of two things: that the poet and reader (and all of humanity) are imprisoned; or that the sun, which is setting behind the clouds, is imprisoned. If the latter, Keats may be influenced by the sun behind the skeleton ship in Coleridge's "The Rime of the Ancient Mariner":

> And straight the Sun was flecked with bars,
> (Heaven's Mother send us grace!)
> As if through a dungeon grate he peered
> With broad and burning face. (176–80)

If the poet, reader, and the rest of humanity are imprisoned, there would be possible justification for the negative connotations of "Conspiring" in line 3 of Keats's poem. There Autumn is "Close bosom-friend of the maturing sun; / Conspiring with him how to load and bless / with fruit the vines [. . .]" (2–3). Beyond immediate positive purpose, the sun colludes with all seasons to "imprison" humanity in time. About this, of course, the sun and seasons are not free but are themselves similarly constrained.

The sense of "barred" as indicative of constraint—an indication increased by association with "Conspiring" and "cells"—adds to the connotations of mutability throughout the poem, which virtually all critics and readers have noticed. It darkens them by adding the element of enforcement and implied oppositional desire. The overall meaning of the poem is slightly altered, its effect strengthened. Negative connotations increase the impression of abundance by contrast to it, as seasoning increases the taste of food, as darkness makes light brighter. In the poem, physical, emotional, and sonic abundance remains the primary reality owing to emphasis on awareness of the present moment, which is secured by imagery of touch and kinesthesis. This suits Keats's stated preference for experience over philosophical thinking—"O for a Life of Sensations rather than of Thoughts!" Immediate tactile sensation here results in an experience of fullness and peace, which resists thoughts of winter and death that time inevitably brings. The imagery of constraint gives special emphasis to awareness in, and of, the present and highlights a heretofore unappreciated thematic aspect of the poem. It implies that inner freedom of awareness and attention is available to the poet and reader, and to anyone else, in any physically contextual situation. As Richard Lovelace put it, "Stone walls do not a prison make, / Nor iron bars a cage."

Source: Thomas Dilworth, "Keats's 'To Autumn,'" in *Explicator*, Vol. 65, No. 1, Fall 2006, pp. 26–28.

Stuart M. Sperry

In the following essay, Sperry views "To Autumn" as Keats's "most mature comment on the nature of the poetic process."

The fallacy of using any single work, such as *The Fall of Hyperion*, either to predict or limit the shape of Keats's career or the direction of his evolution, had he lived, is nowhere better demonstrated than in the lyric he transcribed the same day he announced the final abandonment of *Hyperion*—the ode "To Autumn." As John Middleton Murry long ago observed, the two works are almost total contrasts in tone and spirit. With its struggle for ascent through doubt and self-questioning to a point of visionary comprehensiveness above the human world, the longer work is fired with a Miltonic ardor and intensity. In its condensed but unhurried perfection, its contemplation of the actual, the ode is much closer to Shakespeare. The two works, to be certain, share one supreme concern: their common involvement with process. However as treatments of that theme they differ immeasurably. *Hyperion* fails through the inability to evolve a framework for transcending process, for reconciling man to the knowledge of sorrow and loss. "The Autumn" succeeds through its acceptance of an order innate in our experience—the natural rhythm of the seasons. It is a poem that, without ever stating it, inevitably suggests the truth of "ripeness is all" by developing, with a richness and profundity of implication, the simple perception that ripeness is fall.

> THE AWARENESS OF IMPERMANENCE AND ULTIMATELY OF DEATH IS NO LESS MOVING BECAUSE IT MUST BE MOMENTARILY SUPPRESSED IN A WAY THAT MAKES US RECOGNIZE THE IMPOSSIBILITY OF ANY DIRECT CONFRONTATION."

The perfection of the ode lies chiefly in the care and subtlety of patterning within its three-part structure. The patterns are ones that partly connect "To Autumn" with the odes of the spring and partly mark a new development and vary in complexity. As critics have often pointed out, the three stanzas successively proceed from the last growth of late summer through the fullness of high autumn to the spareness of an early winter landscape, just as they suggest the progress of a single day through to its close in sunset. As Bush, among others, has noted, the imagery of the first stanza is mainly tactile, that of the second mainly visual, that of the last chiefly auditory. In these and other respects the ode displays a deliberate symmetry and balance the earlier odes do not possess. At the same time it makes a more even and practiced use of devices developed in its predecessors. The personification of the season, introduced at the beginning of the first stanza in a way reminiscent of the opening of the "Urn," is developed in the second into a full series of tableaux, and then is briefly and elegiacally revived at the outset of the third before the ode returns us to the simple sounds and images of the natural landscape. There remains, too, but in a more subtle way, the pattern of lyric questioning, from the submerged "how" of the first stanza, to the rhetorical "who" at the outset of the second, to the more imperative "where" at the commencement of the third, that marks the gradual emergence into consciousness of the recognition the season both epitomizes and expresses. One must add, following Bate's observation that "'To Autumn' is so uniquely a distillation," that the ode is Keats's last and most mature comment on the nature of the poetic process. For its whole development, from the imagery of ripening and storing in the first stanza, through that of winnowing and slow extraction in the second, to the subtle, thin, and tenuous music with which the poem rises to its close, represents his final adaptation of his favorite metaphor for poetic creation. The analogy Shelley makes explicit in his "Ode to the West Wind" is not less moving or real because it is left implicit in Keats's hymn. If the "wild West Wind" and its "mighty harmonies" express Shelley's sense of a universal force of spiritual creativity, the autumnal sounds that are borne away on "the light wind" that "lives or dies" at the end of Keats's ode converge to produce a music that is poignantly natural.

The ironies that pervade the odes of the spring are by no means missing in "To Autumn." However they are now resolved within an image that transcends them—the image of autumn itself. Virtually from its beginning the ode compels us to conceive of the season in two different ways: as a conventional setting or personified abstraction that has been depicted poetically and pictorially from time immemorial with a fixed nature and identity of its own; and as a seasonal interval, a mere space between summer and winter that can never be abstracted from the larger cycle of birth and death.

> Season of mists and mellow fruitfulness,
> Close bosom-friend of the maturing sun;
> Conspiring with him how to load and bless
> With fruit the vines that round the thatch-
>   eves run.
> (1–4)

The homely, welcoming personifications seem to proclaim a role that is familiar and established. Nevertheless, as B. C. Southam has observed, the opening line, with its allusion both to "mists" and "mellow fruitfulness," already points to different and contrasting aspects of the year.

While the first stanza concentrates upon the natural world through images of growth and process, the second stanza shifts to a more artful and stylized conception by presenting autumn as a figure captured and framed within a series of perspectives that are recognizably conventional. However the two conceptions of autumn, as process and abstraction, continually modify and interpenetrate each other. To take only one example, there is the depiction in the second stanza of autumn

> sitting careless on a granary floor,
> Thy hair soft-lifted by the winnowing wind;
> Or on a half-reap'd furrow sound asleep,
> Drows'd with the fume of poppies, while thy
>   hook
> Spares the next swath and all its twined
>   flowers.
> (14–18)

The picture is more than an intermingling of activity and stasis. For a moment the figure of the season is involved with and actually worked upon by the very processes she emblemizes, even while she remains careless and impervious to the changes they imply. Such juxtapositions convey a sense of irony of the most delicate and subtle kind.

Throughout the ode the play of irony is developed by the way in which the major patterns alternate and run counter to each other. In the first stanza the sense of process and maturing is carried forward by such active verbs as "load," "bend," "fill," "swell," "plump," "set budding." At the same time another pattern of words, concentrated near the end of the stanza, suggests the contradictory idea of a repletion that has already been attained: "fruit*ful*ness," "all," "more, / And still more," "later," "never," "e[v]er." In the second stanza, which, as Bate has written, is "something of a reverse or mirror image of the first," autumn is personified in a series of fixed poses—as thresher, reaper, gleaner, watcher—that, in their immobility, suggest an ideal of completion. Nevertheless the effect is in a measure counterbalanced by a sustained use of partitives—"oft[en]," "Sometimes," "care*less*," "half," "next," "sometimes," "last," "hours by hours"—as well as by the movement and diversity implied by such different positioning prepositions and adverbs as "amid," "abroad," "across."

It is in the last stanza that these various oppositions achieve a resolution unlike any in the odes of the spring. The questioning with which the stanza begins becomes more direct and pressing, forcing into conscious recognition the knowledge that has all the while been growing latently throughout the ode:

> Where are the songs of Spring? Ay, where
>   are they?
> *Think not* of them, thou hast thy music too.
> (23–24)

The awareness of impermanence and ultimately of death is no less moving because it must be momentarily suppressed in a way that makes us recognize the impossibility of any direct confrontation. Still, such awareness is not finally rejected but rather tempered and reflected in the light of the "soft-dying day," where the imagery of the spring ("bloom," "rosy") is briefly reborn amid the tonalities of autumn, just as it is echoed in the "wailful choir" of gnats that "mourn" and in the distant "bleat[ing]" of the lambs. For it is, in the end, the *music* of autumn that works within the poem its saving mediation, that gathers together and resolves the various antinomies within a larger movement. It is a music that is alternately "borne *aloft*" or "*sinking*" as the "light wind *lives* or *dies*." It composes itself from the sounds of the "*small* gnats" as well as from those of "*full-grown* lambs," from the "*loud*" bleating of the sheep to the "*soft*" treble of the robin. It draws together the song of the red-breast, as Arnold Davenport has noted, "characteristically a winter bird," and the call of the swallow, "proverbially the bird of summer [who] leaves the country when summer is over." It combines the cadences of change and continuity, of life and death. It rises from earth, "*from* hilly bourn" and "*from* a garden-croft" to ascend "*in* the skies." In its gradual withdrawal and attenuation ("treble," "whistles," "twitter"), it suggests the inevitable end of a natural cycle of growth, maturity and distillment in a ghostly and ethereal dissipation.

One aspect of the ode, especially of its final stanza, deserves to be commented on in more detail: the way it returns for a major element of its technique to the early verse, to sonnets like "How Many Bards" and "After Dark Vapours." The connection is suggested by Reuben Brower's remark that "To Autumn" reveals "how a succession of images, becoming something more than mere succession, imperceptibly blends into metaphor." For the final stanza of the ode remains the most perfect expression of the poet's habit of cataloguing (though the latter term now seems crude and inadequate to describe the effect "To Autumn" achieves). The beginning of the stanza deliberately eschews the invitation to conscious reflection, avoiding the moral sentiment or epitaph that constitutes the chief resolution of a whole tradition of the pastoral mode. Instead the stanza gains its end by offering us one more succession of precise impressions, a series of images that extends its texture of associations and reverberations as it unfolds. It elaborates a music that is entirely earthly and natural, yet filled with further implications. It never removes us from the characteristic world of Keats's poetry, a world of

> leaves
> Budding—fruit ripening in stillness—autumn
>   suns
> Smiling at eve upon the quiet sheaves.
> ("After Dark Vapours," 9–11)

Yet it imperceptibly creates a further range of meaning, the final awareness, if not of "a Poet's death," of a settled ripeness of experience we strive to articulate within such set terms as "maturity" or "resignation" or "acceptance." It preserves decorum

by remaining to the last a poetry of sensation; yet it leaves us with a full sense of the ultimate values. It takes us as far as we have any right to require toward a poetry of thought.

Source: Stuart M. Sperry, "Epilogue: 'To Autumn,'" in *Keats the Poet*, Princeton University Press, 1973, pp. 336–42.

SOURCES

Bate, Walter Jackson, "The Ode 'To Autumn'," in *Keats: A Collection of Critical Essays*, edited by Walter Jackson Bate, Prentice-Hall, 1964, p. 156; originally published in *John Keats*, Harvard University Press, 1963.

Bridges, Robert, "A Critical Introduction to the Poems of John Keats," in *John Keats: Odes: A Casebook*, edited by G. S. Fraser, Macmillan, 1971, p. 54.

Bush, Douglas, *John Keats: His Life and Writings*, Collier Books, 1966, pp. 176–78.

Flood, Allison, "T. S. Eliot Named the Nation's Favourite Poet," in the *Guardian* (London, England), October 8, 2009, http://www.guardian.co.uk/books/2009/oct/08/ts-eliot-nations-favourite-poet (accessed January 22, 2010).

Gittings, Robert, ed., *Letters of John Keats*, Oxford University Press, 1970, pp. 37, 38, 43, 70, 291–92, 326.

Keats, John, "To Autumn," in *Keats: Poetical Works*, edited by H. W. Garrod, Oxford University Press, 1973, pp. 218–19.

Marriott, Sir J. A. R., *England since Waterloo*, 15th ed., Methuen, 1965.

Motion, Andrew, *Keats*, Farrar, Straus and Giroux, 1997, pp. 460, 462.

Owen, F. M., "John Keats: A Study," in *John Keats: Odes: A Casebook*, edited by G. S. Fraser, Macmillan, 1971, p. 40.

Ridley, M. R., *Keats' Craftsmanship: A Study in Poetic Development*, University of Nebraska Press, 1933, p. 289.

Swinburne, A. C., "Miscellanies," in *John Keats: Odes: A Casebook*, edited by G. S. Fraser, Macmillan, 1971, p. 48.

Van Ghent, Dorothy, *Keats: The Myth of the Hero*, revised and edited by Jeffrey Cane Robinson, Princeton University Press, 1983, p. 173.

Vendler, Helen, *The Odes of John Keats*, Belknap Press of Harvard University Press, 1983, p. 256.

FURTHER READING

Gaull, Marilyn, *English Romanticism: The Human Context*, W. W. Norton, 1988.
>   This is a study of the literary movement of which Keats was a part. It gives sharp insight into the social and cultural environment and the main historical events as well as the work of Keats and the other great English romantic poets.

Keats, John, *Bright Star: Love Letters and Poems of John Keats to Fanny Brawne*, introduction by Jane Campion, Penguin, 2009.

> This book was timed to coincide with the September 2009 release of the movie *Bright Star* about Keats's relationship with Fanny Brawne. It includes all the letters he wrote to her as well as the sonnet that was supposedly inspired by her.

Walsh, John Evangelist, *Darkling I Listen: The Life and Death of John Keats*, Palgrave Macmillan, 1999.

> This is a detailed study of the last few months of Keats's life, which he spent fatally ill in Rome. Walsh believes that this period has never been fully examined, and he has much to say about Keats's tragic relationship with Fanny Brawne and the diagnosis and treatment of his illness.

Wolfson, Susan, ed., *The Cambridge Companion to Keats*, Cambridge University Press, 2001.

> This is a collection of sixteen articles by scholars of Keats. They present his work in a variety of contexts, including biographical and literary. Topics include Keats's relationship to the visual arts, his use of language, his letters, his sources and allusions, how Byron read Keats, and more. It also includes a glossary of literary terms and a chronology.

SUGGESTED SEARCH TERMS

John Keats

Keats AND Autumn

Keats AND creativity

Keats AND odes

Peterloo massacre

Keats AND romanticism

John Keats poems

John Keats biography

John Keats AND Lamia, Isabella, The Eve of St. Agnes, and Other Poems

What I Expected

STEPHEN SPENDER

1933

Sir Stephen Spender's poem "What I Expected" was published in 1933 and is included in one of his earliest poetry collections, simply titled *Poems*. Spender was one of a group of 1930s poets known as the Oxford Poets, the Pylon Poets, and the Auden Group. These were poets who defined themselves as politically radical and socially conscious and concerned with the state of humanity and humankind. Spender felt that poetry should reflect the concerns of the world and that it should reflect the ideology of the poet. "What I Expected" is a thirty-two-line, four-stanza, free-verse poem that explores the poet's disillusionment with the world in which he lives. As a member of the Pylon Poets, Spender's poetry would have been expected to acknowledge the turbulent political and social landscape of the 1920s and 1930s. This includes themes such as loss of innocence and disillusionment, both of which are found in "What I Expected."

"What I Expected" has been included in many anthologies, including the *Norton Anthology of Modern Poetry*. Spender also included the poem in his 1985 volume *Collected Poems: 1928–1985*, and it appears in a later Spender collection, *New Collected Poems*, published in 2004.

AUTHOR BIOGRAPHY

Spender was born February 28, 1909, in Kensington, London, England, one of four children in a

Stephen Spender (*Ulf Andersen / Getty Images*)

(1930) and *Poems* (1933), which included the poem "What I Expected." The following year, a second edition of *Poems* was published with several additional poems added to the collection. That same year, Spender's narrative poem *Vienna* was also published.

In 1936, Spender married Agnes Marie Pearn, a student at Oxford, whom he had only known briefly. His first play, *Trial of a Judge: A Tragedy in Five Acts*, was published in 1938, and another poetry collection, *The Still Centre* was published in 1939. Spender and his wife divorced in 1940. That same year, Spender saw the publication of two additional poetry collections, *Selected Poems* and *I Sit by the Window*. In 1941 Spender married Natasha Litvin, a pianist with whom he would have two children and to whom he would be married for the next 54 years. Spender continued to write poetry, plays, essays, and an autobiography in 1951, *World within World: The Autobiography of Stephen Spender*. In 1962 Spender was made a Commander of the British Empire and received the Queen's Gold Medal for Poetry in 1971. He was knighted in 1983. Spender's book *Collected Poems: 1928-1985* received a nomination for the *Los Angeles Times* Book Award in poetry in 1986. Over the years, Spender wrote or contributed to more than seventy books. He collapsed at his home in London, England, and died of natural causes on July 16, 1995.

privileged household. His father, Edward Harold Spender, was a journalist. Spender's mother, Violet Hilda Schuster, was a poet and painter. His mother was chronically ill and died when he was twelve years old. His father died only a few years later in 1926, while Spender was still a teenager, leaving him dependent on his maternal grandparents for support. Spender attended several grammar schools and with his grandmother's financial help enrolled at University College, Oxford. While at Oxford, he met W. H. Auden, who became both a friend and an important influence on Spender's poetry. In 1928, while still at Oxford, Spender published his first collection of poems, *Nine Experiments; Being Poems Written at the Age of Eighteen*, on his own hand press. Spender left Oxford without graduating just before his senior year. With the financial help of his maternal grandmother, he began to devote all of his time to travel and writing poetry. His grandmother also funded frequent trips to Germany, where Spender wrote many of the poems published in his next two poetry collections, *Twenty Poems*

POEM TEXT

What I expected was
Thunder, fighting,
Long struggles with men
And climbing.
After continual straining   5
I should grow strong;
Then the rocks would shake
And I should rest long.

What I had not foreseen
Was the gradual day   10
Weakening the will
Leaking the brightness away,
The lack of good to touch
The fading of body and soul
Like smoke before wind   15
Corrupt, unsubstantial.

The wearing of Time,
And the watching of cripples pass
With limbs shaped like questions
In their odd twist,   20

The pulverous grief
Melting the bones with pity,
The sick falling from earth—
These, I could not foresee.

For I had expected always   25
Some brightness to hold in trust,
Some final innocence
To save from dust;
That, hanging solid,
Would dangle through all   30
Like the created poem
Or the dazzling crystal.

POEM SUMMARY

Lines 1–8

In the first stanza of "What I Expected," Spender opens with a statement that immediately puts forth his expectation that a lifetime of hard work will be rewarded. The poem's title implies the kind of cause-and-effect relationship that creates fairness in a person's life. The speaker explains in the first three lines that he had expected to work hard. He had anticipated difficult struggles and the kind of challenging effort that is required if he wants to succeed. The narrator expected to have to fight for what he wanted and that perhaps there would be storms, representative of controversy and conflict. The thunder of battle was not unexpected, as he explains in line 2. He has always understood that the struggle would be difficult and long, as he tells his readers in line 3; the climb is uphill, he writes in line 4. The first complete sentence of "What I Expected" ends at line 4. This opening sentence has defined the poet's expectations of hard work and struggle, as well as a willingness to sacrifice as required. These lines also denote the speaker's strength and ambition, which have no bounds. In the opening lines of this poem, the writer has acknowledged the necessity of hard work and struggle as necessary components of reward.

Beginning at line 5, the speaker explains his expectation of reward, to which he will be entitled after he has made sufficient sacrifice. He claims he is willing to make repeated efforts that should ensure his success, since after working so hard, he will have grown strong with the effort. After a difficult climb to the pinnacle, he will triumph, he explains in line 7, when the mountain of obstacles placed before him begins to crumble and his climb has ended. Then he will have earned a well-deserved rest and his reward.

MEDIA ADAPTATIONS

- Spender reads "What I Expected" in *Stephen Spender Reading His Poems*, recorded by Caedmon in 1958.

- Another audio recording is *Stephen Spender Reads a Selection of His Poetry*, by Argo (1965). In this recording he reads "What I Expected."

- *Stephen Spender Reading His Poetry* was recorded by Caedmon in 1972. In this recording he once again reads "What I Expected."

- In *The Still Centre*, Spender reads a selection of his poems, including "What I Expected." This cassette recording was made in 1994 just before Spender's death and released in 1997 by Faber-Penguin Audiobooks.

- An interview of Spender by Dick Cavett is available as *Words and Wars*, online at http://www.salon.com/audio/nonfiction/2001/01/04/stephen_spender/index.html. In this interview, Spender talks about poetry and politics.

Lines 9–16

The beginning of the second stanza suggests that the speaker's life, or perhaps the world in general, has not turned out the way that he had expected it would. He had not foreseen that the climb to the top would be so arduous or so long. He describes the piling on of time in line 10 and in line 11 complains that the weariness of each passing day only serves to accumulate over time, until he has lost his enthusiasm for the struggle ahead. His desire to succeed and his willingness to struggle have been eroded by the sheer magnitude of the struggle, which has consumed more energy than he had anticipated. In line 12 the vibrancy with which he had begun his effort has dimmed and with it his enthusiasm for the struggle.

One reason for the speaker's loss of optimism is suggested in line 13, when the speaker writes that there is less virtue in the world. There are fewer positive qualities visible around him. Whether the poet refers to a lack of morality in people or the lack of accomplishments of others is not clear at this point in the poem. In line 14, he suggests that his disappointments might be dependent on the failings of humanity, which account for his disillusionment with humankind and with the world in which he lives. This interpretation is further supported by lines 15 and 16, in which the poet describes morality as having been as insubstantial as vapor, which is easily blown away by a breeze or wind. The goodness of humankind, thus, is no more substantial or real than a bit of blowing air. The speaker has begun to realize that humanity is depraved and untrustworthy. In this final line of the second stanza, the poet leaves his readers with a depressing image of dishonor and the poet's belief that there is no justice in a world that fails to reward hard work, while corruption flourishes.

Lines 17–24

In the first line of stanza 3, the speaker notes that the passage of time can be exhausting. With time, reality brings clarity, which dims the brightness and promise of the future. The reality of disease and injury can incapacitate, as he writes in line 18. This devastation of the world is not what the poet had expected. The vision of bodies beaten down by defeat and the passage of time were not what he expected. Those people whose humanity has been defeated by time appear before him as witnesses who challenge him. Their presence disputes his long-held belief that hard work will result in rewards. Instead the speaker witnesses something different, a distortion of reality in which much of humanity is mangled, misconstrued, and distorted. These are the bodies with twisted limbs that he imagines in line 20.

In line 21, the speaker tells of a crushing anguish and despair at what he has discovered. He is no longer the innocent that he was in the first stanza. He is experienced now in the disappointments that the world has foisted upon him. In line 22, he suffers such grief that he can only express it as a pain so great that he can no longer bear to see the wretchedness before him. Humanity literally dissolves into nothingness. This destruction was not something he had expected, as the poet explains in line 24. He could not have envisioned a world such as this one, in which people can be cast aside and destroyed so easily. He had not anticipated a world in which humankind had so little value.

Lines 25–32

In the final stanza, the speaker recalls the days of innocence in which he had expected a brighter world, one filled with promise and possibilities. He had thought that there was a larger protection on which he could count. Although the he never mentions God, his faith had earlier sustained him. In line 26, the brightness is the promise that he has seen in his faith, his trust in a greater goodness. In line 27, he attributes this faith in a greater good to innocence. His innocence was the last thing to fall to cynicism. He had held on to a belief in goodness and an expectation of a better world in which the righteous are rewarded, but even that final innocence has dissolved in the grimness of reality.

In line 29, the poet moves toward the concluding thoughts of "What I Expected." He refers back to line 26 and mentions the brightness, the promise of reward and a better existence, in which he had continued to believe. The speaker has tried to hold onto his faith, and that faith has, as line 30 suggests, continued to entice and tempt him into believing in a better world. In line 31, he tells his readers that poetry also returns him to a state of innocence, a time in which he believed in possibilities and still does believe. When he completes a poem, he recreates that state of innocence, the brightness of promise, and an expectation that the world can really be as wonderful as he had thought it would be when he was young. His creativity is a beacon that erases all doubt. The final line of the poem completes the metaphor begun in line 26. The possibility of the world that he had envisioned is like the creation of a poem, a visible representation of the poet's talent or the breathtaking brilliance of perfection that is a crystal, perfectly reflecting light and beauty.

THEMES

Innocence and Experience

"What I Expected" opens with the speaker's statement of innocence. His innocence was a time in the past when he still believed in the possibility of success and when he saw the world and his future as full of promise. This was an innocent time in which anything was possible. The speaker acknowledges that there would be struggles. Many of these struggles would be akin to climbing a steep mountain, but there was no doubt that he would succeed in reaching his goals. In fact, he anticipates that the struggle for success will make him stronger. He will grow and mature as he attempts to reach his goal. The speaker chooses to reach beyond what can be easily grasped. In his innocence, he thinks that nothing is beyond his reach, if only he is willing to

TOPICS FOR FURTHER STUDY

- Spender is one of several notable twentieth-century poets. W. H. Auden, Louis MacNeice, Philip Larkin, and Cecil Day Lewis were also important British poets and colleagues of Spender. Choose one of these poets to study, and write a research paper in which you discuss the poet, his work, and his legacy as a poet.

- In 1933, when "What I Expected" was published, Adolf Hitler was the newly elected chancellor of Germany. With a small group of three or four of your classmates, research the worldwide response to Hitler's election. Concentrate on the first six months of 1933 in particular. Begin with a search of the online newspaper archives found in your school library's LexisNexis and ProQuest databases. Prepare a multimedia presentation of your material. Consider using PowerPoint slides of photos and old newspaper clippings or clips from documentaries or popular films made about Hitler's rise to power.

- Arnold Adoff writes poems for children and young adults. In Adoff's poetry collection, *Slow Dance Heartbreak Blues*, he focuses on poetry about teenagers and their concerns. Read one of Adoff's poems for teenagers and consider how effective his poetry is in exploring the problems of teenagers. You might consider his poem "Listen to the Voice in Your Head," in which Adoff deals with disappointment and the realization that the poem's speaker will never achieve what he hopes. You should also consider how Adoff's poem differs in tone and content from Spender's poem. Prepare an evaluation of the differences that you noted and present your findings as a comparative poster presentation to your classmates.

- Spender's poem is a reminder that many modern poets have cared deeply about the social problems of the world in which they live and have felt an obligation to use poetry to illuminate the needs of humanity. "What I Expected" was composed early in the 1930s. Research the economic and social problems that were common in London in the late 1920s and early 1930s. In particular, focus on the plight of World War I veterans, who returned from the war with severe physical and emotional injuries. Then prepare a PowerPoint slide presentation in which you discuss what you have discovered using PowerPoint for photos, illustrations, and data graphs, which you will then explain to your classmates.

- Many poets, including Spender, have created audio recordings of themselves reading their poems. These audio recordings become priceless artifacts after a poet has died, since they remain the only way to really "hear" a poem as the poet intended it to be heard. Create your own audio recording of Spender's poetry. Choose at least two or three of Spender's poems and read them aloud into a recorder. Ask at least two of your classmates to read the same poems and record their readings, as well. Then listen carefully to the recordings that you have made and write a short reaction paper in which you discuss the differences that you noted in these readings. Consider whether the different readers emphasized particular words, whether each reader paused at different words or lines, and whether the tone of the poems has changed with each reading and reader's interpretation.

- Spender's poem is about disillusionment and disappointment. Write your own poem that explores a disappointment that you have experienced. Use the same opening sentence that Spender uses in "What I Expected." When you have completed your poem, write a brief evaluation of your work, comparing it to Spender's poem. In your written critique of your poem, consider what you learned about the difficulty of writing poetry about life's disappointments.

make the effort. He believes that a strong effort will be rewarded, and he is willing to make that effort. In his innocence, he believes that the world is just, that life will treat him fairly, and that if he deserves a reward he will achieve it. The reality of the world has not yet shown itself to him, and he remains as innocent of the real world as a sheltered child who is cared for by loving parents. In the first stanza of "What I Expected," the speaker is still full of optimism and willingly embraces a world filled with opportunity and success; however, by line 13 of the second stanza it becomes obvious that the speaker's innocence has been shattered.

In the final stanza of "What I Expected," the speaker is far more experienced at life. He has matured and now realizes that the world is not an ideal place where fairness and justice triumphs. In carefully examining the world in which he lives, he has seen the struggle of humankind and understands that life has not been fair. In this final stanza, the speaker recalls his earlier innocent self and his belief that the goodness of light has shone on all of humanity. Although the speaker realizes his folly, he has discovered a way to recapture the innocence of his earlier life. Creating poetry lifts his spirits and mentally and emotionally transports him to a place where he can experience the innocence of his youth. Innocence is too essential to the poet's life to be given up completely. Seemingly, the poet has found a way to balance innocence and experience.

Disillusionment

"What I Expected" explores the disillusionment that the speaker experiences when the realities of the world intrude on the idealized image of the world that he had created for himself. In the second stanza the poet begins to explain that his life and the world in general are not what he had expected. He had believed in virtue and a reward for hard work. Instead, he sees around him the failures of humankind and the inhumanity with which man treats his fellow man. What he had thought about the goodness of humanity has proved to be as temporal as the passing breeze. In the real world, corruption is rewarded while hard work achieves nothing. This is especially disillusioning to the poet. He notes in the second stanza the passing of time, which has only shown him that life consists of more failures than successes. In the third stanza, the speaker sees people beaten down by oppression and injustice, their bodies unable to bear the disappointments of the world. The destruction of humanity was not what

In the first stanza, the speaker talks about climbing and straining. (Image copyright Galyna Andrushko, 2010. Used under license from Shutterstock.com)

he has expected, when in his innocence he had believed that anything was possible if only he would make the effort. Disillusionment came when idealism and inexperience were replaced by realism and knowledge.

STYLE

Free Verse

Free verse is verse that is free of formal structure, rhyme, or meter. In using free verse the poet is not restricted by a need to shape the poem to a particular meter; this allows the poet the opportunity to create poetry of complex and varied rhythm and syntax. Free verse is most often associated with modern poetry, although poets have been creating poetry free of rhyme and meter for several hundred years. There is no pattern of meter in "What I Expected." Some lines are four syllables, some are five, and others are six or seven. However, the lines have an informal rhyme pattern. In stanzas one, two, and four, lines 2 and 4 rhyme. Spender sacrifices the rhyme in stanza three to emphasize the twist of the bodies and limbs. It is important to remember that free verse is never totally free of stylistic conventions. Spender does use a stanza paragraph of eight lines per stanza, and he does rely on some basic repetition of phrasing and punctuation, but in general, "What I Expected" is free of conventional rules of meter or rhyme.

Modern Poetry

The label "modern" as applied to poetry, novels, and other forms of literature refers to a movement characterized by a conscious effort to break away from tradition. Developed in the early twentieth century in response to the horrors of World War I, modern poetry attempts to create a new world by changing perceptions of the old world. Modern literary works identify the individual as more important than either society or social conventions. Modern poetry privileges the mind and the poet's inward thoughts. The imagination of the poet often prefers the unconscious actions of the individual. Modernism is also about the loss of innocence. "What I Expected" is representative of modern poetry in that it allows Spender the freedom to express concerns about humanity and a person's role in the world. For Spender, modern poetry offers the opportunity to express outrage at man's inhumanity and the loss of innocence that he feels as he witnesses a world that has not lived up to his expectations.

Pylon Poets

The Pylon Poets were a 1930s group of socially liberal poets who included Spender, W. H. Auden, Louis MacNeice, and Cecil Day Lewis. These poets were known for their use of industrial imagery. The title of the group was derived from Spender's 1933 poem "The Pylons." In the poem, the pylons are intrusive and dominate the landscape. The idea is that humankind and technology need to live in peace, but the needs of man are always more important than those of industry and technology. The application of this term to "What I Expected" reveals Spender's disillusionment with society, which seems not to value humankind.

Repetition

Repetition of a word, sound, or phrase is useful in emphasizing ideas in a poem. This stylistic device is one way to express several ideas of similar importance in a similar manner or to establish the importance of a particular idea. Spender uses repetition in "What I Expected" to emphasize ideas and to create tension. For example, the speaker states what he expected in line 1; this phrase is structurally repeated in line 25. A modification of this phrase appears in line 9 when the poet begins to

explain that he had not foreseen the realities of the world. Spender then repeats a variation of line 9 in line 24, when he again acknowledges what he had not foreseen. All of stanza 1 expresses what the poet had expected, while all of stanza 4 recalls once again the poet's expectations. This use of repetition focuses the reader's attention on these words and actions and calls attention to that which has changed.

Tenor and Vehicle

Tenor and vehicle are terms used by I. A. Richards, a twentieth-century literary critic, to describe two parts of a metaphor. A metaphor simply identifies one object with another object. The tenor is the subject, and the vehicle is the object used for comparison. It is necessary for a metaphor to have both a tenor and a vehicle. If both are not present, then no metaphor exists and a sentence is just a sentence. A vehicle makes the tenor, an idea that might be obscure, clear to the reader. In "What I Expected," Spender begins and ends the poem with metaphors. The first metaphor is a familiar one, in which the man's success in life is likened to the effort needed to climb a mountain. Success awaits at the top of the mountain. All that is required is the strength and desire to climb to the top. In the final stanza the brightness of a promised world is similar to the beauty of a created poem that perfectly captures the poet's strengths and thoughts. It is also like a piece of brilliant crystal, which hangs in beauty to reflect light and the brightness wished for in line 26.

HISTORICAL CONTEXT

A Worldwide Depression

During the early 1930s, the Great Depression created severe poverty and homelessness across the United States and throughout the world. Within a year of the stock market crash in October 1929, the unemployment rate in the United States reached 25 to 30 percent. By the end of 1930, an estimated twenty-one million people were unemployed in the world. Unemployment in Germany was at 25 percent of the workforce by the beginning of 1932 and over 40 percent by the end of that year. In 1933, unemployment in Great Britain was between 22 and 25 percent of the workforce. Coal, steel, iron, and shipbuilding industries in Northern Ireland, Scotland, Wales, and northern England

COMPARE & CONTRAST

- **1930s:** British unemployment rises above 12 percent by 1928. In Wales, many working-class families are receiving government assistance of seven dollars a week.

  Today: Unemployment in Britain continues to rise in 2009. Nearly 20 percent of eighteen- to twenty-four-year-olds are out of work and actively seeking a job.

- **1930s:** A study reports that by 1929 90 percent of children living in London's East End suffer from rickets, a sign of severe malnutrition, usually resulting from starvation or famine.

  Today: A recent study reveals that in London, four out of ten children live in poverty. In the inner city, the number of children living in poverty jumps to 50 percent.

- **1930s:** In October 1931, the Japanese invade Manchuria, in northeastern China. The Japanese military hopes that invading China will provide cheap slave labor and other economic benefits that will help offset the effects of a severe economic depression in Japan.

  Today: In 2008, Russia invades the independent state of Georgia. At one time both countries were part of the Soviet Union. South Ossetia, a section of Georgia comprised pri-

marily of Russian citizens, is seeking independence from Georgia.

- **1930s:** In 1932, Mahatma Gandhi begins a fast as part of his campaign of civil disobedience and protest against the British government's treatment of India's lowest caste, the "untouchables."

  Today: The United Nations Human Rights Council in Geneva is preparing to recognize caste-based discrimination as a human rights violation. It is estimated that 260 million people globally are victims of this kind of discrimination. India has declined to back the UN proposal.

- **1930s:** By 1934, a "Milk in Schools" program significantly improves the nutrition of British schoolchildren by providing them with one-third pint of milk each day. At least half of the children receive their milk free or at low cost.

  Today: Although free milk for children was mandated by law in 1946, the act was abolished in the early 1970s by Prime Minister Margaret Thatcher. Currently free milk is provided only to children under age five and to children with medical waivers.

---

were hit especially hard. Spender writes in his autobiography, *World within World: The Autobiography of Stephen Spender*, that he "felt hounded by external events," particularly the rising unemployment in England and the United States and throughout Europe. These countries were still feeling many of the economic effects of World War I. In this respect, Great Britain was in a slightly better economic position than many other countries, since Great Britain's war debt was not as large as that of other European countries. This is because England had financed the war primarily through the sale of foreign assets and thus did not suffer as severely in the Depression as other countries. During the early years of the Depression, Spender lived in Germany,

where the Depression had hit especially hard and the effects were more visible to him. Unemployment in Germany, which chiefly affected men, led to a diminished sense of self-worth caused by men's inability to support their families. It is little wonder that membership in the German Nazi Party, which promised to create jobs and improve the economy, rose from 17,000 in 1926 to more than a million in 1931.

A Time of Turmoil

Spender was particularly interested in German culture and sympathetic to the economic devastation that followed World War I. Spender's maternal grandparents, who supported him after the death

A clock represents "the wearing of Time." (Image copyright pjmorley, 2010. Used under license from Shutterstock.com)

of his mother and later his father, were German Jewish bankers who had converted to Christianity. Spender first went to Germany for extended periods of time to escape censorship in England. In the late 1920s, Germany had a reputation for tolerance, but with rising economic instability, Germany's image of tolerance was only a thin veneer that hid rising anti-Semitism. Germany was a country in economic turmoil. Germany owed an enormous debt as punishment for World War I, which added to the economic and political instability of that country. In January 1933, Adolf Hitler was elected chancellor of Germany, and within months he had seized all power as dictator. After he became dictator, he began targeting several groups for a euthanasia program, labeled the T-4 program, that would eliminate those he considered nonproductive members of German society. These included the elderly and those with physical and mental disabilities. Eventually homosexuals and members of minority ethnic and religious groups, such as Gypsies, Jews, and Jehovah's Witnesses, would be arrested and used for slave labor or exterminated. Within months of Hitler's rise to power, he had issued orders that all Germans were to boycott Jewish businesses. In Berlin, pro-Nazi university students lit a bonfire and burned 20,000 books, many written by Jewish authors but some simply because their content was in conflict with Nazi ideology. Throughout 1933 artists and composers began to flee Germany, which had demanded that all art must glorify Nazism. Spender could not have known how much destruction Hitler would bring upon Europe, but even by 1933, when "What I Expected" was published, it had become clear that Hitler's Germany was on its way to becoming an oppressive country in which Jews and other minorities would be scapegoated and victimized. Although Spender was not religiously Jewish, one of his grandparents was a Jew, so Germany would no longer be safe for Spender. He returned to England in 1933.

Germany was not the only place where oppression and inhumanity coexisted. In the Soviet Union, Communist Party leader Joseph Stalin's Five Year Plan was creating a barbaric system of slave labor. Early in the 1930s, Stalin ordered that all peasants who were wealthy or even slightly successful were to be deported to labor camps in Siberia, where people were fed starvation diets. Millions of people were sent to these labor camps. Sixty thousand labor camp detainees would die digging the Baltic–White Sea Canal, which was finished in 1933. Stalin's attempt to create a system of collectivized farming, beginning in 1929, would lead to a famine in Russia and the Ukraine during 1932 and 1933, which resulted in the deaths of an estimated 14 million people. Meanwhile in El Salvador, a 1932 effort by starving peasants to rise up against oppressive wealthy landowners resulted in 30,000 deaths. Within only a few years, Spain would be embroiled in a civil war, the Japanese would invade China, and Germany would begin a march across Europe. The disillusionment that permeates "What I Expected" was easily fed by the inhumanity that seemed to be spreading across the world in the early years of the 1930s.

CRITICAL OVERVIEW

When Spender died in 1995, several obituaries celebrated his life as poet, journalist, and lecturer. Spender's socially conscious poetry from the 1930s is often considered his best work, as is noted in the obituary published in the London *Times*. The obituary points out that "at his best he records the helpless anguish of the Thirties more directly than any other English Poet of the period,

with the true voice of feeling." The 1930s were a time of economic hardship and political oppression. The obituary notes that Spender's poetry of this period reveals his "compassion for the deprived and the defeated." Similarly, Robert Taylor, writing for the *Boston Globe*, refers to Spender as "a writer who gave haunting expression to the tensions and anxieties of the 1930s."

In an obituary written for the London *Guardian*, Frank Kermode celebrates Spender's multifaceted life. Kermode, who is best known as a literary critic, writes that Spender had for sixty years been "one of the most famous names in 20th-century literature." Among his talents, Spender is defined as "prolific in almost every literary form: novelist, playwright, essayist, political commentator, editor, translator, literary critics, memoirist, occasionally a professor, and, always in his own mind, a poet before anything else." Kermode claims that Spender's knowledge about the relationship between art and politics was among the best of the young writers of the 1930s. Although Spender is not as famous as Auden, Kermode sees the poet as leaving a legacy every bit as significant as Auden's.

In memorializing Spender for the London *Independent*, Peter Porter calls Spender "the symbol of youthful promise in poetry," whose "idealism and innocence" survived changing fashions of poetry. Porter specifically mentions "What I Expected" as an example of the kind of poetry that "shares with early Auden the excitement of a new and terse lyricism." Although "What I Expected" is not mentioned in the review of *Poems* that was published in the *New York Times* in 1934, the social significance of the poems in this collection are not ignored by the reviewer. Columnist Peter Monro Jack focuses on the social consciousness of Spender's poetry, as well as its lyrical beauty. Jack refers to Spender's poetry as "more exciting poetry than we have had for years," and specifically cites Spender's lyricism as "sensitive and immaculate." Jack praises how Spender "moves from one complete lyric to the next, a slow spiritual logic in sensuous shapes, revealing the courage and hope emerging from his nostalgic distress." Spender's poetry clearly reveals that the poet "is haunted by images of hunger" that he sees on the streets. Selections from *Poems* were reprinted in 1955 in Spender's *Collected Poems: 1928–1953*, and reviewer Dudley Fitts for the *New York Times* notes that these poems recall what it was like to be alive in the 1930s. Fitts writes that there are poets whose work is more fluent and engaging than Spender's, but there is no poet who has "his intensity, his special integrity." Given Spender's concern for humanity, he would no doubt be pleased to have earned a legacy defined by integrity.

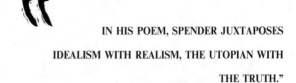

IN HIS POEM, SPENDER JUXTAPOSES IDEALISM WITH REALISM, THE UTOPIAN WITH THE TRUTH."

CRITICISM

Sheri Metzger Karmiol

Karmiol teaches literature and drama at the University of New Mexico, where she is a lecturer in the university honors program. In this essay, she discusses the importance of tension between the ideal and the real in Spender's "What I Expected."

Many students probably think that television and film provide one of the easiest ways to learn about what is happening in the world, and perhaps that is true. However, if such media can so easily illuminate the world, what, then, is the role of poetry in bringing knowledge to people? Why is the mere visualization of destruction insufficient to change the world? The answer lies in the ability of poetry to create tension between the ideal and the real, as the poem leads readers toward an understanding of the depth of human tragedy. Whereas popular media challenges people with painful images but leaves them bereft of answers, poetry brings healing in the face of inexplicable pain. Spender's poem "What I Expected" challenges readers to explore the depths of the poem to discover the disagreeable truths about the world. But the poem offers much more than unpleasant facts and images. "What I Expected" also provides an optimistic ending and the promise of healing. Spender's images of pain and inhumanity offer explication and catharsis, but only if the reader is willing to make the necessary effort to explore the tension between the ideal and the real.

The broadcast media often assaults viewers with images of horror. When the images are too intense, viewers may turn aside or cover their eyes, but the images remain. The story behind the horror is often unexplored; only the images linger in the viewer's consciousness. Nothing is demanded of the viewer, who functions as voyeur. Sometimes poetry can be like a news show and demand nothing from the reader. When poetry is divorced from social consciousness, the poem may appear to be extraordinarily beautiful, with individual words that are lovely and sweet to the eye and ear but demand nothing in return. Upon reading the poem, the reader cannot remember a single word. The poem was captivating but without depth. That is not the case with "What I Expected." Spender creates images of grief and pain, particularly in stanza 3, in which the poet focuses on the devastation of humanity. Crippled limbs are mangled, distorted in pain. The speaker feels crushing grief at what he sees. He had not been prepared for so much devastation; nor had he expected to witness the incomprehensible inhumanity of humankind. It is impossible to remain a neutral voyeur when reading this poem. The ability to involve the reader is one of the strengths of socially conscious poetry. In a 1980 interview with Peter Stitt, published in *Paris Review*, Spender notes the need of the poet to delve deeper into the inhumanity of humankind. According to Spender, journalists often show only one side of a conflict. They show suffering, but sometimes what they report is not unlike propaganda, since it often shows only the superficial pain, leaving out the depth of understanding and causation. The poet, however, has a different obligation, says Spender. He claims that to really understand suffering it is necessary to "penetrate to the depths of the suffering" and witness suffering "on a deeper level." This is what the poet attempts to do in his poem. When the poet witnesses this depth of suffering, he understands that the suffering is on both sides, not just on the part of those who are most visibly injured. When this depth of suffering is understood, the poet is able to create poetry that explores what it is "that human beings do to one another." Thus in "What I Expected," the reader emerges from the poem as a witness to the poet's depth of grief, as well as his knowledge about the depth of suffering.

The reader is witness to the depth of suffering only if a careful reading of the poem takes place. The ability to balance ideology and reality is one of the strengths of poetry. "What I Expected" reveals the tension between two worlds and the conflicted spirit of the poet. There is the world that

WHAT DO I READ NEXT?

- *New Collected Poems of Stephen Spender* (2004) contains seven decades of Spender's poetry. The poems are arranged chronologically and divided according to their publication as separate books.

- *The Thirties and After: Poetry, Politics, People, 1933–1975*, published in 1978 by Spender, contains a selection of his essays, book reviews, and journal excerpts, which serve to create a brief history of the poet's life.

- Spender's 1951 memoir, *World within World: The Autobiography of Stephen Spender*, is considered one of the most innovative of its time. In this book, Spender reveals many of the controversies associated with his early life. He is also honest in divulging incidents that do not always cast him in a favorable light.

- Spender wrote the initial draft of *The Temple* in 1928 but did not submit the novel for publication until 1988. This novel is set in Germany in the 1930s and is a thinly disguised story of Spender's experiences in Germany in the late 1920s.

- W. H. Auden's *Selected Poems* (2007), edited by Edward Mendelson, provides readers with a selection of the poetry written by one of Spender's most important contemporaries.

- *Unsettling America: An Anthology of Contemporary Multicultural Poetry* (1994), edited by Maria Gazette Gillan and Jennifer Gillan, is a collection of poetry that explores inequity, discrimination, and social injustice. This multicultural view of injustice pairs well with Spender's concerns about inhumanity and oppression.

- *Poetry for Young People: Edna St. Vincent Millay* (1999), edited by Frances Schoonmaker and illustrated by Mike Bryce, is designed for a young-adult audience. This is a collection of beautifully illustrated poetry by Millay, who was an important female contemporary of Spender. Millay was equally concerned about the inhumanity of war and the costs of conflict paid in human lives.

the poet expected and the world that disappointed. In his poem, Spender juxtaposes idealism with realism, the utopian with the truth. In her essay "Constructing Meaning When Reading Poetry: An Expert-Novice Study," Joan Peskin begins with a simple claim that "poetry communicates universal human truths." She acknowledges, however, that for many people, poetry can be "difficult to comprehend." In fact, poetry can be very challenging, but it can awaken senses and illuminate worlds that readers might never experience otherwise. According to Peskin, poetry "is an instrument to make us see life and live it more intensely." "What I Expected" does this. The poem allows readers to see the perversions of humanity in the poet's disillusionment. He creates images of anguish and despair, of bodies twisted and cast aside, and of a humanity that seems not to notice the destruction left in its wake. This is the reality that rejects the idealistic. Poetry accomplishes this through language, with carefully chosen words such as "weakening," "pulverous," and "melting." Of course, the news media can show reality as well, but what is not shown is the dream of utopia displaced by that truth. On the news screen the voyeur sees the end result of immorality, of war, or of catastrophe. The viewer feels the victim's pain and may weep at the loss shown. Then the viewer moves away from the screen, and the story and visions are forgotten. However, the poet does not move away. Instead, through the words of a poem, the poet can reveal the depth of suffering and the loss of a dream, which lingers with the reader.

Unfortunately, suffering is all too often easy to find. The poet's creativity does not exist in a vacuum. In a 1977 interview with Richard Dana, Spender talks about the intersection of politics, radicalism, and poetry. According to Spender, this intersection was a topic much discussed in the 1930s, when Spender was writing "What I Expected." This was when fascism was spreading across Europe, and many leaders were plotting the destruction of their fellow humans. Spender understands that poetry responds to the political and social world in which it is written, and if written with honesty, a poem reveals the truth of oppression and corruption. Spender tells Dana that "to be a poet or an artist, you had to have *human* sympathies. Sympathy for human beings." "What I Expected" is the sort of poem that has sympathy for human beings. Spender infuses "What I Expected" with sympathy for life's victims. The poet describes destruction, anguish, and despair so heartbreaking in its reality that the poet's own dreams have been lost. It is only in the final stanza that the poet is able to recapture his dreams in the creation of a poem.

Spender writes in "What I Expected" that he had been an innocent, unprepared for the realities of the world. He had expected rewards for hard work, as he explains in the first stanza of his poem. He had expected justice and goodness in the world. He had not expected that there would be so much evil that it would wear on him, eating away at the success he had expected would fill his days. The reality of the world weakens his will and diminishes his innocence and the joy that he felt in the past when he still believed in the possibilities of goodness. What he sees seeping away is his own humanity, but then in the final stanza, the poet writes that he is able to recapture his faith in humanity when he creates a new poem. The creation of poetry changes the poet, and in turn, the poem transforms the world. In his 1954 book, *Literary Essays*, Ezra Pound argues that poets have a social obligation to create poetry that changes the world. Pound claims that it is the duty of the poet to make people aware of their own humanity. Poetry gives readers a way to understand the world. In meeting this obligation, poets create poetry that possesses the emotional complexity required to inspire men to infuse the world with justice and goodness. Spender reveals his own disillusionment as a way to arouse the moral consciousness of his reader. He is using poetry as a way to create the humanity that has been lost.

Dreams of success and personal accomplishment provide a goal for continued hard work. What people cannot foresee is how reality might replace dreams and negate hard work. Spender recognizes the difficulty in trying to achieve one's dreams when reality weakens the will to succeed. However, Spender does not advocate giving up. Throughout "What I Expected" the reader learns of inhumanity and crushing defeat, but in the final stanza, the poet continues to try to achieve his goals. He understands that his success has the power to create a better world. The unexpected is part of life, but it need not be a cause for defeat. Robert Browning claims in "Andrea del Sarto" that "a man's reach should exceed his grasp." It is easy to be successful when life is easy and the world is fair and just. Browning thought that people should continue to keep working harder to achieve that which is just beyond their grasp. Poetry can make the impossible seem possible. Poetry inspires readers to reach beyond the easy

The poem mentions "the watching of cripples pass/With limbs shaped like questions."
(Image copyright Tatiana Morozova, 2010. Used under license from Shutterstock.com)

and change what initially appears to be too difficult to change. The tension between the ideal and the real is absent in popular media; however, it is an essential element that Spender is able to create in his poem "What I Expected." As Browning suggests, poetry tempts humankind to keep reaching out and to offer a hand of assistance to those who need help.

Source: Sheri Metzger Karmiol, Critical Essay on "What I Expected," in *Poetry for Students*, Gale, Cengage Learning, 2011.

Paul Dean

In the following essay, Dean reviews both a biography of Stephen Spender and Spender's volume New Collected Poems, *and argues that Spender had "little gift for sustained thinking."*

There have been two previous biographical studies of Sir Stephen Spender (1909–1995). The first, by Hugh David (1992), was a hatchet job which caused the family great distress. The second,

HE LIKED WHAT HE LIKED BECAUSE HE LIKED IT: HIS APPROVAL WAS SELF-VALIDATING. THIS MEANS THAT, IF WE ARE NOT DRAWN TO HIM PERSONALLY, WE SHALL FIND IT HARD TO SHARE HIS ENTHUSIASMS OR TO RESPECT HIS JUDGMENTS."

David Leeming's *Stephen Spender: A Life in Modernism* (1999), was more respectable, but it was still too frank about Spender's bisexuality for the comfort of some. This is odd, since Spender was open about the matter himself in his autobiography, *World Within World* (1951), and his autobiographical novel *The Temple*, first drafted in the early 1930s but published, in a revised version, only in 1988. It will be noticed that these accounts stop early in Spender's life, and it seems there was a feeling that the undeniable happiness of Spender's second marriage should not be overshadowed, in the public mind, by the admission that he continued to feel strong, even passionate, attachments to younger men.

John Sutherland, who knew Spender well during the latter's brief professorship at University College, London, has written, as his subtitle proclaims, not just "an" but the authorized biography. He has had access not only to the family papers but also to Spender's widow and his two surviving siblings. This gives his picture of Spender's childhood and youth, in particular, unrivaled interest and authority, even if his account of the later years is circumspect in places and needs supplementing by Leeming's book.

Nevertheless, Sutherland's "official" status also obliges him to maintain, and perhaps even to believe, that Spender is a significant poet. The belief cannot survive a reading of the *Collected Poems* in Michael Brett's new edition, which, for the first time, gives us Spender's entire output in unrevised form. Spender's own ruthlessly selective "collected" poems is about half the length of Brett's, and one has to grant him a degree of self-criticism, but what he left in was not much better than what he dropped. Sutherland's disdain for "the sterile hand of F. R. Leavis and his fanatically purist disciples"

(I'd be interested to meet a half-hearted purist, by the way) is entirely misplaced. Spender's current standing in England, as a minor satellite of Auden, known through a few anthology pieces but largely of historical interest only, is perfectly fair. His criticism is that of a gentleman amateur, who can speak strongly of his own experiences and acquaintances and who has a broad, generous sympathy with European modernism—the modernism of Rilke (whom he translated) and Pasternak as well as of Eliot and Auden. His freedom from donnish pedantry is a blessing, but he had little gift for sustained thinking, whether in prose or poetry.

In 1976, when Spender was sixty-seven, he embarked on a relationship with a twenty-year-old student at the University of Florida in Gainesville. He wrote about this in some of his last poems, "Letter from an Ornithologist in Antarctica" and "Farewell to my Student," which contains these lines:

Perhaps Bellini
Delved from antiquity such an image
Of a twenty-year-old Triton, against waves
Blowing on a conch;
And Seurat, centuries later, in the profile
Of a hallooing boy against the Seine.

But then you turned to me and said
With that mild glance, a third thing to
remember:
"You are gone already, your thoughts are
    far
from here
At least three thousand miles away
Where you will be tomorrow."

Then ten years passed till, today, I write
these lines.

One notices here that Spender offers two pictures, drawn from Bellini and Seurat, which most readers will identify, and then parallels them with a flat reminiscence. The external images are expected to animate a memory he can only report, not evoke or make moving for a third person. To be blunt, he is parasitic upon other men's creativity. The poem achieves at best a clumsy authenticity. In this it is representative of Spender's work when it is not simply bad. I realize that I am asking the reader to take a great deal on trust here, given that Brett's *Collected Poems* runs to nearly four hundred pages, but great swathes of the volume are barely readable. Spender's alternative to gawky plainness was a wildly undisciplined use of metaphor, often toppling over into the grotesque, the risible, or the meaningless. A frequently cited anecdote in *World Within World* documents a conversation with Eliot:

> At our first luncheon he asked me what I wanted to do. I said: "Be a poet." "I can quite understand you wanting to write poems, but I don't quite know what you mean by 'being a poet.'"

Sutherland's comment is, "Stephen knew what he meant." Precisely: that was just the trouble.

Spender's father, Harold, was another trouble, a figure he spent his whole life trying to exorcise. One of his best poems, "The Ambitious Son," was prompted by his father's death. It has a sureness of touch and a controlled fury very rare for him:

> Old man, with hair made of newspaper
>   cutting
> And the megaphone voice,
> Dahlia in the public mind, strutting
> Like a canary before a clapping noise...
>
> Soon you lay in your grave like a crumpled
>   clown
> Eaten by worms, by quicklime forgotten,
> Fake, untragic...

Harold Spender, a double First from Oxford, a moderately successful journalist, lecturer, and Liberal loyalist, married into money, was painfully conscious of being supported by his wife, and idolized his eldest son, Michael—a frigid prig incapable of humor, who despised his siblings. Harold wrote Stephen off as "flabby" and "unmanly." In turn, Stephen indicted Harold's "ignorant windbaggery...everything my father touched turned to rhetorical abstraction" (a fault from which his own poetry is not free). Harold Spender was a cultural philistine, propelling his children past Renoir nudes in the galleries with a cry of "Boiled lobsters, don't look!" He was appalled to find Stephen reading that dangerous radical, Bernard Shaw. It was left to Spender's maternal grandmother, who kept a beady eye on the accounts, to introduce him to Chekhov, Ibsen, and Strindberg, thus ensuring that his concept of modern literature would be European and not parochial.

At preparatory school Spender was bullied and miserable, comparing himself to St. Stephen the martyr. Only the music master was kind to him, and he retained a cultivated interest in music all his life. University College School, London, proved a more liberal and humane environment, but the boy was repressed and morbidly self-conscious: "I had learned that the whole of civilization was based on the concealment of physical acts," he wrote, and again: "My body seemed skewered on the gaze of everyone I passed in the streets." He began to contribute poems to the school magazine, and to read Freud and Joyce in reaction against his father's Victorianism.

In 1927 he went up to University College, Oxford (Shelley's old college—the comparison was duly made) to read History, but changed after two terms to Politics, Philosophy, and Economics. Here Spender rediscovered the unpleasantly arrogant and oafish types of his prep school days. The college was filled with hearty sportsmen, whose reaction to the reproductions of Klee and Gauguin in his rooms may be imagined. He fell in love with a fellow undergraduate only to be informed that he was a bore. Rescue came when he was introduced to W. H. Auden, then an undergraduate at Christ Church but already hailed as the best poet of his generation. Auden was cruel, telling Spender that he was valuable because he was "infinitely capable of being humiliated," and also, less reliably, that his great height had come about because "you want to escape from your balls." Nevertheless, to be accepted, even maliciously, by Auden, guaranteed that Spender became known as a poet, and a pamphlet of his work was published. He neglected his studies so much that he failed to obtain even a pass degree, an achievement which took something like genius in 1920s Oxford. He did not care: "I don't want to be efficient and have a trained mind any more than I want to be a motor-car."

The subsequent events—his sexual liberation in the twilight of Weimar Germany, his disastrous first marriage, his support for the Communists in the Spanish Civil War, his fire-fighting activities during the Blitz, his postwar work in Berlin for the Allied Control Commission, his role in UNESCO, his stream of lectureships at home and abroad—are all chronicled by Sutherland with, at times, excessive attention to detail. About half the book is taken up with the period up to 1940, a deliberate imbalance because Spender is so much a man of the 1930s. His later career was as a teacher of creative writing, a cultural influence through his editorship of *Horizon* and *Encounter* (which he long refused to believe was indirectly funded by the CIA), and, of course, as a reader of his own work.

He continued to write poems but felt increasingly ignored, and he never escaped the baleful influence of Auden, whose prodigious abilities could only be resisted by a profounder creativity than Spender possessed. Others in Auden's circle, such as Christopher Isherwood, found their own voice through prose. Spender's prose was at least workmanlike but he had no ear for cadence, no sense of the aesthetic organization of a sentence or paragraph. Besides, he was so set on "being a poet." He knew what he owed to Auden and managed to give it moving expression in a late poem, "Auden's Funeral," in which he remembers Chester Kallman putting on a record of "Siegfried's Funeral March" at the wake:

> Down-crashing drums and cymbals cataclysmic
> End-of-world brass exalt on drunken waves
> The poet's corpse borne on a bier beyond
> The foundering finalities, his world,
> To that Valhalla where the imaginings
> Of the dead makers are their lives.
> The dreamer sleeps forever with the dreamed.

The slightly fusty diction, the Miltonian inversion of "cymbals cataclysmic," and the Tennysonian lilt are oddly touching.

In the end, the irony is that Spender remained in some ways a Victorian like his rejected father. The scion of a high-minded Liberal family, with a tireless social conscience and a great capacity for friendship, he may well ultimately have valued human beings more than literature—in one sense, an entirely honorable position, but it enfeebled his writing. He found the variety of modernism represented by the "Movement" poets trivial, and (fortunately for him) literary theory passed him by completely. He looked to America to provide the true inheritors of the titans of his youth, admiring Roethke and Anne Sexton (whom he taught), less convinced by Lowell. But, never having acquired much intellectual discipline, he tended to react by intuition alone. He liked what he liked because he liked it: his approval was self-validating. This means that, if we are not drawn to him personally, we shall find it hard to share his enthusiasms or to respect his judgments. John Sutherland, who clearly does like him and cherishes his memory, never really asks himself how he might persuade the unconverted, while Michael Brett unintentionally presents much of the evidence for the opposition.

On the day of his death, Spender was working on a lecture he had agreed to give about Robert Graves. He was amazed, he told his wife, at Graves's gullibility, but perhaps this "was all an act." "These," Sutherland adds, "were his last recorded words." Spender had always had a nose for fakes, from his father onwards. He himself,

> IN SPENDER'S POLITICAL VERSE—HIS CALL TO REFORM OR REVOLUTION—HE FOUND A REAL FORCE AND INSPIRATION."

although often, as he would admit, muddled and self-contradictory, emerges from Sutherland's book as an honest man trying to be true to his impressions and to live a dignified life. It is just a pity that the poetry remains, even after one has tried one's hardest to find merits in it, so largely dead on the page. Thanks to these two books, however, he has had what he once said he wished for: "I want a few poems to survive and some memoir of myself as distinct from any group."

Source: Paul Dean, "Being a Poet," in *New Criterion*, Vol. 23, No. 6, February 2005, pp. 61–64.

Willis D. Jacobs

In the following essay, Jacobs evaluates Spender as a poet and concludes that he is a minor poet, not of the stature of Percy Shelley or John Keats.

Has ever distinguished poet attempted so much and accomplished so little? Of course if one counts the sheer bulk of Stephen Spender's work—poems, essays, criticism, travelogue, autobiography, humorous squibs, lectures, and what not (he is tireless)—one is overwhelmed by the quantity done; yet the thought persists that we have from such an enormous mountain precious little mouse.

This is all the more puzzling because Spender is clearly gifted with sensitivity, intelligence, knowledge, courage, and industry. Is his comparative failure as poet due to insufficiency of poetic talent or to certain personal and literary flaws which cripple his gifts in the act? These are embarrassing questions, and only a real affection for the poet *manqué* and sympathetic human being that is Stephen Spender could encourage one to decipher this mystery.

Here is a man once hailed as the Shelley of our times. That was twenty and more years ago, and Spender is called our Shelley no more. Here is a man once the pride and enthusiasm of young political rebels and aspiring young poets. The first have abandoned him as he abandoned them; the second have turned, long since, to Dylan Thomas for what once they hungered to find in Spender. It is indeed too many years since Spender was welcomed as a brilliant new light in the world of poetry; he is now seen as both a much older man—as we all are—and a much lesser poet. This last is sad and perhaps not fully chartable, but Spender once appeared to possess such ability and still possesses such admirable qualities as artist and man that he deserves a tentative examination to discover, if may be, why his success as poet has been moderate, or, perhaps, even tepid.

Reading affectionately through the poetry of this likeable and noble man, one does encounter here and there lines, even brief poems, of some charm and warmth. The pathos comes as one notes the brevity and scarcity. Frequently in longer works one winces over poem after poem spoiled as an entity by bathos, eruptions of false notes, and dismaying errors in taste—both in language and in the very structure of the poems.

His success, when he succeeds, generally arrives in stanzas of no more than twelve or fifteen lines, and yet there it is a success that leaves one touched, even haunted, but convinced that this is a pretty little talent, not a warm, rich, enduring gift. Such a successful poem, on its level of the not quite immemorial, is his "Discovered in Mid-Ocean." In this poem reminiscent of the Daedalus legend are a number of ramifications: Spender himself as an Icarus, political or poetical, aspiring to the stars, but failing and falling and wrecked; implications of man as artificer, whose mechanical inventions (like the aircraft here) serve both to raise him and destroy him; insinuations of man as creator of weapons (perhaps a warplane here), destroying others with them, and himself destroyed in them. In short there is richness here, and one notes that, appreciates it, remembers the poem—and feels that it misses any true greatness. It is too mild and too timid. Spender's political poems are strident; his personal lyrics are weary.

Shelley too has some lines about a man lost at sea. His words seem almost commonplace:

Many a green isle needs must be
In the deep wide sea of Misery,
Or the mariner, worn and wan,
Never thus could voyage on—
Day and night, and night and day,
Drifting on his weary way...

But as one reads these simple words he feels a force of emotion—a surge of soul—flooding the lines. It is the great heart beat of Shelley. With Spender, however, there is generally a tiredness.

The heart beats, but sadly, sluggishly. His is the lyrical poetry of the defeated. Not that defeat creates only weak verse; Thomas Hardy proves otherwise. Defeat is a powerful motive and noble quality too. Spender's defeat is the sapless defeat of mere and unstruggling surrender; from it comes poetry of wistfulness, not poetry of grief—poetry of charm, not poetry of passion and strength. Stephen Spender is the wistful poet.

He has written an excellent poem called "What I Expected." If society is changed, he tells us, it is not by a dramatic moment, but by the daily straining of suffering men, and meanwhile from them drop away courage, hope, and faith:

What I expected was
Thunder, fighting,
Long struggles with men
And climbing...

What I had not foreseen
Was the gradual day
Weakening the will
Leaking the brightness away...

This is moving, but once more the theme is of the hurt man, wincing at his hurt. I lost and it hurts; the world has changed and it hurts. Can superb poetry be written from this velleity? "Within my head, aches the perpetual winter Of this violent time," Spender sighs; and since we too have been frozen and betrayed by the ignoble days of this world we understand and feel affection for this spokesman of our dismay. Yet his simple wistfulness and regret have not led to poetry of the first rank.

In Spender's political verse—his call to reform or revolution—he found a real force and inspiration. For a period he discerned in Communism the means to a democratic and peaceful world. His political verse, however, was generally flawed by either crass tendentiousness or venal technique. That political verse can be effective and poetically true is apparent; one has only to recall Shelley again, or William Morris even in his blunter moments:

For that which the worker winneth shall
then be his indeed,
Nor shall half be reaped for nothing by him
that sowed no seed.

The political verse of Spender is eloquent and imperfect. "The writer who grasps anything of the Marxist theory," he once wrote, "feels that he is moving in a world of reality and in a purposive world." This conviction lent him force but not poetic sureness. The wistfulness and hurt in the poetry that follows his Communist period probably have a dual cause—his disenchantment with that political doctrine, and his shamed awareness that he had often betrayed the integrity of poetry in his effort to preach. He had, thus, not really a poet's firm hand or great faith; he was poetaster instead. He had failed politically and poetically; he failed politically because, he had became convinced, he had mistaken the nature of Communism; he failed poetically because he was not a *natural* poet, one who knows spontaneously and strongly what poetry must be and what perjuries it must never allow itself. Spender became aware, that is, that he was a man with great yearning to be a poet, sensitivity to ideas and words, and insufficient poetic talent.

Once the political afflatus is past, the writer himself can see and flush at the poetic falseness at the end of "The Landscape Near an Aerodrome." A landing aircraft is described with eye, ear, and love:

> More beautiful and soft than any moth
> With burring furred antennæ feeling its
> huge path...
> Gently, broadly, she falls,
> Scarcely disturbing charted currents of air.

The plane passes over the bleak suburbs of the city, reaches the aerodrome, and frees its passengers. Up to the final stanza this is a poetically notable work. When Spender describes the wind-sleeve of the airport he does so with "l's" that picture its reaching height: "sleeves set trailing tall"—with the hissing of the wind in the "s's" as well. Describing the passengers peering down at the land he refers to their "eyes trained by watching"—creating an effective ambiguity: "eyes-strained by watching." Describing the frayed factory area, where amid ugliness men labor at producing objects of luxury like aircraft for others to enjoy, he puts his rage and hurt into monosyllables, the way men speak in pain: "Here they may see what is being done." Near the airport, chimneys poke into the sky, and Spender provides the words and letters that create the sight: "Chimneys like lank black fingers." The industrial area itself is called the "outposts of work," with the military term "outposts" indicating that the workers there suffer a life of military subservience, command, and regimentation. All this is poetically right. From the words we receive not only idea but picture, and not only idea and picture but an emotional response to both. Up to the last stanza the work is a beautiful and thoughtful poem contrasting the comfort of the few to the squalor

of the many, the luxurious indolence of some to the drab cheerlessness of others. The poem has made its statement. But then comes—as so often with Spender's political verse—the jarring note, the poetical flaw. The final lines are:

> Then, as they land, they hear the tolling bell
> Reaching across the landscape of hysteria
> To where, larger than all the charcoaled
> batteries
> And imaged towers against that dying sky,
> Religion stands, the church blocking the
> sun.

Religion, we are suddenly told, blocks out the light; as an institution, the church abets industry to bring darkness to man. This may be so; but to say it here, at this time, in this poem, is poetically false. This is not a poem about the church; to thrust it in as an afterthought is a structural flaw that bespeaks an earnest and dedicated young man but also an imperfect artist.

So too with the bathetic poem called "The Funeral." In this appears an image of striking beauty—but in the wrong place and contrary to the sense of the poem as Spender conceived it. Spender is saying (as he has every right to say) that our times have new heroes, better heroes than those of our traditional past. These new heroes are the men whose labor produces the physical wealth of the world. Such men are more valuable, he says, than a classical culture "Mourned by scholars who dream of the ghosts of Greek boys." But in the same poem we are asked to mourn the death of a contemporary hero—a Stakhanovite: "This one excelled all others in making driving-belts." This disparity in language and imagery makes the Stakhanovite absurd. The beauty of the Greek image—its long vowels, the sweetness and solemnity of its sounds—engenders nobility and loveliness in the past, in the very era Spender is terming inferior through the rest of the poem. Spender's language contradicts his intention, and he is not artist enough to recognize and excise the fatal anomaly. He too, despite himself, mourns the ghosts of Greek boys more than he does the nameless fabricator of driving-belts, and so his language bears witness. Enamored with a lovely statement, he employs it, though its gravity and melody dwarf the other lines and turn to absurdity the expression Spender sought to make before it.

Similarly the poem called "Not Palaces" ultimately disappoints because of false tone. It is a call to youth to change the world, to strive for economic betterment and human brotherhood. It is a cry for justice, equality, and love. Yet it ends:

> Our program like this, yet opposite:
> Death to the killers, bringing light to life.

The paradox of stimulating brotherhood and love by wide-scale murder ("Death to the killers") is not resolved. Worse, it is not seen. What matters here is not so much the logical confusion; rather it is the artistic failing, the structural flaw whereby the final lines strike a note of murderous vindictiveness in a poem purportedly expressing high idealism and love of humankind. The contradiction is redoubled within the poem. In the new society, Spender writes at the beginning, there will be no people "ordered like a single mind." Some few lines later, nonetheless, he states: "Our goal which we compel: Man shall be man." If there is a difference between *order* and *compel,* surely it is the latter which is the more stern and inflexible. Spender, in short, asserts within a few lines that in his new world man will be *freed* for individual life and then *compelled* to accept goals set by others. Once more we have a contradiction which makes one feel that both as thinker and poet Spender is too frivolous.

What Spender often lacks, it appears, is the "fundamental brainwork" which D. G. Rossetti declared indispensable for a poet. Emotion he has; intelligent control over the structure and language of his poem he too frequently has not. Randall Jarrell had something like this idea in mind when he remarked of Spender:

> Stephen Spender is, I think, an open, awkward, emotional, conscientiously well-intentioned, and simple-minded poet. To like his poems as much as we shouldn't, we need to respond to what they are meant to be, not to what they are—and it is surprisingly easy to do this. Most of his virtues and vices cluster around the word *sincere.* One likes his *Collected Poems* neither for their development (most of his experience and intelligence are excluded from the poems, so any great development is impossible) nor for their general excellence, but for a few touching, truthful poems that seem the products of observation, moral insight, and inspiration. (*Harper's,* Oct. 1955, p. 100)

Once we approach Spender on his true level, we can enjoy him, even though we will occasionally wince. He is no Shelley; he has neither the power nor the instant swoop of that falcon. He is not even Auden; he has not the easiness and breadth of that bright-eyed sparrow. He lacks the gorgeous plumage of a Wallace Stevens. At his best, Spender is the poet who knows that our world, our sex, and our sorrows are ever with us and ever too much for us. He is essentially an elegist. Even his poems of celebration incline toward sadness. "I Think Continually of Those" appears an exhortation to action and the apotheosis of those

> who in their lives fought for life,
> Who wore at their hearts the fire's center.

It is a poem glowing with imagery from Freud and D. H. Lawrence—imagery not only of birth but equally of short life and of swift oncoming destruction. The blaze of the sun and the heat of fire burn throughout the poem. Those who were truly great are dead (perhaps Marx and Lenin, perhaps Shelley and Lawrence). They traveled but "a short while towards the sun"—consumed by the fire of their passage and by the blazing goal they approached. They "left the vivid air signed with their honor," but their life was brief as they flared into death.

In another place, Spender reminds us:

> You were born; must die ...
> The miles and hours upon you feed.
> They eat your eyes out with their distance
> They eat your heart out with devouring need
> They eat your death out with lost significance.

And says finally that the song of life is "Of love, of loneliness, of life being death."

To be at one's best the wistful elegist of man's loneliness and death is no dismal fate for a poet, even if it is not the highest either. Essentially that is Spender's achievement. He feels "The furious volleys of charioteering power Behind the sun, racing to destroy." He hears "the groaning of the wasted lives." He knows the horror of "incommunicable grief." He reflects

> That the kingdom of heaven on earth must always
> Reiterate the garden of Eden,
> And each day's revolution be betrayed.

Behind each man's mask Spender discerns the timorous, uncertain child. He recognizes that child, for he of course is the child. Like the child he seeks some warmth, some haven: "Come home at last; come, end of loneliness."

It is not a mean thing to be a minor poet. Stephen Spender belongs not with Shelley and Keats, but he can interest and please those who fondly remember poets as disparate as Fulke Greville, Sir John Davies, and Wilfred Owen.

Source: Willis D. Jacobs, "The Moderate Poetical Success of Stephen Spender," in *College English*, Vol. 17, No. 7, April 1956, pp. 374–78.

SOURCES

"About the Great Depression," in *Modern American Poetry*, http://www.english.illinois.edu/maps/depression/about.htm (accessed December 29, 2009).

Applebaum, Anne, "World Inaction: Russia Invades Georgia while the West Watches," in *Slate*, http://www.slate.com/id/2197155/ (accessed December 29, 2009).

"British Unemployment Rises to just under 2.5 Million," in *Earth Times*, http://www.earthtimes.org/articles/show/294194,british-unemployment-rises-to-just-under-25-million.html (accessed December 28, 2009).

Browning, Robert, "Andrea del Sarto," in *The Florentine Edition*, edited by Charlotte Porter and Helen A. Clarke, 12 Vols., Smith, Elder, 1910; reprinted in *The Major Victorian Poets: Tennyson, Browning, Arnold*, edited by William E. Buckler, Houghton Mifflin, 1973, p. 313.

Cook, Judith, et al., "The Contribution Made by School Milk to the Nutrition of Primary Schoolchildren," in *British Journal of Nutrition*, Vol. 34, 1975, pp. 91–103.

Courtney-Thompson, Fiona, and Kate Phelps, eds., *The 20th Century Year by Year*, Barnes & Noble, 1998, pp. 99–130.

Dana, Richard, "Stephen Spender: A Conversation," in *American Poetry Review*, Vol. 6, No. 6, November/December 1977, p. 17.

"The Depression of the 1930s," in *British Broadcasting Corporation*, http://www.bbc.co.uk/schools/gcsebitesize/history/mwh/britain/depressionrev1.shtml (accessed December 29, 2009).

Fitts, Dudley, "Tragic Celebration," in *New York Times*, March 13, 1955, p. BR5.

Gregory, James, "The Great Depression 1930-1939," in *National Geographic Eyewitness to the 20th Century*, National Geographic Society, 1998, pp. 125–43.

Harmon, William, and Hugh Holman, *A Handbook to Literature*, 11th ed., Pearson Prentice Hall, 2009, pp. 241, 340, 350–51, 467–68, 547.

"On Air: Is the Indian Caste System a Human Rights Abuse?," in *World Have Your Say*, http://worldhaveyoursay.wordpress.com/2009/09/29/should-india-be-left-to-reform-at-its-own-pace/ (accessed December 28, 2009).

Jack, Peter Monro, "Two Radical Young English Poets," in *New York Times*, September 23, 1934, p. BR2.

Jennings, Peter, and Todd Brewster, eds., *The Century*, Doubleday, 1998, pp. 147–78.

Kermode, Frank, "Grand Old Man of Letters," in *Guardian* (London, England), July 17, 1995, p. 12.

"London Child Poverty Commission Final Report," in *London Child Poverty Commission Final Report*, February 2008, http://213.86.122.139/docs/capital-gains.pdf (accessed December 28, 2009).

Peskin, Joan, "Constructing Meaning When Reading Poetry: An Expert-Novice Study," in *Cognition and Instruction*, Vol. 16, No. 3, 1998, p. 235.

Porter, Peter, "Obituaries: Sir Stephen Porter," in *Independent* (London, England), July 18, 1995.

Pound, Ezra, *Literary Essays*, edited by T. S. Eliot, New Directions, 1954, p. 297.

"Pylon School," in *Jrank.org*, http://www.jrank.org/literature/pages/5471/Pylon-School.html (accessed December 30, 2009).

"Sir Stephen Spender; Obituary," in *Times* (London, England), July 18, 1995, p. 19.

Spender, Stephen, "What I Expected," in *Poems*, Faber and Faber, 1933, pp. 25–26.

————, *World within World: The Autobiography of Stephen Spender*, Modern Library, 2001, pp. 3–36, 150.

Southerland, John, "The 1930s," in *Stephen Spender: A Literary Life*, Oxford University Press, 2004, pp. 105–49.

Stitt, Peter, "The Art of Poetry XXV," in *Paris Review*, No. 77, Winter/Spring 1980, p. 139.

Taylor, A. J. P., *English History: 1914-1945*, Oxford University Press, 1990, pp. 122–23.

Taylor, Robert, "Appreciation; Spender Spoke Up When It Mattered," in *Boston Globe*, July 18, 1995, p. 33.

Trager, James, *The People's Chronology*, Henry Holt, 1992.

"Weimar Republic and the Great Depression," in *History Learning Site*, http://www.historylearningsite.co.uk/weimar_depression_1929.htm (accessed December 29, 2009).

FURTHER READING

Anreus, Alejandro, Diane L. Linden, and Jonathan Weinberg, eds., *The Social and the Real: Political Art of the 1930s in the Western Hemisphere*, Pennsylvania State University Press, 2006.

> This book is an anthology of different representations of art created in the 1930s. The art includes paintings, sculpture, graphic arts, and photography.

Clavin, Patricia, *The Great Depression in Europe, 1929–1939*, Palgrave, 2000.

> This book is a comparative study of the effects of the Great Depression on Europe. The author compares the effects of the Depression on individual countries and discusses how each country chose to respond.

Fritzsche, Peter, *Germans into Nazis*, Harvard University Press, 1999.

> Fritzsche explores German life as it began its transformation into a Nazi state and attempts to discover the reasons so many Germans embraced Nazism. This study focuses on German society rather than Hitler as the foundation of the Nazi state.

Hatt, Christine, *World War I, 1914–18*, Franklin Watts, 2001.

> This book is a history of World War I, designed for young-adult readers. This history of the war includes many photographs and maps. The aftermath of World War I had a major impact on the poets of Spender's generation.

Hynes, Samuel, *The Auden Generation: Literature and Politics in England in the 1930s*, Princeton University Press, 1982.

> Hynes presents a study of the poetry created during the political and social crisis of the 1930s. The emphasis is on the poetry of W. H. Auden, Cecil Day-Lewis, Louis MacNiece, George Orwell, Michael Roberts, and Stephen Spender.

Sutherland, John, *Stephen Spender: A Literary Life*, Oxford University Press, 2005.

> This biography of Spender's life relies on the poet's personal letters and journals, as well as Spender's own autobiography. This is a very readable and often compelling examination of Spender's life.

Whitehead, John, *A Commentary on the Poetry of W. H. Auden, C. Day Lewis, Louis MacNeice, and Stephen Spender*, Edwin Mellen Press, 1992.

> Whitehead offers essays about a selection of the poetry written by these four poets. The author discusses possible sources for the poems and places them within their historical context.

Yapp, Nick, *1930s: Decades of the 20th Century*, Langenscheidt, 2008.

> This book is part of a photographic series that emphasizes specific decades of the 20th century. The photographs offer a visual representation of the political and social conflicts and the personalities important to this decade. Photographs are drawn from the Getty collection.

SUGGESTED SEARCH TERMS

Stephen Spender

Stephen Spender poems

Stephen Spender biography

What I Expected

What I Expected AND Stephen Spender

1930s British poetry

Oxford Poets AND Stephen Spender

Pylon Poets AND Stephen Spender

Auden Group AND Stephen Spender

disillusionment AND Stephen Spender

When In Rome

MARI EVANS

1970

"When In Rome" by Mari Evans was published in 1970 in her collection *I Am A Black Woman*. It is one of Evans's best known and most widely anthologized poems. It is a poem of conflict between a housemaid named Mattie, and her employer, and involves themes of race and class difference as well as unspeakable frustration. It was published during the height of the Black Arts movement, a particularly significant time for African American literature. Evans, a prolific writer for the movement, has been an outspoken advocate for equal rights. Her writing frequently deals with issues of race. "When In Rome" can be found in *Reality in Conflict: Literature of Values in Opposition* by Edmund J. Farrell.

AUTHOR BIOGRAPHY

Evans was born in Toledo, Ohio, on July 16, 1923. Growing up, her father was her greatest influence. In her essay "My Father's Passage," she recalls an formative moment in her early life that sparked her interest in writing: her father saved a story by Evans that was published in her school newspaper when she was in fourth grade. Evans remained in her hometown throughout her college years and studied fashion design at the University of Toledo. However, fashion did not sustain her interest and she soon shifted her focus to writing. Her first

writing-related job was as an assistant editor at a manufacturing firm.

Although Evans is best known for her poetry, she claims that she never intended to be a poet and began writing poetry unintentionally. Her first volume of poems was published in 1968 as *Where Is All the Music?* This volume was more personal and introspective and less politically charged than her later work.

Evans's extensive academic career began in 1969 when she was hired as an instructor of African American literature and writer-in-residence at Indiana University-Purdue University Indianapolis. From 1970 to 1978 Evans was an assistant professor and writer-in-residence at Indiana University. During this period she completed a writing fellowship at the prestigious MacDowell Colony in New Hampshire. From 1972 to 1973 she was a visiting assistant professor at Northwestern University in Chicago in conjunction with her position at Indiana University. Her career progressed with positions as visiting assistant professor at Purdue University (1978–1980), Washington University in St. Louis (1980), and Cornell University (1981–1983), where she received a National Endowment for the Arts Creative Writing Award in 1981. She continued as assistant professor and distinguished writer at Cornell (1983–1985), associate professor at State University of New York at Albany (1985–1986), visiting distinguished writer at University of Miami Gables, and writer in residence at Spelman College (1989–1990).

During Evans's academic career she continued to write and publish her work. In 1970 her second and most widely known book of poetry, *I Am a Black Woman*, was published. *I Am a Black Woman* earned Evans the first annual award for the most distinguished volume of poetry published by a black writer from the Black Academy of Arts and Letters. The poems in this volume, including "When In Rome," are more indicative of Evans's lifelong interest in social and political issues than was her first book, *Where is All the Music?* These poems are largely realistic and related to community issues such as civil rights legislation. Evans's third book of poetry, *Nightstar: 1973-1978*, was published in 1981 and was even more overtly political and experimental than *I Am a Black Woman*. Her most recent book of poems, *A Dark And Splendid Mass*, was published in 1992.

In addition to poetry, Evans has also written essays, plays, short stories, and children's books. She has given countless lectures and was the producer, writer, and director of the acclaimed television program *The Black Experience* from 1968 to 1973. She also wrote music and lyrics for thirteen songs for her play *Eyes*, a stage adaption of Zora Neale Hurston's *Their Eyes Were Watching God*. Over the expanse of her life Evans has engaged in social activism and community involvement. She believes it is the poet's duty to observe the voices of the community and convey them through poetry. In recognition of her influential career, she was featured on the Ugandan postage stamp in 1997.

POEM SUMMARY

"When In Rome" is a poem of thirty-four lines organized into five stanzas. The poem represents an interaction between two distinct personas: Mattie, an African American maid or house servant, and her unnamed female employer. Each stanza is comprised of a statement by Mattie's employer and Mattie's internal response to that statement, except for stanzas 3 and 4 which follow this pattern when considered together. In one long, enjambed sentence that continues throughout the poem, Mattie's employer offers her various foods. When a sentence or clause is enjambed, it continues over multiple lines of a poem.

Stanza 1
In the first five lines the employer gently urges Mattie to take whatever she would like from the icebox. In lines 5 through 8 Mattie responds that she would rather have a different type of food, such as meat, than what her employer has to offer her. The parentheses enclosing Mattie's response indicate that it is directed not to her employer but rather to herself. It would be disrespectful for a servant to openly respond to an employer in the way that Mattie does. Her response is either in her head, or in a whisper quiet enough that her employer cannot hear it.

Stanza 2
In lines 9 through 11, Mattie's employer begins to list some of the foods that are in the icebox for Mattie to eat. She offers her endives and cottage cheese, but what Mattie would rather have is some soul food. In lines 12 and 13 Mattie exasperatedly responds, again to herself. It is evident that Mattie is not enthusiastic about the food her employer offers her.

Stanzas 3 and 4

In lines 14 through 21 Mattie's employer offers her sardines but exclaims that she should not eat the anchovies as they are too expensive. Up to this point in the poem, Mattie's employer appears to be a generous woman, but here it becomes clear that Mattie cannot actually take anything she would like from the icebox. The more expensive or higher quality foods are reserved for people in the house other than servants. In lines 22 through 25 Mattie sarcastically responds to herself, indicating that she would not even consider eating the anchovies because they are not substantial enough to make up a meal. Anchovies are generally used as a garnish or seasoning on other foods and are not usually eaten by themselves. All of the foods the employer has offered Mattie so far are light, snack-type foods that Mattie considers insufficient to fill up a human.

Stanza 5

In lines 26 and 27 Mattie's employer concludes that there should be plenty in the icebox to satisfy Mattie's hunger. Mattie again sarcastically responds that just looking at the food is enough to fill her up. She does not mean this literally, she means that she would rather look at the food than actually eat it because it is not appealing to her. Mattie knows that this type of food will not fill her up and she looks forward to going home so that she can eat what she considers to be proper food. In lines 33 and 34 Mattie concludes by alluding to the well-known idiom from which the title of the poem is also taken: "When in Rome, do as the Romans do." This means that when you are in an unfamiliar culture or environment, you should adhere to the customs of that environment. Mattie realizes that when she is in her employer's house she will have to eat foods that seem unappetizing and insubstantial to her, but she looks forward to going home so that she can eat the types of food she likes.

THEMES

Black-White Relations

Evans's poems often deal with African American civil rights issues. Although "When In Rome" does not specifically deal with civil rights, the theme of black-white relations is certainly present in the poem. The fact that Mattie is black and her employer is white is significant considering the setting of the poem. Although it is not explicitly

stated, the poem probably takes place sometime between the 1950s and 1970, prior to or during the civil rights movement in the United States. During this time, African Americans were still widely viewed as inferior because of their race, especially in the South. Segregation laws were not eliminated in the United States until the Civil Rights Act of 1964, and discrimination was widely practiced until then and in many places even after that point. Although Mattie's employer is not overtly rude or discriminatory towards her, the dynamic between the two women is suggestive of the racial inequalities of an earlier time. For example, Mattie's parenthetical interjections are to herself, not her employer, because to express dissatisfaction with the food that was offered to her would be considered disrespectful and could even cause her to lose her job.

Ethnic Identity

"When In Rome" is stylistically and thematically a poem of contrast between Mattie and her employer. Much of the contrast between these two personas stems from the fact that they clearly embody two distinct ethnic identities. The theme of ethnic identity is manifest in the poem in several ways. One way is through the women's speech. Because Mattie and her employer speak in different dialects, it is apparent that they come from different cultural backgrounds. A dialect is a particular way of speaking that varies in some way, usually in vocabulary or pronunciation, from standard or literary English. Dialects are sometimes used to indicate a person's class, geographic location, or ethnicity. Mattie's employer speaks in a standard English, suggesting that she is most likely a white woman from the upper or middle class. Mattie's dialect is much more informal and grammatically incorrect, incorporating words such as *ain't* instead of *isn't*, *yes'm* instead of *yes ma'am*, and *lives* instead of *live*. These diction choices in the context of Evans's poetry indicate that Mattie is probably a working-class African American woman.

The fact that Mattie and her employer have different taste in food also indicates that they are from different ethnic backgrounds. Mattie's employer thinks that cottage cheese, endive, and sardines are normal and acceptable snacks, but because Mattie is from a different culture these foods seem unfamiliar, strange, and unappetizing to her.

The contrast between these two ethnic identities is significant because it creates tension in the poem. Because Mattie is employed by a person of different, and what at the time was the dominant

TOPICS FOR FURTHER STUDY

- Evans was an important figure in the Black Arts movement. Research the Black Arts movement, as well as the Chicano art movement that began in the 1960s. In each movement, how did art reflect the political or social goals of the broader movements that they were a part of? Who were some of the most important artists, and works of each movement? How can art be an effective way to prompt social or political change? Create a Web site comparing and contrasting these two artistic movements. Be sure to include photographs of the artwork, as well as captions explaining their relevance.

- Read Mari Evans's young-adult novella *I'm Late: The Story of Laneese and Moonlight and Alisha who Didn't Have Anyone of Her Own.* Are any of the themes of "When In Rome" present in the novella? Write a paper explaining your findings.

- "When In Rome" is a poem written in free verse. Pick a topic related to one of the themes of the poem and write your own free verse poem. Post your poem on a Web site and allow your classmates to comment on its theme and style.

- Evans has been a political activist for most of her life, as well as an advocate for activism among young people. Watch the interview with Evans found at http://blackademics.org/december-interview-mari-evans or find your own interview with her online or in a print source. Imagine that you had the opportunity to interview Evans yourself. Write three questions you would ask her, as well as three pieces of advice you think she would offer to young people today.

- Although Evans's style is unique and distinctive, her poetry is sometimes reminiscent of that of her contemporaries. Choose a poem that you enjoy by one of Evans's contemporaries, Maya Angelou, Margaret Walker, or Nikki Giovanni, and write a paper comparing and contrasting it to "When In Rome." How are the style, themes, and content similar or different?

- The rhythm of Evans's syncopated poems are often similar to the rhythms of free-form types of music such as jazz. Using a music editing program such as Garage Band, set the words of "When In Rome" to a jazz song that you think suits the tone of the poem, or create your own song to set the poem to using a computerized song-writing program.

---

ethnicity, she is forced to adhere to norms of a different culture while she is at work. She cannot eat the type of food she would like to or behave as she normally would if she were at home.

Frustration

Although Mattie's sarcastic tone is somewhat joking and comedic, it also evokes genuine frustration. Under normal circumstances she would not eat the type of food she is offered, but due to her position as a maid, she is unable to explain this to her employer and request something different. It is expected that she will be grateful and satisfied with whatever her employer offers her. Mattie's sarcastic internal response in lines 22 through 25 in particular indicates her frustration. She is surprised and even a bit offended that her employer would warn her against eating the anchovies, because to Mattie anchovies do not even remotely constitute a proper meal or snack. Mattie's frustration is further indicated in lines 31 through 34 when she somewhat jokingly expresses concern for her own health. Although Mattie's sarcasm makes her response somewhat humorous, her irritation is clear.

Much of Mattie's frustration probably stems from the fact that as a maid she will most likely be

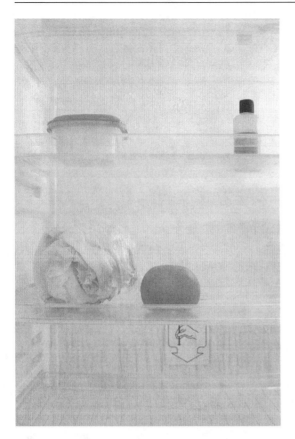

In the poem, the maid is shown a nearly empty refrigerator and told to make herself lunch. (Image copyright Tifonimages, 2010. Used under license from Shutterstock.com)

on her feet doing physical labor all day. While light snacks such as endive or cottage cheese may be plenty to sustain Mattie's employer, they are not enough to provide energy for someone constantly doing difficult physical tasks. Mattie's job is probably all the more difficult if she is hungry and fatigued.

STYLE

Dialogue Poem

"When In Rome" is a dialogue poem, meaning that it is structured as a conversation between two personas. Each of the five stanzas begins with an address to Mattie by her employer and ends with Mattie's rhetorical response to her, excepting stanzas 3 and 4, which follow this pattern when considered together. In poetry, the way a poem is arranged is just as important as what is being said. "When In Rome," like many of Evans's

other poems, has distinctive spacing and punctuation. In this poem the spacing and punctuation help to distinguish the two speakers. Mattie's lines are indented and enclosed in parentheses, while her employer's lines are not. The parentheses indicate that Mattie's responses are not spoken out loud, but rather are said in her head or quietly to herself. Moreover, Mattie's employer's lines (lines 1–5, 9–11, 14–21, 26–27) comprise a single enjambed run-on sentence, while Mattie's lines are brief interjections to her employer's speech. Thus, the ellipses used in lines 8, 13, and 34 of Mattie's interjections indicate moments that something is occurring in Mattie's thought process that cannot be expressed verbally.

Free Verse Poetry

"When In Rome," like many of Evans's poems, is written in free verse. Free verse is a category of poetry that was first popularized in the nineteenth century by poets such as Walt Whitman, Ezra Pound, T. S. Eliot, and Wallace Stevens, but gained major popularity in the United States sometime between 1950 and 1970, the same time period that Evans was writing prolifically. Free verse poems do not use a formal pattern of rhyme or meter. Similar to many free verse poems, "When In Rome" is syncopated, meaning that it follows no predictable metrical pattern but that it still has a distinct, albeit irregular, rhythm. The stanzas do not have a consistent number of lines, nor do the lines have a consistent number of syllables. Although some lines in the poem do rhyme (for example lines 5 and 8, 11 and 13) the rhymes are sporadic.

In addition to irregular meter and rhyme scheme, "When In Rome" also displays complex and fragmented typography. As with many free-verse poems, there seems to be no logical pattern to how the words are organized into lines or stanzas. The discordant, almost telegraphic organization of this poem is typical of Evans's style. "When In Rome" could be compared to an improvisational jazz song in its irregular beat and organization. Just as jazz music embodies a free style that was a departure from traditional music, Evans's poems often depart from norms of traditional poetry.

HISTORICAL CONTEXT

Evans's poetry is associated with the Black Arts movement, which took place from the mid-1960s to the mid-1970s. The Black Arts movement was

COMPARE
&
CONTRAST

- **1960s–1970s:** In 1965, respected publisher LeRoi Jones symbolically relocates from the mainstream neighborhood of New York's Lower East Side to Harlem, a district that was once a thriving community for African American artists and is now in decline. By 1970 he is fully ensconced in the neighborhood and has founded the Black Arts Repertory Theatre/School.

  Today: Former President Bill Clinton moves his office to Harlem in 2001 in an attempt to revitalize the still predominantly African American district. According to Clinton, his aim is "to help promote economic opportunity" in the area. Such revitalization efforts are helping to restore Harlem.

- **1960s–1970s:** After the passing of the Civil Rights Act of 1964 and the Voting Rights Act of 1965, the civil rights movement loses momentum but maintains a latent presence.

  Today: African American equality is still a much debated issue. Despite the election of the first African American president in 2008, as recently as 2006 less than one percent of Fortune 500 companies are led by African American CEOs.

- **1960s–1970s:** Evans receives attention following the publication of her second volume of poetry, *I Am A Black Woman*. Evans also expands her career with positions at several universities. She becomes a significant figure in the Black Arts movement.

  Today: Although Evans has led a more private life than many other participants of the Black Arts movement, she continues to write and publish material relevant to the black experience. Since 2005 she has published a collection of poems, a collection of essays, and a young-adult novel, all related to African American interests. Her work is published in over thirty textbooks and is translated into many languages, including German, Swedish, French and Dutch.

---

born out of and espoused ideals of the civil rights movement, such as racial equality, economic self-sufficiency, and political representation. The artistic branch of the black power movement is said to have begun in 1965 when, after the assassination of Malcolm X, LeRoi Jones, (Amiri Baraka) a highly influential and respected yet also controversial black writer, publisher, and music critic, moved from Manhattan's Lower East Side to the predominantly African American neighborhood of Harlem and joined forces with other African American activists to found the Black Arts Repertory Theatre/School (BARTS). It was from Jones's poem "Black Art" that the name of the movement was derived. During the movement, the African American presence in the arts, particularly literature, experienced its greatest growth since the Harlem Renaissance of the early twentieth century. Prior to the Black Arts movement the English literary canon had been dominated by white, male authors.

Although this is still true to some extent today, during the Black Arts movement there was a significant burgeoning of African American poetry, literature, theater, and visual art that reached a wider audience than it ever had before. The work of the black artists of the movement was produced for a black audience and spoke to the particular condition of being an African American. Evans's work fits definitively within this category. In Robert L. Douglas's book, *Resistance, Insurgence and Identity: The Art of Mari Evans, Nelson Stevens and the Black Arts Movement*, he says of Evans's work:

> It is [Evans's] Black ideology that explains her primary concern for Black people, and it is from this Black ideology, this Black Identity that the content of most of her poetry is born. It is also this Black Identity that demands that Evans search through a wide range of literary devices to choose elements from an idiom rooted in the Black experience.

An African American maid waits on her white employers, circa 1950s (© Bettman / Corbis)

The Black Arts movement was an inherently political one. In his 1968 essay, "The Black Arts Movement," published in the *Drama Review*, Larry Neal described it as the "aesthetic and spiritual sister of the Black Power concept." The black power movement, with which Evans's work has also been associated, took place in the late 1960s and early 1970s. Black power supporters endorsed varying degrees of radicalism. Some adherents advocated black nationalism (the idea that African Americans should have a unified national identity and pride),or black separatism (the idea that African Americans should have autonomy from whites by maintaining separate institutions), and the use of violence to achieve their goals when necessary. Although the black power movement was born out of the civil rights movement, the ideologies of two are frequently seen as being at odds with each other, as many supporters of black power were critical of the nonviolent approach championed by civil rights leader Martin Luther King, Jr. Several of Evans's poems have been directly linked to the black power movement. For example, Douglas interprets the speaker of her poem "My Man Let Me Pull Up Your Coat..." to be Malcolm X, whose ideals provided the foundation of the black power movement.

CRITICAL OVERVIEW

Despite Evans's prolific writing career, there has not been an abundance of criticism concerning her work. However, a number of critics who have written about Evans's work, such as David Dorsey, praised her masterful form and style as well as the didactic value of her poems. If a poem is didactic, it is intended to teach its audience a lesson or a moral, as Evans's poems often do. In Dorsey's essay "The

Art of Mari Evans," published in *Black Women Writers*, he remarks that Evans's 1970 book of poetry, *I Am a Black Woman*, exhibits deliberate "control of the reader's experience for didactic effect." He goes on to note the "subtle design of individual poems" as well as "the careful manipulations of familiar Black perceptions and rhetoric."

Robert P. Sedlack similarly emphasizes the social significance of *I Am a Black Woman* in his essay "Mari Evans: Consciousness and Craft," published in the *College Language Association Journal* by stating that "The admiration of black life styles in such poems as 'When In Rome' are obviously characteristic attitudes of the black renaissance of the 1960s." However, he also insists that Evans is "more than a social commenter who epitomizes the black experience. . . . She is also a skillful poet who conveys this experience by means of traditional poetic techniques adapted to her unique subject matter." That is, Evans's poems are highly regarded because they are not only socially important and sometimes controversial but also stylistically innovative and potent. Sedlack concludes that Evans "fuses a deep consciousness of her world with a high degree of craftsmanship to create a fine collection of poems."

Solomon Edwards also lavishes praise upon Evans in his essay "Affirmation in the Works of Mari Evans," published in *Black Women Writers*. Edwards likens Evans's "masterwork of poems," *I Am A Black Woman*, to Maya Angelou's *I Know Why the Caged Bird Sings* and Margaret Walker's *For My People*. Edwards lauds Evans's pride in black culture and affirmations of black identity. However, he also notes that her poems are relatable to people of various cultural backgrounds. According to Edwards, *I Am A Black Woman* solidified her status as an influential writer of her era. He claims that Evans, "In what at times appeared to be an almost one-woman crusade . . . has unabashedly affirmed the heights of looking, living, loving, thinking, responding, being, and thriving Black."

CRITICISM

Rachel Porter

Porter is a freelance writer and editor who holds a bachelor of arts in English literature. In the following essay, she argues that the stylistic elements of Mari Evans's "When In Rome" emulate the conflict between the two personas in the poem.

> IN ONE QUICK REMARK SHE CALLS ATTENTION TO THE DISTANCE AND THE DIFFERENCE BETWEEN HERSELF AND MATTIE: SHE IS THE ONE WHO EMPLOYS, PROVIDES, AND SETS RULES, WHILE MATTIE IS THE ONE WHO LABORS, TAKES, AND FOLLOWS RULES."

Although the action of "When In Rome" is distinctly mundane and "everyday," this poem is decidedly a poem of conflict, albeit a conflict that is suppressed rather than overt. The fact that the tension between the two personas, Mattie and her employer must be muted is a result of their relative social positions. As an African American woman with limited employment options, it would be detrimental for Mattie to outwardly express her frustrations. Therefore, all of Mattie's comments of annoyance are addressed to herself or muttered under her breath. Mattie's sense of frustration and inability to express herself is mirrored in stylistic elements of the poem, which also seem to emit a sense of smothered agitation. When the poem is read aloud it has a fairly steady rhythm and pleasing acoustic qualities. Likewise, when quickly glanced at, the poem appears to be organized; it looks visually balanced. Yet, when the technical elements of the poem are scrutinized, the poem reveals itself to be highly irregular. This subtle discordance of stylistic elements reflects and heightens the sense of repressed tension between Mattie and her employer.

The poem, like the relationship between Mattie and her employer, appears harmonious on the surface. Much of this effect is established by its strong rhythm. Although the poem does not have a regular meter, every two or three lines can be group together as a section of four stresses, making the poem easy to read aloud to a steady beat. For example, lines 1 and 2 have four stressed syllables between them: the first syllable of Mattie, dear, box, and full. Likewise, lines 3–5 have four stressed syllables between them: take, the middle syllable in whatever, like, and eat. The entire poem can be broken down in this fashion. Doing so divides the poem in logical places, such as in between stanzas

WHAT DO I READ NEXT?

- *Shimmy Shimmy Shimmy Like My Sister Kate: Looking at the Harlem Renaissance Through Poems*, published in 1996, is an young-adult anthology compiled by poet Nikki Giovanni. It includes work by some of Evans's contemporaries, such as Gwendolyn Brooks, as well as that of other well-known African American poets, including Richard Wright and Langston Hughes. The poems included in the collection are interspersed with commentary by Giovanni, who explains why each poem is relevant in the context of the Harlem Renaissance.

- *Arise Chicano! And Other Poems* by Angela de Hoyos was published in 1975. This debut work from de Hoyos is comprised of strong Chicano-nationalist poetry. De Hoyos, a contemporary of Evans, was a major figure in the Chicano movement of the 1970s.

- *Continuum: New and Selected Poems*, published in 2007, is the most recent collection of Evans's poems. It includes poems that have not been previously published in addition to some classic poems from her earlier collections such as *I Am A Black Woman*.

- *The Book of African American Women: 150 Crusaders, Creators, and Uplifters*, edited by Tonya Bolden and published in 2004, is a collection of short biographies of African American women. It includes profiles of actresses, journalists, slaves, teachers, and businesswomen, some who are famous and some whose stories have never been told.

- *Drive: The First Quartet*, published in 2006, is a five-part collection of poems by Chicana writer Lorna Dee Cervantes. The five distinct collections range from political protest poems to personal remembrances of childhood. Many of these poems explore similar themes pertinent to Evans's work, such as feminism, activism, and race issues.

- *Push*, a novel by Sapphire, was published in 1999. The novel is an examination of the emotional and psychological damages that can result from being an underprivileged and economically challenged woman living in the inner-city. It is the story of Precious, an African American teenager living in Harlem, who has had a particularly brutal life. Throughout the novel Precious finds ways to make her life more bearable, including poetry writing as an outlet.

or in between Mattie's employer's comments and Mattie's thoughts. Despite the fact that within the sections of four beats the stressed and unstressed syllables do not follow a repeated pattern, each of these sections ends with a stress, which helps to maintain the sense of steady rhythm. Additionally, except for two instances (*full* in line 2, and *anchovies* in line 19), each of the concluding words of a group of four stresses is a rhyming word. There are no rhyming words that do not conclude a section of four stresses. Evans's marking off of the groups of stresses with rhyme enhances the sense of rhythm and steady cadence in the poem. The rhythm of the poem is noticeably interrupted in lines 17–21, perhaps reflecting the suddenness of Mattie's employer's sharp admonishment to Mattie to stay

out of the anchovies. Aside from this section, the rhythm of the poem is constant throughout.

This balanced quality is mirrored in the poem's construction as a dialogue. There is a steady back and forth between Mattie's employer's comments and Mattie's internal responses throughout the poem. All of these elements create a pleasing, harmonious, and almost musical effect when the poem is read aloud. Unlike many poems written in free verse, the pauses in the poem seem natural and are not jarring. In short, aside from the brief interruption of lines 17–21, the poem does not display any auditory signs of disharmony or upset. Moreover, the poem, despite being structured in an irregular fashion, is fairly symmetrical. All of the lines are quite short (none consisting of more than six words), and of the thirty-four lines, sixteen are indented and eighteen are not. Thus, the poem initially seems organized in both a visually and acoustically pleasing way.

However, in conjunction with these elements of aesthetic cohesion, many disruptive stylistic elements—indicators of tension between the two personas—are also embedded within the poem. One such element is the punctuation of the poem, which is notably suggestive of conflict. All of the punctuation marks in the poem, barring the exclamation mark in line 21, qualify Mattie's comments. All of Mattie's comments are enclosed in parentheses, which indicates that Mattie must stifle them either by whispering them to herself or simply thinking instead of verbalizing them. Although Mattie possesses concerns and frustrations, she must contain them; it would be inappropriate for her to complain to her employer about the food that has been provided for her. Mattie's comments are also frequently marked with ellipses (lines 8, 13, and 34)—a technique that seems to indicate moments in which Mattie is thinking wistfully, perhaps of other types of food to eat or of being at home away from her employer and her questionable provisions. Mattie's exclamatory remark in lines 22–23 is immediately followed by a sarcastic question in lines 24–25 that is interrupted by a dash. The dash denotes a moment of either amusement or indignation for Mattie; she finds it difficult to believe that her employer actually thinks that she would eat anchovies for a meal. To Mattie, eating anchovies for a snack or meal is preposterous. However, again, she cannot outwardly express these emotions. She must think them without making a facial expression that would give her true feelings away. On the other hand, her employer's speech is virtually void of punctuation. This indicates that, unlike Mattie's, her speech is uninhibited. She is simply passing information to Mattie in a matter of fact way, without feeling agitated or having to stifle comments.

The irregular meter adds to the underlying sense of disunity that the punctuation, in part, creates. The meter is just regular enough to make areas of the poem that are irregular seem highly so. Several groups of lines in the poem follow a strict iambic pattern, for example lines 6 through 8. Other groups of lines nearly follow an iambic pattern but have one dactylic foot (lines 12–13) or an extra unstressed syllable (lines 26–27). An iamb is a metrical foot with an unstressed syllable followed by a stressed syllable, whereas a dactyl is a metrical foot

with a stressed syllable followed by an unstressed. Therefore, a dactyl interspersed among iambs is a slight disruption of the rhythm. Yet some parts of the poem, particularly lines 17–19 and 22–23, are so conspicuously arrhythmic and not iambic that they stand out. These two sections also constitute the highest point of tension in the poem: the aforementioned strong warning from Mattie's employer not to eat the anchovies followed by Mattie's emphatic and shocked response. Preceding this point in the poem Mattie's employer has appeared to be a fairly generous (if somewhat clueless) woman, freely offering Mattie whatever she would like from the icebox. However, in lines 17–21 it is revealed that there are some foods she considers too delicate or expensive for the help, such as Mattie, to eat. In one quick remark she calls attention to the distance and the difference between herself and Mattie: she is the one who employs, provides, and sets rules, while Mattie is the one who labors, takes, and follows rules. From Mattie's reaction it is evident that her employer's insistent warning was unnecessary. Mattie has no desire to eat anchovies, and is almost insulted by her employer's insinuation that she would eat them. According to Mattie, anchovies are more suitable for a bird to eat than a person. The height of arrhythmia in the poem is therefore reflective of the height of stress between Mattie and her employer.

Another jarring feature of the poem's style is its line breaks, which seem unpredictable and sometimes arbitrary. The line breaks occur in unnatural or awkward places rather than at the end of sentences or between clauses. Reading the poem aloud according to the line breaks produces an almost stuttering effect and undermines the sense of continuity that the otherwise fairly steady rhythm provides. The line breaks seem to undermine the natural cadence that is not always present in free verse poetry. However, it could also be said that the line breaks of "When In Rome" have the effect of syncopating the steady rhythm, causing the poem to read in a way that seems improvisational and imitative of jazz rhythms. Many of Evans's poems possesses jazz-like rhythms and influences, but it is particularly interesting that Evans should choose to render a scene of conflict in a musical intonation. In so doing, perhaps Evans is imposing a distinctly African American sensibility onto a scene of cultural imposition. In any case, the syncopated rhythm that is inflicted by the line breaks is another telling indicator that under the surface tensions exist in the poem.

The maid is offered sardines for lunch, in spite of her need for more substantial fare. *(Image copyright Picsfive, 2010. Used under license from Shutterstock.com)*

Aside from the obviously enjambed arrangement of the poem, its elements of stylistic disunity are not immediately noticeable upon first read. Just as Mattie must suppress her true emotions and maintain an outward appearance of tranquility, the stylistic indicators of the frustrations in the poem are suppressed: buried under a strong rhythm, a catchy rhyme scheme, and the back-and-forth pendulum-like movement between Mattie and her employer's comments. The stylistic elements of "When In Rome" mirror Mattie's emotion of inexpressible frustration, and thus, what initially seems to be a simple depiction of an everyday scene between a house maid and her employer is actually emblematic of underlying tensions between two women from different cultures whose relationship is defined by clear hierarchies of power. It is significant that the conflict of the poem is based on something that is at once seemingly trivial and inherently culturally specific (food) because Mattie is in a position where her culture is disregarded and maybe even disvalued. The fact that Mattie's employer does not even consider or simply ignores the fact that Mattie might be accustomed to different types of food is telling of the overall treatment Mattie probably receives. Therefore, although "When In Rome" appears to be a slice-of-life depiction of a fleeting interaction between a maid and her employer, stylistic elements suggest deeper issues of displacement, cultural misunderstandings, suppression, and inexpressible frustrations.

Source: Rachel Kathryn Porter, Critical Essay on "When In Rome," in *Poetry For Students*, Gale, Cengage Learning, 2011.

David Dorsey

In the following excerpt, Dorsey argues that the didactic (or teaching) purpose of Evans's work is also a part of the artistic structure of her poetry.

I

There is no basis for confusion about Evans's perception of the political situation of Afro-Americans. She has stated it clearly and consistently in print since 1968: We are a colonized nation, albeit "the fanciest of all oppressed people." Her answer: political unity, and for that, accurate political comprehension.

The emphasis on adequate comprehension of one's political condition follows from Evans's analysis of colonization. She does not emphasize the purposes of the oppression, which are, arguably, self-evident, but rather the means and methods. Evans outlines three "areas of [the colonized person's] vulnerability," the mind, the body, and the environment. The schema is surprisingly inclusive. In it the social structures designed to control the body are largely economic (low wages, job discrimination, easy access to drugs, incarceration, etc.). The more general structures are environmental: selective schooling, housing, etc.; control of transportation, communications, police and justice, arms, "private enterprise," all production, etc.

But it is control of the colonized mind which Evans puts first, and which concerns us most. First in the list of mechanisms is establishment of the colonizer as standard and model for all that is real, right and beautiful. Second is a pattern of mystification through concepts ("naming"). The positive-valued concept "citizenship" has corollaries in negative concepts of "subversion," "conspiracy," "high-risk," "negroes," etc. By such concepts the only legitimate forms of redress are ones in which the colonizer has all ultimate discretion: negotiation, elections, lawsuits, etc. Third, Evans lists the means and patterns of controlling all other values through education and the media, including publishing. In addition to perversion of the inherently neutral means for shaping a people's values, Evans points to the introduction of destructive institutions of dependency such as welfare and internal divisive strata (distinctions based on color, class, education, and employment).

Evans believes that constructive response can stand firm only on solid ground. The only solid ground is accurate and thorough comprehension of the political condition. However, an accurate understanding of the Black condition requires emancipation from colonization of the mind. Anyone thus emancipated will feel no unquestioned commitment to white men's values and perceptions, no matter how basic, sincere, syllogized, or strident. In the most profound sense, the colonized who wish to be free must define reality, espouse values, and practice behavior which finds no confirmation in the society at large, no approval either from whites

or, to the extent that they are bemused, from Blacks. To pursue freedom from colonialism one must willingly have radical (root-level) quarrel with institutionalized views. One must willingly be rebellious, independent, in thought and when necessary in deed.

Despite this vision of immense resources marshaled against a people, and of precious perspicacity required in defense, Evans suggests that Afro-Americans have sufficient institutional and intellectual means to diminish or eliminate their colonization. In the demystification of the colonized mind, the arts are "useful vehicles for piercing delusion, disseminating information, substituting values, instituting new forms of thought, and a matrix for a national political unity. . . ." The Black political writer is "that creative person who, politically informed, and critical, has made certain political observations and analyses and has arrived at certain constantly expanding or narrowing political conclusions; he feels impelled to share this compendium of political views with the target audience."

Such quotations emphasize the sense of purpose which impels the "political writer." But elsewhere Evans has shown that even artists with no conscious political intent inevitably write with political significance. We must understand "political" to include all the structured links between the individual and his community and nation.

We have, therefore, in Evans's published essays, a sober and, I believe, accurate analysis of the "political" context in which Black Americans compose, and the social significance of published compositions, that is, the politics of literature. Her position is not, of course, unique.

Indeed commitment to the betterment of Black life is the only criterion shared by everyone who attempts to define or defend the Black aesthetic.

This anomaly (for purpose cannot alone define an aesthetic) arises primarily in answer to the colonist's attempt to ascribe a generic aesthetic failing to literature which does not reinforce colonial values and colonial perceptions of reality. Black critics, therefore, are repeatedly forced to defend the legitimacy (and inevitability) of "message" in literature, and to delineate the social realities and moral prescriptions appropriate to the literature of a colonized people.

But didacticism is merely the easiest arena in which these opposing gladiators do combat. Form, the structure which is the quintessence of art, is culture-bound. People find beauty in the forms their experience has taught them to embrace. There are no universal formal criteria in literature, as there are no universal scales in music. Even our reaction to new forms is based on their relation to familiar structures. To say that the shapes of beauty are established by cultures implies that the shapes of beauty embraced by Afro-Americans are not the same as those of Euro-Americans. But the formal canons of Euro-American—that is European—literature are among the most codified in human history. Ever since Aristotle they have been subjected to intensive description and analysis. Furthermore, even without the incentive of colonialism, they have been perceived as "universal" principles which characterize art itself, rather than the art of one quite atypical group of related cultures.

By contrast, Black American formal criteria have little tradition of analysis and codified theory which are independent of European concepts and values.

One structural principle of Black art which contrasts with current white preferences concerns didacticism itself. From even the most trivial anecdotal jest to grand works of poetry and fiction, the Black audience demands a meaning, a message. As a requirement of *form,* didacticism is certainly not necessary, but certainly quite natural. A literary composition, like a musical composition, is temporal, the reader's apprehension of its shape evolves as a progression of successive revelations over a period of time. In such "temporal" arts the aesthetic experience is an experience of suspense; the parts gradually combine into an integral, identifiable whole. The demand for a moral is a demand for a single, explicit thought as the ultimate unifying principle for the shape of the whole, for the propriety of its parts and proportions. As examples of a contrasting principle of unity, one may consider most fiction of *The New Yorker* magazine, where clear didactic import is carefully eschewed; instead unity is based on a finely articulated evocation of a single specific mood, attitude, *esprit de coeur.*

When the aesthetic canon demands a moral, there are innumerable forms in which the "point" may emerge. Paradoxically the most suspenseful may be the direct opening announcement of significance. In such cases adroitly handled, the narrative which follows seems at first irrelevant, and in the end utterly apt. But the gradual budding and blossoming of a moral and its sudden epiphany after mystifying incantations are equally common patterns.

Didacticism is necessary. Constructive didacticism is *not.* To say that aesthetic criteria are culturally determined implies that they are conventional. Therefore the didactic content which is most likely to be approved is also circumscribed by convention. Conventional (and therefore variously colonized) didactic messages are most commonly and most easily used to satisfy the structural need for message. Fortunately, wine of any value may be poured into bottles of any shape. The aesthetic canons of the Black community can be employed for constructive and deliberate "political writing" as successfully as any restatements of colonized perceptions and distractions. As Evans has said:

> In the battle for the Black mind, Black political writers, *using community predilection as a plateau,* must forge from what is casual community need, the nucleus for effective political evolution. (Italics mine)

In four different genres Evans demonstrates an extremely precise mastery of Black aesthetic principles and employs those principles in producing works which conform to her own criteria for political writing. It is crucial to recognize that this does not mean the sum of audience experience is the intended lesson. The lesson is integral to the aesthetic experience. Some lesson, in fact, is inevitable. The aesthetic experience is not diminished by a clearly discerned, consciously imposed, and constructive lesson. Evans's works provide instructive models of how didacticism functions as an integral formal element of literary structure.

II

...The same principle applies in poetry. Evans's first volume of poetry, *Where Is All the Music?* (1968), contains twenty-one poems, of which all but five are reprinted in *I Am a Black Woman. Music* is a collection of brief lyrics sketching, engraving, a particular, immediate feeling. The subject is always personal: loneliness, lassitude, familial and romantic love, fortitude. There is no compelling reason to regard the collection as "political" or even "didactic." Nevertheless in the substructure of each poem is an implicit but easily articulated statement, a thought. It is instructive to observe how form is used to intensify both the evocation of emotion and the articulation of the thought.

Evans frequently employs typography to compel reaction synchronized to the poem's meaning. (By "meaning" I suggest the full range of "thought" and affective content combined.) This can easily be observed by careful attention to alterations of dactyls/anapests with iambs/trochees and attention to verse ends in "The Sudden Sight."

> The sudden sight
>
> My eye
> walked lightly over their faces
> until it stopped
> short
> at him
> and my breathing was not the same
> ever again
> even after we became
> lovers the sudden
> sight—
> and my breathing
> was not the same

"The way of things" contrasts "when 'we' drank together looking into each other's eyes" with "'now . . . I' sit drinking alone." It ends with its title:

> and
> that is
> the way of things

Such a coda, which explicitly states or reverses the implicit thought, is a poetic form especially common in Black poetry. In this poem it is an utterly superfluous generalization. Its presence, I suggest, is best explained as expression of the *formal* canon which demands a moral, a thesis, a thought.

The general vision which pervades *Music* is a portrait of immediate feelings and moments for a single, recurrent persona, usually speaking in the first person. Love is celebrated, even in its unhappy eventualities. There is a strong refrain of enduring disappointed love and loneliness. (Note for example the past tense in "The Sudden Sight.") Sometimes the endurance is, of course, couched in defeat.

The more ambitious *I Am a Black Woman* (1970) is divided into sections. The first section's poems all concern personal romantic love. The only characters are me and you (him). The second section, introduced by a photo portrait of a pregnant woman, continues the love affair; almost all its poems long for the departed lover, save the last, entitled "And the Hotel Room Held Only Him." Poems of the next section, "Let Me Crook My Arm Around Them, the Millions, the Childbodies," all treat the victims of social (dys)order, usually explicitly children. The next section is a series of vignettes: individuals of the Black ghetto. The final and longest "chapter" is the most overtly political. Its title is programmatic: "A Black Oneness, a Black Strength." This whole sequence is framed by the introductory poem, "I Am a Black Woman," whose last stanza is repeated as the book's conclusion.

This arrangement leads a reader from the easiest and most egocentric identification or empathy to ever widening fields of vision and association. The only poem, however, which makes global allusions is "Uhuru Überalles! . . . and the sound of weeping)," which begins the section on the dispossessed. The poems which seem intended to evoke a behavioral response to identifiable issues, stand on the values and perceptions ingested, unnoticed, while reading the earlier poems. Poems which would otherwise be devoid of political resonance gain it by this construct. For example, the first love poem, "If there be sorrow," adjures: If one regrets dreams and goals unattained, the list must include "love withheld/restrained." As one progresses through the book, the "love" in question develops from a mere affair to racial unity.

For this design to work with greatest subtlety and effect, each poem must be utterly complete alone; its links with the others are supplied by the reader's inferences. This is even true in the few cases of closely linked poems. Their forms and tone do not mirror each other; each is distinct. The most noticeable case of such a sequence is "The 7:25 Trolley," "When in Rome," and "BeATrice Does the Dinner." The first reports a housemaid's thoughts on awakening. The second reports a dialogue: the employer's statements and the housemaid Mattie's thoughts. In the third we have Mattie's words and thoughts upon arriving home.

The book's design also requires an evolution of form. Throughout there are diction, the rhythm and the tone of conversation; the speaker addresses the individual reader, and intimately. However the exercise of comprehension and the emotive activity sought from the reader gradually intensify. The triad just mentioned occurs in the middle of the book. "The 7:25 Trolley" is the first poem in which the poet cannot be the speaker. It begins:

> ain't got time for a bite to eat
> I'll have to run to catch my trolley at the end
> of the block
> and if I take
> my coffee
> there
> she looks at the cup and she looks at the
> clock
> (Sure hope I don't miss my car . . .
> my house looks like a hurricane

The reader is required to discern that the speaker is a maid, that "she" refers to the employer, that "there" is on the job, that looking at the cup and clock is her employer's ugly and unanswerable reprimand. The indentations which begin with parenthesis and end with three periods repeat the immediate danger as refrain to the stanzas, which describe the general, burdensome circumstances. None of these inferences is difficult to make, but no such "work" has been needed for earlier poems. On the other hand, our sympathy for the maid is so generalized, so traditional, that even her employer could share it. This is only a political poem by virtue of what is to follow.

"When in Rome" requires a little more work and, because the employer is more fully attacked, more commitment. It begins:

> Mattie dear
> the box is full
> take
> whatever you like
> to eat
> (an egg
> or soup
> . . . there ain't no meat)

Here the reader must interpret a visual form: the employer's spoken words at the margin, the maid's thoughts indented in parentheses. (Incidentally, each party uses "bad grammar" which is, for her dialect, fully idiomatic and proper. A certain linguistic sophistication is needed to avoid misinterpreting this element of the realism as derogatory.)

As so frequently in Black rhetoric, the function of the rhyme here is humor. Through rhyme, not only does Mattie "answer" the employer, but the employer also condemns herself:

> there's sardines
> on the shelves
> and such
> but
> don't
> get my anchovies
> they cost
> too much!

Mattie's language, values, burdens, and humor are all familiar to the "target audience" and lead to the reader's amusement. The didactic result is a condemnation of a person, a type or class, and a socioeconomic institution, but this message is thoroughly rooted in our own preconceptions.

With such poems midbook, we may first contrast the first poems. Throughout Evans eschews meter, or at least metrical format of the print. Instead the pauses required by the printed line's end, by indentations, or by isolations precisely control the reader's sequences of perceptions and responses. The "introspective," or "personal," or "love" poems, however, often have such regular rhythm that they conform to metrical patterns.

In these poems all is gentle, graceful, pastel. Sentence structure and diction are simple. Images are elegant. Emotions are quiet, whether pleasant or sad.

> the fluid beauty [song]
> which once fled my soul
> to hang quicksilvered
> in the mote-filled
> air

Oxymoron is tender, juxtapositions fine:

> joy lies discarded
> near and I
> am naked
> in my silence

A hesitant parting "into blackness softly" portrays by its visual pattern the swing of the apartment door, the movement downstairs, the emergence into night air. More than all else, the reader is soothed, comforted, with a very passive delight.

The concluding section of the book is anything but quiet. It begins with "The Great Civil Rights Law A.D. 1964," built (as are many of Evans's poems) with two contrasting stanzas; "they called/Grateful meetings" introduces the first, which is answered by "i/will not sit/in Grateful meetings." The grammar is elliptical, particularly with several parallel verb phrases depending on an unrepeated single pronoun subject. The imagery too is overtly rhetorical (e.g., "dipped for centuries in Black blood"). The metaphor of "Beads" for "Civil Rights" requires some comprehension of African history. In short, even the least subtle critic would recognize this as a "political poem."

More strident poems follow. "Status Symbol" ridicules the "New Negro" honored with a key to the white john. Overtly cynical, the tone contrasts with the earlier, gentle teasing in "The Emancipation of George Hector (a Colored Turtle)." For the speaker here, the New Negro, unwittingly reveals that the mountain of Black labor and revolt has produced minimal results.

The monologues "The Insurgent" and "The Rebel" have the direct simplicity found in the first section of the book. However, here the tone is appropriately determined, defiant, and sardonic. "Black Jam for Dr. Negro" is spoken by a street-corner brother resisting bourgeois proprieties: "...my ancient/eyes/see your thang/baby/an it aint/shit/..." Here "ancient" demonstrates again one of Evans's didactic devices. In the midst of the totally familiar is inserted a word which carries with it uncontested a whole ideological thesis. The speaker is acknowledging a link to African history and culture. In the context characterization, rhythm, and rhetoric demand an adjective. The charm of the poem as vignette requires that the speaker evince some form of unpedantic wisdom. "Ancient" supplies all these needs while reinforcing one subsidiary didactic intent. The "message" is inseparable from everything else.

In "Flames," the concluding lines refer almost directly to "I Can No Longer Sing," and therefore are an example of how the varied subjects, moods, and tones of the poems are woven into a single statement, an overall view of the Black community and one's duty in it.

Control of the reader's experience for didactic effect is well illustrated by "princeling," with its disarming, affectionate diminutive as a title. It consists of a refrain, "swing sweet rhythm," occurring four times, and followed each time by a brief phrase. The first is more puzzling than disturbing; 'charcoal toes' is presumably affectionate in this lullaby, but in strangely poor taste. The second case is also puzzling, but destroys placidity: 'blood-dripped knees.' The third explains all, and adds to the meaning of 'swing': 'Exorcised penis' tells us we are witnessing a lynching. The gradual evolution from serenity and charm to brutal savagery seems a complete experience, but the refrain is repeated, and followed by "My God—my son!" The reader is forced to see the sight through a parent's eyes. This concluding tangent, by digressing in form, affective content, surprise and meaning, is a subtle example of the didactic conclusion so prevalent in Black poetry. To the extent that the last line alludes to the lynch victim as Christ ('God' and 'son' may be taken in apposition) the poem also borrows from a recurrent motif of Afro-American art and letters. In any case again we have the lesson rooted in the familiar and sprouting in the unexpected.

It is not necessary to demonstrate further the subtle design of individual poems in *I Am a Black Woman*, nor even the careful manipulation of familiar Black perceptions and rhetoric. It is

necessary to emphasize that the thematic unity depends on an ever expanding concept of love which comes to embrace the whole community. It also comes to require hate, courage, freedom, unity and, finally, truth. The penultimate poem demands an end to fantasy, "unwisdom," "blowing the mind"; demands that one "Speak the Truth to the People" "To BUILD a strong black nation." The last poem returns to the language of warm pastel to ask, "Who can be born black and not exult!," in the joy, the challenge? (In *Nightstar* this poem is expanded by the insertion of a stanza emphasizing need of the Black community "to come together" in knowledge, power, and majesty.)

The single, title poem which encloses all the others can now be identified as thematic. It announces that the putative speaker of every poem is the Black Woman, over the centuries of her exploitation, in all the facets of her existence. The poem claims to be "written in a minor key" (what I have called "pastel"), but the second stanza in a clear, marching, major key sings of Nat Turner, Danang and napalm. The last stanza, which is repeated to close the book, returns to quiet assertion:

> I
> am a black woman
> tall as a cypress...
> Look
> on me and be
> renewed

Like *I Am a Black Woman*, *Nightstar* (1981) is arranged in titled sections which progress from the most individually personal to the most communally political. But *Nightstar* marks a considerable advance in the variety of architectonics. Structures range from manipulation of very traditional blues poems (e.g., "Blues in B♭,") and satiric caricatures ("Justice Allgood") to highly original constructions such as "Odyssey," whose narrative rests on considerable asyndeton, anacoluthon, anaphora, and a challenging fusion of literal and metaphorical images. Nevertheless two constants apply throughout the book. There is no case of a structure traditional to European (read: white) verse; there is no case of diction alien or condescending to Black speech. The personae of the poems vary more than in early volumes. The Black male, the individualistic female professional, the male revolutionary, Black prisoners, Midwestern pioneers male and female, Evans speaks through them all.

Moreover, *Nightstar* displays many more varied and experimental techniques which, consequently, yield more varied and more precise articulation of poetic statement. Several of these techniques require comment.

Nightstar expands the use of typography. The design of "conceptuality" reinforces imagery, signals progression and paradox in the thought, and imposes the intended rhythms and pauses.

> I am a wisp of energy
> flung from the core of the Universe
> housed
> in a temple
> of flesh and bones and blood
>
> in the temple
> because it is there
> that I make my home
> Free
> of the temple
> not bound
> by the temple
> but housed
>
> no distances
> I am everywhere
> energy and will of the universe expressed
> realizing my oneness my
> indivisibility/I
> I am
> the One Force
> I . . .

Lines 3 to 5 build the temple which is being discussed; lines 2 and 16 swell beyond the temple in accord with the thought. "Free" by its isolation underscores its meaning. (The capital is fortuitously at the beginning of a sentence but deliberately honorific.) Lines 11–13 visually explain the assertion "housed but not confined." The enjambment between lines 17 and 18 surmounts the "divisibility" of separate verses, just as line 21 shows the singularity asserted in line 20. The picture made by the print on the page thus helps to explain an abstract "conceptuality."

In "Eulogy for All Our Murdered Children" there is a receding pattern of indentations used to suggest parallel levels of outrage and revenge. Capitals indicate special emphases which determine both meaning and rhythm. (Both these devices recur elsewhere.) Several poems of the final, revolutionary section are printed on a vertical axis, with one image or thought per line. This layout confers pause and emphasis for each and every unit in a way which would be impossible otherwise. Frequently parallel indentation marks parallel grammatical constructions of accumulated

materials. Spacing between stanzas is arbitrary only in the blues form; in other poems it always marks development: thesis-antithesis, change of speaker, evidence-conclusion, instances-principle, etc., etc. There are more different uses to which design is put than there are poems; every poem displays its own significant arrangements.

Another element of design obviously poetic, but subtly didactic in Evans's employ is idiom. Many poets use idiom *to divorce* the reader from the speakers/subjects, and to cast on them a condescending charm. As in her children's books, Evans's adult works use idiom *to identify* the reader with the speakers/subjects. "Daufuskie (Four Movements)" consists of one poem setting the scene and mood, and three portraits. We have already observed idiom in the second, "The People Gather." The most intensive example is "Janis," with regular repetition of very few and unconfusing features of local sound and idiom. Whether we have such a case or one like "Do We Be There Waiting," whose title contains its only dialectal phrase, the crucial factor is the same: the grammar as a whole, and the premises of the thought, are strictly natural, native, to the reader. Identification with the spirit of the poem is so irresistibly, unambivalently attractive that one does not hesitate over the elements which imply a commitment to the community as a specifically *Black community*.

"Do We Be There Waiting" ends with the parallel format discussed above, with anaphora and reiteration highly characteristic of Black rhetoric, and with a climactic suspense. (By climactic suspense, I mean a grammatical or other element of the conclusion which leads one to anticipate further statement and as a result to regress and reinterpret.) The poems which exhort preparation for revolt and defense also command identification by regularly using "we," not "you," and never including assertions which invite demur.

The diversity of speakers and the greater diversity of portraiture and structure in *Nightstar* express a remarkably consistent vision. First, the eye is extremely accurate in detail:

> glistening morning grass/silverside/exposed
> Maria Pina/sullied sagging fake-furred
> in a proper pleated bosom/dubonnet and
>   white lacedcollared

The same eye sees metaphors with the same precision:

> . . . I and the tree stood watching
> roots in parting grasses

icesplitting the cold quiet/.44 magnum
    jetfurnaces

when white sand threatened
overwhelmed   our   battlements   and   our
    greening

Second, the vision is unclouded by the compassion and censure it engenders. "Curving Stonesteps in the Sun" portrays with sympathy and no justifying excuses the ex-convict, "baad mothuhfuhya" who "came for his/personal property/just a drunk/ enough/and mean."

"The Writers" asks where did our erstwhile revolutionary writers go, and answers that they now sleep with "Miss Annie." The censure is long, sharp, and unmuted. But immediately before the first occurrence of the accusatory refrain, they are described with irretractable praise:

With the wisdoms learned from bluesteel
butts from cement crypts and
With their ancient sealed potential

Thus the vision encompasses unsparing praise and censure simultaneously. There is no paradox here. Rather the emotional and intellectual precision will not accept the kind of simplification which doesn't accommodate both when both are appropriate.... When both are appropriate! In attacking oppression no eviscerating ambiguity can be found. "Daufuskie: Jake" is a lament for "the best damn cap'n in the world." His boat has capsized, yet the speaker's conviction and grief are too intense for us to question the epithet. The result of this sort of complexity is an indirect but compelling didacticism which leads the reader to the same inclusive level of feeling and thought.

Third, as we have implied, Evans's vision assumes rather than argues the integrity, beauty, and promise of Black life. For instance, in the Nicodemus quartet of Midwestern Black pioneers, the focus is on the trials, strengths, and individuality of the characters. We are told incidentally or not at all that they are Black. But their grandeur reflects on all Blacks. (For this, of course, the poet eschews any hint that the characters are distinct from "ordinary people." Even such paeans as "Face on the Sun-warmed Granite" and "Remembering Willie" emphasize the heroism of ordinary men; the readers cannot allow themselves to be less.)

This piecemeal comment on the technique and thought of *Nightstar* cannot suggest the humane grace that pervades the book. The disassembly is meant to demonstrate instead that mechanical means, poetic design, and didactic import are so

> I ORIGINALLY WROTE POEMS BECAUSE CERTAIN THINGS OCCURRED TO ME IN PHRASES THAT I DIDN'T WANT TO LOSE. THE CAPTURED PHRASE IS A JOYOUS WAY TO APPROACH THE MOLDING AND SHAPING OF A POEM."

interconnected that to separate them is to dismember an organism. And in the case of *Nightstar*, this means dismembering both a poem and a book.

Source: David Dorsey, "The Art of Mari Evans," in *Black Women Writers 1950–1980: A Critical Evaluation*, edited by Mari Evans, Double Day, 1984, pp. 170–89.

Mari Evans

In the following essay, Evans discusses her writing process, calling herself an essentially political writer, one who attempts to be as clear as she can be in her writing, but also one who writes within poetic language.

Who I am is central to how I write and what I write; and I am the continuation of my father's passage. I have written for as long as I have been aware of writing as a way of setting down feelings and the stuff of imaginings.

No single living entity really influenced my life as did my father, who died two Septembers ago. An oak of a man, his five feet eight loomed taller than Kilimanjaro. He lived as if he were poured from iron, and loved his family with a vulnerability that was touching. Indomitable, to the point that one could not have spent a lifetime in his presence without absorbing something beautiful and strong and special.

He saved my first printed story, a fourth-grade effort accepted by the school paper, and carefully noted on it the date, our home address, and his own proud comment. By this action inscribing on an impressionable Black youngster both the importance of the printed word and the accessibility of "reward" for even a slight effort, given the right circumstances. For I knew from what ease and caprice the story had come.

Years later, I moved from university journalism to a by-lined column in a Black-owned weekly and, in time, worked variously as an industrial editor, as a research associate with responsibility for preparing curriculum materials, and as director of publications for the corporate management of a Job Corps installation.

I have always written, it seems. I have not, however, always been organized in my approach. Now, I find I am much more productive when I set aside a specific time and uncompromisingly accept that as commitment. The ideal, for me, is to be able to write for long periods of time on an eight-hour-a-day basis. That is, to begin to write—not to prepare to write, around eight-thirty, stop for lunch, resume writing around twelve-thirty and stop for the day around four-thirty when I begin to feel both fulfilled and exhausted by the effort. For most Black writers that kind of leisure is an unaccustomed luxury. I enjoyed it exactly once, for a two-week period. In that two weeks I came face to face with myself as a writer and liked what I saw of my productive potential.

When I began to write I concentrated on short stories, but I was soon overwhelmed by the persistency of the rejection slips. Everything I sent out came back, and although many of the comments, when there were comments, were encouraging, the bottom line was that none were accepted.

I drifted into poetry thought by thought; it was never intentional. I had no "dreams of being a poet." I began to write about my environment, a housing project, and to set down my reactions to it—to the physical, the visual aspects of it; to the people I touched in passing, to what I understood of their lives—the "intuited" drama and poignancy a brown paper bag away. It was not from wisdom that I followed that path, it was Langston spoke to me.

When I was about ten I took a copy of his *Weary Blues* from a shelf and, eyes bright with discovery, mouth shaped in astonishment, rhapsodized, "Why he's writing about me!" He was my introduction to a Black literary tradition that began with the inception of writing in the area of Meroe on the African continent many millennia ago.

He was the most generous professional I have ever known. What he gave me was not advice, but his concern, his interest, and, more importantly, he inspired a belief in myself and my ability to produce. With the confidence he instilled, what had been mere exercise, almost caprice—however compulsive—became commitment and I accepted writing as my *direction*. I defined it as craft, and inherent in that definition was the understanding that as craft, it was a rigorous, demanding

occupation, to be treated as such. I felt that I should be able to write on demand, that I could not reasonably be worthy of the designation "writer" if my craft depended on dispensations from something uncontrollable, elusive, and unpredictable called "inspiration." I set about learning the profession I had chosen.

A state employment agency referred me to an assistant editor's vacancy at a local chain-manufacturing plant. Watts was already in the air, minority employment quotas were threatening in the background, and the company opted to hire me. In their ninety years of operation I would be the first Black to cross their sacred office threshold for any purpose except to clean. The salary would be almost 50 percent less than what I had previously earned, but I took the job. Writing, as a profession, would start here.

The director of the plant's information system was far from flattered at having as assistant editor the first Black employee to work anywhere in the company other than the foundry or delivery. There was much crude humor at his expense, with me as the butt, and a good deal of it within my hearing. Almost his first act was to call maintenance and have my desk turned away from him, so that I faced the wall. An auspicious beginning.

I am cautious, Cancerian, rarely leaping without the long look, but having looked am inclined to be absolutely without fear or trepidation. It was a gamble, undertaken in the heart of Klan territory; it paid off.

He knew how to write. His first draft was as clean as my final copy, and I resented that so much that even his hassling became a minor annoyance. I revised and revised and revised, and only part of it was voluntary. In time, he began to allow me a certain creative freedom, and I became enthralled with industrial editing.

Time softened the hostility but nothing ever changed the fact that I was a Black woman in a white job.

Those three years, however, underscored for the principle that writing is a craft, a profession one learns by doing. One must be able to produce on demand, and that requires great personal discipline. I believe that one seldom really perfects. I cannot imagine a writer who is not continually reaching, who contains no discontent that what he or she is producing is not more than it is. So primarily, I suppose, discipline is the foundation of the profession, and that holds regardless of anything else.

To address specifics: I insist that Black poetry, Black literature if you will, be evaluated stylistically for its imagery, its metaphor, description, onomatopoeia, its polyrhythms, its rhetoric. What is fascinating, however, is that despite the easy application of all these traditional criteria, no allegation of "universality" can be imposed for the simple reason that Black becomes catalyst, and whether one sees it as color, substance, an ancestral bloodstream, or as life-style—historically, when Black is introduced, things change.

And when traditional criteria are refracted by the Black experience they return changed in ways that are unique and specific. Diction becomes unwaveringly precise, arrogantly evocative, knowingly subtle—replete with what one creative Black literary analyst, Stephen Henderson, has called "mascon words," it reconstitutes on paper; "saturation" occurs. Idiom is larger than geography; it is the hot breath of a people—singing, slashing, explorative. Imagery becomes the magic denominator, the language of a passage, saying the ancient unchanging particulars, the connective currents that nod Black heads from Maine to Mississippi to Montana. No there ain't nothin universal about it.

So when I write, I write reaching for all that. Reaching for what will nod Black heads over common denominators. The stones thrown that say how it has been/is/must be, for us. If there are those outside the Black experience who hear the music and can catch the beat, that is serendipity; I have no objections. But when I write, I write according to the title of poet Margaret Walker's classic: "for my people."

I originally wrote poems because certain things occurred to me in phrases that I didn't want to lose. The captured phrase is a joyous way to approach the molding and shaping of a poem. More often now, however, because there is a more constant commitment to my conscious direction, I choose the subject first, then set about the task of creating a work that will please me aesthetically and that will treat the subject with integrity. A work that is imbued with the urgency, the tenderness, the pathos, needed to transmit to readers my sense of why they should involve themselves with what it is I have to say.

I have no favorite themes nor concerns except the overall concern that Black life be experienced throughout the diaspora on the highest, most rewarding, most productive levels. Hardly chauvinistic, for when that is possible for our Black family/nation it will be true and possible for all people.

My primary goal is to command the reader's attention. I understand I have to make the most of the first few seconds his or her eye touches my material. Therefore, for me, the poem is structure and style as well as theme and content; I require something of my poems visually as well as rhetorically. I work as hard at how the poem "looks" as at crafting; indeed, for me the two are synonymous.

I revise endlessly, and am not reluctant to consider a poem "in process" even after it has appeared in print. I am not often completely pleased with any single piece, therefore, I remember with great pleasure those rare "given" poems. "If There Be Sorrow" was such a piece, and there were others, but I remember "Sorrow" because that was the first time I experienced the exquisite joy of having a poem emerge complete, without my conscious intervention.

The title poem for my second volume, *I Am a Black Woman*, on the other hand, required between fifteen an twenty revisions before I felt comfortable that it could stand alone.

My attempt is to be as explicit as possible while maintaining the integrity of the aesthetic; consequently, work so hard for clarity that I suspect I sometimes run the risk of being, as Ray Durem put it, "not sufficiently obscure." Since the Black creative artist is not required to wait on inspiration nor to rely on imagination—for Black life *is* drama, brutal and compelling—one inescapable reality is that the more explicitly Black writers speak their truths the more difficult it is for them to publish. My writing is pulsed by my understanding of contemporary realities: I am Afrikan first, then woman, then writer, but I have never had a manuscript rejected because I am a woman: I have been rejected more times than I can number because the content of a manuscript was, to the industry-oriented reader, more "Black" ergo "discomforting" than could be accommodated.

Nevertheless, given the crisis nature of the Black position at a time of escalating state-imposed repression and containment, in a country that has a history of blatantly genocidal acts committed against three nonwhite nations (Native Americans, the Japanese of Hiroshima/Nagasaki, the inhabitants of Vietnam), a country that has perfected the systematic destruction of a people, their land, foliage, and food supply; a country that at the stroke of a presidential pen not only revoked the rights and privileges of citizenship for 110,000 American citizens (identifiable, since they were nonwhite) for what they "could" do, but summarily remanded those citizens to American internment camps, I understand that Black writers have a responsibility to use the language in the manner it is and always has been used by non-Black writers and by the state itself: as a political force.

I think of myself as a political writer inasmuch as I am deliberately attempting the delivery of political concepts and premises through the medium of the Black aesthetic, seeing the various art forms as vehicles.

I am consumed with the need to produce theater pieces and presently have five; two have been produced, one has been in professional workshop. And I have a novel in progress.

As a Black writer embracing that responsibility, approaching my Black family/nation from within a commonality of experience, I try for a poetic language that says, "This is *who* we are, where we have been, *where* we are. This, is where we must go. And *this,* is what we must do."

Source: Mari Evans, "My Father's Passage," in *Black Women Writers 1950–1980: A Critical Evaluation*, edited by Mari Evans, Doubleday, 1984, pp. 165–69.

Gloria T. Hull

In the following excerpt, Hull considers the work of African American women poets after the Harlem Renaissance, including Mari Evans in a group of "important new names."

...Looking back over this group of seven female poets of the Harlem Renaissance and assessing their impact and collective worth, we can begin to see why they are not better known or more highly rated. In the first place, they did not produce and publish enough: Grimké no book, Spencer no book, Fauset no book, Newsome no adult book, Bennett no book, Helene Johnson no book—which means that six of the seven did not collect a single volume of their work. And the one who did, Georgia Johnson, is not the best poet—though she was the most popular. And even here, her popularity was probably weakened by the fact that most of her poetry is uncharacteristic of the new themes and forms of the Renaissance. Except for Helene Johnson perhaps, this same factor was operative in the cases of the other six writers.

Furthermore, since the Renaissance was a predominantly masculine affair, these poets did not benefit from being insiders. Though Fauset held

her quiet literary gatherings, these women—as women—did not fraternize with the male writers and artists. Nor did they have much opportunity to do so. Fauset lived in New York, and Bennett and Helene Johnson were there for a while—but, on the whole, they were not based in the city which was the cultural center of the Renaissance. In fact, most of them were at one time or another a part of the Washington, D.C., social and literary circle which revolved around Georgia Johnson, whose husband had a government appointment in the Capitol. Thus, they were out of the mainstream in more ways than one.

For these reasons, then, these poets represent a group of talented individuals who did not produce enough, or, in a worldly-wise fashion, parley their talent into "fame." So, lamentably, they end up being "interesting," "minor"—a kind of secondary wave which helped to make up the Renaissance tide.

After this glorious and busy period, the country and Black literary activity went into a slump. What poetry there is, is tinged with depression, socialism, and sometimes protest. Between 1930 and 1945, the major poet was Margaret Walker and the most important poetic event the appearance of her 1942 volume *For My People*, brought out as No. 41 of the Yale Series of Younger Poets, making her the first Black poet to appear in that prestigious group. At the time of its publication, Walker was a twenty-seven-year-old Professor of English at Livingstone College in Salisbury, North Carolina, her first teaching position after she had received a Master of Arts degree from the University of Iowa's School of Letters two years earlier.

For My People is divided into three sections. The first seeks to define the poet's relationship to "her people" and her native Southland, and it begins with the well-known title poem, a work which anticipates the material and the manner of the rest of the section:

> For my people everywhere singing their slave songs repeatedly: their dirges and their ditties and their blues and jubilees, praying their prayers nightly to an unknown god, bending their knees humbly to an unseen power.

The form of "For My People" is the most immediately striking thing about it. Drawing on free verse techniques, on the Bible, on the Black sermon (her father was a preacher), Walker fairly overwhelms the reader with her rhetorical brilliance. She continues this same method and approach in the poems in the collection—reciting her heritage of "Dark Blood," tracing Black people's blind belief in gods from Africa to America, singing of her "roots deep in southern life," and decrying the fact that she is not as strong as her grandmothers were in "Lineage," one of the simplest and nicest poems in this group:

> My grandmothers are full of memories
> Smelling of soap and onions and wet clay
> With veins rolling roughly over quick hands
> They have many clean words to say.

Part II of *For My People* is made up of ballads about Black folk heroes known and unknown, famous and infamous. Traditional subjects are "Bad-Man Stagolee" and "Big John Henry." But no less worthy are "Poppa Chicken," the "sugah daddy/Pimping in his prime"; the "Teacher," who was a "sap" about women; and "Gus, the Lineman," who "had nine lives/And lived them all." Two of the best of these ballads have heroines as their central figures—Molly Means, "a hag and a witch:/Chile of the devil, the dark, and sitch," and Kissie Lee, a tough, bad gal, whose account ends like this:

> She could shoot glass doors offa the hinges, She
> could take herself on the wildest binges. And
> she died with her boots on switching blades On
> Talladega Mountain in the likker raids.

In these tall tale and ballad narratives, Walker adheres pretty closely to the traditional ballad stanza, varying it with four-beat couplets and spicing it up with dialect speech which she is successful at orthographically representing.

The final section, composed of only six poems, is much shorter than the first two. These are sonnets (with the form freely handled) in which Walker gazes back on her childhood, writes about experiences she has had since leaving the South (such as talking to an Iowa farmer), and expresses needs and struggles common to all human beings. Her craftsmanship is not always smooth in this section, but some of her best lines conclude the poem entitled "Whores":

> Perhaps one day they'll all die in the streets or
> be surprised by bombs in each wide bed; learning too late in unaccustomed dread that easy
> ways, like whores on special beats, no longer
> have the gift to harbor pride or bring men
> peace, or leave them satisfied.

On the whole, *For My People* is a good book. Unlike many volumes of poetry, one can read it from cover to cover without getting bored or inattentive—probably because of the narrative interest of Part II. Walker is best with these poems and with her unique "for my people" style, but not as sure or deft in her handling of the sonnets.

The volume was (and is) significant for many reasons. First, its mood coincided with the Depression and hard times of the 1930's, and also with the social consciousness and militant integrationism of that and the following decade. In style, it was different in a worthwhile way from what had been written during the Renaissance. Her attention to Black heroes and heroines was also timely and helped to communicate the "Negritude" of the volume and the delving for roots which is one of its major themes.

After Margaret Walker's *For My People*, Gwendolyn Brooks published *A Street in Bronzeville* in 1945 and went on to win the Pulitzer Prize (the first Black to do so) in 1950 for her 1949 volume *Annie Allen*. From this point on, Black women are well-represented in poetry. In the 1950's and early 60's, Margaret Danner, Naomi Madgett, and Gloria Oden are significant. In the 1960's, poetry exploded (as did Black America) and in this second Renaissance, women were not left out. Walker, after a twenty-eight-year poetic silence, published two more books of poems. Brooks, also of an earlier period, has gone through changes and remained current, productive, and good. And important new names have appeared, including Audre Lorde, Sonia Sanchez, Lucille Clifton, Nikki Giovanni, Mari Evans, June Jordan, and Alice Walker. These writers show all of the characteristics of the poetry of the Black sixties while revealing, at the same time, their wonderful woman/human selves. They are a large and exciting group and, as a group, are of a higher order or quality and achievement than the comparable group of Black male poets.

Whereas, in the thirty years from 1915 to 1945, one could name only about fourteen female poets, the number swells to near fifty for the almost thirty years following—and it is constantly growing. When proportionate figures are compared, more of the Black women who are writers are primarily posts than are the men, showing that more women than men have turned to this form of creative and literary expression. In it, they have wrought well.

Source: Gloria T. Hull, "Black Women Poets from Wheatley to Walker," in *Negro American Literature Forum*, Vol. 9, No. 3, Autumn 1975, pp. 91–96.

Frances S. Foster

In the following excerpt, Foster discusses how African American poets such as Mari Evans seek to establish identity through their art.

> **THE ULTIMATE CRITERION FOR BLACK LITERATURE IS NOT SO MUCH HOW ONE SAYS A THING AS WHAT IT IS THAT HE IS SAYING. HE MUST SPEAK THE TRUTH—I.E., BLACK REALITY BASED UPON THE BLACK EXPERIENCE."**

Traditional notions of the Afro-American woman consist of four images: Topsy, Peaches, Caldonia, and Aunt Chloe. Topsy the child is black with big eyes, long skinny legs and at least fifteen short plaits, more imp than human, and possessing none of daddy's-little-girl's enchantments. The older Peaches is luscious, sly, and loose. She definitely will become a mother— maybe, a wife—and eventually will wind up as Caldonia, the matriarch, fat, loud, and emasculating. Only when her sexual capabilities have seemingly departed, and age has diluted her temper, is any noticeable degree of a nonphysical attribute even implied. The stereotyped Black woman at this time has donned a flowered dress and rundown shoes and become the stalwart Christian or the Voodoo crone.

But traditional notions concerning the Black woman are changing. Too many exceptions have become too obvious to be ignored. Both her allies and her enemies have some measure of responsibility for assigning her new dimensions of personality and power. Daniel P. Moynihan has discovered that she as matriarch is the source and perpetuation of all that ails the Black man, and thus is the key to American society's racial harmony. Woman's Lib groups are convinced that she is their fellow victim of anti-feminism; that, indeed, her oppression is more sexual than racial. Eldridge Cleaver (1968: 205), having gotten over his white woman worship, now recognizes her as "Queen—Mother—Daughter of Africa/Sister of My Soul/Black Pride of My Passion/My Eternal Love." James C. Kilgore's (1970) call for Black men to create an area within Black literature which meets the long ignored need of "Black feminine narcissism" shows a discovery that Black women may have more desires than sex and domination. And H. Foy (1970) has some degree of respect when he says, "The sisters is mean man. I mean like . . . they into something."

But, most responsible for the weakening of stereotypes, and closest to defining the reality of Black womanhood are those who fostered that new psychological image which created the new public images—the Black women themselves. Black women in and of a changing world have given increasing thought and energy to the subjects of identity and roles. Toni Cade (1970a: 7) reflects a preliminary conclusion when she says, "The first job is to find out what liberation for ourselves means, what work it entails, what benefits it will yield." Her anthology of writings by and about Black women is evidence not only of an increasing number of women's efforts to discover and to define themselves through the realities of their Black experience, but also of an increasing influence upon society in general, which, for example, would cause a major white company to decide the financial potential great enough to publish such a collection.

. . . The Black writers now seek to formulate concepts of art based on realities as they know them and ignoring any criterion which does not acknowledge a validity or universality that includes more than white Western concepts. Their writing is about Black people for Black people by Black people. Any white audience is ignored.

Black writers seeking to create a people's literature from a Black perspective do have a tradition to build upon. That literary tradition is primarily oral: folk tales; songs, especially the blues; sermons; the dozens; and the rap are all expressions of creativity, discussions of ideals, adventures in rhyme, figurative language, and connotations. Some Black artists in the past have recognized the validity of this literature. Examples are James Weldon Johnson, who tried to transcribe the poetry of the sermon; Langston Hughes, who recognized the poetry of the blues; and Zora Neale Hurston, who collected and recorded folk tales. Miss Hurston also anticipated the later Black women writers in her novel, *Their Eyes Were Watching God,* which has a realistic Black female protagonist and deals with the life of common Black people.

The writers attempt to use the language of the Black people to record their traditional literature and to create new literature in that tradition. One basic problem stems from the inability of traditional words and spellings to express the actual experience. Carolyn Rodgers discusses the problems of the connotation of "Standard" English to the Black and the inexactness of any written language in "The Literature of Black." She says

"Standard" or white English carries connotations of its source, the oppressor, and, having been designed to symbolize his life style, is often inadequate for ours. Yet transcribing oral communications is difficult in any language because "words are feelings given of sound/sound that is not words." Sonia Sanchez is one of those who attempt to convey sounds through innovative writing techniques. "On Seeing Pharoah Sanders Blowing" simultaneously imitates Sanders' horn and the audience's reaction when "set 3" begins:

> ah ah ah
> oh
> aah aah aah
> ooh.

Attention is especially given to using the real language of the people because Black literature—first of all—is utilitarian; in other words, it is designed to meet the needs and desires of both its creator and its audience. Thus, literary elitism must be avoided. Situations, persons, and the communication of such must be realistic and early understood. In "reflections of a 69th street Pimp after reading a really good black poem," Helen King declares a poem is successful when

> Inside a Black Poem
> There Be REAL People
> And Thought/Words
> That I Can
> Real-l-l-ly Dig!

Black art is not a luxury to be isolated and viewed by a select group of persons. It is an attempt to communicate realities. It is an attempt to meet the needs and desires of all Black people. It strives to inform them of their past and its implications, to identify their enemies, and thus to give them the strength and vision to bring about the necessary changes in their existence.

In the stress upon utilitarianism, artistic beauty is not ignored or disparaged. It is redefined. Beauty is determined by the accomplishment of its purpose of expressing reality to fulfill a need which may be spiritual, intellectual, material. Along with this goes the knowledge that a sense of identity and self-respect is beautiful. The awareness that Blackness is beautiful leads to the knowledge that beauty is also Black.

Black art being utilitarian is, by necessity, temporal. As situations and reality change, the needs and desires change; thus the forms, techniques, and subjects of art must change to accurately record reality. Mari Evans (1970a) discriminates between

Black writing as being a general expression of truth designed to promote basic unity within the Black family/nation and revolutionary Black writing, which is concerned exclusively with the Black revolution, but her comments concerning the role of "revolutionary Black literature" are generally indicative of contemporary attitudes toward all Black literature. She says it is "Temporal, in the positive sense that it is utilitarian, it may survive only as historical records of the ritual role of the writer in stimulating and maintaining the fervor of revolutionary intent and purpose at its apogee." In other words, the concern of Black literary artists is not with creating monuments that will outlive their usefulness.

The ultimate criterion for Black literature is not so much how one says a thing as what it is that he is saying. He must speak the truth—i.e., Black reality based upon the Black experience. Exactly how this Black reality may be indubitably recognized is unclear, but Carolyn Rodgers (1970) suggests one criterion: "if the Black Spirit flows RIGHT through a piece of work it will excite me. It should excite any Black who reads it. *Excite* meaning, some level of yes, indeed, interest or feeling." Along with this goes a belief that if a Black knows truth, he will realize the value that helping his brothers has over more esoteric adventures. Thus, all topics which could conceivably answer some Black need or desire are accepted as relevant.

The contrast of this new Black aesthetic with traditional white criteria is seen clearly in the attitude toward political subjects. Whereas whites have always included their politics in their art but denied its presence and have denounced as propagandistic and nonaesthetic any politics not in line with theirs, Blacks are quite frank about political writings. The Black writer is first of all a Black in a society which uses politics to control and words to legitimate its efforts. Thus, to analyze, define, and exhort political concepts is a necessary and proper goal of a Black writer. This is not to say that the Black aesthetic confuses political rhetoric with art, nor that it encourages sloganeering. Carolyn Gerald (1969) clarifies the difference when she states

> the fiction or poetry of survival is rendered through imagery, through symbols, through experiment with different rhythms, with different syntactical forms, with a different vocabulary, through the indirectness of its statement about our condition.

The writings of the Black woman adhere to these basic concepts. Within these boundaries, however, there are certain subjects which are primarily directed to other Black women. These include attempts to establish an identity as woman and to present more honest evaluations of the Black woman's place in society.

In their search for identity, they seek to destroy negative stereotypes—some of which have been believed by the women themselves. The search includes a realization of their ancestral roots and goes historically through American slavery to Africa. In her poem, "I Am A Black Woman," Mari Evans knows she is

> beyond all definitions still
> defying place
> and time
> and circumstance

as she chronicles her memories of mates who leapt from slave ships and of sons who are in Da Nang.

... In conclusion, Black women, victims of double discrimination, are seeking liberation which begins with a psychological freedom and manifests itself then in a new life style. Black women as never before are aware of their Blackness, with its historical influences upon their physical and psychological existence and of alternatives for the future. The comprehension and statement of this awareness varies from individual to individual, but in general is based upon the knowledge that the oppressive past and present do not have to mirror the future, that realization of themselves, their situation and the causes for this condition, is the first step toward liberation, but that positive steps, beginning with Black unification, must be taken to change their situations. A good example of this new philosophy is found in the women writers involved in the Black literary attempt to realize and to promulgate Black truth. The emerging conclusions are, at times, seemingly contradictory, ambiguous, idealistic, or simplistic. They are, however, an attempt, a beginning. They are unfinished, but they must always be so, for the world changes and Realities relevant to changing things must be changing. Once a formalized and final definition is stated, one can be sure it is out-of-date or its subject is dead. The definitions advanced today may possibly be realized as being as mythological as yesterday's versions. One thing is clear. Today, beliefs in Topsy, Peaches, Caldonia, and Aunt Chloe must somehow be reconciled with a Black woman who says I,

> with these trigger tire/d fingers
> seek the softness in my warrior's
> beard [Evans, 1970b: 11].

Source: Frances S. Foster, "Changing Concepts of the Black Woman," in *Journal of Black Studies*, Vol. 3, No. 4, June 1973, pp. 433–54.

SOURCES

Ballen, Nicole, et. al, "Journey 5, 1967–Today: From Crisis, A Search for Meaning," in *This Far By Faith*, http://www.pbs.org/thisfarbyfaith/journey_5/p_1.html (accessed April 6, 2010).

Boyd, Herb, "Acclaimed Poet Mari Evans on Being a Black Writer," in *Crisis*, March/April 2007, http://findarticles.com/p/articles/mi_qa4081/is_200703/ai_n19198407/ (accessed April 6, 2010).

Cooper, G. Burns, "Molecules and Crystals of Free Verse: Lines and Phrases," in *Mysterious Music: Rhythm and Free Verse*, Stanford University Press, 1998, pp. 92–115.

Dorsey, David, "The Art of Mari Evans," in *Black Women Writers 1950–1980: A Critical Evaluation*, edited by Mari Evans, Doubleday, 1984, pp. 170–89.

Douglas, Robert L., "The Poetry of Mari Evans," in *Resistance, Insurgence and Identity: The Art of Mari Evans, Nelson Stevens, and the Black Arts Movement*, Africa World Press, 2008, pp. 83–180.

Edwards, Solomon, "Affirmation in the Works of Mary Evans," in *Black Women Writers: 1950–1980: A Critical Evaluation*, edited by Mari Evans, Doubleday, 1984, pp. 190–200.

Evans, Mari, "My Father's Passage," in *Black Women Writers: 1950–1980: A Critical Evaluation*, edited by Mari Evans, Doubleday, 1984, pp. 165–69.

Gordon, Ed, "Black CEO One of Four on Fortune 500," in *National Public Radio*, April 11, 2006, http://www.npr.org/templates/story/story.php?storyId=5336052 (accessed April 6, 2010).

Hinojosa, Maria, and Brian Palmer, "Harlem Street Jam Welcomes Clinton to New Office," in *Inside Politics*, July 31, 2001, http://archives.cnn.com/2001/ALLPOLITICS/07/30/clinton.office/ (accessed April 1, 2010).

Neal, Larry, "The Black Arts Movement," in *Drama Review*, Vol. 12, No. 4, Summer 1968, pp. 29–39.

Peppers, Wallace R., "Mari Evans," in *Dictionary of Literary Biography*, Vol. 41, *Afro-American Poets Since 1955*, edited by Thadious M. Davis, Gale Research, 1985, pp. 117–23.

Reed, Daphne S., "LeRoi Jones: High Priest of the Black Arts Movement," in *Educational Theatre Journal*, Vol. 22, No. 1, March 1970, pp. 53–59.

Sedlack, Robert P., "Mari Evans: Consciousness and Craft," in *College Language Association Journal*, Vol. 15, 1972, pp. 465–76.

Ya Salaam, Kalamu, "The Black Arts Movement," in *African American Literature Book Club*, http://aalbc. com/ authors/blackartsmovement.htm (accessed April 6, 2010).

FURTHER READING

Algarin, Miguel, *Aloud: Voices from the Nuyorican Poets Cafe*, Henry Holt, 1994.

The Nuyorican Poets Café was a nonprofit multicultural organization that stemmed from the Nuyorican art movement. It was founded a few years after the Black Arts Movement in the early 1970s in New York City. To this day the café has a reputation for performance poetry and poetry slams. This book, compiled by Algarin, one of the founders of the café, includes work from some of the most predominant artists that have performed at the café.

Chapman, Abraham, ed., *Black Voices: An Anthology of African American Literature*, New American Library, 2001.

Chapman's compilation includes significant works of major African American writers of the twentieth century, such as James Baldwin, W. E. B. DuBois, Langston Hughes, and Leroi Jones. The anthology also includes biographical information about the writers as well as critical essays.

Clarke, Cheryl, *"After Mecca": Women Poets and the Black Arts Movement*, Rutgers University Press, 2004.

In *"After Mecca"* Clarke explores the lives of some of the most influential female poets of the Black Arts movement, such as Gwendolyn Brooks, Nikki Giovanni, Audre Lorde, Alice Walker, and many others. She also explores the roles these women played in the feminist and lesbian-feminist social movements.

Feinstein, Sascha, and Yusef Komunyakaa, eds., *The Jazz Poetry Anthology*, Indiana University Press, 1991.

This collection explores the influence of jazz music on poetry of the twentieth century by examining the work of poets such as Langston Hughes, Carl Sandburg, and Leopold Senghor. A connection between jazz rhythms and Evans's poetry has often been noted.

Wall, Cheryl A., *Women of the Harlem Renaissance*, Indiana University Press, 1995.

Wall's book examines the lives and works of many frequently overlooked women of the Harlem Renaissance, the African American artistic movement that preceded the Black Arts Movement. Wall gives expansive information on these women and their works, focusing particularly on Jessie Redmon Fauset, Nella Larsen, and Zora Neale Hurston.

SUGGESTED SEARCH TERMS

Mari Evans

Mari Evans biography

Mari Evans AND poet

Mari Evans AND When In Rome

Mari Evans AND I Am a Black Woman

Mari Evans AND Black Arts Movement

Mari Evans AND free verse

Mari Evans AND activism

Glossary of Literary Terms

A

Abstract: Used as a noun, the term refers to a short summary or outline of a longer work. As an adjective applied to writing or literary works, abstract refers to words or phrases that name things not knowable through the five senses.

Accent: The emphasis or stress placed on a syllable in poetry. Traditional poetry commonly uses patterns of accented and unaccented syllables (known as feet) that create distinct rhythms. Much modern poetry uses less formal arrangements that create a sense of freedom and spontaneity.

Aestheticism: A literary and artistic movement of the nineteenth century. Followers of the movement believed that art should not be mixed with social, political, or moral teaching. The statement "art for art's sake" is a good summary of aestheticism. The movement had its roots in France, but it gained widespread importance in England in the last half of the nineteenth century, where it helped change the Victorian practice of including moral lessons in literature.

Affective Fallacy: An error in judging the merits or faults of a work of literature. The "error" results from stressing the importance of the work's effect upon the reader—that is, how it makes a reader "feel" emotionally, what it does as a literary work—instead of stressing its inner qualities as a created object, or what it "is."

Age of Johnson: The period in English literature between 1750 and 1798, named after the most prominent literary figure of the age, Samuel Johnson. Works written during this time are noted for their emphasis on "sensibility," or emotional quality. These works formed a transition between the rational works of the Age of Reason, or Neoclassical period, and the emphasis on individual feelings and responses of the Romantic period.

Age of Reason: See *Neoclassicism*

Age of Sensibility: See *Age of Johnson*

Agrarians: A group of Southern American writers of the 1930s and 1940s who fostered an economic and cultural program for the South based on agriculture, in opposition to the industrial society of the North. The term can refer to any group that promotes the value of farm life and agricultural society.

Alexandrine Meter: See *Meter*

Allegory: A narrative technique in which characters representing things or abstract ideas are used to convey a message or teach a lesson. Allegory is typically used to teach moral, ethical, or religious lessons but is sometimes used for satiric or political purposes.

Alliteration: A poetic device where the first consonant sounds or any vowel sounds in words or syllables are repeated.

Allusion: A reference to a familiar literary or historical person or event, used to make an idea more easily understood.

Amerind Literature: The writing and oral traditions of Native Americans. Native American literature was originally passed on by word of mouth, so it consisted largely of stories and events that were easily memorized. Amerind prose is often rhythmic like poetry because it was recited to the beat of a ceremonial drum.

Analogy: A comparison of two things made to explain something unfamiliar through its similarities to something familiar, or to prove one point based on the acceptedness of another. Similes and metaphors are types of analogies.

Anapest: See *Foot*

Angry Young Men: A group of British writers of the 1950s whose work expressed bitterness and disillusionment with society. Common to their work is an anti-hero who rebels against a corrupt social order and strives for personal integrity.

Anthropomorphism: The presentation of animals or objects in human shape or with human characteristics. The term is derived from the Greek word for "human form."

Antimasque: See *Masque*

Antithesis: The antithesis of something is its direct opposite. In literature, the use of antithesis as a figure of speech results in two statements that show a contrast through the balancing of two opposite ideas. Technically, it is the second portion of the statement that is defined as the "antithesis"; the first portion is the "thesis."

Apocrypha: Writings tentatively attributed to an author but not proven or universally accepted to be their works. The term was originally applied to certain books of the Bible that were not considered inspired and so were not included in the "sacred canon."

Apollonian and Dionysian: The two impulses believed to guide authors of dramatic tragedy. The Apollonian impulse is named after Apollo, the Greek god of light and beauty and the symbol of intellectual order. The Dionysian impulse is named after Dionysus, the Greek god of wine and the symbol of the unrestrained forces of nature. The Apollonian impulse is to create a rational, harmonious world, while the Dionysian is to express the irrational forces of personality.

Apostrophe: A statement, question, or request addressed to an inanimate object or concept or to a nonexistent or absent person.

Archetype: The word archetype is commonly used to describe an original pattern or model from which all other things of the same kind are made. This term was introduced to literary criticism from the psychology of Carl Jung. It expresses Jung's theory that behind every person's "unconscious," or repressed memories of the past, lies the "collective unconscious" of the human race: memories of the countless typical experiences of our ancestors. These memories are said to prompt illogical associations that trigger powerful emotions in the reader. Often, the emotional process is primitive, even primordial. Archetypes are the literary images that grow out of the "collective unconscious." They appear in literature as incidents and plots that repeat basic patterns of life. They may also appear as stereotyped characters.

Argument: The argument of a work is the author's subject matter or principal idea.

Art for Art's Sake: See *Aestheticism*

Assonance: The repetition of similar vowel sounds in poetry.

Audience: The people for whom a piece of literature is written. Authors usually write with a certain audience in mind, for example, children, members of a religious or ethnic group, or colleagues in a professional field. The term "audience" also applies to the people who gather to see or hear any performance, including plays, poetry readings, speeches, and concerts.

Automatic Writing: Writing carried out without a preconceived plan in an effort to capture every random thought. Authors who engage in automatic writing typically do not revise their work, preferring instead to preserve the revealed truth and beauty of spontaneous expression.

Avant-garde: A French term meaning "vanguard." It is used in literary criticism to describe new writing that rejects traditional approaches to literature in favor of innovations in style or content.

B

Ballad: A short poem that tells a simple story and has a repeated refrain. Ballads were originally intended to be sung. Early ballads, known as folk ballads, were passed down through generations, so their authors are often unknown. Later ballads composed by known authors are called literary ballads.

Baroque: A term used in literary criticism to describe literature that is complex or ornate in style or diction. Baroque works typically express tension, anxiety, and violent emotion. The term "Baroque Age" designates a period in Western European literature beginning in the late sixteenth century and ending about one hundred years later. Works of this period often mirror the qualities of works more generally associated with the label "baroque" and sometimes feature elaborate conceits.

Baroque Age: See *Baroque*

Baroque Period: See *Baroque*

Beat Generation: See *Beat Movement*

Beat Movement: A period featuring a group of American poets and novelists of the 1950s and 1960s—including Jack Kerouac, Allen Ginsberg, Gregory Corso, William S. Burroughs, and Lawrence Ferlinghetti—who rejected established social and literary values. Using such techniques as stream of consciousness writing and jazz-influenced free verse and focusing on unusual or abnormal states of mind—generated by religious ecstasy or the use of drugs—the Beat writers aimed to create works that were unconventional in both form and subject matter.

Beat Poets: See *Beat Movement*

Beats, The: See *Beat Movement*

Belles- lettres: A French term meaning "fine letters" or "beautiful writing." It is often used as a synonym for literature, typically referring to imaginative and artistic rather than scientific or expository writing. Current usage sometimes restricts the meaning to light or humorous writing and appreciative essays about literature.

Black Aesthetic Movement: A period of artistic and literary development among African Americans in the 1960s and early 1970s. This was the first major African-American artistic movement since the Harlem Renaissance and was closely paralleled by the civil rights and black power movements. The black aesthetic writers attempted to produce works of art that would be meaningful to the black masses. Key figures in black aesthetics included one of its founders, poet and playwright Amiri Baraka, formerly known as LeRoi Jones; poet and essayist Haki R. Madhubuti, formerly Don L. Lee; poet and playwright Sonia Sanchez; and dramatist Ed Bullins.

Black Arts Movement: See *Black Aesthetic Movement*

Black Comedy: See *Black Humor*

Black Humor: Writing that places grotesque elements side by side with humorous ones in an attempt to shock the reader, forcing him or her to laugh at the horrifying reality of a disordered world.

Black Mountain School: Black Mountain College and three of its instructors—Robert Creeley, Robert Duncan, and Charles Olson—were all influential in projective verse, so poets working in projective verse are now referred as members of the Black Mountain school.

Blank Verse: Loosely, any unrhymed poetry, but more generally, unrhymed iambic pentameter verse (composed of lines of five two-syllable feet with the first syllable accented, the second unaccented). Blank verse has been used by poets since the Renaissance for its flexibility and its graceful, dignified tone.

Bloomsbury Group: A group of English writers, artists, and intellectuals who held informal artistic and philosophical discussions in Bloomsbury, a district of London, from around 1907 to the early 1930s. The Bloomsbury Group held no uniform philosophical beliefs but did commonly express an aversion to moral prudery and a desire for greater social tolerance.

Bon Mot: A French term meaning "good word." A *bon mot* is a witty remark or clever observation.

Breath Verse: See *Projective Verse*

Burlesque: Any literary work that uses exaggeration to make its subject appear ridiculous, either by treating a trivial subject with profound seriousness or by treating a dignified subject frivolously. The word "burlesque" may also be used as an adjective, as in "burlesque show," to mean "striptease act."

C

Cadence: The natural rhythm of language caused by the alternation of accented and unaccented syllables. Much modern poetry—notably free verse—deliberately manipulates cadence to create complex rhythmic effects.

Caesura: A pause in a line of poetry, usually occurring near the middle. It typically corresponds to a break in the natural rhythm or sense of the line but is sometimes shifted to create special meanings or rhythmic effects.

Canzone: A short Italian or Provencal lyric poem, commonly about love and often set to music. The *canzone* has no set form but typically contains five or six stanzas made up of seven to twenty lines of eleven syllables each. A shorter, five- to ten-line "envoy," or concluding stanza, completes the poem.

Carpe Diem: A Latin term meaning "seize the day." This is a traditional theme of poetry, especially lyrics. A *carpe diem* poem advises the reader or the person it addresses to live for today and enjoy the pleasures of the moment.

Catharsis: The release or purging of unwanted emotions—specifically fear and pity—brought about by exposure to art. The term was first used by the Greek philosopher Aristotle in his *Poetics* to refer to the desired effect of tragedy on spectators.

Celtic Renaissance: A period of Irish literary and cultural history at the end of the nineteenth century. Followers of the movement aimed to create a romantic vision of Celtic myth and legend. The most significant works of the Celtic Renaissance typically present a dreamy, unreal world, usually in reaction against the reality of contemporary problems.

Celtic Twilight: See *Celtic Renaissance*

Character: Broadly speaking, a person in a literary work. The actions of characters are what constitute the plot of a story, novel, or poem. There are numerous types of characters, ranging from simple, stereotypical figures to intricate, multifaceted ones. In the techniques of anthropomorphism and personification, animals—and even places or things—can assume aspects of character. "Characterization" is the process by which an author creates vivid, believable characters in a work of art. This may be done in a variety of ways, including (1) direct description of the character by the narrator; (2) the direct presentation of the speech, thoughts, or actions of the character; and (3) the responses of other characters to the character. The term "character" also refers to a form originated by the ancient Greek writer Theophrastus that later became popular in the seventeenth and eighteenth centuries. It is a short essay or sketch of a person who prominently displays a specific attribute or quality, such as miserliness or ambition.

Characterization: See *Character*

Classical: In its strictest definition in literary criticism, classicism refers to works of ancient Greek or Roman literature. The term may also be used to describe a literary work of recognized importance (a "classic") from any time period or literature that exhibits the traits of classicism.

Classicism: A term used in literary criticism to describe critical doctrines that have their roots in ancient Greek and Roman literature, philosophy, and art. Works associated with classicism typically exhibit restraint on the part of the author, unity of design and purpose, clarity, simplicity, logical organization, and respect for tradition.

Colloquialism: A word, phrase, or form of pronunciation that is acceptable in casual conversation but not in formal, written communication. It is considered more acceptable than slang.

Complaint: A lyric poem, popular in the Renaissance, in which the speaker expresses sorrow about his or her condition. Typically, the speaker's sadness is caused by an unresponsive lover, but some complaints cite other sources of unhappiness, such as poverty or fate.

Conceit: A clever and fanciful metaphor, usually expressed through elaborate and extended comparison, that presents a striking parallel between two seemingly dissimilar things—for example, elaborately comparing a beautiful woman to an object like a garden or the sun. The conceit was a popular device throughout the Elizabethan Age and Baroque Age and was the principal technique of the seventeenth-century English metaphysical poets. This usage of the word conceit is unrelated to the best-known definition of conceit as an arrogant attitude or behavior.

Concrete: Concrete is the opposite of abstract, and refers to a thing that actually exists or a description that allows the reader to experience an object or concept with the senses.

Concrete Poetry: Poetry in which visual elements play a large part in the poetic effect. Punctuation marks, letters, or words are arranged on a page to form a visual design: a cross, for example, or a bumblebee.

Confessional Poetry: A form of poetry in which the poet reveals very personal, intimate, sometimes shocking information about himself or herself.

Connotation: The impression that a word gives beyond its defined meaning. Connotations may be universally understood or may be significant only to a certain group.

Consonance: Consonance occurs in poetry when words appearing at the ends of two or more verses have similar final consonant sounds but have final vowel sounds that differ, as with "stuff" and "off."

Convention: Any widely accepted literary device, style, or form.

Corrido: A Mexican ballad.

Couplet: Two lines of poetry with the same rhyme and meter, often expressing a complete and self-contained thought.

Criticism: The systematic study and evaluation of literary works, usually based on a specific method or set of principles. An important part of literary studies since ancient times, the practice of criticism has given rise to numerous theories, methods, and "schools," sometimes producing conflicting, even contradictory, interpretations of literature in general as well as of individual works. Even such basic issues as what constitutes a poem or a novel have been the subject of much criticism over the centuries.

D

Dactyl: See *Foot*

Dadaism: A protest movement in art and literature founded by Tristan Tzara in 1916. Followers of the movement expressed their outrage at the destruction brought about by World War I by revolting against numerous forms of social convention. The Dadaists presented works marked by calculated madness and flamboyant nonsense. They stressed total freedom of expression, commonly through primitive displays of emotion

and illogical, often senseless, poetry. The movement ended shortly after the war, when it was replaced by surrealism.

Decadent: See *Decadents*

Decadents: The followers of a nineteenth-century literary movement that had its beginnings in French aestheticism. Decadent literature displays a fascination with perverse and morbid states; a search for novelty and sensation—the "new thrill"; a preoccupation with mysticism; and a belief in the senselessness of human existence. The movement is closely associated with the doctrine Art for Art's Sake. The term "decadence" is sometimes used to denote a decline in the quality of art or literature following a period of greatness.

Deconstruction: A method of literary criticism developed by Jacques Derrida and characterized by multiple conflicting interpretations of a given work. Deconstructionists consider the impact of the language of a work and suggest that the true meaning of the work is not necessarily the meaning that the author intended.

Deduction: The process of reaching a conclusion through reasoning from general premises to a specific premise.

Denotation: The definition of a word, apart from the impressions or feelings it creates in the reader.

Diction: The selection and arrangement of words in a literary work. Either or both may vary depending on the desired effect. There are four general types of diction: "formal," used in scholarly or lofty writing; "informal," used in relaxed but educated conversation; "colloquial," used in everyday speech; and "slang," containing newly coined words and other terms not accepted in formal usage.

Didactic: A term used to describe works of literature that aim to teach some moral, religious, political, or practical lesson. Although didactic elements are often found in artistically pleasing works, the term "didactic" usually refers to literature in which the message is more important than the form. The term may also be used to criticize a work that the critic finds "overly didactic," that is, heavy-handed in its delivery of a lesson.

Dimeter: See *Meter*

Dionysian: See *Apollonian and Dionysian*

Discordia concours: A Latin phrase meaning "discord in harmony." The term was coined by the eighteenth-century English writer Samuel Johnson to describe "a combination of dissimilar images or discovery of occult resemblances in things apparently unlike." Johnson created the expression by reversing a phrase by the Latin poet Horace.

Dissonance: A combination of harsh or jarring sounds, especially in poetry. Although such combinations may be accidental, poets sometimes intentionally make them to achieve particular effects. Dissonance is also sometimes used to refer to close but not identical rhymes. When this is the case, the word functions as a synonym for consonance.

Double Entendre: A corruption of a French phrase meaning "double meaning." The term is used to indicate a word or phrase that is deliberately ambiguous, especially when one of the meanings is risque or improper.

Draft: Any preliminary version of a written work. An author may write dozens of drafts which are revised to form the final work, or he or she may write only one, with few or no revisions.

Dramatic Monologue: See *Monologue*

Dramatic Poetry: Any lyric work that employs elements of drama such as dialogue, conflict, or characterization, but excluding works that are intended for stage presentation.

Dream Allegory: See *Dream Vision*

Dream Vision: A literary convention, chiefly of the Middle Ages. In a dream vision a story is presented as a literal dream of the narrator. This device was commonly used to teach moral and religious lessons.

E

Eclogue: In classical literature, a poem featuring rural themes and structured as a dialogue among shepherds. Eclogues often took specific poetic forms, such as elegies or love poems. Some were written as the soliloquy of a shepherd. In later centuries, "eclogue" came to refer to any poem that was in the pastoral tradition or that had a dialogue or monologue structure.

Edwardian: Describes cultural conventions identified with the period of the reign of Edward VII of England (1901-1910). Writers of the Edwardian Age typically displayed a strong reaction against the propriety and conservatism of the Victorian Age. Their work often exhibits distrust of authority in religion, politics, and art and expresses strong doubts about the soundness of conventional values.

Edwardian Age: See *Edwardian*

Electra Complex: A daughter's amorous obsession with her father.

Elegy: A lyric poem that laments the death of a person or the eventual death of all people. In a conventional elegy, set in a classical world, the poet and subject are spoken of as shepherds. In modern criticism, the word elegy is often used to refer to a poem that is melancholy or mournfully contemplative.

Elizabethan Age: A period of great economic growth, religious controversy, and nationalism closely associated with the reign of Elizabeth I of England (1558-1603). The Elizabethan Age is considered a part of the general renaissance—that is, the flowering of arts and literature—that took place in Europe during the fourteenth through sixteenth centuries. The era is considered the golden age of English literature. The most important dramas in English and a great deal of lyric poetry were produced during this period, and modern English criticism began around this time.

Empathy: A sense of shared experience, including emotional and physical feelings, with someone or something other than oneself. Empathy is often used to describe the response of a reader to a literary character.

English Sonnet: See *Sonnet*

Enjambment: The running over of the sense and structure of a line of verse or a couplet into the following verse or couplet.

Enlightenment, The: An eighteenth-century philosophical movement. It began in France but had a wide impact throughout Europe and America. Thinkers of the Enlightenment valued reason and believed that both the individual and society could achieve a state of perfection. Corresponding to this essentially humanist vision was a resistance to religious authority.

Epic: A long narrative poem about the adventures of a hero of great historic or legendary importance. The setting is vast and the action is often given cosmic significance through the intervention of supernatural forces such as gods, angels, or demons. Epics are typically written in a classical style of grand simplicity with elaborate metaphors and allusions that enhance the symbolic importance of a hero's adventures.

Epic Simile: See *Homeric Simile*

Epigram: A saying that makes the speaker's point quickly and concisely.

Epilogue: A concluding statement or section of a literary work. In dramas, particularly those of the seventeenth and eighteenth centuries, the epilogue is a closing speech, often in verse, delivered by an actor at the end of a play and spoken directly to the audience.

Epiphany: A sudden revelation of truth inspired by a seemingly trivial incident.

Epitaph: An inscription on a tomb or tombstone, or a verse written on the occasion of a person's death. Epitaphs may be serious or humorous.

Epithalamion: A song or poem written to honor and commemorate a marriage ceremony.

Epithalamium: See *Epithalamion*

Epithet: A word or phrase, often disparaging or abusive, that expresses a character trait of someone or something.

Erziehungsroman: See *Bildungsroman*

Essay: A prose composition with a focused subject of discussion. The term was coined by Michel de Montaigne to describe his 1580 collection of brief, informal reflections on himself and on various topics relating to human nature. An essay can also be a long, systematic discourse.

Existentialism: A predominantly twentieth-century philosophy concerned with the nature and perception of human existence. There are two major strains of existentialist thought: atheistic and Christian. Followers of atheistic existentialism believe that the individual is alone in a godless universe and that the basic human condition is one of suffering and loneliness. Nevertheless, because there are no fixed values, individuals can create their own characters—indeed, they can shape themselves—through the exercise of free will. The atheistic strain culminates in and is popularly associated with the works of Jean-Paul Sartre. The Christian existentialists, on the other hand, believe that only in God may people find

freedom from life's anguish. The two strains hold certain beliefs in common: that existence cannot be fully understood or described through empirical effort; that anguish is a universal element of life; that individuals must bear responsibility for their actions; and that there is no common standard of behavior or perception for religious and ethical matters.

Expatriates: See *Expatriatism*

Expatriatism: The practice of leaving one's country to live for an extended period in another country.

Exposition: Writing intended to explain the nature of an idea, thing, or theme. Expository writing is often combined with description, narration, or argument. In dramatic writing, the exposition is the introductory material which presents the characters, setting, and tone of the play.

Expressionism: An indistinct literary term, originally used to describe an early twentieth-century school of German painting. The term applies to almost any mode of unconventional, highly subjective writing that distorts reality in some way.

Extended Monologue: See *Monologue*

F

Feet: See *Foot*

Feminine Rhyme: See *Rhyme*

Fiction: Any story that is the product of imagination rather than a documentation of fact. Characters and events in such narratives may be based in real life but their ultimate form and configuration is a creation of the author.

Figurative Language: A technique in writing in which the author temporarily interrupts the order, construction, or meaning of the writing for a particular effect. This interruption takes the form of one or more figures of speech such as hyperbole, irony, or simile. Figurative language is the opposite of literal language, in which every word is truthful, accurate, and free of exaggeration or embellishment.

Figures of Speech: Writing that differs from customary conventions for construction, meaning, order, or significance for the purpose of a special meaning or effect. There are two major types of figures of speech: rhetorical figures, which do not make changes in the meaning of the words, and tropes, which do.

Fin de siecle: A French term meaning "end of the century." The term is used to denote the last decade of the nineteenth century, a transition period when writers and other artists abandoned old conventions and looked for new techniques and objectives.

First Person: See *Point of View*

Folk Ballad: See *Ballad*

Folklore: Traditions and myths preserved in a culture or group of people. Typically, these are passed on by word of mouth in various forms—such as legends, songs, and proverbs—or preserved in customs and ceremonies. This term was first used by W. J. Thoms in 1846.

Folktale: A story originating in oral tradition. Folktales fall into a variety of categories, including legends, ghost stories, fairy tales, fables, and anecdotes based on historical figures and events.

Foot: The smallest unit of rhythm in a line of poetry. In English-language poetry, a foot is typically one accented syllable combined with one or two unaccented syllables.

Form: The pattern or construction of a work which identifies its genre and distinguishes it from other genres.

Formalism: In literary criticism, the belief that literature should follow prescribed rules of construction, such as those that govern the sonnet form.

Fourteener Meter: See *Meter*

Free Verse: Poetry that lacks regular metrical and rhyme patterns but that tries to capture the cadences of everyday speech. The form allows a poet to exploit a variety of rhythmical effects within a single poem.

Futurism: A flamboyant literary and artistic movement that developed in France, Italy, and Russia from 1908 through the 1920s. Futurist theater and poetry abandoned traditional literary forms. In their place, followers of the movement attempted to achieve total freedom of expression through bizarre imagery and deformed or newly invented words. The Futurists were self-consciously modern artists who attempted to incorporate the appearances and sounds of modern life into their work.

G

Genre: A category of literary work. In critical theory, genre may refer to both the content of a given work—tragedy, comedy, pastoral—and to its form, such as poetry, novel, or drama.

Genteel Tradition: A term coined by critic George Santayana to describe the literary practice of certain late nineteenth-century American writers, especially New Englanders. Followers of the Genteel Tradition emphasized conventionality in social, religious, moral, and literary standards.

Georgian Age: See *Georgian Poets*

Georgian Period: See *Georgian Poets*

Georgian Poets: A loose grouping of English poets during the years 1912-1922. The Georgians reacted against certain literary schools and practices, especially Victorian wordiness, turn-of-the-century aestheticism, and contemporary urban realism. In their place, the Georgians embraced the nineteenth-century poetic practices of William Wordsworth and the other Lake Poets.

Georgic: A poem about farming and the farmer's way of life, named from Virgil's *Georgics*.

Gilded Age: A period in American history during the 1870s characterized by political corruption and materialism. A number of important novels of social and political criticism were written during this time.

Gothic: See *Gothicism*

Gothicism: In literary criticism, works characterized by a taste for the medieval or morbidly attractive. A gothic novel prominently features elements of horror, the supernatural, gloom, and violence: clanking chains, terror, charnel houses, ghosts, medieval castles, and mysteriously slamming doors. The term "gothic novel" is also applied to novels that lack elements of the traditional Gothic setting but that create a similar atmosphere of terror or dread.

Graveyard School: A group of eighteenth-century English poets who wrote long, picturesque meditations on death. Their works were designed to cause the reader to ponder immortality.

Great Chain of Being: The belief that all things and creatures in nature are organized in a hierarchy from inanimate objects at the bottom to God at the top. This system of belief was popular in the seventeenth and eighteenth centuries.

Grotesque: In literary criticism, the subject matter of a work or a style of expression characterized by exaggeration, deformity, freakishness, and disorder. The grotesque often includes an element of comic absurdity.

H

Haiku: The shortest form of Japanese poetry, constructed in three lines of five, seven, and five syllables respectively. The message of a *haiku* poem usually centers on some aspect of spirituality and provokes an emotional response in the reader.

Half Rhyme: See *Consonance*

Harlem Renaissance: The Harlem Renaissance of the 1920s is generally considered the first significant movement of black writers and artists in the United States. During this period, new and established black writers published more fiction and poetry than ever before, the first influential black literary journals were established, and black authors and artists received their first widespread recognition and serious critical appraisal. Among the major writers associated with this period are Claude McKay, Jean Toomer, Countee Cullen, Langston Hughes, Arna Bontemps, Nella Larsen, and Zora Neale Hurston.

Hellenism: Imitation of ancient Greek thought or styles. Also, an approach to life that focuses on the growth and development of the intellect. "Hellenism" is sometimes used to refer to the belief that reason can be applied to examine all human experience.

Heptameter: See *Meter*

Hero/Heroine: The principal sympathetic character (male or female) in a literary work. Heroes and heroines typically exhibit admirable traits: idealism, courage, and integrity, for example.

Heroic Couplet: A rhyming couplet written in iambic pentameter (a verse with five iambic feet).

Heroic Line: The meter and length of a line of verse in epic or heroic poetry. This varies by language and time period.

Heroine: See *Hero/Heroine*

Hexameter: See *Meter*

Historical Criticism: The study of a work based on its impact on the world of the time period in which it was written.

Hokku: See *Haiku*

Holocaust: See *Holocaust Literature*

Holocaust Literature: Literature influenced by or written about the Holocaust of World War II. Such literature includes true stories of survival in concentration camps, escape, and life after the war, as well as fictional works and poetry.

Homeric Simile: An elaborate, detailed comparison written as a simile many lines in length.

Horatian Satire: See *Satire*

Humanism: A philosophy that places faith in the dignity of humankind and rejects the medieval perception of the individual as a weak, fallen creature. "Humanists" typically believe in the perfectibility of human nature and view reason and education as the means to that end.

Humors: Mentions of the humors refer to the ancient Greek theory that a person's health and personality were determined by the balance of four basic fluids in the body: blood, phlegm, yellow bile, and black bile. A dominance of any fluid would cause extremes in behavior. An excess of blood created a sanguine person who was joyful, aggressive, and passionate; a phlegmatic person was shy, fearful, and sluggish; too much yellow bile led to a choleric temperament characterized by impatience, anger, bitterness, and stubbornness; and excessive black bile created melancholy, a state of laziness, gluttony, and lack of motivation.

Humours: See *Humors*

Hyperbole: In literary criticism, deliberate exaggeration used to achieve an effect.

I

Iamb: See *Foot*

Idiom: A word construction or verbal expression closely associated with a given language.

Image: A concrete representation of an object or sensory experience. Typically, such a representation helps evoke the feelings associated with the object or experience itself. Images are either "literal" or "figurative." Literal images are especially concrete and involve little or no extension of the obvious meaning of the words used to express them. Figurative images do not follow the literal meaning of the words exactly. Images in literature are usually visual, but the term "image" can also refer to the representation of any sensory experience.

Imagery: The array of images in a literary work. Also, figurative language.

Imagism: An English and American poetry movement that flourished between 1908 and 1917. The Imagists used precise, clearly presented images in their works. They also used common, everyday speech and aimed for conciseness, concrete imagery, and the creation of new rhythms.

In medias res: A Latin term meaning "in the middle of things." It refers to the technique of beginning a story at its midpoint and then using various flashback devices to reveal previous action.

Induction: The process of reaching a conclusion by reasoning from specific premises to form a general premise. Also, an introductory portion of a work of literature, especially a play.

Intentional Fallacy: The belief that judgments of a literary work based solely on an author's stated or implied intentions are false and misleading. Critics who believe in the concept of the intentional fallacy typically argue that the work itself is sufficient matter for interpretation, even though they may concede that an author's statement of purpose can be useful.

Interior Monologue: A narrative technique in which characters' thoughts are revealed in a way that appears to be uncontrolled by the author. The interior monologue typically aims to reveal the inner self of a character. It portrays emotional experiences as they occur at both a conscious and unconscious level. Images are often used to represent sensations or emotions.

Internal Rhyme: Rhyme that occurs within a single line of verse.

Irish Literary Renaissance: A late nineteenth- and early twentieth-century movement in Irish literature. Members of the movement aimed to reduce the influence of British culture in Ireland and create an Irish national literature.

Irony: In literary criticism, the effect of language in which the intended meaning is the opposite of what is stated.

Italian Sonnet: See *Sonnet*

J

Jacobean Age: The period of the reign of James I of England (1603-1625). The early literature of this period reflected the worldview of the Elizabethan Age, but a darker, more cynical attitude steadily grew in the art and literature of the Jacobean Age. This was an important time for English drama and poetry.

Jargon: Language that is used or understood only by a select group of people. Jargon may refer to terminology used in a certain profession, such as computer jargon, or it may refer to any nonsensical language that is not understood by most people.

Journalism: Writing intended for publication in a newspaper or magazine, or for broadcast on a radio or television program featuring news, sports, entertainment, or other timely material.

K

Knickerbocker Group: A somewhat indistinct group of New York writers of the first half of the nineteenth century. Members of the group were linked only by location and a common theme: New York life.

Kunstlerroman: See *Bildungsroman*

L

Lais: See *Lay*

Lake Poets: See *Lake School*

Lake School: These poets all lived in the Lake District of England at the turn of the nineteenth century. As a group, they followed no single "school" of thought or literary practice, although their works were uniformly disparaged by the *Edinburgh Review*.

Lay: A song or simple narrative poem. The form originated in medieval France. Early French *lais* were often based on the Celtic legends and other tales sung by Breton minstrels—thus the name of the "Breton lay." In fourteenth-century England, the term "lay" was used to describe short narratives written in imitation of the Breton lays.

Leitmotiv: See *Motif*

Literal Language: An author uses literal language when he or she writes without exaggerating or embellishing the subject matter and without any tools of figurative language.

Literary Ballad: See *Ballad*

Literature: Literature is broadly defined as any written or spoken material, but the term most often refers to creative works.

Lost Generation: A term first used by Gertrude Stein to describe the post-World War I generation of American writers: men and women haunted by a sense of betrayal and emptiness brought about by the destructiveness of the war.

Lyric Poetry: A poem expressing the subjective feelings and personal emotions of the poet. Such poetry is melodic, since it was originally accompanied by a lyre in recitals. Most Western poetry in the twentieth century may be classified as lyrical.

M

Mannerism: Exaggerated, artificial adherence to a literary manner or style. Also, a popular style of the visual arts of late sixteenth-century Europe that was marked by elongation of the human form and by intentional spatial distortion. Literary works that are self-consciously high-toned and artistic are often said to be "mannered."

Masculine Rhyme: See *Rhyme*

Measure: The foot, verse, or time sequence used in a literary work, especially a poem. Measure is often used somewhat incorrectly as a synonym for meter.

Metaphor: A figure of speech that expresses an idea through the image of another object. Metaphors suggest the essence of the first object by identifying it with certain qualities of the second object.

Metaphysical Conceit: See *Conceit*

Metaphysical Poetry: The body of poetry produced by a group of seventeenth-century English writers called the "Metaphysical Poets." The group includes John Donne and Andrew Marvell. The Metaphysical Poets made use of everyday speech, intellectual analysis, and unique imagery. They aimed to portray the ordinary conflicts and contradictions of life. Their poems often took the form of an argument, and many of them emphasize physical and religious love as well as the fleeting nature of life. Elaborate conceits are typical in metaphysical poetry.

Metaphysical Poets: See *Metaphysical Poetry*

Meter: In literary criticism, the repetition of sound patterns that creates a rhythm in poetry. The patterns are based on the number of syllables and the presence and absence of accents. The unit of rhythm in a line is called a foot. Types of meter are classified according to the number of feet in a line. These are the standard English lines: Monometer, one foot; Dimeter, two feet; Trimeter, three feet; Tetrameter, four feet; Pentameter, five feet; Hexameter, six feet (also called the Alexandrine); Heptameter, seven feet (also called the "Fourteener" when the feet are iambic).

Modernism: Modern literary practices. Also, the principles of a literary school that lasted from roughly the beginning of the twentieth century until the end of World War II. Modernism is defined by its rejection of the literary conventions of the nineteenth century and by its opposition to conventional morality, taste, traditions, and economic values.

Monologue: A composition, written or oral, by a single individual. More specifically, a speech given by a single individual in a drama or other public entertainment. It has no set length, although it is usually several or more lines long.

Monometer: See *Meter*

Mood: The prevailing emotions of a work or of the author in his or her creation of the work. The mood of a work is not always what might be expected based on its subject matter.

Motif: A theme, character type, image, metaphor, or other verbal element that recurs throughout a single work of literature or occurs in a number of different works over a period of time.

Motiv: See *Motif*

Muckrakers: An early twentieth-century group of American writers. Typically, their works exposed the wrongdoings of big business and government in the United States.

Muses: Nine Greek mythological goddesses, the daughters of Zeus and Mnemosyne

(Memory). Each muse patronized a specific area of the liberal arts and sciences. Calliope presided over epic poetry, Clio over history, Erato over love poetry, Euterpe over music or lyric poetry, Melpomene over tragedy, Polyhymnia over hymns to the gods, Terpsichore over dance, Thalia over comedy, and Urania over astronomy. Poets and writers traditionally made appeals to the Muses for inspiration in their work.

Myth: An anonymous tale emerging from the traditional beliefs of a culture or social unit. Myths use supernatural explanations for natural phenomena. They may also explain cosmic issues like creation and death. Collections of myths, known as mythologies, are common to all cultures and nations, but the best-known myths belong to the Norse, Roman, and Greek mythologies.

N

Narration: The telling of a series of events, real or invented. A narration may be either a simple narrative, in which the events are recounted chronologically, or a narrative with a plot, in which the account is given in a style reflecting the author's artistic concept of the story. Narration is sometimes used as a synonym for "storyline."

Narrative: A verse or prose accounting of an event or sequence of events, real or invented. The term is also used as an adjective in the sense "method of narration." For example, in literary criticism, the expression "narrative technique" usually refers to the way the author structures and presents his or her story.

Narrative Poetry: A nondramatic poem in which the author tells a story. Such poems may be of any length or level of complexity.

Narrator: The teller of a story. The narrator may be the author or a character in the story through whom the author speaks.

Naturalism: A literary movement of the late nineteenth and early twentieth centuries. The movement's major theorist, French novelist Emile Zola, envisioned a type of fiction that would examine human life with the objectivity of scientific inquiry. The Naturalists typically viewed human beings as either the products of "biological determinism," ruled by hereditary instincts and engaged in an endless struggle for survival, or as the products of "socioeconomic determinism," ruled by social and economic forces beyond their control. In their works, the Naturalists generally ignored the highest levels of society and focused on degradation: poverty, alcoholism, prostitution, insanity, and disease.

Negritude: A literary movement based on the concept of a shared cultural bond on the part of black Africans, wherever they may be in the world. It traces its origins to the former French colonies of Africa and the Caribbean. Negritude poets, novelists, and essayists generally stress four points in their writings: One, black alienation from traditional African culture can lead to feelings of inferiority. Two, European colonialism and Western education should be resisted. Three, black Africans should seek to affirm and define their own identity. Four, African culture can and should be reclaimed. Many Negritude writers also claim that blacks can make unique contributions to the world, based on a heightened appreciation of nature, rhythm, and human emotions—aspects of life they say are not so highly valued in the materialistic and rationalistic West.

Negro Renaissance: See *Harlem Renaissance*

Neoclassical Period: See *Neoclassicism*

Neoclassicism: In literary criticism, this term refers to the revival of the attitudes and styles of expression of classical literature. It is generally used to describe a period in European history beginning in the late seventeenth century and lasting until about 1800. In its purest form, Neoclassicism marked a return to order, proportion, restraint, logic, accuracy, and decorum. In England, where Neoclassicism perhaps was most popular, it reflected the influence of seventeenth- century French writers, especially dramatists. Neoclassical writers typically reacted against the intensity and enthusiasm of the Renaissance period. They wrote works that appealed to the intellect, using elevated language and classical literary forms such as satire and the ode. Neoclassical works were often governed by the classical goal of instruction.

Neoclassicists: See *Neoclassicism*

New Criticism: A movement in literary criticism, dating from the late 1920s, that stressed close textual analysis in the interpretation of works of literature. The New Critics saw little merit in historical and biographical analysis. Rather, they aimed to examine the text alone, free from the question of how external events—biographical or otherwise—may have helped shape it.

New Journalism: A type of writing in which the journalist presents factual information in a form usually used in fiction. New journalism emphasizes description, narration, and character development to bring readers closer to the human element of the story, and is often used in personality profiles and in-depth feature articles. It is not compatible with "straight" or "hard" newswriting, which is generally composed in a brief, fact-based style.

New Journalists: See *New Journalism*

New Negro Movement: See *Harlem Renaissance*

Noble Savage: The idea that primitive man is noble and good but becomes evil and corrupted as he becomes civilized. The concept of the noble savage originated in the Renaissance period but is more closely identified with such later writers as Jean-Jacques Rousseau and Aphra Behn.

O

Objective Correlative: An outward set of objects, a situation, or a chain of events corresponding to an inward experience and evoking this experience in the reader. The term frequently appears in modern criticism in discussions of authors' intended effects on the emotional responses of readers.

Objectivity: A quality in writing characterized by the absence of the author's opinion or feeling about the subject matter. Objectivity is an important factor in criticism.

Occasional Verse: poetry written on the occasion of a significant historical or personal event. *Vers de societe* is sometimes called occasional verse although it is of a less serious nature.

Octave: A poem or stanza composed of eight lines. The term octave most often represents the first eight lines of a Petrarchan sonnet.

Ode: Name given to an extended lyric poem characterized by exalted emotion and dignified style. An ode usually concerns a single, serious theme. Most odes, but not all, are addressed to an object or individual. Odes are distinguished from other lyric poetic forms by their complex rhythmic and stanzaic patterns.

Oedipus Complex: A son's amorous obsession with his mother. The phrase is derived from the story of the ancient Theban hero Oedipus, who unknowingly killed his father and married his mother.

Omniscience: See *Point of View*

Onomatopoeia: The use of words whose sounds express or suggest their meaning. In its simplest sense, onomatopoeia may be represented by words that mimic the sounds they denote such as "hiss" or "meow." At a more subtle level, the pattern and rhythm of sounds and rhymes of a line or poem may be onomatopoeic.

Oral Tradition: See *Oral Transmission*

Oral Transmission: A process by which songs, ballads, folklore, and other material are transmitted by word of mouth. The tradition of oral transmission predates the written record systems of literate society. Oral transmission preserves material sometimes over generations, although often with variations. Memory plays a large part in the recitation and preservation of orally transmitted material.

Ottava Rima: An eight-line stanza of poetry composed in iambic pentameter (a five-foot line in which each foot consists of an unaccented syllable followed by an accented syllable), following the abababcc rhyme scheme.

Oxymoron: A phrase combining two contradictory terms. Oxymorons may be intentional or unintentional.

P

Pantheism: The idea that all things are both a manifestation or revelation of God and a part of God at the same time. Pantheism was a common attitude in the early societies of Egypt, India, and Greece—the term derives from the Greek *pan* meaning "all" and *theos* meaning "deity." It later became a significant part of the Christian faith.

Parable: A story intended to teach a moral lesson or answer an ethical question.

Paradox: A statement that appears illogical or contradictory at first, but may actually point to an underlying truth.

Parallelism: A method of comparison of two ideas in which each is developed in the same grammatical structure.

Parnassianism: A mid nineteenth-century movement in French literature. Followers of the movement stressed adherence to well-defined artistic forms as a reaction against the often chaotic expression of the artist's ego that dominated the work of the Romantics. The Parnassians also rejected the moral, ethical, and social themes exhibited in the works of French Romantics such as Victor Hugo. The aesthetic doctrines of the Parnassians strongly influenced the later symbolist and decadent movements.

Parody: In literary criticism, this term refers to an imitation of a serious literary work or the signature style of a particular author in a ridiculous manner. A typical parody adopts the style of the original and applies it to an inappropriate subject for humorous effect. Parody is a form of satire and could be considered the literary equivalent of a caricature or cartoon.

Pastoral: A term derived from the Latin word "pastor," meaning shepherd. A pastoral is a literary composition on a rural theme. The conventions of the pastoral were originated by the third-century Greek poet Theocritus, who wrote about the experiences, love affairs, and pastimes of Sicilian shepherds. In a pastoral, characters and language of a courtly nature are often placed in a simple setting. The term pastoral is also used to classify dramas, elegies, and lyrics that exhibit the use of country settings and shepherd characters.

Pathetic Fallacy: A term coined by English critic John Ruskin to identify writing that falsely endows nonhuman things with human intentions and feelings, such as "angry clouds" and "sad trees."

Pen Name: See *Pseudonym*

Pentameter: See *Meter*

Persona: A Latin term meaning "mask." *Personae* are the characters in a fictional work of literature. The *persona* generally functions as a mask through which the author tells a story in a voice other than his or her own. A *persona* is usually either a character in a story who acts as a narrator or an "implied author," a voice created by the author to act as the narrator for himself or herself.

Personae: See *Persona*

Personal Point of View: See *Point of View*

Personification: A figure of speech that gives human qualities to abstract ideas, animals, and inanimate objects.

Petrarchan Sonnet: See *Sonnet*

Phenomenology: A method of literary criticism based on the belief that things have no existence outside of human consciousness or awareness. Proponents of this theory believe that art is a process that takes place in the mind of the observer as he or she contemplates an object rather than a quality of the object itself.

Plagiarism: Claiming another person's written material as one's own. Plagiarism can take the form of direct, word-for-word copying or the theft of the substance or idea of the work.

Platonic Criticism: A form of criticism that stresses an artistic work's usefulness as an agent of social engineering rather than any quality or value of the work itself.

Platonism: The embracing of the doctrines of the philosopher Plato, popular among the poets of the Renaissance and the Romantic period. Platonism is more flexible than Aristotelian Criticism and places more emphasis on the supernatural and unknown aspects of life.

Plot: In literary criticism, this term refers to the pattern of events in a narrative or drama. In its simplest sense, the plot guides the author in composing the work and helps the reader follow the work. Typically, plots exhibit causality and unity and have a beginning, a middle, and an end. Sometimes, however, a plot may consist of a series of disconnected events, in which case it is known as an "episodic plot."

Poem: In its broadest sense, a composition utilizing rhyme, meter, concrete detail, and expressive language to create a literary experience with emotional and aesthetic appeal.

Poet: An author who writes poetry or verse. The term is also used to refer to an artist or writer who has an exceptional gift for expression, imagination, and energy in the making of art in any form.

Poete maudit: A term derived from Paul Verlaine's *Les poetes maudits* (*The Accursed Poets*), a collection of essays on the French symbolist writers Stephane Mallarme, Arthur Rimbaud, and Tristan Corbiere. In the sense intended by Verlaine, the poet is "accursed" for choosing to explore extremes of human experience outside of middle-class society.

Poetic Fallacy: See *Pathetic Fallacy*

Poetic Justice: An outcome in a literary work, not necessarily a poem, in which the good are rewarded and the evil are punished, especially in ways that particularly fit their virtues or crimes.

Poetic License: Distortions of fact and literary convention made by a writer—not always a poet—for the sake of the effect gained. Poetic license is closely related to the concept of "artistic freedom."

Poetics: This term has two closely related meanings. It denotes (1) an aesthetic theory in literary criticism about the essence of poetry or (2) rules prescribing the proper methods, content, style, or diction of poetry. The term poetics may also refer to theories about literature in general, not just poetry.

Poetry: In its broadest sense, writing that aims to present ideas and evoke an emotional experience in the reader through the use of meter, imagery, connotative and concrete words, and a carefully constructed structure based on rhythmic patterns. Poetry typically relies on words and expressions that have several layers of meaning. It also makes use of the effects of regular rhythm on the ear and may make a strong appeal to the senses through the use of imagery.

Point of View: The narrative perspective from which a literary work is presented to the reader. There are four traditional points of view. The "third person omniscient" gives the reader a "godlike" perspective, unrestricted by time or place, from which to see actions and look into the minds of characters. This allows the author to comment openly on characters and events in the work. The "third person" point of view presents the events of the story from outside of any single character's perception, much like the omniscient point of view, but the reader must understand the action as it takes place and without any special insight into characters' minds or motivations. The "first person" or "personal" point of view relates events as they are perceived by a single character.

The main character "tells" the story and may offer opinions about the action and characters which differ from those of the author. Much less common than omniscient, third person, and first person is the "second person" point of view, wherein the author tells the story as if it is happening to the reader.

Polemic: A work in which the author takes a stand on a controversial subject, such as abortion or religion. Such works are often extremely argumentative or provocative.

Pornography: Writing intended to provoke feelings of lust in the reader. Such works are often condemned by critics and teachers, but those which can be shown to have literary value are viewed less harshly.

Post-Aesthetic Movement: An artistic response made by African Americans to the black aesthetic movement of the 1960s and early '70s. Writers since that time have adopted a somewhat different tone in their work, with less emphasis placed on the disparity between black and white in the United States. In the words of post-aesthetic authors such as Toni Morrison, John Edgar Wideman, and Kristin Hunter, African Americans are portrayed as looking inward for answers to their own questions, rather than always looking to the outside world.

Postmodernism: Writing from the 1960s forward characterized by experimentation and continuing to apply some of the fundamentals of modernism, which included existentialism and alienation. Postmodernists have gone a step further in the rejection of tradition begun with the modernists by also rejecting traditional forms, preferring the anti-novel over the novel and the anti-hero over the hero.

Pre-Raphaelites: A circle of writers and artists in mid nineteenth-century England. Valuing the pre-Renaissance artistic qualities of religious symbolism, lavish pictorialism, and natural sensuousness, the Pre-Raphaelites cultivated a sense of mystery and melancholy that influenced later writers associated with the Symbolist and Decadent movements.

Primitivism: The belief that primitive peoples were nobler and less flawed than civilized peoples because they had not been subjected to the tainting influence of society.

Projective Verse: A form of free verse in which the poet's breathing pattern determines the lines of the poem. Poets who advocate projective verse are against all formal structures in writing, including meter and form.

Prologue: An introductory section of a literary work. It often contains information establishing the situation of the characters or presents information about the setting, time period, or action. In drama, the prologue is spoken by a chorus or by one of the principal characters.

Prose: A literary medium that attempts to mirror the language of everyday speech. It is distinguished from poetry by its use of unmetered, unrhymed language consisting of logically related sentences. Prose is usually grouped into paragraphs that form a cohesive whole such as an essay or a novel.

Prosopopoeia: See *Personification*

Protagonist: The central character of a story who serves as a focus for its themes and incidents and as the principal rationale for its development. The protagonist is sometimes referred to in discussions of modern literature as the hero or anti-hero.

Proverb: A brief, sage saying that expresses a truth about life in a striking manner.

Pseudonym: A name assumed by a writer, most often intended to prevent his or her identification as the author of a work. Two or more authors may work together under one pseudonym, or an author may use a different name for each genre he or she publishes in. Some publishing companies maintain "house pseudonyms," under which any number of authors may write installations in a series. Some authors also choose a pseudonym over their real names the way an actor may use a stage name.

Pun: A play on words that have similar sounds but different meanings.

Pure Poetry: poetry written without instructional intent or moral purpose that aims only to please a reader by its imagery or musical flow. The term pure poetry is used as the antonym of the term "didacticism."

Q

Quatrain: A four-line stanza of a poem or an entire poem consisting of four lines.

R

Realism: A nineteenth-century European literary movement that sought to portray familiar characters, situations, and settings in a realistic manner. This was done primarily by using an objective narrative point of view and through the buildup of accurate detail. The standard for success of any realistic work depends on how faithfully it transfers common experience into fictional forms. The realistic method may be altered or extended, as in stream of consciousness writing, to record highly subjective experience.

Refrain: A phrase repeated at intervals throughout a poem. A refrain may appear at the end of each stanza or at less regular intervals. It may be altered slightly at each appearance.

Renaissance: The period in European history that marked the end of the Middle Ages. It began in Italy in the late fourteenth century. In broad terms, it is usually seen as spanning the fourteenth, fifteenth, and sixteenth centuries, although it did not reach Great Britain, for example, until the 1480s or so. The Renaissance saw an awakening in almost every sphere of human activity, especially science, philosophy, and the arts. The period is best defined by the emergence of a general philosophy that emphasized the importance of the intellect, the individual, and world affairs. It contrasts strongly with the medieval worldview, characterized by the dominant concerns of faith, the social collective, and spiritual salvation.

Repartee: Conversation featuring snappy retorts and witticisms.

Restoration: See *Restoration Age*

Restoration Age: A period in English literature beginning with the crowning of Charles II in 1660 and running to about 1700. The era, which was characterized by a reaction against Puritanism, was the first great age of the comedy of manners. The finest literature of the era is typically witty and urbane, and often lewd.

Rhetoric: In literary criticism, this term denotes the art of ethical persuasion. In its strictest sense, rhetoric adheres to various principles developed since classical times for arranging facts and ideas in a clear, persuasive, appealing manner. The term is also used to refer to effective prose in general and theories of or methods for composing effective prose.

Rhetorical Question: A question intended to provoke thought, but not an expressed answer, in the reader. It is most commonly used in oratory and other persuasive genres.

Rhyme: When used as a noun in literary criticism, this term generally refers to a poem in which words sound identical or very similar and appear in parallel positions in two or more lines. Rhymes are classified into different types according to where they fall in a line or stanza or according to the degree of similarity they exhibit in their spellings and sounds. Some major types of rhyme are "masculine" rhyme, "feminine" rhyme, and "triple" rhyme. In a masculine rhyme, the rhyming sound falls in a single accented syllable, as with "heat" and "eat." Feminine rhyme is a rhyme of two syllables, one stressed and one unstressed, as with "merry" and "tarry." Triple rhyme matches the sound of the accented syllable and the two unaccented syllables that follow: "narrative" and "declarative."

Rhyme Royal: A stanza of seven lines composed in iambic pentameter and rhymed *ababbcc*. The name is said to be a tribute to King James I of Scotland, who made much use of the form in his poetry.

Rhyme Scheme: See *Rhyme*

Rhythm: A regular pattern of sound, time intervals, or events occurring in writing, most often and most discernably in poetry. Regular, reliable rhythm is known to be soothing to humans, while interrupted, unpredictable, or rapidly changing rhythm is disturbing. These effects are known to authors, who use them to produce a desired reaction in the reader.

Rococo: A style of European architecture that flourished in the eighteenth century, especially in France. The most notable features of *rococo* are its extensive use of ornamentation and its themes of lightness, gaiety, and intimacy. In literary criticism, the term is often used disparagingly to refer to a decadent or over-ornamental style.

Romance: A broad term, usually denoting a narrative with exotic, exaggerated, often idealized characters, scenes, and themes.

Romantic Age: See *Romanticism*

Romanticism: This term has two widely accepted meanings. In historical criticism, it refers to a European intellectual and artistic movement of the late eighteenth and early nineteenth centuries that sought greater freedom of personal expression than that allowed by the strict rules of literary form and logic of the eighteenth-century neoclassicists. The Romantics preferred emotional and imaginative expression to rational analysis. They considered the individual to be at the center of all experience and so placed him or her at the center of their art. The Romantics believed that the creative imagination reveals nobler truths—unique feelings and attitudes—than those that could be discovered by logic or by scientific examination. Both the natural world and the state of childhood were important sources for revelations of "eternal truths." "Romanticism" is also used as a general term to refer to a type of sensibility found in all periods of literary history and usually considered to be in opposition to the principles of classicism. In this sense, Romanticism signifies any work or philosophy in which the exotic or dreamlike figure strongly, or that is devoted to individualistic expression, self-analysis, or a pursuit of a higher realm of knowledge than can be discovered by human reason.

Romantics: See *Romanticism*

Russian Symbolism: A Russian poetic movement, derived from French symbolism, that flourished between 1894 and 1910. While some Russian Symbolists continued in the French tradition, stressing aestheticism and the importance of suggestion above didactic intent, others saw their craft as a form of mystical worship, and themselves as mediators between the supernatural and the mundane.

S

Satire: A work that uses ridicule, humor, and wit to criticize and provoke change in human nature and institutions. There are two major types of satire: "formal" or "direct" satire speaks directly to the reader or to a character in the work; "indirect" satire relies upon the ridiculous behavior of its characters to make its point. Formal satire is further divided into two manners: the "Horatian," which ridicules gently, and the "Juvenalian," which derides its subjects harshly and bitterly.

Scansion: The analysis or "scanning" of a poem to determine its meter and often its rhyme scheme. The most common system of scansion uses accents (slanted lines drawn above syllables) to show stressed syllables, breves (curved lines drawn above syllables) to show unstressed syllables, and vertical lines to separate each foot.

Second Person: See *Point of View*

Semiotics: The study of how literary forms and conventions affect the meaning of language.

Sestet: Any six-line poem or stanza.

Setting: The time, place, and culture in which the action of a narrative takes place. The elements of setting may include geographic location, characters' physical and mental environments, prevailing cultural attitudes, or the historical time in which the action takes place.

Shakespearean Sonnet: See *Sonnet*

Signifying Monkey: A popular trickster figure in black folklore, with hundreds of tales about this character documented since the 19th century.

Simile: A comparison, usually using "like" or "as," of two essentially dissimilar things, as in "coffee as cold as ice" or "He sounded like a broken record."

Slang: A type of informal verbal communication that is generally unacceptable for formal writing. Slang words and phrases are often colorful exaggerations used to emphasize the speaker's point; they may also be shortened versions of an often-used word or phrase.

Slant Rhyme: See *Consonance*

Slave Narrative: Autobiographical accounts of American slave life as told by escaped slaves. These works first appeared during the abolition movement of the 1830s through the 1850s.

Social Realism: See *Socialist Realism*

Socialist Realism: The Socialist Realism school of literary theory was proposed by Maxim Gorky and established as a dogma by the first Soviet Congress of Writers. It demanded adherence to a communist worldview in works of literature. Its doctrines required an objective viewpoint comprehensible to the working classes and themes of social struggle featuring strong proletarian heroes.

Soliloquy: A monologue in a drama used to give the audience information and to develop the speaker's character. It is typically a projection of the speaker's innermost thoughts. Usually delivered while the speaker is alone on stage, a soliloquy is intended to present an illusion of unspoken reflection.

Sonnet: A fourteen-line poem, usually composed in iambic pentameter, employing one of several rhyme schemes. There are three major types of sonnets, upon which all other variations of the form are based: the "Petrarchan" or "Italian" sonnet, the "Shakespearean" or "English" sonnet, and the "Spenserian" sonnet. A Petrarchan sonnet consists of an octave rhymed *abbaabba* and a "sestet" rhymed either *cdecde, cdccdc,* or *cdedce.* The octave poses a question or problem, relates a narrative, or puts forth a proposition; the sestet presents a solution to the problem, comments upon the narrative, or applies the proposition put forth in the octave. The Shakespearean sonnet is divided into three quatrains and a couplet rhymed *abab cdcd efef gg.* The couplet provides an epigrammatic comment on the narrative or problem put forth in the quatrains. The Spenserian sonnet uses three quatrains and a couplet like the Shakespearean, but links their three rhyme schemes in this way: *abab bcbc cdcd ee.* The Spenserian sonnet develops its theme in two parts like the Petrarchan, its final six lines resolving a problem, analyzing a narrative, or applying a proposition put forth in its first eight lines.

Spenserian Sonnet: See *Sonnet*

Spenserian Stanza: A nine-line stanza having eight verses in iambic pentameter, its ninth verse in iambic hexameter, and the rhyme scheme ababbcbcc.

Spondee: In poetry meter, a foot consisting of two long or stressed syllables occurring together. This form is quite rare in English verse, and is usually composed of two monosyllabic words.

Sprung Rhythm: Versification using a specific number of accented syllables per line but disregarding the number of unaccented syllables that fall in each line, producing an irregular rhythm in the poem.

Stanza: A subdivision of a poem consisting of lines grouped together, often in recurring patterns of rhyme, line length, and meter. Stanzas may also serve as units of thought in a poem much like paragraphs in prose.

Stereotype: A stereotype was originally the name for a duplication made during the printing process; this led to its modern definition as a person or thing that is (or is assumed to be) the same as all others of its type.

Stream of Consciousness: A narrative technique for rendering the inward experience of a character. This technique is designed to give the impression of an ever-changing series of thoughts, emotions, images, and memories in the spontaneous and seemingly illogical order that they occur in life.

Structuralism: A twentieth-century movement in literary criticism that examines how literary texts arrive at their meanings, rather than the meanings themselves. There are two major types of structuralist analysis: one examines the way patterns of linguistic structures unify a specific text and emphasize certain elements of that text, and the other interprets the way literary forms and conventions affect the meaning of language itself.

Structure: The form taken by a piece of literature. The structure may be made obvious for ease of understanding, as in nonfiction works, or may obscured for artistic purposes, as in some poetry or seemingly "unstructured" prose.

Sturm und Drang: A German term meaning "storm and stress." It refers to a German literary movement of the 1770s and 1780s that reacted against the order and rationalism of the enlightenment, focusing instead on the intense experience of extraordinary individuals.

Style: A writer's distinctive manner of arranging words to suit his or her ideas and purpose in writing. The unique imprint of the author's personality upon his or her writing, style is the product of an author's way of arranging ideas and his or her use of diction, different sentence structures, rhythm, figures of speech, rhetorical principles, and other elements of composition.

Subject: The person, event, or theme at the center of a work of literature. A work may have one or more subjects of each type, with shorter works tending to have fewer and longer works tending to have more.

Subjectivity: Writing that expresses the author's personal feelings about his subject, and which may or may not include factual information about the subject.

Surrealism: A term introduced to criticism by Guillaume Apollinaire and later adopted by Andre Breton. It refers to a French literary and artistic movement founded in the 1920s. The Surrealists sought to express unconscious thoughts and feelings in their works. The best-known technique used for achieving this aim was automatic writing— transcriptions of spontaneous outpourings from the unconscious. The Surrealists proposed to unify the contrary levels of conscious and unconscious, dream and reality, objectivity and subjectivity into a new level of "super-realism."

Suspense: A literary device in which the author maintains the audience's attention through the buildup of events, the outcome of which will soon be revealed.

Syllogism: A method of presenting a logical argument. In its most basic form, the syllogism consists of a major premise, a minor premise, and a conclusion.

Symbol: Something that suggests or stands for something else without losing its original identity. In literature, symbols combine their literal meaning with the suggestion of an abstract concept. Literary symbols are of two types: those that carry complex associations of meaning no matter what their contexts, and those that derive their suggestive meaning from their functions in specific literary works.

Symbolism: This term has two widely accepted meanings. In historical criticism, it denotes an early modernist literary movement initiated in France during the nineteenth century that reacted against the prevailing standards of realism. Writers in this movement aimed to evoke, indirectly and symbolically, an order of being beyond the material world of the five senses. Poetic expression of personal emotion figured strongly in the movement, typically by means of a private set of symbols uniquely identifiable with the individual poet. The principal aim of the Symbolists was to express in words the highly complex feelings that grew out of everyday contact with the world. In a broader sense, the term "symbolism" refers to the use of one object to represent another.

Symbolist: See *Symbolism*

Symbolist Movement: See *Symbolism*

Sympathetic Fallacy: See *Affective Fallacy*

T

Tanka: A form of Japanese poetry similar to *haiku*. A *tanka* is five lines long, with the lines containing five, seven, five, seven, and seven syllables respectively.

Terza Rima: A three-line stanza form in poetry in which the rhymes are made on the last word of each line in the following manner: the first and third lines of the first stanza, then the second line of the first stanza and the first and third lines of the second stanza, and so on with the middle line of any stanza rhyming with the first and third lines of the following stanza.

Tetrameter: See *Meter*

Textual Criticism: A branch of literary criticism that seeks to establish the authoritative text of a literary work. Textual critics typically compare all known manuscripts or printings of a single work in order to assess the meanings of differences and revisions. This procedure allows them to arrive at a definitive version that (supposedly) corresponds to the author's original intention.

Theme: The main point of a work of literature. The term is used interchangeably with thesis.

Thesis: A thesis is both an essay and the point argued in the essay. Thesis novels and thesis plays share the quality of containing a thesis which is supported through the action of the story.

Third Person: See *Point of View*

Tone: The author's attitude toward his or her audience may be deduced from the tone of the work. A formal tone may create distance or convey politeness, while an informal tone may encourage a friendly, intimate, or intrusive feeling in the reader. The author's attitude toward his or her subject matter may also be deduced from the tone of the words he or she uses in discussing it.

Tragedy: A drama in prose or poetry about a noble, courageous hero of excellent character who, because of some tragic character flaw or *hamartia*, brings ruin upon him- or herself. Tragedy treats its subjects in a dignified and serious manner, using poetic language to help evoke pity and fear and bring about catharsis, a purging of these emotions. The tragic form was practiced extensively by the ancient Greeks. In the Middle Ages, when classical works were virtually unknown, tragedy came to denote any works about the fall of persons from exalted to low conditions due to any reason: fate, vice, weakness, etc. According to the classical definition of tragedy, such works present the "pathetic"—that which evokes pity—rather than the tragic. The classical form of tragedy was revived in the sixteenth century; it flourished especially on the Elizabethan stage. In modern times, dramatists have attempted to adapt the form to the needs of modern society by drawing their heroes from the ranks of ordinary men and women and defining the nobility of these heroes in terms of spirit rather than exalted social standing.

Tragic Flaw: In a tragedy, the quality within the hero or heroine which leads to his or her downfall.

Transcendentalism: An American philosophical and religious movement, based in New England from around 1835 until the Civil War. Transcendentalism was a form of American romanticism that had its roots abroad in the works of Thomas Carlyle, Samuel Coleridge, and Johann Wolfgang von Goethe. The Transcendentalists stressed the importance of intuition and subjective experience in communication with God. They rejected religious dogma and texts in favor of mysticism and scientific naturalism. They pursued truths that lie beyond the "colorless" realms perceived by reason and the senses and were active social reformers in public education, women's rights, and the abolition of slavery.

Trickster: A character or figure common in Native American and African literature who uses his ingenuity to defeat enemies and escape difficult situations. Tricksters are most often animals, such as the spider, hare, or coyote, although they may take the form of humans as well.

Trimeter: See *Meter*

Triple Rhyme: See *Rhyme*

Trochee: See *Foot*

U

Understatement: See *Irony*

Unities: Strict rules of dramatic structure, formulated by Italian and French critics of the Renaissance and based loosely on the principles of drama discussed by Aristotle in his *Poetics*. Foremost among these rules were the three unities of action, time, and place that compelled a dramatist to: (1) construct a single plot with a beginning, middle, and end that details the causal relationships of action and character; (2) restrict the action to the events of a single day; and (3) limit the scene to a single place or city. The unities were observed faithfully by continental European writers until the Romantic Age, but they were never regularly observed in English drama. Modern dramatists are typically more concerned with a unity of impression or emotional effect than with any of the classical unities.

Urban Realism: A branch of realist writing that attempts to accurately reflect the often harsh facts of modern urban existence.

Utopia: A fictional perfect place, such as "paradise" or "heaven."

Utopian: See *Utopia*

Utopianism: See *Utopia*

V

Verisimilitude: Literally, the appearance of truth. In literary criticism, the term refers to aspects of a work of literature that seem true to the reader.

Vers de societe: See *Occasional Verse*

Vers libre: See *Free Verse*

Verse: A line of metered language, a line of a poem, or any work written in verse.

Versification: The writing of verse. Versification may also refer to the meter, rhyme, and other mechanical components of a poem.

Victorian: Refers broadly to the reign of Queen Victoria of England (1837-1901) and to anything with qualities typical of that era. For example, the qualities of smug narrowmindedness, bourgeois materialism, faith in social progress, and priggish morality are often considered Victorian. This stereotype is contradicted by such dramatic intellectual developments as the theories of Charles Darwin, Karl Marx, and Sigmund Freud (which stirred strong debates in England) and the critical attitudes of serious Victorian writers like Charles Dickens and George Eliot. In literature, the Victorian Period was the great age of the English novel, and the latter part of the era saw the rise of movements such as decadence and symbolism.

Victorian Age: See *Victorian*

Victorian Period: See *Victorian*

W

Weltanschauung: A German term referring to a person's worldview or philosophy.

Weltschmerz: A German term meaning "world pain." It describes a sense of anguish about the nature of existence, usually associated with a melancholy, pessimistic attitude.

Z

Zarzuela: A type of Spanish operetta.

Zeitgeist: A German term meaning "spirit of the time." It refers to the moral and intellectual trends of a given era.

Cumulative Author/Title Index

Aurora Leigh (Browning): V23
Auto Wreck (Shapiro): V3
Autobiographia Literaria (O'Hara): V34
Autumn Begins in Martins Ferry, Ohio (Wright): V8

B

Babii Yar (Yevtushenko): V29
Baggott, Julianna
  What the Poets Could Have Been: V26
Ballad of Birmingham (Randall): V5
Ballad of Orange and Grape (Rukeyser): V10
Bang, Mary Jo
  Allegory: V23
Baraka, Amiri
  In Memory of Radio: V9
Barbara Allan (Anonymous): V7
Barbarese, J. T.
  Walk Your Body Down: V26
Barbie Doll (Piercy): V9
Barot, Rick
  Bonnard's Garden: V25
Barrett, Elizabeth
  Sonnet 43: V2
The Base Stealer (Francis): V12
Bashō, Matsuo
  Falling Upon Earth: V2
  The Moon Glows the Same: V7
  Temple Bells Die Out: V18
Bass, Ellen
  And What If I Spoke of Despair: V19
Baudelaire, Charles
  Hymn to Beauty: V21
The Bean Eaters (Brooks): V2
Because I Could Not Stop for Death (Dickinson): V2
Bedtime Story (MacBeth): V8
Behn, Robin
  Ten Years after Your Deliberate Drowning: V21
Bell, Marvin
  View: V25
La Belle Dame sans Merci (Keats): V17
The Bells (Poe): V3
Beowulf (Wilbur): V11
Berry, Wendell
  The Peace of Wild Things: V30
Berryman, John
  Dream Song 29: V27
Beware: Do Not Read This Poem (Reed): V6
Beware of Ruins (Hope): V8
Bialosky, Jill
  Seven Seeds: V19
Bidart, Frank
  Curse: V26

Bidwell Ghost (Erdrich): V14
Biele, Joelle
  Rapture: V21
Birch Canoe (Revard): V5
Birches (Frost): V13
Birdfoot's Grampa (Bruchac): V36
Birney, Earle
  Vancouver Lights: V8
A Birthday (Rossetti): V10
Bishop, Elizabeth
  Brazil, January 1, 1502: V6
  Filling Station: V12
  The Fish: V31
  The Man-Moth: V27
The Black Heralds (Vallejo): V26
A Black Man Talks of Reaping (Bontemps): V32
The Black Snake (Oliver): V31
Black Zodiac (Wright): V10
Blackberry Eating (Kinnell): V35
Blackberrying (Plath): V15
Blake, William
  The Fly: V34
  The Lamb: V12
  A Poison Tree: V24
  The Tyger: V2
A Blessing (Wright): V7
"Blighters" (Sassoon): V28
Blood Oranges (Mueller): V13
The Blue Rim of Memory (Levertov): V17
Blumenthal, Michael
  Inventors: V7
Bly, Robert
  Come with Me: V6
  Driving to Town Late to Mail a Letter: V17
Bogan, Louise
  Words for Departure: V21
Boland, Eavan
  Anorexic: V12
  It's a Woman's World: V22
  Outside History: V31
Bonnard's Garden (Barot): V25
Bontemps, Arna
  A Black Man Talks of Reaping: V32
Borges and I (Borges): V27
Borges, Jorge Luis
  Borges and I: V27
The Boy (Hacker): V19
Bradstreet, Anne
  To My Dear and Loving Husband: V6
  Upon the Burning of Our House, July 10th, 1666: V33
Brazil, January 1, 1502 (Bishop): V6
The Bridegroom (Pushkin): V34
Bright Star! Would I Were Steadfast as Thou Art (Keats): V9
Brock-Broido, Lucie
  After Raphael: V26

Brodsky, Joseph
  Odysseus to Telemachus: V35
The Bronze Horseman (Pushkin): V28
Brontë, Emily
  Old Stoic: V33
Brooke, Rupert
  The Soldier: V7
Brooks, Gwendolyn
  The Bean Eaters: V2
  The Explorer: V32
  The Sonnet-Ballad: V1
  Strong Men, Riding Horses: V4
  We Real Cool: V6
Brouwer, Joel
  Last Request: V14
Brown, Fleda
  The Women Who Loved Elvis All Their Lives: V28
Browning, Elizabeth Barrett
  Aurora Leigh: V23
  Sonnet 43: V2
  Sonnet XXIX: V16
Browning, Robert
  My Last Duchess: V1
  Porphyria's Lover: V15
Bruchac, Joseph
  Birdfoot's Grampa: V36
Bryant, William Cullen
  Thanatopsis: V30
Bukowski, Charles
  The Tragedy of the Leaves: V28
Burns, Robert
  A Red, Red Rose: V8
Business (Cruz): V16
The Bustle in a House (Dickinson): V10
But Perhaps God Needs the Longing (Sachs): V20
Butcher Shop (Simic): V7
Byrne, Elena Karina
  In Particular: V20
Byron, Lord
  Childe Harold's Pilgrimage: V35
  The Destruction of Sennacherib: V1
  She Walks in Beauty: V14
  When We Two Parted: V29

C

The Canterbury Tales (Chaucer): V14
Cargoes (Masefield): V5
Carroll, Lewis
  Jabberwocky: V11
  The Walrus and the Carpenter: V30
Carruth, Hayden
  I, I, I: V26
Carson, Anne
  New Rule: V18

Cumulative Nationality/Ethnicity Index

Cumulative Nationality/Ethnicity Index

On Being Brought from Africa to America: V29
To His Excellency General Washington: V13

Serbian

Lazić, Radmila
Death Sentences: V22

Spanish

García Lorca, Federico
Gacela of the Dark Death: V20
Lament for Ignacio Sánchez Mejías: V31
HaNagid, Shmuel
Two Eclipses: V33
Machado, Antonio
The Crime Was in Granada: V23

Williams, William Carlos
The Red Wheelbarrow: V1

Sri Lankan

Ondaatje, Michael
The Cinnamon Peeler: V19
To a Sad Daughter: V8

Swedish

Sandburg, Carl
Chicago: V3
Cool Tombs: V6
Jazz Fantasia: V33
Moon Rondeau: V36
Hope Is a Tattered Flag: V12
Svenbro, Jesper
Lepidopterology: V23
Tranströmer, Tomas
Answers to Letters: V21

Vietnamese

Huong, Ho Xuan
Spring-Watching Pavilion: V18
Thomas, Dylan
Do Not Go Gentle into that Good Night: V1
Fern Hill: V3
The Force That Through the Green Fuse Drives the Flower: V8

Yugoslavian

Lazić, Radmila
Death Sentences: V22
Simic, Charles
Butcher Shop: V7
Classic Ballroom Dances: V33
Prodigy: V36

Cumulative Nationality/Ethnicity Index

Subject/Theme Index

Shame
  Hawthorne: 51, 54
Silence
  To Autumn: 305
  Prodigy: 206
  Snow-Bound: 255
Simplicity
  *I Built My Hut beside a Traveled
    Road:* 127, 132
  Prodigy: 213
  Snow-Bound: 269
Skepticism
  Song to the Men of England: 286,
    287
Slavery
  An Hymn to Evening: 79–85
  An Hymn to the Evening: 72–75
  Snow-Bound: 257
Social class
  Moon Rondeau: 180
  Song to the Men of England: 275,
    279–280, 286
  When In Rome: 333, 340
Social commentary
  Hawthorne: 49
Social criticism
  Self in 1958: 233, 235
Social reform
  Song to the Men of England: 274,
    276, 286, 289–293
Socialism
  Song to the Men of England: 275,
    276
Solitude
  *I Built My Hut beside a Traveled
    Road:* 117
Sorrow
  Snow-Bound: 257, 268, 269
Space. *See* Distance
Spirits (Supernatural beings) 190
  Prayer to the Masks: 201
Spirituality
  Snow-Bound: 247
Stereotypes (Psychology)
  When In Rome: 357
Storytelling
  Birdfoot's Grampa: 19, 22, 24–25,
    31, 33, 35–38
Strength
  *I Am Not One of Those Who Left
    the Land:* 99
  Moon Rondeau: 183, 185, 187
  Prayer to the Masks: 199
Struggle
  *I Am Not One of Those Who Left
    the Land:* 102
  The Idea of Ancestry: 151
  Self in 1958: 235, 240, 245
  What I Expected: 314, 315

Suburban life
  Self in 1958: 228–229, 231–232, 240
Success
  What I Expected: 314, 317
Suffering
  *I Am Not One of Those Who Left
    the Land:* 0, 93, 114
  The Idea of Ancestry: 157
  Prayer to the Masks: 190
  Prodigy: 216
  Self in 1958: 242
  What I Expected: 322, 323, 328
Suicide
  Self in 1958: 240–243
Superiority
  Birdfoot's Grampa: 31
Survival
  *I Am Not One of Those Who Left
    the Land:* 99, 102, 109, 110
  The Idea of Ancestry: 157
  Self in 1958: 245
Symbolism
  To Autumn: 307
  *I Built My Hut beside a Traveled
    Road:* 121
  The Idea of Ancestry: 149
  Moon Rondeau: 165
  Prayer to the Masks: 190, 192,
    197, 201
  Prodigy: 206
  Self in 1958: 238
Sympathy
  Moon Rondeau: 187
  What I Expected: 323

T

Taoism
  *I Built My Hut beside a Traveled
    Road:* 119, 124–127
Technology
  Birdfoot's Grampa: 22, 25, 29
Tension
  Self in 1958: 237
  What I Expected: 322
  When In Rome: 335, 340, 342, 343
Terror
  *I Am Not One of Those Who Left
    the Land:* 105
  Self in 1958: 242, 244
Time
  All Shall Be Restored: 10
  To Autumn: 296
  *I Built My Hut beside a Traveled
    Road:* 128
  The Idea of Ancestry: 160
  Snow-Bound: 257, 258, 267
Tradition
  Hawthorne: 60
  Prayer to the Masks: 190, 196, 198

Transformation
  All Shall Be Restored: 5
  *I Am Not One of Those Who Left
    the Land:* 113, 114
  Prayer to the Masks: 201–202
  Prodigy: 205
  Self in 1958: 245
Transience. *See* Impermanence
Translation
  *I Am Not One of Those Who Left
    the Land:* 91, 96, 102
  *I Built My Hut beside a Traveled
    Road:* 128
  Prayer to the Masks: 199
Triumph
  What I Expected: 314
Trust (Psychology)
  Snow-Bound: 266
Truth
  To Autumn: 304, 308
  Hawthorne: 47
  *I Built My Hut beside a Traveled
    Road:* 119, 120–121, 126
  The Idea of Ancestry: 153
  Snow-Bound: 256, 271
  What I Expected: 330
  When In Rome: 357
Tyranny
  Song to the Men of England: 275,
    276, 284

U

Understanding
  *I Built My Hut beside a Traveled
    Road:* 126
Unhappiness
  *I Am Not One of Those Who Left
    the Land:* 106
Utilitarianism
  When In Rome: 356
Utopianism
  Song to the Men of England:
    276–277

V

Violence
  *I Am Not One of Those Who Left
    the Land:* 99, 101
Virtue
  An Hymn to the Evening: 68, 70, 71
  *I Am Not One of Those Who Left
    the Land:* 93
  Prayer to the Masks: 190
  What I Expected: 314, 317

W

Warning
  When In Rome: 342
Wars
  All Shall Be Restored: 7

Cumulative
Index of First Lines

As virtuous men pass mildly away
(A Valediction: Forbidding
Mourning) V11:201

As you set out for Ithaka (Ithaka)
V19:114

At five in the afternoon. (Lament for
Ignacio Sánchez Mejías)
V31:128–30

At night the dead come down to the
river to drink (The Dead)
V35:69

At noon in the desert a panting
lizard (At the Bomb Testing
Site) V8:2

At six I lived for spells: (What For)
V33:266

Ay, tear her tattered ensign down!
(Old Ironsides) V9:172

B

Back then, before we came (On
Freedom's Ground) V12:186

Bananas ripe and green, and ginger-
root (The Tropics in New York)
V4:255

Be happy if the wind inside the
orchard (On the Threshold)
V22:128

Because I could not stop for Death—
(Because I Could Not Stop for
Death) V2:27

Before the indifferent beak could let
her drop? (Leda and the Swan)
V13:182

Before you know what kindness
really is (Kindness) V24:84–85

Below long pine winds, a stream
twists. (Jade Flower Palace)
V32:145

Bent double, like old beggars under
slacks, (Dulce et Decorum Est)
V10:109

Between my finger and my thumb
(Digging) V5:70

Beware of ruins: they have a
treacherous charm (Beware of
Ruins) V8:43

Bright star! would I were steadfast as
thou art— (Bright Star! Would
I Were Steadfast as Thou Art)
V9:44

But perhaps God needs the longing,
wherever else should it dwell,
(But Perhaps God Needs the
Longing) V20:41

By the rude bridge that arched the
flood (Concord Hymn) V4:30

By way of a vanished bridge we cross
this river (The Garden Shukkei-en)
V18:107

C

Cassandra's kind of crying was
(Three To's and an Oi) V24:264

Celestial choir! enthron'd in realms
of light, (To His Excellency
General Washington) V13:212

Come with me into those things that
have felt his despair for so
long— (Come with Me) V6:31

Complacencies of the peignoir, and
late (Sunday Morning) V16:189

Composed in the Tower, before his
execution ("More Light! More
Light!") V6:119

D

Darkened by time, the masters, like
our memories, mix (Black
Zodiac) V10:46

Dear Sirs: (In Response to Executive
Order 9066: All Americans of
Japanese Descent Must Report
to Relocation Centers) V32:129

Death, be not proud, though some
have called thee (Holy Sonnet
10) V2:103

Devouring Time, blunt thou the
lion's paws (Sonnet 19) V9:210

Disoriented, the newly dead try to
turn back, (Our Side) V24:177

Do not go gentle into that good night
(Do Not Go Gentle into that
Good Night) V1:51

Do not weep, maiden, for war is kind
(War Is Kind) V9:252

Does the road wind up-hill all the
way? (Up-Hill) V34:279

Don Arturo says: (Business) V16:2

Drink to me only with thine eyes,
(Song: To Celia) V23:270–271

(Dumb, (A Grafted Tongue) V12:92

E

Each day the shadow swings (In the
Land of Shinar) V7:83

Each morning the man rises from
bed because the invisible (It's
like This) V23:138–139

Each night she waits by the road
(Bidwell Ghost) V14:2

Even when you know what people
are capable of, (Knowledge)
V25:113

Everything has been plundered,
betrayed, sold out, (Everything
Is Plundered) V32:113

F

Face of the skies (Moreover, the
Moon) V20:153

Falling upon earth (Falling Upon
Earth) V2:64

Farewell, thou child of my right
hand, and joy; (On My First
Son) V33:166

Far far from gusty waves these
children's faces. (An
Elementary School Classroom
in a Slum) V23:88–89

Fast breaks. Lay ups. With
Mercury's (Slam, Dunk, &
Hook) V30:176–177

First, the self. Then, the observing
self. (I, I, I) V26:97

Five years have past; five summers,
with the length (Tintern Abbey)
V2:249

Flesh is heretic. (Anorexic) V12:2

For a long time the butterfly held a
prominent place in psychology
(Lepidopterology)
V23:171–172

For Jews, the Cossacks are always
coming. (The Cossacks) V25:70

For three years, out of key with his
time, (Hugh Selwyn
Mauberley) V16:26

Forgive me for thinking I saw (For a
New Citizen of These United
States) V15:55

Frogs burrow the mud (Winter)
V35:297

From my mother's sleep I fell into
the State (The Death of the Ball
Turret Gunner) V2:41

From the air to the air, like an empty
net, (The Heights of Macchu
Picchu) V28:137

G

Gardener: Sir, I encountered Death
(Incident in a Rose Garden)
V14:190

Gather ye Rose-buds while ye may,
(To the Virgins, to Make Much
of Time) V13:226

Gazelle, I killed you (Ode to a Drum)
V20:172–173

Glory be to God for dappled
things— (Pied Beauty) V26:161

Go, and catch a falling star, (Song)
V35:237

Go down, Moses (Go Down, Moses)
V11:42

God save America, (America,
America) V29:2

Grandmothers who wring the necks
(Classic Ballroom Dances)
V33:3

Gray mist wolf (Four Mountain
Wolves) V9:131

Cumulative
Index of Last Lines

I didn't want to put them down. (And What If I Spoke of Despair) V19:2

I have been one acquainted with the night. (Acquainted with the Night) V35:3

I have just come down from my father (The Hospital Window) V11:58

I hear it in the deep heart's core. (The Lake Isle of Innisfree) V15:121

I know why the caged bird sings! (Sympathy) V33:203

I never writ, nor no man ever loved (Sonnet 116) V3:288

I rest in the grace of the world, and am free. (The Peace of Wild Things) V30:159

I romp with joy in the bookish dark (Eating Poetry) V9:61

I see Mike's painting, called SARDINES (Why I Am Not a Painter) V8:259

I shall but love thee better after death (Sonnet 43) V2:236

I should be glad of another death (Journey of the Magi) V7:110

I stand up (Miss Rosie) V1:133

I stood there, fifteen (Fifteen) V2:78

I take it you are he? (Incident in a Rose Garden) V14:191

I, too, am America. (I, Too) V30:99

I turned aside and bowed my head and wept (The Tropics in New York) V4:255

I would like to tell, but lack the words. (I Built My Hut beside a Traveled Road) V36:119

If Winter comes, can Spring be far behind? (Ode to the West Wind) V2:163

I'll be gone from here. (The Cobweb) V17:51

I'll dig with it (Digging) V5:71

Imagine! (Autobiographia Literaria) V34:2

In a convulsive misery (The Milkfish Gatherers) V11:112

In balance with this life, this death (An Irish Airman Foresees His Death) V1:76

in earth's gasp, ocean's yawn. (Lake) V23:158

In Flanders fields (In Flanders Fields) V5:155

In ghostlier demarcations, keener sounds. (The Idea of Order at Key West) V13:164

In hearts at peace, under an English heaven (The Soldier) V7:218

In her tomb by the side of the sea (Annabel Lee) V9:14

in the family of things. (Wild Geese) V15:208

in the grit gray light of day. (Daylights) V13:102

In the rear-view mirrors of the passing cars (The War Against the Trees) V11:216

In these Chicago avenues. (A Thirst Against) V20:205

in this bastion of culture. (To an Unknown Poet) V18:221

in your unsteady, opening hand. (What the Poets Could Have Been) V26:262

iness (l(a) V1:85

Into blossom (A Blessing) V7:24

Is Come, my love is come to me. (A Birthday) V10:34

is love—that's all. (Two Poems for T.) V20:218

is safe is what you said. (Practice) V23:240

is still warm (Lament for the Dorsets) V5:191

It asked a crumb—of Me ("Hope" Is the Thing with Feathers) V3:123

It had no mirrors. I no longer needed mirrors. (I, I, I) V26:97

It is our god. (Fiddler Crab) V23:111–112

it is the bell to awaken God that we've heard ringing. (The Garden Shukkei-en) V18:107

it over my face and mouth. (An Anthem) V26:34

It rains as I write this. Mad heart, be brave. (The Country Without a Post Office) V18:64

It was your resting place." (Ah, Are You Digging on My Grave?) V4:2

it's always ourselves we find in the sea (maggie & milly & molly & may) V12:150

its bright, unequivocal eye. (Having it Out with Melancholy) V17:99

It's the fall through wind lifting white leaves. (Rapture) V21:181

its youth. The sea grows old in it. (The Fish) V14:172

J

Judge tenderly—of Me (This Is My Letter to the World) V4:233

Just imagine it (Inventors) V7:97

K

kisses you (Grandmother) V34:95

L

Laughing the stormy, husky, brawling laughter of Youth, half-naked, sweating, proud to be Hog Butcher, Tool Maker, Stacker of Wheat, Player with Railroads and Freight Handler to the Nation (Chicago) V3:61

Learn to labor and to wait (A Psalm of Life) V7:165

Leashed in my throat (Midnight) V2:131

Leaving thine outgrown shell by life's un-resting sea (The Chambered Nautilus) V24:52–53

Let my people go (Go Down, Moses) V11:43

Let the water come. (America, America) V29:4

life, our life and its forgetting. (For a New Citizen of These United States) V15:55

Life to Victory (Always) V24:15

like a bird in the sky ... (Ego-Tripping) V28:113

like a shadow or a friend. *Colombia.* (Kindness) V24:84–85

Like Stone— (The Soul Selects Her Own Society) V1:259

Little Lamb, God bless thee. (The Lamb) V12:135

Look'd up in perfect silence at the stars. (When I Heard the Learn'd Astronomer) V22:244

love (The Toni Morrison Dreams) V22:202–203

Loved I not Honour more. (To Lucasta, Going to the Wars) V32:291

Luck was rid of its clover. (Yet we insist that life is full of happy chance) V27:292

M

'Make a wish, Tom, make a wish.' (Drifters) V10: 98

make it seem to change (The Moon Glows the Same) V7:152

May be refined, and join the angelic train. (On Being Brought from Africa to America) V29:223

may your mercy be near. (Two Eclipses) V33:221

midnight-oiled in the metric laws? (A Farewell to English) V10:126

Monkey business (Business) V16:2

More dear, both for themselves and for thy sake! (Tintern Abbey) V2:250

Rises toward her day after day, like a terrible fish (Mirror) V1:116

S

Sans teeth, sans eyes, sans taste, sans everything. (Seven Ages of Man) V35:213

Shall be lifted—nevermore! (The Raven) V1:202

shall be lost. (All Shall Be Restored) V36:2

Shall you be overcome. (Conscientious Objector) V34:46

Shantih shantih shantih (The Waste Land) V20:248–252

share my shivering bed. (Chorale) V25:51

she'd miss me. (In Response to Executive Order 9066: All Americans of Japanese Descent Must Report to Relocation Centers) V32:129

Show an affirming flame. (September 1, 1939) V27:235

Shuddering with rain, coming down around me. (Omen) V22:107

Simply melted into the perfect light. (Perfect Light) V19:187

Singing of him what they could understand (Beowulf) V11:3

Singing with open mouths their strong melodious songs (I Hear America Singing) V3:152

Sister, one of those who never married. (My Grandmother's Plot in the Family Cemetery) V27:155

Sleep, fly, rest: even the sea dies! (Lament for Ignacio Sánchez Mejías) V31:128–30

slides by on grease (For the Union Dead) V7:67

Slouches towards Bethlehem to be born? (The Second Coming) V7:179

so like the smaller stars we rowed among. (The Lotus Flowers) V33:108

So long lives this, and this gives life to thee (Sonnet 18) V2:222

So prick my skin. (Pine) V23:223–224

so that everything can learn the reason for my song. (Sonnet LXXXIX) V35:260

Somebody loves us all. (Filling Station) V12:57

Speak through my words and my blood. (The Heights of Macchu Picchu) V28:141

spill darker kissmarks on that dark. (Ten Years after Your Deliberate Drowning) V21:240

Stand still, yet we will make him run (To His Coy Mistress) V5:277

startled into eternity (Four Mountain Wolves) V9:132

Still clinging to your shirt (My Papa's Waltz) V3:192

Stood up, coiled above his head, transforming all. (A Tall Man Executes a Jig) V12:229

strangers ask. *Originally?* And I hesitate. (Originally) V25:146–147

Surely goodness and mercy shall follow me all the days of my life: and I will dwell in the house of the Lord for ever (Psalm 23) V4:103

syllables of an old order. (A Grafted Tongue) V12:93

T

Take any streetful of people buying clothes and groceries, cheering a hero or throwing confetti and blowing tin horns . . . tell me if the lovers are losers . . . tell me if any get more than the lovers . . . in the dust . . . in the cool tombs (Cool Tombs) V6:46

Than from everything else life promised that you could do? (Paradiso) V20:190–191

Than that you should remember and be sad. (Remember) V14:255

that does not see you. You must change your life. (Archaic Torso of Apollo) V27:3

that might have been sweet in Grudnow. (Grudnow) V32:74

That then I scorn to change my state with Kings (Sonnet 29) V8:198

that there is more to know, that one day you will know it. (Knowledge) V25:113

That when we live no more, we may live ever (To My Dear and Loving Husband) V6:228

That's the word. (Black Zodiac) V10:47

The benediction of the air. (Snow-Bound) V36:248–254

the bigger it gets. (Smart and Final Iris) V15:183

The bosom of his Father and his God (Elegy Written in a Country Churchyard) V9:74

the bow toward torrents of *veyz mir*. (Three To's and an Oi) V24:264

The crime was in Granada, his Granada. (The Crime Was in Granada) V23:55–56

The dance is sure (Overture to a Dance of Locomotives) V11:143

The eyes turn topaz. (Hugh Selwyn Mauberley) V16:30

the flames? (Another Night in the Ruins) V26:13

The frolic architecture of the snow. (The Snow-Storm) V34:196

The garland briefer than a girl's (To an Athlete Dying Young) V7:230

The Grasshopper's among some grassy hills. (On the Grasshopper and the Cricket) V32:161

The guidon flags flutter gayly in the wind. (Cavalry Crossing a Ford) V13:50

The hands gripped hard on the desert (At the Bomb Testing Site) V8:3

The holy melodies of love arise. (The Arsenal at Springfield) V17:3

the knife at the throat, the death in the metronome (Music Lessons) V8:117

The Lady of Shalott." (The Lady of Shalott) V15:97

The lightning and the gale! (Old Ironsides) V9:172

The lone and level sands stretch far away. (Ozymandias) V27:173

the long, perfect loveliness of sow (Saint Francis and the Sow) V9:222

The Lord survives the rainbow of His will (The Quaker Graveyard in Nantucket) V6:159

The man I was when I was part of it (Beware of Ruins) V8:43

the quilts sing on (My Mother Pieced Quilts) V12:169

The red rose and the brier (Barbara Allan) V7:11

The self-same Power that brought me there brought you. (The Rhodora) V17:191

The shaft we raise to them and thee (Concord Hymn) V4:30

the skin of another, what I have made is a curse. (Curse) V26:75

The sky became a still and woven blue. (Merlin Enthralled) V16:73

The spirit of this place (To a Child Running With Outstretched Arms in Canyon de Chelly) V11:173